American Submariners

Volume I: Pre-Civil War

Louis S. Schafer

Copyright © 2018 Littleberry Press LLC

All rights reserved.

ISBN: 1-940750-22-9
ISBN-13: 978-1-9407502-2-4

DEDICATION

This book is gratefully dedicated to two of the most
important people I have ever known

Anita,
the one true love of my life,
who taught me how to mature into manhood
and
become a gentleman;
who encourages me to be a scholar;
and who has the gentle disposition and absolute dignity to never tell
everyone we know that she is light years out of my league.

Dad,
this one's also for you.
With your passing, though the world still turned,
it was filled with much more angst and far less wisdom.

TABLE OF CONTENTS

Acknowledgements i
Prologue: Since the Beginning 1
1. Richard Norwood: *Bermuda Tub* 29
2. Edward Bendall: *Diving Tub* 51
3. Robert Willis: *Diver Hoy* 73
4. William Phips: *Phips Diving Bell* 91
5. David Bushnell: *American Turtle* 113
6. Joseph Belton: *Belton Submarine* 135
7. Robert Fulton: *Nautilus* 161
8. Silas Plowden Halsey: *Renowned Halsey* 187
9. Robert Fulton: *Mute* 215
10. Cornelius Berrian & Richard Berrien: *Turtle* 249
11. Thomas Johnstone: *Eagle* and *Etna* 269
12. Lodner D. Phillips: *Marine Cigar* 289
13. Brutus de Villeroi: *Alligator* 315
14. James Buchanan Eads: *Mississippi Diver* 353
15. Lambert Alexandre: *Explorer* 379
16. J. Avery Richards: *Deep-Sea Diving Bell* 399
17. Edgar Foreman & Henry Sears: *Nautilus* 427
18. Johnny B. Green: *Lake Erie Diver* 465
19. Benjamin S. Maillefert: *Aerostatic Tubular Diving Bell* 489
20. Elliot P. Harrington: *Lake Erie Sub* 511
21. George Henry Felt: *Felt Submarine* 535
Chapter Bibliographies 565
Index 589

ACKNOWLEDGEMENTS

You know how it always goes, don't you? You open a book, turn to the acknowledgement section, and discover that it's happened once again. The writer has mentioned everyone else and not you.

And so it goes; at least, for the vast majority of folks.

Since we have, perhaps, not yet found one another; have only a miniscule passing acquaintance; have never been, and never will be, the very best of friends; have not seen or spoken to one another in at least a year or more; are in some way estranged from one another; are separated by time and space; or will never have the pleasure of saying "hello,"
I cannot find my way to acknowledging the tremendous influence all of you have had on my writing.

So,
let me apologize for the hundreds upon hundreds
of
slights, oversights, omissions, and blunders.

Portrait of Leonardo da Vinci

Prologue
Since The Beginning

"The Great Turk having besieged Venice, the lord Leonardo Da Vinci, at the head of his soldiers, cried out to him: 'Surrender within four hours or you will be sunk!' Yet after four hours, the said lord, the Great Turk not having accepted to surrender, sunk his galleys without the latter's realizing how! And it was a marvel to behold the Turkish vessels sinking into the water with their oarsmen and their cannons, and to hear the cries, curses and blasphemies! The armies of the Serenissima captured many prisoners, and after the battle, the said Leonardo was carried on their shoulders, causing the pride of the Italian nation, and the said lord was greatly honored by the Serenissima, for having been the savior of Venice, and they gave him, as agreed, half the ransoms of the prisoners..."[1]

Since the beginning of recorded history, people have pondered the question of whether or not any man-made devices are truly new. Instead, many have argued that so-called "prototype" creations have merely been "redefined," or evolved with the passage of time. It has even been said that the vast majority of modern day novelties were, in all actuality, designed and engineered many hundreds of years ago. Hence, from that perspective, modern man has simply played the role of plastic surgeon, giving such "inventions" nothing more than a "nip-and-tuck," a nose job, or a face-lift.

When it comes to diving beneath the earth's waterways, seas, and oceans, there is much evidence to support this theory. For centuries, human beings have dived *apne* - that is to say, they have gone down beneath the surface of the water while simply holding their breath. In Greek, *pneo* means "breathing," while the prefix *a-* stands for "no" or "without." From an historical perspective, the primary purposes of diving were to explore new life forms; to procure wealth found in sponges, corals and pearls; and to locate and salvage sunken treasure.

These same motivations continue to the present day. Free diving, without equipment in depths of up to forty meters, is not unusual. Divers engaging in this practice need to be extremely fit, well trained, and self-disciplined. Nevertheless, the life expectancy of apne divers is not very high, for the risks are considerable, and fatigue and wear become part of the longevity equation.

Sir Edmond Halley, Secretary to the Royal Society in England, recorded that divers in search of sponges in the Archipelago were accustomed to placing in their mouths a piece of sponge dipped in oil, which enabled them to dive for longer periods of time. Quite obviously, such a practice did not assist them in prolonging their ability to go without breathing, as Halley further suggested. More likely, the practice provided a means of assisting the diver to see more clearly. Experiments have most recently proven that, in still water, light is transmitted freely to greater depths, while waves cause less light and disturbed vision. By ejecting a little oil from his mouth sponge, a diver was able to calm the waves and, thus, force unobstructed lighting for better submerged vision.

Though free diving, by its nature, has lung-capacity limitations and other human restrictions, practitioners eventually established depth records exceeding two hundred meters. Over time, mechanically minded problem solvers attempted to uncover additional solutions that would allow them to remain under water much longer. Over time, four simple devices evolved: the breathing tube, diving armor, the diving bell, and the submarine. Virtually every diver from that point forward incorporated technological innovation based on one or multiples of these innovative concepts.

An Assyrian bas-relief carving, believed to have been fashioned around 885 BC, shows what appears to be divers using small breathing sacs underwater, allowing them to sneak up on their enemies. They also appear to be wearing a type of protective eye wear, as well as rubberized head gear. As time passed, other inventive souls attempted to use a variety of innovative means—including reeds, tanks, diving bells, and vessels—to accomplish similar feats.

At the British Museum in London, an exhibit known as *Art and Empire: Treasures From Assyria,* is comprised of more than 250 art objects, including sculptures, cylinder seals, military equipment, wall reliefs, decorative ivories, and metal vessels. These items came from excavated palaces and temples located in Nimrud and Nineveh in northern Iraq. One gypsum carving in particular depicts two of three divers using breathing tanks to remain submerged. Its resemblance to the earlier mentioned carving seems more than coincidental.

Discovered among the hieroglyphics of ancient Egypt, archaeologists have found further indications that early civilization attempted to survive under the water by breathing through papyrus reeds extending to the surface. Later, among men and myth of history and fable, the very first diving legend mentioned by name was Glaucus, a young fisherman. One day, while exploring the rocky river bottom, he hauled in his catch, and on emptying his net noticed the fish he had brought to shore hours earlier were reviving and escaping back into the water. Wondering what was causing this, he took a closer look and realized he had emptied his catch on a patch of strange herbs on the riverbank. Legend has it that Glaucus picked a handful of these herbs and, upon tasting them, had an overwhelming urge to enter the river:

> "And the sea-bottom, also, has its zones, at different depths, and peculiar forms in peculiar spots, affected by the currents and the nature of the ground, the riches of which have to be seen, alas, rather by the imagination than the eye; for such spoonfuls of the treasure as the dredge brings

up to us, come too often rolled and battered, torn from their sites and contracted by fear, mere hints to us of what the populous reality below is like. And often, standing on the shore at low tide, has one longed to walk on and in under the waves, as the water-ousel does in the pools of the mountain-burn, and see it all but for a moment; and a solemn beauty and meaning has invested the old Greek fable of Glaucus the fisherman, how he ate of the herb which gave his fish strength to leap back into their native element, and, seized on the spot with a strange longing to follow them under the waves..."[2]

What Glaucus didn't realize was that he had just eaten a plant known as "dog's tooth," a rare and sacred herb to Helios, the Titan of the sun. The herb was typically fed to Helios' horses to keep them fresh, healthy and best of all, immortal. It is said that Glaucus plunged into the blue abyss and became "the blue old man of the sea," diving deeper and deeper into the ever-darkening ocean. Eventually, he found the watery palace of the now-retired Titans, Oceanus and Tethys. Oceanus, who was the original Titan that ruled the salty seas in the days when the earth first began, and his wife, Tethys, the Titaness of Fresh Water, were a kindly, elderly divine couple who took the depressed and lost Glaucus in. Back on land, legend has it that Glaucus never resurfaced.

Glaucus Changed into a Sea-God, Bernard Picart (1731)

Evidence of man's ongoing intrigue to conquer the depths of the seas would continue onward through the generations, for records of attempts to utilize underwater diving apparatus go back to the earliest writings in history. The

Greek philosopher, Aristotle, for example, in his *Problematum*, mentions repeated attempts to build a submersible tank to "enable the divers to respire equally well by letting down a cauldron, for this does not fill with water, but retains the air, for it is forced straight down into the water."[3]

> "...in order that these fishers of sponges may be supplied with a facility of respiration, a kettle is let down to them, not filled with water, but with air, which constantly assists the submerged man; it is forcibly kept upright in its descent, in order that it may be sent down at an equal level all around, to prevent the air from escaping and the water from entering..."[4]

Exactly how long such devices had existed prior to Aristotle's writings is unknown, but around 480 BC, Scyllias, a sculptor, and his daughter Hydna became a part of this underwater story. Legend notes that Scyllias had long been an expert swimmer who had taught his infant daughter the skills of diving well into the deepest parts of the sea. Well known in local circles, the pair had been hired by Xerxes to recover treasure from a shipwreck. After the salvage operation had been a success–and at the same time being allowed to keep a good share of the treasure–father and daughter decided that they wanted to return to Greece. But Xerxes wouldn't let them go, since the pair knew far too much about the Persian plan of attack against Scyllias' homeland.

One day, as the ships were anchored and mustering for the attack, a violent storm arose giving Scyllias and Hydna the opportunity to attempt an escape. But before doing so, they wanted repay the Persians for their hospitality. With knives in hand, the pair dove into the sea and silently swam among the boats, cutting their moorings. Tossed about by the wind and waves, the ships crashed together; some sank and a great many others were damaged:

> "Now the Persians had with them a man named Scyllias, a native of Scione, who was the most expert diver of his day. At the time of the shipwreck off Mount Pelion he had recovered for the Persians a great part of what they lost; and at the same time he had taken care to obtain for himself a good share of the treasure. He had for some time been wishing to go over to the Greeks; but no good opportunity had offered till now, when the Persians were making the muster of their ships. In what way he contrived to reach the Greeks I am not able to say for certain: I marvel much if the tale that is commonly told be true. 'Tis said he dived into the sea at Aphetae, and did not once come to the surface till he reached Artemisium, a distance of nearly eighty furlongs. Now many things are related of this man, which are plainly false; but some of the stories seem to be true. My own opinion is that on this occasion he made the passage to Artemisium in a boat. However this might be, Scyllias no sooner reached Artemisium than he gave the Greek captains a full account of the damage done by the storm, and likewise told them of the ships sent to make the circuit of Euboea..."[5]

Thanks to Scyllias and Hydna, the Greeks later defeated the Persian fleet at Salamis, perhaps saving western civilization from Persian domination. For their patriotic act of bravery, statues of them were later erected at Delphi. In fact, according to the historian Pausanias, Nero "carried off the statue of Hydna" to his palace in Rome, so that he might have her beauty all to himself.

Alexander the Great being lowered in a glass submersible, 16th Century Islamic drawing

Aristotle, in *Problematum*, also told the tale of Alexander the Great, who ruled Macedonian and was the conqueror of the discovered world in his time. At the siege of Tyre in 332 BC, he ordered divers to destroy any submarine defenses the city might undertake to build. While in none of these records does it actually say he had any kind of submersible vessel, a number of historians believe that he descended in a device which kept its occupants dry and admitted light. Most likely, he was lowered in a vehicle that would become known as the "diving bell," which was also noted in the Roman twelfth century *Alexandria*. In its iambic lines of twelve syllables of verse (hence the term Alexandrine), the author relates the tale that Alexander had built "a very fine barrel made entirely of white glass." At the age of eleven, Alexander entered the glass case, reinforced by metal bands and had himself lowered into the sea by a chain measuring over 600 feet in length. Two companions accompanied the adventurer, and all were stunned by the bright lights emanating from the diving machine. Alexander is quoted as observing, from what he had seen underwater, that "...the world is damned and lost. The large and powerful fish devour the small fry."

Over time, verbal legend changed to written history. Roberto Valturio, an Italian engineer and writer born in Rimini about 1405, was best known as the author of a military treatise titled *De Re militari*. Valturio dedicated this treatise to his Patron and Condottiero, Sigismondo Pandolfo Malatesta, popularly known as the "Wolf of Rimini" and considered by his contemporaries as one of the most daring military leaders in all of Europe. When the treatise was finished around 1465, Malatesta distributed copies to European rulers, including King Louis XI, Francesco Sforza, and Lorenzo de Medici. The codex served as compilation for a number of recommendable strategies during wartime, including an armored vessel, a dragon tower on wheels, an armored combat wagon, and a uniquely designed four-propeller powered submarine. Fortunately, one copy of Valturio's treatise found its way into the extensive library of Leonardo da Vinci. It contained a detailed sketch of his proposed vessel.

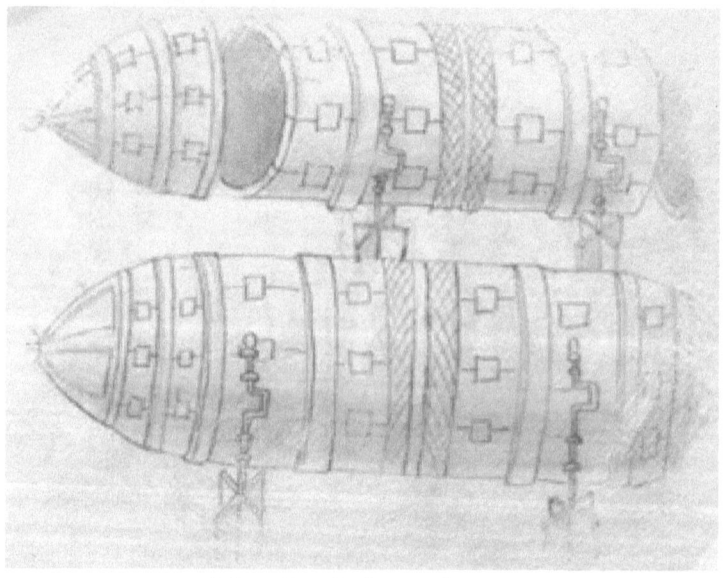

Robert Valturio's submarine drawings

During the second half of the fifteenth century, the multi-sided genius of artist and engineer, Leonardo da Vinci, the Florentine Renaissance inventor, produced blueprints for a host of modern day inventors. His creations included detailed plans for road vehicles, flying machines, rapid-fire guns, and even an ingenious diving apparatus. Earlier in his illustrious career, he had set out to solve the problems of underwater diving by designing a wet suit with a snorkel-like breathing tube quite similar to that of the early Egyptians.

Leonardo's design for an underwater breathing apparatus consisted of cane tubes joined by leather, with steel rings to prevent them being crushed by the water pressure. The tubes were attached to a face-mask and at the other end to a bell-shaped float to keep the openings above water. Other drawings for his diving suits included a coat with a pouch to hold a leather wineskin to store air and a urination bottle so the diver could remain underwater for a long period.

Eventually, in 1490, Leonardo conceived an elaborate scheme to construct a totally submersible vessel. Though some historians believe that the construction phase of this unique device was carried out to its completion, scant records indicate that this is highly unlikely. Though some historical documents convey that he lacked the patience and even temperament necessary to develop his somewhat outrageous concepts into tangible terms, others claim that he purposely kept his plans for an underwater warship a secret. The latter records further indicate that he "was afraid that it would make war even more frightful than it already was."

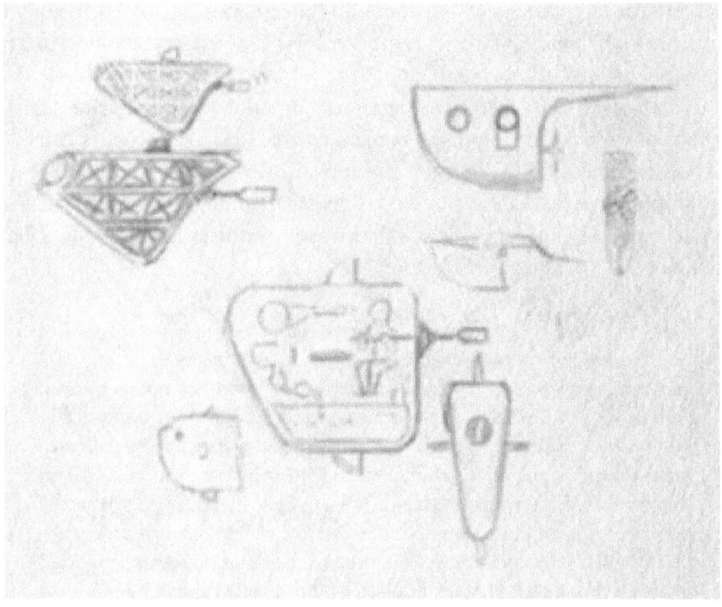

Leonardo da Vinci's rudimentary submarine drawings

Still, Leonardo's design concepts, along with his many scientific observations, were written down in literally thousands of pages of drawings. Interpretation of them was difficult, however, for not only were they sketchily annotated in an odd mirror writing, each page of his words were written from right to left. He died with his work unpublished, carrying many of his secret concepts with him to the grave. Decades later, however, his inventive schemes would be resurrected, scrutinized, and redefined.

In 1505, Olaus Magnus, Bishop of Uppsala in Sweden, detailed a personal sighting of a pair of "leather boats" near the Cathedral of Asloe:

> "I myself saw, in 1505, two such small boats made of leather, which were suspended, as a trophy, over the western entrance of the cathedral church of Opslo, sanctified to the Holy Halvard...where they were hanging on the wall for everyone to see. It was told, that King Hakon had taken them, when he with a warfleet passed the Greenlandic coast, in same moment they [those in the leather boats] were trying to sank [sic] his ships into the sea... For the Inhabitants of that Countrey [sic] are wont to get small profits by the spoils of others, by these and the like treacherous Arts, who by their thieving wit, and by boring a hole privately in the sides of the ships beneath (as I said) have let in the water and presently caused them to sink."[6]

According to Magnus' almost unbelievable account, the wooden underwater crafts were used by pirates of "Gruntland" (Greenland) during their numerous assaults on local merchant ships. Supposedly, the invaders were able to attack their enemies both from beneath and at the surface of the water.

In 1535, thirty years after Magnus documented his submarine sightings, an Italian physicist, Guglielmo de Lorena, created and used what is considered to be the first successful diving suit. The apparatus, weighing about 200 pounds, was nothing more than an upside-down bell-shaped device worn on the shoulders and supported by slings. More than three centuries later, it would be described in detail in a magazine article:

> "This machine he states to have been a round tub-like vessel made of oak, two fingers thick, five palms long, and three wide, open at one end, and the other securely fastened; it was guarded with six hoops of iron, and at the open end or lower portion with one of lead, in order that it might sink easily; the outside was pitched and greased with tallow to make it water-tight; and it was provided with a thick piece of glass (set in so closely that the water could not possibly leak in), through which the person descending might see the objects in the water. This instrument appears to have been placed over the head of the diver, who was supported by iron bands attached to the interior, which, clasping the shoulders, held him firmly, but allowed the use of his arms. For greater security there was also attached a girth, which, descending down the back, passed between the legs, and was fastened in front by a buckle, which could be easily and speedily unclasped. In this manner the person rested astride on the band attached to the machine; but as nothing passed below the middle of his arms, he was enabled to work under the water..."[7]

AMERICAN SUBMARINERS: PRE-CIVIL WAR

With his invention, de Lorena hoped to salvage sunken treasure aboard a pair of ancient roman ships lost in Lake Nemi, near Rome. Among other riches, these ships were rumored to be carrying a cargo of Emperor Caligula's gold. Although he made at least two salvage attempts, the bell-shaped headgear was unable to hold enough oxygen to thoroughly explore the shallow-water wrecks. Exasperated, and unable to determine a solution, the diver eventually gave up on his quest.

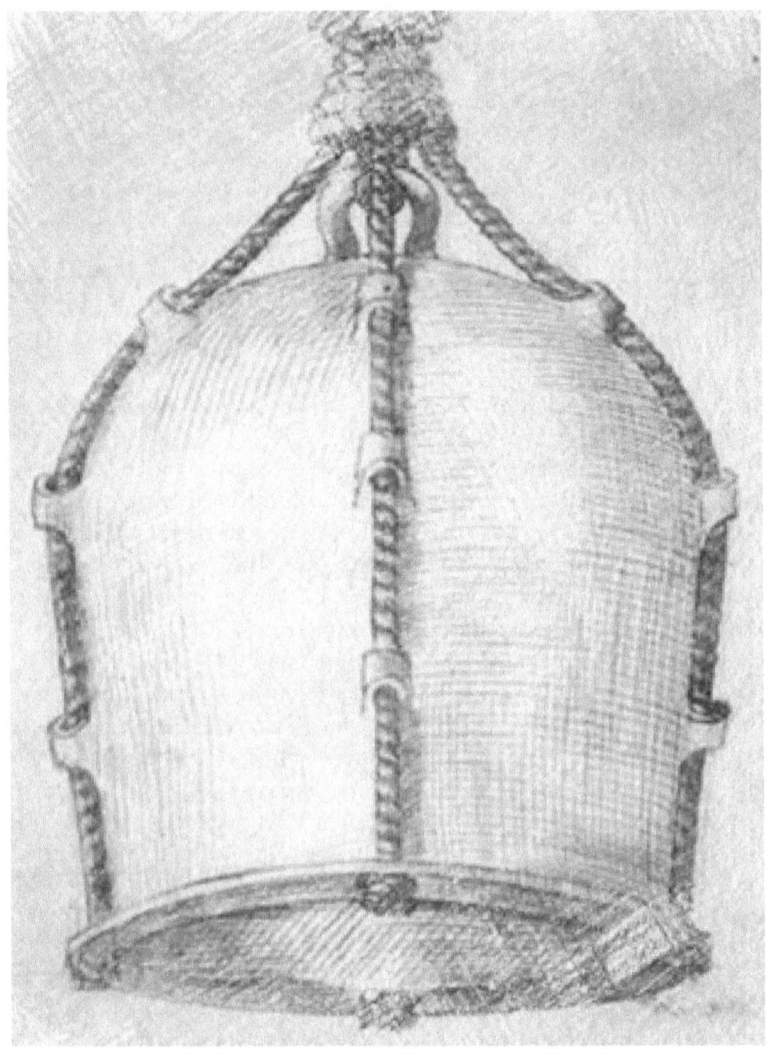

John Taisnier diving bell, called the "Aquatic Kettle"

A few years later, John Taisnier, a mathematician, lawyer, musician, and poet laureate of Cologne, who held an office in the household of Holy Roman Emperor Charles V, described how he planned to use a large diving bell to descend into the murky depths of the Tagus River south of Toledo, Spain:

> "Were the ignorant vulgar told that one could descend to the bottom of the Rhine, in the midst of the water, without wetting one's clothes or any part of one's body, and even carry a lighted candle to the bottom of the water, they would consider it as altogether ridiculous and impossible. This however I saw done at Toledo in Spain, in the year 1538, before the emporer Charles V and almost ten thousand spectators. The experiment was made by two Greeks, who, taking a very large kettle suspended by ropes with the mouth downwards, fixed beams and planks in the middle of its concavity, upon which they placed themselves, together with a candle. The kettle was equipoised by means of lead fixed round its mouth, so that when let down towards the water no part of its circumference should touch the water sooner than another, else the water might easily have overcome the air included in it, and have converted it into moist vapour..."[8]

In his interpretation of Taisnier's eyewitness account, P. Gaspar Schott refers to the apparatus as "cacabus aquaticus," or an "aquatic kettle." In fact, he further describes the use of a "lorica aquatica," or "aquatic armor," which was used to walk under water away from the diving bell.

Next came John Dee (1527-1608), a Welsh mathematician, astronomer, astrologer. occultist, navigator, magician, and consultant to Queen Elizabeth I. During his lifetime, Dee wrote a number of pamphlets on the varied subjects of philosophy, religion, and invention. Among his works, he offered details into the design of "mills, mining, pumps, cranes, bellows, gunnery, engines of war, mechanical clocks, and even the idea of a diving bell." Yet, there is no historical record that his design of a diving vessel was ever put into physical form.

Forty years would pass before William Bourne, an English mathematician, innkeeper and former Royal Navy gunner, who has been often credited with inventing the first navigable submarine, would address the problems associated with underwater exploration and salvage. It was 1578 when Bourne, who authored a number of important navigational manuals, described his vision of a self-styled craft that could travel undetected while completely submerged. In extremely fractured English, he described an enclosed vessel constructed of waterproofed leather and wood:

> "It is possible to make a shippe or boate that may goe under the water unto the bottome, and so to come up againe at your pleasure. Any magnitude of body that is in the water, if that quality in biggnesse, having alwaies but one weight, may be made bigger or lesser, then it shall swimme when you would, and sinke when you list: and for to make anything doo

so, then the jointes or places that doo make the thing bigger or lesser must bee of leather; and in the inside to have skrewes to winde it in and also out againe: and for to have for to have it sinke, they must winde the thing in to make it lesse, and then it sinketh unto the bottom: and to have it swimme, then to winde the sides out againe, to make the thing bigger, and it will swimme according unto the body of the thing in the water. And to make a small shippe or barke, or boate, do this, the barke being made of purpose, let there be good store of balast in the bottome of hir, and ouer the ballast, as lowe as may be, let there be a close orloppe [deck], such a one as no water may come into it, and then in like manner, at a sufficient height, to have another close orloppe, that no water may come through it; and that being done, then bore both sides full of holes between the two close orloppes; and that being done, then make a thing like the side of the barke or shippe, that may go vnto the side of the shippe, the one for the one side and the other for the other side, and that must be made so close and tight, that no water may come through it: and that done, then take leather, such a quantitie as is sufficient for to serve your purpose, and that leather must bee nailed close, with such prousion that no water may soake through it, and to be of that largenesse, that the thing may goe close vnto the barke or shippe side when you would and come in againe, to let sufficient water in, that it shall not be able to swimme. And now, this being done you must make prousion of skrewes, or other engines, to winde the two things on the inside that done, then for the hatch or skotel, that you must goe in or out, you must have leather round about it, that you may bring that together as a purse mouth, and so with a small skrewe, you may wind it so close together, that being in the bottome of the water, there shal no water come in: and that being done, you must have one mast, that must bee of sufficient biggnesse, that it must have hole bored through the one end vnto the other, as a pompe [pump] hath: and that done, then when that you list to sinke, then you must sound the deepness of the water, and foresee that the water will not rise higher than the top of the mast, for the hole that goeth through the mast must give you ayre, as men cannot live without it: And when you would sinke, then with your skrewes winde the two sides inwards, and water will come into the holes, and so the shippe or barke will sink vnto the bottome, and there it may rest at your pleasure: and when you would have it swimme, then with the skrewes winde out the things on both the sides, and that will thrust the water out againe at the holes, and so it will rise and come up above the water and swimme as it did before."[9]

Bourne's description was more a general principal than a detailed plan, though his concept of underwater rowing would be made a reality years later by Dutchman, Cornelius Jacobszoon Drebbel.

Though the inventor remained unnamed—out of privacy, ignorance, disrespect, or jealousy—it might have been William Bourne's vision that was later described by Francis Bacon, an English philosopher, statesman, scientist, jurist, and author. Although his political career would end in utter disgrace, Bacon remained extremely influential through his works. He was knighted in 1603, and earned the titles of Baron Verulam in 1618 and Viscount Saint Alban in 1621. During this same year, Bacon offered a description of a diving bell–as well as a submarine–the former of which had been used to salvage Spanish galleons lost along the coastlines of both Scotland and Ireland in 1588:

> "This vessel is made of metal, hollow like a cask, and being let down with its bottom parallel to the surface of the water, it carried along with it all the air it contains to the bottom of the sea; and having three feet to stand upon, somewhat short of the height of a man, the diver, when he wants to breath, conveys his head into the cavity of the vessel, where being refreshed with air, he afterwards continues his work. And we have heard, that a boat, or small ship, was lately contrived, wherein men may row under water..."[10]

Before the sixteenth century had come to an end, a Scotsman named John Napier of Merchistoun (1550-1617) announced that he, too, had a detailed outline for a diving vessel. In his own words, he had constructed a number of other contrivances as well, which would "render Britain safe from all her enemies." Napier's "secret inventions" included: a burning mirror, which would completely consume and enemy's ships "at whatever appointed distance"; a second mirror, constructed on a different principle, which would produce similar effects; an innovative piece of artillery, which would sweep a whole field clear of an enemy; a chariot which would resemble "a moving mouth of mettle and scatter destruction on all sides"; and, finally, "devises of sayling under water, with divers, other devises and stratagems for harming of the enemyes....by the Grace of God, and worke of expert craftsmen, I hope to perform....for defence of this Iland."[11]

Although Napier did not have the opportunity to put his submarine design into physical form before dying of the gout in 1617, a similar design was sponsored by Magnus Pegelius, who began his career as a professor of mathematics and astrology in Rostock, Germany. After marrying the daughter of the Mayor of Rostock in 1589, Level's work turned toward medicine. He would not only become the father of blood transfusion, but he would develop intravenous injection methods and design the forceps birth. Throughout his lifetime, however, he acquired a tremendous interest in daring, futuristic topics of invention. His book, entitled *Thesaurus Rerum Selectarum Magnarum, Dignarum, Utilium, Marinus, per Genere Humane*, was written in 1604, and detailed projects that included the theoretical conditions for the construction of airships, submarines, ship bridges, automatic firearms, water bath and arts, a memory of art, as well as the idea of evolution of species.[12] Magnus' diving vessel was launched in 1605, but the designer made one serious oversight: he failed to consider the tenacity of underwater mud, and the craft was buried at the bottom of the River Thames during its initial underwater trials.

AMERICAN SUBMARINERS: PRE-CIVIL WAR

German Franz Kessler, who was born about 1580, grew up to become a rather prominent portrait painter, scholar, inventor and alchemist. Beginning in his early twenties, he began writing a number of books and pamphlets, including information about stoves, as well as pamphlets on how-to make sundials, on using a "proportional instrument" (a simple calculator), and on using "Napier's bones" (another calculator). Furthermore, he wrote a book called *Unterschiedliche bisshero mehrern Theils Secreta oder verborgene, geheime Kunste*, or *Various until now mostly Secreta or hidden, secret arts*, which was published in Oppenheim in 1616. The first five chapters of this work dealt with communicating via a crude Aldis lamp. In the same year that his book was published, he constructed an improved diving bell apparatus.

Depiction of Franz Kessler's diving suit

Kessler's arrangement was another inverted wine barrel, although his was attached to safety ropes tied securely to a floating vessel at the surface. He, too, descended with the aid of weights, which could readily be released whenever he wished to resurface. Covered with leather to make it airtight, the vessel could move about on the bottom using the inventor's legs for walking, and also boasted a pair of portholes for viewing purposes. Although test dives proved successful, Kessler's contraption was never put into widespread use.

During the period of time that corresponds with the Pilgrims establishing the early colony of Plymouth, Massachusetts, in 1620, Cornelius Jacobszoon Drebbel, a Dutch chemist, made further progress in the actual construction of a workable underwater vessel. Described as "a native of Alkmaar, a very fair and handsome man, and of gentle manners," he busied himself in the design of a craft very similar to the one described earlier by Bourne.

Between 1620 and 1624, while "lodged by the king in Eltham Palace and supplied with funds from the royal treasury," Drebbel actually put three prototype underwater vessels into physical form. For propulsion, his submarines were rowed by a group of men, who could remain submerged for up to three hours at one time. Claiming that fresh air was easily provided by vent pipes extending to the surface, it was recorded that:

> "...King James himself journeyed in one of them on the Thames. There were on this occasion twelve rowers besides the passengers, and the vessel during several hours was kept at a depth of twelve to fifteen feet below the surface."[13]

Cornelius Jacobszoon Drebbel submarine

Another historian of the times, Cornelius Vander Wonde, who resided in Drebbel's hometown, had this to say of the ingenious inventor:

> "He built a ship in which one could row and navigate under water from Westminster to Greenwich, the distance of two Dutch miles; even five or six miles or as far as one pleased. In this boat a person could see under the surface of the water and without candlelight, as much as he needed to read in the Bible or any other book. Not long ago this remarkable ship was yet to be seen lying in the Thames or London river."[14]

It is now known that the simple tube that Drebbel described would have been, for all intents and purposes, quite useless. In fact, there are a number of similar stories in fiction and history in which characters go underwater while breathing through an ordinary tube. However, physics dictates that this type of arrangement is not as viable as many early inventors supposed. Human lungs are not physically capable of drawing a vacuum. In fact, modern day experiments prove that the comfortable depth limit of such an action is limited to about sixty centimeters–or two feet–below the surface. An effective snorkel that is helpful in free diving is typically much shorter. Longer hoses and deeper depths simply cannot work, unless fresh air is somehow pumped into the hose with pressure. There is no absolute historical evidence that such an arrangement was employed prior to the seventeenth century, so Van Drebbeel had either miscalculated or had withheld the complete details of his arrangement. Either way, he apparently took the truth of the matter with him to the grave.

In the decade that followed Drebbel's death in 1633, two French clerics took up the gauntlet of submarine science. Minim monk, Marin Mersenne, and Jesuit priest, Georges Fournier, collaborated in the design of an underwater craft that would be armed, had wheels for moving around on the flat seabed, and housed a phosphorescent system for lighting while submerged. And, though such an illuminating substance may also have been used by Drebbel to provide sufficient light to "read in the Bible or any other book," it is unknown how his passengers, which supposedly included King James and twelve rowers, managed to secure enough oxygen to survive. Again, it is likely that fantasy has been mixed with history.

A workable answer to the oxygen problem was provided around 1650, when German-born Otto von Guericke invented a vacuum pump consisting of a piston and an air gun cylinder with two-way flaps designed to pull air out of whatever vessel it was connected to. The ingenious machine was used to investigate the properties of the vacuum in a number of experiments. Guericke's scientific and diplomatic pursuits would eventually intersect when, at the Reichstag in Regensburg in 1654, he was invited to demonstrate his device before the highest dignitaries of the Holy Roman Empire. One of them, the Archbishop Elector Johann Philip von Schonborn, bought von Guericke's apparatus from him and had it shipped to his Jesuit-run College at Wurzburg. One of the professors at the College, Father Gaspar P. Schott, entered into friendly correspondence with von Guericke and, at the age of 55, the inventor's work was first published as an appendix to a book written by Father Schott, *Mechanica Hydraulico-pneumatica*, published in 1657. Later, this book would come to the attention of Robert Boyle, a seventeenth-century Irish-born philosopher, chemist, physicist, and inventor, who embarked on his own experiments using air pressure and the vacuum. In 1660, Boyle published *New Experiments Physico-Mechanical touching the Spring of Air and its Effects*.

Thirty years after the daring Drebbel excursions, in 1653, a forty-nine-year-old French inventor remembered only as Monsieur de Son designed and constructed a wooden-clad submersible craft in Holland. Born in 1604, likely near Reims, it was said that he started out as an engraver, later turning his attention to mechanics, metal work, and mathematics. Although his early life remains a mystery, history has uncovered the fact that, during the 1640's, de Son had been preoccupied with the design another type of "war machine":

> "We are told here of a man from Reims who has been in your England, who has a machine of 32 square feet, which he maintains can fly in the air anywhere he wants to, accompanied by 8 or 10 men."[15]

By 1643, de Son was jokingly referred to in France as "that new Icarus, who wanted to leave Paris, fly in his machine to Constantinople to have lunch, and return the same night to have dinner."[16] As of March of 1648, he was still—or perhaps again—working on perfecting his flying machine. Friends and neighbors scoffed at his outrageous ambitions.

By early 1653, however, reports of a new submersible vessel began to filter throughout much of Europe. Known by locals as the "Rotterdam Boat," it was intended for deployment in underwater assaults against the formidable British naval fleet. One contemporary observer believed that de Son's latest invention was a sign of divine intervention for the Dutch:

> "Now the world becomes more subtle day by day, and many new and miraculous arts and practices are being invented, both to the benefit and to the downfall of mankind, and now the extremely damaging war between the United Provinces and the new Republic of England has occurred, it seems as if God wants to end this bloody war, waking up in a miraculous way the spirit of Monsieur de Son."[17]

His vessel, de Son boasted, could destroy thirty men-of-war in the course of a single battle. He further claimed that that his miraculous diving ship could take on one hundred enemy ships in three or four hours time. Even in the harbor, enemy ships would not be safe from his so-called "Terror Terroris," which could track them down, sneak up on them, and crack them open like walnuts. This was, by no means, a conventional warship.

AMERICAN SUBMARINERS: PRE-CIVIL WAR

Drawing of Monsieur de Son's *Rotterdam Boat*

Aside from its incredible strength and stealth, the "Lightning of War"—as it was known by some—was unlike all others because of its unbelievable swiftness. Totally independent of the weather, be it storm, thunder, lightning, or crashing waves, the ship could sail at a pace of fifteen-miles-per-hour, or 180 miles in a day, 1,260 miles in a week, and 5,040 miles in a twenty-eight day period, "which would be almost the entire circumference of the world." Indeed, de Son boasted that, like his flying machine, his submarine vessel could leave Rotterdam in the morning, travel 475 kilometers and arrive in Dieppe, France, before sunset, enjoy a hearty meal there, and return to Rotterdam the same night. All in all, she would be "as quick as a Swallow, or any other light bird changing its course in the sky."

Yet, ultimately, de Son's vessel was perceived by both contemporaries and later historians as a complete and utter failure. Amid the negative sentiment, the inventor disappeared quietly from Rotterdam sometime after 1655, and three years later his abandoned submarine was sold as firewood. The designer and his "Foolish Ship" were ridiculed in prose and poetry during the coming years, and in time became part of submarine lore.

Meanwhile, in Holland, the Superintendent of the Fire Brigade, Jan van der Heyden, and his brother Nicholas took firefighting to its next level with the fashioning of the first fire hose in 1673. These 50-foot lengths of leather were sewn together like a bootleg. Even with the limitations of pressure, the attachment of the hose to the gooseneck nozzle allowed closer approaches and more accurate water application. Van der Heyden was also credited with an early version of a suction hose, using wire to keep it rigid. Earlier fire hoses were fabricated of leather, fastened together with copper rivets and washers and, as can be imagined, it was heavy, stiff, and commonly leaked. If early American submariners were to incorporate the combination of pump and hose in their vessels, this issue of leakage would need to be solved.

Jean de Hautefeuille, a French physicist who is credited with devising a primitive internal-combustion engine in 1678 which was to use gunpowder as a fuel, believed that "it is not possible for man to breathe air at normal atmospheric pressure when he is himself underwater at depth…" He went on to explain:

> "The first reason is taken from M. Pascal's teaching of the equilibrium of liquids in which he shows in what fashion water acts on submerged bodies pressing in on them from all sides, and in which he demonstrates that a compressible body introduced into water must be compressed inwards towards the center, something he proves by various examples. No great degree of intelligence is required to grasp that a bag or tube attached to the mouth of a man under water will act in the same fashion. A man's lungs are a sort of bellows and in order to inflate them the man must raise the column of water, which is pressing down on him from above. However, this column, being very heavy and the strength of his muscles being very inadequate, he finds he cannot raide the column of water and therefore he cannot breath…"[18]

However, de Hautefeuille further hypothesized that Cornelius Jacobszoon Drebbel's key to success…

> "…was probably the machine which I had imagined, consisting of a bellows with two valves and two tubes resting on the surface of the water, the one bringing down air and the other sending it back. By speaking of a volatile essence which restored the nitrous parts consumed by respiration, Van Drebbel evidently wished to disguise his invention and prevent others from finding out its real nature."[19]

Giovanni Alfonso Borelli (1608-1679) was a Renaissance Italian physiologist, physicist, and mathematician. He contributed to the modern principle of scientific investigation by continuing Galileo's custom of testing hypotheses against observation. Trained in mathematics, Borelli also made extensive studies of Jupiter's moons, the mechanics of animal locomotion and, in microscopy, of the constituents of blood. He is also considered to be the one of the first men to contemplate a self-contained underwater breathing apparatus along with an early submarine design. The exhaled gas would be cooled by sea water after passing through copper tubing. The helmet would be constructed of brass, with a glass window and 0.6 meters (2 feet) in diameter.

Some curious submarine information was recorded in a little-known volume published in Edinburgh in 1688 by George Sinclair, "sometime Professor of Philosophy in the College of Glasgow." Historical records indicates that Sinclair had been born in the Haddington area, and was Professor of Philosophy at the University of St Andrews before moving to Glasgow in 1655. He resigned in 1667 when University professors were required to submit to the Episcopal form of church government. He then became a mineral surveyor and engineer, and eventually turned to teaching in Edinburgh, where he was also employed to supervise a project to bring fresh drinking water into the city. He published several important books on mathematics and practical physics. One such work was a scarce work on navigation, astronomy, and the salvaging of sunken ships.

Entitled *The Principles of Astronomy and Navigation*, Sinclair's booklet spoke of the real life undersea adventures undertaken by an ingenious man, the Marquis of Argyle. As the now accepted historical record indicates, the Marquis had secured from the Duke of Lennox, Lord High Admiral of Scotland, a formal gift of the ship *Florida*, originally known as *Brod Martolosi*. Yet, there was one major obstacle concerning this large vessel of the Spanish Armada; it had been destroyed and sunk in the Bay of Tobermory near the Inner Hebridean of the Island of Mull on November 5, 1588. In an effort to recover riches that he then legally owned, the Marquis "employed James Colquhoun, of Glasgow, a man of singular knowledge and skill in all mechanical arts and sciences." He later described the risky operation in sparse detail:

> "This man, not knowing the diving-bell, went down several times, the air from above being communicated to his lungs by a long pipe of leather. He only viewed and surveyed the ship, but I suppose buoyed nothing up..."[20]

Sinclair pointed out that the weight of the vessel was identical with the displacement, and suggested that air containers, called "arks," open at the bottom, could be secured to the submerged wreck and air admitted, either by pumping through leather pipes, or by divers introducing it with the aid of inverted buckets or inflated skins. He further wrote that, in about 1664, Lord Argyle employed an ingenious gentleman from Forfarshire, England, the Maule of Melgum. Using his own version of a diving bell, Maule managed to salvage three pieces of ordinance; one of brass, one of copper, and one of iron. The writer explained that the diver was surprised to discover that bullets employed for these weapons "were of stone, instead of metal."

By 1690, Sir Edmond Halley had patented his own version of the diving bell, which included weighted barrels of air that could be lowered and connected to the interior of the bell by a pipe; a hole in the bottom of the barrel would allow the air to be replaced by water. As the bell was very heavy and not very maneuverable, he further considered using divers fitted with glass helmets and connected to the bell by a breathing tube:

> "The bell I made use of was wood, containing about 60 cubic foot in its concavity, and was of the form of a Truncate-Cone, whose diameter at top was three foot, and at bottom five. This I coated with lead so heavy that it would sink empty, and I distributed the weight so about its bottom, that it would go down in a perpendicular situation and no other. In the top I fixed a strong but clear glass, as a window to let in the light from above, and like wise a cock to let out the hot air that had been breathed: and below, about a yard under the bell, I placed a stage which hung by three ropes, each of which was charged with about one hundred weight,

to keep it study. This machine I suspended from the mast of a ship, by a sprit which was sufficiently secured by stays to the masthead, and was directed by braces to carry it over board clear of the ship side, and to bring it again within-board as occasion required."[21]

Both the barrels and the bell–the latter with men in it–were lowered to a depth of more than sixty feet (18.3 meters) for nearly ninety minutes. Overall, the dive was considered to be a sound success.

Drawing of Sir Edmond Halley's diving bell. air barrel, and diving suit

Between 1690 and 1692, a French physicist named Denis Papin–who was later credited with inventing the pressure cooker–designed and built a pair of workable submarines. The first was a strong and heavy metallic square box, equipped with an efficient apparatus that pumped air into the hull to raise the inner pressure. In theory, when the air pressure reached the required level, holes would be opened manually to let in some water. This first machine was destroyed accidently before even being tested in water.

The second design, constructed in 1692, had an oval shape and worked on similar principles. It included a waterproof hatch at the top, where a diver could enter, and holes beneath that would allow him to admit and discharge water for ballast, all of which was controlled by a pump from within. According to sources, a spy of German Gottfried Wilhelm Leibniz, named Haes, reported that Papin had some success with his second design on the River Lahn.

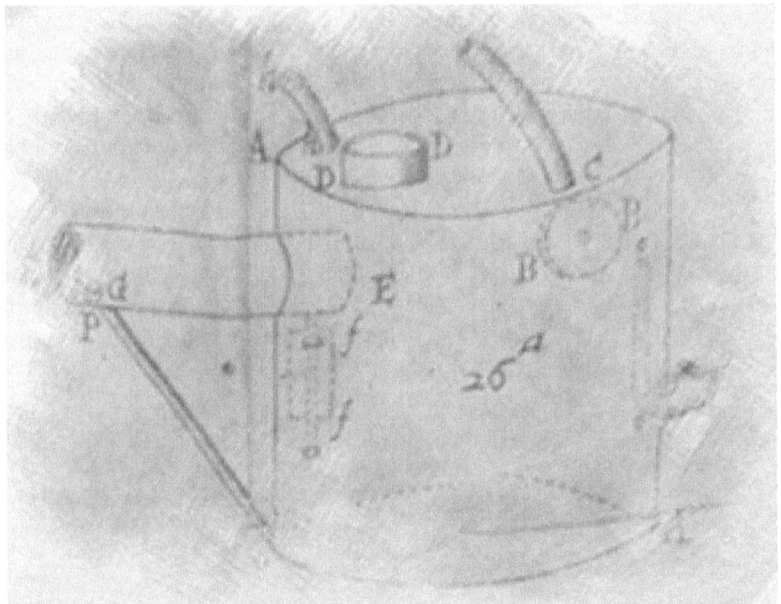

Dr. Denis Papin's diving kettle, 1692

The next reputed contributor to the submarine puzzle was the English-born Bishop of Chester, John Wilkins, an exceedingly interesting historical character. His life is detailed in the preface of the fifth edition of his primary scientific manuscript, *Mathematical Magick: or the wonders that may be perform'd by Mechanical Geometry*, published posthumously in 1707.

From this writing, we learn that Wilkins was likely born in 1614, and entered New Inn, Oxford, at the amazingly young age of thirteen. After graduating–not at New Inn, but at Magdalen Hall–he served as a Chaplain, first to Lord Say and then to Charles, Count Palatine of the Rhine. In 1648, he received the degree of Doctor of Divinity, and in 1656, married the sister of Oliver Cromwell. Eventually, after becoming Head of Trinity College in Cambridge and then Dean of Ripon, he became Bishop of Chester. During this illustrious career, it seems that he found ample time to author a number of small, yet significant, books. Among them was the aforementioned *Mathematical Magick*. This little publication, which details a number of mechanical concepts, contains one chapter entitled "Concerning the Possibility of Framing an Ark for Submarine Navigation: The Difficulties and Conveniences of such a Contrivance."

Although Wilkins gives credit for the submarine's idea to Marin Mersenne, who he explains "doth so largely and pleasantly descant upon the making of a ship wherein men may safely swim under the water," he undoubtedly details Bourne's concept without giving him credit. Indeed, Wilkins also outlined Bourne's leather attachments; his collapsible oars; his water-ballasting methods; and even his air-purification system.

In 1715, Englishman John Lethbridge constructed a "diving engine," which was nothing more than an oak cylinder reinforced with iron hoops, and possessing a glass viewing port. Inside, a diver could stay submerged for thirty minutes at sixty feet (18.3 meters), while protruding his arms into the water to conduct salvage work. The suit remained water-tight by means of greased leather cuffs sealed around the operator's arms.

Nearly sixty years later, the first diving death in history was recorded in England. In 1774, a gentleman named James Day, a millwright from East Anglia, constructed a diving vessel–indeed, instead of a "submarine," Day built a stationary "diving sloop"–in which he submerged himself to a depth of thirty feet, remaining there for several hours. Writer Nikolai Detlef Falck described Day in his 1775 publication:

> "His temper was gloomy, reserved and peevish; his disposition penurious; his views pecuniary; and he was remarkably obstinate in his opinion and jealous of his fame. But withal, he was allowed to be penetrating in his observations; acute in his remarks; faithful to his patron; and unshaken in his resolutions."[22]

With this small bit of success, Day sent a letter to an investment friend named Christopher Blake, seeking a financial partnership that would enable him to build a much larger plunging vessel. He further explained that he hoped to take the new submersible down at least three hundred feet, remaining at the bottom for a minimum of twenty-four hours. Day further stated that wagers placed on how long he could remain submerged would not only repay Blake for his investment risk, but might even make the pair fairly wealthy. Blake renegotiated the terms, stipulating that the inventor needed to consider modifying the depth to no greater than 120 feet for a maximum of twelve hours. Blake further reasoned that the enterprising pair should not forgo "any expense to fortify the chamber...against the weight of such a body of water." Day readily agreed, and the began his quest to locate a suitable and affordable vessel that could be altered to meet his needs.

By March of 1774, Day had found an inexpensive 50-ton, 31-foot-long wooden ship, lying at anchor near Plymouth Sound, which he agreed to purchase for 340 pounds sterling. Described by one historian as an "odd, solitary individual, addicted to dark water" and possessing a penchant for gambling, Day's unique submersible would not function so much like a "submarine," but rather a completely stationary "diving sloop, which he named the *Maria*." Constructing a wooden diving chamber from her timbers, the new submersible measured approximately twelve feet in length, nine feet wide, and eight feet deep, all of which projected above the level of *Maria's* main deck. Topside, she boasted a rudimentary system of signals that would allow Day to communicate readily with the outside world, thus enabling him to advise onlookers about his "state of health" during his underwater excursion:

> "On the deck of the chamber were fixed three buoys of different colours ... the white was to denote his being very well; the red, indifferent; and the black his being very ill..."[23]

Unfortunately, however, perhaps due to the immense water pressure or some other unpredicted problems aboard the *Maria*, John Day would never be able to incorporate the signals.

Drawing of cross-section of the *Maria*

On June 20, 1774, John Day brought the larger vessel out into Plymouth Sound near Drake's Island, where he planned to descend to a record-depth of 132 feet. To accomplish this almost unbelievable task, the inventor had attached thirty tons of milestones to his fifty-ton craft. Acting as ballast, the heavy load-milestones were each drilled through the center and strung onto wooden rods extending from the hull of his vessel. Some detail of this unique arrangement was recorded for posterity:

> "The vessel had a false bottom, standing on feet like a butcher's block, which contained the ballast; and, by the person in the vessel unscrewing some pins, she was to rise to the surface, leaving the false bottom behind."[24]

Pulling the plugs which allowed the *Maria*'s hull to fill with water, Day waited for the vessel's deck to become awash. Though the ship was loaded down with ample supplies, including food, blankets, and candles, Day found that the immense ballast weight was still not sufficient to force the boat beneath the surface. To solve the buoyancy issue, he ordered workmen to continue heaving heavy stones onto the top of the sloop. Eventually, the craft did, indeed, begin to sink. As Day jumped aboard, he gleefully waved to the onlookers on shore. Eye-witness ccounts say that "she went down stern foremost, and is supposed to have bulged directly, as a very great rippling appeared instantly after her sinking."[25]

From a nearby barge, Christopher Blake looked on "with a pensiveness that seemed to forebode to his mind an evil omen, and a solemn silence seized all the witnesses of the extraordinary and awful sight." Sadly, Blake's feelings would prove to be right, since John Day had forgotten one small detail: there would be no way for him to unload the extra stones, since he would be locked safely within the vessel's watertight belly. Furthermore, once he was submerged, there would be no way of communicating with those on the surface. History records that Day's diving craft went down at precisely "2:00 p.m. on Tuesday, June 28," 1774. What occurred next was also recorded by the *Annual Register*:

> "A day for the final determination was fixed; the vessel was towed to the place agreed upon; Mr. Day provided himself with whatever he thought necessary; he went into the vessel, let the water into her and with great composure retired to the room constructed for him, and shut up the valve. The ship went gradually down in 22 fathoms of water... He had three buoys or messengers, which he could send to the surface at option, to announce his situation below; but, none appearing, Mr. Blake, who was near at hand in a barge, began to entertain some suspicion. He kept a strict lookout, and at the time appointed, neither the buoys nor the vessel coming up, he applied to the Orpheus frigate, which lay just off the barge, for assistance. The captain with the most ready benevolence supplied them with everything in his power to seek for the ship. Mr. Blake, in this alarming situation was not content with the help of the Orpheus only; he made immediate application to Lord Sandwich (who happened to be at Plymouth) for further relief. His Lordship with great humanity ordered a number of hands from the dock-yard, who went with the utmost alacrity and tried every effort to regain the ship, but unhappily without effect... Many and various have been the opinions on this strange, useless, and fatal experiment, though the more reasonable part of mankind seemed to give it up as wholly impracticable. It is well-known, that pent-up air, when overcharged with the vapours emitted out of animal bodies, becomes unfit for respiration; for which reason, those confined in the diving-bell, after continuing some time under water are obliged to come up, and take in fresh air, or by some such means recruit it. That any man should be able after having sunk a vessel to so great a depth, to make that vessel at pressure, so much more specifically lighter

than water, as thereby to enable it to force its way to the surface, through the depressure of so great a weight, is a matter not hastily to be credited. Even cork, when sunk to a certain depth will, by the great weight of the fluid upon it, be prevented from rising."[26]

About a quarter hour after going down, the crowd of onlookers gathered, noticing that the surface of the water was "suddenly agitated, as if boiling...but various are the accounts of this; some of the men told me it was like a kind of eddy that always ensues on the sinking of anything; but Mr Black thinks it was attended with a violent ebullition of air."[26]

Despite the obvious indications, the crowd looked on with anticipation of John Day's return to the surface, which was scheduled to take place precisely at 2:00 pm on June 21. Yet, there was no sign of the couragious inventor. As daylight hours turned to dusk, and then night, disappointment gradually turned to concern. Early the next morning, a massive rescue effort was undertaken:

"Lord Sandwich ... ordered up all the aid which the dock-yard could afford, for weighing her up; three days passed under the continual endeavours of two hundred men, lighters, cables, and other requisite materials; but in vain; he was left to be numbered amongst the dead."[27]

Meanwhile, a close associate of John Day's, Dr. Nikolai Detlef Falck, was visiting in London at the time of the inventor's excursion. Though Day had not reappeared at the appointed hour, Falck reassured the onlookers there there was nothing to worry about, theorizing that the enterprising diver would be quite safe from underwater temperatures, as well as man-eating fish, just as long as he was inside the craft's "watertight chamber." Therefore, there would be no major hurry in attempting a rescue of the ingenious inventor. Time passed.

Falck leisurely waited until the following month before journeying to Plymouth. Once there, he put his rescue operation in motion. With a detailed plan, a contrivance to find the *Maria*, a number of volunteers, a good deal of recovery equipment, and a map of Plymouth Sound, Falck went to work.

Falck's overall ambition was to locate, rescue, and–if necessary–resuscitate his close friend:

"...having been fortunate enough to restore to life persons that have been drowned, (the method of which I have fully stated in my Seaman's Medical Instructor) I own that my sanguine expectations were flattered, notwithstanding the length of time he had remained in this suspense, since we have had instances of some extraordinary recoveries, with circumstances less favourable than here."[28]

On July 30, 1774, Falck was convinced he had, indeed, located the sunken *Maria*. Incorporating "a marine searcher (of my own contrivance," which resembled a pointed sounding lead made of iron, he believed that he could distinguish wood from stone at great depth beneath the water. His efforts continued until October 21, 1774. Eventually, the weather turned foul and, as Falck later wrote, "My private affairs required my attention at home." The physician returned to London, planning to return to Plymouth to locate the lost inventor once the weather improved.

Drawing of recovery equipment and map of Plymouth Sound

But, alas, though parts of the *Maria* were located, she could not be raised, for Falck's plans fell through and Day was never seen again. For centuries now, John Day and the *Maria* have rested at the bottom of Plymouth Sound, lost and nearly forgotten. As a final tribute, Falck later wrote:

> "...she (*Maria*) was sunk at two o'clock...and Mr. Day descended with her into perpetual night."[29]

Sketch of Richard Norwood

AMERICAN SUBMARINERS: PRE-CIVIL WAR

- 1 -
Richard Norwood: *Bermuda Tub*

"In the year of our Lord 1639, the 49th year of my age, a day which I had set apart to give unto the Lord by fasting and praying privately... I was born in October in the year of our Lord 1590 at Stevenage in Hertfordshire, which I reckon amongst the many favors of God towards me, who vouchsafed me to be born in those days of the glorious sunshine of the Gospel in the reign of that blessed Queen Elizabeth of famous memory, the second year after the great overthrow of the Spanish Armada which came to invade England: even in the most prosperous and happy age that ever England enjoyed."[1]

Just before Christmas, 1613, a brilliant, twenty-three-year-old Englishman stepped off a ship onto the "Isle of Devils." His advice had been very beneficial to the captain when the vessel they were on ran aground on one of the outer reefs, for young Richard Norwood knew precisely how to extricate the ship from its trappings. The shallow waters surrounded the British overseas territory, which was nestled in the North Atlantic and located off the east coast of the New World. Its nearest landmass was an unsettled region that would later become known as Cape Hatteras, North Carolina, which was about 1,030 kilometers (640 miles) due west-northwest. The islands were also about 1,239 kilometers (770 miles) south of present-day Cape Sable Island, Nova Scotia, and 1,770 kilometres (1,100 miles) northeast of the southern tip of Florida.

Bermuda, then known as Somers Isles, had been discovered in 1505 by Spanish sea captain, Juan de Bermúdez. He had claimed the apparently uninhabited islands for the Spanish Empire. Although he paid but two visits to the archipelago, Bermúdez never stepped foot on the islands themselves, claiming that he did not want to risk sailing through the dangerous shallow-water reefs encircling them. Subsequent Spanish explorers or, perhaps, some other European visitors are believed to have released the feral black pigs that had already become abundant on the islands when British settlers arrived.

The islands remained virtually unknown to English explorers until 1593, when Henry May was shipwrecked there aboard a French vessel, the *Edward Bonaventura*. Then, in 1609, the Virginia Company, a pair of English joint stock ventures chartered by King James I on April 10, 1606, which had already established Virginia and Jamestown on the American mainland two years earlier, was about to accidentally establish a more permanent settlement on Bermuda. On

June 2, 1609, the Admiral of the Company, Sir George Somers, had set sail from Plymouth, England on the *Sea Venture*, the flagship of the seven-ship fleet, (towing two additional pinnaces) destined for Jamestown, Virginia. The fleet carried a total of five- to six hundred colonists bound for the New World.

On July 25, out of the northeastern sky "a dreadful storm and hideous began to blow...swelling and roaring," blackening the skies as to "beat all light from Heaven." Thos was a violent "tempest" that, in its "restless Tumult," would not relent. Though the experienced eight seamen manning the *Sea Venture* struggled valiantly "to hold the whipstaff" and steer the vessel, "there was not a moment in which the sudden splitting or instant oversetting of the ship was not expected." The winds and rains, it seemed, would never abate, as "fury added to fury, and one storm urging a second more outrageous than the former."

The *Sea Venture* fought the storm for four days and nights. Not surprisingly, Sir George Somers' flagship found itself separated from the others. Similarly sized ships had survived such weather in the past, but she had exhibited one major critical flaw; she had only recently been constructed, and her timbers had not yet set. The caulking was forced from between them, and the ship had begun to leak severely, "having spewed out her oakum before we were aware." All hands were applied to bailing, but the water continued to rise in the hold, "and we almost drowned within whilst we sat looking when to perish from above." Frantically, the ship's guns were jettisoned–though two would be salvaged from the wreck in 1612–to raise her buoyancy, but this only delayed the inevitable. The ordeal caused "much fright and amazement, startled and turned the blood...of the most hardy mariner."[2]

In spite of all their efforts, on the fourth morning the vessel seemed to be covered by ocean water "from stern to stern like a garment or a vast cloud." Simultaneously, all on board realized the inevitability of their doom. The howling wind seemed to drown out their prayers, so that there was "nothing heard that could give comfort, nothing seen that might encourage hope." Just after midnight on Friday, July 28, the passengers and crew were prepared to give up and, after shutting down the hatches, "commending our sinful souls to God, committed the ship to the mercy of the gale."

Not believing his eyes, Sir George Somers spied land as the light dawned aboard the sinking *Sea Venture* on the morning of July 28. By then, the water in the hold had risen to nine feet, and crew and passengers had been driven past the point of exhaustion. Somers deliberately drove the ship onto the reefs of what proved to be Bermuda in order to prevent it from foundering. This allowed all 150 people and the dog aboard to reach shore safely, at what they later named Discovery Bay. Not seeing them again, those who continued on to Virginia presumed that Somers and the others had died in the storm, which had battered the relief fleet and damaged its supplies.

The settlers and seamen were forced to spend the next ten months in Bermuda, living on food they could gather on the island and fish from the sea.

During their time on the islands, the crew and passengers constructed a makeshift church and houses, the start of the Bermuda colony. Somers and Sir Thomas Gates oversaw the construction of two small ships, built from local Bermuda Cedar and the salvaged spars and rigging of the wrecked *Sea Venture*. During that building period, the *Sea Venture*'s longboat was fitted with a mast and sent out to find Jamestown. Neither it, nor its crew, was ever seen again.

When the pair of vessels, christened the *Deliverance* and the *Patience*, finally departed from Bermuda in May of 1610 and set sail for Jamestown, they left several people behind, some to maintain Somers' claim to the islands for England, some who had died. Those aboard the two ships included Sir Thomas Gates, the military commander and future governor of Jamestown, William Strachey, whose account of the wrecking later inspired William Shakespeare's *The Tempest*, and John Rolfe, who would found Virginia's tobacco industry, and who left a wife and child behind buried in Bermuda. Rolfe would one day find a new bride in the Powhatan princess Pocahontas.

Meanwhile, it was decided that Bermuda would be ruled as an extension of Virginia by the Virginia Company until 1614, when its successor, the Somers Isles Company, took control. It would be more than a century before the islands became a British colony, following the 1707 unification of the parliaments of Scotland and England, which created the Kingdom of Great Britain. The island's first capital city, St. George's, was established in 1612.

Richard Norwood had arrived only a year and a half behind the first boatload of stranded settlers, which had included Bermuda's first governor, Richard Moore. Norwood had been sent to the islands as a "technical specialist," meaning that he had been hired as a pearl diver in search of what proved to be Bermuda's non-existent pearls. When that job proved hopeless, it was absolute sheer chance that launched him on a career that would give him a very special place in both Bermuda and American history as its first mapmaker, surveyor, and diving bell inventor. Though few would remember his significance to history, he was a man of exceptional ability in those occupations, as well as in the many other pursuits in which he would engage during his extensive lifetime.

Richard's heritage can be traced back across hundreds of years and several generations, to his eleventh great-grandparents, Sir Stephen and Joan (Fedive) de Northwode. Stephen had been born in about 1165 and, though Joan had been raised in Ashwellthorpe, County Norfolk, more than a hundred miles to the north, the two were married in 1208 and resided in his hometown of Eddintune (Addington), a village in the county of Kent. It was recorded that, in 1220, "Sir Stephen de Northwode, Knight, was seized of 310 acres of land, 500 acres of marsh in the Isle of Shepeye, and four score and ten acres of marsh with their pertenencies in Upcherche, and of the manors, lands and tenements in the county of Kent. And he had a son, by name Sir Roger, who succeeded by inheritance, to those manors, lands, and tenements, after the death of the said Sir Stephen..."[3]

The Isle of Sheppey—meaning "isle of sheep"—was nestled off the northern coast of Kent in the Thames Estuary. Roger de Northwode, Richard's only known son, was born there in about 1225, and it was where he married Bona Fitz Bernard about a quarter century later. Already a wealthy man due to his inheritance, his marriage also secured his wife's possessions, which included the manors of Shorne and Thorneham. During his lifetime, Roger would hold the prestigious posts of Warden of the Cinque Ports and Baron of the Exchequer. It was also cited in historical records that, in September of 1265, when he was serving as steward of the Archbishop of Canterbury, he was made "a knight commissioned in Kent to take the lands of the rebels into the king's hands."[4]

Before his death on November 9, 1286, Roger de Northwode "took an interest in the old monastery of St. Sexburge for it had been long neglected. He made many repairs and donated to the monastery, wherefore among the servants of God, he is to this day called the restorer of that house."[5]

John de Northwode, son of Roger and Bona, was born in about 1254, and later married Joan de Badlesmere, "lady of the manors of Horton near Canterbury, and Beausfelde near Dover in the county of Kent; she possessed also certain tenements in Southwerke, in the county of Surrey, and rents in the city of London. Sir John and Joan issued Sir John, the eldest son, James, Thomas, Richard, Simon, and Humphrey. The said James died without heir of his body."[6]

It would be five Northwood generations, two hundred years, and two name changes—Northwode to Northwood, and then to Norwood—before John Norwood II, Richard's fourth great-grandfather, was born in 1455. It was he that would leave the family history behind on the Isles of Sheppey when he married Eleanor Giffard in 1486. It was through that marriage that Leckhampton Court, a fourteenth century manor house in faraway Gloucestershire, came into his possession. One or more of the Norwood family members would live there for 300 years.

Richard's intellect and love of learning was, in all probability, inherited from his grandfather, Roger Norwood, who was born in about 1530. Records indicate that, by 1548, he had become a fellow of Merton College, one of the constituent colleges of the University of Oxford. In 1554, Roger was chosen usher to the headmaster of Berkhamsted School in Hertfordshire. This was the same school that grandson Richard would attend years later.

While at Berkhamsted, Roger married Elizabeth Monoxe, daughter of Richard Monoxe, a London salt trader, and his wife Sicely. The wedding took place in the parish of Berkhamsted, St. Peter's Church, on July 15, 1554. Their first two sons, named John and Edward respectively, were born there, the second surviving only two months. Roger moved his family in 1561 to the tiny village of Astwood, meaning "eastern wood," an estate he inherited from his father in Buckinshire, just a few miles west of Bedford.

Richard's father, Edward, was born soon after the move to Astwood. Although he was raised a gentleman, Edward would apparently live in genteel poverty most of his adult life. The family moved about a great deal, sometimes as a result of financial problems, sometimes to avoid the legal ramifications of being a debtor. Probably any property of value belonging to his father Roger had gone to Edward's older brother, John, when his will was read in 1593.

Richard Norwood was the second child and only son of the four children of Edward and his wife, Sybil Mathew, of Towcester. Soon after their marriage they moved to the village of Stevenage, Hertfordshire. Richard was just three years old when his grandfather died.

Richard's formal education began at the age of five or six, when he joined his older sister, Elizabeth, in attending a "dames school" near Cannix, kept by a Mrs. Langton and her daughter. There he was instilled with a deep religious interest that would remain with him all of his life. After two years of gaining a solid foundation of the basics, he joined the classrooms of several "uninteresting schoolmasters," who made no impression on him whatsoever, and he soon "lost all interest in learning." Furthermore, he became discouraged by the fact that he had a speech impediment that seemed to hamper his progress and acceptance by other young learners, who often tended to tease him incessantly. The speech impediment remained problematic for several years thereafter, though it was slight and he eventually overcame the embarrassing psychological and social impacts.

Edward Norwood decided to move his family from Stevenage to Berkhamsted. Once again, he was having financial problems with his farm and decided to go where Richard could attend, what he considered, a more rigorous school. Richard looked back upon this move in later years as pretty much an act of God, for which he was eternally thankful. He was about ten when the family relocated and, quite surprisingly, Richard took to the new school, founded in 1541 by John Incent, Dean of St Paul's Cathedral, like a duck takes to water. Quickly, he became one of the brightest students there in, excelling in Latin and Greek, and earning the commendation of his master, Thomas Hunt:

> "Until ten years of age I lived with them at Stevenage, being taught to read (and I think) entered in writing and my accidence. Afterwards I lived with them at Berkhampstead till twelve years of age, where was a grammar school, a free school, where I went through the Latin Grammar and other books appertaining, and entered into the Greek."[7]

Unfortunately, however, before Richard turned thirteen, his father came upon hard times once again and moved the family. "At what time my parents went from thence to Shutlanger and from thence to Stony Stratford." The elder Norwood's financial difficulties were not unique, for thousands of men all across England seemed to be continually migrating from one village to the next. The major causes included not only an increasing population, but the rising rents and food prices, as well as the gradual collapse of the textile industry. The result was that migrants desperate for ways to keep body and soul together trekked long distances, and (were) "overshadowed by the tramping curse of necessity."[8]

To add insult to injury, Richard's father could no longer afford to even pay for his childrens' education, due to "much decaying in his estate." Initially, Thomas Hunt had decided to keep young Richard enrolled in the Berkhamsted school, at least for an additional month while he tried to secure a patron who would agree to support the bright youngster's continued education in exchange for a future apprenticeship. The patron that he had in mind, however, opted to choose another youngster to support, who happened to be a very close friend of Richard's named Adolphus Speed. It is interesting to note that Adolphus' father, perhaps thankful for his son's unforeseen opportunity, included Norwood's map of Bermuda in one of his books on world geography many years later.

Discouraged, Richard came to a sort of crossroads in his young life, torn between education, a mariner's life, and a newly discovered talent. His personal writings described his feelings:

> "At Stratford when I was near fifteen years of age, being drawn in by other young men of the town, I acted a woman's part in a stage play. I was so much affected with that practice that had not the Lord prevented it I should have chosen it before any other course of life…I think that acting a part in a play, the reading of playbooks and other such books…and the vain conceits which they begat in me was the principal thing that alienated my heart from the word of God which afterwards grew to that height that scarce any book seemed more contemptible to me than the word of God…"[9]

The day that young Richard was forced to depart from the Berkhamsted School would be remembered as one of the unhappiest of his entire life. Not only did it end his formal education, but it placed a major roadblock in his aspirations to attend the university of his choice–or any university at all–for he failed to earn any type of scholarship. Undaunted, Richard's learning did not stop, however, for he would spend the next ten years getting as much practical experience as humanly possible. Somehow, he became a self-educated expert in a number of the same subjects he would have pursued at the university. Had Richard actually graduated from some institution of higher education, however, it is probable that Bermuda and America would never have had the benefit of his contributions to its early development and the history of diving.

At the age of fifteen, Richard was apprenticed with a London fishmonger, "who also dealt in sea-cows…a stern man." The job was quite demanding and he disliked the work, but he became extremely intrigued with what the friends of the fishmonger told him about maritime affairs, navigation and foreign lands:

> "I was so much affected that I was most earnestly bent both to understand the art which seemed to me to reach [as it] were to heaven, and to see the World…"[10]

Before Richard was even seventeen years old, the fishmonger's family had come down with the plague, and the teenager was also stricken with the illness. As soon as he recovered, he found a chance to get an apprenticeship with a sea captain sailing back and forth between London and Newcastle. He had taken along a math textbook of his father's and was so interested with it that he completed all the work in just three weeks. After suffering an injury, he tried to leave the apprenticeship service of his master, and was thrown in jail for failure to complete his apprenticeship contract. Luckily, another skipper wanted his services and bailed him out of jail.

After a very brief sojourn as a soldier in Holland, much of the next year, 1609, was spent traveling by land and by sea to the Germany, Belgium and Italy. He sometimes accepted handouts and slept in barns, receiving the "bulk of his support from English Catholic outposts." Still, he was having his late teenage adventure, even traveling to see Mt. Aetna and Naples. Still down and out, Richard reached the point where he was penniless, just like his father had always seemed. Feeling befriended by a group of Roman Catholic priests, he considered seriously converting to the Roman Catholic faith. Upon his return to the fatherland, however, a Church of England clergyman, whom he later referred to as "the wily fiend," drew him back to Anglican Calvinist beliefs, where he remained a staunch church member for the next few years.

In August of 1610, twenty-year-old Richard sailed on a number of occasions to the eastern shores of the Mediterranean and back. To help pass his free time during these voyages he was able to borrow a great many books on mathematics. Often, in fact, he opted to forfeit his shore leave in order make more time to study and learn. He tells in his *Journal* how, while forced to lay over for three weeks at Yarmouth, he went through Robert Record's treatise on arithmetic, *The Ground of Arts*. So involved was he in studying mathematics that he almost forgot to eat and actually caught "a spice of the scurvy." During the following years, Norwood would make several voyages to the Mediterranean and, on his first trip, was fortunate to find a fellow passenger with an extensive mathematical library, among which was Leonard Digges's *Pantometria*. On following trips Norwood himself took along mathematical books, including Euclid's *Elements* and Clavius' *Algebra*. As a result, he had mastered algebra, geometry, and trigonometry by the age of twenty. In March of 1612, he purchased his freedom, being charged "only forty pence for the privilege" and enabling him to pick and choose what he would do next.

Richard next joined a piracy expedition as master-mate sailing out of Limehouse, working occasionally as tutor in navigation. The ship was scheduled to go to Persia via the Cape of Good Hope. Initially named the "Cape of Storms" by Portuguese navigator, Bartolomeu Dias, it was situated at the convergence of the warm Mozambique-Agulhas current from the Indian Ocean and the cool Benguela current from Antarctic waters. Before departing, another ship that was part of the expedition was scheduled to join them at Lymington.

But something happened at the Lymington River port that provided Richard the opportunity to show what a good diver and problem solver he had learned to be, leading to his first appointment by the Virginia Company for similar work in Bermuda. One of the cannons being loaded on this other ship slipped from its sling and fell deep into the water. The gun was completely covered with silt, making it almost invisible. Richard volunteered to retrieve it and, in doing so, devised a makeshift diving bell out of a large, wooden hogshead. Most likely, he had simply used the knowledge he had gained from the works of Cornelius Jacobszoon Drebbel and John Dee, both highly regarded in such undersea endeavors. Placing the contraption upside-down over his head, he was lowered slowly down by ropes. Within minutes he had located the silt-covered gun, attached cables to its sides, and had it hauled back up to the surface. To those in charge of the expedition, Richard was a "God-send," who had saved them a great deal of time and money.

Historical records indicate that the planned expedition, which had hoped to establish direct trade with Persia, never got underway. It was canceled when one of the principal shareholders, Prince Henry, son of King James I, died unexpectedly on November 6, 1612. The change in plans was quite fortuitous for young Richard, who otherwise would likely have missed his life-changing opportunity to sail to Bermuda with a group known as the Bermuda Adventurers:

> "And then a plantation having a little before begun in the Bermudas...the Company that were adventurers for that place having heard of me and how I had gone under water at Lymington, etc. and being informed also that there was great store of pearls in Summer Islands and that the best could not otherwise be recovered but by diving, they sent for me and agreed with me to go thither, promising me a large part of whatsoever should by such means be recovered by myself or others..."[11]

Richard Norwood made his way back to London, having now been away from home for seven years. Having been nothing more than an apprentice, he admitted that he had "never...received wages." He spent the months leading up to his departure to the Isles of Somers in a partnership with a well-known math teacher named John Goodwin. The partnership lasted four or five months, until Goodwin married, and it had proven to be a strong friendship for Richard. He continued teaching for another four months, until he received an offer from the Virginia Company to make good use of his diving bell as a Bermuda pearl diver. It was an offer that the adventurous Norwood could not refuse.

Meanwhile, during his months in London as a teacher, the lure of stage plays proved irresistible. In fact, his autobiography tells us that he "frequented" the Fortune Theater, going "often to stage plays wherewith I was as it were bewitched in affection and never satiated." The creative side must have taken over for a time, for he even "began to make a play and had written a good part of it." That autobiography, misleadingly entitled *The Journal*, was actually written years later, in 1640, long after he had become a devout Puritan. It was written around "catalogues" of sins and divine mercies organized shortly after his "conversion" in 1616, with his stint of attending plays quite prominent among his stated sins:

> "It happened after some time that I fell out with the players at the Fortune (which was the house I frequented) about a seat which they would not admit me to have, whereupon out of anger, and as it were to do them a despite, I came there no more that I remember."[12]

It is believed by historians that Richard probably had few, if any, intellectual equals among his contemporaries. He had already distinguished himself as a mariner, navigator, and diver and would later prove his genius as a mathematician, textbook writer, schoolmaster and historian, as well as surveyor and mapmaker. He had many other interests, too, such as nature and religion and would one day write a journal of his early life. Its detail and clarity would prove invaluable for historians. The original document, passed down through generations of his descendants, is now the prized possession of the Bermuda Archives.

The summer before Richard arrived on the islands, the Virginia Company sold full title to the islands to a group of investors. They were anxious to have a precise survey made so that the land could be equally divided among shareholders. Departing for Bermuda in early November of 1613, Norwood suffered the choppy waters for seven grueling weeks:

> "It was Christmas...when they reached Bermuda, but disappointment awaited them both in the size and quality of the pearls found and in the insufficient supply of food. Fortunately for Norwood, Governor Moore took very favourably to him and his hunger was frequently appeased by his dining with the Governor. This did not make him any the less anxious to return to England and he eagerly awaited the arrival of the next ship. On this, a Company known as The Bermuda Adventurers had sent a Mr. Berkeley for the purpose of making a survey of the island. This was not carried out because of a great plague of rats that had spread from a few that had escaped from a Spanish grain ship, causing Mr. Berkeley to return to England."[13]

The refusal of Berkeley to remain in Bermuda was a lucky break for Richard. Since his pearl-diving job was now non-existent, he was delighted when the governor appointed him to do the survey. Yet, while he prepared to conduct his business in an attempt to earn an adequate living for his family, he and a number of other Bermuda colonists suffered the debilitating effects of a slow starvation:

> "Being destitute of foode [sic], many dyed [sic], and we all became very feeble and weake [sic], whereof some being so, would not; others could not stirre [sic] abroad to seeke [sic] relief, but died in their houses: such as went abroad were subject, through weaknesse [sic], to be suddenly sur-

prised with a disease we called the Feages, which was neither paine [sic] nor sicknesse [sic], but as it were the highest degree of weaknesse [sic]; depriving us of power and abilitie [sic] for the execution of any bodilie [sic] exercise, whether it were working, walking, or what else."[14]

In search of food for himself and his family, Norwood realized that desperate measures would be needed. "To carry out this gigantic task, Richard cut down a tree and hollowed it out to form a boat. He then went in search of food, which he found in the form of palmetto berries. Having found a source to satisfy his hunger he made his first journey of the coastline of the islands early in 1614." The exploratory portion of the job, which included the coastlines of more than one hundred islands, was both tedious and time consuming.

As Norwood was in the midst of making his initial survey of all island coastlines, the charter for Bermuda was issued in June of 1615. King James I had authorized the Somers Island Company to "establish all manner of orders, laws, directions, instructions, forms and ceremonies of government and magistracy fit and necessary for…the inhabitants there."[15]

In May of 1616, the first resident Somers Company Governor, Daniel Tucker, a former Jamestown settler, was appointed in Bermuda. In Norwood's eyes, Tucker's three-year term would prove to be of mixed success. Almost immediately, he made himself extremely unpopular by instituting the same disastrous martial law and compulsory work regimes he had experienced in Virginia. The settlers were further incensed when he used public labor and timber to construct a handsome, extravagant mansion for himself.

Yet, with Norwood as his chief surveyor, life in Bermuda would soon be permanently transformed. The new governor assigned had given him the task of dividing the land into eight "tribes"–Devonshire, Hamilton, Paget, Pembroke, Sandys, Smith's, Southampton and Warwick–later known as parishes, with each named for one of the wealthy adventurers living there. Individual tribes were then further subdivided into four hundred 25-acre plots of land known as "shares." St. George's and St. David's islands, as well as a small eastern portion, would remain unallocated "general" land. The overall result was that Bermuda shifted from a common corporate venture to a more public-private partnership, one in which investors became individually responsible for cultivating land given to them. In effect, the Norwood survey created the concept of private property.

Merchant and shipbuilding families living throughout the colony of Bermuda now began to construct wharves, storehouses, and workshops near their homes. Each "share" designated by Norwood's survey had at least one, after sometimes two, water access points in order to accommodate local boat travel. Bermudians quickly adapted their water frontage into staging points, where their personal sloops could load, unload, be refitted, and be repaired. Over time, waterside hamlets were established, evolving into substantial commercial ports. They included Flatt's Inlet, as well as the protected shores of Bailey's Bay, Salt Kettle, Ely's Harbor, Crow Lane, Shelly Bay, and Mangrove Bay.

Norwood and his assistant, Charles Caldicott, had accomplished the work with amazing accuracy and skill despite the crudeness of their instruments. Yet, as they vigorously surveyed each nook and cranny of Bermuda, Richard noted that settlers began to clear and farm shares as quickly as he laid them out. In fact, a few overly eager planters had even proceeded to do so prior to his arrival. Overall, his work rendered "an unsettled and confused chaos...[into] a convenient disposition, forme and order to become indeed a plantation."[16]

Norwood also noted a vital shift in attitude among Bermudian settlers as his survey was completed. Prior to 1615, these emigrants "had noe [sic] heart to build or plant" on company land. Yet, now settlers "built for themselves and families not tents or cabins, but more substantial houses," and they "planted not onlie [sic] such things as would yeeld [sic] them their fruits in a yeare [sic], or half a year, but all such too as would afford them profit after certain years"[17]

Upon his return to England in 1617, Richard gathered his data together, checked and double-checked his calculations, drew the final draft of his map and supervised the printing of it in London. It was published in 1622, the same year that, at age 32, he married Rachel, daughter of Francis Boughton of Sandwich, County Kent. The map that he devised would remain in use through the centuries with only minor corrections. No copy of this map is now known to exist, but in 1624 and 1625, Samuel Purchas reprinted the Newbery version. Norwood's work in 1614 through 1617 was only the beginning, for his future influence on both Bermudan and American history would continue.

Meanwhile, on April 30, 1621, Virginia Company officials decided to send Norwood, now respected as an experienced surveyor, to the Virginia colony to lay out particular (or privately sponsored) plantations. On May 21, 1621, Company officials noted that Norwood had been highly recommended by Captain William Tucker for his expertise, and stated that he had expressed an interest in going to Virginia. Plans were made to meet with Norwood to discuss how he would be compensated.

On April 8, 1623, Richard wrote to inform his father that he had arrived in Virginia on April 1 aboard the *Margaret and John*, which had met up with the *Abigail*. Norwood further stated that he was half-starved when he landed, and that he found that many people living there were terribly ill:

> "It was the first of Aprill [sic] before we came to Virginia, and we were halfe [sic] starved for want of Victualls [sic]: for we were kept with stinking Beane [sic] and water: one portion of bread and a quart of peace porridge was the allowance for 5 men a day, wch [sic] caused 9 or 10 of our Passengers to leave the shipp [sic] and stay in the West Indies..."[18]

By April 24, 1623, things had grown so bad for Norwood and some of his fellow passengers on the *Margaret and John* that they sent a petition to the governor, complaining about the terrible shipboard conditions they had been forced to endure on the voyage to Virginia.

By then, Norwood had purchased a share in the Virginia Company, and records indicate that he had submitted an application for patented lands in Virginia on the 7th of May. Similar patents were approved for a number of people, enabling each to "transport 100 persons" to Virginia; Norwood was 64th on the list. But it does not appear that he remained there for an extended period. He may have made several return visits to Bermuda, and even Virginia, but according to his own statements he was, for some years before 1630 and after, a resident in London. Records indicate that he lived near Tower Hill, where he continued to be employed as a teacher of mathematics. He also spent time writing books, and occasionally doing surveys for various estates.

Richard and Rachel Norwood would have four children, all of which were born in England during the 1620s. Andrew, their oldest son, was born about 1623, and Matthew followed two years later. Next, they would have two daughters, with Elizabeth being born in about 1627, and Anne about 1628. As near as can be determined, there is no record of Richard pursuing any diving adventures during this decade, though the idea was always on his mind.

During his years in London, Richard wrote several books, which became very popular. The first of these was *Trigonometrie or the Doctrine of Triangles*, published in 1631 by W. Jones and Company, which was destined to have seventeen editions and reprints over a period of fifty-five years. Essentially, it was intended essentially as a navigational aid to seamen. In it, Norwood explained the common logarithms, the trigonometrical functions, the spherical triangles, and their applications to the problems confronting the navigator. He posed practical problems of increasing complexity; his explanations were clear; and he enabled the navigator to determine his course with the aid of a plane or Mercator chart and the logarithmic and trigonometric formulas. He emphasized great circle navigation by giving the formulas involved and thus facilitated the, calculations. In his *The Seasman's Practice* (1637), he set out a great circle course between the Lizard (the southernmost point in Great Britain) and Bermuda.

It was also during that year that John Speed's *A Prospect of and the Most Famous Parts of the World* was published containing Richard's 1622 map of the Bermuda Islands. On the back of it was Norwood's "Description of the Islands," in which he offered a detailed description of Sir George Somers' shipwreck and a history of the islands for the next ten years. In keeping with his great interest in, and knowledge of, botany and zoology, Norwood also gave details of the configuration of the islands, the vegetation, soil, climate, native birds and fish, and discussed whales, turtles, prickly pears and a great many insects.

On April 2, 1632, Richard Norwood was "granted special" patents by King Charles I for "special means to dive into the sea and other deep waters, there to discover, and thence by an engine to raise or bring up such goods as are lost or caste away by the shipwreck." This contraption was, in essence, a large, open-ended wine cask, weighted down at its open end, which was inverted and lowered into the water, thus trapping breathable air in its closed end. With his fourteen-year license, Norwood became the first to patent an idea relative to submarine exploration.

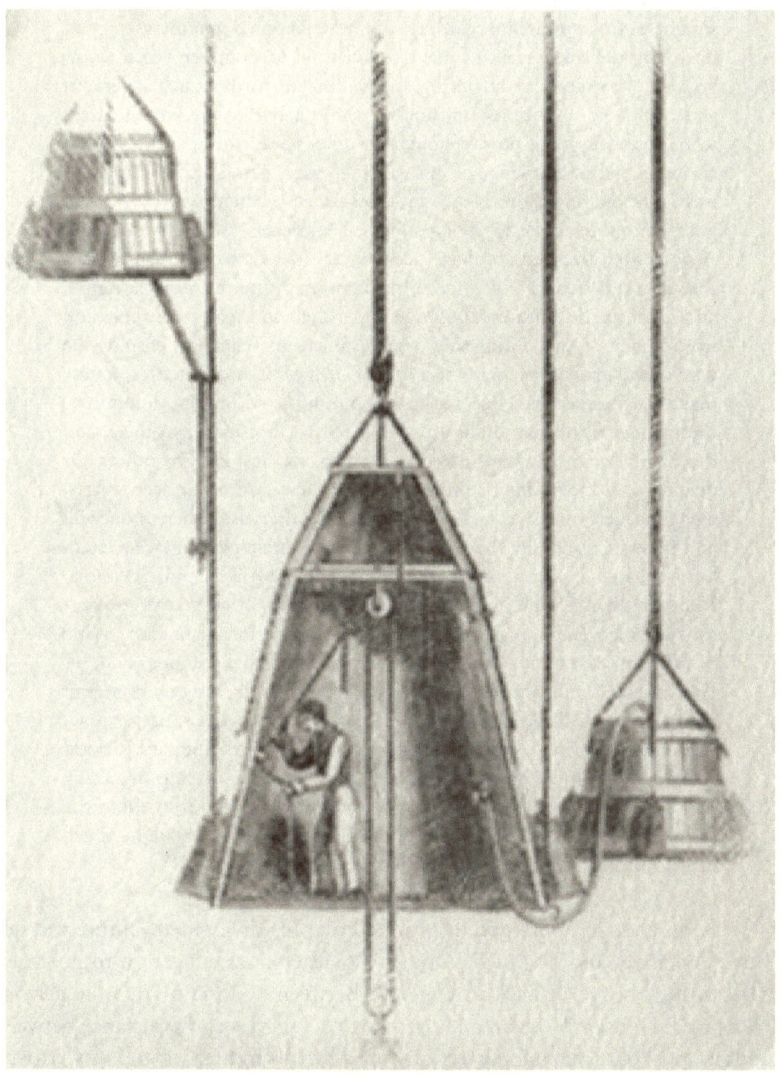

Sketch of Norwood's *Bermuda Tub*

Soon widely referred to as the *Bermuda Tub*, the invention was detailed in *Treaties and Conventions, Letters, and the Journal of Public of any kind by the King of England*. Translated from Latin, it read in part:

> "Whereas our well-beloved subject, Richard Norwood, hath informed us, that he at his great charge (expense) and by his industry and indeavor,

hath found out a special means to dive into the sea or other deep waters, there to discover, and thence by an engine to raise or bring up such goods as are left or cast away by shipwracke or otherwise, and hath humbly besought us to be pleased, according to our accustomed goodness, to grant unto him the sole benefit of the said invention for fourteen years. Know ye, that we graciously favouring and willing to further such ingenious and profitable inventions, and finding the practice of the same tendeth to the publick good, do therefore, and other good causes and considerations hereunto moveing, of our especial grace, certain knowledge and meer motion, for us, our Heires and Successors, by their patents, give and grant unto the said Richard Norwood, his Executors, Administrators and Assigns, full, free and absolute Licence, Libertie, Power, and Authoritie, that the said Richard Norwood, his Executors, Administrators, Assignes, and Deputies Substitutes, and none other, shall and may at all times and from tyme to tyme, during the terme of fourteene years next ensuing the date of this patent, at their and every of their wills and pleasures, frame, make use, exercise, practice, set up and put in use within our dominions, the manner of diveing by him newly invented, not used by others, and the Engine or Instruments invented by him, and not used by others, for diveing, and for raising or bringing out of the sea or other deep waters, any goods left or cast away by shipwracke or otherwise; whereof our will and pleasure is, and by theire patents by our more especial grace, certain knowledge and mere motion; wee doe, for us, our heirs and successors, straightly charge, inhibit and prohibit all and every other person and persons whatsoever, of what Estate, Degree or Condition he or they or any of them be, that none of them other than the said Richard Norwood, his Executors, Administrators, Substitutes, Workmen or Assigns, or any of them, do or shall during the said term of fourteene yeares, use or practice, directly or indirectly, the instrument or engine by the said Richard Norwood invented, and not used by anie other, for diveing or raising or bringing out of the sea or other waters, anie such goods, without the Licence, Consent and Agreement of the said Richard Norwood, his Executors, Administrators or Assigns or some or one of them..."[19]

Soon enough, Norwood determined that his diving bell venture was not all that lucrative, and he opted to put his mathematics education to good use by becoming a surveyor back in England. Between 1633 and 1635, he personally measured–partly by chain and partly by pacing–the entire distance between London and York, making corrections for all the windings of the way, as well as for the ascents and descents. He also, from observations of the sun's altitude, computed the difference of latitude of the two places and, while doing so, calculated with a high degree of accuracy the length of a degree of the meridian. His result was only 600 yards too great, making it the nearest approximation that had then been made in England up to that time. Isaac Newton noted Norwood's work in his *Principia Mathematica*, first published on July 5, 1687.

In 1635 Richard's father died at the Charterhouse Hospital in London, where he was listed as "a pensioner." It is uncertain whether or not this indicated that he was nearly penniless, but the elder Norwood must have had at minimum a small bit of wealth, because Richard acted as executor of his father's estate, which wasw divided up among the family.

Over the course of the next couple of years, while continuing to dream about salvaging treasure and weaponry from the ocean floor, Norwood became incensed with the views of some of the bishops whose innovations he opposed. When the Bermuda Company advertised for a schoolmaster, Richard applied for and got the job. His reasons for wishing to leave England were complex, and required a great deal of personal soul searching:

> "...the times were dangerous in England, by reason of many innovations in Religion brought in by the Bishops (the Lord be blessed for that happy reformation wch we heare and hope of) and at that time I was in danger my selfe to have bene called in question, wch occasioned me to move the honorable Company for this place."[20]

In 1637 Norwood's book, *The Seaman's Practice*, was published by G. Hurlock, and it quickly became one of his best known works, thought of as the standard book on practical navigation. Ii would enjoy continual publication for more than three-quarters of a century and, in 1700 the seventeenth edition was printed, twenty-five years after Norwood's death.

The most remarkable thing about this book was the fact that, until it came out, navigators had a very imperfect concept of the length of a degree or a nautical mile. Norwood's work to determine these concepts began by his observing the meridian altitude of the sun at a point near the Tower of London in June of 1633. He repeated this procedure two years later in the middle of the city of York. He used a sextant with a five foot radius and, by carefully measuring distances between his observation points and making corrections to allow for deviations, he came up with a figure only two-thirds of one percent off what is recognized today as the correct distances discovered through modern scientific measurement. This was a brilliant deduction on Norwood's part, considering the crudity of his instruments and the fact that no-one else had attempted to do the measurements so vital in navigation.

Toward the end of 1637, the Norwood family set sail for their return to Bermuda. At that time, his children ranged in age from nine to fourteen and, if all shared their parent's cabin, it would have been fairly crowded. Rachel was opposed to spending weeks at sea under those conditions and urged Richard to make other arrangements. He managed to get the two boys put into the Reverend Nathaniel White's cabin. Sharing his space with those boys did not please the clergyman at all, and it led to bad feelings between the two men that lasted the rest of their lives. For years to come White waged a bitter vendetta against Richard, mainly on religious issues. In reality, he simply did not like the man.

Richard's third book, *Fortification or Architecture Military: Unfolding the Principall Mysteries Thereof, in the Resolution of Sundry Questions and Problems*, came out in 1639, and in it he detailed his surveying work in the Netherlands. Even in the seventeenth century, plagiarism was a widespread problem for writers. Norwood was continually annoyed in finding that a great many of the proofs of his writing were stolen by literary pirates while still in the hands of the printer, and there was absolutely nothing he could do about it.

Richard's first Bermuda school is believed to have been in Devonshire Parish, although the exact location is unknown. Originally named "Cavendish Tribe" and later "Devonshire Tribe," it was named for William Cavendish, 1st Earl of Devonshire. Unfortunately, Richard's arrival in the islands was at a time when extremists in politics and religion were in power. Even though he was a moderate in both areas, he was constantly under attack by both the "conservatists" and the radicals.

Furthermore, Richard noted that, after years of hardship during which settlers had endured not only political instability with a rotating governor, but there was still what he referred to as the "wonderfull [sic] annoyance of silly rats" to deal with. In fact, upon his arrival he had found that the entire colony had been, quite literally, "besieged by rats that devoured crops and swam across channels from island to island" like miniature free divers. Still, the good news was that it was now "possible for those settlers who had reached Bermuda in the 1610s and 1620s to plant crops and live modestly."

As the months went by, Reverend Nathaniel White began to openly criticize Richard's anti-Laudian religious beliefs, and he publicly denounced him as a failure as a schoolmaster, saying that none of Richard's pupils could conjugate a verb or decline a noun. White also claimed that Norwood should stick to teaching and not air his views on religion, about which White inferred that Richard knew nothing.

Meanwhile, Norwood complained to the Bermuda Company about the "new practices" that White had brought into the islands. He singled out White's "universal Catechizing," which he found deeply offensive, as well as his "adaptation of new forms of worship," for which Richard could find no scriptural foundation. Yet, most of all, he objected to White's weekly "Loblolly Feasts," promoted as religious revivals.

Even without White's constant harassment, Richard found that the education of young boys was no easy task. Enrollment fluctuated constantly, and attendance was not regular, particularly at shipping or planting time. He felt that he had to work as hard as if he had twice the number of steady students.

In spite of the criticism levied by White, Bermudians benefited greatly from having Richard Norwood as their schoolmaster, He was an internationally acknowledged expert in theoretical navigation, and his *Seaman's Practice* was among the most widely read books on the subject. He was able to blend practical experience gained from sailing aboard English ships in his youth with extensive mathematical knowledge. He could demonstrate his ingenious method of using the *Bermuda Tub* nearly anywhere. And, his advice on ways to keep a reckoning at sea using astronomical observations and mathematical calculations, as well as his directions for charting coastlines, were particularly insightful.

Norwood graduated no less than twenty-three scholars in 1642, his first year of teaching, and it is estimated that he taught between fifteen and twenty boys annually over the course of his three decades of teaching. Hence, as Bermuda's leading schoolmaster, he taught theoretical navigation to more than 500 youngsters between 1642 and the early 1670s. He also shared with them his one-of-a-kind extensive library and chart collection, letting them practice their skills with his personal cross-staffs, quadrants, and other surveying, navigational, and scientific instruments. Overall, it is believed that a great many ship captains had "been instructed by Ould Norwood, who lived here many years."[21]

Some good fortune, as well as a bit of reinforcement for his hopes of one day striking it rich beneath the surface of the ocean, came Richard's way in 1645 when he was given £150 as his share of a privateering venture, during which he "confiscated" booty from the Spanish Main with his *Bermuda Tub*. In those days this was considered a real windfall.

In 1644, another person entered Richard's life that was as much an irritant to him as Reverend White. John Witter, whom Richard had no use for, secretly courted and married Richard's daughter, Elizabeth, then only seventeen years old. Described as "an Irishman and a Surgeon," he made the arrangement legal when "she was invited to a wedding about eight miles from her home and arranged for her own marriage to take place at that time." Records further indicate that "Capt. Wood gave her in marriage and the ceremony was performed by the Reader of the Tribe." She had always been forbidden to even spend any time alone with Witter, and the marriage was a real emotional and devastating blow to her father.

Richard's troubles only began there, as Witter and Norwood were constantly engaged in verbal confrontations with one another. Witter kept bringing Richard up on frequent charges based on various pretexts. Each time, Richard was forced to travel all the way from Devonshire to the court in St. Georges to answer these bogus and annoying charges. It was not easy to travel back and forth, and it cost Richard much time away from his teaching duties. Although Norwood would always claim that Witter treated his daughter abominably, the marriage lasted and Elizabeth bore John seven children. All were mentioned in their grandfather's will.

Anne, Richard's younger daughter, also made a marriage disappointing to her father, for she married Richard Bowen, a man that both of her parents considered "socially beneath them." Whether this was the reason for Anne's apparent estrangement from Richard is not clear, but Anne was bequeathed a mere £5 and part of her mother's wardrobe when Richard died, whereas, Elizabeth and Andrew Norwood received the major share of the estate.

Since Bermuda was so very far away from England, the islanders did not learn of King Charles I's execution until March of 1649, two months after the king's death. Almost immediately the Bermuda Company, which had evolved from being Royalist in sentiment until 1647 to supporting Cromwell from then on, ordered that Governor Turner by removed from office and that he be replaced by a commission of three men. Those men were to have been William Wilkinson, Richard Norwood, and Captain Thomas Leacraft. But the latter had died before the appointment was official.

Wilkinson, who was a strong leader of the Independents in the church, was a councilor of Sandy's Tribe strongly opposed by the more moderate or conservative churchmen. Norwood refused to serve without him and when it reached a stalemate, Turner was asked to serve a little longer. He did not wish to, but agreed, only to be ejected two months later for being, what Bermudians described, as "too moderate."

Richard continued to find himself in the middle of violent confrontations between Reverend White's extreme Independents and the conservatives of the church party. In 1649 those who opposed Norwood managed to have a grand inquest held regarding his school. The group reported it to be unsatisfactory, and the lifelong educator was asked to resign. And so he did.

Just about the time that Richard resigned as schoolmaster, another problem began to plague him. By 1651, witch-hunting had reached Bermuda, just as it had in England and the mainland of America. In May of that year, a woman named Jeane Gardiner, the wife of Ralph Gardiner, and was put on trial by Captain Josias Forster, Governor, accused of having "affected a woman with magic." Furthermore, she was accused of having "threatened she would cramp" Tomasin, a mulatto woman, who later claimed to have been struck blind and dumb for two hours. Gardiner was brought to trial, and she was subjected to the ordeal of water. After being "throwne [sic] twice in the sea…she did swyme [sic] like a corke [sic] and could not sinke [sic]." She was judged guilty of witchcraft and executed on Monday, May 26, 1651. During that trial, Anne Bowen, Richard's daughter was mentioned as a suspect and tried with her, but for lack of evidence, escaped any severe penalties. Richard was so concerned at the very real possibility that he might become a suspect that he hid his mathematical manuscripts on Boaz Island.

By the early 1650s, the practice of wrecking—or salvaging—goods from sunken vessels was as old as the Bermuda settlement itself, dating back to the ship that Norwood had arrived on in 1614. During his earliest years on the island, Richard had shown planters and fisherman how to use his diving bell to salvage old Spanish and Portuguese wrecks as they were discovered, and how to methodically "work over" new vessels that "came to grief on the island's reefs."

In fact, in nearly every instance of shallow-water marine salvage work, Bermudians employed Richard Norwood's primitive diving bell arrangement. This was to become the ubiquitous polymath's third historical contribution to early Bermuda and American history, along with surveying the one hundred islands that comprised Bermuda and educating two generations of mariners.

In the mid-1650s, Norwood and his trained "free divers" and mariners had fully incorporated his improved diving bell apparatus to expand their salvaging operations into Bahamian and Turks and Caicos waters, where a number of Spanish wrecks lay scattered across shallow reefs. One crew, in fact, recovered "nearly twenty-six hundred pounds of silver plate and coin" in 1657 from a Spanish vessel that had sunk near Eleuthera Island. By the early 1680s, five years after Norwood's death, Bermudian wreckers and Norwood's "Bermuda Tub" diving bell design would be well known throughout the entire Caribbean.

Meanwhile, the two men that followed Richard as head schoolmaster didn't last long. The first, Percival Goulding, Jr., hired "in May 1655, took possession of the School in Devon Tribe, and the Library comprising about sixty-seven works of solid learning and divinity in folio, 52 volumes in quarto, and about 28 in Octavo of which not a trace exists, the remembrance has vanished like the books themselves."[22]

Though it may well have been Richard who had confiscated the school's library, Goulding still proved to be completely incompetent. Richard was even asked to return, but feeling insulted, he refused. The next man appointed was the Reverend Jonathan Burr, who undertook to "teach, writing, ciphering and Latin for nothing, and navigation for a fee." Burr, too, was also considered a failure and, in 1661, at the age of 71, Richard was prevailed upon to return to his school. The Company had made an inquiry just prior to his rehiring, and had informed the governors that "a learned schoolmaster was one of the greatest needs of the colony," since at least one-third of the men could not even write their own names, and those who had had some instruction were educated only to the most rudimentary level. Mysteriously, the missing library reappeared with Richard's return, though he stayed on as head schoolmaster for just a few more years. Finding it more and more difficult to walk as he grew older, he retired to manage his fifty-acre estate in Pembroke, purchased in 1657. There he would decide to build his own school, and started teaching once again.

After a number of land disputes began cropping up, the council engaged Norwood to resurvey the islands for a fee of £50. That was in 1662, and he finished the work a year later when he was seventy-three years old. His book of this survey was entitled the *Domesday Book of Bermuda*, and it settled many questions and furnished the basis for all future legislation on property assessments. Amazingly, the publication described every property and listed the owner or tenant of every acre in Bermuda in 1663.

Richard Norwood died on November 3, 1675, while residing in Bermuda, just three months after his 85th birthday. His wife, Rachel, had died a few years earlier. His will was dated April 1, 1674, and its inventory was dated January 25, 1676. In part, it offered the following details:

> "...Imprimis I make constitute and ordaine my well beloved sonne Andrew Norwood living at Barbadoes, together with my loving daughter Elizabeth Witter living in Summer Islands, myne Executors of this my

Last Will and Testament, I doe give and bequeath unto my said sonne & daughter my dwelling house, schoole house, store house, and all other edifices or outhouses to the same belonging, and my two shares of land in Pembroke Tribe, wch I bought of Mr Forester, whereupon I have built the said house; moreover I bequeath unto my sonne and daughter aforesaid foure of my Bond Servants, viz Negro Tom and his wife called Besse & their two negroe sonnes, the one called Dick and the other Tom..."[23]

The family bible went to his daughter, Elizabeth, along with "Crookes Booke of Annatomy." His other daughter, Ann Bowen, received five pounds sterling, as well as "that part of my wifes wearing apparel wch fell to her by lott." James Witter, brother of his daughter's husband, received "what other Booke or Bookes of mine not exceeding the value of three pounds that he shall desire... and the hive of beese [sic]." Other than his properties, books, and other accumulated wealth mentioned in this early part of his will, Richard's estate also included "five black adults, one old Indian woman, one Indian negrow [sic] girle [sic] called Nann, and four other black children."[24]

Within the extensive *Domesday Book of Bermuda*, Richard had drawn a new map, and left copies of the original and the book to his daughter, Elizabeth, as a source of income. She was to charge an inspection fee of 6d each time they were consulted, a fee that helped to pad the family income for years thereafter.

Although Anne Norwood was almost ignored in her father's will, it was one of her descendants who discovered Richard's hand-written journal in New York City more than 250 years later. Luckily, this distant relative realized its historical value, and it was preserved in the Bermuda Archives. Unfortunately, another of Richard's descendants, two hundred years after his death, found some of his mathematical manuscripts and, fearing that her children might be "infected by the contaminating stuff," burned them.

Only Richard's daughters remained in Bermuda and, thus, the Norwood name stopped there. Son Matthew was a senior captain serving the Bermuda Company and had emigrated. He would publish two books of his own, *The Seaman's Companion* (1671) and *Norwood's System of Navigation* (1685). He had apparently inherited his father's intelligence and talent, because the books were popular and in use for many years. It was Andrew who followed in his father's surveying footsteps, laying out two towns on Staten Island, New York. He raised his family in New England, and later lived part of the time, in Barbados.

Richard Norwood's proud home and school house have long since disappeared from the Bermuda landscape. And, though there is no known grave commemorating America's first inventor of a diving vessel, the Norwood House on Bailey's Bay, as the present house is known, is said to be one of the loveliest on the islands.

Portrait of Edward Bendall

AMERICAN SUBMARINERS: PRE-CIVIL WAR

- 2 -
Edward Bendall: *Diving Tub*

"If the diving-bell had by ingenious or philosophical men been earlier invented, I doubt that no instance of its successful application can be found before this."[1]

Since historians first began to record important events, it has occurred to those who are considered the very best at writing to blend both public happenings with private, lesser-known lives. To readers, the connection between historical fact and biography leads to the creation of human interest, which has become the most sought after of all readings. Such is the case with the remembrance of American underwater inventors and explorers, whose lives must come from somewhere obscure and travel somewhere enticing, keeping in mind that the existence of one individual must be set against the backdrop of a sense of the times and the places in which he lived and died. In a sense, we must hope to tell his story in such a way that the reader feels as if he or she knew him both personally and intimately.

America–or New England, for that matter–in its earliest days was a place that was so small that we might readily know the names of almost every man, woman, and child who lived there. In its heyday, Boston, in particular, presented just such an opportunity of knowledge. Though a modern day historian would find it literally impossible to track a specific individual's comings and goings–say, what time he crawled out of bed each morning and what his favorite meal might have been–it is possible to gain a very real sense of what type of person he was. In fact, this intimate personal acquaintance is far more valuable to history than anything else. Hence, what follows is an attempt to get to know one man named Edward Bendall, Jr. as personally as is historically possible.

Today, those who stroll through downtown Boston eastward along Freedom Trail will soon find themselves looking up at the historical Faneuil Hall, which has stood near the waterfront since its construction in 1742. Beyond here is the Marketplace, a veritable collection of old and new world charms coming together to form an exquisite array of shopping options. Beyond, still walking eastward, are the wharves, forming the edge of famous Boston Harbor.

In 1640, just ten years after the city was founded, a pedestrian would have had a totally different visual experience. Back then, the sea seemed more immediate, more menacing, more ominous. The shoreline stretched away endlessly in both directions: on the left it followed the leading pathway of North Street; and on the right it ran gallantly along, keeping pace with what is now Merchant's Row. Down close to the seashore stretched the first coastal highway, along which stood the homes of numerous worthy residents who failed to go down in history with any sort of notoriety, fortune, or fame.

To the left along North Street lived a shoemaker named George Burden, and in front of his house stood a stone wharf, or stepping-off place, for people coming ashore. George had been born around 1611 in England, and was likely–though we cannot prove it–that "Georg Burden," son of William Burden, carpenter, who was baptized at All Saints Church, Newcastle upon Tyne, Northumberland on April 22, 1610; that "Georg Burden," whose father, William, had married Christabell, who everyone simply referred to as "Bell"; and that "George Burden," who married Anne Soulby at St. Nicholas Church, Newcastle upon Tyne, both of whom came to Boston, lived there, worked there, and died there. It was beyond that stepping-off place, at the end of the lengthy pier, where the folks of Boston could often see that "Georg Burden," shoemaker, standing in front of a large wooden kettle holding water, wherein he moistened and softened his leather almost every afternoon beneath the summer sun.

Further along, toward what would later become North Washington Street, stood the home of Valentine Hill. Whether or not he owned a part of the wharf cannot be determined by historical record, although he and others were granted a large tract near the "Dock" to develop wharves, with the privilege of collecting for tonnage. Furthermore, we do know is that he was born near London about 1603, that he became a popular "mercer," and that he was ordained a deacon "by ye laying on of ye hands of ye presbytery" on May 7, 1640. Eventually, he would take his entire family to New Hampshire, "due to his declining finances."

Nearby stood the house of Isaac Grosse, brewer of fine ales, who was also a proud "husbandman," or small landowner. Beyond that lived George Foxcroft, whose modest house was sandwiched between the cove on the north and the fledging enterprise of a butcher to the south. Born to Richard Foxcroft and Alice Hodson Foxcroft in Cambridge, England, his name appeared in a list of members of the Fishmongers Company as "merchant of Coleman Street," indicating also that he was a parishioner of John Davenport's church. In 1644, permission was granted by the Court to "take planks, etc., from Foxcroft's estate to pay a debt due by his agent."

In the opposite direction stood the home of Robert Nash, butcher, who slaughtered his animals on the street in front of his home, gutting and cleaning them for all his neighbors to see and hear. There, from iron hooks, he would hang their bloody carcasses to dry. Needless to say, Robert was not the most well liked of Boston gents. Further south in the same direction stood the home of Edward Bendall, dock owner who, like most of the others, had come here aboard John Winthrop's fleet. Though history would falsely refer to him as "Jr.," he was actually at least the third in succession with the same first name.

Bendall, while still a young man, would have an active life as ship chandler and broker, Collector of Customs, commissioner for the sale of prize ships, proprietor of a ferry boat to Noddle Island and to ships at anchor in the harbor, a tireless real estate speculator, contractor for transporting ordinance and all sorts of supplies to Castle Island, and for raising sunken ships. Yet, who was this this man, and why has he been largely forgotten by American history?

The Bendall family had a long and, sometimes, lawless ancestry. In ancient Anglo-Saxon England, the earliest clan with that surname resided in Salop County (Shropshire), where the name was taken from the parish of Benthall, situated near the towns of Brosley and Much Wenlock. Historically, Benthall had long been associated with an ancient family of the same name, who had resided there since the twelfth century. The country manor estate co-existed with the Parish, and stood proudly just a few miles south of the historic Ironbridge Gorge, formed by the River Severn thousands of years earlier.

In 1166, King Henry II established trial by jury, known as a "grand assize," or traveling criminal courts to be conducted around England and Wales. Comprised of twelve knights who would hear and decide each case, this arrangement initiated a means of settling all disputes, and provided a means for itinerant justices to set up county courts. The Assizes of October 1272, held in Shropshire, not only disclosed something of the lawlessness of the period within the Benthall family, but offered insight into why a specific branch migrated to, and settled in, faraway Suffolk County:

> "The Jurors of the Wenlock Liberty reported how Roger de Eyton and Petronilla de Eyton his daughter had previously accused, in the County Court, Robert de Benethall, Hugh his brother, and John de Kantreyn of rape and robbery, and Phillip de Benethall of aiding and abetting. The case, it appears, had been carried from the County Court to the hearing of the King, but had not yet been settled."[2]

From the proceedings that were conducted, it appears that on June 9, 1269, Petronilla appeared in court in an effort to help prosecute the four defendants for rape, and for "breaking the King's Peace." The sheriff was ordered to arrest them all and keep them in safe custody until October 6, when they were to appear before the King's Court. On that day, Petronilla again appeared in support of the charges of rape and robbery. The Sheriff, however, reported that Robert de Benethall and John de Kantreyn could not be found. He was again ordered by the court to "outlaw them," display wanted posters throughout the region, have them arrested, and "have their bodies in court" on November 18.

During the six-week interim, however, the parties involved in the crime–including the victim's father and missing defendants–"subsequently accorded among themselves," thus somehow settling the dispute. It is likely that bribes were offered and money changed hands. Yet, since the King's Peace had already been violated, the Jurors were compelled to follow through with the prosecution and court hearing. Eventually, they acquitted all defendants of the robbery charge, but found them all guilty of a forcible attack on Roger de Eyton's house at Broseley, and the abduction and forcible rape of his daughter. Hugh de Benthall and John de Kantreyn were immediately arrested, retained in custody, and placed in lockup. Meanwhile, Philip de Benethall had temporarily escaped, but did not get far:

> "At the same Assizes, the Stottesden Jurors reported that Roger Fitz Denys of Burwardesle, having accused Philip Mouner of Benthall of robbery, and being in pursuit of him, the latter turned to defend himself on the bridge of Brug, and was killed in the conflict which ensued."[3]

Robert de Benethall, however, was nowhere to be found and, according to the assize records, was never prosecuted fully for his crimes. Time passed, as a "Robert Benthall" suddenly appeared in the Kersey area of Suffolk County, nearly 200 miles to the southeast.

Meanwhile, generations of Benethalls–which evolved into "Benthall"– continued to live and thrive in the Shropshire region. The present-day Benthall Manor, in fact, was constructed by William Benthall in 1535, and stood on the very site of an earlier 12th century medieval manor house where the three family members were accused of their horrendous robbery and rape. The carvings in the entryway, drawing room, and smaller sitting room, displayed the arms of William Benthall himself, impaling those of Agnes, daughter of Thomas Cassey, of Whitefield, Gloucestershire, and then the wife of brother Lawrence Benthall.

Edmund de Benethall, grandfather of William, had been next to the Prior, the fourth person admitted as a burgess of the Borough of Wenlock, on the grant of the incorporating 8th Charter of Edward VI. The son, grandson, and great-grandson of William served the office of Bailiff in the years 1554, 1593, and 1637 respectively. Though the family name was destined to become extinct in Shropshire, it mysteriously reappeared in Devon and Dorset by younger branches. Eventually, one family branch had taken root in faraway southeast England. The name itself, with spelling variations of Bendell, Bendal, Bendel, Bendle, and Bentall, was first recorded in Suffolk County, when it was written in the *Domesday Book*.

Edward Bendall I of Suffolk County–or at least the first one known–was the son of Thomas Bendall. Born in the spring of 1566, he was baptized on April 15 at the Anglican church of St. Mary the Virgin, in the ancient wool and cloth market town of Hadleigh Heath. His father died and was laid to rest in the church cemetery when Edward was less than two years old, and his early years of education were spent at nearby Bury St. Edmunds Grammar School. As a young lad, he apprenticed as a carpenter and builder, learning the trades of woodworking and "pargeting" (plastering).

The name "Hadleigh Heath" was believed to have originated from the Norse "Haethlega," fittingly referring to "a heath-covered place," though the area was inhabited much further back in time. The remains of a 1st century Roman villa can still be found to the east of the present town, and there is evidence of a fifth century pagan Saxon occupation in the area. However., it was in the ninth century that the town came to prominence as one of the Viking King Guthrum's royal towns, and it is believed by some that he died in Hadleigh and was buried in St. Mary's Churchyard. In the tenth century, Hadleigh was given by another Viking ruler to the priory of Canterbury, and from then on the town was an "ecclesiastical peculiar" under direct control of the Archbishop Of Canterbury rather than the Bishop of the local Diocese.

By the time the Normans completed the Doomsday Survey in 1086, East Anglia was the most thriving region, and Suffolk was the most densely populated. In 1252, the grant of a weekly Monday market and an annual fair had been secured from King Henry III by the Lord of Toppesfield. A descendant later bequeathed these rights to twenty-four trustees in 1438, and it became the "Hadleigh Market Feoffment."

In the late fifteenth century, one of the most notable Rectors of Hadleigh Heath, Archdeacon Pykenham, planned the construction of a huge brick palace on a site between the church and the river. The Bendall family, as well as other skilled craftsmen, were solicited for the immense project, which was estimated to take several years. The fifty-two-foot "Deanery Tower" was the initial result. Completed in 1495, it was intended to be the grand entrance gateway to his new palace. Unfortunately, the Archdeacon died in 1497, and his dream never reached fruition.

The town of Hadleigh continued to thrive throughout the fifteenth and sixteenth centuries, still relying heavily upon the cloth industry. The acting government of the community–albeit without formal powers–lay in the hands of the "Chief Inhabitants," comprised mainly of the most wealthy and influential Trustees of Hadleighs' two major "feoffments" (charities administering land and property of great value).

Over the past 300 years or so, the town had grown to be extremely wealthy as a result of that steadfast wool and cloth industries. This had led to the building of the spectacular parish church on the site of the old wooden Saxon church between the thirteenth and fifteenth centuries, the Guildhall and dozens of other fine dwelling houses. A great number of these houses had been constructed by Bendall ancestors, particularly Edward I, as well as by his sons, who had remained in Hadley and carried on the family trade. Like father, like son, the second Edward Bendall II–our Edward Bendell III's father–had been born about 1585, in the same small village and, he too, apprenticed in the trade of carpentry. He married first Sarah in 1605 at the church of St. Clement Danes, Strand (later renamed Middlesex) County.

But, the best of times were long past for the residents of Hadleigh. The heavy felted broadcloth upon which much of the wealth of Hadleigh Heath–and indeed many local economies–had been built was fading out of fashion, being overtaken in popularity by the "new draperies" fostered by Dutch immigrants who settled in the larger towns of Colchester and Norwich. Failing to adapt, by the end of the sixteenth century the cloth industry was in serious decline.

After giving birth to a daughter, Grace, in 1605, in nearby Groton, Edward and Sarah had a son. Edward, named after his father and grandfather, was baptized on October 18, 1607, in Kersey, also in Suffolk County. The three townships where the majority of Bendall family members had resided for generations–Hadleigh, Groton, and Kersey–were within walking distance of one another, less than seven miles total distance apart. Younger brother, William, would be born in the summer of 1611 and, like his older siblings, would by baptized at Kersey's St. Mary Church, near the shrine of Our Lady of Kersey. Sadly, illness got the better of Edward's younger brother, who died and was buried in this same churchyard on October 12, 1619, when he was just eight years old.

By the time that young Edward Bendall had grown to adulthood, he had become weary of the Church of England. He young wife, Anne Bendall–whose given name, we do not know–agreed to sail with him to America with a group organized by neighbor and fellow Puritan, John Winthrop. Born in nearby Edwardston, Suffolk, on the January 12, 1588, John was the son of Adam Winthrop of Groton Manor, and Anne Browne Winthrop. In December of 1602, he matriculated at Trinity College, Cambridge, but he did not graduate. The years after his brief course at the university were devoted to the practice of law, in which he achieved considerable success, being appointed, about 1623, an attorney in the Court of Wards and Liveries, and also being engaged in the drafting of parliamentary bills. Though his residence was at Groton Manor, much of his time was spent in London. Meanwhile he passed through the deep spiritual experiences characteristic of Puritanism, and made wide acquaintance among the leaders of the Puritan party. On August 26, 1629, he joined in the "Cambridge Agreement," by which he, and his associates, including the Bendalls, pledged themselves to remove to New England.

In late March of 1630, Winthrop and his fellow Puritans–Edward and Anne Bendall among them–boarded one of eleven ships in Southampton harbor and prepared to set sail, planning their first stop at the Isle of Wight off the English coast:

> "Riding at the Cowes, near the Isle of Wight, in the *Arbella*, the ship three hundred and fifty tons whereof Capt. Peter Milbourne was master, being manned with fifty-two seamen and twenty-eight pieces of ordnance... upon conference it was agreed that (in regard it was uncertain when the rest of the fleet would be ready) these four ships should consort together; the *Arbella* to be Admiral, the *Talbot* Vice-Admiral, the *Ambrose* Rear Admiral, and the *Jewell* a Captain; and accordingly articles of consortship were drawn between the said captains and masters.; whereupon Mr. Cradock took leave of us, and our captains gave him a farewell with four or five shot...About ten of the clock we weighed anchor and set sail."[4]

They were all scheduled to depart for the New World on March 29, but unfavorable winds and strong seas would keep them anchored until April 8.

Winthrop, his three sons, and eight servants traveled aboard the flagship *Arbella*, a 350-ton ship formerly known as the *Eagle*, but now renamed for the wife of Isaac Johnson, the highest-born passenger of the fleet. Records strongly indicate that Edward and Anne Bendall were also aboard the *Arbella*, though history did is not absolute. Winthrop was deeply saddened to leave his own wife behind, but they agreed to think of each other every Monday and Friday between five and six each afternoon during communion. In addition to the Winthrop party, the *Arbella* carried twenty-five of the most important passengers, seventy tradesmen, fifty-two seamen and fifteen officers.

The remainder of the 700-person expedition was spread among the ten other ships, with the *Talbot*, *Ambrose*, and *Mayflower*–not the *Mayflower* of Pilgrim fame, but another ship of the same name–carrying most of the passengers. Although they carried some passengers, the other ships–*Jewel*, *Charles*, *Trial*, *Success*, *Whale*, *Hopewell*, and *William and Francis*–transported mostly livestock; 240 cows and sixty horses, as well as freight for the new settlement in New England. The first four sailed ahead of the others, and the remaining seven followed about three weeks behind in early May.

On the very first day of the expedition, the four ships came upon what they thought might be a band of pirate ships. They hurriedly dismantled cabins to make room for the cannons, armed the men with muskets, and threw overboard most of the ships' bed mats, as the items were liable to catch fire. After much prayer and preparation, the small flotilla stood ready to do battle. Luckily, the suspicious ships were friendly, and the passengers would later regret getting rid of their sleeping materials so hastily. Two days later, the southernmost tip of Cornwall dropped behind them, and they had left England entirely behind. A week out of port, the group lost sight of the *Talbot* in one of the many storms the fleet faced during the crossing. They would not see it again until July 20, when it straggled into the New World twenty days after the rest of the fleet.

In his journal, John Winthrop divulged that Lady Arbella and the other "gentlewomen" dined in the great cabin, where they would also sleep. Besides Lady Arbella, there were wives of George Phillips, William Coddington, Thomas Dudley, Simon Bradstreet, and Increase Nowell, and two daughters of Richard Saltonstall. We know these two daughters were attended by a maid, since it was reported the maid "fell down at the grating by the cook room, but the carpenter's man, who occasioned her fall unwittingly, caught hold of her with incredible nimbleness, and saved her; otherwise she had fallen into the hold."[5]

For Edward and Ann Bendall, conditions on board the ship were horrible, although they were certainly no worse off than any other passenger. In fact, all eleven ships were veterans of the Mediterranean wine trade, and thus they were specially chalked and drier than most ships below decks. However, they could hardly be called comfortable. Above decks, the forecastle deck (on the forward part of the ship) housed the ship's crew, and the poop deck (at the rear) housed the officers. Most of the space in between was used for storage. The men made jury-rigged cabins for the women and children and hung hammocks from the ceiling for themselves. There was no ventilation below decks, no heat, no light at night, and only the most basic sanitary and cooking facilities. Since fresh water could not be kept clean and potable during long sea voyages, the ships carried beer for passengers to drink during the crossing. The *Arbella* alone carried forty-two "tuns," equal to about 10,000 gallons of ale. For food, they consumed salt pork.

Throughout much of the passage, the Bendalls huddled below decks and tried to weather the storms. Winthrop occasionally convinced the seasick passengers to come out on deck and get a breath of fresh air. Winthrop offers a novel cure for seasickness:

> "In the afternoon less wind, and our people began to grow well again. Our children and others, that were sick and lay groaning in the cabins, we fetched out, and having stretched a rope from the steerage to the mainmast, we made them stand, some on one side and some on the other, and sway it up and down till they were warm, and by this means they soon grew well and merry."[6]

He also found that a splash of salt spray often cheered up the passengers. Storms blew up with regularity and cost the expedition precious resources, in material and in morale. One storm alone killed nearly seventy cows. Two servants aboard the *Ambrose* died in the crossing and a crewman on the *Jewel* perished as well.

By no means were all the passengers on the *Arbella* saints. In fact, one group of crewmembers grew far too rowdy for the pious passengers:

> "This day our captain told me, that our landmen were very nasty and slovenly, and that the gun deck, where they lodged, was so beastly and noisome with their victuals and beastliness, as would endanger the health of the ship. Hereupon after prayer, we took order, and appointed four men to see to it, and to keep that room clean for three days, and then four others should succeed them, and so forth on."[7]

On June 6, 1630, after sixty days at sea, the expedition sighted the jagged coast of America at Cape Sable. Two days later, the group first laid eyes on New England, spotting Mount Desert along the modern-day Maine coastline. On June 11, the ships cruised by the Isles of Shoals, where they could see a cluster of fishing boats working the seas, and they worked their way down to Cape Ann before anchoring for the night. The next morning, the *Arbella* sailed between Bakers Island and Little Island and into the mouth of Salem harbor.

As their ship laid anchor off Plum Cove, the weary passengers walked out on deck, gaining their first glimpse of the shacks and hovels of Salem, a colony that at the time represented the finest New England had to offer in the way of civilization. After leaving their families and country behind, following two months at sea being tossed about by North Atlantic storms and eating food scraps, they could finally see that the hardest part of the trip lay behind them. For Edward and Anne Bendall, the lengthy journey was now complete, though precisely where they would live had yet to be settled.

By mid-afternoon on June 12, 1630, Governor John Endicott had come on board and had escorted the ladies and gentlemen to the shore:

> "We supped with a good venison pasty and good beer and at night we returned to our ship but some of the women stayed behind. In the meantime most of our people went on shore, which lay very near us, and gathered stores of fine strawberries..."[8]

Though the first batch of the nearly 400 new settlers were relieved to finally be in New England, the settlement that greeted them could hardly have been described as "welcoming." Another 600 settlers would arrive in the next three weeks, and there was much work to be done before the area would be hospitable. Only about 300 settlers lived in the community and on its surrounding land when the Bendalls arrived, all on a few hundred cleared acres around Salem. They lived in shacks and wigwams, based on the Indian design. Beyond the clearings lay uncharted forest, home only to Indians and wild animals. The last winter had claimed more than eighty of the settlers, and they had few encouraging words for the new arrivals. The French and Spanish colonies nearby would occasionally attack the English settlements, and Indians were a constant threat. All in all, the situation looked grim for John Winthrop's Puritans.

The new colonists opted to leave Salem, climbing back on board their ships and making their way twenty miles down the coast to Boston Harbor. Some went to the Dorchester or the Charlestown area, while others traveled a bit further south to Rocksbury. According to records, one of the most pressing problems the settlers faced in their first months was finding a source of drinking water. The English had been raised to only trust spring water, and Charlestown's single spring could not provide for the entire colony. After Isaac Johnson and his wife, Lady Arbella, died of disease possibly related to the water, Winthrop began to look for alternatives. He found an even better location across the harbor on the Boston peninsula. William Blackstone had emigrated there from England several years prior and had lived ever since on an expansive estate. Winthrop and most of Charlestown moved across to the new peninsula in early October, even bringing with them the frame house Winthrop had begun constructing.

Starvation became an increasingly drastic concern for the colonists as the winter began. By the end of November, Winthrop alone had buried seven of his own servants. While some of the settlers remained resolute, others in the party were less so. Winter began in earnest the day before Christmas, when a giant storm struck the colony. Frostbite exacted a heavy price from the colonists, and several huts were lost that winter after the fires inside grew too large and caught the thatched roofs. In Winthrop's journal, he relates the story of six colonists marooned on Cape Cod in December. Only two survived. The entire colony might have been lost that first winter except that the *Lyon* arrived in February bearing with it a hold full of food–most importantly, it brought lemon juice to ward off scurvy. When the ship prepared to leave again, it carried with it eighty passengers who hoped to leave New England behind forever. The Bendalls remained behind, determined to survive.

And survive they did, although more than 200 of their friends and neighbors perished during that first winter. An equal number fled the colony when the winter ended. Over the second summer, while Winthrop laid out plans for a 600-acre farm and a large stone house on the Mystic River, Edward Bendall had begun the construction of the family home near the waterfront. As the colony expanded, it came to need a variety of businesses to support it. While many of the colonists found they could make a good living as "carpenters, joiners, bricklayers, sawers, and thatchers," others grew and sold crops to the newly arriving immigrants. A few took to fishing, with Edward among them. Though no record has been left behind, he evidently became intimately familiar with the harbor, which determined his course in life.

In researching diaries, personal histories, court records, and land deeds, we find a glimpse into Edward Bendall's life. First and foremost, he and his wife were devout members of the First Church of Boston, as evidenced by one historical record in which the name of "Jane Scarlett widdowe ye mother of our brother Edward Bendall" can be found, as well as that of Robert Turner, "our brother Edward Bendall's man-servant."

Created in 1630 when the settlers on the *Arbella* arrived in Charlestown, Massachusetts, John Wilson was installed as the first minister of the church. Born into a prominent English family from Sudbury in Suffolk County, situated some ten miles west of the Bendall family estate, Wilson's father was the chaplain to the Archbishop of Canterbury, and thus held a high position in the Anglican Church. As with many other Puritan divines, he had come to New England with his friend, John Winthrop, in 1630. During the winter of 1630-31, Edward was admitted to his church as member #77. In 1632, Edward joined other members of his congregation in the construction of a meetinghouse across the Charles River near what would become State Street in Boston, and Wilson was officially installed as minister there.

In a scant few notes left behind by William Pynchon, acting colony clerk, we find the following passage, allowing us to understrand the direction of Edward Bendall's chosen career:

> "Paid out of the Common Treasury Oct 9, 1632: paid Edward Bendall for lighterage of ordinance..."[9]

AMERICAN SUBMARINERS: PRE-CIVIL WAR

And further records state:

> "...paid to Edward Bendall for lighterage of ordinance and 280 bullets out of the Griffen, being 4 tides..."[10]

Although wharves had to be built for unloading purposes, the lack of natural dock facilities was balanced by the advantages of the Boston harbor, where five hundred ships could easily ride at anchor. Apparently, by his second year in New England, Edward had settled upon the business of "lighterage," or the process of transferring cargo by means of a lighter vessel, thus reducing a heavily laden vessel's draft in order to enter shallow waters. His business property consisted of a stone house and warehouse adjoining it, standing just west of Change Avenue, and facing Faneuil Hall Square. The dock was then used as a cove for shipping, and was the center of Boston's mercantile business.

Edward Bendall was allowed to take the "Freeman's Oath" on May 14, 1634, which gave him full citizenship in the Massachusetts colony:

> "I, Edward Bendall, being by God's providence, an Inhabitant, and Freeman, within the Jurisdiction of this Commonwealth; do freely acknowledge myself to be subject to the Government thereof: And therefore do here swear by the great and dreadful Name of the Ever-living God, that I will be true and faithful to the same, and will accordingly yield assistance and support there unto, with my person and estate, as in equity I am bound; and will also truly endeavor to maintain and preserve all the liberties and privileges thereof, submitting myself to the wholesome Laws and Orders made and established by the same. And further, that I will not plot or practice any evil against it, or consent to any that shall so do; but will timely discover and reveal the same to lawful Authority now here established, for the speedy preventing thereof. Moreover, I do solemnly bind myself in the sight of God, that when I shall be called to give my voice touching any such matter of this State, in which Freemen are to deal, I will give my vote and suffrage as I shall judge in mine own conscience may best conduce and tend to the public weal of the body, So help me God in the Lord Jesus Christ."[11]

Under the first Massachusetts charter, only freemen had the right to hold public office or vote in town meetings. Though he was never called upon by his fellow citizens to serve as Governor, Deputy to the General Court, or Captain, Edward did not shirk any duty that he was asked to perform. On March 21, 1636, Boston officials ordered "all fences belonging to the cornfield shall be made sufficient, and they shall be overseen and looked to." He and John Button, local miller, were chosen to oversee the fences in the mill field surrounding Button's windmill on Copp's Hill. The following year, on October 16, 1637, "Ralph Hudson and Edward Bendall are chosen Constables for this towne for this next yeare."[12]

By late 1636, Edward and Anne Bendall's deep devotion to their long-held religious had shifted from the teachings of John Wilson and the First Church of Boston to those of another church leader, John Cotton. Serving as a minister at St. Botolph's, a parish church that was part of the Church of England in Boston, Lincolnshire, Cotton had spent the better part of the past twenty years attempting to do away with the ceremony and vestments associated with the established Anglican Church and preach in a simpler, more consensual manner. While many English ministers had been removed from their pulpits for their Puritan practices, Cotton thrived because of supportive aldermen, lenient bishops, and his very conciliatory and gentle demeanor. By 1632, however, the Anglican Church had greatly increased its pressure on the non-conforming clergy, and William Laud, Bishop of London, summoned Cotton to the Court of High Commission. Cotton immediately knew for whom the bell tolled and went into hiding. In 1633, he and his wife embarked for Boston, in the company of Thomas Hooker, Edmund Quincy, and John Haynes–all soon to become prominent leaders.

Cotton was highly sought as a minister in Massachusetts and was quickly installed as the second pastor of the Boston church, sharing the ministry with John Wilson. However, Wilson had a much different approach to the pulpit and, within six months, the two church leaders were at odds. The disagreement grew, becoming known as the Antinomian Controversy–or the "Free Grace" Controversy, lasting from 1635 to 1638. The most notable of the free grace advocates, often called "antinomians," was the charismatic Anne Hutchinson.

After Cotton had been compelled to emigrate in 1633, William and Anne Hutchinson, two of his Boston, Lincolnshire, congregation, followed a year later with their eleven children. The Hutchinsons soon became well established in the growing settlement of Boston. Anne was a midwife, and very helpful to those needing her assistance, as well as forthcoming with her personal religious understandings. Soon she was preaching to women at her house on a weekly basis, providing commentary on recent sermons. These meetings became so popular that she began offering meetings for men as well. Pregnant, and in need of her midwifery services, Anne Bendall had introduced her husband to the outspoken woman.

When Edward and Anne Bendall had given birth to their first child, a son, on July 5, 1635, they opted to name him Freegrace. Apparently, it was now their strong conviction that, under the gospel dispensation of grace, moral law was of no use or obligation because faith alone was needed for salvation. In simpler terms, the Bendall's point of view was that everyone received eternal life the moment they believed in Jesus Christ as their personal Savior and Lord. Sadly, Freegrace had been born frail and sickly, and he died within days of his birth. Certainly, the Bendall family faith was being tested to the hilt.

By the time that spring had arrived in 1636, Anne found herself with child once again. On September 30 of that year, a second son was born, which they again named Freegrace. By then, Edward had become somewhat outspoken about his criticisms of the teachings of the First Church of Boston that he, along with a number of other followers of Anne Hutchinson and her brother-in-law, John Wheelright, found themselves at a religious crossroads. Ultimately, many of these individuals would be "disarmed," meaning they were ordered to turn in all of their weapons to the authorities. This was a serious penalty, because by law adult men were required to carry a weapon to all public meetings and gatherings. Others were "disfranchised," losing their ability to vote, a privilege which came with the status of being a freeman. Still others were "dismissed," or removed, from the church, though allowed to re-establish their membership elsewhere. A few were even "excommunicated," totally disowned by the church, and removed from fellowship with the local body of believers. In a few extreme cases, a few were "banished" and ordered to leave the jurisdiction of the colony. Banished citizens went to two places in New England: south to Rhode Island or north to New Hampshire. At least two colonists went back to England, never to return.

Having attended Anne Hutchinson's Free Grace prayer meetings on the site of the old corner bookstore and signing a petition openly supporting John Wheelright, Edward Bendall was fined forty shillings, disarmed of his weapons, and thrown in prison in 1637. His wife, Anne, convinced him that their future livelihood was in Boston, and that they should not leave the Massachusetts colony. He eventually agreed and recanted his support for Hutchinson and Wheelright, admitting that his punishment was fully deserved. Though he was soon released, it would take him several months to earn the respect and trust of his fellow townspeople once again. Just a few months later, still suffering ridicule from the "disgrace" on Christmas Day, 1637, Anne died of consumption, and Edward was heart-broken.

Colonial Boston did not neglect to recognize that adequate ferry facilities were necessitated by her shallow harbor and lack of bridges. The rolling Charles River separated the Shawmut settlers from the Charlestown people. A mile or two beyond the Charles, on the far side of the Mystic, lay Winnissimet (Chelsea). Inhabited Noddle's Island, completely cut off from the mainland, also stood some distance out in the harbor. By 1631, although the "Great Ferry" was in operation between Boston and Charlestown, additional means of transport were still needed.

By then, Edward's property near the harbor had become known as "Bendall's Dock," and it was from the shore in front of his warehouse that, in December of 1637, he was permitted to run a "ferry boat to Noddle's Island," and to the "ships riding before the town." By the time of Anne's death, he had constructed a house, the first made of brick in Boston, surrounded by a garden on two acres of land. The Bendall estate was situated at the corner of Tremont Row and Tremont Street. It seems that life, despite the loss of his beloved, went on. All total, his business and personal holdings had, by then, consumed about $10,000 of his hard earned money.

By late 1638, Edward had exchanged vows once again, this time with Mary, whose family name has long since been forgotten. On August 18, 1639, the couple gave birth to a daughter, who they named Reform, perhaps referring to the Puritan efforts to change the Anglican Church so that it would resemble "the best reformed churches" on the Continent.

As time passed, Edward's estate and his business dealings, expanded. On January 8, 1638, the Boston Town Records indicate that he was granted thirty-five acres at Muddy River, a series of brooks and ponds that ran through sections of Boston's Emerald Necklace. The property was nestled along the south boundary of Brookline, where the river flowed into the tidal Charles. On March 26, 1639, Richard Parker of Boston, a well-known merchant, sold to Edward one half the "wharf, crane and warehouse lying in Boston," which Parker had purchased the day before from several Boston residents. On May 1 of that same year, Parker leased to Bendall the other half of the wharf, and "one great lighter with its tackling and appurtenances...and advantages that shall be gotten by one servant called Thomas Hedger in and with the said lighter to be employed."[13]

The Bendall's also operated a small farm and orchard on present day Deer Island, and the terms of the lease from the City of Boston indicate why the island is so barren of trees. As part of the agreement, Bendall allowed the inhabitants of the city to "cut wood from the primeval forest...as freely as they wished."

The English merchant ship, *Mary Rose*

By mid-July, 1640, the *Mary Rose*, an English merchant ship trading with the colonies, had berthed in Charlestown harbor. She had arrived with a warlike cargo consisting of large guns and two barrels of gunpowder, all for equipping the fortifications then being constructed. Almost immediately, the crew became notorious for mocking the Puritans for their religious beliefs. Aboard their vessel, they were seen to laugh at, and make fun of, the colonists' ways. On shore, Thursday, July 23, had been set aside as a day of fasting on behalf of English reform, but the captain and crew refused to partake.

Four days later, on July 27, the townspeople looked out across the harbor in horror as the vessel from Bristol exploded, went up in flames, and sank within moments, taking at least sixteen men down with her, including her Captain, ten crewmen, and five visiting businessmen. Governor John Winthrop later wrote about the tragic event:

> "Being the second day of the week, the *Mary Rose*, a ship of Bristol, of about 200 tons, her master one Captain (John) Davis, lying before Charleston, was blown in pieces with her own powder, being 21 barrels; wherein the judgment of God appeared, for the matter and company were many of them profane scoffers at us, and at the ordinances of religion here; so as, our churches keeping a fast for our native country, etc., they kept aboard at their common service, when all the rest of the matters came to our common assemblies; likewise the Lord's day following; and a friend of his going aboard next day and asking him, why he came not on shore to our meetings, his answer was, that he had a family of his own, etc., and they had as good service aboard as we had on shore. Within two hours after this (being about dinner time) the powder took fire (no man knows how) and blew all up, viz., the captain and nine or ten of his men, and some four or five strangers. There was a special providence that there were no more, for many principal men were going aboard at that time, and some were in a boat near the ship, and others were diverted by a sudden shower of rain and others by other occasions. There was one man saved, being carried up in the scuttle, and so let fall in the same into the water, and being taken up by the ferry boat, near dead, he came to himself the next morning, but could not tell anything of the blowing up of the ship, or how he came there. The rest of the dead bodies were after found, much bruised and broken. Some goods were saved, but the whole loss was estimated at 2000 [pounds sterling]. A 20 shilling piece was found sticking in a chip, for there was about 300 [pounds sterling] in money in her, and 15 tons of lead, and 10 pieces of ordinance..."[14]

The "one man saved," who Winthrop wrote about, was Thomas Jones, a tailor, who had gone out to the *Mary Rose* along with Edward Bendall to secure several yards of kersey and baize belonging to one of his customers from the Agaminticus, Maine, region. His goods, and the goods of a number of other area merchants, were believed to be lost forever beneath the harbor's sometimes "treacherous and unforgiving waters." Yet, Jones was fortunate, for the hero who pulled him from the dangerous waters as he was hanging on for dear life to one of the ship's hatchways was none other than Edward Bendall himself.

Knowing the Puritan beliefs of Boston in 1640, we should not be surprised that the majority of citizens considered such calamities devout providence–the manifestation "of the rod of God"–and retribution for past sins and offenses. In fact, in the majority of opinions throughout the colony, the *Mary Rose* was "sunk in a moment" by God's punishment. John Endicott, who had brazenly cut the cross out of an English flag one day as the militia carried it through the streets of Salem, sent this scathing summation of remarks in a letter to Governor John Winthrop shortly after the explosion:

> "Hearing the remarkable stroak [sic] of God's hand upon the shippe [sic] and shippe's [sic] companie [sic] of Bristol, as also of some Atheisticall passages and hellish profanations of the Sabbaths and deridings of the people and ways of God, I thought good to desire a word or two of you of the truth of what you have heard. Such an extraordinary judgement [sic] would be searched into, what God's meaning is in it, both in respect of those whom it concerns were especially in England, as also in regard of ourselves. We have heard of several ungodly carriadges [sic] in that shippe [sic], as first in their way overbound they would constanlie [sic] jeere [sic] at the holie [sic] brethren of New England, and some of the mariners would in a scoff ask when they should come to the holie [sic] Land? After they lay in the harbor Mr. Norrice sent to the shippe [sic] one of our brethren upon business, and hee [sic] heard them say, 'This is one of the holie [sic] brethren,' mochinglie [sic] and disdainfullie [sic]. That when some have been with them aboard to buy necessaries, the shippe [sic] men would usually say to some of them that they could not want any thinge [sic], they were 'full of the Spiritt [sic].' That the last Lord's Day, or the Lord's Day before, there were many drinkings aboard with singings and musicke [sic] in tymes of publicke [sic] exercise. That the last fast the master or captain of the shippe [sic], with most of the companie [sic] would not goe [sic] to the meetings, but read the book of common prayer so often over that one of the companie [sic] said he 'had worn that thread bare,' with many such passages. Now if these or the like be true, as I am persuaded some of them are, I think the truth hereof would be made knowen [sic], by some faithfull [sic] hand in Bristoll or elsewhere, for it is a very remarkable and unusuall [sic] stroake [sic]..."[15]

Thomas Lechford, a Boston lawyer, who was not a friend of–nor a believer in–the steadfast Puritan ways, considered the explosion aboard the *Mary Rose* not so much a "special providence," but simply a horrible accident. Later, he wrote the following letter to a close friend:

> "And now, Worthy Sir, what news can I write you from us, but such as is heavy and sad in every respect? Yesterday being the 27th of July, a tall ship riding at anchor before Charlestowne, that brought hither provisions from Bristoll, called the *Mary Rose*, was (most part) blown up with gunpowder which she had in her for her defence [sic], (and the rest sunke

[sic] down immediately,) through some careless rummaging with candle light in the hold; wherein died a brave mariner Captain Davis, with ten others, seamen, and two or three of the country being on boarde [sic]. Fourteen others of the ship's company being on shore, through the mercy of God escaped; I never heard such a fearful blow: it shook the house wherein I was being a mile off, as an earthquake. A sad and doleful accident, and much laid to heart by me. This was at one o clocke [sic] in the afternoone [sic]. God of his mercy grant that we the living may lay it to heart and repent indeed, lest we likewise perish..."[16]

Almost immediately, the consequences surrounding the sinking of the *Mary Rose* became far less religious and much more mercantile in nature, for not only had she taken lives, but a valuable cargo, down with her. One of the items lost was a sum of gold equal to about $1,500. Ironically, Edward Bendall had taken his lighter boat out to the anchored vessel, tied it to the side, and stepped aboard just a few hours before the explosion. It was that excursion that happened to put him in the right place at the right time to save Thomas Jones' life:

"Edward Bendall of Boston in New England aged about thirty-two years sworne [sic] sayth upon his oath that upon the very day the Ship *Mary Rose* was blowne [sic] up in Charles River this deponent in behalf of Mr. John Oliver of Newberry in New England was going aboarde [sic] the said ship in the morning before the same was blown up to demand and take order to fetch away a certaine [sic] pack of goods sent in the said ship to the said John Oliver and by the way this deponent met with Mr. Danett, one of the merchants of the said ship, coming ashor [sic] and told him this deponent's errand; whereupon Mr. Danett sayd [sic] that if he had knowne [sic] this deponent was to have received it he should have had it before that tyme [sic] and therefore at this time bad this deponent trouble himself no further about it; the said Mr. Danett promising that he would at high water or the next tyde [sic] send the said packe [sic] ashore to this deponent in the long boate [sic] of the said ship..."[17]

Realizing that the was "much damnified" by the sunken *Mary Rose*, the General Court of Massachusetts granted her owners "above a year's time" to unclog the harbor and recover her lost "ordinance, ballast, much lead, and other goods" in whatever way they might contrive. Contracting with a private citizen of Boston to accomplish this seemingly impossible task, the court further recorded that:

"Edward Bendall having order to cleare [sic] the ryver [sic] of it and if he cleare [sic] the harbor, hee [sic] is to have all wch [sic] he can get up; if not he is to have the one halfe [sic] and the country is to have the other halfe [sic]. For the clearing of the harbor he hath liberty till the first of the 8th M, 1642; and he is to give account to the treasurer, from time to time, and to leave the full haulfe [sic], or give good security."[18]

As further incentive, Bendall was given "liberty to make use of any of the cables, and other things belonging to the worke [sic], as he needeth..."[19]

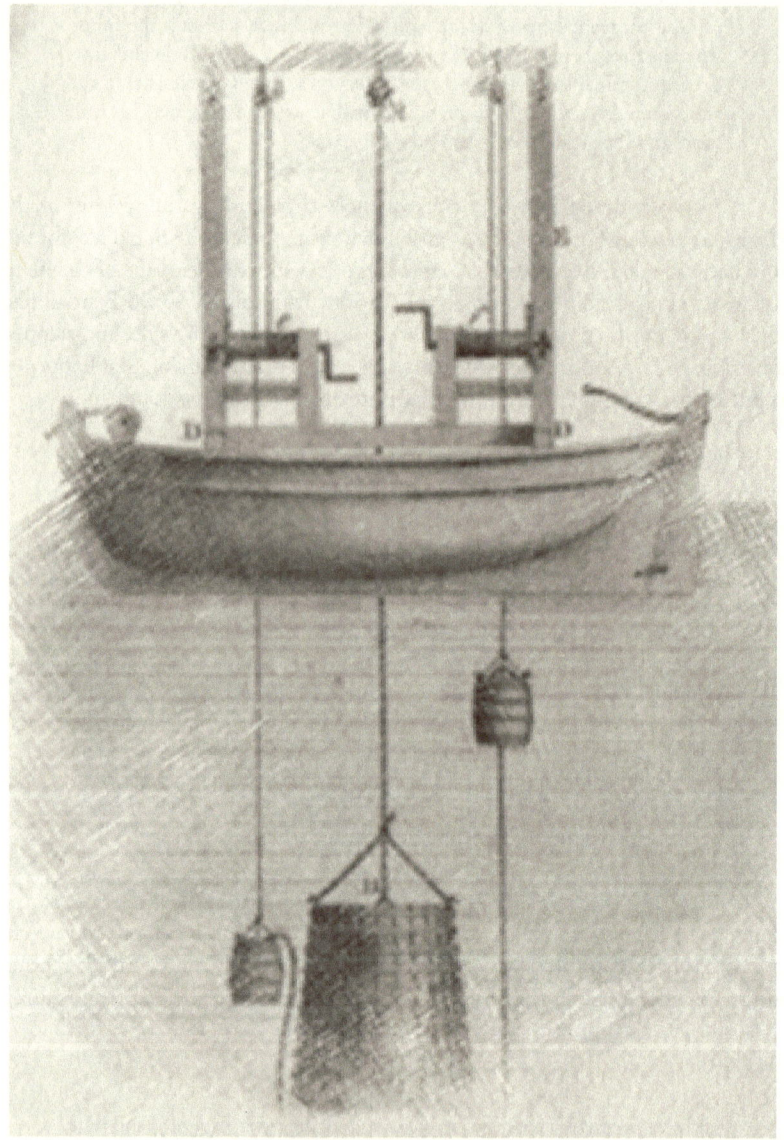

Edward Bendall's *Diving Tub*

Carefully considering the task at hand, Edward Bendall eventually came to the realization that he needed more than mere cables to get the job done. Though portions of the harbor could be as shallow as six feet deep at low tide, the predominant ship channel where the *Mary Rose* had gone down–known later as the "Devil's Back Ledge"–was estimated to be thirty to forty feet deep, and the current was believed to be fairly strong. To tackle the problem, he designed an enormous hogshead diving bell, comprised of "two great tubs, bigger than a butt, very tight, and open at one end, upon which were hanged so many weights as would sink it to the ground (bottom)" of the harbor. This was essentially a large wine cask, capable of holding between "108 to 140 gallons," inverted and weighted around its edges so that it could be lowered into the harbor with air trapped inside. Bendall, working the harbor floor, could enter the tub and breathe for a few minutes, then return to work without having to swim to the surface. Through experimentation, he determined that it would require approximately 600 pounds of lead ballast to submerge his *Diving Tub*. During one of his manned test dives, he discovered the wreckage of the *Mary Rose* resting on rocky terrain, surrounded by a great deal of thick kelp.

Edward Bendall's salvage plan was simple. He would climb aboard his sinkable vessel and, while sitting on a crosspiece within the tub, would be slowly lowered to the bottom. Once near the wreck, he could make fast the "cables and other things" to the ordinance. Next, he would move the ballast and lead into a net or tub, so that they could easily be brought up to the surface and placed aboard his lighter vessel, which would be positioned directly above.

On the appointed day, Bendall removed his clothing, climbed naked inside the *Diving Tub*, sat on a crude bench, and waited as he was lifted over the edge of his lighter and slowly lowered beneath the surface by strong chains. In one hand he held a signaling cord, which he would pull whenever he wished for them to bring him back up. A second cord would be used to signal the crew to move him from place to place diagonally. It was estimated that he had enough oxygen to remain submerged for up to half an hour at a time. When it came time to resurface, a long pole would be thrust into the depths, placed beneath the sunken vessel, and used to ensure that the open end would remain downward. This would maintain trapped, clean oxygen within the *Diving Tub*.

Bendall's exit from his submersible was, perhaps, the most ticklish of all processes. When the tub had been drawn back up so that the open end remained just a little below the surface, an assistant above would knock on the top of the *Diving Tub* to notify the inmate that it was time to escape. If the tub had been drawn completely out of the water with its operator inside, pressure would have caused him to be sucked violently out of the vessel, risking great bodily harm. Instead, when he heard the knock, Bendall dropped from his seat into the water, seized the aforementioned pole, wriggled from beneath the *Diving Tub*, and pulled himself upward to the surface. Likely, this was an exhausting exercise to complete every half-hour or so when his oxygen had been depleted.

As the great cannons were hoisted to the surface, one-by-one, drawn up by the hefty cables, there was a great deal of curiosity among all onlookers. Words whispered among their ranks included legendary conversations about "thirty pounds put down the muzzle of one of these guns." After all weaponry had been brought up safely, they were searched one-by-one and, low and behold, they removed a wad of rope-yarn from one of them that weighed an estimated thirty pounds. Having some difficulty unwrapping the "foul and wet" wad, which had been underwater for more than two years, they tossed it aside, believing the tale of hidden wealth to be nothing more than fiction. Yet, they would soon discover their grave mistake:

> "...and about 8 or 9 days after, coming to try one of the guns, and finding this wad lying there, they thrust it in after the powder, and shot it off into the channel, but perceived part of it to break and fall short, and the rest fell into the middle of the channel. But the next low water there was taken up several pieces of gold and some silver. This was in a place where people pass daily, and never any found there before that time."[20]

Those who found the money refused to hand it over to Edward Bendall, though the diver claimed that it was legally and rightfully his as salvaged cargo, "whereupon, he brought his action (to court), and the money was adjudged to him."

Edward Bendall's salvage expedition proved to be an immense success, for he brought to the surface everything he found, including the sunken ship itself, which was later repaired and placed back into service.

Apparently, life went on for the Bendalls of Boston, though little more was written about the salvage of the *Mary Rose*. In May of 1644, after having given birth to a daughter, Reforme, and two sons, Hopefor and More Mercy, his second wife, Mary, died. At the time, all of Edward's children were still quite young. Freegrace, the oldest, was just seven years of age, and not yet old enough to help his father with the heaviest of chores. His half-sister, Reforme, was four years old, far too young to be left home in the care of Freegrace and her younger siblings. Hopefor, who had been born in October of 1641, was almost three, and his younger brother, More Mercy, was not yet one. Without much choice, their father was forced to search for adequate childcare while he struggled to make a living. Though he petitioned the Massachusetts General Court for permission to utilize a local Indian squaw to mind his children, the request was denied.

Unable to maintain such a large homestead, Edward sold his property on Tremont Row to David Yale in 1645. There, the buyer's son, Elihu, founder of Yale University, was likely born. A later occupant to the house built by Bendall was the great-grandfather of Peggy Shippen, the wife of Benedict Arnold.

Records further indicate that Edward applied for a patent for his innovative *Diving Tub* from the Massachusetts General Court on May 2, 1649, but was duly denied. Apparently, that same year, "he was appointed, by the General Court, collector of customs and registrar of horses intended for exportation." For "every horse so entered" he was to be paid "six pence," and if a ship's captain refused to pay the tax, they would "for such offence forfeit the sume of forty shillings to the informer, & forty shillings to the Treasurer."

By then, Edward had taken a third wife, Jane Gower, the widow of Captain John Gower of London. To the couple were born two more children; Ephraim, a son, in early June of 1648, and Restore, another son, who was christened in Boston on December 30, 1649. The marriage and his growing family was, in all likelihood, what led Edward, his wife, and their children to leave New England and return to London permanently in 1653.

Freegrace Bendall, Edward's eldest, remained behind with his wife, Mary (Lyell). The two of them tragically drowned in a boating mishap on June 6, 1676, while returning from Noddles Island, leaving their twelve young children to be raised by his brother. Meanwhile, Edward's second son, Hopefor, took the orphans back to England and followed in the footsteps of his father, becoming a noteworthy sea captain for the East India Company, a member of the Royal Africa Company, and the Company of Mine Adventurers of England.

At Dursley and the adjoining parish of Cam, the families of Bendall have been numerous for centuries. Just previous to the emigration of Edward to New England there was recorded the marriage of three Edward Bendalls at Cam. Yet, like the man himself, the name of Edward Bendall had disappeared from all Boston records by 1660. The house that he had once owned on the cove was, in late 1653, seized for a debt to Stephen Lynde of London:

> "...Bendall of Boston acknowledged himself indebted to Symon Lynd of Lond. Merch in the summe of one hundred sixty one pounds of lawfull money of England, to be pd unto the sd Symon or his assigned..."[21]

There is some confusion as to exactly when Edward Bendall died and where he was laid to rest. Although some historians mistakenly place his death around 1682, there is clear evidence that it occurred shortly after his return to London. On January 26, 1660, we find a Suffolk County, England, deed of ownership bestowed upon "Jane Bendall, wife of Edward Bendall, deceased, (that) authorizes Capt. Samuel Scarlett as her lawful attorney." Whatever the case, he has been largely forgotten among the annals of American submarine and diving history. Perhaps, a single sentence left behind in Boston's plethora of historical archives is the most fitting epitaph that we can attribute to one man's legacy:

> "The land upon which ye house doth stand was a gift of the Towne to Freegrace Bendall, in consideration of several good services down to the Towne by the sd Bendall's father..."[22]

Robert Willis sketch

- 3 -
Robert Willis: *Willis Diving Bowl*

"For the church was the first thing that was spoiled; then the abbot's lodging, the dormitory and refectory, with the cloister and all the buildings around, within the abbey walls... all things of price were either spoiled, plucked away or defaced to the uttermost... it seemed that every person bent himself to filch and spoil what he could. Nothing was spared but the ox-houses and swincotes and other such houses or offices that stood outside the walls–these had greater favour shown to them than the church itself"[1]

Michael Sherbrook, a priest and rector in Wickersley, witnessed the pillaging first-hand during the dissolution of monasteries, priories, convents, and friaries. When he was a much older man, he wrote about the momentous events of his youth; of the reigning monarch who appropriated their income, disposed of their assets, and separated most of England from Papal authority. Specifically, Sherbrook was referring to the destruction of Roche Abbey, but it might have been Lewes or Fountains, Glastonbury, Tintern or Walsingham, or any of dozens of other holy places. They were all names that continue to haunt religious historians today, much like their ruins haunt the English landscape. These were the monasteries suddenly, and for many, shockingly destroyed by King Henry VIII during the Time of Dissolution, from 1536 to 1541. The destruction was played out with a mix of violence, heroism, sinfulness, political wrangling, and genuine theological disputation. What was lost included immaculate architecture, paintings, treasures, and religious habits of the monasteries themselves, along with historical records of the commoners who lived near them. One of these sacred places was the Benedictine Abbey of Evesham, County Warwickshire, England.

At the time of dissolution, Robert Wyllys was chaplain at the Chapel of All Saints, situated but a short walk from the Abbey of Evesham. Appointed officially in March of 1545, he had long been a vicar in the nearby village of Cropthorne. The Abbey survived far longer than most, partly due to its size and partly to the fortitude of men like monk John Alcester, one of Wyllis' closest and most beloved friends. Only about twenty Benedictine abbeys and priories had survived into the year 1540, and by the end of that year not one remained.

Alcester kept a personal record of events as they unfolded in 1540, written by hand at the end of the *Book of Maccabees* in his personal 1537 edition of Matthew's version of the Bible:

"...the monastery of Evesham was suppressed by Kyng Henry the viii the xxxi yere of his raygne the xxx day of Januer at Evensong tyme the convent beyng in the quere [choir] at thys verse [in the Magnificat] Deposuit potentes and wold not suffur them to make an ende. Phillypp Ballard beyng Abbot at that tyme and xxxv Relygius men at that day alyre in the seyde monastry..."[2]

Preserved, somehow, in spite of the dissolution, "it is thought that within two months of the suppression of the Abbey, Alcester's Bible was taken from him."[3]

Meanwhile, long-held religious convictions of the entire Wyllys family were forced to shift, as Robert's "sentiments were moulded by the then vacillating religion of the state; which–affected one day by Henry's faith as a Catholic, and influenced on the next by his hatred to the papal rule–must have left one certain class of its ministers in doubt as to the exact measure of Protestantism which they were expected to assume." The confused chaplain and his wife would later be interred in the church itself, with a small brass plate forever imploring all passers-by in the Latin language to pause and "pray for the souls of Robert Wyllys and Agnes his wife; upon whose souls may God have mercy."

Chaplain Robert Wyllys, an early ancestor of Robert Willis of diver fame, originated in the villages of Evesham, Napton, Priors Marston, and Fenny Compton, all nestled within miles of one another in County Warwick in the West Midlands region of England. The genealogy of the family was discovered in the *Visitation of Warwick*, written in 1619. Though the dates of births, baptisms, and deaths of the earliest members are nowhere to be found, historical estimates bring us back to one Richard "Willes" of Napton, our Robert's eighth-great-grandfather, who was born about 1350. The family of Richard's wife, "Jona (Jeames), daughter and heir of John Jeames," can be traced back a great deal further, perhaps another six generations, to about 1180 or earlier.

By the mid-1300s, the Willes (as it was then being spelled) family "possessed much property," and in the succeeding centuries "were the owners of several manors." Like so many other English surnames, Willes was of ancient Norman origin. Old and Middle English lacked any definite spelling rules, and the introduction of French Norman added an unfamiliar ingredient to the English linguistic stew. French and Latin, the languages of the court, also influenced these spellings. And finally, Medieval scribes generally wrote names and words phonetically, so one and the same individual was often referred to by different spelling variations–even within a single document. As the reader can clearly see, the names of the earliest Willes' of England were often written as Willice, Willys, Wyllys, Wyllis, Willust, and even Wallis. Eventually, an American historian would settle upon "Willis."

During the latter half of the fourteenth century, Richard and Jona Jeames Willes resided in the tiny village of Napton, a tiny market town situated some three miles east of Southam in County Warwick, England. Granted its market charter by King Edward II, it had grown throughout the Middle Ages to become one of the largest settlements in the region. The toponym Napton had been derived from the Old English *cnaepp* meaning "hilltop" and *tun* meaning "settlement" in the Old English language. In 1086 the *Domesday Book* first recorded the village as Neptone. The hill on which the village was built stood just over 500 feet above sea level, commanding the remainder of the parish, which for the most part was at a height of about 300 feet.

Richard Willes and Jona had at least one known son, named Thomas, who survived to adulthood. Born in about 1382, he remained in the small village of Napton to raise the next generation of Willes sons and daughters, naming his firstborn Richard after his grandfather. According to surviving records, the younger Richard was baptized during the second decade of the 1400s at the parish church of St. Lawrence. When he married, Richard took up residence three or four miles south of Napton in the village of Priors Marston, where one of his sons, Thomas, was born in about 1435. Eventually, a third Richard Willes, diver Robert's third-great- grandfather, would be born in about 1467. At the beginning of the second decade of the 1500s, he married "Joane, daughter of Grant of Norbrooke, County Warwick," who was one year his senior, and the two of them took up residence on an estate in nearby Fenny Compton. Its name originated from the Anglo-Saxon *Fennig Cumbtuun* meaning "marshy farmstead in a valley."

Over time, Richard became quite a wealthy "gentleman, lord of the Mannour of Fenny-Compton," where he was appointed one of the King's Justices of the Peace. One son, William, was born in about 1512. When father Richard died in 1531 at the age of sixty-four, he was laid to rest next to Joane, his wife, at nearby Priors Marston.

A son from the next generation, named William, had been born in Fenny Compton in about 1512. Following his betrothel to Anne Clarke in 1532, niece of Sir John Clarke of Northampton, William had at least three known sons. Ambrosius was born in 1533 in the Wyllys family manor, followed by younger sibling, Richard, who was born in about 1535. Records indicate that a third son, whom they named Robert, was born about 1538. Eldest son and heir, Ambrose, married Agnes, daughter of William Coles of Great Preston, in county Northumberland; second son, Richard, married Hester, daughter of George Chanibre, of Williams Cot, County Oxford; and third son, Robert, who was born in the mid-1540s at Fenny Compton, whom history failed to closely track. We do know, however, that this third son was our Robert Willis's grandfather, and that he had at least one son who was destined to be educated at Oxford.

John Willis, diver Robert's father, was born in about 1588 in Warwickshire, and later moved to Somersetshire when he married his wife, Mary, in 1612. There, the young couple befriended Dorothy Wadham, a wealthy Somerset widow who had recently used money left by her husband, Nicholas, to endow an Oxford college. In a period of only four years, she had gained royal and ecclesiastical support for the new college, negotiated the purchase of a site, appointed the west country architect William Arnold, drew up the college statutes, and appointed the first warden, fellows, scholars, and cook. On April 20,

1613, John Willis was accepted at the newly established Wadham College, where he was immediately selected Scholar. He would earn his B.A. on February 25, 1616, and his M.A. on July 7, 1620.

Though getting on in years, Dorothy Wadham kept a close eye on her personally selected fellows and scholars. Soon after he earning his first degree, John Willis incurred her anger when he "absented himself from college without leave." It was not recorded where he went or what he might have been doing, but it is known that he young wife was then in the process of giving birth to their first child, a son that they would name Robert. Still, Dorothy Wadham was displeased with his behavior and, "while willing to overlook the absence if the college agrees, is quite resolute that he shall reap no advantage thereby." Wadham's secretary, William Arnold, recorded her sentiments on March 16, 1617:

> "I wish from my hearte I could write you news of my mistris recovery... she be altogether bedrinded, for she is not able to sitt up longer than her bed is makinge... My mistris hath been moved to dispense with Sr Willis that she grant him time of a year for his return... But by no means will she that he shall have any allowance from the house departing as he did..."[4]

But the College–or, perhaps, John Willis's scholarly friends–refused to accept the fact that he had lost his entire income, and the next year, on April 8, 1618, they not only convinced Dorothy Wadham to allow him to return to Gloucester Hall at the College, but at his full allowance. Undoubtedly, "he returned to college by the time specified, and in less than a year," on September 24, 1619, "we find him presented to the college vicarage of Hockleigh (Hockley) in Essex," a small village just east of London.

Hence, records have narrowed the timeline down so that we can determine that Robert Willis was born in the early months of 1617, while his mother was living with relatives in County Somerset and his father was absent from his college post without permission. A younger brother, John, Jr., would be born nine years later, in 1626 and, though the two of siblings would grow to adulthood in the same households on the outskirts of London, living in both Hockley and Ingatstone, their gap in age and interest would lead them in much different pathways. While Robert discovered an unquenchable fondness for shipbuilding and sailing on the open waters, John, Jr., followed in his father's educational and career footsteps. Earning his own B.A. on October 17, 1648, and his M.A. on July 27, 1650, from Wadham College, the younger brother became a man of the cloth as both reverend and rector at St. Nicholas church, serving the sister towns of West Horndon, Herongate, and Ingrave for forty years.

Meanwhile, older brother, Robert, avoided all formal education, spending much of his free time near River Crouch, just a few miles north of the Willis home. By the age of fourteen, he had become a fishmonger, already trained at selecting and purchasing, handling, gutting, boning, filleting, displaying, merchandising and selling his product, primarily salmon, brown trout, chub, dace, roach, barbel, perch, pike, bleak, and flounder. By seventeen, Robert had secured a job aboard a local barge and, in good conditions, traveled daily from Oxford to London and back, carrying timber and wool, foodstuffs and livestock, battling with the millers all along the way.

Meanwhile, across the Atlantic, Boston had recently become the capital of Massachusetts and the first city of New England, primarily because of a freshwater spring. In 1629, John Endicott had built a house in Charlestown for Massachusetts' new governor, John Winthrop. Salem, where Endecott had been living, was passed over as a capital, in part because its rocky soil couldn't save its small group of pre-Winthrop settlers from starvation. By contrast, Charlestown offered better farmland, as well as a protected harbor and the Charles River. Winthrop was living in the house that Endicott built by July of 1630, but Winthrop's fellow settlers were soon dying from disease in Charlestown. Even the limited medical knowledge of 1630 included the understanding that fresh water was a key to health. Charlestown's one fresh-water spring was accessible only during low tide. Winthrop and his sick companions relocated across the Charles to Boston "drawn there by a spring with abundant fresh water."[5]

By the end of 1630, Winthrop had brought 150 settlers to Boston. By 1640, Boston's population would grow by eight times that many, to a robust and active 1,200 citizens. During that decade of expansion, life went on in the tiny hamlet of Fenny Compton. In the early 1630s, George Wyllis was one of those who immigrated to Massachusetts and, in 1636, dispatched a purchasing steward named William Gibbons, who had been given the task of securing property near Hartford, Connecticut. Meanwhile, his first cousin, Robert, was living with his wife, Sarah, and his widowed father, a clerk, in the Stepney area of London. Restless, twenty-one-year-old Robert longed to make his fortune in New England, and his cousin was willing to help him defray the expense of the journey. A son, John Willis, had already been born in late January of 1638 and, following his christening on February 10 at Saint Dunstan Church, Robert, Sarah, and their newborn boarded a ship in London bound for Massachusetts. Though Robert and Sarah made the arduous passage safely, young John was not as fortunate. Dying of pneumonia during the crossing, he was buried at sea.

Every successful colony prior to Massachusetts Bay had been oriented around extracting wealth from the new world and bringing that resource back to Europe. Spanish settlers in the south were driven by silver and gold, which enriched the conquistadors, who returned to Spain and funded the vast Hapsburg military machine. The Dutch colony in New Amsterdam and the Swedish colony in what would later become Delaware were essentially trading posts oriented towards acquiring furs from Native Americans. And the Virginia settlements would soon become filled with plantations, growing tobacco and shipping it to the old world. These were all extractive settlements built around an obvious source of wealth, which could be readily exploited, and from which many of these early settlers would return to the old country once their individual fortunes had been made.

Robert Willis must have found the Massachusetts Bay Colony to be fundamentally different from all others, particularly the Boston area. The earliest settlers brought by John Winthrop–as well as those who arrived later–sought material prosperity certainly, but they had every intention of living permanently in Massachusetts. After all, these Bostonians–including Robert–saw Stuart London as a terribly sinful city, not as an ideal spot to retire. Moreover, the New World had no obvious source of wealth. As John Smith wrote in 1616, New England's "main staple, from hence to bee extracted for the present to produce the rest, is fish," and Robert soon learned that there was no reason to remain in Massachusetts to fish there. After all, fleets from Europe had been exploiting New England's fish population for decades before 1630. And, while Virginia extended the simple extractive model of Latin America and the previous trading posts, Massachusetts Bay created a whole new model with the goal of building a new society. New England offered cheap land to be sure, but no natural export, and Robert Willis would be forced to look elsewhere for his personal income.

When the Willis' arrived in the spring of 1639, the Massachusetts Bay economy already operated as something similar to a colonial "Ponzi scheme." Earliest settlers provided food and other necessities to later settlers, who had brought their life's savings from England. As such, the capital needed for "old settlers" to purchase commodities from England was provided by newer settlers, who bought simple agricultural products at inflated prices. But, in order to remain strong, this model required a steady ratio of incoming new settlers to old residents. By 1640, there were already too few people coming from England to support the economy, and Bostonians like Robert Willis needed to find an alternative source of funds to buy the products they needed. By 1641, he had become a shipwright, an occupation that traced its roots to before recorded history.

Designing and building ships had, for centuries, remained one of the oldest professions. Archaeological evidence indicates that humans arrived on Borneo at least 120,000 years ago, probably by sea from Asia-China mainland during an ice age period when the sea was lower and distances between islands shorter. The ancestors of Australian Aborigines and New Guineans also traveled across the Lombok Strait to Sahul by boat over 50,000 years ago. Later, during the 4th millennium BC, evidence from Ancient Egypt indicates that the early Egyptians learned how to assemble planks of wood into a ship hull as early as 3000 BC. Over time, they figured out how to assemble planks of wood with treenails, using pitch for caulking the seams. The *Royal Ship of Khufu*, a 43.6-meter wooden vessel sealed into a pit in the Giza pyramid complex at the foot of the Great Pyramid of Giza around 2500 BC, became a full-size surviving example that may have fulfilled the symbolic function of a solar barque.

By the late Middle Ages, the "cog," a single-masted and a square-rigged vessel, was widely used along the coastal waters of Europe, in the Baltic, and also in the Mediterranean. Given the conditions of the Mediterrenean, but not exclusively restricted to it, galley type vessels such as this were extensively used there, as were various double-masted vessels, including the "caravels" with their lateen sails. From about 1515, Portugal had trade exchanges with Goa in India, consisting of three four-masted sailing ships, then known as "carracks," leaving Lisbon with silver to purchase cotton and spices in India. Soon, as America was being settled, shipyards became large industrial complexes, with ships financed by groups of investors. It would be a worthy profession for Robert Willis to diligently learn and pursue.

The difficult task of training apprentices in the shipbuilding trade in Massachusetts fell on the shoulders of Alexander Adams, a master-craftsman born in Colchester, County Essex, England, in 1614. Due to a restrictive English law preventing ship owners and shipmasters from leaving the mother country, all shipwrights were forced to secure special permission before leaving England. Records indicate that Adams had come to New England with Captain Thomas Hawkins, who had, indeed, received such permission to travel to America on May 8, 1632, so it must have been in late June or early July of that year that the two of them had arrived in Boston.

Adams, it was written, "was a large man, of a ruddy countenance and a kind and genial nature." He was a shipwright by trade, and he was closely associated with others in the trade, including Nehemiah Bourne, Elias Parkman, and Captain Thomas Hawkins. All of these men had come to Dorchester and settled at Rocky Hill (now Savin Hill), and they had soon learned that, among the major problems of local shipbuilders was a scarcity of labor, as well as a tendency among workmen to shift from one yard to another. Adams would help to begin stabilizing conditions by training more than thirty young apprentices over the course of the next thirty-five years. One of his earliest and most industrious students was Robert Willis.

Like Captain Hawkins, Nehemiah Bourne–son of the shipwright, Robert Bourne of London–had been forced to obtain special permission to come to America. Securing that right, he had arrived in 1638, becoming a freeman and friend of Governor Sir Henry Vane. There, in the first few years of residency, he manufactured and exported ship masts and tar from the New England to the homeland to earn a living. After working in Dorchester for a brief stint, Bourne established his own yard in the North End of Boston. In 1640, he began construction on the first large ship to be built in that city. Named the *Trial*, she would be a 160-ton square-rigged vessel. It was at that time that he hired Robert Willis to assist him in her construction, and she was completed in 1641.

Meanwhile, a daughter, Sarah, was born in Boston to Robert and Sarah Willis on January 10, 1642. Still, early records did not yet indicate Robert's chosen career; he was only recorded as "an inhabitant of Boston in 1642."

Nonetheless, Robert Willis eventually became well respected among most Boston-based shipwrights. Another fledgling shipyard, situated just north of

Copp's Hill, was owned and operated by Benjamin Gillan. Some of the vessels turned out there, with Robert Willis employed as a master ship's carpenter, were of remarkable size. One example was the *Welcome*, a 300-ton vessel built by Valentine Hill during the early 1640s. In beauty and size, the 400-ton *Seafort*, designed and built by the aforementioned Thomas Hawkins, was launched in 1644. By the time she was completed, Robert Willis had honed his skills as a shipbuilding apprentice. But her glory was only brief, for within a few months of her launching the *Seafort* ran aground and sank near the Strait of Gibralter:

> "The sound of a ship's timbers scraping, breaking against rock is terrifying. The *Seafort*...would have shaken hard enough to break bones and crush skulls... Barefoot, bewildered, half naked, the passengers who could still stand ran out on deck in the pitch darkness. But as the heavy seas pushed the Seafort off the rocks and toward the coast, they were powerless to do anything but gather their valuables together and pray. The ship broke up before reaching the shore. Men, women, and children were pitched into the sea and left clinging to the wreckage. Those broken timbers and spars are what saved them—those, and the initiative of one of the seamen, who swam to the shore with one end of a rope and helped them to the safety of the beach where, as the sun rose over a scene of exhaustion, misery and loss, the local people came down and stole anything of value they could find. Nineteen people drowned in the wreck..."[6]

All of the dead were close friends and neighbors of Robert and Sarah Willis. Captain Thomas Coytmore was one; barber and surgeon, Abraham Pratt, and his wife, Jane, were two others. Yet, miraculously, Robert Willis' closest friend, Thomas Hawkins, was among the survivors.

As the months passed, all types of vessels were sliding down the ways of the local Boston shipyards. There was a continuous demand in the fishing and coasting trade for shallops, fitted with mainmast, foremast, and lugsails. The Medford yards, where Willis spent the majority of his working hours, constructed sleek brigantines and barks, which were designed square and usually weighed less than fifty tons.

Medford, some six miles northwest of Boston, also dispatched a number of sloops and ketches during the 1640s. The deck cabins of the sloops, placed at the stern, gave the appearance of the poop-deck of an earlier era. Another characteristic of these unique vessels was the single mast carrying fore-and-aft mainsail boom, and a yard or two of topsail. These broad-beamed vessels often did duty in carrying firewood to Boston and Charlestown, while the Medford ketches became the common type of ship used by Bostonians in the West Indies trade two-masted, rigged with a square sail on the mainmast and a lateen on the mizzen. Smaller sloops, called "lighters," used for river and shallow harbor navigation, were built at Rock Hill Landing, near West Medford. A number of these were purchased and used by diver, Edward Bendall, who must have been a personal friend of Robert Willis.

AMERICAN SUBMARINERS: PRE-CIVIL WAR

The increase in maritime activity around Boston, with its desperate need for improved waterfront facilities, demanded the gradual "filling in" of marshes and swamp areas covering the Peninsula, and the "pushing out" of the water mark to the deeper waters of the harbor. The area of solid ground representing navigable water frontage was limited, and the merchants recognized quite early on that a more uniform waterfront was needed. Bounties were established for persons who showed their public spirit by extending the shoreline. In 1643, for example, the town granted the North Cove–an area now partly occupied by the North Station–to Henry Symonds, George Burden, and others, for the purpose of erecting "corn mills" along its shores. The new owners opened and deepened a channel from Mill Pond to the Great Cove on the other side of the Peninsula, which became known as Mill Creek.

As discussed earlier, the original waterfront and the center for shipping was principally located in the vicinity of Dock Square, near the present Faneuil Hall. Here the first Town Dock was established in the early 1630s, and it was, for a considerable time, the focal point of all marketable produce. The merchant Edward Bendall was so prominently connected with the activities of this wharf that it became widely known as "Bendall's Dock." It was Bendall who contrived a primitive sort of diving bell, the first used in the harbor, and raised the *Mary Rose*, which had blown up in August 1641, from an explosion of gunpowder on board and had obstructed the harbor for almost a year. Robert Willis was there to witness the entire salvage operation, from start to finish.

Meanwhile, with the outbreak of civil war in England in early 1642, Nehemiah Bourne, Robert Willis, and a number of others eventually returned to support the their homeland's cause, with Bourne becoming an army major. By 1645, both Bourne and Willis were back in Boston, each escorting their respective wives to England once again by the spring of 1646. There, Bourne's abilities in getting new vessels constructed with limited resources and the help of his close friend, Robert Willis, got him promoted to a navy commission as Rear Admiral. Meanwhile, Willis's wife gave birth to their third child. Sadly, their second, a son named Samuel, died and was laid to rest on August 21, 1646, at St. Dunstan, Stepney, Middlesex, England. Their last child, Mary, would be born back in Boston on July 18, 1653.

Still attempting to eek out a meager living in any way that he could, Robert Willis traded goods for a house on a few acres in Boston, in an effort to secure an adequate home for his wife and children. On February 10, 1653, he made a legal contract with John Ellisonn, trading six hundred pounds of sugar for a modest home:

> "Recd of Robert Willis ye full sum and quantety of six hundred pownds of muscavadoes shuger wch is in full of all bills, bonds or any other accompts or debts what soeuer yt hath beene between him & mee or his or my assignes from ye begining of ye world to this present day & more espetially in full of one bill vndr, the said Willis his hande of five pownds

sterling pble to mee in september last past & further I doe hereby engage my selfe my heyres Exequitors Administrators or assigns yt if ye said some of five pownds sterling to be paid to Captain John Allen or recouered by him as hee is my Lawfull Atturney of or from any of ye said Willis his heyrs or assigns. Then I will make ye said Robert Willis good payment of soe much muscauadoes suger as I have recd from him–to him, his heyres, Exequiters or Assignes in witness–Whereof I have here unto sett my hand & seale this tenth of february 1653–(signed) John Ellisonn"[7]

Meanwhile, as he climbed further up the political ladder, Nehemiah Bourne never forgot his close friend, Robert Willis. Early in 1655, he recommended Willis as a more than capable man to raise the guns of a recently sunk naval ship, the *Liberty*. Bourne further explained that the New England gentleman had been "very instrumental in weighing [raising] severall guns and other goods that were sunke in 5 or 6 fathoms of water, and where there came a considerable tide. He is not a man of art, but of experience...he should be allowed his charges and a boat to attend him."[8]

This recently lost vessel had been launched in 1633 as the *Charles*, one of the finest vessels in the navy of King Charles I, but was renamed the *Liberty* by the Commonwealth government early in 1650 to symbolize the change from royal tyranny to republican freedom. This ideological gesture was, however, to backfire when the forty-four-gun ship ran aground on a sandbank off Harwich a few months later and was lost.

Bourne must have been convincing, for Robert Willis was employed by the Royal Navy to make salvage attempts to this wreck every summer season from 1655 to 1658. He would also work on two other naval wrecks; the forty-four-gun *Sussex*, which had blown up off Portsmouth in December of 1653 after loose gunpowder had been accidentally ignited; and the fifty-gun *Laurel*, which ran aground due "to the great negligence of her chief officers" and was lost on a sandbank off Great Yarmouth in May of 1657. But, of the three, it was the *Liberty* that offered the greatest likelihood of success, and so it was at Harwich that Willis concentrated his efforts.

In the early spring of 1655, a hulk was moored some distance out in Harwich Harbor, to be used in Willis's salvage operation, "to which guns, stores, and crew might be transferred when a ship was to be hove down to be cleaned (salvaged), and Robert Grassingham, as master-shipwright and master-attendant, and   , as storekeeper, were the first civil officers attached to the establishment."[9]

On March 25 of that same year, a letter was dispatched from navy commanders to Robert Blackborne, Secretary of the Admirality: "Send a letter of Robert Grassingham from Harwich, that he and Robt. Willis have spent 3/ (3 shillings) in hiring men and boats to find the *Liberty*, but without effect; some men have offered to search for a week, on payment of 10/ (10 shillings) if they find her, and 5/ (5 shillings) if they do not."[10]

Willis, meanwhile, was based at the naval dockyard at Deptford, situated along the River Wylye, where his diving vessel, suitably called the *Diver Hoy*, would be fitted out at the beginning of each diving season (a hoy being the generic term for a particular sort of small coastal vessel). It was agreed that he and his crew would be paid wages by the navy. Willis urged his employers to offer more than the standard rate, since he was having a great deal of difficulty convincing able-bodied men to serve with him, "the vessel being so small, and the employment so short and dangerous, having to lie day and night among the sands." These men would be equipped with sweeps, grapples, hooks, and other equipment used by salvage crews. But they also would use a crude diving-bell to assist with the salvage work. Such operations tended to make even experienced divers a bit nervous, particularly in the often churning waters off Harwich.

Like Bendell before him, Robert Willis needed to utilize equipment that was already handy as his diving apparatus. His vessel of choice, however, was shaped less like Bendell's "bell" and more like an oversized "pudding bowl." Standing about five feet high and made of lead, it would be securely attached to four cables leading down to a square lead platform situated just a few feet below the vessel. The plan was for Willis to stand on this platform as it was carefully lowered into the frigid water, with only his head and upper torso out of the water. Although history did not record the intricate details of each dive, it is likely that he wore some type of watertight leather suit to insulate himself from the cold.

Once he reached the desired depth, seldom more than twenty-five feet down, Willis' initial task would be to use a wooden stave fashioned with an iron hook to "catch onto and clear debri" from around the sunken *Liberty*. At times, he would find it necessary to attach a heavy rope dangling from above to heavier pieces of the wreckage, in order to move them away from those items that were to be salvaged. Since submerged time would be limited to about forty minutes per dive–by both the diminishing supply of oxygen and the cold water–Willis would be forced to return to the surface on a regular basis.

On April 8, 1655, the following letter was sent to Navy Command, describing Robert Willis's rendezvous with Robert Grassingham:

> "Has entered on board the hulk at Harwich, but has neither provisions nor lodgings but the deck. Is informed if he can so subsist for a month, he may receive 15s. to supply his next month's necessaries, which will cost him 6s. or 7s. a week, besides other expenses; 3s. 9d. a week is not enough for him as for others belonging to the hulk, as they live in the town and have relatives, while he is a stranger; left his voyage and lost his passage for New England, and now has 15s. a month abated of his usual wages in New England, if confined to 3s. a week. Noted that he is to have 7s. a week for diet."[11]

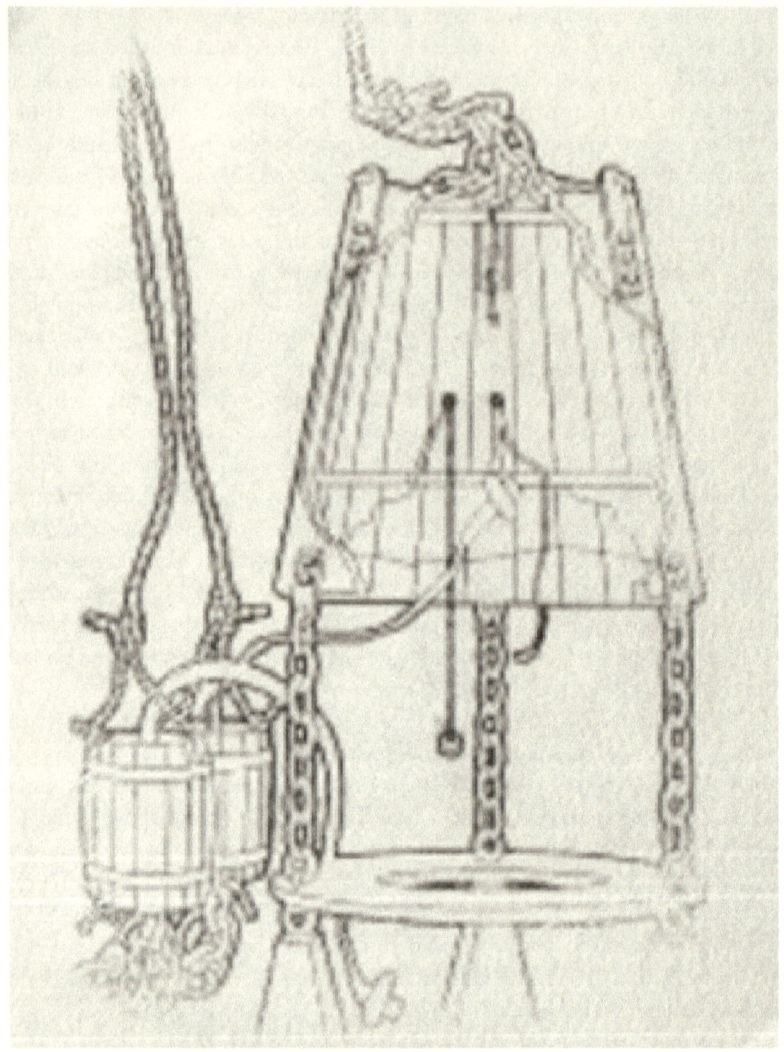

Sketch of the *Willis Diving Bowl*

Raising guns from the shifting sands off Harwich was certainly not an easy task, for the work was arduous and often quite perilous. Yet, at the beginning of Willis' efforts everything seemed simple enough. In the spring of 1655, the water was clear, and he could see some of the guns from the surface. On May 7, Robert Grassingham reported on Willis's progress to his naval commanders: "Sent Robt. Willis out with some boats, and he found the *Liberty*, laden with ballast, lying upright in 15 feet at low water; he surveyed her and found she was going to pieces, but hopes to recover her guns, anchors, and cables."

Now, all Willis needed to do was make his first salvage attempt. Yet, he decided–rather foolishly perhaps–to leave what he had found until the summer months, when he thought that the water might be even clearer. Yet, when summer came, strong winds from the south and west had thickened the water so that visibility was no longer optimal. At that time of year, when "once in a fortnight...he did see downe, hee found that these winds had covered them [the guns] with sand." Willis learned his lesson about salvaging guns in shifting sands the hard way, since the good conditions of spring, 1655, were not to reappear for a few of more years.

In October of 1655, Robert Willis received thirty pounds on his account, for his wages "and to make engines." It quickly occurred to him that, due to the dangerous turbulence and cloudy waters, his diving bowl would be the most useful "engine" for him to use. In the meantime, continuous bad weather meant that his first two seasons were virtual failures, for he managed to bring up only a copper kettle and a sacker (a small bronze cannon), for which–and for all subsequent bronze raised–he received payment of twenty shillings a hundredweight on top of his wages. Early in January, 1656, despite bringing very little of value back to the surface, it seemed as if Royal Navy personnel were quite satisfied:

> "Recommend Robt. Willis, a diver, for encouragement. He was employed to recover the guns of the *Liberty*, and although prevented further action through the storms, he brought up a sacker of 18 cwt., and a copper kettle of 3 cwt., which he delivered into the stores at Harwich. His family are in New England, and depend upon him."[12]

Later in 1656, Willis managed to recover "a quantity of cordage" sunk aboard a wooden Dutch vessel. By then, he had also made severa; attempts at salvaging goods aboard the *Sussex*, which had been burned and sunk in choppy waters off the coast of Portsmouth. Reportedly, persistant foul weather prevented him from having any sort of success in the latter adventure. Meanwhile, a number of successful test dives were conducted with his diving bowl from the decks of the *Diving Hoy* near Deptford and at Harwich Harbor. Slowly but surely, his crew was becoming more proficient with employing a submersible vessel for salvage operations.

Much like his Boston predecessor, Edward Bendall, Robert Willis soon discovered that individual expeditions using a diving vessel were limited to about forty minutes before all fresh oxygen was depleted. His contraption was a large cable-suspended chamber, open at the bottom, and lowered underwater from Willis's *Diving Hoy*, to be operated as a base or a means of transport for a small number of divers. The pressure of the water kept the air trapped inside the bell. Unlike future submarines, the *Willis diving bowl* was not designed to move under the control of its operator, nor could she operate independently of her tether.

On April 28, 1656, the following communication was dispatched to the British Navy Commander, Robert Blake, regarding Willis' concern about the kidnapping and impressments of the men in his well-trained diving crew, as well as his authority over their behavior. Apparently, the diver was a bit worried about the sailors in his charge disobeying direct orders:

> "Being ready to sail, desires an order to keep his men from being pressed, as also one to Grassingham and Browne at Harwich, to supply him with a wherry ready manned, so that if he finds his company refractory or negligent, he may discharge and give them tickets, and hire others; also payment of 20s disbursed."[13]

For the most part, 1656 proved quite fruitless in the salvage business for Robert Willis, who continued to be paid in spite of little positive results. Records indicate that, as late as October 17 of that year, there was issued an "order to pay the wages of the company of the *Diver Hoy* at Deptford" The transplanted New Englander now began to worry about the future of his employment. Yet, both "good" luck and "bad" luck came for the Willis expedition when another British ship was lost. On the night of May 30, 1657, "while the pilot and master were below" deck, the six-year-old, 102-foot long, 46-gun fourth-rate frigate *Laurel*, weighing a modest 489 tons, struck a sandbar on the Newark Sands, off Yarmouth, England, and sank in shallow waters. Constructed and launched in Portsmouth in 1651, she had carried the flag of Rear-Admiral Samuel Howett in the Battle of Portland in 1653 under the command of Captain John Stokes, and was also present at the battle off the North Foreland the following June. Later, in May of 1655, her "160 seamen, 30 soldiers and 40 guns" had formed one of William Penn's fleet, under the command of Captain William Crispin, that had participated in the capture of Jamaica. With her sinking, Robert Willis was legally charged with salvaging all of her guns and any other valuables that she took to the bottom with her. History, however, did not record whether or not he was successful in this venture.

Apparently, Robert Willis faired much better during the 1657-salvaging season, and confidence in him remained quite strong. On March 17, the British Navy issued an "order for fitting out the *Diver Hoy*, and sending Robt. Willis, the diver, to Harwich, to recover the guns of the *Liberty*, cast away off Harwich, and furnishing him with materials and instruments." By the middle of May, the *Liberty* could "now clerely be discovered upon the shelfe whereon she lies as a wrack." Though her guns were not yet visible, by July he had found two of them, and was "in hopes of recovering more, but they must be gained by waiting an opportunity." Such opportunities did, indeed, present themselves, for in September of 1657 "a trew account" showed that Willis had raised four more guns totaling 101 hundredweight. With each successful recovery, the gun would be sent to be identified and stored until payment could be made. One such transaction was indicated by a letter sent from Joseph Falkener, Ordinance Officer, to Robert Blackborne, British Secretary to the Customs Commissioners:

"Has received into the stores from Robt. Keeble, Master of the *Mary* at Harwich, a piece of brass ordnance, weighing 40 cwt., which was one of the *Liberty's* guns that was cast away. With the Admirality Commissioners' for 40 (shillings) to Keeble for the service, if he recovered the gun, and if Willis, the diver, was not concerned therein. 10 Sept."[14]

In 1658, Willis was once again slow to show any progress, but was, as usual, confident in the future. "As yet," he reported on June 7, "I have got never a goon [gun] by reason of soe much blowing weather. I am not yet without hopes for I have been once downe [in the bowl]...and with an iron felt two or three goons in the sand, but the recovery of them depends upon the Providence of God in calme weather." A week later, the navy's agent at Harwich was also optimistic and thought that Willis was "likely to do much good on the guns, if fair weather presents. He made his gear fast to a great one yesterday, but in heaving it up, his gear gave way three times, so he sent in for better ropes." Such documented comments are all that exist to suggest just how difficult this salvaging work truly was.

Weather conditions improved later in the season, and Willis was able to raise two anchors, a copper furnace, and at least five bronze guns. He also found four culverins and one huge cannon of two and a half tons which, at twenty shillings per hundredweight, provided him with a handsome sum to support his family back in New England.

Robert Willis, the *Diver Hoy*, and his *Diving Bowl* disappeared for a time from the official records at the end of the 1658 salvage season, but it seems likely that he remained ready for duty at Deptford. In fact, he was on hand to exhibit his diving skills when the diarist John Evelyn went down river with other members of the Royal Society for some entertainment in July of 1661. "We tried our diving-bell, or engine, in the water-dock at Deptford, in which our curator continued half an hour under water; it was made of cast lead, let down with a strong cable."[15]

The members of the Royal Society were interested in just about every technological advancement then known to man, and developments in the ability to work under water were certainly intriguing. They conducted experiments in breathing in a confined space, and under water with birds and other animals; they asked the great scientist, Robert Hooke, to "procure glasses fit to see under water, as far as the thickness or turbidness of the water would permit." And they seem to have had regular demonstrations of the Willis Diving Bowl.

In August of 1662, Robert Willis, still described as "the diver," made a reappearance in the public records in a letter to the Navy Commissioners. He was back up at Harwich, working on the same wreck as in the 1650s, now subtly renamed the *Charles*–again to reflect the Restoration of King Charles II. On the first day of August, 1663, it was reported that "Robert Willis, diver, to the Navy Comrs. Account of his endeavour to recover guns from the wreck [of the *Charles*]. Is much hindered by the weather, the buoys having got foul of the wreck, which is in the middle of the sand. Has buoyed one gun, and has hopes of another. Has taken up a piece of cable, a crow of iron, &c., to show that he has not been idle."[16]

Willis further reported that he "swept the track of the *Charles*, but the sea has been so turbulent that he has not dared to lie over her." The next year, 1664, he would have further trouble with the weather, and he had to report no success in recovering the guns of the *Charles*. Beyond that, historical records indicate that he was afraid that "the hand of God or the power of darkness is against him." Clearly, this worried comment suggested that his New England Puritan background was getting the better of him. Indeed, the man who had seemed so confident and competent, though unlucky, in the 1650s now seemed to have lost his nerve. "Yesterday there came a strange dreadful fish and swam round about the Diving *Hoy*, and setting the water of each side the *hoy*, and faced us, to all our men's admiration that saw it...it had long gray whiskers, five or six inches long at the least, and some say it had long hair hanging down to the shoulders; but it looked gasfully [ghastly]."[17]

When Samuel Pepys, Chief Secretary to the Admiralty, was unanimously elected a member of the Royal Society in February of 1665, his useful connections with the British Navy were recognized, and he was almost immediately asked "to bespeak a man, at Deptford, for diving." Pepys was pretty busy that year and he seems to have neglected to carry out this commission, for a few months later "the President was desired to put Mr. Pepys in mind of the diver for the diving experiments in this season."[18]

The stress placed upon Robert Willis, both from outside sources and personally, led not only to his increasing fear that his Majesty might be growing displeased with his lack of success, but to a diagnosable illness. Unable or unwilling to continue his salvaging work, he inquired, in fact, as to precisely "how long he was to stay." A letter was sent to Major General, John Leverett, on his behalf:

> "In ansr [sic] to the peticon [sic] of Robert Willis, who on the 15th July, '65, was on the service of the country at ye Castle, & suffered under ye Solemne stroke of thunder yt tooke away Capt Davenport, & is not as yet capable to worke in his callinge, petitioning for reliefe, the court judgeth it meete to refferr him to Major Generall Leverett, who hath power in this case, & in like cases hath given reliefe & supply to such as suffered in the same."[19]

This is nearly the last we hear of Robert Willis, although Boston Vital Records report him living with his wife, Sarah, and daughters, Sarah and Mary, in late, 1665. Apparently, he had "retired" permanently from the business of salvaging and no one else seems to have replaced him at Deptford as a regular navy diver, though one would have thought that such an appointment would have been useful to future recovery operations.

Sir William Phips

- 4 -
William Phips: *Phips Diving Tub*

"The diarists John Evelyn and Narcissus Luttrell used identical words to describe the proceeds of the voyage, 'a vast treasure.' How vast was it in reality? According to the historian W.R. Scott, who was followed by such eminent authorities as J.H. Clapham and Maynard Keynes, it was sufficient to alter the course of England's financial history. (William) Phips's treasure, Scott argued, encouraged the formation of many more joint-stock companies and thus contributed substantially to the expansion of the market in stocks in the early 1690s and thereby to the foundation of the Bank of England."[1]

When history speaks about the European settling of North America, the word "first" creeps into the discussion very quickly–the first ever, the first permanent settlement, the first permanent settlement still in existence today, the first settlement with women and children, the first child born, the first Spanish/French/English, etc., etc., etc. While the discussion may force us to define our terms more carefully–a valuable exercise in itself–we should begin the topic of the "first American underwater explorer" as a European who crossed the Atlantic, disembarked, settled with the intention of staying, found suitable work and a home site, and began to consider what mysteries were hidden below the surface of the water. For clear answers to this, we must most certainly begin at the beginning.

Isabella was a small town that Columbus ordered his men to build on the northeastern shore of Hispaniola, in present-day Dominican Republic, during his second voyage to the New World in 1493. Hunger and disease soon led to mutiny, punishment, disillusion, and more hunger and disease. The struggling town barely survived until 1496, when Columbus ordered a new town built on the island as the Spanish capital, now known as Santo Domingo. Hence, history recorded Isabella as the first of the Indies, claimed Antonio de Herrera, the seventeenth-century historian who compiled this early record of New Spain from state archives.[2]

Meanwhile, Jamestown has justifiably been called "the first permanent English settlement" in the New World, though it was, indeed, a hard-won designation. As historian Alan Taylor recounts, of the first 104 colonists who landed in April of 1607, only thirty-eight survived that first harsh winter. Of the 10,000 who left England for Jamestown in its first fifteen years, only twenty percent were still alive, and still in Jamestown, in 1622. The early months of the colony's existence were chronicled by John Smith, Edward Wingfield, and George Percy, the latter of which twice served as the settlement's governor. After writing several accounts to justify his controversial actions as governor, Percy left Jamestown for good in 1612.[3]

To American school children of many generations, the term "colonist" has spurred images of stalwart Pilgrims setting sail on the *Mayflower* to land at Plymouth Rock–an epic tale of adventure and determination. And, for the most part, the story is true. Unlike the single men–the courtiers, soldiers, and adventurers–who built Isabella, Jamestown, and many other early European settlements, the Pilgrims were skilled, hardworking, and self-disciplined. In addition, they came as families, unique in all Atlantic coast settlements up to that time. Historians have learned this from the journal of the settlement's longtime governor, William Bradford, who detailed the colonists' difficult first year after landing in November of 1620 up to the first harvest in the autumn of 1621.[4]

As far as history has recorded these and all other events, Europe was closely aligned with America, and to define the "first American underwater adventurer" is, quite literally, quite difficult. The combining of the basic simple machines used for underwater exploration–the tube and the barrel–began in the mid-seventeenth century. European astronomer, Edmond Halley, well known for the comet he described, had an immense interest in numerous aspects of physics. As such, he addressed the varied issues and defects of the diving bell design up to that time, and suggested a number of solutions. Building on previous designs of the diving bells, in fact, he integrated the principles of the tube into a more versatile system. In simple open bell diving, the diver would leave the bell and swim "apne." But in Halley's system, the diver would first don a bucket-shaped cap attached to a lengthy hose, the open end of which was kept by a diving tender inside the bell.

Pre-Halley, any diver who departed from the safety of his bell could only breathe when he was more or less level with the air-bubble in the bell. Though withstanding the overpressure when swimming upward was feasible, swimming down deeper than the magic sixty centimeter limit below the air-bubble's deepest end meant that the diver would be forced to close both nose and mouth in order to avoid unacceptable suction pressure on his lungs. Furthermore, the diver's breathing would rapidly reduce the oxygen content of the submerged air-bubble, putting a limit to his diving time. Halley's system provided for replenishing of the oxygen supply by adding air that was compressed in a stored barrel. One early American understood all of this long before Edmond Halley. Known to American and English history as Sir William Phips, his background and life were both intriguing and complex.

Digging back into the Phips family roots, we learn that the name is believed to have originated in Greece, and is quite literally interpreted to mean "a lover of horses." The Ancient chronicles of England reveal the early records of the surname Phipps as being of Norman origin, and one of the oldest names interwoven into the history of Great Britain. Research using ancient manuscripts indicates the first Phipps' were found in southwestern Britain, where they were seated from very early times and were awarded lands by Duke William of Normandy for their distinguished assistance at the Battle of Hastings in 1066. From that point forward, the name emerged as a notable English family in western Wiltshire, where family members were recorded with great antiquity, being seated as Lords of the Manor and Estates in that shire. Tradition held that they were descended from the Norman family Phillips of Picton Castle in Herefordshire, and that they branched off to Haywood House in Westbury, Wiltshire, and also to Leighton House in that same region.

Most frequent spellings and misspellings of the surname have included Phips, Phipps, Fipp, Fipps, Fips, and Phip. Other variations found in English records prior include Phyps, Phypps, Phyips, Fypps, Fyps, Phyppi, Fippi, Phippe, Phipe, Pipe, Fippe, Fyppe, Phyppe. It is doubtful that all members of the Phips family line originating in Great Britain, nor that all British-born Phips' are related. The name is patronymic, and would have sprung up independently in many areas of the country in the late Middle Ages when surnames became more common and began to be passed from one generation to the next. Tracking Sir William Phips, American underwater explorer, is certainly a challenge.

The first known mention of this particular Phips/Phipps family ancestry is found in an early deposition of one Johannes Phipps, who lived in Somersetshire, the next county east of Wiltshire. The name appeared in an obscure document, dated 1292, and stated that Johannes was sixty years of age at the time, placing his birth about 1232. More than 250 years would pass when, in 1493, a second Johannes Phipps appeared in another obscure historical record, in which he gave the family home to his son, Richard. It seems, without question, that this second Johannes was a descendant of the first Johannes, since both owned property and resided in the same small village of Cameley.

Across decades, Cameley remained an out-of-the-way, quiet hamlet lying restfully within the Chew Valley less than twenty miles due west of Westbury, Wiltshire, England, and ten miles directly south of Bristol. Nestled along the Cam Brook, the town was described in 1086 as having been named for "the curved river meadow" from the Celtic term "cam" and the Old English "leah."

About 1150, control of the Cameley manor town was handed over to Bath Abbey by the Alnes (or d'Alneto) family. Later, in the last years of the twelfth century it was held by the Marisco family, better known for their connection with Lundy, and then passed into the control of the Knights Templar, which was confirmed in a grant of 1201. During the thirteenth and early fourteenth centuries the manor would again come under the control of the de Marisco family. The parish church known as St. James, which was constructed in the late twelfth century from blue lias limestone dug from local caverns, was where the earliest Phipps family members were christened, married, and laid to rest in the church cemetery.

King Arthur, son of Uther Pendragon, was said to have been born along the north coast of England's southwestern peninsula, where he lived briefly with his queen, Guinevere, and the Knights of the Round Table. Later, the entire entourage was believed to have relocated much further east to a place known only as "Camelot." Some believed it to be near Queen Camel; others, at Cameley; still others somewhere in the twenty miles in between the two villages. On his itinerary of 1542, John Leland, English poet and antiquarian, wrote:

> "At the very south ende of the chirch of South-Cadbyri standeth Camallate, sumtyme a famose toun or castelle, apon a very torre or hille, wunderfully enstregnthenid of nature... The people can telle nothing ther but that they have hard say that Arture much resortid to Camalat."[5]

Johannes Phips' son, Richard, born around 1475 in Cameley, married Margaret at Saint James, the same church where generations of Phips children had been christened. The couple–who were William Phips' third great-grandparents–would remain in the tiny village throughout all of their marriage, living on the family estate and raising their growing brood. Among them was youngest son Thomas, who was born in 1515. As he approached the age of thirty, Thomas fell in love with and married Anne, a fifteen-year-old lass who would give him three sons before she turned twenty. Robert was born in 1545, Richard in 1548, and William just one year later.

Eldest son Robert, great-grandfather of Sir William, had been brought into this world 150 miles north of Cameley in Nottingham, while Anne was staying with relatives. In 1570, at the age of twenty-five, he took Isabel Brounley as his wife, solemnly declaring his love and devotion to her at the Church of Saint Mary the Virgin in Nottingham. They would have seven sons, among them William.[6]

About 1578, diver William's grandfather, William Phips, who would become a noted blacksmith, was born in the village of Mangotsfield, a small parish five miles northeast of the large seaport of Bristol situated in southern Glouchestershire, England. History records that the community was first mentioned in what would later become known as the *Domesday Book*, a record of the great survey of much of England and Wales completed in the year 1086. Executed by King William I–better known as William the Conqueror–it was written that "while spending the Christmas time of 1085 in Gloucester, William had deep speech with his counselors and sent men all over England to each shire to find out what or how much each landowner had in land and livestock, and what it was worth."[7]

The birth of seven of grandfather William's children was recorded at Mangotsfield between 1597 and 1614. Although James Phips was not among them, he was likely born in 1608 or 1609 (when there is a gap both in the parish registers and in the dates of birth of the seven children). Further north, son James was baptized in Nottingham on August 29, 1610, during another family visit.

AMERICAN SUBMARINERS: PRE-CIVIL WAR

James' early years are shrouded in mystery. We do know that, on March 1, 1626, the fifteen-year-old was apprenticed to John Brown, a blacksmith, for a standard term of seven or eight years. Brown's family had originated in nearby Barton Regis, an early Norman manor held by the king in Gloucestershire, so the two families may have known each other long before the apprenticeship. There is no record of James Phips becoming a freeman of Bristol, however, which would have been recorded after completion of his apprenticeship if he had still been in the city. Hence, the presumption is that he and Brown departed from Bristol and migrated to America together before 1634. Evidence indicates that Brown had likely first visited this "brave New World" some years earlier.

John Brown was likely the first permanent settler in Maine. Town records of Bristol recorded that he had been apprenticed to Robert North as a blacksmith in 1611. Early Maine records show that a John Brown, described as "a blacksmith from Bristol," and his wife, Margaret Haywood Brown, were living in Pemaquid, Maine, by 1622 and, over the next seventeen years, raised a family of four daughters and one son. We can safely assume, therefore, that John Brown, the blacksmith in Pemaquid, was the same man to whom James Phips was apprenticed in Bristol. It is conceivable that John Brown was instrumental in getting Sir William Phips' father to migrate to the Maine coast, possibly as his personal assistant. During his apprenticeship, James received instruction and experience in the working of metals. He saw–and even worked on–a number of heavy, clumsy, matchlock muskets, which were often brought into Brown's shop for minor repairs. Outside of London and Birmingham there were few gunsmiths until the era of mass production, and many country blacksmiths like Brown were forced to become skillful at this trade out of sheer necessity. As fate and historical happenstance would have it, this gun-smithing skill was passed on to James Phips, and he used it to design his own doglock gun mechanism.

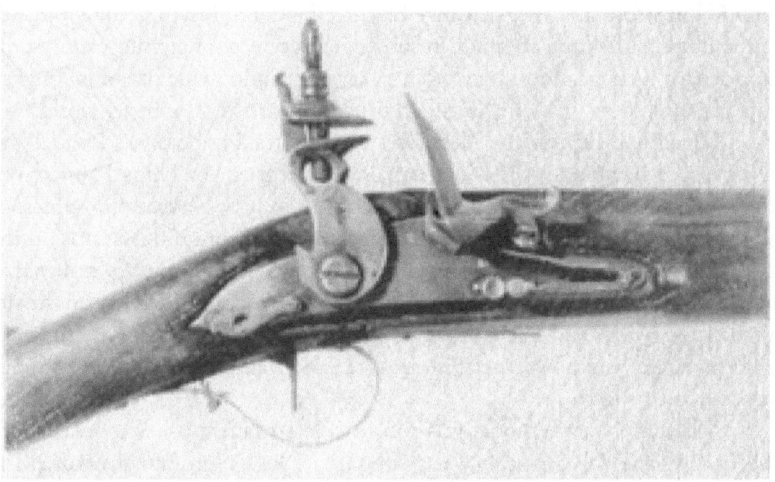

Drawing of doglock mechanism designed by William Phips

Much like the later flintlock, the Phips design contained a flint, a frizzen, and a pan, yet exhibited an external catch as a half-cock safety known as a "dog." With an overall length of fifty-seven inches and a 41.5-inch barrel, it soon became one of the more popular weapons in the Colonies.

James and John Brown eventually settled in the coastal region of what is now present day Woolwich. Known then as the Indian place-name "Nequasset," it was situated along the jagged coastline. The entire region was purchased in the autumn of 1639 by John Brown and his business partner, Edward Bateman, from an Indian named Robin Hood, or Manowormet. Sales records indicate they paid for "Negwasset, in America...1 hogshead of corn and 30 pumpkins," which included all property between Sagadahoc and Sheepscot rivers, Great Pond to the north and the Nequasseg River to the south. Eight years earlier, Bristol merchants Robert Aldworth and Gyles Elbridge had been granted the patent to the Pemaquid region further to the east. James Phips completed his apprenticeship to Brown in Bristol in 1634, and John White, a sugar refiner who had apprenticed to Aldworth in 1628, most likely became a freeman of Bristol in 1636.

In 1646, Phips and White purchased a piece of property from Bateman that would become known as "Phips Point." Situated on the western side of Sheepscot River, they had presumably began living there in 1639, at the time of the Brown and Bateman purchase from the Indians, since they were employed by Bateman at that time.

Sometime during this murky historical period a trading post was established at Nequasset, possibly even by Aldworth and Elbridge; there is an accounting of it from 1646 on by Francis Knight, their selling agent, but how much earlier it was operating is not known. It was in that same year, however, that Thomas Elbridge, inheritor of the Pemaquid patent, arrived in the region. John White's son later deposed that Elbridge had long been a frequent visitor to the Phips and White complex in subsequent years, strongly suggesting some type of a business relationship. Certainly, given the minuscule size of its English population, mid-coast Maine during this period was a very compact world.

Precisely where in the Nequasset area the trading post was located was never recorded, although it could certainly have been on Phips Point, given this prominent location and the excellent access to it by water from numerous directions. At present, the documentary record is as silent on this as it is on the date of the trading post's establishment. It is, however, important to realize that archaeological research indicates the real possibility of English activity on the site by the later 1630s, and that this activity may have been, at least in part, generated by the fur trade. Whether historical research will ever solve these complex puzzles remains to be seen.

The Phips family home was constructed by father James sometime between 1639 and 1646, and it was a substantial post-in-ground structure. The foundation core consisted of a fifteen-foot by seventy-two-foot longhouse, divided into four rooms, with the southernmost twelve-foot by fifteen-foot section serving as a byre, or cow shed. While the building had a stone hearth, evidence indicates that it had a wattle-and-daub smoke hood. A second round of post-in-ground construction some time later resulted in an ell-shape to the building, or perhaps more properly stated, an attached "wing" to the home. This was possibly the home of Phip's partner and co-land-owner, John White. This addition was more substantially built than the core, for its fourteen-foot by five-foot hearth was constructed on a carefully laid fieldstone footing, as opposed to the hearth of the first structure which amounted to thin flagstones laid on grade. This second structure measured approximately twenty feet by sixty feet. An earth-fast outbuilding was situated approximately twenty feet south of the longhouse, measuring 29.5 feet by 13.5 feet. A drainage ditch was located outside the two uphill sides of the building to divert water away from it. This building served as a small storage facility.

William Phips was born on the Phips' homestead on February 2, 1651, the son of James and Mary Jane Upchurch Phips. As a child, he was described as being "willful, fearless, generous, robust, and of great physical strength." His father died when he was just six years old, and his mother was remarried to a close neighbor and business partner, John White. Although Cotton Mather in his biography of son William claimed that he was one of twenty-six children–twenty-one of which were boys–this number is likely an exaggeration. His mother was known to have had six children by James Phips, and eight by White, although there may have been more that did not survive infancy. As mentioned, his father's ancestry was of gentry in Nottinghamshire, and son William was a first cousin of Sir Constantine Henry Phipps, Lord Chancellor of Ireland. According to Mather the youngster tended sheep until the age of eighteen, giving him the nickname of the "Shepherd Boy of Woolwich."

Afterward, William began a four-year apprenticeship as a ship's carpenter at Clarke and Lake Shipyard at Arrowsic (Spring Cove), Maine. During all of these formative years, he received no formal education, although he did learn to read and write a few basic words. Thus, his literacy skills were quite rudimentary, and once he had achieved fame he often relied upon his personal secretary for assistance in this area.

Meanwhile, it was an historical period of time for pirates, wreckers, corsairs, and buccaneers on the high seas. Of the nations that loomed powerful and wealthy across the ocean was the great land of Spain. By 1640, this formidable nation had long been sending huge fleets to America to harvest and steal its silver and other precious metals. Two in particular were dispatched annually: one sailing in the early spring for Vera Cruz, a port of New Spain, and the other in the autumn for Terra Firme in South America. On arriving, each unloaded their European cargoes and took on vast amounts of silver "which made up over 90 percent by value of their return cargoes," and some of it the property of Philip IV, King of Spain.

The flagship of one of these fleets was the *Nuestra Señora de la Concepción* (*Our Lady of the Immaculate Conception*), one of the best known of all Galleons, boasting three main masts and all the rigging pertaining to them, enormous quantities of gear, tons of goods, six hundred men, women, and children, and all the commissary to feed such a large population. Among their ranks were the most illustrious, including clergymen, their princely attire, and all of their dozens of servants. The flagship had, indeed, made its lengthy voyage with its fleet, and "had had few problems—a couple of ships requiring running repairs in the Atlantic, one bad storm, and once clash with corsairs." She arrived safely at Vera Cruz on June 24, 1640, unloaded her varied stores and, after what some believed to be too long in port, departed on July 31, 1641. Without major impact, she eventually made port in Savanna, Cuba, on August 27, 1641.

Prior to setting sail on its final leg, there were heated discussions and disagreements among her officers and men: Juan de Campos, the Captain General, wanted to leave immediately, hoping to arrive home on the expected date; others, somewhat superstitious, claimed that it was already beyond August 20, believed to be the last safe date to set sail. In the end, the Captain General had his way, and the date of departure was set for September 20, a full month beyond the mystical ill-fated deadline. The *Concepción*, loaded down with tons of bullion, never reached her destination, for she ran into a terrifying fall hurricane, struck a reef called the North Riff in a position listed on maps as the Abrojos (open your eyes), north of Hispaniola, and sank to the bottom of the ocean. Most of the hundreds of passengers aboard swam to a nearby sand bar, where they created makeshift rafts from the wreckage. Two hundred of them left the others behind in an attempt to float to Santo Domingo, with only a few dozen reaching safety. Bad weather prevented a salvage effort for several months, and by the time the weather cleared the sandbar had been washed away and the rescuers could not locate the wreckage site.

Meanwhile, young William Phips grew to adulthood. After his formal apprenticeship ended in 1673, he traveled to Boston, believing that he "was born for greater matters." There, he continued to employ his ship making and carpentry skills. About a year passed before he met and married Mary Spencer Hull, widow of John Hull. Mary's father, Daniel Spencer, was a merchant and landowner with interests in Maine, and Phips may have known her from a very early age. She found him to be a "tall, handsome, romantic," and soon exhibited "genuine affection" and love toward him. Their story, in fact, may have been a classic "love at first sight."

From the few descriptions that survived the centuries, William appeared to others to be a gentleman of "giant physical strength and endurance"; a man who was "tall beyond the common set of men...and thick as well as tall, and strong as well as thick." Some said that he was capable of "quelling a mutiny by the mere force and bearing of his personality"; that "he would contrive a weighty undertaking, and then pursue it unto the end."

By 1675, Phips had established a shipyard on the Sheepscot River at Merrymeeting Bay in Maine. The venture was financially successful, turning out a large number of small boats. Phips, however, had grander goals, and constructed his first large merchant ship in 1676. As he was preparing for its maiden voyage in August of that year, planning to deliver a load of lumber to Boston, a band of Indians descended upon the area. Rather than loading his cargo, he took on board as many of the local settlers as his hull and deck could hold. Hence, on August 14, 1676 the Phips and White families, along with a number of Wiscasset area refugees, sailed away on the vessel just completed by William, minutes before the complex went up in flames. As with much of Maine, the first Anglo-American settlement on Phips Point came to an abrupt end.

Phips had been forced to leave behind his shipload of lumber in order to make room for family and friends aboard his ship to remove them from danger to Boston. The group of British merchants with whom he had contracted abruptly ended their working relationship with him and took his ship as payment, since the lumber was gone he could not repay them in any other way:

> "The depths of Phips's loss can be measured by the series of lawsuits he faced during the eighteen months following his hurried departure from Maine. Although many New Englanders, particularly ships' captains and aspiring merchants like Phips, were frequently in court fighting civil cases, Phips had rarely been involved in such proceedings. His avoidance of them suggests that he had managed on the whole to meet his obligations and had dealt with people who did likewise. All of this changed with his reversal of fortune in 1676. First, Francis Dodson successfully sued for payment of twenty-three pounds that Phips owed him for stoning a cellar. The contract had been signed in March 1676, when Phips was still solvent and had apparently decided to build a house in Boston. Elizabeth Hammond then sued Phips for three pounds that was owed from the sale of beef on the Kennebec the previous year, and Daniel Turell, Jr. sued Phips for the sum of thirteen pounds, nine shillings; the nature of the latter debt was not stated, but it may have been for hardware for the ship Phips had built, because Turell was an anchorsmith. Finally Phips was involved in a suit and countersuit with Thomas Joles over settlement of the contract to build the ship. When Phips lost the case and was ordered to pay eighty-five pounds, he became enraged. 'In a deceitful and felonious way,' alleged his opponents, he seized the award from the hands of Joles's attorney, John Walley, 'and threw it into the fire and burnt it.' In January 1678 the court sentenced Phips to pay the eighty-five pounds to Walley and a five-pound fine to boot. By the time he appeared before the court, Phips had regained his composure, and when he apologized for his behavior the court cut his fine in half."[8]

Although he was, for the most part, financially ruined, Phips was celebrated as a hero to the citizens for saving their lives. Actions, rather than wealth or education, spoke volumes, and he had now gained their undivided respect.

Soon enough, Phips had managed to establish a second shipyard in Boston, supported by a new group of investors who knew and trusted his skills. His mother and stepfather eventually returned to Maine for a brief time, hoping to rebuild their settlement, and the couple would remain there until his stepfather died. His mother would eventually return to Boston, where she would remain, assisted by her son's financial support, care, and stability.

Around 1677, it was reported that William Phips took command of a Boston trading vessel bound for the West Indies. While there, he was introduced to the art of diving, and first heard about a lost sunken treasure from an "old native of Haiti." He was intrigued by the idea of discovering a vast fortune beneath the ocean, and recovering whatever wealth he might find. It was a concept that would motivate him as a deep-sea adventurer for the remainder of his life.

Meanwhile, on October 4, 1679, his mother, Mary, and stepfather, John White, decided to transfer a handsome piece of property situated at Jeremysquam Neck, Maine, to twenty-eight-year-old William. John and William Haynes served as witnesses to the legal document of ownership transfer, and the couple stated that it was done simply "for love and affection" of Mary's son. The sliver of land was situated on Westport, a twelve-mile-long island lying in the middle of the Sheepscot and Back rivers, within site of Phips Point. Like the rest of the surrounding property, this piece had originally been purchased from the Abenaki Indians by John Brown and Edward Bateman.

In 1680, William had happened upon a little-known treatise written by George Sinclair, a professor at Glasgow University. Though he could not read the words himself, one of his assistants shared the language, which detailed the theory and techniques for using diving bells to find and salvage treasure.

In 1682, armed with this rudimentary understanding of how to locate and salvage cargo from sunken ships, William shifted his attention toward treasure hunting. Making a voyage to the Bahamas as owner and captain of a small vessel, the *Resolution*, he was determined to seek lost riches near New Providence. Reportedly, he "had little success in finding any wreckage" and, after several days of diving, he decided to make an attempt in another location. Yet, "success" is often measured in the opinion of men who seek vast riches, and a 1682 court case determined that, indeed, Phips had salvaged cargo of some value during his Bahama exploits. In fact, four of Phips's former crew members sued him and the two quartermasters of the *Resolution* for nonpayment of half of their share in a venture that was, without question, this initial voyage. The Massachusetts Court of Assistants, sitting as a court of admiralty, ordered the four to receive "the half-shares of twenty-seven pounds each." A voyage in which a full share was worth fifty-four pounds would certainly qualify as a profitable enterprise. It was enough to prompt the royal customs official, Edward Randolph, to mention, in August of 1683, Phips's "late successful returns" as a treasure seeker, while a Spanish narrative of 1687 reported that Phips had "for some years followed the art of discovering shipwrecked vessels, not without considerable success."[9]

Even more determined than ever to find "untold wealth," Phips turned his attention to tales of a 680-ton sunken Spanish galleon known as the *Nuestra Señora de la Concepción*, which had gone down during a violent storm on the shoals north of Hispaniola more than four decades earlier. Realizing he needed a good deal more equipment and men for such a large-scale recovery, he traveled to England in 1683, seeking an audience with King Charles II. There he was introduced, with the help of extended family connections, to Sir John Narborough, a rear admiral and commissioner of the Royal Navy. Narborough had the ear of the king, and the political connection soon bore fruit.

Phips's success in making the politically correct contacts was, indeed, one of the more remarkable portions of his story. Historians might question how a simple, uneducated carpenter from a "despicable plantation" on the fringe of empire could possibly gain the backing of high-ranking naval officers and the crown itself. However, now that Phips's family tree has been untangled, the explanation is not so difficult to comprehend. To wealthy New Englanders, Phips may have been an outsider of humble origins, but in England his family connections were sufficiently respectable to enable even a poor cousin to muster introductions that would smooth his entry into an official culture in which connections of family and locality were crucial to his success. Indeed, he simply was related to all the right people.

In June of 1683 the Admiralty agreed to fit out and lend the American treasure hunter the *Rose of Algiers*, a twenty-two-gun 180-ton frigate, for the purpose of traveling throughout the high seas searching for gold and other treasure. The king personally took a twenty-five percent share–in addition to the crown's established ten percent–but also assigned two agents, Charles Salmon and John Knepp, to the ship to ensure it was used for the intended purpose. Edward Randolph, traveling with the vessel to New England as an appointed royal emissary, reported to Sir Robert Southwell, a long-standing English diplomat and confidante of the king:

> "Since mine to you of ye 28th last the *Rose* frigott [sic] of 20 gunns, an Algereen [sic] prize is fitted out to sea and bound to the Spanish wreck off the Bahama Islands under the conduct on one Phips...a New England man who upon his late successful returnes [sic] in that undertaking is entrusted by his Majesty & commissionated [sic] for the whole business. He is to call at Boston to take in his diving tubs (bells) & other necessaries & to return to England to account for & share the purchase upon which ship I am now directed to take my passage..."[10]

Securing an able-bodied crew to agree to go for a share of the prize– which was all that William could offer in way of payment at this time–was quite difficult, so his crew ended up being a motley bunch. The cook was given a fixed stipend contributed by each member of the crew, and was the only one exempted from any share in the recovered treasure. The common sailors were to be given a share each, equaling one of the Captains, and every boy was promised half a share. The mate and other officers were each to have something more than a regular share. And the doctor on board was provided for in the same way as the sailors. Each of the ship's company was obligated to contribute two pence monthly for the purpose of supplying his medicine chest. Orders were given for the crew to behave in a way befitting a Royal ship, which included the charge "to fire a gun morning and evening to set and discharge the watch, and to make all other vessels strike there colors and topsails in honor of their Royal ship." Finally, as commander of the ship, Phips agreed to furnish all the instruments required for locating the wreck and salvaging its treasure, but was to be reimbursed only when the share of the treasure was divided. The Captain, as well as each of his crewmembers, was obliged to give security in the amount of a hundred pounds, ensuring that the contract would be adhered to faithfully.

William Phips sailed from London on September 5, 1683. It was soon discovered that the crew had not brought enough provisions, so they were forced to anchor in the River Sharon in Ireland while Phips went to Limerick to purchase additional supplies. While he was away, the crew decided to supplement the stores themselves by shooting some sheep and chickens belonging to local farmers. Since this didn't sit well with the local magistrate, some of the crew was arrested and thrown in jail; still others were detained for selling hats they had taken with them from home. Before the voyage had even really begun, Phips was forced to free his men. Finally, after a few more weeks, the *Rose of Algiers* was fully provisioned, watered, and recaulked. On the voyage to America, one of the King's envoys, John Knepp, kept a secret journal of their exploits. Evidently, he was very upset about the crew's behavior, and "started off by grumbling that the only bed he was assigned was a lid of a chest." He also complained that, unlike a well-disciplined Royal Navy ship, there was far too much drinking, swearing, and cavorting. Half in jest and half seriously, the crew openly talked about marooning him.

On October 22, 1683, William Phips and his crew reached Boston Harbor, where they remained anchored for a few weeks, with the crew drinking and brawling in the local taverns while Phips loaded his diving tub and hired more men. Whenever other ships–either out of ignorance or obstinance–refused to dip their flags in respect to the *Rose of Algiers*, as was mandated by British rule, Phips ordered a shot be fired across their bows. Shortly thereafter, a boat would be dispatched from the *Rose* demanding six shillings, eightpence for the cost of the shot. This situation came to a head when Captain Thomas Jenner of the *Susannah and Thomas*, which had sailed out of London, was fired on for the fifth time and refused to pay for the shot. Jenner, described as "a rough, covetous tarpaulin (who) understood his business well enough, and had some smatterings of Divinity in his head,"[11] was extremely angered by Phips' arrogance; so much so that he took Phips to court, claiming he had read Phips' orders in London and they contained no power to operate as a man of war. Governor Simon Bradstreet agreed and upheld Jenner's complaint, sentencing a stubborn Phips to pay five pounds to the county and five pounds to Jenner with costs.

Meanwhile the ship's crewmembers were also in dire straits with the townspeople of Boston. Two of them were badly beaten by the town constables in a tavern and, when Phips turned up to collect his men from lockup, it was reported that he told the constables to "kiss his arse," and that he did not "care a turd for the governor." He soon found himself in front of an angry court magistrate once again, who was not amused by his actions and words. He boldly declared that it had been the constables who had started the disagreement. Folowing a stern warning, the three were allowed to return to their ship.

Somewhat naturally, Mary Phips was quite alarmed by her husband's shenanigans, realizing that Knepp's report was going to do her husband a great deal of harm once it arrived in England and was placed in the hands of the King. Consequently, she was extremely insistent that William make certain that John Knepp was on board when they set sail for the Caribbean. King's agent, Charles Salmon, got wind of all of this and, when he discussed it with Knepp, the latter jumped to the conclusion that if he did sail aboard the *Rose of Algiers*, he was unlikely to return safely. Accordingly, he made absolutely certain that he would "accidentally" miss the ship when Phips finally set sail.

At the same time, a second ship, William Warren's *Good Intent*, was preparing to go on a treasure hunting expedition to the same area in the Caribbean that Phips was planning to search. Phips couldn't beat him, so he joined him; after failing to convince Massachusetts authorities that they should prevent Warren's voyage, Phips entered into an agreement with him. In exchange for his divers and supplies, Warren would receive shares from any treasure found.

When William Phips and crew left Boston Harbor on January 14, 1684, John Knepp was nowhere on board. Despite his absence, it was reported by Salmon that the crew continued to behave badly. Twice during the voyage there were mutinies, with Phips' men attempting to turn the expedition into piracy rather than a treasure hunt. The first was quelled with his bare fists; the second time Phips aimed the ship's cannons at the perpetrators, yelling: "Stand off, ye wretches, at your peril." The guilty parties were quickly sorted out and left off at Jamaica. Meanwhile, King Charles II, having read Knepp's reports of the illicit conduct of Phips and the crew, immediately gave orders for their detention and arrest to his Massachusetts agents "if it appears that Phips or his seamen have a design to defraud the King of the ship with the plate and bullion thereon." Yet, arrest was no longer an option, since Phips had already set sail by the time the agents received the notice.

By March 16, 1684, two hundred pounds worth of treasure had been hauled in by the *Phips Diving Tub*; considered only a miniscule amount, it had been discovered in the Bermuda Triangle near Jamaica. Meanwhile, Mary's fears proved well founded, for her husband, William, was summoned back to London in August of 1684, with King Charles II expecting a thorough explanation for

Knepp's report. The accounting for the expedition indicated that the voyage was a total loss. The shares of the men were small, and the crown, which had spent 700 pounds to fit the ship, only received 471 pounds in return. The voyage back to America was further complicated by a stop in Bermuda, where Phips agreed to transport to England, Henry Bish, a staunch opponent of Bermuda's Governor Richard Coney whom Coney had had arrested. When they arrived in England, Bish had Phips arrested on charges that the shipmaster had transported him against his will, and it took the intercession of the king to secure Phips' release.

It was believed that King Charles II, fed up with Phips' disloyal behavior, was now more than willing to abandon the entire salvage operation. Yet, fate seemed to be smiling down on Phips, for, shortly after his arrival back in London, King Charles II died on February 6, 1685. Still, his successor would prove difficult to convince of the expedition's worthiness, for the king's brother, King James II, had virtually no interest in treasure hunting.

Not to be discouraged, William Phips sought out financial new backers. He did not have much luck at the start, but then the Duke of Albemarle–encouraged by his madcap wife, the former Lady Elizabeth Cavendish–agreed to put up a quarter of the capital. Not to be outdone, Sir John Narborough's interest was revived, and he agreed to put up an eighth. He could certainly afford it, for his second wife–another Elizabeth–had brought him a large dowry to add to the fortune in prize money he had reaped from three successful expeditions against the Barbary corsairs. The partners bought a frigate, diplomatically renaming the 200-ton, 23-gun *Bridgewater* the *James & Mary*, sold the other shares to five more investors, secured a Royal Patent, and off Phips sailed for a second attempt at fame and fortune. To accompany the *William & Mary*, the 45-ton *Henry of London* sloop was dispatched as a sister-ship. She was commanded by Francis Rogers, who had been Phips' second mate during the previous voyage. As Daniel Defoe later described the entire operation, "'twas a mere Project, a Lottery of a Hundred Thousand to One odds." And yet, it proved to be one of the greatest commercial successes of the 17th century.

Phips sailed from London in September of 1686, arriving off Hispaniola in November. Weather conditions were poor, and the search was delayed for a few months. On January 20, 1687, as she floated along the Ambrosia Bank, the shallow draft sloop *Henry of London*'s crew spotted what was later described as a "sea feather"–a pretty plume-like coral–well below the surface. On attempting to capture it and bring it aboard, they discovered that it grew from the encrusted muzzle of a cannon on the hulk of a rotting ship. Unknowingly at first, they had found the wrecked 1641 Spanish vice admiral, *Nuestra Señora de la Limpia y Pura Concepción*, wedged tightly between rocks in seven or eight fathoms (about forty feet) of boiling shoal water. She had lain there undisturbed for forty-six long years. Until midmorning on January 22, 1687, the divers pulled up treasure, but a threatening sky warned them it was time to sail back to Puerto Plata to inform William Phips of their find. It was reported that Phips wept at the news.

AMERICAN SUBMARINERS: PRE-CIVIL WAR

On February 22, Phips, four trained divers, and a pair of diving tubs arrived at the site. Much like Edmond Halley's design, the *Phips Diving Tub* resembled an upside-down truncated cone, measuring five feet across its open bottom and about three feet across its closed, airtight top. The slanted sides of the Tub stood precisely five feet in height. Hanging beneath the Tub was a platform, fasted to the bottom edges in four places by stout hemp rope. This floor was intended to stand on as Phips crawled up into the vessel.

Diving Tub similar to that of William Phips

Once inside, William Phips sat upon a bench, where he would remain perfectly dry. Here, at ete level, was a glass porthole, which not only let light in but allowed the diver to see out. In a number of earlier test dives, Phips had learned that the deeper the tub sank, the higher the water level rose within.

It wsa recorded that the Phips divers pulled up treasure from dawn to dusk for fifty-eight days, losing eight Sundays, nine days to extremely bad weather, and one day on March 10 when the divers were terribly ill. The four divers worked so diligently, without much rest, that it was recorded they sometimes "came up coughing blood." They had managed to bring up more than thirty-seven tons of treasure, including 63,000 pounds of silver, 347 pounds of gold, and chests of pearls, rubies, emeralds, and diamonds. They had picked clean all that could be easily reached, leaving the coral encrusted after-hold that was wedged between the two huge rocks untouched. Concern for hurricanes and pirates forced them to return to England before the job was complete:

"...Phips finally called an end to the operation and returned to England with treasure that would equal $50 million in today's currency..."[12]

William Phips and crew arrived back in London on June 6, 1687. For his valiant efforts, Phips received his 1/16 share, which equaled £11,043, or about $80,000; he also was given a gold chain and medal, valued at $5,000. The Duke of Albemarle presented his wife, Lady Mary, with a gold cup worth about $400. King James II's share was approximately £20,700. The expedition's financing partners received the remainder. All in all, the find was described as changing the very future of England, returning wealth to a nation in desperate need.

King James II awarded William Phips the title of "Knight of the Bachelor Order," making him the first American ever knighted. He was also given the post of Provost Marshal General (chief sheriff) of the Dominion of New England, serving under Sir Edmund Andros. In September of 1687, Phips returned to the wreck, though he did not command the venture. Admiral John Narborough elected to personally lead the expedition, which was supported by King James II, who purchased shares and provided a navy frigate for security. The expedition was not very successful, since the sunken ship had already been found by other treasure hunters, and the arrival of the English had scattered more than twenty smaller ships in search of riches. Treasure worth only £10,000 was recovered during this final expedition before Narborough's death in May of 1688, which brought the entire operation to an abrupt end. Phips had, in fact, left the salvage site in early May, sailing for Boston to take up his post as provost marshal.

Nearly 300 years would pass before the job would be finished. During "Operation Phips" in 1977, treasure seeker, Burt Weber, and his crew attempted to find the *Concepcion* and bring up the remaining treasure Phips had been unable to bring up. The initial attempt failed, but after an English researcher uncovered Phips' ship log giving the precise location of the vessel, a second attempt was made in 1978 that proved to be a success. Every working day for nine long months they brought treasure up, including, porcelain predating the Ming dynasty, unmarked silver, three ancient astrolabs once used in navigation and said to be worth $100,000, chains of gleaming gold, a unique ivory doll, a traveling trunk with a false bottom concealing silver coins neatly stacked four to six deep, buckets of silver and gold coins, and crates of exquisite ancient pottery. This most recent recovery was estimated to be worth $200 million.

A spectacular dinner was held at the Swan Tavern in London, in celebration of William Phips' successful salvage expedition. The food was sumptuous and the wine flowed freely, and everyone in attendance "made merry into the late hours of the night." Despite the unparalleled success of the venture, Spain would long argue that the rediscovered horde them, an argument that would cause political unrest between the two powerful nations for a number of years.

Sterner moralists were of the steadfast opinion that it might only be fair that members of a marauding expedition should not enjoy the fruits of their illegal gains. In retrospect, history has recorded that many of them did not. As stated, Rear Admiral, Sir John Narborough, died at sea in 1688; the Duke of Albemarle, Christopher Monck, passed away at the age of thirty-five the following October; and two other investors would die within a few years. Meanwhile, those investors that remained were plagued by lawsuits. It seemed that those who "meddled with the riches of the dead" were destined to be bitter and unsatisfying. But what of Phips?

Though Sir William Phips would never again search for treasure beneath the ocean surface, he was destined to gain notoriety for a number of totally different types of exploits. He returned to America amid a hero's welcome. Tanned from the southern sun, majestic in his captain's clothes, he first began constructing the brick house of his dreams. Next, he joined the Congregational Church of Boston, where he met Cotton Mather, who was destined to become his official biographer. And, on April 20, 1690, he was given the prestigious post of leading a naval force that was charged with capturing French-held Port Royal.

Soon enough, history also recorded that Phips was not well suited for the Provost Marshal General post in Boston. He had no administrative or legal experience, and he had no significant political connections either with the Andros administration or with local politicians.

Sir William would return to England in February of 1691 to seek financial and political support for yet another expedition. Securing no such support he, instead, joined with Increase Mather and other agents to gain a new charter for Massachusetts. A number of Mather's requests concerning the charter were rejected, but William and Mary placated Mather by allowing him to nominate the colony's next governor. The monarchs appointed Phips the first royal governor, at Mather's suggestion, under a newly issued colonial charter for the Province of Massachusetts Bay. The charter greatly expanded the colony's bounds, including not just the territories of the Massachusetts Bay Colony, but also those of the Plymouth Colony, islands south of Cape Cod including Martha's Vineyard and Nantucket, and the present-day territories of Maine, New Brunswick, and Nova Scotia.

On reaching Boston on May 14, 1692, Phips found the colony gripped by witchcraft hysteria, which he detailed in a letter dated October 12, 1692:

> "When I first arrived I found this province miserably harrassed with a most Horrible witchcraft or Possession of Devills which had broke in upon severall Townes, some score of poor people were taken with preternaturall torments some scalded with brimstone some had pins stuck in their flesh others hurried into the fire and water and some dragged out of their houses and carried over the tops of trees and hills for many Miles together; it hath been represented to mee much like that of Sweden about thirty years agoe, and there were many committed to prison upon suspicion of Whichcraft before my arrival. The loud cries and clamours of the friends of the afflicted people with the advice of the Deputy Governor and many others prevailed with mee to give a Commission..."[13]

Within a three-month period that he was away, more than 125 people had been arrested on charges of witchcraft, and were held in prison pending the inauguration of the new government. Phips established a special Court of Oyer and Terminer to hear the accumulated cases on May 27, appointing Lieutenant Governor William Stoughton as the chief judge. The court notoriously admitted spectral evidence—alleged demonic visions—and denied the accused access to legal counsel, and a number of people were convicted and executed based on such evidence. Although the court was terminated in September of 1692, accusations and arrests continued, including charges against some fairly high profile individuals, including Phips own wife. Phips finally put an end to the proceedings by first suspending the trials, and then in May of 1693 releasing about 150 prisoners charged with witchcraft.

Meanwhile, French and Indian raids had resumed in the years following Phips' 1690 expeditions, so he sought to improve the province's defenses. Pursuant to his instructions from London, in 1692 he oversaw the construction of a stone fort, which was dubbed Fort William Henry, at Pemaquid (present-day Bristol, Maine), where a wooden fort had been destroyed in 1689. The expense involved in this effort made it unpopular in the province. Attempts by Phips to coordinate defenses with neighboring provinces were marred by difficulties often emanating from his rough personality and temper. He persuaded Major Benjamin Church to lead a 450-man expedition against the Indians within the Maine territory. In August of 1693, Phips reached an extremely tenuous peace agreement with the Abenaki people, one of the Algonquian-speaking peoples of northeastern North America; it was eventually subverted by French interests to bring the Abenaki back on the warpath, and had no lasting impact.

Phips' governorship was marked by political factionalism, and his lack of connections to existing local powers hurt him. To add insult to injury, Joseph Dudley, a Massachusetts native (and former dominion official) was in London, scheming to replace him. Phips frequently quarreled with friends, foes, and other government officials. His biographers describe his behavior as "blustering aggressiveness," and his contemporaries complained of his "lowness of education." He argued with neighboring governors over military issues, and even went as far as to aggravate a border dispute with neighboring Rhode Island. He twice got into physical altercations with other government officials, situations that Dudley and his other opponents highlighted to the Lords of Trade. He was also accused of violating the Navigation Acts–which he was, as governor, supposed to enforce–in what his opponents described as "illegal and self-serving commercial activities." Phips' repeated attempts to justify his actions included attacks on his enemies, many of whom were on good terms with the colonial secretary, William Blathwayt. Nonetheless, Blathwayt continued to support him, as did Increase Mather, but this was not enough to overcome the many complaints lodged against him.

Dislike, mistrust, suspicion, antagonisms, animosity, and religious zealots gave rise to a great number of personal enemies. Sir John William Fortescue, a military historian of the British army who served as the Royal Librarian and Archivist of Widsor Castle for more than two decades, referred to Phips as "ignorant, brutal, covetous and violent," and that his appointment to the Government of Massachusetts was "a very grave misfortune."

Later, John Clarence Webster, a long-time medical doctor who specialized in gynecology and obstetrics, conducted extensive medical research at the University of Chicago. He resigned his position there in 1919, apparently leaving medicine entirely, returned to his home in Shediac, New Brunswick, Canada, and took up the study of history. Among other appointments, Dr. Webster was to become a Trustee of the Public Archives of Nova Scotia, a Member of the Historic and Monuments Board of Canada, and the Honourary Curator of Fort Beausejour Museum. After studying the life of William Phips, perhaps more thoroughly than any other historian, he summed up the man's life in the following manner:

> "His education had been elementary, his mental endowment was limited, and he was fond of boasting of his self-made career in rather a coarse manner. He was inclined to be rude and hot tempered and on one occasion, while he was governor [Boston], did not hesitate to cane the collector of the port and a Captain in the Royal navy, actions which indicated that he was quote unfitted for such a position. The truth is that Phips was a self-made man of the roughest type. He owed everything to his luck in recovering treasure from a sunken vessel; for this he received a title and obtained the favour of royal parasites who gladly took from him the lion's share. He returned to Massachusetts a marked man, possessing wealth

and the king's favour. His capture of Port Royal was the result neither of boldness, ability, nor military qualities. The place fell without any defence. The terms of capitulation were much better than they need have been, had he taken precautions to ascertain the true state of affairs. When he realized that the Governor and Father Petit had scored over him, instead of accepting the situation like a gentleman, he sought and found an excuse to break the terms, and behaved like a cad, even taking the money and personal effects of the Governor, which the Council at Boston later forced him to give back."[14]

Meanwhile, a number of other malcontents wanted Phips either hanged or, at the very least, recalled to London to answer charges. A lengthy list of grievances, signed by those who knew him intimately, was forwarded to King William III and Queen Mary.

On July 4, 1694, Phips received an official summons to appear before the Lords of Trade in London. He spent much of the summer at Pemaquid, overseeing the frontier defenses, while Lieutenant Governor William Stoughton oversaw the gathering of evidence for the hearing. He sailed for England on November 17, and arrived in London on January 1, 1695. There, he was arrested on exaggerated charges, levied by Joseph Dudley, that he had conspired to withhold customs monies. Dudley had hoped that the £20,000 bail would prevent Phips' return to Massachusetts, but Phips was bailed out by Sir Henry Ashurst.

Perhaps it was stress that caused William Phips to fall gravely ill with a fever while preparing his defense, and he died unexpextedly on February 18, 1695, before his charges were heard. He was buried in Bristol, England, at the far east end of the yard of the Church of St. Mary Woolnoth, near the corner of King William Street and Lombard Street. Overcome with grief, his wife, Mary, had a fitting monument erected to honor her dead husband. It was white and adorned with a carving depicting an urn between two cupids, the figure of ship and a boat at sea, with persons in the water. It also exhibited seven medals, some with Spanish impressions, including the royal castle. Finally, there was the figure of a sea-quadrant, a cross-staff, and the Phips' family coat-of-arms, all of which surrounded the following inscription:

> "Near this place is interred the body of Sir William Phips, Knight; who in the year 1689, by his great industry, discovered among the rocks near the banks of the Bahamas, on the north side of Hispaniola, a Spanish plate ship, which had been under water 44 years, out of which he took gold and silver, to the value of 300,000 pounds sterling, and with fidelity equal to his conduct brought it all to to London, where it was divided between himself and the rest of the adventurers; for which great service he was knighted by his then Majesty King James the 2nd; and afterward by the command of his present Majesty and at the request of principal inhabitants of New England, he accepted the government of Massachusetts, in which he continued at the time of his death; and discharged his trust with

that zeal for the interest of his country, and with so little regard to his own private advantage, that he justly gained the good esteem and affections of the greatest and best part of the inhabitants of that Colony."[14]

The original marker was later removed. Eventually, in 1892, his remains were relocated to Manor Park Cemetery in London, where they still rest today.

Depiction of David Bushnell

- 5 -
David Bushnell: *American Turtle*

"Considering Bushnell's machine as the first of its kind, I think it will be pronounced to be remarkably complete throughout in its construction, and that such an invention furnishes evidence of those resources and creative powers, which must rank him as a mechanical genius of the first order..."[1]

Just as numerous detailed innovations of aviation were initially conceived when America was in the tedious process of creeping toward independence, so, too, were the foundation principles of underwater vehicles. Ursula Southeil–better known as "Mother Shipton," a "seer" from 16th century England–may have been the first to predict precisely what was in store for future generations when she blatantly proclaimed: "Under water men shall walk, shall ride, shall sleep, shall talk."

That rather startling prediction, made more than four hundred years ago, paved the way for a remarkable American inventor named David Bushnell (1740-1824), who launched an odd-looking submersible craft in the summer of 1775 which has come to be known as the *American Turtle*. His "water machine," the first of its kind in this country's lengthy history, was destined to become the cornerstone in America's search for the "perfect" underwater vessel.

When and where the Bushnell family name originated will, in all likelihood, never be fully known. Evidence indicates that it was first recorded in Berkshire County, England, in an area situated west of Reading, along Kennet River. Prior to the Norman Conquest, the individual family name of "Bushnell"–or any of its probable spelling variations–did not seem to exist; at least not among the middle classes.

The ancestral line of submarine inventor, David Bushnell, can be traced back to Joan Busshenell, his eighth great-grandmother, a widow found in the taxation subsidy roll dated January 15, 1524, who was then residing in Tilehurst, Berkshire County, England. Her son, William Busshenell, left a will dated August 31, 1563, expressing a desire to be buried in the "Tylehurst churchyard," and bequeathing to his "son John, a cow, a brass pot, a kettle, and one-half his tools; son William a bullock, a sheep, an old pan and one-half his tools; dau. Alice a cow, a pot and a kettle; dau. Joan two bullocks, a heifer, a kettle, and a gown; servant Joan Pinke a petticoat cloth and as much wool as will make her a pair of hosen." John, William's eldest son, was David's sixth great-grandfather.

Situated along the north shore of the River Thames, the tiny hamlet of Tilehurst was first recorded in 1291 in Pope Nicholas III's taxation lists. With the dissolution of the monasteries, King Henry VIII had granted the Manor of "Tylehurst," which had long been a part of the Reading Abbey, to Francis Englefield. Four years later, in the spring of 1549, twenty-four-year-old "Yeoman" Nicholas, son of John and Alice Bushnell, married Elizabeth at the St. Thomas Chapel in nearby Thatcham. Situated some twelve-and-one-half miles west of Tilehurst, it was here that the newly-married Bushenells decided to live with Elizabeth's aging parents and raise a family.

Francis Bushnell, Sr., David's fourth great-grandfather, was the first child and eldest son of Nicholas and Alice, born in Thatcham, Berkshire County, England, in early 1550. During the span of the next decade, he was followed by brothers John, Roger, Richard, Thomas, and William, as well as only sister, Joan. His father's will, dated April 10, 1591, bequeathed "to the poor of Thatcham, 10s; to his eldest son Francis, his messuages and lands in Thatcham, and Henwick, called Auberies, and in Midgham, and 3 acres in North Field near Thatcham, including the piddles (Pightels) therounto belonging, to him and the male heirs of his body, with contingent remainders to his sons Roger and Richard, entail male, and to the said Roger and Richard 20s each a year; to Joan Bushnell, dau. of Francis Bushnell a bullock and a cow, his overseers to have charge of the same until her age of 21..."

Francis Bushnell, Jr., David's great-great-great-grandfather, was born about 1580 in Thatcham, and was married first to Ferris Quenell on May 13, 1605, in Horsham, Sussex County, England. When Ferris died just a few weeks prior to her 41st birthday, while giving birth to their twelfth child, she was laid to rest with her stillborn daughter, Elizabeth, on March 10, 1628. Records indicate that Francis was married second to Joan Kinward on June 2, 1629, residing in that same region for the next ten years.

All indications are that Francis, Jr., was an artisan by trade, making an adequate living as either a painter or decorator, for in 1610, it was written that "Frauncis Bushnell was paid ve (five shillings) for cullering the funt (of the church or alter) in Horsham." His name would be mentioned again on August 15, 1625, in the will of his father as a beneficiary and executor. By 1626, Francis and his family had "subscribed" to the church at Horsham, Sussex County, England, for "by a seating list of this church dated 1626...a Seate under the new gallery stayers for Pharis Bushnell, the wife of Frauncis Bushnell, to belong to him and his heirs for ever."

"For ever," it seems, lasted just over a dozen years, for Francis, Jr., departed from England bound for America in May of 1639, along with his second wife, Joan, and two daughters from his first marriage, Rebecca and Sarah. Their ship was named the *St. John*, and she was one of two vessels that sailed under the leadership of Reverend Henry Whitfield. When these vessels were about ten days out, a covenant was signed and, in July, the ships entered the calm harbor waters of Quinnipack, the first from across the ocean to reach that port. Those aboard joined together to purchase land from the Mohegan Sachem Uncas, and named their settlement Guilford, after a hamlet in England, where many of them had originated. The words of the covenant read:

> "We, whose names are hereunder written, intending by God's gracious permission to plant ourselves in New England, and if it may be, in the southerly part, about Quinnipiac: We do faithfully promise, each to each for ourselves and families, and those that belong to us; that we will, the Lord assisting us, sit down and join ourselves together in one intire plantation: and to be helpful each to the other in every common work, according to every man's ability and as need shall require; and we promise not to desert or leave each other or the plantation, but with the consent of the rest, or the greater part of the company who have entered into this engagement. As for our gathering together in a church way, and the choice of officers and members to be joined together in that way, we do refer ourselves until such time as it shall please God to settle us in our plantation. In witness whereof we suscribe [sic] our hands, the first day of June, 1639."[2]

Francis Bushnell's name appeared third on the list of twenty-five individuals who signed what became known as the "Guilford Covenant," sometimes called the "Plantation Covenant."

Like the majority of seventeenth century New England towns, Guilford was organized around a common or green, with the first homes being nothing more than small huts with thatched roofs, wooden walls and dirt floors. Unlike other villages, it had no protective palisade fence surrounding the community. In their stead, the residents constructed four large stone houses for the township leaders. The home of Reverend Whitfield remains one of the oldest houses in the United States outside of St. Augustine, Florida. These stone houses were strategically located and used for shelter by all during times of emergency. Life in Guilford was extremely primitive, resembling a medieval village for several generations to come.

Earlier, William Bushnell, son of Francis, Jr., had been baptized on February 3, 1610, in Horsham, Sussex County, England. Records indicate that he came to America a full four years before his father, finding passage with his four living brothers–Francis III, Edmond, John, and Thomas–aboard a ship named the *Planter*. Arriving in Boston in 1635, he took up residence in nearby Salem for a few years, before relocating to Guilford, Connecticut, where he began to ply his trades as both a carpenter and miller.

On February 8, 1637, Francis Bushnell III was granted a tract of land of twenty-four acres at Muddy River Hamlet, Massachusetts, so named for the series of murky brooks and ponds that ran through sections of Boston's Emerald Necklace. There must have been six in Francis' family at the time, however, for these lots at Muddy River were granted according to the number of heads in the family. Historians believe that this included Francis, his wife, their two daughters, Elizabeth and Martha, and two of his brothers, most likely Richard and William, David Bushnell's great-great-grandfather. Thus, "those that face the river between the foot of the hill and the river, four acres upon a head and those that are further off, to have five acres upon a head." Accordingly, six heads equalled twenty-four acres.

In 1642, William relocated to Saybrook, Connecticut, where he met and married Rebecca Chapman in 1643. There, according to family tradition, he constructed the first meetinghouse in 1646. As a carpenter and miller, he assisted in helping the town grow over the next decade. In 1659, he was the town rate collector and, on October 3, 1661, was appointed Ensign of the "train band" militia, serving during the Indian wars. By then, he and Rebecca had given birth to eleven children, seven sons and four daughters. The Bushnell family was expanding quickly across the face of America.

William Bushnell, Jr., David Bushnell's great-grandfather, carried on the family trade as a carpenter and miller. On October 1, 1675, he married Rebecca Stratton of Long Island, New York. Five years later, in 1680, the citizens of Saybrook granted him a tract of twenty-four acres at Tilley's Point, where he would build a house and raise his four children. William Bushnell III, David's grandfather, was born there on April 3, 1680. Almost thirty years to the day later, on April 22, 1710, David's father, Nehemiah, was born.

Life must not have been easy during the early-1700s for the townspeople of Saybrook, Connecticut, which was nestled in Middlesex County near the mouth of the mighty Connecticut River, stretching out along the sandy shoreline of Long Island Sound. Agricultural endeavors in this region of young America were nearly unbearable, at times, for the residents were forced to cope with almost insurmountable problems on a daily basis. These issues included tilling the rocky, almost unworkable, ground; using crude farm implements, such as wooden plows, harnesses, and harrows, which required continual repair and replacement; and the constant supervision of growing and demanding families, consisting of a half-dozen children or more. Such was the inevitable environment for young David Bushnell, who was born to Nehemiah and Sarah (Ingram) Bushnell on August 30, 1740.

Hundreds of years earlier, the Algonquin-Nehantic Indians had occupied a village here, which they called "Pashebeshauke," meaning "The Place at the River's Mouth." Early in the 1600s, these same Indians were conquered by the Pequot tribe from the North. In 1614, a Dutch explorer Adriaen Block, became the first European to enter the river Quonitocutt, or "Long Tidal River." The Dutch were active fur traders and claimed the river for the New Netherlands. In 1631, the Earl of Warwick, as president of the Council for New England, had signed the "Warwick Patent," conveying a vast segment of New England to a group of English Lords and Gentlemen. Among them were Viscount Saye and Baron Brook, for whom the town of Saybrook was be named in 1635.

AMERICAN SUBMARINERS: PRE-CIVIL WAR

David Bushnell grew up in the same two-story home built by his grandfather, William Bushnell III. As a child, he attended the local one-room schoolhouse, where he acquired rudimentary academic skills. Soon after he had learned to read, write, and cipher, his formal learning came to a sudden standstill, at least for the time being. It had been his father's opinion that young David's physical prowess was in far greater demand around the family homestead than were his abilities in the classroom.

At home, the ambitious youngster applied all that he had absorbed from his daily observations toward the invention of a number of work-saving devices and machines. He designed a harrow, for example, that possessed "springy teeth," which enabled him to "grasp" onto the heavy, back-breaking stones in the fields. Later, he devised an ingenious plan for insulating the Bushnell family home against frigid temperatures by hauling cart-load after cart-load of grass from the nearby marshes and stuffing it between the inner plank walls and the abode's outside shell.

As he grew from adolescence into manhood, Bushnell passed the time partaking in his favorite hobby—reading. He was described by one close friend as "a very modest, retiring young man, shunning all society and bound down to his books."[3] Later, when he was twenty-seven years old, his father died, and it was Bushnell's fortune to inherit the family estate. Yet, he seemed rather dissatisfied with his lot in life.

Hence, in the autumn of 1770, having harvested the season's crops of corn and beans, David opted to sell the farm, lock-stock-and-barrel, to his brother, Ezra. Next, he took up residence at the home of Elias Tully, who lived in the center of Saybrook. Determined to further his education, David spent the remainder of that year studying under the direction of the Reverend John Devotion, respected pastor of the local Congregationalist Church.

The following summer, David Bushnell presented himself to the board of examiners at Yale University, located in nearby New Haven, Connecticut, and he was duly accepted. During his first year of college, along with another university intellectual, Phineas Pratt, he became somewhat enthralled by the concept of experimenting with exploding submerged gunpowder charges. He felt that, if deployed correctly, such a force might be able to inflict a great deal of damage to an enemy vessel. Together, the enterprising pair conceived of an underwater bomb that housed a time delayed flintlock detonator.

It seems, however, that Bushnell's hypothesis on the subject conflicted with the accepted theories of the day: that the force of any underwater explosion would tend to dissipate harmlessly downward into the water. Thus, his ideas of creating a sound and effective underwater explosive were scoffed at by most learned theorists and scientists. Undaunted by these so-called "experts," David continued his experiments, which would one day prove his assumptions.

His earliest tests with underwater explosives were conducted by employing approximately two ounces of black powder encased in miniature wooden kegs, which he positioned four feet below the surface. These mines eventually managed to evolve into much more forceful charges:

> "The...experiment was made with two pounds of powder inclosed [sic] in a wooden bottle, and fixed under a hogshead, with a two-inch oak plank between the hogshead and the powder; the hogshead was loaded with stones as deep as it could swim; a wooden pipe, descending through the lower head of the hogshead, and through the plank, into the powder contained in the bottle, was primed with powder. A match put to the priming exploded the powder, which produced a very great effect; rending the plank into pieces, demolishing the hogshead, and casting the stones and the ruins of the hogshead, with a body of water, many feet into the air, to the astonishment of the spectators. I afterwards made many experiments of a similar nature, some of them with large quantities of powder; they all produced very violent explosions, much more than sufficient for any purpose I had in view..."[4]

Such experiments with underwater explosives seemed somewhat incongruous to those who were close friends of the thirty-five-year-old student, for he had always presented himself as a frail, gentle, scholarly man, rather than an adventurous inventor. One classmate, from a patriotic assembly of men who were far more intrigued with the romantic notion that they would one day run off to join the Continental Army and risk their lives in the defense of their homeland, expressed the group's mutual lack of confidence by proclaiming: "I pray we are not close by when David blows himself up."

Still, though Bushnell was not cut out to be "soldier material" in the eyes of his friends, he was extremely patriotic. Somewhere in his personal vision of himself, he hoped to one day contribute to the ultimate downfall of the ruling British empire.

During the autumn of 1772, as the American colonists were swept closer and closer toward an armed conflict with Great Britain, Bushnell turned his attention toward the construction of an underwater mine that would be able to destroy any British man-of-war on the high seas. After extensive testing, conducted upon small target crafts set adrift in the Connecticut River, he calculated that it would require approximately 150 pounds of gunpowder to be successful in this dubious venture.

Next, David Bushnell was compelled to determine precisely how his underwater explosives could best be deployed against the British flotilla, which was habitually stationed in the shallow waters along the northeast coastline of North America. Briefly outlined, his initial plan of attack would be to release the keg-mines in an adjoining stream, where they would be carried by God, luck, and the prevailing currents toward the vulnerable wooden hulls of the enemy vessels. To this end, Bushnell had devised a unique fuse, so sensitive that it would instantaneously detonate on contact.

However, the young inventor quickly came to realize that this "chance" method of destruction was not without its shortcomings. Not only was the constant ebb and flow of the ocean currents quite unpredictable, but there would exist a very real possibility that one of these dangerous "floating devils" might accidentally explode against the hull of an unsuspecting American ship.

In the beginning, David Bushnell's solution to this directional problem was to load a lightweight skiff with one or more of his mines. Individually outfitted with timed detonating devices, the craft could then be guided under the cover of darkness and attached by ropes to the sides of an enemy vessel. However, this idea also brought with it a number of problems. First, the explosives-laden craft would be expected to somehow find its way to the target ship, most likely by rowing or towing, and then the perpetrators would be forced to make their escape. Furthermore, the British might very well spot the skiff and its operators before the attack had reached its cataclysmic end, thus foiling the entire "secret" operation.

Sometime in 1774, David happened upon an article printed in the 1747 volume of *English Gentleman's Magazine*, which he discovered on the dusty shelves of the university library. There, on page 581, he read a "description of a diving ship, built by order of his most serene highness Charles Landgrave of Hesse Cassel." Attached to the article were detailed sketches, drawn by Cornelius Jacobszoon Drebbel, a Dutch physician who had also invented an improved microscope, a mercury thermostat, a chicken incubator. David carefully copied each of Drebbel's drawing by hand and excitedly shared them with his close friend, Phineas Pratt, as well as his brother, Ezra.

Born in Alkmaar, Holland, in 1572, Drebbel had studied at both the Latin School and the Academy of Haarlem. His instructors at the Academy had included a number of well-respected, learned men: Hendrick Goltzius, engraver, painter, and humanist; Karel van Mander, painter, writer, and humanist; and Cornelis Corneliszoon, who had invented the wind-powered sawmill. Under their tutelage, Drebbel came to understand a great number of devices that might be utelized in a submersible vessel.

Intriguingly, Drebbel's third and final submarine model, completed and tested in 1624, could transport up to sixteen passengers. Bushnell could clearly determine that its propulsion was based on a simple rowing boat with raised and meeting sides, covered in greased leather, with a watertight hatch in the middle, a rudder and six oars. Under the rowers' seats were positioned large pigskin bladders, connected by pipes to the outside. Rope could used to tie off the empty bladders; in order to dive, the rope was simply untied and the bladders filled. To surface the crew squashed the bladders flat, squeezing out the water.

Incorporating each of Drebbel's submarine concepts one-by-one, the thirty-one-year-old Bushnell began his quest to design a working model of his own during the spring semester in 1775. His, however, would be much smaller, carrying only the operator, and it would be used as an attack vessel. Seeking financial support from the Connecticut colony, David Bushnell was offered "a rather insignificant pittance" to assist in the construction costs. He eventually rejected the Colony's offer of meager funding, calling it extremely "inconsiderable." Instead, he opted to proceed "at his own Risque."

During the months that preceded the outbreak of the Revolution, when America was not yet in its independent infancy stage, there were a number of engineering and scientific problems for Bushnell to overcome if he hoped to construct a formidable version of his attack submarine. They included the designing of a waterproof hull to withstand immense water pressure; horizontal, as well as vertical, mobility; an adequate steering mechanism; variable ballast characteristics; upright stability while the vessel was totally submerged; and an effective explosives delivery system. Yet, despite the seemingly insurmountable odds of success, Bushnell was determined to see his project through to the bitter end.

Returning to Saybrook, David convinced his younger brother, Ezra, to take part in the design and construction of a prototype model, turning to Phineas Pratt to forge its necessary ironwork frame. Isaac Doolittle of New Haven, a well-versed mechanic and clock-maker, was recruited to design a force pump that would enable the vessel to be raised to the surface after submersion. Together, the Bushnell brothers, Pratt, and Doolittle located an insignificant building site on Poverty Island, located near Sill's Point, along the Connecticut River. There, they constructed a small shed, which would be used as the main workshop. They decided to disguise their activities by informing local residents and township officials that they were planning to enter the competitive fishing business. Apparently, Bushnell had convinced each of the other three to do work on speculation, anticipating eventual government financial support.

Next, the creative Bushnell brothers transported huge quantities of oak, tar, cork, rope, brass, and iron to their island hideaway, all beneath the guise of constructing a large fishing vessel. And, despite a lack of technical know-how, the Bushnells' submersible craft was carefully and meticulously constructed:

> "The Body, when standing upright in the position in which it is navigated, has the nearest resemblance to the two upper shells of a Tortoise joined together. In length it doth not exceed 7-1/2 feet from the stem to the higher part of the rudder: the height not exceeding 6 feet. The person who navigates it enters at the top. It has a brass top or cover, which receives the person's head as he sits on a seat, and is fastened on the inside by screws. In this brass head is fixed eight glasses, viz. two before, two on each side, one behind, and one to look out upwards. In the same brass head are fixed two brass tubes, to admit fresh air when requisite, and a ventilator at the side to free the machine from the air rendered unfit for respiration. On the inside is fixed a Barometer, by which he can tell the depth he is under water; a Compass, by which he knows the course he steers. In the barometer and on the needles of the compass is fixed foxfire, i.e. wood that gives light in the dark. His ballast consists of about 900 wt. of lead which he carried at the bottom and on the outside of the

machine, part of which is so fixed as he can let run down to the Bottom, and serves as an anchor, by which he can ride ad libitum. He has a sounding lead fixed at the bow, by which he can take the depth of water under him; and to bring the machine into a perfect equilibrium with the water, he can admit so much water as is necessary, and has a forcing pump by which he can free the machine at pleasure, and can rise above water, and again immerge, as occasion requires. In the bow, he has a pair of oars fixed like the two opposite arms of a wind mill, with which he can row forward, and turning them the opposite way, row the machine backward; another pair fixed upon the same model, with which he can row the machine round, either to the right or left, and a third, by which he can row the machine either up or down; all which are turn'd by foot, like a spinning wheel. The rudder by which he steers, he manages by hand, within board. All these shafts which pass through the machine are so curiously fix'd as not to admit any water to incommode the machine. The magazine for the powder is carried on the hinder part of the machine, without board, and so contrived, that when he comes under the side of the Ship, he rubs down the side until he comes to the keel, and a hook so fix'd as that when it touches the keel it raises a spring which frees the magazine from the machine and fastens it to the side of the Ship; at the same time, it draws a pin, which sets the watchwork agoing which, at a given time, springs the lock and the explosion ensues. Three magazines are prepared; the first, the explosion takes place in twelve, -- the second in eight, -- the third in six hours, after being fixed to the ship. He proposes to fix these three before the first explosion takes place. He has made such a trial of the effects of the explosion of gunpowder under water, since Dr. [Benjamin] Franklin did me the honor to call upon me, as has exceeded his most sanguine expectations, and is now convinced his magazines will contain three times so much powder as is necessary to destroy the largest ship in the navy."[5]

Though the craft would later be referred to as the *American Turtle*, the *Marine Turtle*, and the *Marine Torpedo*, the Bushnells apparently never christened the ship, calling it simply a "submarine vessel."

The *American Turtle* measured seven feet deep from the top of its crown to the bottom of its detachable keel, four feet long, and three feet at her thickest width. Her hull was constructed of warped oak planking held together by strong iron bands, somewhat like barrel staves, and all of her joints were meticulously waterproofed with an ample application of tar and cork. In the opinion of those who saw her, she was shaped to resemble something halfway between an egg and a clam standing on end.

The vessel was designed as a one-man vehicle, whose operator would have his work cut out for him. First, he would be forced to enter through a crude conning tower fashioned into a snug brass hatchway measuring twenty inches in diameter and seven inches high. Shaped like a derby hat, the opening was situated at the crest of her domed hull. This opening could be sealed with a hinged lid once the operator entered, making the vessel safely airtight.

From his perch, which was nothing more than an oak beam attached above the lead ballast and two flood tanks to reinforce the craft's structure, Bushnell could peer out of a half-dozen glassed portholes no larger than half-dollars, which had been neatly cut into the conning tower. To propel the submarine in a forward or reverse motion, the operator's right hand would work a crank situated in front of him, which, in turn, would spin a pair of heavy oak blades on the outside. Simultaneously, his left hand would control the rudder, allowing the craft to turn in either direction. It was his left foot that would operate the ballast chamber, opening and closing a valve: "through which water entered at his pleasure. When he had admitted a sufficient quantity, he descended very gradually; if he admitted too much, he ejected as much as was necessary to obtain an equilibrium, by the two brass forcing pumps, which were placed at each hand..."[6]

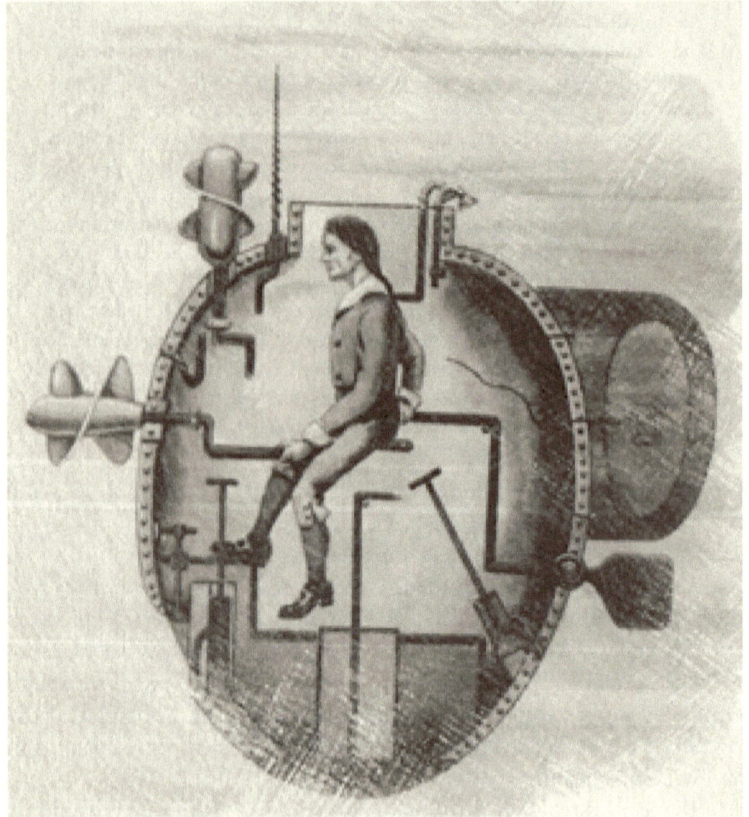

David Bushnell's *American Turtle*

Finally, by turning a hand-operated auger stationed to the front of the conning tower, the operator would be able to attach the submarine's deadly 150-pound torpedo explosive to the belly of an enemy vessel:

"Behind the submarine vessel was a place, above the rudder, for carrying a large powder magazine. This was made of two pieces of oak timber... and was secured in its place by a screw turned by the operator. A strong piece of rope extended from the magazine to the wood screw...and was fastened to both. When the wood screw was fixed and was to be cast off from its tube, the magazine was to be cast off likewise by unscrewing it, leaving it hanging to the wood screw. It was lighter than water, so that it might rise up against the object to which the wood screw and itself were fastened. Within the magazine was an apparatus constructed to run any proposed length of time under twelve hours; when it had run out its time, it unpinioned a strong lock, resembling a gun lock, which gave fire to the powder. This apparatus was so pinioned that it could not possibly move, till, by casting off the magazine from the vessel, it was set in motion."[7]

Estimating that the air supply within the *American Turtle* would be severely limited to a maximum of thirty minutes of breathing time, David Bushnell installed twin oxygen pipes, to be used anytime the submarine was at or near the surface. With one of these "snorkels" admitting fresh oxygen, and the other expending foul air, he reasoned that the operator could remain submerged almost indefinitely. An added attraction concerning this primitive breathing apparatus proved the ingenuity of the *American Turtle*'s creator: valves at the upper ends of the two pipes closed automatically whenever water began to enter.

Bushnell also understood that the depth perception by the operator was extremely essential to a successful mission. Hence, he devised an ingenious gauge to measure underwater pressure and depth. Constructed of simple glass tubing, it was sealed at its upper portion and open at the lower end. Whenever the American Turtle descended, a floating cork would be forced upward inside the tube. By measuring the depth accurately from the surface at intervals, Bushnell was able to etch calculation depth marks into the glass. Finally, by incorporating cold light, which was emitted by a phosphorescent chunk of wood, the operator would be able to read the gauge from within the vessel's conning tower.

Using a magnetic compass, illuminated by sunlight at a depth no more than three fathoms (eighteen feet), and by the same phosphorescent wood at greater depths, Bushnell would be able to maintain a correct course for his submarine. This was essential, he knew, because the lone operator would need to remain totally submerged during his mission for the sake of secrecy.

Ballasted with 900 pounds of lead, the craft was also equipped with an emergency device in the form of a detachable keel weighing nearly two hundred pounds. Whenever operations were going as planned, the lead keel would provide stability; however, if something were to go wrong while submerged, the operator could disconnect the keel from within the *American Turtle*'s belly, thus forcing the vessel to resurface very rapidly.

When Bushnell was totally convinced of his submarine's abilities, the *American Turtle* was placed carefully aboard a small sloop-of-war and transported to Long Island Sound for more extensive testing. After gently lowering her into the water, the inventor gingerly climbed aboard through the brass hatchway and closed the trap. He then allowed the craft to admit just enough water into her ballast tanks to take her down into depths exceeding the height of his snorkeling pipes.

David Bushnell had some difficulty operating the vehicle's broad propeller, though he swam submerged for nearly forty-five minutes. Finally, after nearly losing consciousness from the lack of fresh oxygen, he found enough energy to work the forcing pumps to expel the water in the ballast tanks. Almost immediately, he came to the surface, opened the hatchway, and gulped down an enormous breath of fresh air. The inventor had, most assuredly, learned two important facts from this, his maiden voyage: the *American Turtle* was certainly capable of carrying out her intended mission; yet, he, himself, was not physically able to operate the vessel for the necessary length of time that it would take to complete such an arduous adventure.

David's brother, Ezra, willingly volunteered to take to the helm of the *American Turtle*, and was subsequently put in charge of carrying out the attack against the British fleet. Following a series of additional trial and error runs in the depths of the Connecticut River near Poverty Island, word got out concerning the submarine's limited success. Hearing of the intriguing machine, Governor Jonathan Trumbull, of Connecticut, asked for a full-fledged demonstration, to be supervised by Major-General Israel Putnam and witnessed by other high-ranking army personnel. "Old Put," as he was affectionately known, was, indeed, impressed with the craft's possibilities, and he took it upon himself to secure ample funding to continue the testing phase.

In short order, plans were drawn up to have the *American Turtle* transported to Boston Harbor, where she would be deployed in an offensive against Great Britain's blockading fleet. However, the journey was delayed by the failure of a ballast tank installed aboard the submarine and, by the time new parts had been cast and machined, autumn had arrived in earnest.

Ordinarily, the season would have been of little consequence; yet the phosphorescent glow of the fox-fire wood, which Bushnell had employed to illuminate his instruments, could no longer be used. Fox-fire was only seasonal, with the phosphorescence being killed by the frost, and the mission would have to be put on hold until the following spring.

During the third and fourth months of 1776, the precious wood was once again abundantly available, and Bushnell was given the go-ahead for his all-important mission. However, the *American Turtle* was now suffering from other unexpected ailments. After having been in storage throughout the cold New England winter months, her joints had become loose and leaky, and needed to be resealed. Aside from that, brother Ezra was out of practice when it came to her operations, and he required more time for preparation.

Finally, after several weeks of added delay, the submarine was once again restored to her original condition, and Ezra Bushnell had received the well-needed practice. A sloop-of-war was made ready to transport the vessel within close range of the Boston Harbor blockading fleet. Yet, before the crew and vessel were able to leave port, more untimely news came their way: the British Navy had altered their strategy of blockade, relocating their entire squadron further up the North American coastline to Halifax, Nova Scotia. After four long years of waiting, Bushnell's patience would again be tested.

The inventor's tough moral character and hopeful anticipation prevailed, however, when it was later decided to ship the *American Turtle* to New York Harbor, in order to break up the British blockading fleet anchored there. In a letter dispatched to John Adams, it was clear that others within the American ranks were not only losing patience with all the delays in the submersible's arrival, but they were not yet totally convinced of the *American Turtle*'s capabilities:

> "The famous water machine from Connecticut is every day expected in Camp. It must unavoidably be a clumsy business as its weight is about a ton."[8]

Hidden aboard a sloop-of-war, the submarine was transported southward in early spring of 1776, and the Bushnell brothers, along with their craft, took up residence with the local American defensive land battery.

Ten more days were scheduled for training exercises before a full-scale attack could be conducted. Ezra would need that much time, at least, to become comfortable with the tricky currents and tides of New York Harbor. Just a few days after the 4th of July, General Israel Putnam gave the enterprising pair permission to commence an attack upon the next British warship that anchored within range in the harbor. Almost obligingly, Lord William Howe, commander of the British naval forces in North America, brought his proud flagship, the sixty-four gun *HMS Eagle*, a short distance off the coast of Staten Island on July 12. Due to its proximity to Hell Gate, a turbulent area in the East River, the area where she had dropped anchor had been named for the monster Charybdis. According to Greek mythology, Charybdis was the daughter of Poseidon, the god of the sea. As a young nymph, she flooded lands to add to her father's kingdom until Zeus, the supreme ruler of the gods, turned her into a monster. In any case, that part of the channel had been formed by faults deep underground, and contained some of the deepest water in New York Harbor. Its hazardous reefs bore quaint, though telling, names such as "Hen and Chickens," "Pot Rock," "Bread and Cheese," and "Bald Headed Billy."

Ominous poor luck struck once again before they could put their plans in motion, however, as David Bushnell's brother, Ezra, became deathly ill, and was bed-ridden with a dangerously high fever. The mission would have to be put on hold a bit longer, and the inventor realized that, perhaps, fate was not on his side. As the weeks slipped by, it seemed inevitable that America's one-man submarine force would not see action, for Ezra Bushnell grew far too weak to operate the underwater vessel's energy-draining controls.

Finally, to Bushnell's delight, Brigadier General Samuel Parsons of Lyme, commander of a brigade of Connecticut Continentals, took an interest in the tiny submersible. "Find three volunteers for extra hazardous duty," he ordered, "and have them report to me at once." One of the three replacements was Ezra Lee, also of Lyme, who professed to be unafraid of anything on land or at sea.

During the next several weeks, Bushnell outlined the submarine's intricate details to Lee. On several outings, the oak-ribbed craft nearly met with disaster on the muddy bottom of the Connecticut River, despite the fact that a heavy cable had been attached to her hull as a salvation line. Eventually, the pair made sufficient progress and, by mid-summer of 1776, Bushnell had grown nearly certain that the volunteer would be successful in his attempt at sinking a British warship. In the meantime, the *HMS Eagle* continued to anchor herself patiently in the harbor. Finally, as August gave way to early September, Bushnell was completely convinced of Lee's knowledge and preparation for the mission. All was ready for an offensive.

Depiction of the *HMS Eagle*

Just after midnight, on September 6, 1776, a sliver of moon illuminated the skies, and the waters surrounding New York Bay reflected the soft light like a mirror. The *American Turtle* was checked and rechecked, while a one hundred, fifty pound charge was carefully put into position above her rudder. She was then lashed securely to a pair of whale-boats at Whitehall Stairs, near the defensive battery stationed at the tip of Manhattan. Muffled oars were prepared to drag her out onto the shiny bay toward the looming black hulk of the *HMS Eagle*, Admiral Lord Howe's flagship, moored just off of the island now occupied by the Statue of Liberty. Under the command of one Captain Duncan, the *Eagle* was unsuspectingly positioned southwest of their base, about two miles from the darkened shore. Ezra Lee was extremely optimistic:

AMERICAN SUBMARINERS: PRE-CIVIL WAR

"Aye. The gunpowder is securely affixed. The inside is, for the moment at least, dry. And I am aching to awaken Admiral Lord Howe with a peal of American thunder such as he has not heard before...let us be away and to our task."[9]

Halfway between the mainland and Staten Island, the rowers stopped to cut their lines and, for the first time in the history of American naval warfare, an undersea craft began its fateful mission to destroy an enemy vessel. Slowly, carefully, Lee approached his unsuspecting target:

"When I rowed under the stern of the ship I could see men on the deck and hear them talk. I then shut down all doors, sunk down and came up under the bottom of the ship. Up with the screw but found it would not enter. I pulled along to find another place, but deviated a little to one side and immediately rose with great velocity and came above the surface two or three feet between the ship and the daylight, then sunk again like a porpoise. I hove about to try again, but on further thought I gave out, knowing that as soon as it was light the ship's boats would be rowing in all directions, and I thought the best generalship was to retreat as fast as I could, and my compass being no use to me I was obliged to rise up every few minutes to see that I sailed in the right direction..."[10]

Time, along with the relentless tide, was running out on the covert mission, as Lee diligently attempted to steer the *American Turtle* toward the safety of shore. Finally, after it became clear that he was making little headway, he lightened the craft and increased his chances of success by ejecting all of the ballast water. Yet, now nearly one-third of the submarine's decipherable hull floated above the surface of the bay, which placed her within direct sight of the enemy troops stationed on nearby Governor's Island. He later recalled what happened next in a personal diary entry:

"When I was abreast of the fort on the island, 300 or 400 men got up on the parapet to observe me; at length a number came down to the shore, shoved off in a 12 oar'd barge with 5 or 6 sitters and pulled for me. I eyed them, and when they got within 50 or 60 yards of me I let loose the magazine in hopes that if they should take me they would likewise pick up the magazine, and then we should all be blown up together..."[11]

As Ezra Lee began to make his escape, the British seamen rowed cautiously toward the strange-looking object bobbing up and down on the calm surface. All the while, the mine's clockwork mechanism had been ticking away. Just moments before the curious sailors drew up alongside the deadly explosive, the device released its flintlock trigger. The charge went off with a deafening roar, and a geyser of water rose high into the air. Quickly, nearby British warships slashed their anchor cables, moving the entire blockading fleet further out into the harbor. In their confusion, some vessels sideswiped other vessels, causing extensive damage and utter chaos within the British ranks.

No direct hit had been inflicted by the explosive; yet it was a moral victory, if nothing more, for David Bushnell and the American forces. After all, they had managed to accomplish, to a degree, precisely what they had set out to do. In essence, the most formidable blockading squadron in the world had effectively been displaced away from the port city.

Unfortunately, on the eve of the submarine's first combat mission, Ezra Bushnell, the inventor's beloved brother, died. For the next several days, still grieving from his loss, David spent long hours inspecting every movable part of the *American Turtle*. He lubricated those areas which demanded either oil or grease; he tightened and recaulked all hull openings; and he repitched all of the seams around the craft's exterior. Then, on September 15th, it was decided to attempt a second attack on the *HMS Eagle*, which was now anchored further out in the deeper waters of the Lower Bay.

Fate once again intervened, however, as the heavy currents and tides made accurate directional movements against the enemy literally impossible. After fighting the dangerous ebb and flow for several anxious moments, Lee was barely able to bring the *American Turtle* safely back to the shore.

A third and final attempt was conducted at mounting an offensive against a British war vessel later that month. But, while moving the submerged submarine along the North River, just opposite the township of Bloomingdale, tricky currents once again frustrated the mission. In the end, David Bushnell was forced to give up all hope of ever sinking a British ship.

Eventually, the *American Turtle* and her inventor were placed aboard a swift sloop, bound for the Connecticut coastline. However, just prior to departing from the Long Island Sound area, a British frigate spied the sloop moving suspiciously across the water and managed to sink it with a few well-placed cannon shots. The *American Turtle* went down with the tiny sloop, but the entire crew, including Bushnell, managed to swim to safety.

The incident marked the end of the inventor's submarine exploits during the American Revolution. Despite the loss, however, Bushnell's expertise continued to be respected by many high-ranking officials, including the newly-appointed president, George Washington:

> "Bushnell is a man of great Mechanical powers--fertile of invention--and a master in execution--He came to me in 1776 recommended by Governor Trumbull (now dead) and other respectable characters who were proselites to his plan.--Although I wanted faith myself, I furnished him with money, and other aids to carry it into execution.--He laboured for sometime ineffectually, & though the advocates for his scheme continued sanguine he never did succeed--One accident or another was always intervening.--I then thought, and still think, that it was an effort of ge-

nius; but that a combination of too many things were requisite, to expect much success from the enterprise against an enemy, who are always upon guard.--That he had a machine which was so contrived as to carry a man under water at any depth he chose, and for a considerable time & distance, with an apparatus charged with Powder which he could fasten to a ships bottom or side & give fire to in any given time (sufft. for him to retire) by means whereof a ship could be blown up, or sunk, are facts which I believe admit of little doubt--but then, where it was to operate against an enemy, it is no easy matter to get a person hardy enough to encounter the variety of dangers to which he must be exposed. 1 from the novelty 2 from the difficulty of conducting the machine, and governing it under water on acct. of the Currents &ca. 3 the consequent uncertainty of hitting the object of destination, without rising frequently above water for fresh observation, wch., when near the Vessel, would expose the adventurer to a discovery, & almost to certain death--To these causes I always ascribed the non-performance of his plan, as he wanted nothing that I could furnish to secure the success of it.-- This to the best of my recollection is a true state of the case...."[12]

Never one to give up or give in on his dream, David Bushnell continued his research and experiments in the field of submerged explosives until the final few months of the war. When peace was finally declared on September 3, 1783, the inventor was secretly "mustered" out of the army and away from public scrutiny, receiving five years severance pay in one lump sum. Maurice Delpeuch, in his book *La Navigation Sous-Marine: A Travers Les Siecles* (*Underwater Navigation Throughout the Centuries*), indicates that David Bushnell traveled to Europe in the spring of 1797, hoping to peddle his submarine concept to the French government:

"Then (1797) there appeared an engineer who offered to the Directory a means quite as terrible as it was invisible to force the British to lift their blockade, and not only did this man undertake to drive the enemy from our shores, but he even proposed to carry the war to the shores and ports of Great Britain, heretofore inviolable..."[13]

Undoubtedly, Robert Fulton became closely acquainted with David Bushnell during the time they were both in France engaged in similar pursuits with the French government. But the failure to accomplish results, or to get his ideas accepted by others, deeply disappointed Bushnell, causing him to return to his native country later that same year.

Shortly thereafter, David Bushnell disappeared, dropping entirely out of sight, opting to severe most communications with friends and relatives. His friend and former Yale student, Abraham Baldwin, who later established the University of Georgia, convinced Bushnell to relocate to the deep south. Some historians believed that Bushnell had been captured by British forces; others, that he had been killed in action; still others, that he had simply relocated to the peaceful countryside of France. None of these were historically correct, however, for scant public records prove otherwise.

Years passed, and David Bushnell had not been heard of or seen by those who had known him intimately. For two dozen years or more, he lived a quiet life in the home of Abraham Baldwin, his lifelong friend and fellow soldier. Later, in 1807, when Baldwin died at the age of fifty-two, Bushnell moved thirty miles to the west. Eventually, in 1826, in the inconspicuous hamlet of Warrenton, Georgia, it was recorded that an aging "Dr. David Bush" had passed away. Soon, however, it would be revealed that the frail, old man was, in reality, none other than David Bushnell, who had managed to live the final forty years of his life in total obscurity. During that time, he had secured numerous new friends, had earned a medical degree, and had practiced privately for more than twenty years. In Warrenton, he had been involved in family medicine for the last twenty years, and had taught both religion and science at the local Warrenton Academy. Records indicate that he had never married.

It soon became apparent that David Bushnell had never been able to completely give up his dream of constructing the "perfect" underwater diving machine. At the time of his death, his cluttered workshop was found to possess "some curious machinery," determined to be the disassembled pieces of a wooden diving vessel, very similar, in fact, to the *American Turtle*, which has reportedly never been recovered from the depths of New York Harbor. In his will, Bushnell left the probate of his estate–including his submarine drawings and its parts–to executors, George Hargraves, notary public and justice of the peace in Warren County, Georgia, and Peter Crawford, an avowed Whig and practicing attorney. Hargraves, it seems, had known the truth about Bushnell's secret identity for several years. As indicated in a letter to President Thomas Jefferson on August 4, 1814, he revealed the inventor's identity in a roundabout manner:

> "The enclosed description and drawing of a Torpedo is an original paper which has lately fallen into my possession. Not being a judge of such matters, I shou'd probably have thrown it by as useless paper had I not known the Inventor to be a man of science, and more capable, in my opinion, of judging correctly of the efficacy of such things than any other person I know of–I am induced to send it to you not only because he mentions your name, but because after examining it, shou'd you think it deserving notice, you will have it in your power to forward it to some man of genius capable of making the experiment. Every exertion I think ought to be made at this time to check the predatory warfare carried on by the Enemy on our Sea board, and cou'd any plan be adopted to prevent maritime warfare altogether it wou'd doubtless be productive of great good to the World–From that part wherein your name is mentioned, you will readily conjecture who the Inventor is–: Doctor Ramsay, in his History of the Revolutionary War, mentions him among the ingenious men of that time–I have no objection to your communicating the plan to any one you think proper, but for particular reasons, I beg of you to conceal his name,

and to withhold from publick view that part which may lead to a discovery. Shou's a trial be made I shou'd be highly gratified to know the result. I am now at the Bedford Springs drinking the waters for my health—my place of residence is Warrenton, Georgia..."[14]

Life-size model of the *American Turtle*

Today, a life-size model of the original *American Turtle* from a program known as the Turtle Project is on exhibit at the Connecticut River Museum in Essex, Connecticut. A collaboration between Old Saybrook High School and the Naval Undersea Warfare Center of Newport, Rhode Island, she was designed by Joseph Leary and built by Fred Frese in 1976 as part of a U.S. Bicentennial project. She was christened by Governor Ella Grasso, and then launched in the Connecticut River to be tested for her maneuverability and submersible ability. This demonstration proved, without question, that the little submarine named the *American Turtle* worked as intended and confirmed the ingenuity of early American inventor, David Bushnell.

Undoubtedly, Bushnell had managed to improvise a number of important innovations in his unique submersible. The *American Turtle* was, for example, the first of its kind to use water as ballast for submerging and raising the vessel. To maneuver under the water, she was the first submersible to use a screw propeller of any kind. Furthermore, Bushnell was also the first to equip a submersible with any sort of breathing device. And finally, the weaponry of the *American Turtle*, which consisted of a torpedo, or mine, that could be attached to the hull of the target ship, was also quite innovative. Bushnell was the first to demonstrate that gunpowder could be exploded under water, and his mine was the first time bomb, allowing the operator of the tiny submarine to attach the mine and then to retreat a safe distance before it detonated. Indeed, he paved the way for a number of future American submariners.

Sketch of Joseph Belton (speculated from a photo of his great-grandson)

- 6 -
Joseph Belton: *Belton Submarine*

"...experiments will speak plainer than words, and being conscious of my own abilities [sic], I will engage to shew [sic] experimental all that I have herein asserted, and upon my non performance, I will become obligated to reimburse all that you may advance; so that the whole expence [sic] should then fall upon myself, and not the publick [sic]. And if I performed according to what is asserted, then I should be intitled [sic] to such, as you thought my ingenuity and plan merited [sic], though at the same time Gentlemen, I can assure you, that I am not excited so much with the view of incuring [sic] premiums, as that of sarving [sic] my country in so glorious a cause. And would readily engage, after making a few experiments, to sink, or destroy, the admirals ship now in Boston, or any other ever so difficultly situated, as I can readily conceive, of several other destructive meathod [sic] might be pursued, some by the Machine only, & some by the Gun only, which I shall omit at present, but shall be allways [sic] ready to inlarge [sic] on..."[1]

The surname, Belton, occurs in many historical references throughout England, Ireland, and Scotland, but from time to time, has been recorded as Beltone, Beleton, Beldan, Belden, Belston, Belting, and Beldon. It was not uncommon for one person to be born with one spelling, married with another, and have yet another at his burial.

The Belton name is believed to have emerged in Berwickshire, Scotland, where they held a family seat from very ancient times in the Parish of Dun Barra. Their historical significance originated prior to the Norman Conquest of England by Duke William of Normandy in 1066 A.D. Belton is the anglicized version of Beltown, meaning "beautiful town" or "town of the bells."

The first of the Scottish Beltons to come to the New World was transported aboard the Faulcon de London to the island of Barbados. Commanded by Master Thomas Irish, the ship set sail from London, England, on April 14, 1635, with ten women and sixty-eight men on board, which included "Persons of Quality, Emigrants, Religious Exiles, Political Rebels, Serving-men sold, Apprentices, Children stolen, Maidens pressed, and others who went from Great Britain to the American Plantations." Among them was Joseph Belton, who had left his home in the Parish of Dun Barra, East Lothian, Berwickshire, situated along the southeastern coastline of Scotland.

Born in 1587, forty-eight-year-old Belton had–either by choice or by force–"taken the oaths of Allegeance and Supremacie," promising his lifelong conformity to the Church of England. At the time of his arrival in Barbados, the island was being divided into large and small sugar plantations. However, like the majority of Barbadians, Joseph was not one of the elite few who profited from sugar. In fact, within a few years, his rather meager 30-acre plantation had been swallowed up by one of the eight wealthiest men on the island. The loss of these small parcels of land was, of course, closely correlated to the general exodus of whites from Barbados to the North American mainland. Among them was an aging Joseph Belton, his wife, and children, who found their way to the wilderness of South Carolina in the late 1650s, where they soon disappeared.

About 1712, another Joseph Belton made his way from the village of Wymeswold Parish, situated in the Charnwood district of Leicestershire, England, to North Stonington, New London County, Connecticut. There, in 1716, the twenty-six-year-old, who made his living making and selling rope, married Sarah Stark, the daughter of Aaron and Mehitable (Shaw) Stark. Even before they had wed, the couple had given birth to, what would be, their only son, Jonas. The family resided in nearby Newport, Rhode Island, for a time, where Joseph became a prominent member of the Congregationalists, and clerk of the monthly, quarterly and yearly meetings of Newport for the next decade.

The area had a rich history. In 1524, the Italian navigator Giovanni Verrazzano and his crew became the first Europeans conclusively known to visit Narragansett Bay. More than a century later, in 1636 or 1637, Dutch fur traders paid to use the island of Quentenis as a base for their activities. Within one year, the English had made arrangements to use Conanicut Island for grazing sheep.

In 1657, a consortium of about 100 buyers purchased Conanicut, Dutch and Gould islands. They divided Conanicut Island into roughly one dozen large plots and reserved Dutch Island and parts of Conanicut Island for common use. Benedict Arnold, one of the purchasers, became governor of the colony of Rhode Island the same year. He returned to the office in 1662, 1663, 1669, and 1677. The Native Americans and newly arrived colonists continued to live side-by-side in relative peace for the next four decades. Eventually, conflicts occurred in a number of areas in southern New England, leading to what became known as King Philip's War. Although Conanicut Island remained a haven for many Native Americans, life in the region was dominated by the colonists after 1676.

By 1710, many of Conanicut Island's roads were in place, including North Main Road, the North Ferry Road, the Ferry Road, and a road southwest leading to the beach. Less than two miles to the east of the island, on the other side of East Passage, the community of Newport was blossoming into a vibrant center of maritime commerce. Aquidneck Island and nearby areas were blessed with fertile soil; agriculture was thriving; and the Bay offered fish in seemingly limitless quantities. Abundance led to the desire to transport surplus products to other markets; and by 1715, ships were being built throughout the Narragansett Bay region–in Providence, Newport, Warren, Bristol, East Greenwich, and Warwick–and being sold for use in other colonies and as far away as Europe. And, as Joseph Belton quickly discovered, they all needed an ample supply of strong rope.

In the early spring of 1725, the Joseph and Sarah Belton family relocated to the community of Groton, New London County, Connecticut–then known as "Poquonock Plain"–where Joseph became extremely active in the formation of the church:

> "At a town meeting held in Groton May 5, 1725…voated [sic] that Deacon James Morgan and Lieut James Avery (the present deputy) are chosen agents for the town to answer the petition that is to be proposed to the General Assembly by the North part of the town to be a Society by themselves. The church and parish being virtually established, though not yet sanctioned by law, were supplied with preaching for a few weeks by Mr. Samuel Seabury… He preached here only ten weeks, four Sundays at Captain John Morgan's, four at William Morgan's and two at Ralph Stoddard, when to the surprise of the people, he declared himself an Episcopalian. The North Parish settled no minister…"[2]

Within just a few weeks, Joseph had commenced buying and selling property on a liberal scale. Records indicate that on January 12, 1726, "Samuel Davis of Groton sold and confirmed to Joseph Belton of Newport, R. I., a tract of land with housing and orchard, situated near the meeting house, for £220." Just five days later, on January 17, he had sold a very small portion of that same property to John Lamb for £105, with James and Joshua Morgan as witnesses. Within months he had established the family home near the foot of Candlewood Hill, three miles east of the village on the northern side of the post road.

The community of Groton had been established in 1705, when it separated from New London, Connecticut. About 100 years before the town was established, the Nehântick (meaning "of long-necked waters"), a tribe of New England Native American people, lived in the area between the Thames and Pawcatuck rivers. The Nehânticks were brutally attacked by another band of natives during the Pequot War of 1637. These invaders burned their wigwams, destroyed their cornfields and food supplies, and a few possessions were stolen. A great number of the Nehântick warriors were tomahawked, with about 100 survivors fleeing to Misquamicut in what is now Rhode Island.

Meanwhile, the Pequot Indians, a branch of the Mohawk people, had continued to move eastward into the Connecticut River Valley, displacing existing settlements of indigenous peoples. The Pequots finally rested and made their headquarters in what is now Groton. They built three villages at Groton Heights, Fort Hill, and Mystic.

On January 26, 1729, Joseph's strong testament in family and church were profoundly tested when his wife, Sarah, died unexpectedly. Young Jonas had not yet reached the age of maturity and, as his father's faith was challenged by his mother's death, the youngster turned more and more toward his God and church to find strength. It was during this period that he met and fell in love with Mary Morgan.

Celtic in origin, the name Morgan is older than the advent of the Saxon race or language. Though the derivation cannot be conclusively determined, one English authority on surnames believes it means "by the sea." Still others argue that the "name is allied to the Scotch ceann mor," meaning "big headland." In either case, the name was common at the time of the Conquest, and appears in both the *Domesday Book* and the *Battle Abbey Roll*. Among the Welsh, several sovereign princes and other potentates of the Morgan family line were living as far back as 300 or 400. One of these, known as "Morgan of Gla Morgan," is credited with devising the concept of trial by jury in 725, a process which he referred to as "the apostolic law."

Jonas Belton married Mary, daughter of William and Margaret (Avery) Morgan, on August 7, 1737, in Groton, New London County, Connecticut. Mary's great-grandfather, Captain John Morgan, was born in Llandaff, Glamorganshire, Wales, in 1607. The family appears to have migrated from Llandaff to Bristol, England, sometime prior to 1636. Traditionally, the name of his father was believed to be William, a story that had originated from a book that James owned, dated 1600 and inscribed with "William Morgan, of Llandafif." As further evidence, he also owned some gold sleeve-buttons stamped "W.M." said to have belonged to William Morgan, of Llandaff, Wales.

In March of 1636, James Morgan and two younger brothers, John and Miles, had boarded a ship and sailed from Bristol, England, to Boston, Massachusetts. John Morgan disliked the austerity of the Puritans that he found living there, and decided to move to Virginia, while Miles Morgan moved to Springfield, Massachusetts, and became the progenitor of the Morgan family, later represented by J.P. Morgan of Morgan and Company, Bankers.

Historical records find James Morgan residing Roxbury, near Boston, prior to 1640. He was married on August 6, 1640, to Margery Hill of Roxbury, and together they would give birth to six children, four of which would live to adulthood. James became a freeman in Roxbury on May 10, 1643. In 1650, he, Margery, and their four surviving children moved to Peauot–now New London–where they had a household assigned to them. On December 25, 1656, he sold his homestead on "Cape Ann Lane" and relocated across the River Thames, finally coming to reside in a house that he built on a large tract of land granted to him by the town, situated on the east side, now the south portion of Groton.

During the next few years, James Morgan became a large proprietor and land dealer, buying and selling on speculation. During his lifetime, he would be employed as a local land surveyor, establishing highways, determining boundaries, and settling civil difficulties. Overall, he was said to be "a good neighbor and a Christian man, in whom all appear to have reposed a marked degree of confidences and trust." He was one of the trusted "townsmen" for several years, was one of the first "Deputies" sent from New London Plantation to the General Court at Hartford, and was nine times chosen a member of that assembly.

Undoubtedly, Morgan impressed this grave body of men with his high sense of honesty and integrity of character, for it appears that in a controversy between the General Court and the New London Plantation about boundaries and jurisdiction, it was ordered that the matter be submitted to three arbiters, mutually agreed upon. The General Court would ultimately agree to submit to James Morgan's sole decision, which seems to have satisfied all parties. Though he died in 1685 at the age of 78, he would not be forgotten, for the James Morgan homestead would be passed down through eight generations.

Three generations later, Jonas and Mary (Morgan) Belton gave birth to two children; a son, Ebenezer, born in early 1738, and daughter Mary, born on May 21, 1739. Sadly, Mary died while giving birth to her second child. Jonas remarried in 1742, this time to Elizabeth Smith, and during the next three years they would give birth to three healthy children, Sarah, Joseph, and Hannah.

Joseph Belton, son of Jonas and Elizabeth (Smith) Belton, was born in 1744 in Groton, New London County, Connecticut. During the first few years of his life, a religious revival in Connecticut known as the "Great Awakening" had developed. The Groton township Congregational church, which the Belton family had long attended devoutly, experienced divisions in its congregation. The "Old Lights" wanted to keep things as they were, while the "New Lights" embraced and advocated reforms and worship with far more spirit and fervor. Jonas, Elizabeth, and their five children remained steadfast with the Old Light traditions.

When Joseph was twelve years old, war broke out, and his father, Jonas, decided to join the Connecticut militia. Unlike previous squirmishes involving the British colonists in America, in which fighting broke out in Europe and spread across the Atlantic, this conflict took an opposite route. In 1756, Abraham Wooster, a seasoned captain aboard the sloop-of-war Defense during King George's War in the 1740s, was made a colonel of the Third Connecticut Regiment at the start of what would become known as the French and Indian conflict. Patriotic in the defense of his family and property, Jonas was compelled to serve under Wooster's command. But disease and poor leadership prevented the ragtag militia from mounting an effective campaign, and Wooster was soon replaced by James Abercromby. Described as "one a child could outwit and a popgun terrify," it was fortunate that young Joseph's father managed to survive the war. Yet, he did, and by the late-1750s he had returned home with honor and the military title of "Captain."

Having spent his early youth helping his father and mother on the farm in Groton, Joseph learned the techniques of planting and harvesting. While his father was away fighting the war, he had been employed by various men of his village, as a farm laborer, a tannery apprentice, and quarry worker, earning meager wages along the way in accordance with the custom of his day. He had also attended the town's first school, which was constructed near the first church, tavern and a stagecoach shop at the intersection known as Groton Center corners. Then, sometime around 1760, his had father "erected the Belton Tavern in the clearing a half-mile west of the corners in Groton, a building which remained one of the landmarks of the region for generations, and finally perished by the torch of an incendiary in 1852." For the next five or six years, Joseph would help his father run the tavern, as well as an adjoining hostelry.

Apparently, young Joseph Belton grew up in a home that not only valued and nourished education and patriotism, but also the creative spirit. Evidence suggests the imaginative, inventive side of him bubbled up very early on, for he was extremely fond of drawing and painting throughout his childhood. In 1900, his great-granddaughter, Mercy W. Miner, discussed evidence of this:

> "My husband, Elisha M. Miner's great-grandmother, was Sarah Belton, a daughter of Jonas Belton. How she was connected with Joseph Belton I cannot say, but think probably there must have been a close relationship between them. We have a very crude painting in the house painted by Joseph Belton, no doubt when he was a young boy. It was exhibited at the Groton Centennial in 1881 as a relic, on account of its age. It had always been in the family, and Mr. Miner's mother (an old lady at that time) said then it was over one hundred years old. The picture is painted on a board one-half inch thick, and the dimensions are 27x19 inches. The picture itself is beyond description. The only wonder is that it has been kept all these years. The only way I can reconcile it is that his family must have been very proud of him, and that anything that he had ever done was sacred..."[3]

At the age of 19, Joseph happened to meet the Reverend James Manning, a 1762 graduate from the College of New Jersey (now Princeton University), and a Baptist minister. At the time, Manning and his new wife, Margaret, were in the middle of a year long honeymoon, traveling extensively through the American colonies combining business with pleasure. Having been chosen by the Philadelphia Association of Baptists, Manning was leading an attempt to establish, somewhere, a Baptist college at which "education might be promoted and superior learning obtained, free from any sectarian tests."[4]

In July of 1763, Manning had arrived in the Newport, Rhode Island with a plan for a "liberal and catholic" institution of higher education," to be known as the College of Rhode Island. Rhode Island's leading citizens had previously heard a similar plan presented by the Congregationalist Reverend, Ezra Stiles. He, assisted by the attorney William Ellery, Jr., drew up a charter based on the Reverend Manning's draft and this was presented to the General Assembly. This charter's "catholic" plan was to divide the Corporation's power about equally among Baptists (who would make up a majority of the Trustees) and Presbyterians, while allowing a few seats to Quakers and Anglicans.

In September of 1764, at Newport on Aquidneck Island, the first meeting of the new governing body for the proposed Rhode Island institution of higher education was held. Among the twenty-four officials present was Governor Stephen Hopkins, later to become a signer of the Declaration of Independence, who was named as the institution's first chancellor. Also present were future Rhode Island governor, Samuel Ward, and Nicholas Brown, grandfather of Nicholas Brown, Jr., after whom the newly established College of Rhode Island eventually would be renamed Brown University. Hence, the widespread report that the college was founded "by an assorted group of Revivalist Presbyterians, Congregationalists, Baptists, and Anglicans," is historically inaccurate.

The next year, the Reverend Manning was formally chosen as "President of the College of Rhode Island, and Professor of Languages, and other branches of learning, with full power to act in these capacities at Warren," Rhode Island. Professor Manning was to teach languages, and in addition was to offer instruction in all the "other Branches of Learning." In September of 1765, enrollment began with a single student, fourteen-year-old William Rogers of Newport, who would for the first nine months of its existence be the school's sole pupil. Eventually, nineteen-year-old, Richard Stites, from Connecticut Farms, New Jersey, doubled the enrollment on June 20, 1766. Then, on November 4 of that same year, Joseph Belton was matriculated. Four others followed, so that the first commencement ceremony in 1769 presented seven proud graduates. As a statement of their American patriotism and a protest against the unjust trade laws of Great Britain, it should be noted that, on this memorable occasion, the Reverend James Manning and all seven of his graduating students "were attired entirely in clothing that had been created in the New World from New World materials."[5]

In its September 11, 1769, daily edition, the *Newport Mercury* newspaper reported on the memorable event:

> "On Thursday the 7th Instant was celebrated, at Warren, the first Commencement in the College of this Colony, when the following young Gentlemen commenced Bachelors in the Arts: viz. Joseph Belton, Joseph Eaton, William Rogers, Richard Stites, Charles Thompson, James Mitchell Varnum, and William Williams. About 10 o'clock A.M. the Gentlemen concerned in conducting the Affairs of the College, together with the Candidates, went in procession to the Meeting-House. After they had taken their Seats, and the Audience were composed, the President introduced the Business of the Day with Prayer; then followed a salutatory Oration in Latin, pronounced with much Spirit, by Mr. Stites; which procured him great Applause from the learned Part of the Assembly. He spoke upon the Advantages of Liberty and Learning, and their mutual Dependence upon each other, concluding with proper Salutations to the Chancellor of the College, and to the Governor of the Colony, e&. particularly expressing the Gratitude of all the Friends of the College to the Rev. Morgan Edwards, who has encountered many Difficulties in going to Europe to collect Donations for the Institution..."[6]

At three in the afternoon, with the audience being reconvened following a hearty midday meal, James Mitchell Varnum spoke openly about his feelings toward the British government and the American move toward independence:

> "Had British America been left to the peaceful enjoyment of those privileges, which it could boast of in former reigns, the most romantic genius, in its wildest excursions, had not dreamt of independence. But the late alarming attacks of the parent state upon American freedom...has, with justice, roused the advocates of American liberty to the most vigorous exertions, in defence [sic] of our rights..."[7]

Standing side-by-side-by-side, joining together into one thought, William Williams, William Rogers, and Joseph Belton were even more passionate in their response:

> "Let not the menaces of a British Parliament, in the least affright, nor their fair promises deceive you, into any base compliances. Latet anguis in herba (Latin for "Luring in the grass"). Their evident design is to make us slaves. They are wresting our money from us without our consent. Do not be charmed by the fascinating sounds, Parent-State. Mother-Country, Indulgent-Parent, &c... Their menaces might terrify and Subjugate servile timid Asiatics, who peaceably prostrate their necks to be trampled on by every bold usurper. But my auditors, you have not so learned the principles of liberty...my point is gained; your countenances indicate the patriotic feelings of your breasts, and with one voice...declare, that America Shall Be Free."[8]

After graduation, Joseph Belton returned home with his intense patriotic feelings and inventive thoughts, trying desperately to conjure up some methods of assisting his fellow Americans with the inevitable conflict over independence. Remaining quite close to his siblings–Ebenezer, Mary, Hannah, and Sarah–he often became involved in heated discussions about Great Britain's treatment of the colonies. While a majority of Americans felt they deserved all the rights of Englishmen, the British, on the other hand, felt that the colonies were created to be used in the way that best suited the crown and parliament.

Captain John Avery had married Joseph's sister, Sarah, and often shared his political inclinations with his brother-in-law. In fact, Avery was quite active in a secretive organization that would become known in history as the "Loyall Nine." This well-organized, political group had been formed in 1765 by nine likeminded citizens of Boston to protest the passing of the Stamp Act. They would evolve into the larger "Sons of Liberty." Since they were a close-knit group made up of only nine men, the organization functioned informally and left very little in terms of a paper trail. Their membership consisted of club secretary, Captain John Avery, a distiller by trade, Henry Bass, a cousin of Samuel Adams, Thomas Chase, a distiller, Stephen Cleverly, a brazier, Thomas Crafts, a painter, Benjamin Edes, printer of the Boston Gazette, Joseph Field, a ship captain, John Smith, a brazier, and George Trott, a jeweler. All nine men would go on to become active members of the Sons of Liberty, and four of the nine would be documented as having participated in the Boston Tea Party.

Joseph Belton regularly attended Sons of Liberty meetings and, on several occasions, all members of the Loyall Nine were present. Future president, John Adams, offered a rare glimpse into one of these gatherings:

"Jany. 15, 1766–I spent the evening with the Sons of Liberty at their own appointment, in Hanover Square, near the 'Tree of Liberty.' It is a counting-room in Chase and Speakman's distillery. A very small room it is. There were present John Avery a distiller, of liberal education, John Smith the brazier, Thomas Crafts the painter, Benjamin Edes the printer, Stephen Cleverly brazier, Thomas Chase distiller, Joseph Field master of a vessel, Henry Bass, Geo. Trott jeweler, and Henry Wells. I was very cordially and respectfully treated by all present. We had punch, wine, pipes and tobacco, biscuit and cheese, etc. they chose a committee to make preparation for a grand rejoicing upon the arrival of the news of the repeal of the stamp act."[9]

On March 7, 1767, while his grandson continued his studied at the College of Rhode Island, grandfather Joseph Belton, "for love, goodwill, etc., gave to his granddaughter, Mary Allyn (wife of Joseph Allyn of Groton), and her heirs, 100 acres in Groton, with mansion-house and building." The aging family elder, now nearing seventy-eight years old, must have realized that he did not have long for this world. Yet, he hung on to life that he so dearly cherished, for more than a year later, on May 12, 1768, records indicate that, "for the natural affection he bore his grandson, Joseph Belton…he gave him and his heirs 40 acres in Groton."[10]

After graduating from college, grandson Joseph Belton returned to the family homestead in Groton, Connecticut, just in time to attend his grandfather's wake and burial. Afterward, the young man combined his inventive nature with the mechanical skills he had acquired during his youth to design a concept for an underwater attack vessel to be used against British ships flaunting their power in American harbors.

Sometime during the early-1770s, Joseph Belton moved from his home in Groton, Connecticut, to Philadelphia, Pennsylvania, renting a room from the Ford family at 309 Walnut Street, situated between 3rd and 4th streets. A few blocks eastward, he opened a small machine and gunsmith shop, where he would work on a number of his inventive projects. Pennsylvania's communities began preparing for war as early as 1774, with counties and towns establishing committees of correspondence to consider the growing crisis and to raise volunteer companies of soldiers to prepare for the possibility of war. In June of 1775, the Pennsylvania Assembly formalized the colony's preparations by establishing a Committee of Safety to coordinate the defense of the province and the provisioning of its soldiers. By July, the Committee distributed a pamphlet to encourage and regulate the raising of volunteer companies in counties and townships throughout the province. These companies became known as "associators," and they were "united in this general Association for defending our Liberties and Properties, under the sole denomination of Americans."

As attitudes between American patriots and the British government intensified during the early 1770s, Philadelphian, Benjamin Franklin, put forth the idea of conducting a meeting among colonial delegates to discuss an agreed upon plan of action should war occur. He was unable to convince the colonies of its necessity, however, until the British placed a blockade at the Port of Boston in response to the Boston Tea Party in 1773. The First Continental Congress, as it was called, met briefly in Carpenter's Hall in Philadelphia, Pennsylvania, from September 5 to October 26, 1774. It consisted of fifty-six delegates from twelve of the thirteen colonies, excluding Georgia, which decided that it had its own troubles and needed the protection of British soldiers. Though Joseph Belton was not a delegate, he did have some very close and supporting friends that were present, including Benjamin Franklin, John Adams, and Governor Samuel Ward of Rhode Island.

Meanwhile, the northern colonies were fast becoming a hotbed of sedition in the spring of 1775. Preparations for conflict with the Royal authority had been underway throughout the past winter with the production of arms and munitions, the training of militia, and the organization of defenses. In April, General Thomas Gage, military governor of Massachusetts decided to counter these moves by sending a force out of Boston to confiscate weapons stored in the village of Concord and capture patriot leaders Samuel Adams and John Hancock reported to be staying in the village of Lexington.

The atmosphere was tense, as word of General Gage's intentions spread through Boston, prompting the patriots to set up a messaging system to alert the countryside of any advance of British troops. Paul Revere arranged for a signal to be sent by lantern from the steeple of North Church—one if by land, two if by sea. On the night of April 18, 1775 the lantern's alarm sent Revere, William Dawes and other riders on the road to spread the news. The messengers cried out the alarm, awakening every house, warning of the British column making its way towards Lexington. In the rider's wake there erupted the peeling of church bells, the beating of drums and the roar of gunshots—all announcing the danger and calling the local militias to action.

With remarkable speed, committees of correspondence spread the traumatic news of Lexington and Concord beyond the borders of Massachusetts. By April 24, New York City had the details, and Philadelphia had them by the next day. Savannah, the city farthest from the scene of the engagement, received the news on May 10. Massachusetts' call for a joint army of observation was answered by the three other New England colonies: New Hampshire, Rhode

AMERICAN SUBMARINERS: PRE-CIVIL WAR

Island, and Connecticut. Within two months three small armies had joined the Massachusetts troops at Boston, and a council of war began strategic coordination. These regional forces would pave the way for the creation of a national institution, the Continental Army.

Over the course of his first two years in Philadelphia, Joseph Belton had befriended a number of politically active men, including Benjamin Franklin, Benjamin Rush, George Clymer, and Thomas Paine. By August of 1775, the 30-year-old had detailed his submarine plans in writing, and forwarded them to the state Committee of Safety:

> "Gentlemen... I will make a Machine by the help of which, I will carry a loaded cannon, two or three miles up or down any of our harbours [sic] without any other assistance, and all the way there should nothing appear above the surface much larger than a man's hat, and by attracting [sic contracting] my Machine, would wholely [sic] decend [sic] under warter [sic] for some time, and by expanding, would rise to the surface at pleasure, and by this means, to avoid any discovery when I had arrived within an hundred and fifty, or two hundred yards of a Ship, I could decend [sic] under the surface, and go along side of her bottom against which, I could discharge the Cannon, that should be prov'd large enough to send a ball through any ships side..."[11]

What the *Belton Submarine* might have looked like

Receiving no response for several days, which grew into weeks, Belton was surprised by the Committee's hesitation. Soon, he became convinced that the entire decision-making process was a matter of an unwillingness to risk financing on such an ambitious, unproven concept. With that in mind, he dispatched a second letter to the Committee on September 4, 1775:

> "Gentlemen, Not long since having laid a plan under your consideration, and have not since been able to obtain your Oppinions [sic] on the same. Wheather [sic] you have judged that some conciliatory plan will soon be adopted, for which reason there will be no occasion, to encourage any harsh, or destructive meathod [sic] whatever, if so there is no more to be said. But if otherwise you have concluded, that the plan itself might prove abortive, either through the inability of the undertaker, or the imperfection of the plan itself, and you by encouraging it with the publick's [sic] money, would become liable to be censured by the publick [sic] for so doing, which to remove as well as all other Objections... But to conclude as experiments will speak plainer than words, and being conscious of my own abilities [sic], I will engage to shew [sic] experimental all that I have herein asserted, and upon my non performance, I will become obligated to reimburse all that you may advance; so that the whole expence [sic] should then fall upon myself, and not the publick [sic]. And if I performed according to what is asserted, then I should be intitled [sic] to such, as you thought my ingenuity and plan merited [sic], though at the same time Gentlemen, I can assure you, that I am not excited so much with the view of incuring [sic] premiums, as that of sarving [sic] my country in so glorious a cause..."[12]

Finally, realizing that the Committee might also be hesitant because the entire idea of a submersible vessel might be too difficult to comprehend, Joseph Belton ventured to offer answers to a number of, as yet unspoken, questions concerning the vessel's general operation. Apparently, Belton intended to install peddle-power as a primary mode of propulsion inside the vessel. Yet, whenever she found herself "in a rapid tide with all this machinery," either above or below the surface, the inventor suspected that this rudimentary "man" power would prove insufficient. Hence, in order to avoid being swept away by the current, Belton would simply install a small grappling hook, "which by leting [sic] go, I could stop when and where I pleased."

In addressing the problem of sighting a target enemy ship prior to attack, Belton explained that he intended to install "a thick clear glass in front, and my head just touching the top of my Machine, so that when my eyes was just at the surface, all the Machine that would naturally be above would not be larger than what I have before mentioned." At great distances, he believed that enemy lookouts would be highly unlikely to spot such a small object moving along the surface of the water. Besides, he surmised, there would be no need for an operator to keep constant vigilance at the porthole:

> "...it would be only requisite now and then to see, that I was floating in a true direction for the object I had in view, and the rest of the time, I might be immerged more, so as not to appear larger than a man's fist..."[13]

Aside from seeing, the submarine designer had taken into account the importance of actually "hearing" conversation of the enemy after dark. Indeed, he reasoned that "hearing as well as seeing might in the night be advantageous, so likewise 1 would have a small doar [sic] in front, which I could open & shut at pleasure, by which I could hear perfectly well..."

In considering all of this quite carefully, the inventor further explained that the timing of an attack would be critical. Hence, it would be optimal "begining [sic] to float in the Eavening [sic] at a large distance, just keeping my object in view, which being large I could easily do, when they on board could not possably [sic] discover any thing of me, and if I found that I floated too fast, and was likely to get up before it was dark, and by that means be liable to be discovered, I would drop my grapling [sic] and ride by it, till I thought proper to proceede [sic], by this means droping [sic] up with the tide..."[14]

As he approached an enemy vessel, and "had come with in an hundred yards of the ship" Belton understood that the chances of being spotted would be greatly increased. So, at that point, he would drop his grappling hook and "by pay-out line gently drop up under the wake of her *Bowsprit*, and under her bows, and so long side; and chouse what part I thought most condusive [sic] to effect my purpose."

It seems as if Joseph Belton had considered all possibilities, questions, and problems that might arise during any offensive by his tiny submarine. When it came to the issue of being totally submerged beneath an enemy vessel's belly, and being unable to clearly see a specific vulnerable spot for attack, he would use an intriguing arrangement of machinery:

> "I would have fins like fixed at my feet, & arms which by pushing from me would naturany [sic] expand and take large hold of the water, and when drawn to me would attract & take little or none, by this means I could move considerable fast, & even venture to stem a small tide."[15]

As for armament aboard his vessel, Belton had carefully considered "that one gun would not be sufficient." Instead, he had reasoned that "two or three may be convey'd in the same box, & all discharged by the same lock." This statement, in fact, was the first indication that he had devised a weapon that could fire multiple shots, both above and below the surface of the water. Some members of the Committee wondered whether or not such an innovative gun, firing multiple rounds one after another, might not push Belton's submarine violently and suddenly up to the surface. This, in turn, might force water inside the vessel, causing grave danger to its operator. Yet, Belton had already thought about this possibility, designing a safety mechanism for just such an occurrence:

> "And you may think that by any accident I should suddenly immerge myself I should thereby be liable to be drowned, to which I answer, that the little pipe, which need not exceed two or three inches in length, through

which I have a communication with the air, at the top of this I would have a valve, which should be kept about half open with a feable [sic] spring, which by any sudden immersion the natural pressure of the warter [sic], would shet [sic] perfectly tite [sic], and only take in a spoonfull or two, but allowing I had at sundry times, taken in considerable warter [sic], I could be expanding, & keeping a little motion with my feet, raise myself higher above the surface than common, & by turning a cock just below my chin, I would let out all the warter. For the part which my body was in, it being the part which I expanded, should be perfect tite [sic] of itself, and should have no communication with the appartment [sic] of my head, so that a person in one of these Machines need never be in danger of drowning"[16]

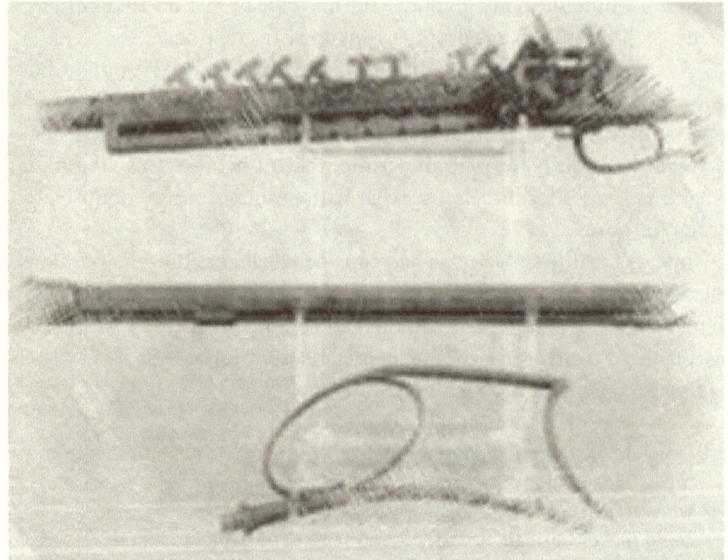

Belton's submarine armament (in pieces)

In an attempt to make one final selling point, Belton preyed upon Congressional patriotism, offering a speech that portrayed the British king as evil incarnate, and the American people as victims of his wrath:

"Methinks this nuse [sic] would appear to our King, as the hand writing did to the grand monarch of old, conscious guilt, of shedding the innocent Blood of his loyal people, would now instantly seize him, convulsive terrour [sic] shake his whole frame, chilling horrour [sic] freeze his blood, (perhaps never more to circulate,) dire dismay & confusion overtake his wicked Counsellors [sic], be the happy means of opening the eyes of the deluded people, and work out a glorious revolution in favour [sic] of us now distressed Americans, fix perminent [sic] our Liberties, reestablish that union which once so happily subsisted between the Parent state and these her Colonies, so great, so noble an undertaken, has often almost reduc'd me to dispare [sic], but being ever supported with the conscious knowledge, that the overruling hand of Providence, attends all the actions of men, and to mannifest [sic] its power, it has often been pleased to make use of small and obscure means, to effect wondrous revolutions, in defecting armies that were engageed [sic] in a wrong cause, (even so small as the sling of a stone.) And as the Plan is form'd not to shed Blood, or to trifle with the lives of men, but merely to destroy some floating, wooden engines, which are sent to our distruction [sic], Methinks Saints and Angles would encourage such a plan, and Heaven itself smile upon it, and if that is for it, who can be against it."[17]

Intrigued by the details and thoroughness of his submarine proposal, evidence indicates that there must have been much discussion and debate by the Pennsylvania Committee of Safety during the next week. Knowing that the inventor would be expecting some type of compensation for the destruction of enemy vessels, some wondered about the ultimate cost. Still others wondered whether or not a prototype had been—or would be—constructed, and how its use might be demonstrated before they agreed to move forward. Finally, others were concerned with Belton's legitimacy and wondered who might vouch for his ability to see the project through to the end. In short order, a response in writing was dispatched, voicing each of these concerns. He responded almost immediately:

"Permit me Gentlemen, once more to trouble you since you have thoughts of encourageing [sic] my plan by Premiums, or by giving a bounty upon every ship which I should distroy [sic] in any of our Harbours [sic], either by sinking or burning, &c. Which bounty is to be twenty pounds upon every gun, which said Ship or Ships doth carry. And likewise, a further encouragement perhaps you will be willing to sertify [sic] (i.e.) If any Ship, or Ships, so sunk, should by any succeeding plan be rais'd & maid fit for service, you will become obligated to give a generous price for the same, or any part thereof which might be serviceable to the Country, all which and in what particular manner you will become obligated to encourage me; please to certify at large; and when communicated, will be acknowledged as a favour [sic] by Your Humble Servant, Joseph Belton.P.S; As you have a number of armed boats to give in charge to such men, as has commanded by sea, I would readily engage in one of those in the defence [sic] of our Country, in which (I think) I could make several experiments that might be of infinite service, provided (I saw) I could imbrace [sic] this engagement without depriveing [sic] myself of the liberty of prosecuting my preconcepted [sic] plan."[18]

Finally, as a personal reference, Joseph Belton offered that "as I am a Stranger to you Gentlemen, my Character (as well as that of my family) may be well known from Governour [sic] [Samuel] Ward, one of the Gentlemen Diligates [sic] from the province of Rhode Island."[19]

Presumably, Joseph Belton received some positive news from the Committee, with Benjamin Franklin, himself, promoting the concept up the political ladder. Founder of the American Philosophical Society, Franklin was a Boston-born printer who had turned his attention to "electric fire" as early as 1746. Months earlier, in August of 1775, Franklin's interest in underwater vessels had been sparked by a letter from his friend, Benjamin Gale, who informed him of a one-man submersible then being constructed in Connecticut by a young Yale student, David Bushnell. Traveling to Boston in October of that year, Franklin had taken the time to visit Bushnell's "secret" workshop near Saybrook. There, he closely examined the young inventor's system of limpet mine warfare, utilizing a hand-propelled, one man submersible. Amazingly, Franklin would soon learn of the uncanny similarities in the Bushnell and Belton designs.

With a positive frame of mind, Joseph Belton went to work in the design and construction phase of his version, believing that he would soon hear good news. However, as the summer weeks turned into autumn, then winter, the inventor became somewhat cash poor. In an attempt to raise money, records indicate that Joseph Belton "late of Groton, now belonging in Philadelphia," sold, for £250, sixty acres to his father, Jonas Belton, of Groton, Connecticut.

Meanwhile, as spring came the following year with no word from the Committee, Benjamin Franklin grew tired of waiting. Subsequently, he dispatched a hand-written letter on Belton's behalf, explaining the details of the scheme to General George Washington. Dated July 22, 1776, the letter was intended as an introduction of Joseph Belton to the future president, outlining the ingenious inventor's plan to construct a submarine to be used against British Admiral, Richard Howe's, warships:

> "The Bearer, Mr. Joseph Belton, some time since petitioned the Congress for Encouragement to destroy the Enemy's Ships of War by some Contrivance of his Invention. They came to no Resolution on his Petition; and, as they appear to have no great Opinion of such Proposals, it is not easy, in the Multiplicity of Business before them, to get them to bestow any part of their Attention on his Request. He is now desirous of trying his Hand on the Ships that are gone up the North River; and, as he proposes to work intirely at his own Expence [sic], and only desires your Countenance & Permission, I could not refuse his Request of a Line of Introduction to you, the Trouble of which I beg you to excuse. As he appears to be a very ingenious Man, I hope his Project may be attended with Success. With the sincerest Esteem & Respect, I have the Honour to be, Your Excellency's most obedient & most humble Servant. B. Franklin."[20]

Indeed, after meeting face-to-face with Joseph Belton, General George Washington liked the idea of constructing submarines to destroy British enemy war ships. On July 30, 1776, in fact, he responded positively to Franklin's introductory letter:

AMERICAN SUBMARINERS: PRE-CIVIL WAR

"Within these few days I have been favour'd with two Letters from you–the first cover'd one to Lord Howe which with equal confidence I should have sent locked under a Seal–the only difference is, that I have had an oppertunity [sic] of perusing Sentiments which cannot but be admired—the Second, recommending the scheme of [ ] to whom I have given every aid in my power to bring his project to maturity. Your Letter to Lord Howe is gone to him, & I have the honour [sic] to be with great esteem & regard Sir Yr Most Obedt & Most Hble Servt. Go: Washington"[21]

Belton must have been delighted to secure the support of Washington, one of the most influential men in America. As the winter of 1776 approached, he went to work in his Philadelphia gun shop, preparing for the construction of his submarine vessel and perfecting the firing mechanism concept of his multiple-shot weapon. Acceptance of his inventions was only a matter of time.

Meanwhile, long-standing arguments over who had jurisdiction over land south of Philadelphia continued, as they had for nearly one hundred years. Initially, William Penn had been granted control of "Pennsylvania," which specifically excluded New Castle and any of the lands within twelve miles of it. Nevertheless, Penn strongly desired an outlet to the sea from his new province. He persuaded James, the Duke of York, to lease him the western shore of the Delaware Bay. So, in 1682, Penn had arrived in New Castle with two documents: a charter for the Province of Pennsylvania and a lease for what became known as "the Lower Counties on the Delaware." Thus began nearly a century of litigation between William Penn and Cæcilius Calvert, 2nd Baron Baltimore, and their heirs, in the High Court of Chancery in London.

In 1751, a line had been surveyed straight across the Delmarva Peninsula beginning at what at least some early Swedish settlers called Cape Hinlopen, which was to be the southern boundary of Delaware. Today, this place is better known as Fenwick Island. Twenty-four miles north was another cape named Cape Henlopen near Lewes, Delaware. Various spellings of henlopen were translated to mean "entering in" or "approaching." The confusion of the names became the crux of the long-standing dispute between the Penns' claim to Delaware and the Calverts' claim to Maryland, the latter arguing that the Lewes' cape should have been the start of the boundary line.

Ironically, it was a map commissioned by Charles Calvert himself in 1732, which showed Cape Hinlopen at Fenwick Island, which was used to decide the matter in court. Calvert had intended the Lewes' cape to be so named, but he only discovered the mistake after he had submitted it to the English high court considering the case. He failed in his later attempts to have the court reject his own map. If the actual Cape Henlopen near Lewes had been used as the start of the line, Delaware would be about one thousand square miles smaller, over a third of its current area.

Most recently, the settlement of the final legal battles had been finished by the heirs agreeing to the survey performed by Charles Mason and Jeremiah

Dixon between 1763 and 1767, with their work resulting in what would become known as the Mason-Dixon line. The final adjudication was not completed until the eve of the Revolution, and the settlement resulted in a major reason for close political alliances between the property owners of the Lower Counties and the Royalist Proprietary government, which remained loyal to Great Britain.

As a resident of Philadelphia, Joseph Belton fully understood the importance of controlling the Delaware River and its lower bay. The Mason-Dixon line, in fact, had formed a boundary between Delaware and Maryland, beginning at the Transpeninsular Line drawn by Charles Calvert. The border between Pennsylvania and Delaware was formed by an arc known as the Twelve-Mile Circle, laid out to clearly delineate the area within the sphere of influence of New Castle. While Belton believed his submarine, with its multi-shot weaponry, would keep the river and bay clear of invading British forces, a handful of English sympathizers were bound and determined not to allow that to happen. Secretly, they made plans to foil Belton's scheme.

As war raged on, Belton divulged a few details of his multi-shot gun to his closest allies of the Second Continental Congress. Then, on April 11, 1777, he forwarded a formal letter to the Congress, sharing the following information to those he thought he could trust:

> "I would just informe [sic] this Honourable [sic] Assembly, that I have discover'd an improvement, in the use of Small Armes [sic], wherein a common small arm, may be maid [sic] to discharge eight balls one after another, in eight, five or three seconds of time, & each one to do execution five & twenty, or thirty yards, and after so discharg'd, to be loaded and fire'd with cartridge as usual, which I am ready to prove by experimental proof and can with equal ease fix them so as to discharge sixteen, or twenty, in sixteen, ten, or five seconds of time, which I have kept as yet a secret, thinking that in two, or three Months we might have an army thus equipt [sic], which our enemy should know nothing of, till they should be maid [sic] to know it in the field, to their immortal sorrow... And if you Gentlemen are desirous to enquire into this improvement, your Humble Servent, is ready to wait upon you at any time, or place, or he may be waited on at the Widow Fords, in Walnut Street, between second & third street....from your most Obedient Humble Servent [sic]; Philidelphia [sic] April 11th 1777, Joseph Belton."[22]

The Congress acted swiftly on Belton's proposal, placing a number of his guns into service, for on May 3, 1777, they passed the following resolution:

> "Resolved that...Belton be authorized and appointed to superintend, and direct the making or altering of one hundred muskets, on the construction exhibited by him and called 'the new improved gun,' which will discharge eight rounds with once loading; and that he receive a reasonable compensation for his trouble, and be allowed all just and necessary expences."[23]

AMERICAN SUBMARINERS: PRE-CIVIL WAR

The inventor read Congress' response with a measured bit of excitement, realizing that he had finally earned their resounding approval for his invention. However, apparently he had expected them to offer a handsome monetary reward as payment for his invention, as well as the time that he had already spent in the weapon's development. For clarification purposes, on May 7, he responded with a second, more detailed letter, expressing his unsatisfied expectations and overall disappointment:

"I have receiv'd your resolve of the first of May, Werein [sic], I am Authorized to superintend, & direct, the altering of one hundred Muskets, & that I receive a reasonable compensation for my trouble (for so superintending & directing) &c. But I see no prospect of having any reward for my Invention, and for the cost and trouble I have already been at, Which has ever been customary through all Nations, to reward usefull [sic] inventions, or discoveries, as I have set for in a paper, Which I had wrote before. I had seen the Resolve, Which I had defer'd the Board of War to lay before your Honours, and to what lengths I would carry the invention and What Service it might render to the States, and provided I should fail in compeating [sic] the armes [sic] as I had therein set fourth, I would have no rewards as I desire not my Counteries [sic] money without rendering Services adiquate [sic] thereto, And still to remove all possible Objections, & to put things on an equitable, & reasonable a futten [sic], as any one I think can desire, I will engage to direct the arming of one hundred men, so as to be equal to two hundred in the field of Battle, or any number equal to double the same number as they are arm'd at present, Which shall be left to the Judgement [sic] of the Commander, or three first Commanding officers of our Army. And if they judge they are not I will be satisfied, & desire, and receive no reward & be intitled [sic] to none, But provided they should judge they were equal I then should be intitled [sic] to a thousand pound from each State–according to resolve of Congress, fo then where one hundred was thus equipt [sic] it would be the same, to the strength of the army, as if there was another hundred raisd & equipt [sic], & what state can raise, cloth & equipt [sic] one hundred men for a thousand pound, or even three thousand then allowing one hundred men to be equipt [sic] for each State, their strength would be the same, as if they had been to the expense of three thousand pounds more, in raising men besides the cost of maintaining them which may be saivd to the State, What then would be the saving in arming three or four thousand for each State, in short the many & ennumerable [sic] advanteages [sic], which it may render, are almost beyond discription [sic], which makes my proposal vastly reasonable, & until it is agreed to, or something simular, I shall beg to be exus'd from superintending & directing the altering of any Muskets, But when it is, it will be undertaken with Alacrity by Your Most Obedient Humbl Ser't, Joseph Belton."[24]

Finally, in an addendum of sorts, Belton offered reassurance to the assembly of Congressmen that there was virtually no danger of his secret weapons falling into the hands of the enemy. However, if it did, he offered a few possibilities if precisely how that might occur. In retrospect, it might have been wiser for him not to speak on the subject whatsoever:

> "...As for the Enemies obtaining & making any use of the invention against us, as some perhaps may imagine, I am no ways apprehensive of at present, for it will be my own folt [sic] if they doe, at least untill [sic] we had what number you please armd [sic], and if they doe then it might be by a deserter from our army, after he had become acquainted with the use of the armes [sic], for were our enemy to take some of the Armes [sic] after they were completed they could not very suddenly use them, untill [sic] they had discovered the true & safe method of Charging, which might puzzle the best of them for Months as it has done me, & perhaps split one or two about their ears, as I have done, Which you may think Gentlemen, as you have seen me discharge, to be very easy, but if any Gentleman in this place will tell me in a week with what, & how I charge I will give him the Invention, And him that alter'd me the gun knows not, and I am confident there is but one upon the Continent beside myself that does know, But from this you may think it will always be difficult, & dangerous, for men to use them, But so far from that, that I would trust any friend that was usd [sic] to a gun, after giving him the materials, & three or four words of direction, to go by himself & Charge, for me to discharge, and who had never seen the gun thus Charg'd before, Many things appear vastly dangerious [sic] & difficult, & are so till they are found out, then as vastly easy & simple so experientia docet omnia, and has taught the forgoing to your HblSert [sic] Jos Belton."[25]

Exhibiting a profound inability to help his own cause, it seems that Joseph Belton persisted in his self-defense of asking for monetary reward by writing another letter to his friend, John Hancock. In it, he specified exactly what he had determined to be equal to "reasonable compensation for my trouble":

> "Perhaps the Congress will sooner Comply with this than what I have heretofore laid before them, (Viz) I will engage to arm any member which shall prove equal to double the same number in Battle, if so then I should be intitled [sic] to five hundred pounds from each State, & if equal to three times their number I should be intitled [sic] to a thousand pound from each Sate, and if equal to four times their number I should be intitled [sic] to fifteen hundred from each State, so on riseing [sic] five hundred for every greater number. Which should be left to four experienced Officers two of which I should have the privelage [sic] of Choosing, And as they brought in so I should receive. And if they judged they were not equal to double their number I would be intitled [sic] to no reward which will be hartily [sic] complied with by Your Most Obiedient [sic] Humble Ser't Joseph Belton."[26]

Apparently, despite claiming that his primary motive was to "serve his country," Belton's persistence bordered on insistence to "name his price"–at least in the opinion of the majority of Congressmen. Indeed, a few were so put off by his demand for an extraordinary allowance that they ultimately decided to put their working relationship with him on hold for a time, thus temporarily rescinding their order for "the making or altering of one hundred muskets."

Records of correspondence with the Second Continental Congress–although communication was now flowing only one way–indicate that Belton was not immediately aware that he had fallen out of good favor with the Congressmen; nor was he told of the assembly's decision to table the project. On June 14, 1777, with Belton beginning to wonder about the lull in their responses, the persistent inventor sent the following letter to their attention:

> "Please to inform the Honourable [sic] Congress, that as I have heretofore asserted to them, that I can discharge sixteen, or twenty balls from one piece, one charging, by once puling tricker [sic], or at two or three diffrent [sic] times, by little more than cocking & priming the same lock two or three different times. And as I mean ever to fulfull all & every one of my Assertions, I propose next munday [sic] about ten O'Clock A.M. (if it be agreeable to your Honours [sic]) in the State House Yard to make the following exhibition (viz) to make five different discharges from one pulling tricker [sic]. Then again by little more than cocking & priming to make five more different discharges, then by little more than cocking & priming again to make six, all which I will warrant to do execution one hundred yards and think I might safely warrant it would two hundred, after which I can charge & fire with cartrage [sic] as usual."[27]

Arriving almost at sunrise at the Pennsylvania State House lawn, located on Chestnut Street between 5th and 6th streets, on Monday, June 16, 1777, Joseph Belton began to arrange his multi-shot contrivance for, what he expected to be, a bevy of onlookers. He was somewhat surprised that to find that, as the ten o'clock hour approached, only a handful of observers had come to witness his "amazing device." Undeterred, he fired his weapons repeatedly, all of which reportedly "came off without a hitch." A number of Congressmen and other observers agreed to endorse his guns for the entire assembly.

Finally, on July 10, 1777, Belton sent a fourth letter to Congress, still vehemently arguing "I ought to be handsomely rewarded by the Publick for my Invention." On this particular occasion, however, he made two grave miscalculations. First and foremost, he compared a fledgling America with the British government when it came to its ability to provide adequate compensation for inventions of this type. And second, he hinted at the fact that, if he was not handsomely rewarded," he would not provide the weapons demonstrated. Each of these "demands" ultimately proved to be too big of a risk:

> "The service that such armes [sic] may render to the Publick at this day & to posterity, I will leave your Honours to Judge. at the same time, I think that Great Britan [sic] has granted many five hundred a year for less

services renderd [sic] to their country, then what this will render to mine, and I look upon this extensive continent to be able to grant five hundreds as well as the little Island of Britan [sic], and as money is stild [sic] the sinews of war, so it may be stild [sic] the sinews of invention, for doubtless many experiments which might have discoverd [sic] something useful to the Publick, has for the want of it, died in Oblivion, And as the present Invention opens a door, into a wide extended field of improvement in every military department, where many useful things present themselves to view, which lies as yet unnotissed [sic], which when I am rewarded as the Invention merits, I shall readily step forth in my Counteries [sic] cause, and exert eery [sic] ingenious nerve to arm my Countery [sic] to the best possable [sic] advantage, for which purpose I beg leave to dedicate these papers to your Honours [sic] serious consideration and your wise determinations, may I hope, be crown'd with salutary consequences..."[28]

Attached to Belton's letter was an endorsement, though not actually "resounding," which had been signed by a handful of Congressmen who had witnessed his demonstration on the State House lawn. Noting the spelling variations, it is evident that the inventor had prepared the communication in his own handwriting:

"Having Carefully examined M. Beltons New Constructed Musket from which He discharged Sixteen Balls loaded at one time, we are fully of Opinion that Muskets of his Construction with some small alterations, or improvements might be Rendered, of great Service, in the Defense of lives, Redoubts, Ships &c, & even in the Field, and that for his Ingenuity, & improvement he is Intitled [sic] to a hansome [sic] reward from the Publick."[29]

The recommendation was signed by the following men: David Rittenhouse, renowned American astronomer, inventor, clockmaker, mathematician, surveyor, scientific instrument craftsman, and public official; Charles William Seale; Major General Horatio Gates, a controversial military figure; George Nash; Thomas F. Proctor; J.W. Strickland; and Benedict Arnold.

The support carried little weight in the majority of Congressmen, which ordered that Belton's petition be referred to the Board of War. According to notes of the Continental Congress, dated Saturday, July 19, 1777, the request was formally denied.

History would provide no known samples of Belton's gun design. It can be theorized, however, that it worked in a manner very similar to a Roman candle, with a single lock igniting a fused chain of charges stacked in a single barrel, packaged as a single large paper cartridge.

Little is heard from Joseph Belton until April 17th of the following year, when a letter was dispatched from to the First Joint Commission at Paris at Passy, an area located in the 16th arrondissement, along the Right Bank.

"Being unfortunately [sic], on a Voyge [sic] from Baltimore to Charles Town, in January last, disabled at sea, through stress of Weather, which occasion'd my faling [sic] into the hands of Capt. Man, and carried into Dover in England, and sent on Board the guard Ship in the Downs, a Prisoner, from Whence at length I obtaind [sic] my liberty by an order from the board of Admiralty, And being in an enimies [sic] Countery [sic], and antious [sic] to return to my friends, I fled into this, in the condition of most prisoners, empty in purs [sic] (at least of such currency as passes here,) and bairly [sic] Cloath'd [sic], relying on the friends of America [sic] for assistance; Which I hope worthey [sic] Gentlemen you will find it convenient to affoard [sic] me assistance, by granting me the lone of about Fifteen Guines [sic], which I will become Obligated to discharge upon my first arrivel [sic] in America, or will give a bill upon my Father who resides in the State of Connecticut, and will call upon the thirteen united states as an endorser to the bill, that is I will deposit as much of the States Currency as shall be equivalent to an endorser. Your Assistance worthey [sic] Gentlemen will be esteemed as a favour [sic] by a Native of Groton in the State of Connecticut, North America, who is Your Most Obedient Humble Servant Joseph Belton."[30]

History has been unable to substantiate how much, if any, of Belton's plea for a loan was based on truth. In fact, there seems to be no record of any ship being "disabled at sea" during a voyage from Baltimore, Maryland, to Charles Town, Massachusetts. Furthermore, no Captain Man can be uncovered in British Revolutionary War history. And finally, it seems a bit astounding that, between January and April of 1778 (a total of, perhaps, 100 days), Belton was captured by enemy forces, immediately taken to Dover, imprisoned aboard a "ship in the Downs" area of the North Sea, contacted the Board of Admiralty, was released, and somehow made his way to Paris, France. In further point of fact, typical passage times from the American east coast to the English mainland "for a well-found sailing vessel of about 2000 tons" were estimated to be between twenty-five and thirty days, with ships logging 100 to 150 miles per day on average.

Traditionally, Passy was home to many of the city's wealthiest residents. Ironically, in December of 1776, Joseph Belton's close associate, Benjamin Franklin, had been dispatched to France as commissioner for the United States. He took with him as secretary his sixteen-year-old grandson, William Temple Franklin. Together, they lived in a home in the Parisian suburb of Passy, donated by Jacques-Donatien Le Ray de Chaumont, who supported the United States during the war. In all likelihood, it was Franklin that had initially helped Belton in his most recent "time of need," perhaps even loaning him money and, most certainly, providing him with a temporary place to live.

Historical records indicate that sometime around the beginning of June, 1778, Joseph Belton departed from Benjamin Franklin's home in Passy and made his way 240 miles west to Nantes, France, where he rented a room from an innkeeper named Mathieu Hamelin. Apparently, Hamelin was a close acquaintance of Franklin's, who had recommended Belton as an honorable man. After remaining at Hamelin's inn for nearly six months, Belton departed from Nantes and returned to Passy without paying his bill, which totaled some 797 francs. He had promised to return within five or six weeks and, when he failed to come back, the innkeeper grew increasingly agitated. By the middle of February, 1779, Hamelin had become completely outraged and disappointed, and he dispatched a letter to Franklin pleading for his assistance in collecting the debt. On Sunday, February 28, Franklin responded with the following words:

> "M. Belton is gone from hence to Flanders, But propos'd to be back in five or six Weeks. I know nothing of his Debts & cannot be accountable for them. But when he returns I will press him to pay you & do what I can to obtain the Money for you. I am, Sir, &c."[31]

Although little is known about Belton's movements after February of 1779, the Commissioners may have taken action on his request for the loan of funds, for on February 13, 1779, they sent Benjamin Franklin a receipt for fifty guineas in payment for a public service performed by him. Whether or not this "public service" had anything to do with Belton cannot be proven, though the assumption can be made from the following receipt:

> "Passy, Feb. 13. 1779; Receiv'd of B Franklin, Fifty Louis d'ors on Account of Public Service to the United States, which I have undertaken to perform.–Jos. Belton."[32]

Either way, we know that Belton did not immediately return to America. Later that year, on September 10, 1779, John Adams, who had been in France between April 1, 1778, and June 17, 1779, responded to a communication from Joseph's father, Jonas, who was extremely concerned that he had not heard from his son in several months. Reassuring the elder Belton, the letter read:

> "I have received your Letter of the 14 of August, and have the Pleasure in Answer to it, to inform you, that I Saw your son, Several Times in France, and in particular, Some time in the Month of February, or Beginning of March last, at Dr. Franklins House, consulting with him about Some of his Philosophical or mechanical Inventions or Projections. He was in good Health. I thank you, Sir, for your complaisant Congratulations, on my Return to my native Country, and am…"[33]

In addition, Jonas Belton dispatched a letter to his son on March 30, 1780, expressing a desire for his safe return to America, and stating that he had learned of Joseph's situation from John Adams.

Apparently, Joseph spent the next four years wandering throughout the European countryside, though little is heard about his specific whereabouts.

Meanwhile, Henry Nock had opened a business in 1772 as a gunlock smith at Mount Pleasant, London. In April of 1775, he formed a partnership with fellow gun-makers, William Jover and John Green, planning to sell firearms made under English Patent No.1095 from 83 Long Acre. By 1779 he had moved to the Whitechapel district of London, and appears at Castle Alley the following year. Shortly thereafter, Nock made a set of gauges for the Gunmaker's Company Proof House, but he had severed his ties with the Company by purchasing his freedom in 1784. This move reflected the sentiments of many gun-makers who worked outside the Company's control over London's inner city area.

Meanwhile, William Jover operated his own gun making business, called "Jover and Son," situated at 337 Oxford Street between 1784 and 1796. Records indicate–though scant, at best–that an American, Joseph Belton, a former "citizen of Philadelphia," came to London from Paris in 1784 and teamed up with Jover to make several examples of a unique multi-shot weapon. However, the pair failed to interest the War Office or the East India Company, although the latter did conduct trials in India in 1786.

Little more was heard of Joseph Belton, his submarine invention, or his gun designs in Europe. Historical records, in fact, cannot absolutely prove when he returned to America. There is some historical indication that he married Catherine Hallick on December 22, 1800, at Paddington, London. Apparently, soon a gentleman by the same name, who once "lived in Passy, Paris, France," made his way to Columbiana County, Ohio, in 1804, where he gave birth to a son, Israel Belton. A few years later, in 1809, that Joseph Belton was laid to rest in an unmarked grave in the east Ohio wilderness. From there, the Belton legacy continued with two more sons of Israel, named John and Joseph, the former being buried near the grave of his grandfather in Saint James Cemetery, New Lisbon, Ohio, and the latter eventually migrating westward to the community of Waveland, Montgomery County, Indiana. He would be buried there, from his wounds while fighting in a conflict between the North and the South.

Of course, no clear and concise connection can be made, for the puzzle of history has lost a few pieces along the way, and it is uncertain precisely where the submarine inventor died or precisely where he was laid to rest. Yet, one particular fact remains quite clear: Joseph Belton was an inventive native of America, who tried desperately to develop a submersible vessel to assist in the cause of winning his country's independence from Great Britain during the Revolutionary War.

Sketch of Robert Fulton

- 7 -
Robert Fulton: *Nautilus*

"...as the component parts of all new machines may be said to be old; but it is that nice discriminating judgment, which discovers that a particular arrangement will produce a new and desired effect...the mechanic should sit down among levers, screws, wedges, wheels, etc. like a poet among the letters of the alphabet, considering them as the exhibition of his thoughts; in which a new arrangement transmits a new idea of the world."[1]

Saturday, February 25, 1815, was a chilly, wet day in Manhattan. Yet, as evening approached, the sun's rays spilled across the landscape, pushing deep shadows behind a group of men wearing funeral badges of mourning as they stepped through the freezing slush. They were on their way to pay last respects to an American icon, Robert Fulton. They came from all directions and from all social backgrounds—"not only from the handsome residences of nearby Wall Street, State Street, and Broadway, but also from the workmen's neighborhoods north of City Hall and from the wharves of the East and Hudson Rivers."

Before the clock struck five on this somber afternoon, a simple mahogany coffin with a small metal plaque engraved "Robert Fulton, age 49" was carried slowly down the front steps of his home, with his widow and four children—the eldest a boy just six years of age—grieving inconsolably. Amid the dull sound of gunfire from the West Battery, the procession, led by every important city official then alive, walked solemnly up Broadway to Trinity Church. There, to the ancient cadence of "ashes to ashes, dust to dust," Fulton's remains were locked within a vault owned by his wife's family.

In the eight rather brief years since his return from Europe, Fulton had become a national symbol, a hero for every man's dream of inventing some newfangled machine that would escort the nation into a wondrous industrial age. His *New York Post* obituary read:

"His is the only loss for which the public has no indemnity. Politicians, historians, poets, etc. are found throughout the United States, and readily succeed each other, but there is no person who will succeed to Mr. Fulton's genius as a mechanic, or be capable of prosecuting those schemes which he left in an unfinished state."[2]

Robert Fulton certainly did not have his roots in a family of creative mechanical geniuses. The family name can be traced to a Norman lineage, from a family called "de Fultowne" that entered Britain with William the Conqueror or shortly thereafter, and settled in Ayrshire, Scotland. Thomas de Fultowne is recorded as having lived in a manor in Ayrshire in 1220. Over time, the name evolved to "Fowlton," and eventually to Fulton.

Robert Fulton's direct family line was of Scotch-Irish descent, and historical record suggests that his ancestors trace their roots to Reverend Doctor Robert Fulton, who is known to have been the chaplain to Lady Arabella Stuart. The said Lady was, in 1614, imprisoned in the Tower of London for the crime of marrying William Seymour, later Marquess of Hartford, without royal approval. The Lady died in the Tower in 1615, and the Reverend Robert subsequently moved to a small farm called "Belsize," located on Seymour lands at Lisburn in County Antrim, Ireland. Members of the Reverend Doctor's Scottish-born family are believed to have settled at Lisburn as early as 1611, when the town was called Lisnagarvy. It was renamed following its destruction during an Irish Catholic uprising in 1641.

During the first half of the 17th century, a branch of the family found its way 160 miles south to Kilkenny, Ireland. While the two regions were not in close proximity to one another, there seems little doubt that the Fultons of Kilkenny were, in fact, a branch of the Fultons of Lisburn. The ancestral pathway is quite readily followed. In 1611, King James I granted Sir Fulke Conway, a Welshman of Norman descent, the lands of Killultagh, making "the landlords of the entire area around Lisburn and Dirriaghy in northwest County Down and southeast County Antrim, Northern Ireland...the Lord Conway Family." Research proves that this same family also held lands in the Kilkenny region. The Reverend Doctor's son, William Fulton–believed to be Robert Fulton's fourth great-grandfather–died in faraway Lisburn in 1638, and his wife, Elizabeth was described as the "widow of William of Deriaghy." The parish and hamlet of Derryaghy was nestled between the Cities of Belfast and Lisburn, precisely where the Reverend Doctor Robert Fulton's Belsize farm was located. Meanwhile, some–if not all–of the widow Elizabeth's five sons–John, Richard, James, Thomas, and William–born in that order between 1623 and 1630, were known to travel between the two Conway estates.

John Fulton, Jr., the son of John the elder, was born in 1653, and married Margaret in about 1674. One year later, John Fulton III, Robert's great-grandfather, was born in Lisburn. During the course of the next decade, brothers Richard, Robert, James, and William were born, each of which grew to maturity in Lisburn. While brother, Robert, was educated at Edinburgh and appointed chaplain on both the ship *Success* and later in Jamaica, the Hearth Money Roll records John, Robert Fulton's great-grandfather, in the parish of Derriaghy in 1666 or 1669. There is no mention of brothers Richard or James, but both Thomas and William appear in the Upper Malone which lies between Derriaghy and Belfast in 1666 and in Belfast itself in 1669. This suggests that the younger brothers had moved away from the original Belsize farm location towards the town of Belfast, which was now beginning to expand.

It appears that John Fulton III had four sons, each of whom were born in Lisburn, County Antrim, and who later relocated to Kilkenny. The eldest was William, born in about 1700, who was followed by James, Thomas, and Alexander. It is known that eldest brother, William, who was Robert Fulton's grandfather, married Mary Smith in 1728, and that the two of them gave birth to at least three sons–David, John, and Robert. Together, the Fulton family arrived in America during the early 1730s and, on July 21, 1734, William received a warrant for 150 acres on "Cunawingo, in Drurymore." Records indicate that the property, which would expand to 393.75 acres, was actually situated along the Conowingo Creek, near the boundary of Drumore and Little Britain townships, in southern Lancaster County, Pennsylvania.

Little is known of the Smith family branch, Robert's fraternal grandmother, prior to the emigration to Pennsylvania. Records do indicate, however, that the family name was "MacDonald," which formed a part of the earliest Scottish emigration across the North Channel into Ireland at the time that King James II ruled England. Near the end of the seventeenth century, Mary Smith's grandfather lived in northeastern Ireland. Just before the battle of the Boyne, as a soldier, King William III was reconnoitering when his horse lost a shoe. There was no farrier nearby to replace it, but MacDonald who, like many other farmers, was something of a blacksmith, offered to repair the loss and shod the horse. From this time forward his neighbors dubbed him "The Smith," a name he readily accepted and handed down to be used as his family name.

When religious persecution became unbearable, among the first to come to America were John and Susanna Smith Fulton, who left their home in Ireland in 1720. During the stormy and unusually long voyage, their son Robert was born. After landing in Philadelphia, the emigrants proceeded westward some thirty miles into Chester County, and settled in Uwchlan Township in a place long known as the "Brandywine Settlement." Shortly after her brother John had arrived with wife, Susanna, his sister Mary Smith Fulton followed.

Meanwhile, other Fulton family members arrived in the area during this same time period. Hugh Fulton appears in West Nottingham Township, Chester County, located about three miles south of Oxford, Lancaster County, in 1726; James and Alexander, two of William's brothers, in 1734; David Fulton came in the autumn of that same year; John arrived in East Nottingham in 1735; and deeds indicate that Thomas, William's youngest brother, owned land in West Nottingham in 1737.

William Fulton died in 1741, leaving his wife, Mary, alone and without income. Her three sons went to live with uncle Alexander for a time, at his nearby home known as Oak Hill, in Little Britain Township. Meanwhile, their mother married James Gillespie in October of 1742, and ownership of the 393.75 acres transferred to him on November 12. Over time, James expanded the property to a total of 545 acres and constructed a mill, the second on Conowingo Creek. The couple later fell into debt, however and the acreage was sold by the sheriff in 1764 in two separate parcels; 182 acres and the mill went to George Ross and James Bickham, while the eastern 363 acres was sold to Robert Fulton, Sr., father of submarine inventor, Robert.

Robert's father, Robert, Sr., was hardly what one could refer to as successful in agricultural endeavors. By 1755, pilgrim Robert had taken up the trade of tailor in Lancaster, Pennsylvania, a newly established frontier community, for a short time to be known as "the largest inland town in America." Not until he was well beyond the age of twenty did the elder Fulton find a suitable wife–or, perhaps, a woman who found him to be a suitable provider.

The elder Fulton's bride, Mary Smith, whom he married in 1759, was from a well-to-do family, and quite educated and respected by that day's standards. Her father, Joseph Smith of Oxford Township, had bequeathed her five pounds in his will, and her brother was a minister in the church. In exchange for a small down payment the newly married couple acquired a large mortgage and a modest brick dwelling along Lancaster's northeast corner of Penn Square, where they would remain for five years. During that time, they had three daughters, and Robert joined nearly every local organization that would have him.

A gregarious man, well liked by friends and neighbors, Fulton senior soon became secretary of the local Lancaster volunteer fire department, a position just as much coveted for its social and political benefits as its importance to the safety of the community. He was also a charter member of the Juliana Library, the third oldest book depository in the country, as well as a founder and celebrated chorister of the First Presbyterian Church. He struggled to make a living as a tailor, often having difficulty collecting money owed him. His lack of education showed in his correspondence:

> "...mr. Bufenton & mrs. Febey Hober...as you are to settle the esteat [sic] of Capton [sic] William Weay, Deses'd, [sic] the last chusday insteat [sic]. I did intend to come down, had my family not been in much truble [sic] by the death of my only son, but as Mr. John Clemston is to go down I mack [sic] no dout [sic] but you will send me the cash for the account I proved and sent you against the estet [sic]. As it is for wearing aperral [sic], it would be the highes [sic] reflecton [sic] on the deses'd [sic], which I would be sorey [sic] to heare [sic] others cast on him, much more myself. Mrs. Hober, you will know with what modistey [sic] I used him at your Father's, and even seemed to hide it frome [sic] them. If others should want I think you shuld [sic] pay the close [sic] that was on his back for honer's [sic] saick [sic]. Therefore, sencable [sic] of the trust the desesd [sic] has reposed in you, I mack [sic] no doute [sic] but you will remet [sic] me the cash in cash; in confidenc [sic] of it, I remaine [sic] with... your most Humble Servent [sic], Robert Fulton."[3]

Apparently, though no written records have survived, the elder Robert had lost a son in infancy, which would have been the elder brother of Robert, the inventor. Life was difficult, and much of the time Robert and Mary Fulton offset his meager earnings as a tailor by trading a few coveted consumer items, particularly rum.

Mary Smith Fulton appears to have been a well-grounded woman, quite steadfast in her support and devotion to marriage and family, and managed to keep her husband moving in the right direction. The few records that have survived the passage of time indicate that her primary concerns were the love and care of her daughters, as well as maintaining a close relationship with members of the family. Furthermore, evidence shows that she was, indeed, in charge of the home front, managing that as well as the outdoor chores and crops.

Robert Fulton's birthplace near Quarryville, in Lancaster County

In February of 1765, Robert and Mary Fulton sold their house and, with the profits, bought a piece of auctioned property near the tiny Conowingo Creek in Little Britain Township, Lancaster County, Pennsylvania. The 394-acre farm, located thirty miles south of Lancaster, included a modest two-story house, solidly constructed with gray and brown stone trim. Once again, the Fulton family was seriously in debt. Curiously, one might wonder why such a sociable gent would opt to remove himself from such an active community and relocate to the quiet of country living. Perhaps, it was Mary who had convinced him that rural life would be better for raising a family; or, perhaps, it was to get her often-wayward husband away from the thirty-two taverns then operating in Lancaster. Little more than nine months later, on November 14, 1765, the Fulton's gave birth to their first son, an active, brown-eyed baby they named him Robert.

Robert Fulton grew up in the modest, colonial era fieldstone, situated seven-and-one-half miles of Quarryville, in the southernmost tip of Lancaster County just a few hundred steps from the state border of Maryland. There exist few written records of young Robert's earliest years, though we do know that the farm did not yield great profit. Somehow, the Fulton family survived the terrible growing season of 1768, during which repeated hailstorms were so tumultuous that their "crops were flattened, fruit trees debarked, poultry decapitated, and windows shattered." In 1771, they were forced to pay an enormous tax of one pound, two shillings, and six pence on a farm that only had four head of cattle, a pair of "prized" horses, one work horse, and a single servant. Prosperity indicated by crops and stock that couldn't be peddled was only imagined wealth; in reality, the family was dirt poor.

In the grim January of 1772, the Fulton's were finally forced to give up the house that they had owned for just seven year in a sheriff's foreclosure sale. Even the beds, furniture, and kitchen utensils were auctioned to the highest bidder. "Only our clothing was excepted," the elder Fulton wrote to his two mortgage holders, who were in the process of disposing of his acreage. He pleaded with them to, at least, leave some small slice of income-producing property:

> "Y [sic] have nothing to by [sic] land back nor money to setup [sic] with in town; besides it is verrey desegreable [sic] to my wife and family to go back, if you would be so good to sell only 200 acckr [sic]...with that land & my head y [sic] could bring up my family..."[4]

His creditors were unforgiving, however, and the Robert Fulton, Sr., was forced to pack up his family and return to Lancaster, where he once again took up the profession of tailoring. Forlorn and broken, he died less than two years later in 1774. Young Robert, his mother, Mary (Smith) Fulton, and Robert's four siblings–Isabella, Elizabeth, Mary, and younger brother, Abraham–found themselves literally locked within an inescapable financial prison. In the numerous historical records left behind throughout his life, Fulton never once mentioned his father. Yet, one well-taught quality that the elder Fulton had managed to impart upon his family was the clear understanding that every individual must give his or her best to ensure survival.

Perhaps the return to Lancaster had been a positive aspect of young Fulton's life. It was a diverse community with five hundred homes and four thousand residents. And it was continually evolving, being " connected to High Street in Philadelphia to the Kings Highway, to the western wilderness by the great Conestoga Road, and to the inland South by ancient Indian trails," all of which brought in a constant flow of different cultures. The town's first settlers were of English origin, but they had quickly been followed by Swiss Mennonites, German Lutherans and Moravians, Jewish fur traders, French Huguenots, freed blacks, slaves, and a strong Scotch-Irish Presbyterian group to which Fulton's father had belonged.

Despite the diversity, Lancaster made absolutely no boasts that it was an American melting pot. Each ethnic group retained its own culture, language, and uniqueness. The Germans held onto their own schools and newspapers; the Huguenots continued to speak only French; The Irish celebrated Saint Patrick's Day; and the English loved their king, at least until the Revolution came. In summation, there were no less than fourteen distinct houses of worship, all steadfastly attended by artisans, mechanics, and folks with unflappable customs. Young Fulton would grow up submersed in a true land of opportunity.

Considering the circumstances, Robert Fulton was fortunate to grow up with immense advantages. They were poor, but not impoverished. They had warm clothing in winter, a roof over their heads, plenty of food on the table, books to read, and the love and affection of family. Later, he wrote about these fond memories in a letter to his eldest sister, Betsy:

> "I remember when we all lived in Lancaster opposite Irving Beefs and when you and Bell were good industrious girls. I was a stripling of a boy about 12 years old. Our mother being at Mr. Craig's in the country I had a battle against the two Sisters. You and Bell had turned me and the cat out of the truckle bed. It was of a winters evening about 8 o'clock. I instantly flew to the tongs and, as I stood in my shirt with uplifted arms ready to knock all your brains out, you were so much astonished at my resolute manner and wickedness as you supposed, that you began to cry and said you were sure I would some day be hanged...I was instantly disarmed and throwing down the tongs I went up to you, took you by the hand and said no Betsy, I shall live to be the protector of you and the family..."[5]

Robert began his formal education at a Quaker elementary school in 1773, under the guidance of schoolmaster Caleb Johnson, a "colorful Tory... and jack-of-all-trades." Avoiding, what he later would term, "painful commitment to studying such topics as reading, writing, and arithmetic," he instead concentrated his attention toward a topic that he considered more worthwhile– mechanical drawing. On one occasion, his mother having suggested to his teacher that the boy was not giving as close attention to his books as was desirable, the honest pedagogue replied that he had done his best, but that Robert had asserted that "his head was so full of original ideas that there was no room for the storage of the contents of dusty books." The boy was then ten years old.

Even at this early age, young Robert exhibited the bent of his genius by the manufacture of his own lead-pencils–hammering out the lead from bits of sheet metal, the writing utensils were considered hardly inferior to any graphite pencils of that time. This was two hundred years after their invention; but the Fabers had been making graphite pencils for more than a dozen years, and the Conte process, later standard, was only invented twenty years later.

In 1777, twelve-year-old Robert Fulton visited the store of a Lancaster neighbor, William Henry, who had been experimenting since 1763 on boats propelled with steam engines on the Conestoga River. Though he had planted the seed in young Fulton's inquisitive mind, his own experiments with steam would not begin until 1786 in England.

In 1778, the citizens of Lancaster, having been forbidden by the town council to illuminate in honor of Independence Day because of the scarcity of candles, Robert invented a skyrocket, and, as he said, proposed to "illuminate the heavens instead of the streets." When it was suggested to him by a friend that this was impossible, he replied, "No, sir; there is nothing impossible." His friends soon nicknamed him "Quicksilver Bob."

While still a teenager, Fulton became an expert gunsmith, and supplied to the makers in his town drawings for stocks, locks, and barrels. He even made computations of proportions and performance that were verified on the shooting-range. He was successful, both as designer of the main features of the gun and in his decorative work, and the makers were always glad to secure his sketches, and to profit by his computations. He even designed an air gun in 1779, at the age of fourteen.

Sketch of Robert Fulton's first paddlewheel boat on the Conestoga River, 1779

It was at about this time that his first ideas of new methods of boat-propulsion seem to have come to him. Finding the labor of "poling" a flat-bottomed boat while on a fishing expedition somewhat arduous, he made a model of a boat to be propelled by a pair of paddlewheels. In 1779, he tried his scheme on the same old fishing-boat, which had so severely taxed his thought processes, and found it so satisfactory that he and a friend used it on their excursions on the Conestoga River.

The boy's youth included the preliminaries to the War of the Revolution and its final successful accomplishment, and the young engineer and artist was one of the most earnest of rebels and a foe of the Tories. These events naturally turned his thoughts to military and naval inventions.

Meanwhile, Robert Fulton's intrigue for painting grew strong, and the development of that natural talent had become so unusual and so promising that he thought it wise to seek a wider field for the employment and application of his time and labor. At the age of seventeen, he departed from the family's rural Pennsylvania homestead, bound for Philadelphia, where he was determined to secure his fame and fortune.

There, in the "city of opportunity," Robert Fulton immediately set up shop as an artist, hawking miniature sketches and paintings to earn an adequate, though less-than-comfortable living. Under the patronage of Benjamin Franklin, however, he did manage to earn enough of a profit to enable him to purchase a small farm in Washington County, Pennsylvania, for his still financially struggling mother.

Close confinement and intensely stressful application began to enfeeble Fulton's strength. Slowly, his health began to fail, with his lungs exhibiting symptoms of such weakness that it was considered unsafe to neglect them. Worrying for his safety, friends insisted upon his going abroad in search of diversion, recreation, and health. He first traveled for a time to the Warm Springs, Virginia, recovering from an illness involving the lungs in a state of serious inflammation, with incipient hemorrhaging being among the more unpromising symptoms.

Meanwhile, John West, the father of budding artist, Benjamin West, had remained an intimate friend of Robert Fulton's father since the days that he had operated and lived at the Square Tavern and Inn in nearby Newtown Township. As a young boy, Benjamin drew during his leisure moments, concentrating particularly on birds and flowers he saw around him. Historical records mention a copy-book, with Reverend Beriah Hotchkin stating that it was in existence at least until 1834. This copy-book was filled with young Benjamin West's drawings made, according to the Reverend, "while at school in Newtown Square." Dr. George Smith further explained that the copy-book had been made "in the way of compensation for assistance given West in arithmetic by another school-boy named Williamson, the youthful artist not having much taste for figures."

Remnants of the Okehocking Indian tribe who frequented the Newtown Township area in the summer months were fascinated by the young boy's sketches of the birds and flowers they knew so well, and they taught him the origins of the red and yellow pigments they employed in making their painted ornaments. West's mother added blue to his palette by giving him some indigo with which she had been dyeing her wool. He had no brush, so he fashioned one from the hair of a cat's tail pulled up through a goose quill.

Earliest known drawing by Robert Fulton, Owned by the Estate of Dr. Joseph Bringhurst

The reputation of this talented and intelligent yet practically untutored boy from the countryside of Newtown Township grew. A Justice of Chester County, Samuel Flower, invited the youth to his home, where a governess, recently arrived from England, instructed him in readings from translations of ancient historians and poets. From this governess, Benjamin West heard for the first time of the Greeks and Romans. George Ross, a lawyer from Lancaster who would later be a signer of the Declaration, was a friend of Flower. He had several children and a beautiful wife, and Flower suggested that they sit for portraits by Benjamin West. They requested John West's approval, which he gave, and young Benjamin went off to Lancaster to complete the commissioned works.

The fame of Benjamin West in London was a favorite topic of conversation of the Fulton household in Lancaster. Meanwhile, sixteen-year-old Robert had already been applying his inventiveness to a number of tasks: he had designed carriages and buildings; he was able to sell his mechanical drawings to local machine shop owners; he had painted tavern signs for local inns; and he had honed his sketching skills using India ink as his tool. And, all the while, he studied the finer points of portrait and miniature painting.

An interesting example of Fulton's earliest artistic talent was a sketch in India ink of a French landscape, depicting a small group of peasant women washing linen by the side of a stream. It was entittled *La Blanchiseuse* (*The Washerwoman*), and signed "Robert Fulton, March 15, 1783." Clearly, it was made during the a time that the eighteen-year-old was visiting Philadelphia, and was likely a copy of a French engravingin a museum where he was taking art lessons. At that time, Charles Wilson Peale was the foremost artist in that city, and it was believed that Fulton was his student.

Therefore, it seemed quite natural that the budding artist would want to study under Benjamin West's expert guidance. Hence, in 1786, a well-rested Fulton packed his bags once again, sailing this time from America to faroff London, England. There, he continued his artistic endeavors, studying under the tutelage of the well-respected painter and future president of London's Royal Academy. The would-be submarine inventor would detail his early experience in the foreign land:

> "...and I must now give some little history of my life since I came to London. I brought not more than 40 Guineas to England and was set down in a strange country without a friend and only one letter of introduction to Mr. West–here, I had an art to learn by which I was to earn my bread, but little to support whilst I was doing it...Many, many a silant [sic] solitary hour have I spent in the most unnerved studdy [sic] anxiously pondering how to make funds to support me till the fruits of my labours [sic] should sufficant [sic] to repay them. Thus I went on for nearly four years."[6]

There are indications that young Robert soon grew homesick, missing not only his mother, but his younger sisters and brother. On June 14, 1790, he dispatched the following letter to his family back in Pennsylvania:

"Dear Mother; I have rec'd yours of January 29th, and am happy to hear of the good health of the family which is the first consideration and nearest my heart. May Heaven continue to shed that blessing on you and I shall be happy. I can easy conceive your garden to be the best in Washington; gardening ever was your delight, besides you have a taste for that kind of cultivation which perhaps the people of your western country are strangers to. Be assured that my (artistic) ideas often hover around the little spot. I think I see it improved by your industrious hand whilst the flowers of spring lend their aid to beautify the scene; but chief of all I think I see you on a Sunday evening contemplatively walking on the grounds and with silent pleasure on the past day. So shall time pass on and pleasure crown the evening of life. Here I could enter into a chain of those ideas which crowd upon a heart sensible of the feelings of a fond mother and the affection due from a child, but I must be silent and only answer your letter. It has given me much pleasure that you do not wish me to hurry home till I complete my study. Indeed it is of so much importance my gaining all possible knowledge that should I now return I might have it to repent of ever after... You tell me Polly is going to be maryed. May she be happy, but I will write to her on the subject... I am just getting ready to go to France for 3 months and am afraid I shall not have time to write to Abraham but give my best love to him and all friends and believe me to be with continued affection, your loving son, Robert Fulton"[7]

In September of 1785 Robert paid $75 for four lots in the community of Washington, Pennsylvania, for his family. In 1786, just after Robert had departed for London, his sister, Isabella, had married Peyton Cooke. Some time later, Margaret Elizabeth Fulton–affectionately called "Peggy" by her older brother–became the wife of Robert Scott, who died a few years later, and Peggy and her children moved into the family farm with her mother. In 1790, Mary Fulton–or "Polly"–married David Morris, a nephew of Benjamin West. Finally, Abraham Smith Fulton, his only brother, opened a school in Washington. In spite of being away for eighteen years, it is clear that his love for them remained strong.

In 1793, when he finally seemed to be at the very brink of securing his lifelong dream of becoming a highly successful painter, Fulton abruptly altered his chosen career direction, opting toward the science of engineering. The only evidence available as to the motivation behind the drastic turn-about was offered in his initial published literary attempt, entitled "A Treatise on the Improvement of Canal Navigation":

"On pursuing a paper descriptive of a canal projected by the Earl of Stanhope in 1793, where many difficulties seem[ed] to arise, my thoughts were first awakened to this subject (engineering)."[8]

Perhaps Fulton could look back to his boyhood days in Lancaster to truly locate his initial inspiration for engineering. It was way back then that early Swiss settlers had fashioned a method of irrigating barren acreage by simply cutting trenches along the side of a nearby hill, wherein water was carried from the highland springs to the thirsty soil below. Hence, the digging of channels in England to form lengthy watercourses would be nothing new, since it had already proven its value decades earlier.

From that moment forward, Robert Fulton expended all of his energy studying the design and construction of other man-made devices. He visited the stone and marble quarries in Devonshire, and discovered that the digging and raising of heavy product was extremely difficult. His first invention was a mill for sawing marble and stone. Next, he designed a machine for spinning flax, perhaps with his aging mother in mind, working her old-time spinning wheel.

Two talents were now having a tug-of-war for the majority of Fulton's attention—art and science. One or the other would be forced to the forefront, demanding all of his time and devotion, while the other would be set aside. To that end, Fulton put away his brushes in favor of engineering design. It was not because he no longer loved art; in fact, he continued throughout the remainder of his life, from time to time at least, to paint. But, there was not enough time for both professions. Still, just as he had previously experienced with art, he seemed to be a natural in this particular new endeavor of inventive thought. Soon, he managed to single-mindedly design the "inclined plane" canal, which would one day replace the more popular lock system.

During the same year that Fulton decided to switch professions, the concept of propelling watercrafts by steam power began to creep into his inventive mind. Such a drastic variation from ships under ordinary sail was, however, also nothing novel during the late 1790's. In fact, Jonathan Hulls had detailed just such an innovative machine in his pamphlet published more than a half-century earlier in 1737. Later, James Rumsey had actually put such a vessel into physical form, exhibiting it along the Potomac River as early as 1785. Eventually, John Fitch, another American, had gone as far as to transport passengers and freight on a regular schedule along the Delaware River in 1790. Despite all of these earlier experiments, Fulton claimed that a better, more practical steam vessel could easily be constructed. He would subsequently prove this theory with his own design during the next few years, concluding:

> "After this I was convinced that society must pass through ages of progressive improvement before the freedom of the seas could be established by an agreement of nations that it was for the true interest of the whole. I saw that the growing wealth and commerce of the United States, and their increasing population, would compel them to look for a protection by sea, and perhaps drive them to the necessity of resorting to European measures by establishing a navy. Seeing this, I turned my whole attention to finding out means of destroying such engines of oppression by some method which would put it out of the power of any nation to maintain such a system, and would compel every government to adopt the simple principles of education, industry, and a free circulation of its produce."[9]

Though the specific date remains unknown, Fulton managed to design and refine a compacted prototype submarine model sometime between 1793 and 1797, which he hoped would one day become a full-scale vessel. It was on December 13, 1797, that he dispatched a letter to the French Directory, proposing that the government finance the construction of his submarine design, while "having in view the great importance of lessening the power of the English fleet." Receiving no immediate response from the Directory, however, he next approached the French Minister of Marine with his innovative concept. In doing so, he suggested that an "outside agency" actually finance the project and requested that a rank in the French Navy be bestowed upon him in exchange for the creative details of his craft. The letter was sent on December 31, 1797:

> "Considering the great importance of deminishing [sic] the power of the British fleets, I have contemplated the construction of a mechanical Nautilus. A machine which flatters me with much hope of being able to annihilate their Navy; hence feeling confident that practice will bring the apperatus [sic] to perfection; The magnitude of the object has excited in me an ardent desire to prove the expirement [sic]. For this purpose, and to avoid troubling you with the investigation of a new project, or the expense of carrying it into effect; I have arranged a company who is willing to bear the expense, and undertake the expedition on the following conditions: First: That the government of France contract to pay the Nautilus Company 400 livres per gun for each British ships over 40 guns which they may destroy; and 2000 livres per gun for all vessels of war under 40 tons which they destroy, that the sum be paid in specie within six months after the distruction [sic] of each vessel. Second: That all prizes of British vessels and cargoes taken by the Nautilus Company; shall be the property of the company; nor meet with any interruption from the agents of government further than to ascertain that they are British property. Third: That the government give to the Nautilus Company the exclusive right to use this invention from all the ports of France, except when it is the desire of government to construct such vessels to act against the enemies of the republic. In such case the government, to be at liberty to build and multiply the mechanical Nautilus, on paying to the company one hundred thousand livers for each Nautilus which they may construct or use in the service of the republic. Fourth: As a citizen of the American States; I hope it may be stipulated that this invention, or any similar invention, shall not be used by the government of France against the American States, unless the government of America first apply the invention against France. Fifth: That if peace is concluded with England within three months from the date hereof, government will pay to the Nautilus Company the amount of the expenses which they may have incured [sic] in the experiments. Such payment to be made within three months after the declaration of peace. Sixth: And whereas fire ships or other unusual means of destroying navies are considered contrary to the laws of war, and persons taken in such enterprise are liable to suffer death, it will be an object of safety if the Directory give the Nautilus Company commissions specifying that all

persons taken in the Nautilus or submarine expedition shall be treated as Prisoners of War, and in case of violence being offered; the government, will retaliate on the British Prisoners in a four fold degree. Citizens hoping that this engine will tend to give liberty to the seas; it is of importance that the experiment should be proved as soon as possible in order that if successful the terror of it may spread before the descent on England, and that it may be brought into use to facilitate that descent."[10]

The presumptions were acknowledged by the Minister of Marine in early January, 1798, who generally accepted them with the following amendments to four out of six of Fulton's clauses:

"(1) The sums proposed as prize money for the destruction of the enemy's ships, being too great, were to be cut in half. (3) The construction of as large a number of Nautilus as deemed necessary was authorised [sic], the place of construction, however, to be far removed from all the war ports. (5) The reimbursement of the expenses of the Company that was asked for in case of conclusion of peace was refused unless due to fear inspired by the construction of the Naxtibs [sic]. (6) Finally, the Minister absolutely refused Fulton's request for commissions in the French Navy, because he did not think that it was "possible to grant commissions to men who made use of such means to destroy the enemy's forces and, even so, that such commissions could be any guarantee to them. For the reprisals with which the French Government could threaten the English Cabinet would be useless, since there existed in England three times more French prisoners than English prisoners in France."[11]

Fulton accepted the amendments with the exception of clause five, which he stipulated should read, "the total sum to be reimbursed to the Company on the conclusion of peace should be a sum not exceeding 25,000 francs" the reason given being that the construction and trial of the *Nautilus* would take three months. Fulton also held to his original demand for commissions for the crew. He proposed to construct his submarine at Paris and test it at Havre. These proposals were submitted to the Minister on January 20, 1798.

Meanwhile, a draft decree was drawn up and submitted by the Minister to the Directory, but it was never issued for, on February 5, 1798 Fulton received from the Minister a letter telling him that all his proposals were totally rejected without explanation.

Remaining self-assured, and refusing to give up on his idea, Fulton decided to simply bide his time until another Minister of Marine was appointed. Eventually, his patience paid off and, on July 23, 1798, he resubmitted his proposal to the new Minister, Admiral Decrea. Boastfully, he argued that his submarine vessel would not only lead to the complete and utter destruction of the English naval forces, but also to total freedom of the high seas for France. This time, the French government was more inclined to take heed of Robert

Fulton's ideas, opting to convene a board of technical experts to further examine the proposal. At about the same time, unwilling to not make a similar offer in his homeland, he wrote a letter to a political friend in America. It read in part:

> "...a free trade, or in other words, a free ocean, is particularly important to America. I would ask anyone if all the American difficulties during this war is not owing to the Naval systems of Europe anda licensed robbery on the ocean? How then is America to prevent this? Certainly not by at-temting to build a fleet to cope with the fleets of Europe, but if possible by rendering the European fleets useless."[12]

Clearly, Robert Fulton's plan to construct a boat that could descend beneath the water would be designed to deliver explosives wherever it was desired. These bombs could be set by timeclocks, so that they would later explode. Initially, he referred to his concept as a "torpedo," a name inspired by a strange fish he had read about in the writings of traveler Sir Thomas Herbert. Described as a "torpedo or cramp fish," Herbert had explained that, when he and his companion picked up the creature in their bare hands, it alarmed them so much that they "trembled," for "it let forth a cold breath upon them, so they would be so frightened that they would let it go."

Drawing of Fulton's *Nautilus*

The initial detailed drawings that Fulton submitted for review by the French depicted a diving boat with iron ribs and a copper sheath, possessing the shape of an imperfect ellipsoid measuring twenty-one feet, three inches in total length. Boasting an extreme beam of six feet, four inches, the vessel–which had already been dubbed the *Nautilus* by its designer–would exhibit an attached, hollowed-out iron keel situated beneath its reinforced hull. This mechanism, explained Fulton, would act as ballast, with a valve permitting the introduction of, and a hand-pump forcing the rejection of, seawater. In theory, taking on only a small amount of water would take the submarine down smoothly, while the expulsion of the same quantity would bring it immediately to the surface.

On the forward portion of the *Nautilus* there would be a watertight spherical compartment, along with a single hatchway for entering and exiting the craft. To power the submarine, Fulton proposed a typical screw propeller. Quite similar to the one designed and implemented by David Bushnell, it would be positioned at the stern, directly in front of the rudder. Such a mechanism, Fulton reasoned, would be operated from within by a hand-crank driving a series of small gears, which, in turn, would revolve a shaft extending through a watertight stuffing box.

While one man would operate the propeller crank, a second would be in charge of filling and emptying the ballast tank. Provided that the underwater craft was in motion, Fulton theorized that he could achieve a particular depth by simply altering the angle of two planes attached to the sides of the steering rudder. Forward movement at the surface of the water would be obtained by a fan-shaped sail, which, along with its supporting mast, could be folded down to deck level and covered with envelopes. In his scientific opinion, Fulton's proposed underwater machine would require a maximum of three men to operate.

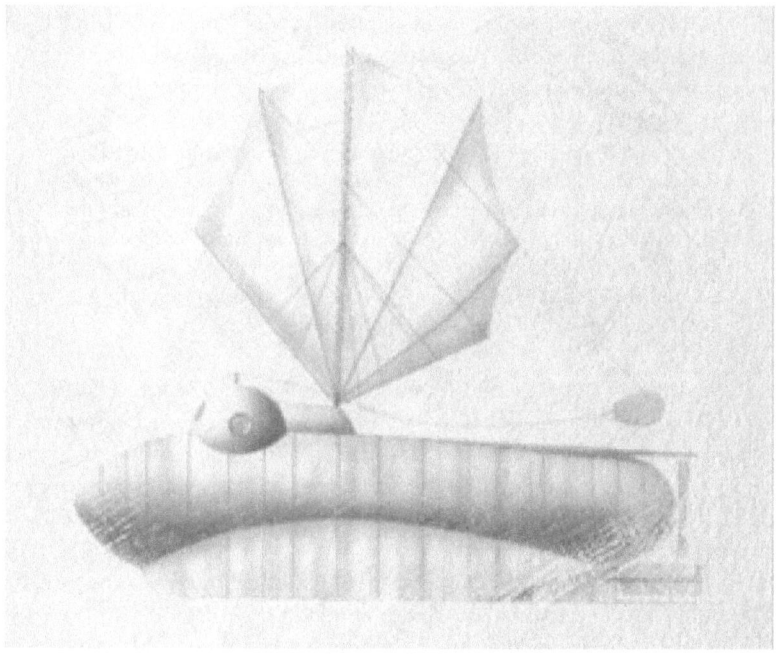

Drawing of Fulton's *Nautilus* under sail

The vessel's proposed weapon delivery system would consist of a vertical spike attached to the extreme peak of the observation dome, through which would pass a leaded cord leading to a stuffing box and a winding spool. With an explosive charge attached to the free end of the cord, the submarine would dive beneath an enemy vessel and "touch" the protruding spike to the underside wooden hull planking. A sharp blow on the opposite end of the spike would drive the detachable fixture into the unsuspecting ship's timbers. The *Nautilus* would then simply move away from the enemy craft, leaving the spike behind and pulling the cord through the spike's hole, much like a thread through the eye of a needle. Slowly, the charge would be guided closer to the hull by way of increasing the distance between the enemy ship and the submerged *Nautilus*. Eventually, when the explosive came in contact with the hull, it would be detonated, thus inflicting a gaping hole through the vessel's under belly.

The board of technical experts, established for the specific purpose of studying Fulton's detailed proposal, was greatly impressed. Though they fully believed it to be a sound concept, they had one small misgiving; the idea of the foldaway sails. In their "expert" opinion, the mast extended too far out in an upward direction, and would undoubtedly cause the floating craft to become unstable in a strong wind. Though seemingly insignificant at the time, the criticism would be only the first of a great many that Fulton would suffer over the course of the next eighteen years.

Robert Fulton was greatly encouraged by the commission's initial endorsement. So certain of the *Nautilus*'s eventual acceptance, he added the following stipulations to his previous proposal:

> "...the French government pay immediately on the receipt of news of the destruction of an English ship of the line, 500,000 francs, with which sum be engaged to build a squadron of 10 Nautilus to be used against the English fleets. That the government was to pay...the sum of 100 francs for each pound of caliber of the guns of English ships destroyed or put out of action by the Nautilus during the war; that is to say, for a 5 pounder gun 500 francs, or for a 10 pounder, 1000 francs."[13]

In spite of the favorable recommendation by the board, however, the proposal was eventually rejected by higher ups within the French government. Refusing to relinquish his dream to construct a fleet of underwater diving vessels, however, Fulton continually badgered French officials with innovative and logical arguments. Finally, after many weeks of persistence and impatience by the outspoken American, the resistant body of lawmakers gave in. Delighted, Fulton immediately traveled to Rouen, where he began the early construction phase of his craft in earnest at the Perrier Boatyard.

During the last week of July 1800, the *Nautilus* was duly launched with little fanfare. Just five days later, she proved herself before a large assembly of onlookers by making an initial plunge to a depth of twenty-five feet:

"...the *Nautilus* was tried on the Seine, above the Hotel des Invalides. Fulton having shut himself up in his boat, with a sailor carrying a lighted candle, descended underwater, remaining there for twenty minutes, and emerged after having gone a considerable distance. He again descended in order to regain the point of departure. He then reappeared at the surface and sailed several stretches, amid the applause of the assembled multitude."[14]

Due to the swift current of the Seine River, however, Fulton decided to move his test dives to the open, less taunting, waters of the open Atlantic Ocean, just off the coast of Havre. There, along with two other crewmembers, he managed to remain submerged for an astounding six hours on a single dive. On that particular outing, the trio had obtained a fresh supply of oxygen through a lengthy tube, whose open end had been supported by a surface float. Apparently, the depth of submersion was just below the surface.

Robert Fulton next decided to investigate his earlier theory that a screw propeller would work much better than a rowing apparatus. With two men continually pumping the oars, the *Nautilus* was able to travel only sixty fathoms in a seven-minute period; yet, with the same two men cranking the propeller, the craft covered an equal distance in approximately four minutes. Still, the inventor was not satisfied with the speed. Hence, he opted to replace the more conventional screw propeller with his own design possessing blades set at angles. Similar to a windmill, this "flier" propeller produced far better results.

Despite the positive outcome of Fulton's tests, the French Minister of Marine remained unconvinced of the submarine's viability. Returning to Paris, the inventor surrounded himself with influential people, whom he hoped would be able to assist him with his quest to convince the French government to finance the construction of an entire fleet of diving vessels. One of his closest companions during this period was the American poet, Joel Barlow, who also happened to be a personal friend of Napoleon Bonaparte, the newly appointed First Consul of France.

Two additional allies of Fulton included reputable scientists in their respective fields: a mathematician named Gaspard Monge and an astronomer named Pierre Simon de Laplace. In order to gain their full support and assistance, he dispatched the following convincing letter to Monge and de Laplace:

"Citizens, Not having had the time to busy myself with the drawings and description of the latest changes that I have thought fit to make in my *Nautilus*, I take the liberty to recommend the model of it to your examination as the best means of enabling you to judge of its form and combinations. Although having exact details of experiments, I shall limit myself to rendering here a succinct account of the most important of them. First experiment: The *Nautilus* is 20 feet long and 5 in diameter and according to the calculations of Cen Guyton it will contain a quantity of air sufficient for 3 men and a candle for three hours. Second experiment: On

24 August, 1800 I plunged in the basin at Havre to the depth of 15 feet having with me two people and a lighted candle; we remained below the surface for the space of one hour without experiencing the slightest inconvenience. Third experiment: On 25 August I tried to manoeuvre [sic] the *Nautilus* by means of wings 4 feet diameter like the sails of a windmill; to this end at first I placed on the bridge two men with oars; they took 7 minutes to row about 90 toises (192 yards), the length of the basin; then I ordered the same 2 men to set the sails and in 4 minutes the *Nautilus* covered the 90 toises to the starting place; I proved by this that the speed of sails to that of oars is about 2 to 1 and that these sails are very suitable to manoeuvre [sic] a boat under water. The success of this experiment has given me several new ideas, which I hope will facilitate much the use of carcasses of powder or torpedoes. Fourth experiment: On 26 August I tried balancing the *Nautilus* under water in such a way as to prevent it rising towards the surface or descending to the bottom, meanwhile advancing. This is executed by means of a pair of wings placed horizontally on the front of the *Nautilus* and which communicate with the interior. By turning these wings from left to right the *Nautilus* is made to descend below the water, in turning them from right to left, it is raised to the surface. My first trial was unfortunate, in not having placed the boat in the necessary trim in order that the wings could act. The next day I had a decided success and I kept my *Nautilus* below water at a depth of about 5 feet whilst it covered a distance of 90 toises, about from one end of the basin to the other. This day I made several movements under water and I observed that the Compass acts as well under water as at the surface. The three people who have been my companions during these experiments are so familiarized with the *Nautilus* and have so much confidence at present in the movements of this machine that they undertake without the least concern these aquatic excursions. Having thus assured myself of the ease of emersion [sic] and of submersion of the *Nautilus* and all its movements as well as the effect on the compass, on 27 August I half filled an ordinary barrel and placed it at anchor in the harbour at about 200 toises (426 yards) from the jetty; I seated myself then in an ordinary boat at the distance of about 80 toises and placed in the sea a torpedo containing about 30 lb. of powder; the torpedo was attached to a small rope of 100 toises; the current going under the barrel, the torpedo passed without touching it; but turning the helm of the boat in which I sat, I made it go obliquely till I saw the torpedo exactly under the barrel; I then drew back the cable till at last the torpedo touched the barrel; at that instant the battery went off, the powder exploded and the barrel was reduced to fragments being lost in a column of water 10 feet in diameter that the explosion threw into the air to the height of 60 or 80 feet. On 12 September I left Havre for La Hogue and in this little voyage, my *Nautilus* sometimes did a league and a half (4.5 miles) per hour, and I had the pleasure of seeing it ride the waves like an ordinary boat. On 15 September I put into a little harbour called Growan near Isigny at 3 leagues from the islands of Marcou. On the 16th the equinoctial gales commenced and lasted 25 days. During the time I tried twice to approach two English brigs, which were anchored near one

of the islands, but both times, whether by accident or design, they set
sail and were quickly at a distance. During one of these trials I remained
during the whole of one tide of 6 hours absolutely under water, having for
the purpose of taking air only a little tube, which could not be perceived
at a distance of 200 toises. The weather being bad, I remained 35 days at
Growan and seeing that no English vessel returned, and that winter approached, besides my *Nautilus* not being constructed to resist bad weather, I resolved to return to Paris and place under the eyes of Government
the result of my experiments. In the course of these experiments there
has come to me a crowd of ideas infinitely more simple than the means
that I have employed hitherto and in an enterprise so new and without
precedent one ought to expect that new ideas should present themselves,
tending to simplify the execution of the great object in view. As to myself
I look upon the most difficult part of the work as done. Navigation under
water is an operation whose possibility is proved, and it can be said that
a new series of ideas have just been born as to the means for preventing
naval wars or rather of hindering them in the future; it is a germ which
only demands for its development the encouragement and support of all
friends of science, of justice and of society."[15]

It was Gaspar Monge who personally brought Fulton's submarine fleet idea to the attention of Napoleon, who, in turn, recommended the scheme to the Minister of Marine. A few days later, Monge and Pierre Simon Laplace managed to arrange a face-to-face meeting between the America inventor and the First Consul. Following much discussion, Napoleon Bonaparte left Fulton with the promise that he would personally take the proposal under consideration.

A week went by with no word from Napoleon or the Minister of Marine. Not known as a man of patience, Fulton grew more restless with each passing hour. Finally, unable to withstand the silence any longer, he dispatched a critical and somewhat threatening letter to the Minister:

"Although I retain the most ardent desire to see the English Government
beaten… the cold and discouraging manner with which all my exertions
have been Treated…will compel me to abandon the enterprise in France
if I am not received in a more friendly and liberal manner."[16]

Clearly, a proud and stubborn Robert Fulton had decided to take a calculated risk by his blatant urging for the construction of his submarine fleet, which, of course, would be financed by the French government. In retribution for the inventor's "threatening contempt," Admiral Decrea, the Minister of Marine, vetoed the proposal emphatically, and explained his reasons in writing to the First Consul.

Monge and Laplace quickly attempted to right the wrong that Fulton had inflicted upon himself, expressly advising him to refrain from writing any more accusatory letters to high-ranking French officials. Meanwhile, they also made a personal plea to Napoleon to ignore the American's blatant written outburst. Furthermore, they managed to convince the First Consul that Fulton had acted out of sheer impatience, and advised him to disregard the Minister of Marine's opinion on the matter. Ultimately, Napoleon not only took their advice, but gave the inventor his personal permission to go full-speed-ahead with the project. In a message dispatched by the First Consul in 1801, it was clear just how interested Napoleon was:

> "I have just read the project of Citizen Fulton, Engineer, which you have sent me much too late, since it is one that may change the face of the world. Be that as it may, I desire that you 'immediately' confide its examination to a commission of members chosen by you among the different classes of the institute. There it is that learned Europe would seek for judges to resolve the question under consideration. A great truth, a physical, palpable truth, is before my eyes. It will be for these gentlemen to try and seize it and see it. As soon as their report is made it will be sent to you, and you will forward it to me. Try and let the whole be determined within eight days, as I am impatient."[17]

From that day on, the submarine's future operation would come under the close scrutiny of a new watchdog committee. Fulton could not have wished for a more positive outcome, for that three-man team would be comprised of none other than his close associates, Monge and Laplace, as well as a respected scholar named Constantin François de Chassebœuf, comte de Volney.

With a simple majority of the investigative committee fully behind him, Fulton hurried off to Havre, having the *Nautilus* transported to nearby Brest. There, it underwent extensive alterations and improvements. Finally, on July 3, 1801, he and three volunteers took the reconditioned vessel down on the first of several test dives:

> "...the engineer, accompanied by three men, went aboard...his boat in the harbour of Brest; he descended to a depth of 25 feet, and remained under water for an hour, moving in all directions at will...he replaced his candle, which consumed too much of the respirable air, by an opening at the top of the boat, fitted with thick glass, which allowed sufficient light to penetrate to enable him to count the minutes by his watch. On the 26th he adapted to the Nautilus a mast, a large sail, and a jib. Suddenly, in the middle of the harbour, he struck the sails and mast and prepared to descend. His preparations consumed in all only two minutes. The boat had a speed under water of one meter per second; it was under perfect control, and could be handled as well as on the surface. The compass at no depth whatever lost any of its magnetic properties."[18]

By then, with the help of a mathematician named Gueyton, Fulton had calculated that a 212-cubic-foot submarine would house enough oxygen to supply four men and two small candles for a minimum of three hours. Yet, with the installation of a window porthole in place of candles for light, that time period would later be greatly extended. As a further innovation to enhance the oxygen supply, he designed and constructed a copper sphere, referred to as a "bomb," in which two hundred cubic feet of compressed air could be stored. Testing the new apparatus, Fulton and two others took the *Nautilus* down into depths of five feet of water, where they remained for six hours without experiencing any difficulty in breathing.

Next on Fulton's widening agenda was the effort to develop an explosives delivery system for his underwater craft. His early mine designs were fashioned from various sized copper cylinders, each containing between ten and two hundred pounds of gunpowder. Furthermore, they were each fitted with an innovative gunlock mechanism, which would trigger the detonating charge whenever they came in direct contact with the hard wooden surface of a ship's hull.

These innovative underwater explosives were demonstrated in front of a small, elite group of spectators, including not only Monge, Laplace, and a few other close allies, but French Admiral Veilaret. The intended target was an abandoned 40-foot sloop. With the *Nautilus* guiding its mine, housing twenty pounds of gunpowder, Fulton submerged at a safe distance of about 600 feet from the sloop and continued on, unseen, beneath the surface:

> "So as to pass near the sloop I struck her with the bomb in my passage... the explosion took place and the sloop was torn into atoms; in fact nothing was left but the buye [sic] and cable, and the concussion was so great that a column of water, smoak [sic] and fibres [sic] was cast from 80 to 100 feet in air."[19]

In the course of his experiments at Brest, Fulton found it to be perfectly comfortable to descend to any depth, and to take any course that he might desire. He actually entered channels at a twenty-five foot depth and explored their soundings, and was only prevented from attempting greater depths by the fact that he had a boat which would not safely withstand the great external pressure. The depth at any given moment was determined by the use of the barometer, and he directed the course by means of the compass. He found the boat as obedient under the surface as it was above. The air-supply was renewed by drawing upon a reservoir in which was compressed 200 times its volume of atmospheric air. Using this as a reserve, the inventor was able to remain under water nearly four-and-one-half hours:

> "The diving-boat, in the construction of which he is now employed, will be capacious enough to contain eight men, and provision enough for twenty days, and will be of sufficient strength and power to enable him to plunge one hundred feet under water, if necessary. He has contrived a reservoir of air, which will enable eight men to remain under water

eight hours. When the boat is above water it has two sails, and looks just like a common boat; when she is to dive, the mast and sails are struck. In making his experiments, Mr. Fulton not only remained a whole hour under water, with three of his companions, but had the boat parallel to the horizon at any given distance. He proved that the compass points as correctly under the water as on the surface, and that while under water the boat made way at the rate of half a league an hour, by means contrived for the purpose."[20]

Furthermore, it was now Fulton's urging that all future submarines be constructed with brass hulls, enabling them to dive to depths of sixty to eighty feet. Aside from the crew, he contended, these reinforced crafts would be able to transport ample provisions of food and other stock, as well as between twenty-five and thrity-five explosives apiece.

Two months went by before Robert Fulton was informed by Monge, Laplace, and Volney that they were highly interested in further developing the details of his latest scheme, and eventually turning them into reality. Furthermore, they proudly informed him that Napoleon Bonaparte, himself, was looking forward to boarding the now widely acclaimed *Nautilus* and accompanying him on a test dive. Shockingly, however, the three-man committee was informed by the upstart inventor that this would not be possible. When asked why, Fulton offered a rambling written explanation on September 20, 1801:

> "I am sorry that I had not earlyer [sic] information of the Consuls [sic] desire to see the plunging boat, when I finished my experiments. She leaked very much and being but an imperfect engine I did not think her further useful...hence I took her to pieces, sold her iron work, lead, and cylenders [sic] and was necessitated to break the greater part of her movements. In taking them to pieces, so that nothing now remains which can give an idea of her combination, but even had she been complete I do not think that she could have been brought around to Paris—You will be so good to excuse me to the Premier Consul, when I refuse to exhibit my drawings to a Committee of Engineers...for this I have two reasons: the first is not to put it in the power of anyone to explain the principles or movements least she should pass from one to another till the enemy obtained information; the second is that I consider this invention as my private property, the perfectionment [sic] of which I will give to france [sic] incalculable advantage over her most powerful and active enemy. And which invention I conceive aught [sic] to secure to me an ample independence, that consequently the Government should stipulate certain terms with me before I proceed to further explination [sic]..."[21]

Though difficult to read, the specific repercussions of the lengthy letter were quite clear; the inventor had dismantled the *Nautilus* and, once again, had managed to place his own personal desires above those of Napoleon. Needless to say, the French First Consul was extremely dismayed with the American's irritating independence, and this time Robert Fulton would not be so easily forgiven. It now seemed that not even his closest political allies–including Monge and Laplace–could alter the course of history.

Sketch of Silas Plowden Halsey

- 8 -
Silas Plowden Halsey: *Halsey Submarine*

"Col. Halsey is recollected as a man of tall and commanding figure, of sanguine temperament, persuasive address, combined with great force and energy of character. He had ten children; the eldest was Jeremiah Shipley Halsey, father of Jeremiah Halsey, lawyer of Norwich, and the youngest, Silas Plowden Halsey, who was lost in a torpedo off New London, in August, 1814, in an attempt to blow up the British ship *Ramillies...*"[1]

The War of 1812 was, perhaps, America's most diversely interpreted war. Historians would long agree that Great Britain's disrespect for American maritime rights–its interference with American trade and its illegal impressment of seamen from American ships–severely strained Anglo-American relations in the years before 1812. But there is considerable disagreement as to why this ultimately led to conflict and what this war actually represented.

One group of historians has long argued that the war was a complete waste of resources and lives. For starters, they say, it was unnecessary. When Britain failed to meet James Madison's demand that it revoke the Order in Council, declaring American commercial vessels subject to interception and seizure, western War Hawks in Congress wanted revenge. Within a week of the declaration, however, Britain did suspend the provocative order–and the cause for war was thus eliminated. With just a bit more patience, or more efficient communication, these historians argue, the war might have been avoided.

In addition, these same historians argue that the war was inconsequential. After three years of fighting, and nearly 6,000 American casualties, the United States and Great Britain agreed to a treaty that resolved none of the substantive issues that had prompted the conflict in the first place. In fact, the argument over trade policies and maritime rights that preceded the war would persist well into the 1820s, almost as though the war had never occurred at all.

Yet, when the U.S. Congress did, indeed, approve the declaration of war against Great Britain in June of 1812, it boasted a very small standing army and navy. It was comprised of only sixteen larger navy vessels, a fleet of small gunboats, fourteen cutters, and a handful of small revenue boats. This rather insignificant group was expected to fight against the world's largest navy and a professional army with a great deal of battle-tested experience. Even with the British Army and the Royal Navy largely engaged in confining and defeating Napoleon Bonaparte's forces in Europe, if the United States had any chance of achieving its aims, a civilian involvement in the fighting would be absolutely necessary if they hoped for success.

The initial step taken by the relatively young U.S. government was to call up each individual state's militia in support of the regular federal army. This was done immediately, although it was an act resisted by several New England states that opposed fighting a war with Britain. This refusal to send their boys and men into harm's way to support a national cause weakened America's military effort, resulting in a dramatic lengthening of the war.

The second step, initiated one week after the declaration of war, was to legislate the use of privately armed vessels known as privateers by granting letters-of-marque, who would come together in an effort to make war on Britain's merchant marine. These privateers would be motivated by a number of factors: profit, patriotism, and protection of their families and personal property.

The last step was known as the Torpedo Act, passed by Congress on March 3, 1813:

> "Be it enacted &c., That, during the present war with Great Britain, it shall be lawful for any person or persons to burn, sink, or destroy, any British armed vessel of war, except vessels coming as cartels or flags of truce; and for that purpose to use torpedoes, submarine instruments, or any other destructive machine whatever: and a bounty of one-half the value of the armed vessel so burnt, sunk, or destroyed, and one-half the value of her guns, cargo, tackle, and apparel shall be paid out of the Treasury of the United States to such persons who shall effect the same, otherwise than by armed or commissioned vessels of the United States."[2]

In essence, the act legalized and encouraged a maritime version of "asymmetric," or guerrilla, warfare along the American coast. Combined, all three of these initiatives equaled an open invitation for U.S. citizens to use inventive force and resistance as a means defending their families, their incomes, and their shores. In actuality, further development and refinement of underwater explosives and submarines would be the inevitable result.

As we know, the idea of using underwater bombs as a means of attacking an enemy ship had been introduced by David Bushnell of Westbrook, Connecticut, thirty-seven years earlier during the American Revolution. Bushnell had designed and built a one-man wooden submarine, which was equipped to attach a waterproof explosive with clockwork detonator to a warship's wooden hull. Operated by Sergeant Ezra Lee of Lyme, Connecticut, Bushnell's *American Turtle* made several attempts to accomplish this in New York Harbor in 1776. The underwater explosive, which Sergeant Lee referred to as a "torpedo," failed to sink any enemy ships, since he was unable to drill a hole into a ship's keel as planned. Bushnell would also be credited with developing floating mines–waterproof kegs of gunpowder–that were used unsuccessfully on the enemy, including the infamous "Battle of the Kegs" along the Delaware River in 1778.

AMERICAN SUBMARINERS: PRE-CIVIL WAR

Battle of the Kegs, 1778

Pennsylvania-born Robert Fulton had recently experimented with submarines and underwater munitions in both France and Great Britain, attempting to blow up vessels with floating mines–or torpedoes–before returning to his homeland of America in 1806. In 1807, Fulton demonstrated a successful torpedo in New York Harbor, and in 1810 he made presentations to the U.S. Navy and to Congress on the practical use of such "infernal" weapons.

Fulton's explosives were copper cylinders containing about 100 pounds of gunpowder, with a brass box holding the flintlock firing mechanism. Recently, in 1812, he had recommended the use of such torpedoes, and the award of prize money for their successful use, to Secretary of the Navy, Paul Hamilton, claiming, "How can government get rid of 74 or 80 Gun Ships so Cheap as by this means?"[3] Apparently, the government was listening, for it was Fulton's demonstrations and urgings that led to passage of the Torpedo Act. One American in particular paid heed to this open invitation to attack British blockaders.

Silas Plowden Halsey was born on January 6, 1787, in Preston, New London County, Connecticut, a small farming community situated in the southeastern portion of the State. He was the seventh of ten children born to the Revolutionary War hero, lawyer, and militia officer, Jeremiah Halsey, and his wife, Esther "Fanny" Park Halsey.

Silas Halsey's roots traveled back several generations. The Halsey family has been mentioned in records as the Lords of the Manor on Tanesley, Cornwall, England as early as 1189. According to Cussant, the historian of Hertfordshire, a branch of the Halsey family settled at Great Gaddesden in 1458 and later became lessees of the Rectory of Gaddesden until March 12, 1545. When Henry VIII dissolved the religious houses, he bestowed the estate upon William Halsey. It was here, in the old mansion known as the Golden Parsonage, that Thomas Halsey, Silas' third great-grandfather, was born in 1591. The Golden Parsonage was situated a short distance from the river Gadde in Hertfordshire, England, about twenty-eight miles north of London.

Sometime after April, 1638, Thomas immigrated to America with his first wife, Elizabeth Wheeler Halsey, and their three sons–Thomas, Isaac, and Daniel. They initially settled in Lynn, Massachusetts, where Thomas purchased 100 acres of land. A number of colonists of Lynn had resolved to leave and to settle in another place and on March 10, 1639, Edward Howell with others contracted for transport to the future Southampton, Long Island. Thomas was not, at the beginning, one of the adventurers in this project, but upon acceptance by the rest of the party and contribution of eighty pounds, he was included as one of them. The final agreement to settle Southampton was dated at Lynn, on April 17, 1640, and the colonists arrived there by December 13, 1640. The settlers gave the local indians sixteen coats and sixty bushels of corn for the land.

In 1649, Elizabeth "Phoebe" Wheeler Halsey became "the first victim to fall at the hands of the hostile tribe of Indians who later raided this colony." Thomas remarried on July 25, 1660, this time to Ann Johnes, widow of Edward Johnes. Before the death of the elder Thomas Halsey, his three sons–second generation Halseys in America–had already become landowners. On April 15th, 1656, Richard Barrett "hath put of his allotment in Sagaponack division to Thomas Halsey Jr." In 1663, John Woodruff sold to Thomas his "lot in Mill Neck over against the piece of land called Cobs Pound, also three roods of ground in fist Neck in the great plaine [sic]" in exchange for "five acres in the ten acre lot furlong in great plaine [sic]." In 1663, in a "proposal by the neighborhood where they desire to have their present division to lie," we find the younger Thomas with "fifty acres adjoining to the rear of his lot at Cobs Pound, eight acres at his land in Mill Neck;" with Isaac on the "north side of Robert Wooley at the west side North sea path," and Daniel with "one hundred and fifty between Mr. Rainer and Joseph against the little plaine [sic]." The three sons again are mentioned in 1657 when a half-pound of powder was to be delivered "out of the Magazine" to each of forty persons, among whom were Thomas, Isaac and David [Daniel]. The sons all survived their father by many years. The younger Thomas died about 1699, Isaac about 1725 and Daniel about 1682.

The land that comprised Southampton, Long Island, equaled only about 6,000 acres and soon became overpopulated, making it necessary for younger generations to seek lands elsewhere. The first Halseys to leave the area were third generation Americans, grandchildren of the first Thomas Halsey to arrive from England. Isaac Halsey's son, Joseph, migrated to Elizabethtown, New Jersey, in early 1694, while his brother, Samuel–and another Halsey named Daniel, who appears to have been a son of the Thomas–migrated to North Carolina. Meanwhile, Daniel's son, William, went to live in New London County, Connecticut, arriving there by 1689.

Jeremiah Halsey, son of second generation Thomas and grandson of pilgrim Thomas, was married three times: first, to Anna Wheeler of Stonington, Connecticut, in 1694; second, to Ruth Stanborough of Southampton, New York, in 1715; and finally, to Deborah, whose surname has been lost in history. He and first wife, Anna, gave birth to ten children, five sons and five daughters; Jeremiah, Anna, William, Jerusha, Nathan, Silas, Mary, Elijah, Experience, and Abigail. Each of these fourth generation Halseys would scatter across the country, impacting American history in their own unique ways.

When the elder Jeremiah died in 1737 at the age of 77, it was discovered that he had left behind a will, bequeathing portions of his estate to his third wife, Deborah; his sons Jeremiah, Nathan, and Elijah; and daughters Experience and Abigail (who were unmarried at the time of his death). Earlier, he had given land in Preston, Connecticut, to his son William, as well as land in Morristown, New Jersey, to son Silas.

William Halsey, of the fourth generation, eventually settled in Preston, Connecticut; Silas, also of the fourth, traveled on to Morristown, New Jersey; in about 1730, A Recompense Halsey found his way to Scotch Plains, and then to Morris County, New Jersey; and records indicate that an Ezekiel Halsey also traveled to and settled in Morristown, New Jersey, in 1753.

So, it came to pass that three generations after the pilgrim Thomas Halsey arrived on American soil, his great grandson, William, married Sarah Stanton on June 19, 1738, in Stonington, New London County, Connecticut. Eventually, they took up residence on the land given to William by his father, near the small farming village of Preston. There, they gave birth to three children, William in September of 1739, Sarah in June of 1742, and Jeremiah in June of 1744--the youngest being submariner Silas Plowden Halsey's father. Each would grow up and receive as much education as the Connecticut public schools had to offer at the time.

Early manifestation of young Jeremiah's patriotism and genius, which would be characterized throughout his entire life, surfaced at an early age when "he sought eagerly for such books as he could command, and directed his attention to the study of the law."[4] After marrying Ester Parke on January 1, 1769, he was admitted to the bar by the County Court at New London, Connecticut, for the June term in 1770, and later entered the practice of his chosen profession in his hometown of Preston. It was there that he practiced law while Ester did her best in raising the first of their children. Eventually, over the course of nearly a quarter century, the number of Halsey children would grow to ten, including Phoebe, Jeremiah Shipley, George Washington, Sally Ayer, William Pitt, Esther, Silas Plowden, Polly, John Jay, and Harriet.

Historical records state that during the Revolutionary War, Jeremiah Halsey was a volunteer Minuteman, risking his life at the Lexington Alarm.

He later joined the Continental Army on May 1, 1775, and, less than two months later, earned the distinction of becoming the first commissioned commander of the United States Navy:

> "Whereas there is at present Sundry Armed Vessels and small Craft on Lake Champlain which have lately been destitute of an officer to take the Command of them... Do therefore reposing special trust in your Loyalty, Courage, Skill and Capacity, Constitute and appoint You the said Jeremiah Halsey to be Commander of all the squadron on Lake Champlain, George, South and East Baye, Wood and Otter Creeks etc. etc. Consisting of Snows, Brigs, Sloops, Schooners, Gundalows, Schows, Pettiaugres, Rowgallys, Cutters, Barks, Cannoes, etc. And Cap of the Armed Sloop *Enterprize* of Twenty Guns & Tou are therefore Required to Repair Imediately on board the said Armed Sloop *Enterprize* and to hoist your flag on board of her–When ready then to Cruise up and down the Lake Champlain, with the said sloop or any other Vessle or Craft, that you shall order. To Guard and Protect the Frontiers of the Province of New York in Particular and the United Collony's in General. You are to Obey the Instructions, that you will from time to time Receive, from me or any other Superior Officer that shall or may be on this Command, for Which this shall be your Siffficient Warrant. Given under my hand and seal at Ticonderoga this 27 of June, Anno Domini One Thousand seven hundred and seventy-five and in the fifteenth Year of his Majesty's Reign...Benjn Hinnman, Collo of 4th Reg and Commander in Chief"[5]

Jeremiah would later serve as a primary engineer at the capture of St. Johns, and was made captain in the Continental Line in December of 1776. He was commissioned once again, this time to the rank of Lieutenant Colonel, in the 27th Regular Militia in January of 1780. After the war, aside from his law practice, Jeremiah became a skilled shipbuilder, earning him even more accolades during peacetime when he designed and constructed a vessel from the trees from his own property:

> "In 1786, a very singular vessel was constructed at Poquetannuck on the river Thames, ten miles from New London, by Jeremiah Halsey. She was double-decked, burden about 150 tons, and built almost wholly of plank, several courses being laid crossing each other at right angles. The only timbers in her were the keel, stem and stern post. She was firm, well-molded, graceful, and on coming down to New London in November excited very general curiosity. She was called a snow and named *Lady Strange*, but many people for her lightness called her the *Balloon*. In a storm which occurred Dec. 3d, while she was fitting for sea, she was driven directly over the sandy point of Shaw's Neck and stranded among the trees of an orchard on Close Cove, but was got off without damage and sailed for Ireland Jan. 19, 1787. She proved to be a good sea vessel and a fast Sailer, and made several voyages from New London, but was afterwards owned in Philadelphia. According to a statement published soon after the death

AMERICAN SUBMARINERS: PRE-CIVIL WAR

of Halsey, the ingenious architect of this vessel, she was examined at Philadelphia when 32 years old, and was at that time staunch and sound."[6]

In 1792, the Connecticut Legislature authorized the construction of a new State House in Hartford. After it had been partially completed, with the allocated funding already spent, Andrew Ward and Jeremiah Halsey proposed to complete it in exchange for the title to a tract of land, 220 miles long and 2.35 miles wide, lying along the border between New York and Pennsylvania. Known simply as the "Gore," the land exchange agreement was quickly approved. When the contract was made binding, Lemuel Hopkins, a well-repected physician and eminent writer, sent a letter to the Governor, exclaiming "on the whole I think that if wild lands, with a dubious title, at a vast distance and covered with Indians, will erect our public buildings, school our children, and expound our Bible, we are a most favored people."[7]

By the end of 1795, the State House was completed, at least enough to be habitable, by the two enterprising men. By the spring of 1796, the building was completely occupied by the Legislature. The interior contained a beautiful stone spiral stair case in the great hall behind the northern arch, designed by Asher Benjamin, and the porticos with their high arches at either front, were outlined with graceful iron work.

Meanwhile, Governor Samuel Huntington had conveyed, as promised, the Gore lands to Ward and Halsey on July 25, 1795. A few days later, on August 4, Colonel Halsey purchased Ward's half interest of the Gore. By then, he had spent more than $35,000–quite a hefty sum at that time–to build the State House and purchase Ward's interest in the lands. He then organized the Connecticut Gore Lands Company and, within a few months, had sold $300,000 worth to anxious investors. Seemingly, the Halsey family was destined to become one of the wealthiest in the State.

Unfortunately, however, Connecticut's title to the Gore lands proved defective, meaning they had absolutely no legal right to convey the lands to Ward and Halsey in the first place. Though the Connecticut Legislature eventually agreed to compensate him with $20,000, Jeremiah Halsey was financially damaged and embarassed by the entire affair. He would never fully recover from the reputational scandal that ensued.

Undoubtedly, young Silas and his siblings grew up among a number of learned men that visited his father quite regularly at the Halsey farm, situated a little south of Preston City. Jeremiah Halsey had built a spacious brick mansion there to accommodate his growing family, though only four of his ten children would outlive him. The Halsey homestead, according to the custom of the times, was a place of generous and welcoming hospitality, particularly to his father's colleagues. Among others who came to visit were two brothers; Calvin Goddard, who would go on to become a successful attorney, mayor of Norwich, Connecticut superior court judge, and U.S. congressman, and Hezekiah Goddard, who would hold a number of elective offices as a member of the Whig party, serving in the general assembly for one term, being twice elected to the court of common council, and serving as city sheriff for nine years. Records indicate that the Goddard brothers not only served as mentors for young Silas and his siblings, but also acted as tutors who educated them in all things vital in life.

Yet, young Silas slowly came to dislike and distain Hezekiah Goddard, who sometimes exhibited an abrupt and uncontrollable temper, as well as little patience for childhood behavior. Hezekiah's anger would often flair up with adults as well. On one such occasion in 1792, when Silas was just five years old, he witnessed a violent confrontation between Hezekiah and the Reverend Paul Park, uncle of Silas' mother, Esther. The 72-year-old Reverend Park, who had been pastor of the First Separatist Church of Preston for more than forty-five years and was well respected by most townspeople, was somewhat taken aback when an angry–and perhaps drunken–Goddard confronted him in front of the church. The disagreement had begun over the fact that Goddard was being forced by local authorities to pay taxes–as all church members were mandated–in support of the church. Records indicate that State of Connecticut law enforcement officials charged Hezekiah with not only refusing to pay those taxes, but with disturbing and breaking the public peace by "tumultuous and offensive carriage" for threatening, assaulting, and actually striking Reverend Park, and calling him "an old knave and a lying villain."[8] It was a scene that young Silas would carry with him for the rest of his life.

Apparently, by February of 1795, Hezekiah Goddard had made peace with the Park family, for Reverend Park officiated at the wedding of Hezekiah and Phoebe Halsey, Silas' eldest sister. Further evidence indicates that Hezekiah had become far more than merely a trusted "family friend and tutor" to the 22-year-old Phebe, for a little more than seven months after their marriage vows had been exchanged, in mid-September of 1795, Phoebe gave birth to their first child, Jeremiah Henry Goddard.

In early January of 1803, Phoebe went into labor with their fourth child, George Goddard. But there were complications during the delivery from which she would never recover. Six weeks later, on February 17, baby George died. Unable or unwilling to recover from her sorrow, Phoebe's strength slowly ebbed away, leaving her bedridden and with no will to live. On March 8, 1803, the attending physician, Dr. Samuel Holden Parsons Lee (Samuel H.P. Lee), would inform the Halsey family that their eldest daughter had passed away. For months thereafter, a heartbroken Silas would often visit his sister's grave at the Preston City Cemetery, sobbing as he read the inscription etched into her tombstone:

> "Sacred to the memory of Mrs. Phoebe Goddard, Wife of Mr. Hezekiah Goddard & Daughter of Jeremiah Halsey Esq, who died March 8th, 1803, in the 31st year of her age. Why should we weep or wail or moan Since God hath took thee for his own"[9]

Silas was unwilling to accept his eldest sister's death as merely fate, blaming his "somewhat vile" uncle Hezekiah for corrupting, mistreating, and belittling her so much that it "led to her early exit from this life."

By the beginning of 1804, Sally Ayres Halsey, Silas' second eldest sister, had taken on the huge responsibility of helping Hezekiah in raising his two surviving children. Eventually, it seems that the widower's relationship with her had followed a similar pathway as that of her older sister, going far beyond that of a grieving "uncle." In fact, records indicate that Sally, too, was already "with child" at the time she and uncle Hezekiah were married on February 1, 1807. A son, Hezekiah Willard, was the result, born on October 21 of that same year.

Sadly, however, within five months of giving birth, Sally became deathly ill with yellow fever. Dr. Samuel H.P. Lee was called in as attending physician once again, and he provided her with, what he claimed to be, his very own special remedy. Yet, a different "Dr. Samuel Lee," who resided in nearby Windham, Connecticut, nearly thirty miles directly north of New London, had actually been the concoction's inventor. Just twenty-three years old in 1796, Lee of Windham had become the first American physician to patent his own miracle cure. But then life became complicated for the accomplished physician.

Coincidentally, another Samuel Lee (Samuel H.P. Lee), then a druggist and reseller of pharmaceuticals, had been legally distributing "Windham Bilious Pills" to a number of his New London County patients, friends, and neighbors for almost a year. Eventually, in the summer of 1798, druggist Samuel H.P. Lee had had a disagreement with his supplier of Bilious Pills–Dr. Samuel Lee of Windham–and had decided to go into the business of remedy production for himself. The physician from Windham accused the druggist from New London of having "fabricated certain pills, resembling in appearance, but of different ingredients." In other words, he claimed that the druggist had violated his patent.

By the spring of 1799, Samuel H.P. Lee had begun advertising himself as the licensed physician that he was, having actually secured his legal admission to the Medical Society of New London six years earlier in 1793:

> "At a meeting of the New London County Convention, at the city of New London, on the 4th Tuesday of September–on application of Doctor Samuel H. Lee, to be admitted a member of this society, Doctor Lee produced letters testifying his having acquired sufficient knowledge to practise [sic] Physick and Surgery, from Doctor Bailey of New York, and sundry other gentlemen. Voted that Doctor Samuel H. Lee be admitted a member of this convention."[10]

Thus began the medical career of Dr. Samuel Holden Parsons Lee. With proven legitimacy, he began selling his own brand of medicine known as "New London Bilious Pills," which could be used to battle a number of ailments. Unlike many other physicians of the times, who hoped to keep their ingredients a secret, Dr. Samuel H.P. Lee published his medicinal recipe in the meeting minutes of the Connecticut Medical Association. His pills were composed of various juices of trees from Southeast Asia, referred to as "gamboges," as well as the juices of a number of aloe plants from the Caribbean. Additionally, Lee had mixed in a bindweed known as "scammony," imported from the eastern Mediterranean region; cascara sagrada, a long-standing native American herbal laxative; ordinary soap; nitrate of potassa, also known as saltpeter, a major ingredient in gunpowder; and mercury, said to be about a ratio of fifteen percent per pill.

In addition to relieving biliousness, Dr. Samuel H.P. Lee claimed that his pills effectively treated the "gravel" (kidney stones), "dropsy" (excessive fluid retention), worms, partial palsy, rheumatism, a variety of "female complaints," convulsions, and what he called "hysterical affections." Most importantly to the Halsey family, the concoction was also said to be "very efficacious in preventing yellow fever" and its symptoms. Aside from all of that, the New London physician was provided "with nearly 30 years of financial success" from his pills.

However, when administered to Sally Halsey Goddard, Dr. Samuel H.P. Lee's remedy caused his patient to vomit violently, sweat excessively, and frequently urinate. Silas looked on in horror and fear as his sister's symptoms continued to worsen without relief; "languor and restlessness, chills and flushes, nausea, extreme pains in the head and back, scurfy, pealing tongue, yellow skin, delirium, and black vomit." Finally–perhaps mercifully–Dr. Lee pronounced Sally dead early Wednesday morning, March 16, 1808.

Tragedy would continue to haunt the Halsey family during the next few years. On November 24, 1809, Silas' eldest brother, William Pitt Halsey–who had most recently served as a Captain aboard the brig *Commerce* and sloop *Caroline* with his older brother, George Washington Halsey–died of yellow fever. He was just a few months in port and only twenty-seven years old. Then, in September of 1811, John Jay Halsey, Silas' youngest brother, was killed by natives at St. Bartholomew Isle in the West Indies. John Jay was only twenty years old at the time, and his body arrived back in Preston, Connecticut, amid family sorrow and a number of unanswered questions. The life of a merchant seaman was proving to be more and more dangerous as time passed.

Still, Silas Halsey's love of the sea was evolving with his growing awareness of her perils. As early as 1804, then seventeen years of age, he had set sail as first mate aboard the brig *Franklin* on a voyage from New London to the Dutch colony of Georgetown, Demerara, in South America. For the next two years, Silas and his crewmates would transport sugar back to the eastern seaboard, with his last departure being on April 18, 1806.

In November of 1806, though he was still only nineteen years old, Silas was placed in command of the sloop *Eliza*, constructed in Glastonbury, Connecticut, in 1801. Under Halsey's command, she would make four voyages to the West Indies and South America. During his final voyage, which departed from New London bound for Berbice, Guyana, on September 15, 1807, Master Halsey was delighted to have on board a new deck boy; seventeen-year-old John

Jay Halsey, his youngest brother. It would be the youngster's first expedition of this magnitude.

During this same period of time, just a few miles from the Halsey homestead, Dr. Samuel H.P. Lee had become one of the founders of the Connecticut whaling business. In the autumn of 1804, he had formed his own shipping company, which would operate out of New London Harbor. In doing so, he had purchased his first ship, the *Dauphin*, with Joseph Barber spending the better part of a year outfitting her in Westerly, Rhode Island, for the enterprise of open-sea whaling. With Captain Laban Williams at the helm, she finally set sail for the Brazil Banks on September 6, 1805, and arrived back in New London Harbor with her first cargo of whale oil nine months later, on June 14, 1806.

With the profits of the *Dauphin*'s first whaling expedition, Samuel H.P. Lee was able to purchase a second ship, constructed in Hanover, Massachusetts, and outfitted in New York, which the enterprising physician added to his fleet of whalers. Named the *Leonidas*, she departed from New London alongside the *Dauphin* in August of 1806. With Laban Williams now captaining the *Leonidas*, and Captain Alexander Douglas in charge of the *Dauphin*, they returned in the spring of 1807, bringing with then more than a combined 2,000 barrels of whale oil.

As Dr. Lee's success in the whaling business continued to be profitable, he intended to add new ships to the line. Next came the *Lydia*, built in Hanover, Massachusetts, and purchased and outfitted in New York in the summer of 1807. Together, all three of his vessels departed from New London bound for the coast of Patagonia. Records indicate that all made a safe return in June of 1808, delivering a combined total of 3,100 barrels of whale oil to their home port. The British blockade, however, would soon put a stop to Dr. Lee's growing business venture.

Meanwhile, Silas Halsey not only captained a number of vessels during this portion of his adult life, but he, like Dr. Samuel H.P. Lee, invested his earnings to become the sole or shared owner of a few profitable ships. In 1808, he purchased the 54-foot, 58-ton sloop *Caroline* from Enoch Bolles. His brother, William Pitt Halsey, would command her for more than a year when, on July 6, 1809, he would be forced to surrender her to British blockaders. Much to the growing anger of his bother, Silas, the illegally-seized ship and her valuable cargo would later be sold in a foreign port.

Silas commanded the schooner *Orion* on a voyage to Tangier in May of 1810. His brother, John Jay, joined him once again, this time as First Mate, aboard the 58-ton vessel, along with four other crewmen. In April of 1811, Silas became part owner of the 65.5-foot, 98-ton brig *Fame*, along with a trio of Coit brothers–Farewell, Erastus, and Benjamin–and noneother than his ex-brother-in-law, Hezekiah Goddard.

By that time in his life, still just twenty-three years old, Halsey had not only grown to love the sea, but it was the only way for him escape the trials and tribulations of his life. Yet, the freedom and financial security it afforded him were repeatedly being challenged by the British naval blockade of the eastern seaboard. Something had to be done to put a stop to the tyranny.

Growing disgust among American seaman hadn't exactly "exploded" when war was declared in June of 1812; it was more of a simmering, slowly building discontent that had taken months and years to come to a boil. Beginning in the late 1790s, in what had become known as the "Quasi War" with France, revenue cutters had comprised one-third of the American naval fleet. For much of that undeclared conflict, these armed vessels served under the control and direction of the U.S. Navy, which Congress re-established in 1798. It marked the first of many times in which cutters were expected to perform combat duties.

After the Quasi War had concluded in 1800, the U.S. government and its citizens tried to remain neutral in the constant conflicts between Britain and France, but the two countries had continued to violate American sovereignty on the high seas. Presidents Jefferson and Madison had used economic pressure to enforce U.S. neutrality by enacting a series of embargoes and trade restrictions, including the Non-Importation Act of 1806, the Embargo Acts of 1807 and 1808, the Enforcement Act of 1809, the Non-Intercourse Act of 1809 and 1810, and Macon's Bill Number 2 in 1810. None of this seemed to be effective, however. Throughout all of this, revenue cutters were called upon to enforce these laws, which would eventually put thousands of Americans out of work, including Silas P. Halsey and Dr. Samuel H.P. Lee.

Within a month of finally declaration of war in June of 1812, British Royal Navy squadrons had begun patrolling off the eastern seaboard. The British Admiralty established an official blockade on November 27, 1812, sending orders to Admiral John Warren, commander-in-chief of the North American Station, to cut off the Chesapeake and Delaware bays from trade. Likely due to winter conditions, as well as the cessation of the sailing season, Warren did not begin true enforcement of the orders until early February of 1813.

On February 4, a British fleet under Rear Admiral George Cockburn anchored its vessels in Hampton Roads, Virginia, beginning a tight blockade of the Chesapeake Bay. In response, on March 15, 1813, U.S. Treasury Secretary Albert Gallatin ordered the Norfolk customs collector to "immediately extinguish" the lights and remove the lamps, oil and "other moveable apparatus" in all lighthouses located in the Chesapeake Bay "for the purpose of preventing the enemy again putting up the lights." As spring approached, the Royal Navy began a deliberate campaign of attacking and burning Chesapeake's coastal towns, designed to weaken the will of the American people. It backfired. This campaign of coastal hostility, attacks, and infiltration only served to cut off local commerce and shipping, prompting lifelong seamen to grow incensed at the British invaders. Quietly, in village taverns, public squares, and other gathering places, men began to discuss effective measures that might be used to beat back British warships and the barges they deployed for shallow water attacks.

AMERICAN SUBMARINERS: PRE-CIVIL WAR

As the confrontations between the United States and Great Britain intensified, these men–who had long made their living shipping goods to other parts of the world–became more and more frustrated. Finally, in late March of 1813, they were given legal permission to take action with passage of the Torpedo Act by the U.S. Congress. In short, the Act made it lawful for "any person or persons to burn, sink or destroy any British armed vessel of war...and to use torpedoes, sub-marine instruments."

Under further provisions of the law, the government had promised to pay to any individual who burned, sank, or destroyed a British warship, a bounty equal to half the value of the destroyed craft, plus half "the value of her guns, cargo, tackle and apparel."[11]

Captain Thomas Masterman Hardy's British squadron established itself firmly off the shores of New London, Connecticut, in April of 1813, and moved in closer once Commodore Stephen Decatur, Jr., Captain Jacob Jones, and Master Commandant James Biddle brought the *United States*, *Macedonian*, and *Hornet* into the Thames River on June 1. With the British warships anchored so near, and British barges seizing so much coastal commerce on Long Island Sound, there were both reason and opportunity for civilians to retaliate. This, in essence, set the stage for New London County citizens to take matters into their own hands. Among them were two men who had met each other amidst totally different circumstances years earlier, Silas Halsey and Dr. Samuel H.P. Lee.

Like Dr. Lee, a great number of Halsey's Connecticut friends and neighbors had formed strong personal grudges against Great Britain in general, and the Royal Navy in particular. In fact, they had had enough. The first attempt at breaking up the blockading fleet came in June of 1813, though it was more of an improvised happening than a well-devised, high-tech mission.

New Yorker John Scudder, Jr., enraged about civilian deaths in the west where his relatives lived, for which he blamed the British and their Indian allies, stepped to the forefront. It hadn't taken much convincing for him to be persuaded by Commodore Jacob Lewis of the New York gunboat flotilla to outfit the coasting schooner *Eagle* as a deadly floating bomb. On June 15, fellow New Yorker, Captain John Lawrence Riker floated the *Eagle* down the Sound, intending to anchor her off Millstone Point in Waterford:

> "Agreeable to your request, I transmit to you a statement of facts relative to the explosion of the schooner *Eagle*, which I presume will forever put to silence the many misrepresentations which have been afloat respecting that affair. Having been the author of the plan, I feel it a duty incumbent on me to state to my fellow citizens the motives by which I was actuated, and the manner in which the plan was fixed and executed, and I leave it to my countrymen to approve or condemn the act. My relatives in the state of Ohio and on the frontiers are numerous–they have suffered much by Indian hostility, excited by the British mandates, and the blowing up of the brave [Zebulon] Pike and his band of heroes, after the enemy had

actually surrendered, was to my mind, an act of such horrid cruelty, that it called loudly for retaliation. These are the principal reasons which induced me to contrive the following plan, which has succeeded in destroying upwards of one hundred of the enemy. Ten kegs of powder were put into a strong cask, with a quantity of sulphur mixed into it. At the head of the cask was fixed two gunlocks, with cords fastened to the triggers, and to the underside of the barrels in the hatchway, so that it was impossible to hoist the barrels without springing the locks each side of the powder–and on the top was placed a quantity of turpentine and spirits of turpentine, which in all probability was sufficient to have destroyed any vessel that ever floated on the water, if she could have got along side, which was the object in view. The *Eagle* left this place for New London on the 15th of June, and in eight or ten days after, she arrived within sight of the enemy, about 11 o'clock a.m. The enemy sent a barge with 20 oarsmen, and as many more in the bow and stern of the boat, to take possession of her. Capt. Riker, who commanded the *Eagle*, states that the enemy got within musket shot, and that a number of shots were exchanged before they abandoned the vessel..."[12]

As the expected British barges had surged in, Captain John Riker retired ashore with just enough resistance that the British cut the anchor cable and towed the *Eagle* off toward Hardy's flagship, the 74-gun *HMS Ramillies*. But wind and tide prevented them from bringing her directly alongside the *Ramillies*, so they finally moored her next to a small vessel about three-quarters of a mile away from the flagship. An officer and his men began to inspect the *Eagle*'s cargo of food and naval stores. Apparently, they did not notice cords running from small flour barrels in the hatch to a large cask in the hold. Those cords were attached to flintlocks on the heads of the cask, which was filled with 400 pounds of gunpowder. At some point they moved the small casks, the cords fired the flintlocks, and the explosives were detonated. The immense explosion was later described in the following way:

"...when the vessel blew up, four boats were seen alongside–and it is the opinion of Captain Riker, and a number of others who were very near the scene, that there could not have been less than 100 men on board and alongside. Some suppose the number to have been 120. After the explosion, there was not a vestige of boats or men to be seen. A boat from the 74 was immediately dispatched, but returned without picking up anything. The body of fire appeared to rise upwards of 900 feet into the air, with a blue streak on the outside, and then burst like a rocket..."[13]

Writing from his flagship, *HMS Ramillies*, Thomas M. Hardy reported the incident to Admiral John B. Warren:

"I beg to acquaint you, that yesterday morning at 10 o'clock, Mr. McIntyre Master's mate was sent from this ship in one of her boats to cut off a schooner that standing for New London, as there was little wind he easily effected his purpose...she was taken possession of at 11 o'clock by our boat under a sharp musquetry from the shore, but without doing any mischief–at 1 pm I was hailed from the schooner by Mr. McIntyre, and informed her name was the *Eagle* of New York, and was laden with naval stores and provisions...at half past 2 o'clock, whilst in the act of furling her sails and taking in moorings, the schooner blew up with a most tremendous explosion, and I lament to say Lieutenant Geddes, and ten valuable seamen fell a sacrifice to this new mode of warfare–three seamen who happened to be on the foretopsail yard are very much burnt...the service will experience a great loss in Lieutenant Geddes, whose gallant and meritorious conduct I have frequently witnessed..."[14]

The Yankee Torpedo, by William Elmes

The British Navy immediately became exceedingly suspicious and overly cautious of all types of craft seen near their ships. Warnings, as well as orders of retaliation, were issued by British naval commanders throughout the region:

"I have warned the schooner '*Sallie,*' of Barnstable, to proceed to her own coast, in consequence of the depredations of the '*Young Teazer*'...but more particularly from the inhuman and savage proceedings of causing the American schooner '*Eagle*' to be blown up...an act not to be justified on the most barbarous principle of warfare. I have directed HBM cruisers on the coast to destroy every description of American vessels they may fall in with, flags of truce only excepted."[15]

Outrage over the very idea of "ungentlemanly" use of explosives quickly spread across the "Great Pond" to Great Britain. In early November of 1813, Thomas Tegg would publish William Elmes' satirical print, "The Yankey Torpedo," depicting a sea-monster discharging flames and missiles against a British ship. An exploding barrel in the drawing alluded to British indignation of the attack by the schooner *Eagle*, while the mention of "torpedo capers under his bottom" referred to other American submarine efforts. Meanwhile, British Admiral Sir John Borlase Warren, who would be responsible for leading a detail of British troops that occupied Havre de Grace and set a fire that destroyed much of that Maryland town, blustered that "the Enemy are disposed to make use of every unfair and cowardly mode of warfare."[16]

Sketch of the *HMS Ramillies*

Throughout the early months of 1813, a group of unidentified New London "proprietors"–merchants and seamen–had come together to finance a project to once again attack the Captain Hardy's *HMS Ramillies*, this time from beneath the surface of the New London Harbor. The clandestine group was well aware that anyone able to actually sink the British flagship would be rewarded handsomely, in the calculated amount of $150,000. Armed with this knowledge, they wanted the very best, most experienced seaman to both captain and crew their nearly completed one-man vessel. It remains unclear to historical record whether or not Silas Plowden Halsey was already one of the investors in the unique project, but there are strong indicators that this was, indeed, the case. After all, there was virtually no one else among the residents of New London that had a stronger motive for revenge than Silas Halsey. Indeed, the grudge he held was quite persistent.

Aside from that, there is also strong evidence that Silas Halsey's financial backers had also received a great deal of technical expertise for the construction of their submersible from one Dr. Samuel H.P. Lee. In fact, who was better qualified provide design assistance than the son of Ezra Lee, who had captained David Bushnell's one-man submersible, the *American Turtle*, thirty-seven years earlier. In fact, in 1813, Dr. Samuel H.P. Lee's 64-year-old father still lived in nearby Lyme, Connecticut, and he often shared intimate details of the tiny vessel that had come so very close to sinking an enemy ship during the great war for independence.

Like the Halseys that migrated from England to Lynn, Massachusetts, and then on to Southampton, Long Island, New York, the Lee family had deep American roots. The first Lee to arrive in America originated from the vicinity of Kenilworth, England. Thomas Lee embarked for the New World with his wife, Phoebe, and their three children–Thomas, Phoebe, and Jane–as well as with the Reverend William Brown, along with his wife and daughter, in 1645. During the passage, Thomas Lee and the elder Mrs. Brown both died of small pox, though the remaining family members arrived safely in Old Saybrook, Connecticut, as the entire region was then called.

Four generations later, Ezra Lee was born in Old Lyme. When he was fourteen years old, his father, Abner, a land speculator, purchased acreage known as "Smith's Neck," situated along a stretch of Old Lyme's marshland on the peninsula where the Black Hall and Duck Rivers meet. The property also included a house and an old barn. Ezra attended school nearby and, being so close the Connecticut River, soon became quite familiar with boats, fishing, and seamanship.

Ezra Lee and Deborah Mather were married in a quiet ceremony at the home of his father on November 14, 1771. Exactly nine months later, on August 5, 1772, the couple gave birth to a son, naming him Samuel Holden Parsons after his uncle. A sister, Elizabeth, was born two years later. Even before young Samuel H.P. had turned three, his father, Ezra, had gone off to fight the war against the British, leaving his wife and two children behind.

Ezra Lee's role in the American Revolution was extensive. By the age of 25, he was already serving in the 6th Connecticut Regiment. Commanded by his brother-in-law, Colonel Samuel Holden Parsons, the regiment had been raised in May of 1775 "for the special defence and safety of the Colony." In June of that same year, the unit joined General George Washington at the Siege of Boston, where Lee took part in the Battle of Bunker Hill. He would remain in Boston until the British evacuated the city in March of 1776.

In August of that same year, Ezra Lee was proud to hear of his brother-in-law's promotion by Congress to the rank of Brigadier General in the Continental Army. Stationed together in Brooklyn, New York, the in-laws found themselves in the thick of the fighting with British troops under Lord Sterling at Battle Hill on August 17, 1776. They took part in the Council of War on August 29, during which the Brigadier General decided to retreat from the region. Brigadier General Parsons Lee successfully transported his men, including Ezra, from Long Island, joining the main body of the army as it withdrew from the city.

On September 6, 1776, Samuel Holden Parsons Lee had enough faith in his brother-in-law to select him as the man who would personally operate America's first submarine in an attack of the British Navy's flagship *Eagle*, then anchored at the mouth of the Hudson River. Following that risky and highly-secretive attack, Ezra Lee became a part of the 1st Connecticut Continental Line, 1st Regiment, which was formed in January of 1777. Still serving under the command of Parsons, Ezra would remain in the unit from 1777 through 1781. Finally, Lee retired from the military in June of 1782, having served his soon-to-be country for seven long years. He received recognition and a pension, which was paid in arrears at a rate of $20 each month, and returned to his family in Old Lyme, Connecticut. By then, his wife, Deborah, had given birth to a second daughter, Polly. His eldest, still their only son, was now ten years old, and extremely proud of his father. He listened closely as the elder Lee told and retold stories of his daring adventures aboard the tiny *American Turtle*.

The entire Lee family remained close-knit throughout the course of the next forty years, living as neighbors and patriotic citizens. Ezra Lee's father, Abner, who had lost his wife to disease prior to the start of the American Revolution, would make his living speculating in numerous parcels of land, much of which was a part of the Black-Hall River area near Lyme. On June 28, 1798, Ezra's father had given his son three very valuable pieces of property near Smith's Neck. A deed stated that the first piece of land was about twenty acres "on which Ezra's house now stands." It was "bounded along the northern edge by the highway, west on the river that runs by Smith's Neck, south on William Lay's land, and east on his Ezra's own land." Here, Samuel H.P. moved in with his wife, Elizabeth Sullivan Lee, and their three-year-old son, Henry Sullivan Lee. The second piece of property given to Ezra by his father was a thirty-acre parcel, described as lying west of Mile Creek Hill, while the last piece was about twelve acres in size, and was nestled along the Flat Rock Hill Road. In 1802, Ezra would return these parcels of land to his father, though the Lee family would continue to live within a few acres of one another.

Though it is unknown to historical record precisely how the information was shared, Ezra Lee managed–most likely through his son, Dr. Samuel H.P. Lee–to offer details of the *American Turtle*'s design, construction, and general operation to the Halsey submarine planners and investors. That information then took the shape of a new one-man submersible that would be used against the British flagship *HMS Ramillies*, the lead vessel blockading New London Harbor in April of 1813.

Although they have never been positively identified, historical records indicate that the group of patriotic Americans that helped to construct the compact *Halsey Submarine* included at least seven men. Aside from one-man captain and crew of the vessel, Silas Halsey, and his financial backer, Dr. Samuel H.P. Lee, there was Jonathan Sizer, a 53-year-old New London County native who owned and operated a small metal smith shop situated along the west side of Bradley Street in Preston City. As a youngster, he had first exhibited his bravery and patriotism by joining the militia as a drummer boy, marching against the British invaders during the American Revolution. Discharged in 1780 because of ill health, he had returned home, where he learned the art of metal-smithing. Eventually, he became quite skilled at making tools and utensils out of ordinary tin, sheet iron, copper, and brass. Recently, on October 15, 1811, he had even been granted a U.S. patent for a newly-designed circular steam boiler, which could be utilized in the process of hardening hats. It was this inventive businessman who would be put in charge of designing the explosive weapon to be used in the attack against the British blockading fleet.

Joining Captain Halsey, financial backer Samuel H.P. Lee, and the experienced metal worker in this venture was twenty-five-year-old, Increase Wilson, who had learned metal-smithing under Sizer's close guidance during the early years of the 1800's. As time went by, however, Wilson had hoped to open his own shop, and kept his eyes pealed for an available business front. Just up the street from Sizer's metal smith shop, on the corner of Bradley and Atlantic streets, had stood a saddlery operated by John Bolles. Legal records indicate that, on January 28, 1809, after the building "was seized for indebtedness," then Sheriff Hezekiah Goddard sold the building to Wilson. The entire block–including Sizer's shop– had been spared by Benedict Arnold's troops during the American Revolution as they set much of New London on fire, because an Arnold informant who lived there had explained that "nothing on the street was worth burning."

As the War of 1812 approached, Bradley Street was comprised of about ten businesses, and was known as "Widow's Row." It was here, in the shadowy confines of the "shop that still smelled of horse leather," that Wilson began to make his fortune in the manufacture and selling of tin cups, which he would peddle to the government throughout the war years; and it was here that scant historical records offer an indication that the shell of the Halsey torpedo weaponry would be constructed by Sizer and Wilson.[17]

Aside from these two enterprising metal smiths, native New Yorkers, John Scudder, Jr., and Captain John Riker, both of whom had recently collaborated in the attack on the British flagship *HMS Ramillies* with the floating explosive packed aboard the schooner *Eagle*, loaned their experience and expertise to the *Halsey Submarine* mission. Others may have been initially identified through a correspondence between Robert Fulton and Commodore Stephen Decatur. In a letter dated August 5, 1813, Fulton not only asked for more details about the vessel, but expressed his doubts as to Halsey's capabilities of destroying an enemy ship:

"What is the kind of torpedo experiment which is preparing at New London? What are the name(s) of the parties...is not Mr. Scudder and Riker concerned in it who were concerned in the *Eagle*? How do they mean to act? Many persons insist that Halsey's project was all a farce to create alarm in the enemy and that he never actually attempted to go to sea in his boat. Did you see him and it? On philosophical principles I have strong doubts that he could not remain so long under water as you suppose or go to a sufficient depth to get under the bottom of a 74 (ton) without the water pressing his machine together and drowning him. At 22 feet under water there would be a pressure of 1400 pounds on each superficial foot of his boat on deck ends and all round. A boat only 2 feet diameter and 10 feet long would have a pressure on her of 45 tons."[18]

Rather candidly in his response to Fulton, Commodore Decatur divulged his very limited knowledge of the entire affair, though he did seem to identify a few other important players:

"The Torpedo expedition fitting here I know nothing about...a Major Frink & Mr. Richard are the proprietors...your man Welden is here... the moon (unless overcast) will prevent any immediate attempt. Any aid in my power I will give him. He appears to be prudent & perservering–I shall offer some more remarks on the submarine business shortly..."[19]

The correspondence between Robert Fulton and Commodore Decatur proved one thing: neither man was involved with–or overly familiar with–Silas Halsey's experiments. Undoubtedly, the individual mentioned by Decatur as "your man Welden" was James Welden, a patriot he had met through a mutual acquaintance, Samuel Swarthwout. Decatur had also confirmed that Welden, whom he considered "prudent & perservering," was not in New London working with Halsey.

The "Major Frink" that Decatur referred to was likely Major Nathan Frink, a forty-three-year-old native of New London County. The expansive Frink family had long been well-respected citizens of nearby Stonington, a coastal village situated a few miles east of Preston City, with a number of them exhibiting their patriotism during an earlier conflict with the British. One of Nathan Frink's uncles, Andrew Frink, had even been a Second Lieutenant during the American Revolution, fighting side-by-side with Captain Jeremiah Halsey in the Fourth Battalion of the Continental Army. No doubt, the two families had been extremely close ever since.

Finally, the "Mr. Richards" referred to in Decatur's correspondence was the New London customs inspector, Nathanial Richards, who the Commodore knew personally. In fact, when Richards had been in danger of losing his job to a replacement, Decatur made a written plea directly to Secretary of the Navy, William Jones, saying that Nathanial Richards had performed a number of services in "the squadron under my command," and that from the "lively & personal exertion he displayed in placing the town in a state of defense on probability of an attack, & his efforts in preventing supplies going to the enemy—I do not hesitate to declare that I believe Mr. Richards, patriotic & deserving." Finally, as to the vital question of political affiliation, "Mr. Richards is reputed by all to be a Republican, & has been unequal in his support of the present administration."[20] The letter was passed on directly to President James Madison, and Richards was able to retain his position.

Throughout late May and much of June 1813, hand-written receipts were dispatched that indicate supplies were purchased either by Silas Halsey personally, or on his behalf, from Joseph White, a Baltimore shipbuilder. Within a four-week period, beginning on May 28, these supplies included 450 feet of plank, twelve pounds of nells [sic], three pounds of candles, five pounds of rosin, three pounds of putty, a leather hose, "a machine for fireing [sic] a pistol," a clock work mechanism, four stuffing boxes, a pump-hood, and a pump handle. In addition, more than a dozen payments were made toward an account set up by Halsey as work progressed in the fashioning of a number of parts to be used aboard his submarine. Finally, on June 25, he secured a number of critical items to finish his vessel, including all equipment necessary to attach an explosive device to the belly of an enemy ship.

By early July of 1813, Halsey was prepared to make his first practice run into the New London Harbor, which would serve as a mock attempt at sinking the *HMS Ramillies*. His submersible had been checked and rechecked to ensure that it was airtight. A water cock had been installed, along with a hand-operated force pump. This arrangement would allow him to let in water whenever he wanted to submerge, and to dispel water whenever he wanted to re-surface. There was also a hand-operated propeller crank that simultaneously served as an auger, so that he would be able to attach a torpedo to the hull of a wooden ship. Surrounding his head was a narrow conning tower with portholes, which would enable Halsey to see some distance beneath the surface. Finally, an air tube attached to a float would extend to the surface, providing a constant supply of fresh air.

Initial tests indicated that the submarine remained stable under the surface and, with its large paddles, maintained an efficient speed. Indeed, this entire arrangement would allow Halsey to move stealthily toward his prey, drill a small hole in the ship's hull, place the explosive, and move away without detection.

Apparently, traitorous blue lights had appeared as warning signals along the coastline and were spotted when Halsey attempted his initial attack on Commodore Hardy's flagship, which came during the last week of June 1813:

> "This change of position has resulted in consequence of several torpedo and submarine expeditions that have been prepared at this place and of which they have been informed. The night before last a Captain Halsey left the harbor in a submarine boat and from the description I have received of it the enemy, had they not been apprized of the precise moment

of attack, would have been in much danger. Captain Halsey had not left the harbor five minutes when a signal from the shore (by firing guns which were answered from the ships) was made. Halsey, I believe, has not been heard from since."[21]

By late July of 1813, 26-year-old Silas Plowden Halsey had gained the reputation in the New London area as "Bushnell the second," which he was referred to by editor Samuel Green of the *Connecticut Gazette*:

"Since the attempt of the renowned Halsey of Preston, in a Torpedoe [sic] the British ships have taken new ground for anchorage; & for some time before tripped their anchors every few hours. The commodore [Hardy] has frankly confessed that the apprehensions of some yankee trick has given him great anxiety. He knew of the *Halsey Torpedoe* [sic], and mentioned the names of persons whom he said were the proprietors. He confesses that the torpedoes are among the acknowledged weapons of national warfare; although personally opposed to them. He never having used even hand grenades in any vessel he has commanded."[22]

Halsey continued to bide his time, waiting for the perfect opportunity to take his vessel out on an attack. During the next few months, he would again plan to attack the *HMS Ramillies*, with either the tide or British intelligence continually thwarting his attempts.

Meanwhile, British crewmen became more and more brazen, often going ashore on Fishers, Plum, Gull, and Gardiners Islands to cavort with the enemy. Commodore Hardy himself regularly dined with John Gardiner on his island. This piece of intelligence was noted carefully by a man named Joshua Penny of East Hampton, Long Island, a longtime friend of the Halsey family. Penny conceived a plan to capture Hardy on one of his visits to Gardiner's home. He took the plan to Commodore Decatur in New London who approved the project and provided additional crewmen for the mission.

Penny had good reason to hold the British Navy in contempt. Born in Southold, Long Island, in 1773, on the eve of the colonies disagreement with King George III, Penny was apprenticed at the age of fourteen to Dr. John Gardiner. But, wishing to go to sea, his service was cancelled at the end of the first year. His first taste of the sea came as a cabin boy on a sloop sailing to Guadaloupe when he was 15, and it convinced Penny that this was the life for him. Within five years, Penny had worked his way to Ireland, where a recruiting sergeant for one of His Majesty's Irish regiments got him liquored up enough to sign enlistment papers. But soon after he was measured for his red jacket, he left town and headed for Liverpool, England. Indeed, he had his "protection" paper proving his U.S. citizenship, protecting him from being impressed by a British "press-gang." But he remained on guard. "I have frequently seen the papers of neutrals torn in pieces by the press-gang and thrown into the fire, declaring their protections good for nothing."[23]

AMERICAN SUBMARINERS: PRE-CIVIL WAR

While the Napoleonic wars—the European struggle between Britain and France following the French Revolution, in which the United States remained neutral—led both belligerents to infringe on the rights of neutral nations, it was the British who attacked American ships most often and impressed U.S. citizens as sailors. For Joshua Penny, Liverpool was far too dangerous, so he decided to move on. "Tired of being haunted by a press-gang, I engaged with captain Matthews of the ship *Budd*, bound to the African slave coast," he wrote matter-of-factly, as if picking up 382 slave prisoners to take to Jamaica was no different, from the seaman's point of view, than hauling any other type of cargo.

Within just a few days of arriving in Port Royal, Jamaica, the entire crew of the *Budd*—four Americans and the rest Scandinavians—was grabbed by a British press-gang and forced aboard the 28-gun brig *Alligator* under the command of Captain Africk. "No sooner was the captain on deck in the morning, than we were ready with our protections. He said, 'Men, I will not look at your protections...my ship is in distress, and I will have men to carry me to England.'"

Once in England, Penny was transferred to the frigate *Stately*, which, with six other warships, headed to False Bay, near Cape Town, which then was controlled by the Netherlands under the aegis of the Dutch East India Company. There, he was then forced to serve on land, though he managed to escape and hide out among the Dutch. A few months later he was recaptured at Cape Town and, after being imprisoned as a deserter, was again impressed aboard various British ships. Becoming terribly ill, he was sent to a hospital at Table Mountain, South Africa, from where he again escaped and lived alone in the wilds of the mountains for more than a year:

> "I had become perfectly reconciled to my condition—had abundance of meat, sorrel, honey and water, and every night could sing my song with as much pleasure as at any period in my life. In fine, I never enjoyed life better than while I lived among the ferocious animals of Table Mountain; because I had secured myself against the more savage English."[24]

Eventually, after surviving on whatever he could find to eat, Penny found his way aboard a merchant ship bound for America, making the long and arduous journey to Long Island. It had been eleven-and-one-half years since he had looked upon his beloved American soil. Eventually, on a warm Sunday morning in early June of 1803, he found himself in Southold at the home of his parents:

> "In short, they had long since buried me. Two of my sisters and one brother had died in my absence...In December I was married. My employments were from this period, either coasting or going to the West-Indies."[25]

When the war broke out, Penny was running a little coasting vessel, which he at once sold and returned to his home at Three Mile Harbor in order, as he said "to avail myself of the first opportunity of doing mischief to those who had so long tortured me."

On the night July 26, 1813, four small crafts—one of which carried Joshua Penny—floated out to Gardiners Island. Penny's landed his vessel and disembarked, waiting patiently for what he and his comrades hoped would be a visit by Commodore Hardy. Unfortunately, the small pinnace that came ashore was from the frigate *Orpheus* rather than the *HMS Ramillies*. It was almost as if Hardy knew beforehand they were about to take him captive. For some reason, Penny chose not to wait for another opportunity at a later date and, instead, captured the seven men and one boy who came ashore. He took their signed paroles for later prisoner exchange, released them, and departed empty-handed.

In reality, Commodore Hardy had known about Penny's plan. Over the course of several months, in fact, he had developed an excellent intelligence system, receiving information about enemy movements from a variety of sources in the New London area, Eastern Long Island and New York City. It wasn't long before Hardy became aware of one more of Penny's schemes. New Yorker, Thomas Welling, had traveled to New London and met with Commodore Decatur, and then with Joshua Penny, to discuss his plans to utilize an ironclad whaleboat filled with explosives to blow up the *Ramillies*. Welling wanted to employ Penny as an expert pilot to captain his attack vessel. Penny agreed.

At about the same time, Silas Halsey was preparing to make another attempt at destroying the *Ramillies* as she was anchored in the harbor. In July of 1813, while the *Ramillies* was lying anchor off New London, the following incident was reported to the local papers:

> "A gentleman at Norwich, U.S. has invented a diving-boat, which by means of paddles, he can propel under water at the rate of three miles an hour, and ascend and descend at pleasure. He has been three times under the bottom of the Ramillies, off New London. In the first attempt, after remaining under some time, he came to the top of the water like the Porpoise for air, and, as luck would have it, came up but a few feet from the stern of the *Ramillies*. He was observed by the sentinel on deck, who sang out 'boat ahoy'—immediately on hearing which, the boat descended without making a reply. Seeing this, an alarm gun was fired on board the ship, and all hands called to quarters—the cable cut and the ship got under weigh with all possible dispatch, expecting to be blown up by a Torpedo. In the third attempt he came up directly under the *Ramillies*, and fastened himself and his boat to her keel, where he remained half an hour, and succeeded in perforating a hole through her copper; but while engaged in screwing a Torpedo to her bottom, the screw broke, and defeated his object for that time."[26]

Though Halsey had apparently escaped, Commodore Hardy would soon learn of Welling and Penny's daring scheme to blow up the *Ramillies*, and of Penny's role in the attempt to kidnap him on Gardiners Island. On August 21,

1813, a Sag Harbor ship captain got word to Hardy that he had overheard boastful remarks made by Penny about using Welling's floating bomb. Quickly, the tables turned, and Penny became the quarry. That night, a raiding party went ashore, dragged him out of bed and escorted him back to the *HMS Ramillies*, where he was held prisoner. Hardy had become so nervous by the repeated attempts to blow him up, that Penny said while he was a prisoner aboard the flagship, "the Captain had her bottom swept every two hours night and day, to keep off the damned Yankee barnacles."

That autumn, Hardy and the *HMS Ramillies* set sail to Halifax, Nova Scotia. It would be nine months before Penny was set free. And when he was, he would long claim that he had been "betrayed into impressment at the hands of the British by a certain man from Sag Harbor, who owed him a grudge," and whom he stated, "sold his country for a penny." This apparently was true, and has contemporary confirmation by Dr. Ebenezer Sage and others. Captain John Fowler, a prisoner on board the *HMS Ramillies*, wrote of Penny's impressment:

> "On the 21st, a sloop from Sag Harbor came to anchor a little way from the shipping; the captain came on board and went on shore with an officer and showed the said officer Mr. Penny's house, and told him Mr. Penny was coming off with a torpedo to blow up the ship the first opportunity. That night a boat's crew, with the first lieutenant went on shore and brought Mr. Penny on board with his shirt torn off his back; he was put in irons in a place where he could see no daylight, on a small allowance of bread and water; he asked for a little salt, but it was not allowed him, nor was he allowed a book to read. The above sloop left Sag Harbor on the 20th."[27]

Commodore Hardy would later have Joshua Penny released in Halifax, Nova Scotia. By mid-January, 1814, Hardy had returned to New London Harbor, anchoring the *HMS Ramillies* within sight of the shoreline. Apparently, despite his absence, the Commodore had continued to maintain excellent intelligence on activities along the Connecticut coastline, the eastern end of Long Island, and New York City. Undoubtedly, his network of spies provided a steady stream of both routine and militarily significant information. Citizens of New London lived in constant fear of a British attack, largely provoked by the presence up the Thames River of Commodore Decatur's three trapped warships–the *United States*, *Macedonian*, and *Hornet*.

Preparing to make a dash to the sea, Decatur moved his ships downstream and waited for favorable tides on the moonless night of December 12, 1813. A pair of seemingly insignificant guard boats led the way toward the mouth of the river. As they approached Avery Point near Groton, an officer aboard one of the boats happened to spot an ominous blue light just below Fort Trumbull on the New London shore. Within moments, a lookout detected a second blue light, this one on the opposite bank close to Groton's Fort Griswold.

An outraged Decatur soon concluded that traitors were using the blue lights to signal the waiting British squadron that the American ships were attempting to escape. With his scheme foiled, Decatur was forced to move his ships back up the river. Within a few days, however, he had briefed the editor of the *New London Gazette* of the signal lights, who, in turn, denounced "the traitorous wretches who dare thus to give the enemy every advantage over those great and gallant men, who...have surrounded the American stars with a luster which cannot be eclipsed."

It is here, in August of 1814, that the trail of Silas Halsey seems to abruptly end. Neither the *New London Gazette* nor the *Connecticut Gazette* printed anything more about the shipmaster from Preston, or what became of him. By 1812, an estimated 2,500 American men had been impressed into the British navy, according to Averill Dayton Geus, author of *"From Sea to Sea: 350 Years of East Hampton History."* This included others from the "East End" of Long Island: Lewis Osborn, John Strong, Reuben Hedges, John Gann, Ben Miller, and Ben Leek. One man, John Sawyer of Sag Harbor, was killed aboard a British ship after being impressed. Even more disappeared from the coastal villages of Connecticut. Speculation is that Silas Plowden Halsey was among them.

When Commodore Stephen Decatur wrote to the Secretary of the Navy, William Jones, in early July, 1813, he stated that "Halsey, I believe, has not been heard from since." He undoubtedly was referring to the fact that there had been no further reports of a Halsey attack upon British navy vessels. Yet, other future historians surmise that Halsey had purposefully disappeared, relocating to some obscure corner of America, in an effort to avoid capture or detection by both Americans and British. Still others believed he had simply been trapped aboard his submersible and perished. Perhaps there were a few family members or close friends who knew the truth, and had taken a vow of secrecy. The war between America and the British ended on Christmas Eve, 1814, and for all intents and purposes, Silas Plowden Halsey seemed to simply vanish without a trace.

Twenty-seven years later, in early 1842, Samuel Colt made his way to New London, Stonington, and Mystic, Connecticut, to investigate several intriguing leads on the attempts of an obscure Connecticut inventor, whom he believed was named Silas "Clowden" Halsey, and his attempt to conduct a torpedo attack against British warships in 1814. There he met with Captain Jeremiah Holmes of Mystic, Luther Sargent, and others, who offered him enough information of the one-man submersible that Colt was able to sketch the vessel and its towing torpedo in some detail. During these discussions, Colt had noted that Halsey had been "lost in New London harbor in an effort to blow up a British 74."

Colt's depiction from the various "eye-witness" accounts shows a well-dressed gentleman standing in the one-man submersible, with his head poking up through a conning tower with a glass viewport. The operator's right hand is firmly grasping the tiller, while his left is free to turn both the propulsion unit and the drilling bit designed to bore a hole in the wooden hull of an enemy vessel. In this way, a contact mine could be attached via a lengthy lanyard and an eye hook. When the submerged boat moved away, the lengthy line would pull the explosive toward the enemy ship covertly until it exploded against the hard surface. Finally, the drawing indicates that there is a "water cock" and a "force pump" situated on the floor of the submarine, as well as an air tube.

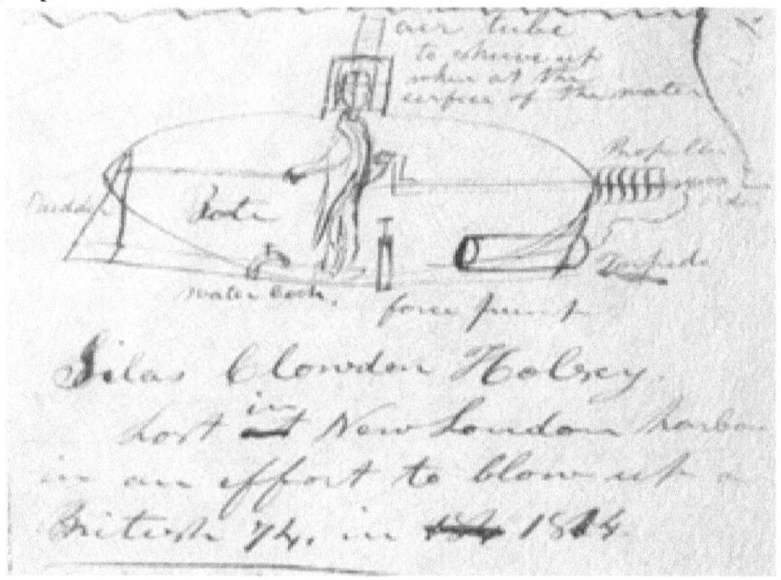

Rudimentary sketch by Samuel Colt of the *Halsey Submarine*

Sixty-eight years later, in his 1882 edition of the *History of New London County, Connecticut*, D. Hamilton Hurd reiterated and elaborated on the information found in Colt's notes, again making the assertion that "Silas Plowden Halsey...was lost in a torpedo off New London, in August, 1814, in an attempt to blow up the British ship *Ramillies*, 74, then blockading the harbor of New London." Later, in his 1907 study of *The Evolution of the Submarine, Mine and Torpedo*, local historian Murray Fraser Sueter indicated that in the biography of Captain Thomas Hardy, nowhere did he indicate that the unnamed operator of the submersible that had attacked the *HMS Ramillies* was taken prisoner or had drowned. In Hardy's own terms, these submarine attacks simply ended.

It is unlikely that we will ever know precisely what became of Silas Plowden Halsey, though we have come to understand his important and dynamic contribution to the history of American submarines.

Sketch of Robert Fulton, c1803

-9-
Robert Fulton: *Mute*

"...I am now busy winding up everything and will leave London about the 23rd inst... The packet, being well manned and provided will be more commodious and safe for an autumn passage, and I think there will be little or no risk... But although there is not much risk, yet accidents may happen, and...I have made out a complete set of drawings and descriptions of my whole system of submarine attack... These with my will, I shall put in a tin cylinder, sealed and leave them in the care of General Lyman, not to be opened unless I am lost. Should such an event happen, I have left you the means to publish these works with engravings, in a handsome manner..."[1]

Thus, Robert Fulton communicated his wishes to his close friend and confidante, Joel Barlow, which he sent on the eve of his final departure from England in September of 1806. He had lived abroad for nearly twenty years, and seemed somewhat anxious and unnerved about the idea of returning home.

Yet, Fulton, as we know, reached America safely, and there was no need for Barlow to publish his life's work on submarines. The manuscripts and drawings were packed away until 1870, when they were sold at auction. For another fifty years or so, "they rested quietly and unknown to the general public," until they were passed on to historian William Barclay Parsons, who made them public in 1922, one hundred, sixteen years after Fulton had placed them inside the cylinder for posterity's sake.

The manuscripts and drawings proved to be invaluable. While it is, without doubt, true that the genius of Robert Fulton as an innovator and inventor was to a certain extent exhibited in his civil constructions, and in his numerous novel devices for the improvement of canals and their navigation, modern day engineers would regard the majority of his contrivances as rather crude and commonplace. Despite the fact that there would be questions of his great skill and talent in this area, however, the study of his plans for the institution of a system of submarine navigation and warfare would certainly have thoroughly removed all doubt.

In the early part of the 19th century–and perhaps even before–Fulton had given much thought to the means available for securing what he considered essential to the independence of all nations–total freedom of the seas. This concept would eventually result in the production of a very complete plan for an underwater warfare system, primarily as an ideal, but also in the attainment of some degree of success in their application.

Acting as if he had completely given up on his ambition to build a fleet of attack submarines, Fulton turned his attention to the design of steam-powered boats. The 36-year-old traveled to Plombieres-les-Bains, in the Lorraine region of eastern France, during the spring of 1802. There, he fashioned a his earliest drawings and completed his plans for the construction of his first steamboat. Many attempts had already been made, and a great number inventors were hard at work contemporaneously with him. Every modern device imaginable–the jet-system, the "chaplet" of buckets on an endless chain or rope, the paddle-wheel, and even the screw-propeller–had been proposed, and all were familiar to the well-read man of science from America. Indeed, as Benjamin H. Latrobe, a distinguished engineer of the time, wrote in a paper presented on May 20, 1803, to the Philadelphia Society, "A sort of mania began to prevail" for propelling boats by means of steam-engines. Fulton was one of those taking this mania very seriously. In September of 1802, Fulton sent the following letter to Fulner Skipwith, detailing his progress:

> "The expense of a patent in France is 300 livres for three years, 800 ditto for ten years, and 1,500 ditto for fifteen years. There can be no difficulty in obtaining a patent for the mode of propelling a boat which you have shown me; but if the author of the model wishes to be assured of the merits of his invention before he goes to the expense of a patent, I advise him to make the model of a boat in which he can place a clock-spring, which will give about eight revolutions. He can then combine the movements so as to try oars, paddles, and the leaves which he proposes. If he finds that the leaves drive the boat a greater distance in the same time than either oars or paddles, they consequently are a better application of power. About eight years ago, the Earl of Stanhope tried an experiment on similar leaves, wheels, oars, and paddles, and flyers similar to those of a smoke-jack, and found oars to be the best. The velocity with which a boat moves is in proportion as the sum of the surfaces of the oars, paddles, leaves, or other machine is to the bow of the boat presented to the water, and in proportion to the power with which such machinery is put in motion. Hence, if the use of the surfaces of the oars is equal to the sum of the surfaces of the leaves, and they pass through similar curves in the same time, the effect must be the same. But oars have their advantage; they return through air to make a second stroke, and hence create very little resistance; whereas the leaves return through water, and add considerably to the resistance, which resistance is increased as the velocity of the boat is augmented. No kind of machinery can create power. All that can be done is to apply the manual or other power to the best advantage. If the author of the model is fond of mechanics, he will be much amused, and not lose his time, by trying the experiments in the manner I propose; and this perhaps is the most prudent measure, before a patent is taken."[2]

AMERICAN SUBMARINERS: PRE-CIVIL WAR

By the spring of 1803, Robert Fulton had managed to construct an actual prototype model. The inventor described the vessel in a letter "to Citizens Molar, Bandell, and Montgolfier":

> "Friends of the art,–I send you here with drawings sketched from a machine that I have constructed, and with which I purpose soon to make experiments in causing boats to move on rivers by the aid of fire-pumps (pompes-a-feu). My first aim, in occupying myself with this idea, was to put it in practice on the long rivers of America, where there are no tow-paths, and where these would scarcely be practicable, and where, consequently, the expenses of navigation by steam would be placed in comparison with that of manual labour, and not with that of horse-power, as in France. In these drawings you will find nothing new, since they are only [those of] water-wheels, a method which has been often tried, and always abandoned because it was believed that a purchase could not be thereby obtained in the water. But after the experiments that I have made, I am convinced that the fault has not been in the wheel, but in ignorance of proportions, velocities, powers, and probably mechanical combinations... Citizens, when my experiments are ready, I shall have the pleasure of inviting you to witness. them; and if they succeed, I reserve to myself the privilege of either making a present of my labours to the Republic, or deriving therefrom the advantages which the law authorizes. At present, I place these notes in your hands, so that if a like project should reach you before my experiments are finished, it may not have preference over my own."[3]

The hull measured sixty-six feet in length, eight feet beam, and was described as being "of light draught." But, unfortunately, the hull was far too weak to hold its heavy machinery, and it splintered in two and sank to the bottom of the Seine during its maiden voyage. Fulton at once set about recovering the wreck, drying her out, and repairing the damages. He was compelled to direct the rebuilding of the entire hull, but the vessel's machinery was but slightly damaged. In June of 1803, the reconstruction was complete, and the vessel was refloated in July.

On August 9, 1803, the refurbished ship was sent out once again, and demonstrated in front of an immense number of spectators. The group included a committee from the National Academy, consisting of Bougainville, Bossuet, Carnot, and Perier. The boat moved slowly, making only between three and four miles an hour against the current, the speed through the water being about 4.5 miles. Still, this was, all things considered, a huge success.

Nearly two months earlier, on June 19, 1803, just a single month after France and Britain had officially gone to war, the British Admiralty issued a top-secret circular to their naval commanders stationed at Downs, Portsmouth, Plymouth, and Sheerness, explaining that "a plan has been concerted by Mr. Fulton, an American resident at Paris, under the influence of the First Consul of the French Republic, for destroying the Maritime Force of this Country..."[4]

However, covert sources in the British government had also discovered by this point that Fulton and Napoleon had had a parting of the ways, and that the American inventor now seemed to be pursuing less hostile endeavors. Rather than take the chance that he might one day resume his submarine projects with the support of the French, however, the British government believed that it would be extremely wise to lure Fulton over to their side. To this end, a gentleman simply calling himself "John Smith" was dispatched to the bustling city of Paris, in order to attempt a private contact with Fulton, though agents were unsure whether or not he had already departed from that country.

Indeed, Fulton was still in France in the autumn of 1803, when he received a message from the mysterious John Smith, asking that he meet an agent of the British government in Holland for the purpose of discussing the character and applications of his submarine invention. Though only the general nature of such underwater war machines was understood by Lord Stanhope, the admiralty had become quite interested in Fulton and had kept track of his earlier successes. And now, government officials hoped to secure a similar invention for use by the British army and navy.

Fulton eagerly proceeded to Holland as arranged, but the contacting agent did not meet him there as planned, and the disappointed inventor returned to Paris. Several months passed before he was again contacted in the spring of 1804, and he was requested to visit London and confer with the new government in power. As a show of good faith, the American inventor shared a transverse cross-section of his submarine.

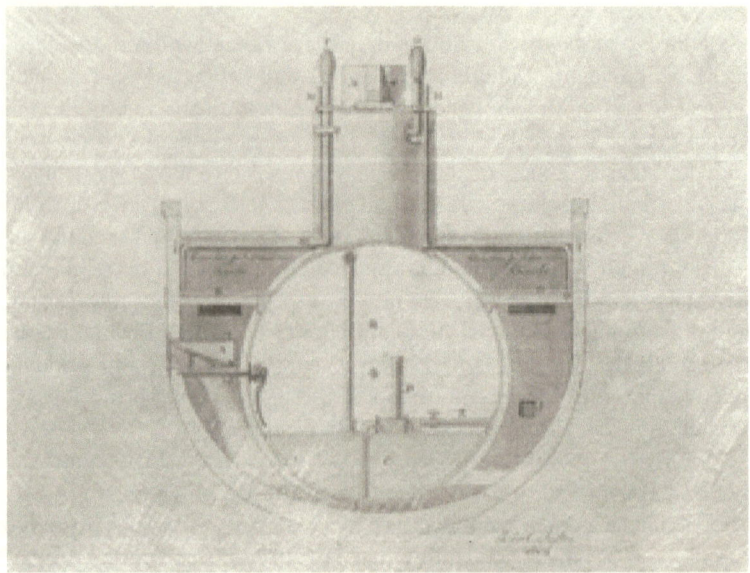

Sketch of the traverse section of submarine, by Robert Fulton

In another detailed drawing, John Smith closely studied five distinct mechanisms that would be incorporated into a prototype vessel. One was a type of forcing section of double facing pumps, which could be utilized to pump water for buoyancy in and out of the submarine. Next to that was a side view of those same pumps. Fulton also offered an end and side view of his proposed windlass, a horizontal cylinder that would be rotated by the turn of a crank to move heavy weights. The final sketch depicted a set of the pump tubes.

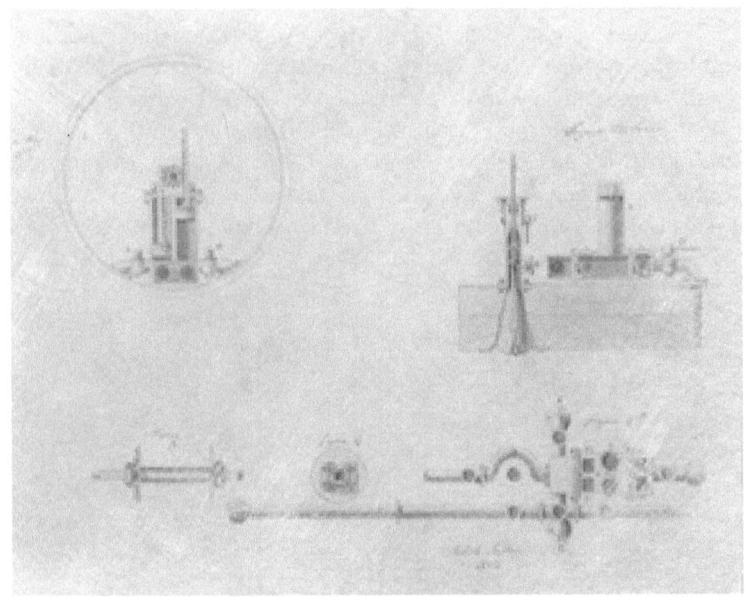

Sketch of pumps and windlass, by Robert Fulton

Though it was far less than Fulton had initially hoped for, Smith offered the displaced American inventor £800 to travel to England and outline his invention to the Ministers. Always the bargainer, Fulton requested ten thousand pounds in exchange for, what he considered, information that could alter the very course of British naval history. As a further demand, he insisted that a committee of British experts be established within a three-week period of his arrival upon English soil, for the sole purpose of investigating his submarine proposal to its fullest. Only then would he agree to actually sell all of his secret designs and drawings–for the "mere pittance" of one hundred thousand pounds.

After a few weeks of deliberation, the English agent informed Fulton that his asking price was far too high. On the other hand, explained the contact, if the inventor would dare to trust the British government with the remaining specific details of his invention, then he might "rely on being treated with the utmost liberality and generosity."[5]

Since it was the only interest in his experiments with submarines at this juncture in his life, Fulton decided to take the agent up on his offer, departing from France and traveling to London on April 28, 1804. Yet, to his bitter disappointment, William Pitt was about to become the new British Prime Minister; and Pitt was most definitely not interested in purchasing an underwater vessel for such an enormous sum of money, particularly since it would be purchased sight unseen. As a compromise, however, he invited Fulton to construct a working craft that could prove its worth against the French fleet.

Presented with no other option, the American inventor hesitatingly agreed. In drawing up the subsequent legal contract for his services, he would be financially compensated with the lump sum of £7,000 in exchange for the diving vessel's completion and proven success. Furthermore, he would be granted full use of his Majesty's dockyard, a salary of £200 per month, and one-half of the estimated value of all enemy vessels eventually destroyed by his underwater craft. Finally, it was stipulated that the agreement would remain legal and valid for no less than fourteen years.

Sketch of glass windows with stop cocks in the submarine, by Robert Fulton

A few features of the Fulton design were quite innovative, with one drawing depicting a mode of placing glass windows in the conning tower section that could be plugged with corks in case of an accident. In another, the inventor had sketched a lid and cap of a dome for observation, as well as a bathometer gauge for measuring depth of the vessel. Needless to say, Prime Minister Pitt's commission was quite impressed.

AMERICAN SUBMARINERS: PRE-CIVIL WAR

Before the construction phase of the first British-backed submarine had begun, however—which Fulton hoped would eventually be used against the French naval forces at Boulogne—Prime Minister Pitt was plagued by opposition to the agreement from his commanders-in-chief. They did not believe that such a vessel would ever become a reality. A commission was appointed in June of the same year, consisting of five distinguished engineers and military men, who examined the Fulton submarine plans. But, with true British conservatism, the commission reported that the design was both flawed and "impracticable." Fulton set out immediately to prove the commission incorrect in their assumption. By this point in time, Fulton understood the concept of a submersible vessel better than anyone in the world. A submarine, he explained to the English ministers, was a propelled ship capable of operating underwater. For stability, surface hulls are broadest above the waterline, whereas underwater hulls would possess more circular cross sections that increase strength and reduce surface area and friction drag.

Fulton's design concept was fundamentally an air space contained by a hull designed to withstand deep ocean pressures and to move easily under the surface. The hull would be a double steel shell, with the inner, or pressure, hull containing all the machinery for propelling and guiding the vessel, plus living quarters for the crew. The outer hull would hold the ballast tanks. When the vessel submerged, these tanks would be opened and flooded with seawater. For surfacing, the seawater would be forced out of the ballast tanks and replaced by compressed air.

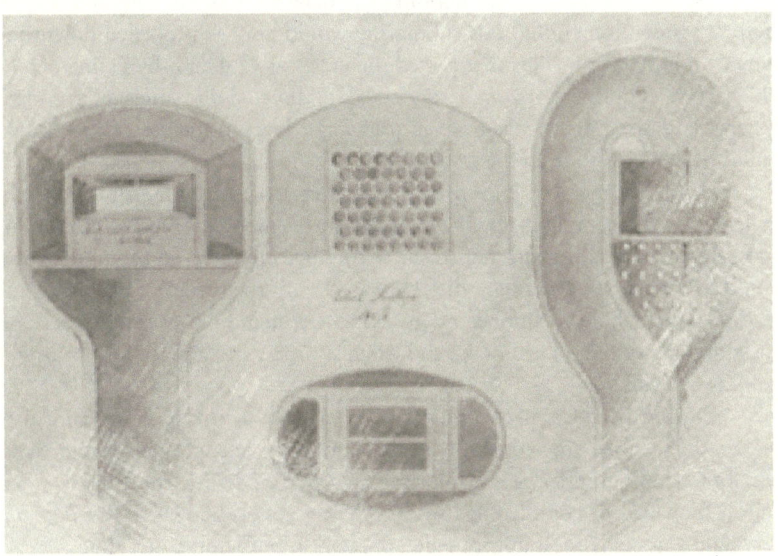

Sketch of the incompressible tanks on the submarine, by Robert Fulton

Two views of the submarine, one under sail and one submerged, by Robert Fulton

Fulton understood that flooding the ballast tanks was only one step in the process of submerging. His submarine would also be propelled downward by rear-mounted propellers that forced the craft forward, and by diving planes, which were movable horizontal rudders that directed the angle of the dive. When the desired depth was reached, the water level in the vessel's trim tanks would be adjusted to keep the craft stable.

While submerged, Fulton further contended, his submersible could be navigated with a simple magnetic compass, supplemented by pre-dive conning tower observations. This fin-shaped superstructure mounted on top of the vessel would further serve as a bridge when the vessel is on the surface. Finally, it could be designed to hold a number of instruments, including: a crude periscope, the snorkel, a system of air intake and exhaust pipes, and a place for his unique "fold-away" sails.

During the next twelve months, the American inventor was forced to take on the tedious, time-consuming task of not only defending his inventive design, but building underwater explosives as well. Yet, despite these distractions, Fulton managed to complete his second diving vessel, known as the *Plunging Boat*, and was ready for a full-scale demonstration in October of 1805:

"It is now twenty years since all Europe was astonished at the first ascension of men in balloons; perhaps in a few years they will not be less surprised to see a flotilla of diving-boats, which on a given signal shall, to avoid the pursuit of an enemy, plunge under water, and rise again several leagues from the place where they descended... But if we have not succeeded in steering the balloon, and even were it impossible to attain that object, the case is different with the diving-boat, which can be conducted under water in the same manner as upon its surface. It has the advantage of sailing like the common boat, and also of diving when pursued. With these qualities it is fit for carrying secret orders, to succour [SIC] a blockaded fort, and to examine the force and position of the enemy in their harbours. These are sure and evident benefits which the diving-boat at present promises. But who can see all the consequences of this discovery, or the improvements of which it is susceptible? Fulton has already added to his boat a machine, by means of which he blew up a large boat...; and if by future experiments the same effect could be produced in frigates or ships-of-the-line, what will become of maritime wars, and where will sailors be found to man ships-of war when it is a physical certainty that they may at every moment be blown into the air by means of diving-boats, against which no human foresight can guard them?"[6]

Fulton's earliest experiments with "infernal" explosives had been conducted in 1797, when he had attempted to build a form of what today would be called the "automobile," or self-moving torpedo. His ingenious machine was intended to drive a cigar-shaped torpedo in a definite direction to a prescribed place, and there to fire the charge. The experiment was not a success, however, and it would be years before he would actually share his ideas with the world.

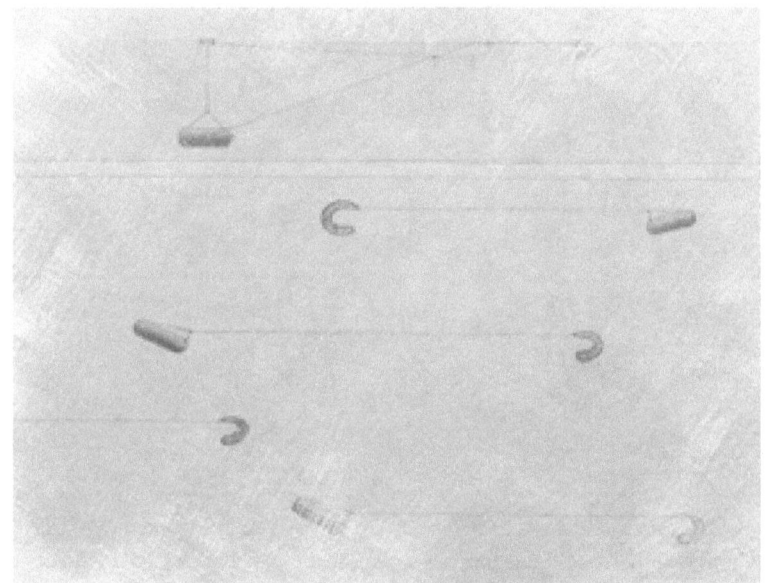

Sketches of Fulton's explosive mines, by Robert Fulton

Robert Fulton did, however, design a "clockwork" type of torpedo that he scheduled for demonstration. On the appointed date, an ordinary rowboat was launched on a mission to destroy an aging Danish brig known as the *Dorothea*, then anchored at Walmar Roads, near Deal. Beneath the shadows of the Pitt castle, the down-sized, two-man surface vessel made its way slowly past a number of skeptical dignitaries. She passed within thirty feet of her target, shooting a harpoon dragging a rope attached to a single seventy-pound explosive charge. Moments later, the mine found its mark, exploding violently against the defenseless brig's wooden hull:

> "Exactly in fifteen minutes from the time of drawing the peg and throwing the carcass into the water, the explosion took place. It lifted the brig almost bodily, and broke her completely in two. The ends sank immediately, and nothing was seen but floating fragments."[7]

Brig *Dorothea*, as she was blown up on October 15, 1805

In further summing up of what was witnessed, it was recorded that the defenseless vessel "went to pieces like a shattered eggshell." Due to the successful demonstration, another aspect of Fulton's experimental work had attracted the attention of the British government: the design of his underwater weaponry.

The inventor's motto had always been, and continued to be, that "the liberty of the seas will be the happiness of the earth;" and his desire to break up all naval warfare pushed him forward in this burgeoning field of study. Finally, Fulton believed, the British government would be forced to accept his invention.

But, sadly, the inventor's British submarine fleet and its weaponry aspirations were short-lived, for the hand of fate dealt a severely cruel blow to his ambitious dreams less than a week later. On October 21, 1805, Admiral Horatio Nelson managed to surround and destroy the combined French and Spanish fleet at Trafalgar. It would go down in history as one of the most convincing British sea victories ever. Ironically, little did the world know that it had also inflicted a devastating defeat to one of America's greatest inventors. In a letter written to the British government in August of 1806, Fulton expressed his feelings:

> "At all events, whatever may be your award, I never will consent to let these inventions lie dormant, should my country at any time have need of them. Were you to grant me an annuity of 20,000 pounds a year, I would sacrifice all to the safety and independence of my country."[8]

In October of that same year, fully realizing that the British no longer desired or needed his inventions, a disheartened Fulton made plans to return to his native America. Though he felt scorned by France, rejected by England, and ignored by his own government, he refused to give up hope of one day constructing an underwater attack force comprised of innovative submersibles.

The voyage across the stark North Atlantic Ocean, including a layover in Halifax, Nova Scotia, took nine-and-one-half weeks. Time, the fresh salt air, and relaxation helped Fulton to get rid of his distraught feelings and, when his ship, the packet *Windsor Castle*, arrived in New York Harbor on December 13, 1806, he was anxious to get on with business. Nearly 500 vessels docked in the harbor that cold and bleak December, and "every thought, work, look, and action of the multitude seemed to be absorbed in commerce." Fulton was happy to be home, and he soon found his optimism. Almost immediately, he presented his plans to the Government of the United States. He received a great deal of encouragement from ex-President Thomas Jefferson, from then President James Madison, and from the Secretary of State and of the Navy under the two Presidents. Critics forced him to defend his earlier decision to offer his vital knowledge to foreign governments:

> "It never has been my intention to hide these inventions from the world on any consideration. On the contrary, it ever has been my intention to make them public as soon as may be consistent with strict justice to all with whom I am concerned. For myself, I have ever the interest of America, free commerce, the interest of mankind, the magnitude of the object in view, and the national reputation connected with it, superior to all calculations of a pecuniary nature."[9]

Fulton had been in America but a few weeks when he collected his detailed drawings went to Washington, to urge the Government to accept his plan for torpedo and submarine warfare, arguing that "in the hands of a righteous nation, they would insure universal peace." He secured a small appropriation, returned to New York City, set up his workshop on Governor's Island, and began explaining it to representatives of the army and navy–and, for that matter, anyone else interested in the subject.

During the spring of 1807, Fulton planned to carry out a series of demonstrations, showing the value of his inventions. During one such event, he invited the magistracy of New York and a party of citizens to witness his torpedoes at work. While he was explaining their mechanism, the intrigued onlookers crowded round him with a discommoding effect. He pointed to a copper case, standing under the gateway close by, to which was attached a clockwork lock. This he set in motion, followed by this remark: "Gentlemen, this is a charged torpedo, with which, precisely in its present state, I mean to blow up a vessel. It contains 170 pounds of powder, and if I would let the clockwork run fifteen minutes, I doubt not that this fortification would be blown to atoms." The circle around Fulton was enlarged in a twinkling, and before five of his fifteen minutes had gone by, there were not more than two spectators left. Even more convincing was his destruction, by a single torpedo on July 20, 1807, of a large brig in the harbor of New York. The vessel had been completely annihilated or, as Fulton himself described, "decomposed."

Later, descriptions of his inventions and of his experiments were published by Fulton in *Torpedo War*, a book addressed to the President of the United States and Members of Congress. The ultimate result was that Congress passed an act permitting the extension of these experiments for several years to come. In fact up to the time of his death, Fulton busied himself–if only intermittently–in the prosecution of his studies, and in submarine warfare experiments. A naval commission was appointed to witness and report on his work, and the American government continued its interest in the subject.

During the winter of 1806-1807, Robert Fulton began to design and construct his first steamboat, selecting Charles Brown, a well-known ship-builder of that time, to complete her construction. The hull of this steamer, which would become the first to establish a regular route and regular transportation of passengers and merchandise in America, would be 133 feet long, eighteen feet beam, and seven feet depth of hold. The engine was designed to measure twenty-four inches diameter of cylinder, four feet stroke of piston; and its boiler would be twenty feet long, seven feet high, and eight feet wide. When completed, her tonnage was computed to be approximately one hundred, sixty.

In early August of 1807, Fulton demonstrated his underwater explosives in front of a large group of approximately 2,000 onlookers along the New York harbor. The extrvaganza was announced in local newspapers, an aging 200-ton brig was secured and anchored offshore, and his percussion torpedoes were prepared for the experiment. The first attempt failed, however, when "the tide drove them (explosives) under the brig near her keel, but in consequence of the locks turning downwards, the powder fell out of the pand and they both missed fire." During a second attempt, the toepedo missed its target entirely, with the explosion taking place "about one hundred yards from her, and threw up a column of water ten feet diameter, sixty or seventy feet high." On his third and final attempt, Fulton's demonstration proved successful, with the brig being totally and utterly destroyed. The onlookers, along with a number of government officials, were quite impressed.

Meanwhile, on August 17, 1807, Fulton and Chancellor Robert Livingston, Jr., together launched the *North River Steamboat* (later known as the *Clermont*), which was scheduled to carry passengers between New York City and Albany. According to writer, Alice Crary Sutcliff, narrating nearly a century later, it was on this journey that, "Just before the boat was about to cast anchor off Clermont, the Chancellor announced the betrothal of Robert Fulton to his young kinswoman, Harriet Livingston."

North River Steamboat replica

Though often somewhat difficult to sort out entirely, relationships throughout history can readily be separated into two parts–the "cousinhood" and the amount removed. The first identifies how close the families are–first cousins, for example, are simply the children of siblings. The amount removed can be thought of as the difference in generations. Harriet was the second cousin, once removed, of Henry Livingston, Jr., and was the daughter of Walter Livingston, who was the son of Colonel Robert Livingston, 3rd Lord of Livingston Manor. Fulton's partner in the steamship venture, Chancellor Robert R. Livingston, Jr., was the son of Robert R. Livingston and Margaret Beekman, both Henry's first cousins, once removed.

Little is known about just how the couple met. Harriet was described at the time as "a pretty lass of twenty four years." She had grown up at the family's country estate of Teviotdale, outside the present-day town of Germantown, being one of nine children. Her father had died when she was fourteen, leaving her imposing mother to raise them all. Nevertheless, Harriet was given a notable education; she spent two years in boarding school at the Moravian Seminary in Pennsylvania, which put her head and shoulders above many of the other girls she would have encountered. She was artistic, musical, and possessed of both lovely blonde hair and a fashionably-strong profile.

Meanwhile, 42-year-old Robert Fulton proudly described the *North River Steamboat*'s maiden journey in a lengthy letter to his life-long friend and confidante, Joel Barlow:

> "My steamboat voyage to Albany and back has turned out rather more favourably than I had calculated. The distance from New York to Albany is one hundred and fifty miles. I ran it up in thirty-two hours, and down in thirty. I had a light breeze against me the whole way, both going and coming, and the voyage has been performed wholly by the power of the steam-engine. I overtook many sloops and schooners beating to windward, and parted with them as if they had been at anchor. The power of propelling boats by steam is now fully proved. The morning I left New York, there were not perhaps thirty persons in the city who believed that the boat would ever move one mile an hour, or be of the least utility; and while we were putting off from the wharf, which was crowded with spectators, I heard a number of sarcastic remarks. This is the way in which ignorant men compliment what they call philosophers and projectors. Having employed much time, money, and zeal in accomplishing this work, it gives me, as it will you, great pleasure to see it answer my expectations. It will give a cheap and quick conveyance to the merchandise on the Mississippi, Missouri, and other great rivers, which are now laying open their treasures to the enterprise of our countrymen; and, although the prospect of personal emolument has been some inducement to me, yet I feel infinitely more pleasure in reflecting on the immense advantage my country will derive from the invention..."[10]

The 1870 book *Great Fortunes* quoted a former resident of Poughkeepsie who described the scene firsthand:

> "It was in the early autumn of the year 1807 that a knot of villagers was gathered on a high bluff just opposite Poughkeepsie, on the west bank of the Hudson, attracted by the appearance of a strange, dark-looking craft, which was slowly making its way up the river. Some imagined it to be a sea-monster, while others did not hesitate to express their belief that it was a sign of the approaching judgment. What seemed strange in the vessel was the substitution of lofty and straight black smoke-pipes, rising from the deck, instead of the gracefully tapered masts that commonly stood on

the vessels navigating the stream, and, in place of the spars and rigging, the curious play of the working-beam and pistons, and the slow turning and splashing of the huge and naked paddle-wheels, met the astonished gaze. The dense clouds of smoke, as they rose wave upon wave, added still more to the wonderment of the rustics."[11]

On Sept. 1, 1807, the *Albany Gazette* announced that the "*North River Steamboat* will leave Paulus's Hook [Jersey City] on Friday, the 4th of September, at 6 in the morning and arrive at Albany on Saturday at 6 in the afternoon." The New York Central train then took only a few minutes more than three hours to make the trip. The same paper on Oct. 5, 1807, announced that "Mr. Fulton's new steamboat left New York against a strong tide, very rough water, and a violent gale from the north. She made headway against the most sanguine expectations, and without being rocked by the waves."

Harriet Livingston, age 24

Amid little fanfare or publicity, Robert Fulton and Harriet Livingston were married on January 7, 1808, in the parlor of the bride's Teviotdale home. Nowhere in Fulton's correspondence from this period was there mentioned any wedding planning whatsoever. The local newspaper carried the announcement in just a few words:

> "Married, on Thursday evening, by the Rev. Dr. Bench, Robert Fulton, Esq. to Miss Harriet Livingston, daughter of the late Walter Livingston, Esq. of the upper manor."[12]

Harriet's brother Robert, married to the Chancellor's daughter Margaret Maria, was away in Paris at the time, and even he simply received the news from the Chancellor as "I give you joy of the marriage of Harriet and Mr. Fulton."

Meanwhile, after the *North River Steamboat*'s first season of operation, her hull was lengthened to 140 feet, and widened to 16.5 feet, thus being completely rebuilt; while her engines were altered in a number of details, Fulton furnishing all of the specific details for the alterations. Two more boats, the *Raritan* and the *Car of Neptune* were added to form the fleet of 1807, and steam-navigation was finally a reality in America, some years ahead of Europe. The Legislature was so impressed with this result that they promptly extended the monopoly previously given Fulton and Livingston, adding five years for every boat to be built and set in operation, up to a maximum not to exceed a total of thirty years.

By then, Fulton was making plans to move his pregnant bride away from his mother-in-law's home in the Hudson Valley down to spend the remainder of her pregnancy with the Barlows in Washington. In a letter to Joel, he wrote:

> "You have not told me Mrs. Barlow's plan for the Summer...Will she wait until our arrival and then form a plan? Say how shall it be ruthlinda [Mrs. Barlow]? Shall we unite our fortunes to Make Kalorama the centre of taste, beauty, love, and dearest friendship... She [Harriet] is very desirous to know whether I think you will love her and I always tell her that depends on how She behaves,"[13]

It is unknown as to whether or not her "behavior" was enough to earn the Barlow's approval. Either way, on October 10, 1808, Harriet gave birth to a son named after both his father and his father's best friend: Robert Barlow Fulton. Throughout his childhood, the youngster would be called by his middle name. According to Fulton, a few weeks later Harriet was "charmingly up running about, please to the soul, gay as a lark, laughing, singing, dancing, playing and plaguing my soul out while I am making these long letters and calculations."

Yet, in reality, Harriet remained ill for several weeks after the birth of her baby boy, and the Barlow household was closed to the typical tide of winter visitors, suggesting that something was terribly wrong. Perhaps having the two families sharing one household was not all that they had hoped.

Meanwhile, while trying to adjust to married life and raising a family, Fulton concentrated his efforts on the design and construction of not only his steamboats, but on underwater explosives. Initially, his explosives were designed as a defense mechanism, deployed to keep enemy ships from anchoring in American harbors. These quite amazing devices could be dropped into the water, where they would sink. However, they were made in such a way that Robert Fulton was able to actually "time" their resurfacing in an exact number of days. Hence, by employing a complex submerged percussion instrument, they would come back to the water's surface after a set amount of time, where they would explode when the hull of an enemy vessel came in contact with the rising bombs:

> "I will now suppose the enemy to be approaching a port; a signal announces them; our boats run out and throw into the channel two hundred Torpedoes, set each to 15 days. Should the enemy sail among them, the consequence will teach future caution; should they cruise or anchor at a distance, what could they do? They not knowing the number of Torpedoes which were put down, nor the day on which they were to rise to the surface, could not have their boats out exposed to our fire, and waiting from day to day for a time uncertain. Whereas, our officers, knowing the number which were put down, and the day they were to rise to the surface, would have their boats ready to take them in, and at the same time replace them with others set for ten, fifteen, twenty, or more days..."[14]

Next, Fulton went to work on an offensive means of delivering these same torpedoes in attack fashion from above ther waterline. Incorporating the same clockwork mechanisms, the bomb would be incorporated by harpooning an enemy vessel in the bow and simply wait for its destruction. Fulton would later explain how this would work during warfare:

> "My experience with this kind of harpoon and gun is that I have harpooned a target of six feet square fifteen or twenty times, at the distance of about thirty to fifty feet, never missing, and always driving the barbed point through three inch boards up to the eye, which practice was so satisfactory, that I did not consider it necessary to repeat it. The object of harpooning a vessel on the larboard and starboard bow is to fix one of the Torpedo-line, then, if the ship be under sail, her action through the water will draw the Torpedo under her; if she be at anchor, the tide will drive it under her, where at the expiration of the time for which the clockwork was set, the explosion will destroy her."[15]

Though he had not completely divulged this plan of attack earlier, Fulton also admitted that this was "the kind of Torpedo and clockwork by which the Danish brig known as the *Dorothea* was destroyed in Walmer Roads, as well as the aging brig in New York Harbor in August of 1807. In each case, the harpoon had been successful in fixing the line to the target vessel, with the tide pushing the explosive against the hull of each ship. Each of these demonstrations, explained Fulton, proved the value of his weapon's design.

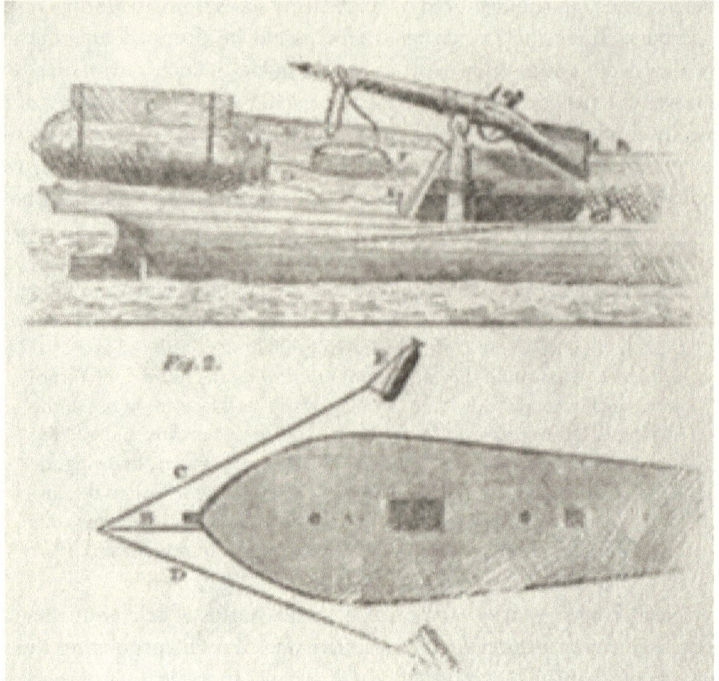

Drawing of Robert Fulton's harpoon design and torpedo

Finally, it was time for Fulton to construct the ultimate weapon; one that could be fired from below the surface, delivering the same clockwork explosive without the enemy ever being aware of the impending attack. Such a torpedo could be easily deployed in conjunction with his newest diving vessel. The first of its kind, though never constructed on a large scale, exhibited a great deal of promise to government officials:

"A gun 2 feet long, 1 inch diameter, was loaded with a lead ball and one ounce of powder; I put a tin tube to the touch-hole, made it water-tight, and let it under water 3 feet. Before it I placed a yellow-pine plank, 4 inches thick, 18 inches from the muzzle. On firing, the ball went through the 18 inches of water and the plank. When the gun is loaded as usual, a tompkin or plug is put in the muzzle, to keep the water out of the barrel... In this experiment the gun being immersed, with the pressure of three feet of water on all its parts, that circumstance might be assigned as a reason for its not bursting. It then became necessary to try the effect with the muzzle in water and the breech in air."[16]

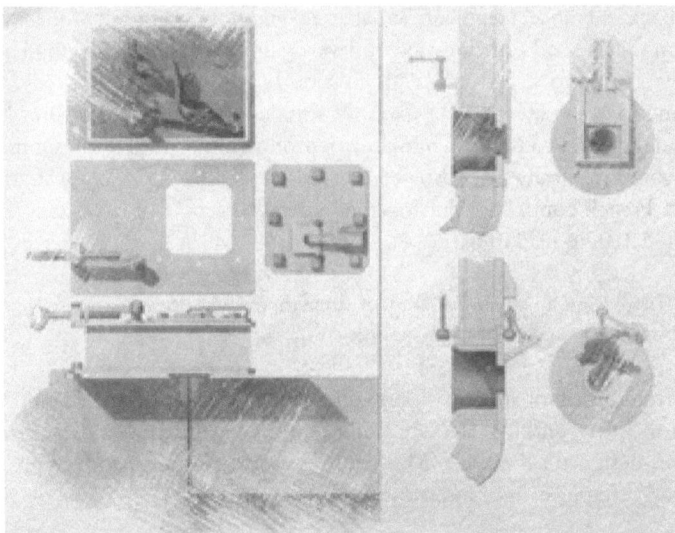

Sketch of Robert Fulton's underwater cannon detonator and muzzle

Time passed. Long after his historical success with the *North River Steamboat*, which had managed to make him a wealthy and well-known public figure, Robert Fulton went to work on designing yet another diving vessel. And he continued his work with torpedoes, never losing sight of his premise that steamboats and torpedoes combined would result in bringing about free trade:

> "I will not admit that it [the steamboat] is half so important as the torpedo system of defense and attack; for out of this will grow the liberty of the seas; an object of infinite importance to the welfare of America and every civilized country...in case we have war and the enemy's ships come into our waters, if the government will give me reasonable means of action, I will soon convince the world that we have surer and cheaper modes of defense than they are aware of..."[17]

By February of 1809, Fulton was gently trying to extricate himself and his bride from the Barlow household without hurting their feelings. On March 16, he signed a three-year lease on a newly constructed house at 75 Chambers Street, less than two city blocks from Cornelius and Richard Berrien's stagecoach manufacturing firm. Situated just north of City Hall, the rather large home with its own stable had cost him $750 plus taxes. Still, the developing neighborhood was rural enough that he could ride freely amid cattle and pigs that roamed the streets. Both the Fultons and Berriens had a "splendid" view of the city prison facility and, between them, the wooden Board of Health building. Fulton found the appropriate servants and purchased a young slave woman, to whom he apparently promised freedom after six years of servatude.

Back in France, Napoleon Bonaparte could not rid himself of the nagging suspicion that he had somehow lost the war against Britain by allowing Fulton's inventive genius to slip through his fingers. In 1809, perhaps to redeem his earlier mistake, the French First Consul commissioned the Coessin Brothers of Paris to design and construct a miniature reproduction of the Fulton submarine, which would ironically be christened the *Nautile*. Following a demonstration at Havre, a French committee put together a detailed report of its success. Dated April 11, 1810, in read in part:

> "There is no longer any doubt that submarine navigation may be established very expeditiously and at little cost..."[18]

From his Manhattan workshop on the opposite side of the Atlantic, Robert Fulton knew nothing of Napoleon's rejuvenated interest and faith in the American-designed submarine. Meanwhile, construction of the inventor's newest prototype continued uninterrupted:

> "...the hull was a foot thick. The deck was covered with iron plates. It was intended that the boat should habitually run on the surface like ordinary boats, but on approaching the enemy, it was to dive quickly under the water."[19]

With an immense amount of steamboat business taking up much of his time, Fulton found that his preparation for an upcoming torpedo demonstration was "a long and tedious job." A harpoon gun that he had promoted with much confidence proved to be neither accurate or powerful. As an alternative method of expending his energy, he designed a six-oared "torpedo boat":

> "Suspended from the bowsprit was a 40-foot pole tipped with a torpedo and so balanced that the operator could elevate or depress it with his right hand while launching the torpedo with his left. Protected by movable spars, the boat looked in plan more like an ungainly water bug than a deadly attack vessel."[20]

In addition, Fulton had designed an amazing gun-powered "hook and chisel" contrivance that the inventor claimed could "cut ship's cables under water by remote control." Yet, even if successful in casting British ships adrift and separating them from their $5,000 anchors, this newest invention did nothing to improve the efficient and safe delivery of underwater explosives.

In 1810, Harriet Fulton gave birth to a daughter Julia, a beautiful, curly-haired angel adored by all who saw her. By the summer of 1812 she would be pregnant with her third child–though she was not too tired to give a "splendid entertainment" on the East River with a band and an eighteen-gun salute. Friends and relatives supposed that the Fulton family could not be happier.

Depiction of Barlow and Julia Fulton

Things were not going all that well, however, within the Fulton household, and a lack of money seemed to be the problem. In July of 1812, arguments between Harriet and her husband were coming to an ugly head. In desperation, she wrote a rather sarcastic and hot-headed letter to Chancellor Livingston:

> "As my husband in his good nature and thoughtless has been disposing of my property without consulting me...I must appeal to you for justice. Know then that when the Steam Ferry boat was commenced he gave to me for present pin money and future support of my Children in case of accidents the whole of the Patent rights to the ferry...Yesterday on claiming this right I was surprised to hear him say he had given you half of it and he was so delicate on this point that I am forced to negotiate with you.Say my dear Sir, have I not a prior right? in honor is it not mine?...indeed my heart is so set on it that your generosity must meet my wishes..."[21]

Not only was Harriet unhappy about that, but it seemed to her that her husband's affections were continually being lavished on his beloved Barlows. The couple had returned to France–from whence they'd originally come–and, despite the distance, they continued to exchange gifts and "necessaries" on a regular basis. According to one historian, "Ruth (Barlow) begged Fulton to send sugar because it was so expensive in France. She expected Harriet to buy English cambirc [a fabric] for her, since none was available there... Still, Fulton comissioned the Barlows to buy French carpets, chandeliers, dinner plates, and other embellishments..." Yet, whenever Harriet got involved in these ventures, the exchange never seemd to go as planned: either the wrong product was purchased or requests were simply ignored. The relationship with the Barlows slowly became an antagonism in Harriet's already dismal marriage to the handsome inventor.

As Robert Fulton's work continued, Commodore John Rodgers, a senior naval officer in the United States Navy who would serve under six Presidents, did everything in his power to stop Fulton from completing his inventions. During the course of their confrontations, Rodgers met him at every turn with objections and ridicule. At one point, the enterprising inventor had unveiled a proposal for a torpedo boat, which particularly made the Commodore's blood boil, and he didn't hesitate to bring forth his animadversions in public:

> "Mr. Fulton exhibited a model of a vessel of three hundred tons, in the presence of Colonel Williams, Captain Chauncey, and myself, and some other gentlemen of similar curiosity, which he called a 'torpedo blockship,' the sides of which were calculated (he said) to be cannon-proof, and the decks proof against musket-shot, yhe former being six feet thick abd the latter six inches. This vessel is intended to be armed with two torpedoes on each side, which are to be applied by means of a spar ninety-six feet long, projecting from the vessel's side, supported at the inner end by a double circular swivel, and at the outward end by guys leading from the mastheads. For the particulars of this singular vessel (which to my mind deserves the mame of 'Nondescript'), I leave the reader to make his own conclusions from the figure annexed, and by which alone he will be enabled to judge whether such torpid, unwieldy, six-feet sided, six-inch decked, fifteen-sixteenths sunk water dungeons are calculated to supercede the necessity of a navy, particularly when the men who manage them are, as is intended, confined to the limits of their holds, which will be under water, and in as perfect darkness as if shut up in the Black Hole of Calcutta!"[22]

The repeated course comments of Commodore Rodgers had, above all others, destroyed what little confidence existed in the arena of public opinion, and Fulton opted to discontinue all further torpedo discussions. Yet, occasionally, his hopes and aspirations would resurface when he received any reassuring commentary. In the Spring of 1812, for example, he received a letter from a gentleman named William Brents, Jr., who lived near Aquia, Virginia, suggesting that he investigate the concept of torpedoes detonated by electricity. Apparently, Brents had offered specific details of their design. Fulton quickly responded:

> "Sir—Every friend of the torpedo is encouragement to me to persevere to their actual practice. I thank you for the hints, and will be much obliged

by any communication you will have the goodness to make of your thoughts or mean of using them. Some years ago, I investigated the mode and practicability of firing by electricity under water; the difficulties are, to preserve long wires from being torn or broken–the enemy might float up a few logs or old boats with graplins and tear away the wires, and thus render the torpedo useless...It will give you great pleasure when I assure you that I believe I possess sufficient mechanical means to put torpedoes under the bottom of our enemy in our harbors or some miles at sea; and all that I want is men practised [sic] to this new mode of warfare, which can be had if Mr. [Stephen Rowe] Bradley's bill passes into a law. But in addition to the models I possess, there are hundreds yet undiscovered for applying torpedoes, hence I thankfully receive any communications from their friends, If successful their benefit to America will be immense, for I still assert, and every reflection confirms my opinion, that these submarine mines must go to the annihilation of military navies, and consequently produce the liberty of the seas, relieve us of all the trouble and expense of our foreign negotiations, and turn the whole genius and resources of our people on the useful arts. Everything, therefore, should be done to prove their value."[23]

On March 26, 1813, as the War of 1812 continued and British blockaders continued to play havoc with American merchant ships, Fulton signed an agreement with Samuel Swartwout, a Poughkeepsie, New York, native. During the war, along with his brothers, John and Robert, Samuel had served briefly as captain of the Iron Grays, a light infantry unit. In November of 1806, he had been arrested as one of four allies of Aaron Burr charged with misprison of treason. Following a hearing in Washington, D.C., he had been released in February of 1807. Afterward, he had been engaged in a number of other enterprises, including farming, dairying, the ferryboat business, railroads, a lumber company, coal mines, and land speculation in New York, New Jersey, Virginia, Illinois, and Texas, where he had launched his most ambitious scheme. He and James Morgan had helped to establish the New Washington Association, which would purchase and develop Texas land.

The contract committed that Robert Fulton would supply Swartwout with a minimum of six torpedo explosives, along with detailed instructions for their deployment by a pair of rowboats commissioned as privateers, which he would also provide. For his part of the bargain, Swartwout promised to carry out "any attack which he may make on an enemy's Vessel or Vessel of War by placing cannon, carronades, Columbiads, or other guns inside of a vessel and firing through her sides and through the sides of the enemy at close quarters."[24] Such an attack operation, it was further agreed, would be carried out for the price of $100 per month, and one-fifth of the bounties for enemy ships destroyed and one-sixth value of all vessels captured. The remainder would belong to Fulton.

It is important to note that one James Welden's signature is affixed to a second agreement between Fulton and Swartwout, and that he is also mentioned as being involved with the privateering scheme. Finally, in order to secure the support of the Secretary of Navy, William Jones, Fulton dispatched the following letter of introduction on May 8, 1813:

> "This will be presented to you by Mr. Swartwout. He will relate to you an expedition with torpedoes in which he has been engaged for me on the Delaware and the reason Governor Haslett assigned for not permitting him to make the attack....I hope you will countenance and aid Mr. Swartwout in carrying my submarine engines into effect. The depredations of the enemy and the times demand every exertion of mind and nerve. Mr. Swartwout is a gentleman of great energy and resource. And I hope any Impression which may have existed against him will not interfere in this case to impede or injure a good cause or an experiment on the enemy which if successful will be of incalculable importance..."[25]

Robert Fulton's instructions for deploying the torpedoes were typically explicit, detailing that it was optimal to employ whaleboats of six or eight oars. Such oars should be "well muffled and painted, like the boats, a faint gray." The men carrying out the attack should wear white flannel overwaist coats and matching caps, which would absorb gray tint from the water and the overcast skies. Dark, rainy nights, when the winds are ruffling the water, would be most favorable for an attack, Fulton explained, "since all hands except the watch would be sheltering between decks."

Fulton's directions, which came complete with sketches depicting the launch of the torpedoes, made the entire operation seem more like an adventure than an attack on the enemy. In order to put the contact torpedoes in position the operator was to take the top of a pine or any other small tree, from which could be fashioned a large barbed float. The torpedo was to be attached to it with a 90-foot length of rope, and the whole device would be dropped within the target vessel's mooring by an auxiliary boat.

Meanwhile, the primary launching vessel could be as far away as a fifth of a mile, and would row in a huge circle, drawing the line tight so that the tree-hook would snag the ship's cable. Calculating the tide and the friction of the waves, the line manipulators would slowly guide the torpedo beneath the keel of the enemy ship. All that was necessary at that precise moment was to pull a second line, releasing the trigger against the percussion detonator.

A few weeks later, Swartwout commenced staking out the Delaware River as agreed, and dispatched two vessels carrying twenty men and four torpedoes into the Delaware estuary. It was not until early May, however, that they spotted their prey, the *HMS Poictiers*, a Vengeur Class 74-gun Royal Navy third rate ship of the line. One of two ships constructed at Upnor, she measured 176 feet long and more than forty-seven feet beam. Most recently, she had been pillaging and burning defenseless settlements all along the shoreline, although the ship's captain, John Poo Beresford, was thought to be a British gentleman while doing so. On March 16, 1813, he had sent the following message the Chief Magistrate of Lewes, Delaware:

> "As soon as you receive this, I request you will send 20 live bullocks with a proportionate quantity of vegetables and hay to the *Poictiers* for the use of Britannic Majesty's squadron now at this anchorage, which will be immediately paid for at the Philadelphia prices. If you refuse to comply with this request I shall be under necessity of destroying your town. I have the honor to be, sir, your very obedient servant, J.P. Beresford Commodore and commander of the British Squadron in the Mouth of the Delaware."[26]

Colonel Samuel Boyer Davis, commander of the American troops in Lewes, refused the demand, and on April 6th and 7th, Beresford shelled the town. A single chicken was killed, and a pig was wounded, in the assault.

Swartwout prepared his torpedoes and was fully prepared to launch an full-scale attack on the imposing *HMS Poictiers*. However, the Governor of Pennsylvania put an abrupt end to the operation, since the British target ship was found to be transporting American prisoners. Needless to say, Robert Fulton was extremely disappointed. On July 28, 1813, Fulton signed a carefully crafted contract with James Welden to attack British blockaders in Long Island Sound. Undoubtedly, Welden would utilize the same "plunging boat" that he and Swartwout had intended to use in the Delaware River against the *HMS Poictiers*. The contract read as follows:

> "Memorandum of an agreement entered into at New York on the twenty eight day of July 1813, Between Robert Fulton of New York of the first part and James Welden also of New York on the second part; the said Fulton hereby agrees to furnish said Welden with a plunging boat, Torpedoes and apparatus for him the said Welden to make an attack on the vessel or vessels of war of the enemys [sic] of the United States in the waters near New London, and should the said Welden succeed to Destroy one or more such vessels, he, his heirs, Executors, Administrators and Assigns shall be entitled to one half of the Reward granted by a Law of Congress dated March third 1813, for destroying vessels of war of enemys [sic] of the United States, and one half such reward shall be for the said Robert Fulton, his heirs, executors, administrators or assigns. And the said Fulton further agrees to supply the said James Welden with the sum not exceeding five dollars a day for two months from this date, at which time the longest term of his cruise of this contract shall cease, but should his cruise end in less than said two months, the said pay of five dollars a day shall cease with the cruise and the said James Welden hereby binds himself to use his utmost exertions to destroy a vessel or vessels of war of the Enemy and to use every prudence to return to said Fulton his boat and all apparatus which shall not be destroyed or lost in an actual attack on the vessels of the enemy and herein contracting parties hereby agree

that this agreement cancels all former agreements between them for the use of torpedoes. Signed, Sealed and Delivered–P. Dubayle (from) Robt. Fulton & James Welden"[27]

It is unknown who "P. Dubayle" was, or what his interest might have been in the submarine agreement. Two days later, on July 30, 1813, an addendum was added to the bottom of the contract, indicating payment by "Robert Fulton (of) two hundred dollars on account of the preceding contract."

The vessel that Welden had contracted to use was a much smaller version of the last submarine conceived by Fulton. She would be dubbed the *Mute*, due to both her highly secretive construction and virtually silent method of attack. When completed, she would measure a full eighty feet long, twenty-two feet wide, and fourteen feet deep. Furthermore, she would be able to transport no less than a battalion of ninety men:

> "He had contrived a vessel which was to have a capacity, by means of an air-chamber like that which was in his '*Nautilus*,' to be kept at a greater or less depth in the water, but so that her deck should not be submerged. That chamber communicated with the water, and was shaped like a diving-bell; but it could at pleasure, by an air-pump, be exhausted of air, and then it would, of course, fill with water; or any requisite quantity of air could be forced into it, so as to expel the water from it entirely. The sides of the vessel were to be of the ordinary thickness, but her deck was to be stout and plated with iron, so as to render it ball-proof, which would not require so much strength as might be at first imagined, because, as no shot could strike it from a vessel but at a very great angle, the ball would ricochet on a slight resistance from a hard substance. She was to be of a size capable of sheltering a hundred men under her deck, and was to be moved by a wheel placed in another air-chamber near the stern, so that when the vessel was to be propelled only a part of the under paddles should be in water; at least, the upper half of the wheel, or more, moving in air. The wheel was to be turned by a crank attached to a shaft, that should penetrate the stern to the air-chamber through a stuffing-box, and run along the middle of the boat until it approaches her bows. Through this shaft rungs were to be passed, of which the crew were to take hold as they were seated upon each side of it on benches. By merely pushing the shaft backward and forward the water-wheel would be turned, and the boat be propelled with a velocity equal to the force of a hundred men. By means of the air-chamber, she was to be kept, when not in hostile action, upon the surface, as common boats are; but when in reach of an enemy she was to sink, so that nothing but her deck would be exposed to his view or to his fire. Her motion when in this situation would be perfectly silent, and therefore he called this contrivance a "mute." His design was that she should approach an enemy, which he supposed she might do in fogs or in the night, without being heard or discovered, and do execution by means of his torpedoes or submarine guns. He presented a model of this vessel to the Government, by which it was approved; and under the

authority of the Executive he commenced building one in this port; but before the hull was entirely finished, his country had to lament his death, and the mechanics he had employed were incapable of proceeding without him."[28]

On December 24, 1813, Robert Fulton invited a group of friends–including prominent merchants, professional men and naval officers–to his home on Chambers Street in New York City. Among those present at the meeting was Major General Henry Dearborn, a leading citizen and soldier who was later to become noted in American political history. As the group listened carefully, Fulton proposed to construct not only the *Mute* submarine, but mobile floating batteries, or heavily built and armed hulks with small sailing rigs.

The first step taken by the group was the founding of the Coast and Harbor Defense Company, with Dearborn as president, Fulton as engineer, and Thomas Morris as secretary. Next, a committee was established to raise funds from Federal, State, and New York City government sources, as well as from individual contributors. The members of this committee consisted of: General Henry Dearborn; Commodore Stephen Decatur; General Morgan Lewis; Commodore Jacob Jones; Noah Brown, shipbuilder; Samuel L. Mitchill; Henry Rutgers; and Thomas Morris. The committee would prove to be somewhat cumbersome, and was later reduced to General Morgan Lewis, Isaac Bronson, Henry Rutgers, Nathan Sanford, Thomas Morris, Oliver Wolcott, and John Jacob Astor. Known as the "Coast Defense Society," they decided to name the prototype vessel *Pyremon*.

The estimated cost to build a battery 130 feet long, with a fifty-foot beam, capable of a speed of five mph, and carrying twenty-four long guns (18-pounder), was $110,000. In an effort to interest the Federal Government, Fulton constructed a model of the proposed vessel and submitted it to some prominent naval officers–Commodore Stephen Decatur, Jacob Jones, James Biddle, Samuel Evans, Oliver Perry, Samuel Warrington, and Jacob Lewis. All gave their support to the Society in a written statement and this recommendation proved helpful to the project in Congress and in the Navy Department.

In the process of presenting a proposed bill to the Senate Naval Affairs Committee, the group requested $250,000 for the construction of the floating battery, and the sum was raised to $1,500,000 for the construction of "one or more" floating batteries. On March 9, 1814, Congress authorized construction of a steam war vessel to be built from Fulton's plans. The Secretary of the Navy William Jones, who supported the project, raised some vital technical concerns regarding the design of the batteries, which Robert Fulton answered with a description of the vessel "as 138 feet on deck, 120 feet on the keel, 55 feet beam (each hull to have a 20-foot beam and the "race" between to be 15 feet wide), draft 8 or 9 feet loaded, and the intended speed was to be 4-1/2 to 5 mph. The ship was to carry twenty-four long guns, the engine was to be 130 hp, and the total cost, $200,000."[29]

In detailed correspondence with the Jones, Fulton stated that Adam and Noah Brown had been chosen to build the hull for $69,800, and that he would design the engine, machinery and boilers for $78,000, a total of $147,800. Fulton intended to have the boilers, valves, fastenings, and air pumps of brass or copper, which would raise the costs for the vessel's machinery fifty-nine percent above that of stationary engines and boilers then in use.

Noah Brown had been born in Salem County in northern New York in 1770, though the family had relocated to New Stamford, New York, when he was just a toddler. In 1780, Noah and his three brothers were captured by Indians, and their father was killed. Regaining their freedom, his mother and her five young children relocated to Darien–then a part of Old Stamford, Connecticut–to live near maternal relatives and close friends.

Noah had begun working as a house carpenter in 1785 at the age of fifteen. In 1792, he went to New York City, where he expanded his wood-working profession as a house joiner. Eventually, in 1804 he began to work in the shipbuilding industry. When the War of 1812 began, he and his brother, Adam, quickly became involved in U.S. Government contracts, building the privateers *Paul Jones*, *General Armstrong*, and *Prince of Neifchatel*. They also converted the ship *China* into the privateer *Yorktown*.

In January of 1813, the Browns went to work with Daniel Dobbins on warships being constructed on Lake Erie. Under the supervision of Master Commandant Oliver Hazard Perry, they had completed a number of vessels in just six months time, including the brigs *Lawrence* and *Niagara*, as well as the schooners *Porcupine*, *Scorpion*, *Tigress*, and *Ariel*. Noah Brown later recalled his days working near Lake Erie:

> "All the above vessels were built by me, and furnished with all materials, and we did not receive any funds from the Government till March 1814, when Commodore Chauncey came to New York and signed our bills."[30]

These vessels would represent the bulk of Perry's squadron in the memorable Battle of Lake Erie, which began on September 10, 1813. The Brown brothers would later return to New York City in early June of 1814, to begin the work on Fulton's steam battery, as well as his most recent plunging boat. Noah mentioned this work briefly in his later writings:

> "We built a vessel called the *Mute* for Robert Fulton, Esq. She was bomb-proof and was to be propelled by machinery under water. We received no compensation for our services, nor yard rent for her..."[31]

Meanwhile, construction of the Fulton steam battery had begun on June 20, 1814, at the yard of Adam and Noah Brown. Progress was measured at a snail's pace, due in large part to a shortage of materials resulting from the blockade and the demand for such material for other shipbuilding at New York. On

November 21, the ship was towed from the Browns' yard on the East River by Fulton's *Car of Neptune* and *Fulton*, each lashed to the sides of the battery, and taken to Fulton's works along the North River. There, Robert Fulton supervised the completion of the vessel and construction of her machinery. Undoubtedly only a little of his time was required in inspection of the Browns' work on the battery, for the two shipbuilders had been closely associated with Fulton throughout the life of the project and were fully capable as ship designers.

The work on the vessel's machinery was another matter, however, for men capable of working metal were scarce, and few workmen could read Fulton's plans accurately. The inventor, therefore, had some of the work done outside of his own plant, particularly the brass and copper work–mostly by John Youle's foundry. As a result, Fulton was required to move from plant to plant almost on a daily basis, keeping each job under constant scrutiny while he personally supervised the workmen. The equipment then available for building such a massive engine was inadequate. In particular, the large steam cylinder presented the largest problem: it had to be recast several times.

The ship was fitted with furnaces, and some of her guns were to be discharged below the water-line. The estimated cost had grown to an enormous $320,000. Yet, her construction was authorized by Congress in March of 1814. In May the vessel was ready for her engine, and the keel was laid on June 20. The following month, she conducted a trial-trip to the ocean at Sandy Hook and back, fifty-three miles round-trip, in eight hours and twenty minutes. In September, with her armament and stores on board, the same route was traversed, with Fulton's vessel hitting an average speed of 5.5 miles per hour. Her engine, having a steam-cylinder measuring forty-eight inches in diameter and of five feet stroke of piston, was furnished with steam by a copper boiler twenty-two feet long, a dozen feet wide, and eight feet high. She turned a wheel, between the two halls, sixteen feet in diameter, with "buckets" fourteen feet long, and a dip of four feet. The sides were four feet, ten inches thick, and her spar-deck was surrounded by musket-proof bulwarks. The armament consisted of thirty 32-pounders, intended to discharge red-hot shot. There was one mast for each hull, fitted with lateen sails. Large pumps were installed, intended to throw streams of water on the decks of the enemy, with a hope of disabling it by wetting its ordnance and ammunition. A submarine gun was to have been carried at each bow, to discharge shot weighing 100 pounds, at a depth of ten feet below water.

The vessel, then known as the *Demologos*, was officially launched on October 29, 1814. She was the first steam warship in the world, and had been constructed with a thick, double hull. She measured 156 feet in length, fifty-six feet across, and twenty feet deep. The paddle wheel, which had been designed to be sixteen feet in diameter, would be driven by a steam engine with a cylinder forth-eight inches in diameter and had five feet stroke. The sides of the vessel were strengthened by massive, heavy timbers, until a thickness of five feet had been reached. When completed, she would boast twenty 32-pounder guns on the gun deck.

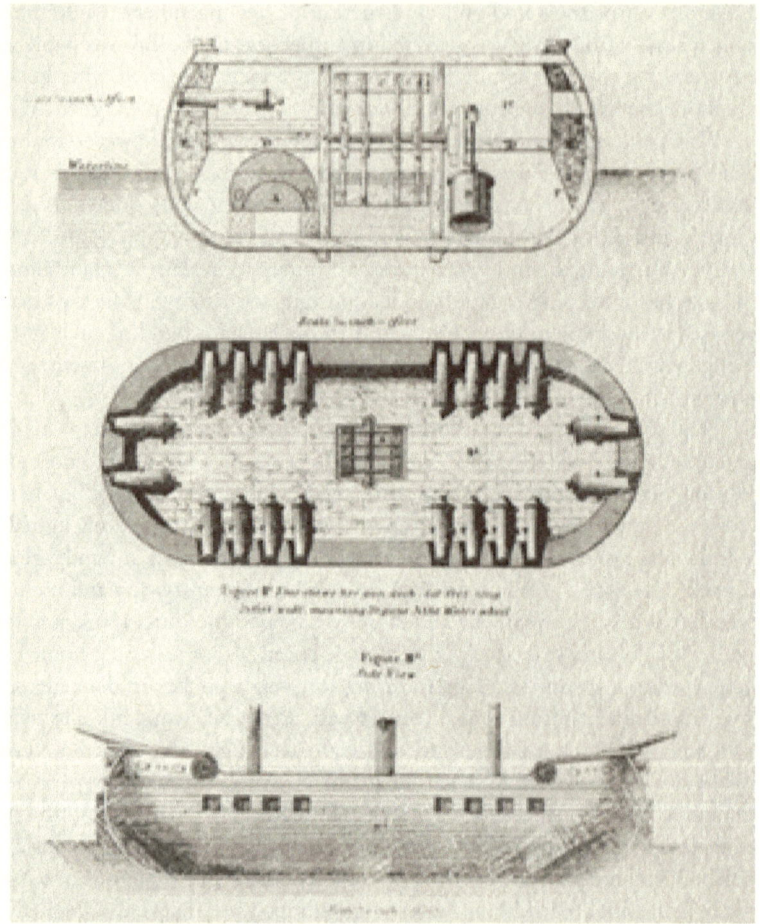

Patent sketches of the *Demologos*

Robert Fulton's design solved several of the problems inherent in warships powered by paddle-wheels, which led to the adoption of the paddle steamer as an effective warship in following decades. By placing the paddlewheel centrally, sandwiched between two hulls, Fulton protected it from gunfire; this design also allowed the ship to mount a full broadside of guns. Her steam engine offered the prospect of tactical advantage against sail-powered warships. In a calm, sailing ships depended on the manpower of their crews to tow the ship from the boats, or to kedge with anchors. *Mute*, with steam, might have found it easy to outmaneuver a ship-of-the-line in calm weather.

Alas, however, Fulton, who was present at the launching of the vessel, would not live to see her in service. He had been to Trenton, New Jersey, to attend a hearing on the steamboat monopoly and, on the way back, the ferry on the North River was caught in the ice. He was attempting to walk across the frozen river when his attorney, Addis Emmet, had fallen through and, in the attempt to rescue him, Fulton had gotten soaked. Indeed, it would be his devotion to the work of the *Demologos'* construction that would lead him to spend many hours on her deck in the cold of winter, while he continued to be troubled with a heavy cold. The cold soon turned to pneumonia, which caused his death on February 23, 1815, at his home in what is now called Battery Place.

Robert Fulton's death resulted in the stoppage of work entirely on the submarine *Mute*, the 80-foot, manually propelled, torpedo boat that Fulton was then having built in the Browns' yard. Conflicting reports indicated that work also ended abruptly on his revolutionary means of underwater vessel, *Demologos*. Others reported that it had slowed dramatically with the success of the *North River Steamboat*. Those close to Fulton, however, knew better, making certain that work on his experimental steam ship continued even after his death.

The *Demologos* was renamed the *Fulton* after his death. Charles Stoudinger, Fulton's foreman or superintendent, was able to complete and install the ship's machinery. On June 10, 1815, the vessel was given a short trial run in the harbor with Stoudinger and the Navy inspector, Captain Smith, on board. This trial revealed the need of some mechanical alterations; sails were not used, and it was found she could stem the strong tide and a fresh headwind.

On July 4, 1815, she was given a second trial. She left Fulton's yard at Corlear's Hook at nine in the morning, ran out to Sandy Hook Lighthouse, bore west and returned home. She had traveled a total of fifty-three miles under steam, reaching her slip at 5:20 in the late afternoon. She was found to steer "like a pilot boat." This prolonged trial run revealed that the stokehold was not sufficiently ventilated, and more deck openings were needed. The windsails used in existing hatches were also inadequate. The paddle wheel was positioned too low and had to be raised eighteen inches, and there were still some desirable modifications to be made in the machinery.

Following one last sea trial the *Fulton* (alias *Demologos*) was handed over to the U.S. Navy in June of 1816, and delivered to Captain Samuel Evans, commandant of the New York Navy Yard. The final settlement showed that the Committee, as Navy agents, had paid out $286,162.12 with $872.00 unpaid, as well as a claim for $3,364.00 by Adam and Noah Brown, making a total of $290,398.12. Her one and only day of active duty occurred on June 18, 1817, when she transported President James Earl Monroe on a tour of New York Harbor. A two-masted lateen rig was added by the orders of her first commander, Captain David Porter. With the name *Fulton*, she appeared in the navy list of ships for a number of years, doing duty as the receiving-ship at the Brooklyn Navy Yard. In 1821 her armament and machinery were removed. On June 4,

1829, her magazine accidentally exploded when a sixty-year-old seaman entered her magazine to get powder for the evening gun:

> "Yesterday afternoon, about half past 2 o'clock, the Magazine of the steam frigate *Fulton the First*, which was lying on the flats about a cable's length from the Navy Yard dock, exploded and dreadful to relate, killed and maimed nearly all on board, estimated from 70 to a hundred. At half past 5 in the afternoon, 25 dead bodies had been brought on shore, and 25 to 30 of the wounded, many of whom are shockingly mangled. Others were yet missing. Among the dead were two women, wives or relatives of the marines and seamen. The magazine was directly under the sick bay and all the invalids there confined, supposed about 15 in number were killed. The officers on board were Lieut. Breckenridge, who was so badly wounded that it was feared he could not survive many hours. His lady, who was on board at the time, was slightly wounded. The accident is supposed to have occurred in consequence of the ignorance of a person named Williams who was employed yesterday to act as gunner, who it is said, went into the magazine with a light, mistaking the place for another apartment. There was but a small quantity of powder in the magazine, caused no greater concussion than the firing of a 44 pounder; yet the three masts of the frigate were blown into the air to the height of 40 to 50 feet, both decks forward of the main mast blown up, the starboard side shattered to pieces and the ship rendered a complete wreck."[32]

Much of Robert Fulton's submarine story would remain unknown for decades. Between the years 1797 and 1804, he had worked in France and England developing a system of submersible warfare. Fulton foresaw the complete freedom of the seas from naval blockade for the free trade of nations and set about a way to obtain this through the use of submarine vessels. He had lived with, Joel Barlow, the American ambassador to France those same seven years; initially to expand on his work of as designer of canals, which he had spent the past four years designing in England. Using Barlow's connection to Napoleon, Fulton had soon found himself designing his *Nautilus*, a boat that was able to plunge beneath the water and fasten a torpedo to an enemy ship's hull.

Although he had successfully demonstrated the destructive power of his *Nautilus* on two distinct ocassions, and had the support of Napoleon's scientific-consultants, Napoleon ultimately decided Fulton was a charlatan and extortionist due to his lack of formal scientific education and unwillingness to disclose drawings of his boats mechanisms.

Harriet Fulton had given birth to her third and fourth children, Cornelie and Mary, in August of 1812 and July of 1813, resprctively. When her husband died, she found herself left to sort out his affairs. She had $9,000 per year left to her from his will–which would be reduced to $3,000 per year if she remarried– and additional money for child support. She and Ruth Barlow, the "darling of her husband's affections," quarreled over payment for the many articles he had asked for from France. Both women accused the other of attempting to sell the materials for profit.

Less than two years after Robert's death, Harriet married an "avaricious English charmer" named Charles Dale. They purchased the Teviotdale estate from her brother, John, and set up housekeeping. But, in 1820, they morgaged the property and traveled to England. They did not take her four children with them, but instead left them with a widowed sister-in-law in nearby Claverack.

Harriet and Charles Dale eventually returned in 1825, and Harriet died the following year. Her teenage children were left as orphans. Her husband, Dale, did very little to care for them, and the only son, Barlow, was left to fight for every penny to care for his younger sisters. "Money have they none," he wrote, "even to buy garments, & what I can save from my small sallary is by no means sufficient for even one of them."

Dale's final act of cruelty was to take everything of value from Teviotdale and order the servants to burn the rest. All the Fulton children managed to save from their parents was their mother's harp, a few of her paintings and portraits, and some personal affects. Eventually, a governement settlement and improved employment would provide enough money from Barlow Fulton for his three siblings, though he would die a batchelor at the age of 32. Thus, no living decendants of Robert Fulton would share the Fulton surname.

Sadly, what became of his family and the eventual explosion of the ship, *Fulton*, was not the legacy that Robert Fulton had hoped for, or dreamed of, throughout his entire life. In reality–and perhaps quite ironically–it was the use of explosives that he had promoted as a means of keeping American naval vessels safe from harm's way.

Perhaps, of all the things that have been written about Robert Fulton's life, Cadwallader B. Colden summed him up most eloquently:

> "Fulton was about six feet high. His person was slender, but well proportioned and well formed. Nature had made him a gentleman and bestowed upon him ease and gracefulness. He had too much good sense for the least affectation. A modest confidence in his own worth and talents gave him an unembarrassed deportment in all companies. His features were strong and of manly beauty. He had large dark eyes, and a projecting brow expressive of intelligence and thought. His temper was mild, his disposition lively. He was fond of society, which he always enlivened by cheerful, cordial manners, and instructed or pleased by his sensible conversation. He expressed himself with energy, fluency, and correctness, and, as he owed more to his own experience and reflections than to books, his sentiments were often interesting from their originality."[33]

Sketch of Cornelius P. Berrien

Sketch of Richard P. Berrien

-10-
Cornelius P. Berrien and Richard Berrien: *Turtle*

"Local history is fleeting and evanescent. Events of one day, even considered of supreme importance at the time, are forgotten the next day, and soon drop into oblivion. Any effort to recall them, after years have passed, entails tireless and exhaustive research amongst the files of musty, old newspapers, private memoranda, public records, and, best of all; the interviewing and arousing the recollections of elderly persons...for their memories are usually very retentive and are seldom found inaccurate."[1]

Following the American Revolution, Alexander Hamilton became the first Secretary of the Treasury and, on April 22, 1790, he submitted a request to Congress asking for permission to build a fleet of sea-going vessels to enforce tariffs and trade legislation. On August 4 of that same year, Congress approved Hamilton's request for these revenue enforcement vessels and, because this new federal maritime fleet had no official name, merchant seamen and lawmakers simply referred to them as "revenue cutters."

Perhaps believing coastline defense was unnecessary and unwarranted, the fledgling federal government had disbanded the Continental Navy in 1785 without allowing for a new navy under the Constitution. Therefore, cutters would become the only federal vessels keeping America safe from coastal invasion and protecting maritime interests of the new nation. Furthermore, for the next fifteen to twenty years, cutters would be the primary defense against attempts to circumvent customs duties on imports, which was the new nation's only source of income besides the sale of public lands.

The various peacetime tasks specifically assigned to the cutters included boarding incoming and outgoing ships and checking their papers; sealing cargo holds of incoming vessels; and seizing those vessels in violation of the law. In addition, cutters would deter smugglers who often tried to unload their cargoes directly on shore out of sight of major ports, as well as punish those who loaded their goods on smaller "coasters" outside the watchful eyes of busy harbors. The cutters interdicted this illegal trade by sailing out of homeports and catching tax evaders in the act as they attempted to bypass federal law.

The coastal region being policed by the cutters was expansive. Long Island alone had a length of 120 miles, with nearly 280 miles of coastline indented with numerous bays and inlets. The entire island varied in width from twelve to twenty-three miles. The level seacoast of the south shore, with its extended views of bay and the broad ocean, contrasted sharply with the hilly north shore and its deep indentations. Residents were spread out across its 1,682 square miles, which also included the outer islands of Coney, Riker's, Berrien, South Brother, Fire, Barren, Shelter, Gardiner, Fisher, and Plum. There were, in essence, literally thousands of nooks and crannies that could hide a smuggler's illicit cargo.

During the decade prior to the War of 1812, British blockaders began to take control of and expand the job of American cutters. Often, they not only detained, confiscated, and destroyed large ships attempting to off-load supplies into American coastal communities, but they attempted to stop coasters from operating. One New Yorker who owned a small shipping operation was Captain Cornelius Penfold Berrien, of Long Island, whose small vessel was illegally seized by Commodore Thomas Hardy's blockading squadron in June of 1813:

> "A capt. Berrian, whose vessel was captured by the British squadron off New London, on remonstrating with capt. Hardy on the small value of his vessel, was told that his [Hardy's] orders were to distress the enemy; 'and that he was determined to punish the coasters, and learn them to vote differently, and turn out the present administration.' This is warm electioneering. They [British], however, permitted capt. B. to ransom his vessel for $500."[2]

How very generous of the British, must have been the sarcastic thought of Captain Berrien. A native son of Newtown Village, New York, he could ill-afford what he considered a steep and unplanned expense to his major source of income. He openly promised, in fact, that he would find a way to retaliate against the "British bastards."

Captain Berrien's homeport of Newtown had been settled by the Dutch in 1652. Initially named Middleburgh, it was situated a short distance from New Amsterdam in New Netherland (Nieuw Nederland). The original Europeans who arrived there were, by and large, from the nearby colony of "Maspat," who had been forced to leave because of ongoing threats and attacks by local Indians. When the British took over New Netherland a dozen years later, in 1664, they renamed Middleburgh as New Town (Nieuwe Stad) Village in order to maintain the Dutch heritage. This would later be simplified to Newtown.

Among the earliest settlers to the region was Cornelius Jansen Berrien, on whose land chance seedlings would produce the "Newtown Pippin," destined to become Colonial America's most famous apple. He was the great-great-grandfather of one of America's least remembered submariners, Cornelius Penfold Berrien. Records indicate that the Berrien family was of French origin, having migrated from their family seat in the Brittany region of Finistère (literally "end of the earth"), France. Historians within this extensive family agree "their ancestor was a Huguenot who, during the civil wars of France, was forced to flee and took refuge in Holland."[3]

Cornelius Jansen, as it appears on the earliest documentation, was born in Ruinen, Drenthe, Netherlands, in about 1638. He was the first to carry the family name to America, arriving in Midwout (Flatbush), Long Island, New York, in 1669, at the age of thirty-one. Settling there with his wife, Jannetje Stryker Berrien and his one-year-old son, John, he would prove to be not only a devoted family man, but a gentleman of sound character, education, and trust. Over the next two decades, the Berriens would give birth to two more sons and two daughters, and be appointed to a number of township offices, even serving for a time as the Deacon of the local Dutch church. In 1683, records further indicate that, by decision of the Colonial Assembly, he served as one member of a committee brought together to consider and levy a special tax within the colony.

Two years later, in 1685, Cornelius Jansen relocated his growing family to Newtown Village, Long Island. In collaboration with his brother-in-law, Abraham Brinckerhoff, he purchased more than four hundred acres of land nestled at the head of Flushing Bay, which they divided nearly in half. In 1688, Cornelius Jansen died unexpectedly at the age of fifty, leaving his family without means of support or survival. At the time that his widow opted to become Samuel Edsall's fourth wife, Cornelius Jansen's five children–John, Pieter, Nicholas, Catherine, and Agnes–ranged in age from twelve to nineteen. Apparently, it was a financial burden that Samuel Edsall was willing to accept.

Cornelius Jansen Berrien's second eldest son, Pieter, who had been born in 1672 in Flatbush, Long Island, would marry his new stepfather's daughter, Elizabeth Edsall, on August 10, 1706. Together, they would give birth to nine more Berrien children, the oldest of which they proudly named Cornelius after Pieter's father. A "surveyor by profession," Pieter was destined to become one of the region's largest and most prosperous landowners, and would be remembered for his generous donation of the property upon which the First Dutch Church of Newtown Village was constructed. The townsfolk would be shocked and saddened, however, when "he died very suddenly while riding from Newtown to his home, April 5, 1737."[4]

Ten years prior to his father's death, in 1727, twenty-year-old Cornelius –the enterprising grandson of pilgrim Cornelius Jansen–had taken his father's advice and had purchased a twelve-acre parcel of land from neighbor Timothy Wood. Surrounded on all sides by New York's East River, it had long been "commonly called the Round Island," later to be renamed Berrien's Island. Berrien Lane, pointing like an arrow toward the western edge of Berrien Island, ran along the shoreline and fronted the expansive Berrien farmhouse, built by Cornelius and Amy Scudder Berrien in the same year that they had acquired the island. At the south end of the lane stood a small schoolhouse, constructed by the Berriens in 1735. It was here, amid pitch pine, scarlet oak, Tupelo, and apple trees, that this third generation of Berriens would raise and educate their three sons and four daughters, each of whom would develop a love affair with the sea. Over time, the family estate would grow to more than four hundred acres.

Berrien family farmhouse

    The fourth generation of American Berriens would continue to become deeply entrenched and dependent upon the coastal merchant trade. The eldest, Cornelius Berrien II, married Elizabeth Penfold in 1765, and grew up to become a ship captain involved with importing goods from Europe, the West Indies, and the Spanish Main. During what historically would become known as the French and Indian War, he was commissioned as first lieutenant aboard the privateer *Tartar*, whose job it was to capture and confiscate the cargo of enemy vessels. And, after the conflict had ended, Cornelius II would engage in the import of goods, owning and commanding a number of his own vessels.

    Like all Long Island natives, Cornelius II fully understood the dangers of the open seas, but was not completely prepared to deal with confrontation and tragedy inflicted by British soldiers in his hometown of Newtown Village. On May 20, 1766, news reached the Berrien family, along with others in the community, of the repeal of the Stamp Act. On the following day, township residents gathered in celebration in an area known as the Fields. A few weeks later, to show their loyalty and gratitude to the king, they assembled once again on his birthday, June 4, and celebrated the memorable event with feasting and hard drinking. A great pole with twelve tar barrels at its top was erected, and twenty-five cords of wood were placed at its base. Then, while a salute of twenty-five guns was fired in another part of the Fields, the great bonfire was kindled and the royal standard raised amid the "boisterous cheers of the crowd." Another pole was raised on this memorable day, bearing the inscription, "The King, Pitt, and Liberty." It was intended to stand proudly as the first "liberty-pole," serving as the rallying point of the citizens for several years to come; the visible sign of the principle of "no taxation without representation."

This liberty-pole was being erected not far from the barracks of the British soldiers, on the north side of Chambers Street. On the tenth of August, a party belonging to the 28th Regiment cut the pole down. The next day, while citizens were assembled on the Commons preparing to erect yet another, they were attacked by the soldiers, and several of the Sons of Liberty were severely injured. Among them was John Berrien, Cornelius II's younger brother, who would have a noticeable limp for the remainder of his life.

Written complaints were lodged by the Berrien family and the citizens of Newtown Village, though British officials declared that the affidavits submitted were false. As anger grew, British officers refused to reprimand or punish the accused offenders. It was the one major incident that the Berrien family would never forget or forgive.

In 1777, Cornelius II dispatched three ships to the West Indies, under the watchful "command of his brother, Peter, his brother-in-law, John Penfold, and Captain Richardson."[5] While securing a shipment of mules along the Spanish Main, and preparing to return home for the winter, they were unexpectedly attacked by natives. All three captains were killed, and only two crew members survived to share the details of their ordeal. It was the first of many confrontations at sea that would demand revenge by an angry Berrien family of seamen.

Following the Spanish Main attack, Captain Cornelius Berrien II gave up his life at sea and retired to the peaceful Penfold farm near Hellgate. Over the course of the next quarter-century, he would dabble in the practices of raising crops and animal husbandry, never forgetting or forgiving the mistreatment and "savagery of foreigners." As time passed, his two eldest twin sons, Cornelius III and Richard, would inherit their father's seafaring ways and tenacious hatred of those who had gotten in his way.

The twins, who had been born on October 5, 1779, grew up in a hard-working family along with their six younger siblings, though much of their pre-adult years were spent amid increasing population chaos. In fact, Long Island Sound itself was a main travel corridor, linking people from Boston to New York, as well as the rest of New England. Eventually, a single rudimentary trail, known as the "Ferry Road," sprang up, allowing merchant vessels to unload and haul their goods inland. In actuality, the trail had originated as a means of connecting various groups of Native Americans to one another before the arrival of Europeans. Eventually, as white settlers continued to arrive by the thousands, it was widened into a wagon route and renamed the King's Highway:

> "The latter was built along the two lines of the Ferry Road, one leading to Jamaica; and the other to Flatbush and Flatlands. There were also a number of branch-roads established, which all were included under the appellation of the Kings Highway. These were: Red Hook Lane, leading

to the Red Hook; Gowanus Lane, running along the line of present Fifth Avenue to Gowanus Cove; the Big Lane, or Church Lane, running from the Flatlbush branch to Flatlands Neck; the Little Lane, or Lott's Lane, running from the Flatbush branch to Canarsie; the Clove Road, leading from Bedford Corners to the salt meadows and to Flatbush Village; the Cripplebush Lane, running from Bedford Corners to the Cripplebush settlement; the Old Bushwick Road, running from the Jamaica branch to the Bushwick Road."[6]

As early as 1788, though there were only six carriage-shops to be found in the entire city of New York, a coach-makers' society was organized, loosely based on the plan of one in London, England. This society would take a prominent role in the rather showy pageant organized in honor of the adoption by the States of the Federal Constitution on July 23 of that same year:

> "The coach-makers, in company with the harness-makers, had a stage drawn by ten horses at the head of their division, accompanied by three postilions, dressed in yellow, with jockey caps and trimmings of the same color. Four workmen were on the stage, busily at work. A flag was stretched across the stage, representing a shop with open doors, in which besides was seen (in paint) a finished coach, with other hands at the workbench. At the door a vessel was represented as laying at the wharf, taking on board carriages for exportation; over the shop the Union flag; over the ship the nine Federal members from this country; in the center, the coach and coach-harness makers' arms; on a blue field three open coaches, supported by Liberty on one side, holding in her left hand the cap of Liberty; on the other side by Peace, holding in her right hand the horn of plenty; Fame blowing her trumpet over their heads; motto, 'The Federal Star shall guide our Car.' A green monument supported by ten pillars, with a Union in the center; crest on the top of the arms, and an eagle soaring from a globe. In addition to the above, the saddlers, harness and whip makers carried in a separate department an emblematic figure of their profession, — a horse decked out with an elegant saddle and harness, with embroidered tassel, led by a groom dressed in character...with a long retinue of bosses and journeymen bringing up the rear."[7]

Apparently, Cornelius and Richard took note of the increasingly busy roadways throughout Long Island and beyond. In fact, by the time the twins had reached adulthood, they had decided that there was a good deal of money to be made in the manufacture and selling of wagons and stagecoaches. They had reached this conclusion by suffering the immense cost in traveling between Long Island and Washington, D.C., by way of Philadelphia and Baltimore:

> "Stage fare from New York to Philadelphia, $5; expenses on the road to Philadelphia, $3.75; expenses in Philadelphia, $7.25...Stage fare from Philadelphia to Baltimore, $8; expenses on the road to Baltimore,–expenses at Baltimore, $4.12...Stage fare from Baltimore to Washington, $3.50; expenses on the road to Washington, $2.25; or $33.87 [total]..."[8]

From experience, young Cornelius and Richard understood that making a journey of just fifty miles–let alone the 225 between their home and Washington, D.C.–was no easy journey. In fact, vehicles for private conveyance were few and far between during the first decade of the 1800s, and it was quite rare for families to even come across a "cheer," as they were referred to, which might be available to purchase. Not only that, but Cornelius and Richard also realized that such carriages were somewhat uncomfortable for lengthy journeys:

> "They were all hung upon springs made of wood generally, with rude bow or standing-tops of round iron, hung around with painted cloth curtains. The linings and cushions, stuffed with 'swingling tow,' sometimes salt hay, were in those primitive times of simplicity and innocence deemed good enough for any American sovereign, and very fortunate was he who could get even a short ride in one…"[9]

By the time that Cornelius Penfold and Richard Penfold Berrien were twenty years old, they had ventured into the coach manufacturing business with two other brothers, Arthur and George Cullum, neighbors and friends from the Newtown Village area. Locating their partnership at 23 Chambers Street in Manhattan, the business was aptly named "Berrian and Cullum, Coachmakers." Brother George Cullum also manufactured and sold horse harnesses.

At the beginning of the 19th century, the Bowery Bay Ward of New York–where the Berrien brothers had been raised–included Berrien and Riker's islands, and was little more than a cluster of taverns, livery stables, and stores. People visiting any part of Long Island were brought to this point by the boats from New York City. They found good horses in the stables if they desired to make the journey on horseback. Stagecoaches, constructed by Berrien and Cullum, as well as other makers, leaving for any point to the island interior started from here. Coaches could be hired for private use and, before the start of any journey, "a good meal could be had at a reasonable price." A dry goods store, hardware store, stationery and bookstore were just a few of the small shops already here; this was the shopping center for the majority of Newtown, Long Island, residents and visitors.

Meanwhile, across the river, life was much different in the area of the city where Cornelius and his brother Richard had located their business. There, along Chambers Street, the firm was centrally located amid the "Bloody Sixth" Ward in lower Manhattan. The busy urban sprawl resembled a small triangle outlined by the famous Five Points, and its boundaries were Broadway on the west, Canal and Walker streets on the north, and Chatham Street and Chatham Square along the east and south.

In 1805, the first brigade of artillery was organized in New York City, and it consisted of the Regiment of Artillery, with Lieutenant-Colonel Peter T. Curtenius designated as commanding officer of the First Regiment. Both Cornelius and Richard Berrien would serve as soldiers in this unit from its inception through 1809. The following year, census records from 1810 indicate that each of the brothers had relocated their homes to Ward Six. Though their personal socio-economic situation continued to be prosperous, the majority of people who lived there were not so fortunate:

> "I suppose there are and have been worse conditions of life, but if I stopped short of savage life I found it hard to imagine them. I did not exaggerate to myself the squalor that I saw, and I do not exaggerate it to the reader. As I have said, I was so far from sentimentalizing it that I almost immediately reconciled myself to it, as far as its victims were concerned. Still, it was squalor of a kind which, it seemed to me, it could not be possible to outrival anywhere in the life one commonly calls civilized. It is true that the Indians who formerly inhabited this island were no more comfortably lodged in their wigwams of bark and skins than these poor New-Yorkers in their tenements. But the wild men pay no rent, and if they are crowded together upon terms that equally forbid decency and comfort in their shelter, they have the freedom of the forest and the prairie about them; they have the illimitable sky and the whole light of day and the four winds to breathe when they issue into the open air. The New York tenement dwellers, even when they leave their lairs, are still pent in their high-walled streets and inhale a thousand stenches of their own and others' making. The street, except in snow and rain, is always better than their horrible houses, and it is doubtless because they pass so much of their time in the street that the death rate is so low among them. Perhaps their domiciles can be best likened for darkness and discomfort to the dugouts or sod huts of the settlers on the great plains. But these are only temporary shelters, while the tenement dwellers have no hope of better housing; they have neither the prospect of a happier fortune through their own energy as the settlers have, nor any chance from the humane efforts and teachings of missionaries, like the savages. With the tenement dwellers it is from generation to generation, if not for the individual, then for the class, since no one expects that there will not always be tenement dwellers in New York as long as our present economical conditions endure."[10]

In the winter of 1797, at the age of eighteen, brother Richard had married Elizabeth Vanderbeek, daughter of Solomon and Geesje Terhune Vanderbeek, whose family had long lived in the township of New Barbadoes, New Jersey. During the next twelve years, they would have five children–three sons and two daughters. In 1806, Richard's twin brother, Cornelius, married Elizabeth Bruen Morris, the only known daughter of John and Sarah Bruen Morris. Over the course of the next two decades, they would give birth to four daughters and four sons. As their respective families grew, Cornelius and Richard also expanded their business interests to include land speculation, often for rather large profit:

> "On City Island, West Chester County, and possession given the first of May next–Several rights of land, with two Dwelling Houses–One 35 feet

in front, 31 feet deep, two stories high, four rooms on the lower floor, two on the upper floor, besides a kitchen and milk room. One, two rooms on the lower floor and a kitchen. Both houses have got good cellars, and the smallest a piazza in front. Part of the land is well cultivated and is fence [sic]; the remainder is well worth improvement. Besides the orchard of good bearing trees, there is on the land a considerable number of others, such as pear, peach and cherry trees, an excellent well of water, and the prospect from either house is delightful, and convenient for a gentleman, farmer, merchant or inn keeper–there is 4 acres of land which produced a plentiful crop this last harvest, owen [sic] again with wheat and rye; the situation is so well shown and frequented, that any further description would be needless, only it may be recommended for a safe and agreeable retreat during the hot months. The terms will be made known by applying to Mr. Richard Berrien at his house in New York, corner of First and Eagle streets, or to that subscriber on the island by whom an indisputable title will be given."[11]

The Common Council of New York City, a body assembled to oversee various projects that might impact its citizens, met on March 8, 1813, to consider a number of proposals, petitions, applications, and recommendations. On the agenda was a memorial written by Richard P. Berrien, which stated that:

"...he (Berrien) had invented a shell which would be directed in a straight line and would lodge after entering the side if a vessel, which he deemed would be very useful in Harbour defence and requesting the Corporation to appropriate a sum for making castings for the purpose of experiments."[12]

The matter was handed over to the Committee of Defence, which would be in charge of overseeing such experiments. Later that year, on May 31, Alderman Nicholas Fish would present accounts of "experiments made by order of the Board on a bomb shell invented by R. Berrian [sic] which were referred to the Comptroller" for payment. For his "experiments in gunnery," Richard was compensated in the amount of $154.75.

To further their financial stability, the brothers devised an ingenious plan; why not purchase one or two small coasters that could haul their merchandize quickly up the eastern end of Long Island and southern coast of Connecticut. Furthermore, they believed that it would be no problem to sneak their wares past blockading British vessels. They were wrong and, as records have indicated, Cornelius was forced to ransom one of his coasters for the seemingly exorbitant fee of $500. Furthermore, their entire cargo of coaches had been stolen by the "British thieves."

Returning to Long Island empty-handed and deeply in debt, the brothers grew increasingly agitated and defiant at the British blockaders, and soon became convinced that drastic action must be taken. John Lawrence Riker, a long-time friend of the Berriens, who had earlier worked with Silas Plowden Halsey in constructing a torpedo explosive, suggested a retaliatory strike using a submersible that could deliver an explosive directly to the hull of an enemy ship. Cornelius Berrien successfully used his influence and reputation to approach the city of New York for assistance in financing the venture:

> "The Common Council...made an appropriation of several hundred dollars to one Berrian, of New York City, to construct a torpedo boat for the purpose of destroying some of the enemy's war vessels in Long Island Sound."[13]

There is no historical record of the Berrien brothers having the means or know-how to design and construct a complex submersible vessel during the War of 1812, let alone a sturdy enough submarine that would be capable of traversing the ninety miles they were later known to travel from Newtown Village to the eastern end of Long Island. Since the mid-1600s, the island's shoals, sandbars and assorted submerged hazards had caused many an unskilled vessel to shipwreck, and this particular journey would require a minimum of twenty-five to thirty hours in the best of conditions. Not only would the brothers need to avoid all of the pitfalls, but there would be literally dozens of British ships on the lookout for any vessel that appeared out of the ordinary. Indeed, to captain such a vessel would take more than one set of eyes from a group of experienced seamen, each of whom had traveled this treacherous coastline on a number of occasions. Undoubtedly, the Berriens were forced to turn to one man for advice and guidance, who would have both the expertise about submarines to plan such a difficult mission and the connections among coastal shipmasters to assemble such an able-bodied crew to be successful. That man was Robert Fulton.

On July 28, 1813, a contractual agreement had been signed between Fulton and James Welden, a close friend and experienced seaman. As indicated earlier, Welden had been referred to in correspondence by Commodore Stephen Decatur, and the submersible that had been agreed upon for use was a prototype version of a vessel known as the *Mute*, later constructed by shipbuilders, Noah and Adam Brown. This much smaller version, able to transport up to a dozen men, was received by Welden in early July of 1813. Records indicate that Welden was already very familiar with her operation, having shared the helm beginning in late March and continuing at least through the second week of May, 1813.

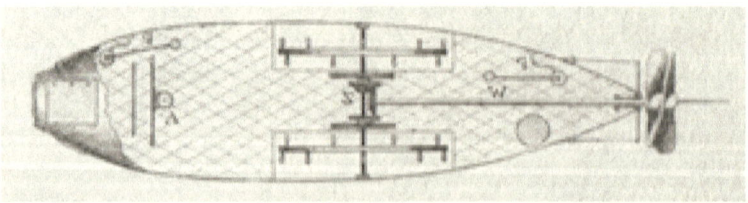

Sketch of the *Turtle* prototype

On August 24, the low-slung torpedo boat was spotted by British barges as she floated down through Long Island Sound from Newtown Village, New York. A message from New London, dispatched on September 1, 1813, stated that "the torpedo from New York was chased on Tuesday of the week previous, nine miles by several British boats, but by frequently diving escaped." This was her first appearance with Cornelius Penfold Berrien sharing control of a diving vessel known as the *Turtle*, the Fulton-designed vessel that could earn him many times the value of his ransomed coaster if he could manage to help sink Commodore Thomas Hardy's flagship, the *HMS Ramillies*, or any other blockader then in Long Island Sound.

The season was getting late and the waters around Long Island much more difficult to navigate, and it was reluctantly decided that an attack would now have to be postponed until spring of 1814. Though the initial mission had not been successful, John L. Riker suggested a few more seasoned volunteers who would be more than willing to risk their lives in order to assist in a breaking up the blockade. One was a man named Jeremiah Holmes, then residing in Mystic, Connecticut, who shared a deep-seated grudge and long-standing resentment toward the British fleet clogging up the Sound.

Holmes had been born in North Stonington in 1782, and had spent the better part of his youth being raised by relatives in Norwich, New York. He had gone to sea at the age of seventeen in 1800, and was imprisoned when the ship he was on traded illegally on the coast of Brazil. After returning home by way of Lisbon, he had sailed on a whaling voyage to the west coast of South America, where he joined a British whaler. A French privateer captured the whaler and, in July 1804, Holmes ended up on the island of St. Helena and was impressed aboard the *HMS Trident*. After three years of being held prisoner on the *HMS Saturn* and several other British warships, where he learned to handle cannons, he had escaped. Returning to America, he had settled in Mystic, Connecticut, married Ann Denison, and continued as a mariner until the war had been declared. In early 1813, Holmes had served on the Mystic privateer *Hero*, used his Royal Navy artillery training to man the guns defending Mystic, and served as lieutenant in the private armed boat *True Blooded Yankee*. Then, early in 1814, Holmes had taken command of a sixteen-oar boat owned by John Mott and Richard S. Williams of New York City, which he named *Young Hornet*.

Once again, John Lawrence Riker would provide the torpedo that armed the *Young Hornet*. For this mission, Riker's explosive design was a thirty-foot tube, just seven inches in diameter, with buoys to keep it horizontal at the water's surface. Filled with seventy-five pounds of "superfine" gunpowder, it would lie along a vessel's waterline and rip a long, gaping hole in the hull. The torpedo also boasted a twelve-foot crossbar with hooked ends that passed through it at one end. When any of its crossbar hooks snagged a ship's anchor cable or the curve of its bow, the crossbar would pivot, causing a spring to trigger the flintlock firing mechanism. It was not easy to handle this awkward weapon. Holmes planned to choose a dark night with the right combination of wind and tide, place his boat in a suitable spot, and then let the torpedo drift down on an enemy ship, adjusting its path with the long line attached to it.[14]

Holmes brought the *Young Hornet* and its torpedo up the Thames River to Gales Ferry, where he gathered his crew of men and discussed his plan with Commodore Decatur. After a couple of nighttime reconnaissance trips downriver, Holmes picked an early March evening in 1814, to attack a frigate *HMS Endymion* anchored off the Dumplings on the north side of Fishers Island. His crew got into position a little too late, and as the torpedo drifted slowly toward the frigate, the heavy, stiff control line sank and got fouled on the bottom, pulling the torpedo down below the surface. Unable to salvage it, Holmes cut the line and departed.

Returning to New York, Holmes had Riker build two more torpedoes and then brought the *Young Hornet* back up the Thames. On the night of March 24, 1814, Holmes and his crew headed back out to attack the 74-gun *HMS La Hogue*, anchored off New London. Circling the ship as they gauged the wind and tide, they anchored several hundred yards to the northwest and let the torpedo drift downwind. When it seemed to be in position, they tried to move eastward to make it strike the ship, but they drifted too close to *La Hogue* in the pitch blackness. When they tried to haul in the torpedo for a second attempt, the crossbar caught on *La Hogue*'s anchor cable. Riker's torpedo exploded in a geyser of water nearly one hundred feet high, but the *La Hogue* miraculously escaped without injury. Her sailors instantly lined the rails and fired their muskets into the darkness, lantern signals were exchanged between ships, and *La Hogue* fired cannons. Even the American militiaman on guard at Eastern Point in Groton fired on the *Young Hornet* as she retired up the Thames into the darkness. Every one of their shots missed the mark, however.

With the British ships off New London all on high alert for torpedo attacks, Holmes decided to take his last torpedo east to Vineyard Sound, another center of British activity. He and his crew spent a week stalking a British frigate, but never got close enough to deploy their explosive. After the failed stalking, the *Young Hornet* headed home to Mystic, and Jeremiah Holmes slid the unused torpedo under his house until he eventually returned it to John L. Riker the following spring.

Meanwhile, in late June of 1814, Cornelius Penfold Berrien and brother Richard brought the submersible *Turtle* out into the choppy waters of the East River, as reported by the *New York Evening Post*:

> "A new invented Torpedo Boat, resembling a turtle just above the surface of the water, and sufficiently roomy to carry nine persons within, having on her back a coat of mail, consisting of three large bombs, which could be discharged by machinery, so as to bid defiance to any attacks by barges, left this city one day last week, to blow up some of the enemy's ships off N. London. At one end of the boat projected a long pole under water,

with a torpedo fastened to it, which as she approached the enemy in the night, was to be poked under the bottom of a 74, and then let go. The boat we understand is the invention of an ingenious gentleman by the name of Berrian."[15]

Covertly, the brothers moved the *Turtle* up past the north end of Riker's Island, north past Powell Cove and Little Bay, and into the open waters of the Sound. Smoothly, the glistening vessel hugged the northern coastline of Long Island, pushing her way past Little Neck Bay, staying well south of Hart Island. She was twenty-three feet long and a full ten feet wide, with a six-foot depth but only a foot of hull exposed above the waterline. Her very strong arched deck was covered with half-inch iron plates and painted a dirty white for the sake of camouflage. In full operation now, her deck was nearly awash, like a turtle, though she more resembled a smooth-backed porpoise:

> "I would give you a description of this torpedo if I could intelligibly and reasonably within bounds. It is upon an entire new construction, cost $1,500 and was projected by an ingenious artist in New York at the expense of a few private gentlemen, and is I think better calculated to effect its object than any hitherto attempted. It is a bomb-proof thing and calculated to go boldly up to a 74 in the daytime and blow her up. The boat will contain about 10 men, a small part of which is above water and of the thickness of 4 or 5 feet of timber and iron bars, she is kept upright by a cast iron keel, weight 1,500, is propelled by a spiral oar at the rate they say of 4 miles an hour. The contrivance of keeping off boarders and exploding their powder under the bottom of the ship is very ingenious and quite original..."[16]

Inside, nine men, likely including Cornelius Penfold Berrien, Richard Penfold Berrien, Joshua Penny, and James Welden, operated a crank mechanism to drive her propeller wheel, moving the vessel slowly forward. She moved past Oyster Bay, then Huntington Bay toward Smithtown without being spotted. Behind her, she towed five Riker-designed torpedoes on separate tethers, an arrangement reminiscent of one of Fulton's earlier designs. After laboring for several hours, the crew aboard the *Turtle* was laboring immensely to round Horton's Point on the north shore of Long Island. It was late in the afternoon on Thursday, June 23, 1814, when she was suddenly spotted by lookouts aboard both the *HMS Maidstone* and *HMS Sylph*.

HMS *Sylph* with the *HMS Maidstone* close behind, B.J. Phillips

The *Sylph* was a fast-moving "sloop-of-war," a small sailing warship with a single gun deck and three masts. She had been constructed in Bermuda in 1812, and was armed to the teeth with sixteen 24-pounder carronades, two lengthy 12-pounders, and a pair of 12-pound carronades. During the past two months, she had been quite active in the interruption of commerce along the Long Island shores, including the capture and destruction of more than a dozen merchant vessels. Still, the *Turtle* was unlike any other vessel she had ever encountered.

Two months earlier, on May 11, 1814, the *Sylph* had captured the merchant sloop *Grace*, and had taken her cargo of iron and dismantled her for fuel. One week later, on May 18, she, along with the frigate *Maidstone*, fired upon a defenseless Swedish vessel. As part of the larger blockading squadron, the *Sylph* and *Maidstone* had joined forces with the *HMS Bulwark* and *HMS Nimrod* to scour the region in search of floating mines.

On May 25, the *Sylph* and *Maidstone* had become engaged in a battle with thirteen small gunboats under the command of Commodore Lewis. After a three-hour battle, the American vessels succeeded in their task of allowing a large contingent of small merchant packets and coasters to pass unmolested past the British warships. At the conclusion of this confrontation, two 74-gun British ships arrived, and the American forces retreated towards Guilford, Connecticut. The *Sylph* and *Maidstone* would continue throughout early June to make trouble on the Sound, until they spotted Captain Cornelius Berrien's *Turtle* moving along the shoreline on the afternoon of June 13, 1814.

The two British vessels sent barges to chase the odd-looking vessel and, if possible, capture her. Tragedy was about to strike the exhausted crew of the small submersible, as she floated just off shore of Horton's Point near Southold:

> "...It appears that they and 7 or 8 others had conducted a torpedo boat to within 7 or 8 miles of this place, where they anchored on account of the wind. While they were here the wind rose to a tempest during which one of the men attempted to swim on shore, his comrades seeing him in danger of drowning cut the cable to give him relief, but the man drowned and the boat drove on shore among the rocks and knocked off her keel, this was in the evening, the next morning a number of the garrison started in boats to assist in getting her off, and about 9 o'clock I observed the two frigates (which lay before the harbor) make sail and steer for the place where the torpedo was. I then remarked that some rascal had given them information, which since proves to be correct; wind and tide prevented the frigates from arriving at the place until the afternoon. As soon as they hove in sight the Captain of the Torpedo after removing the apparatus into the woods, put a barrel of powder into the boat and some straw and set fire to it, but the straw being wet it did not explode under half an hour and not until after the British had landed, who however never went near it [Turtle]. As soon as the ship got within gunshot of the shore they opened a most tremendous fire upon the poor boat, and good old Deacon Mulford's house who together with his family were 3 or 4 miles off at church. Under this fire they landed about 100 sailors and marines who soon drove about a dozen Militia [sic] who had been firing at them into the woods and then went to the deacon's house which stood near the beach and was badly battered with their cannon balls, and after robbing it of 2 or 300 dollars in clothing, breaking the clock and looking glasses, destroying the furniture, doors and windows, proceeded to make war upon his sheep, poultry and pigs...they then went on board and returned to their anchorage."[17]

On Saturday, July 9, 1814, a local newspaper published a brief article about the incident, claiming that "people collected and for some time resisted them (British), and having removed the spiral wheel (by which the boat was moved) and rudder, crank, etc., but being without hope of saving her (*Turtle*), they blew her up–the British are said to have had 4 killed in the affray."[18] As time passed, details of the events on that fateful summer day were told and retold much differently:

> "There followed such a bombardment from some of the ships that the good people of Southold, listening to a sermon by their pastor, the Rev. Jonathan Huntting, rushed from old South Church to see 'what the shooting was about.' There are several versions of the incident at this point. One is that the object had floated westward and northward into the Sound before being discovered by the British and that as they fired in its general direction, it eventually came ashore at Ashamomoque Beach

on the northerly side of Southold town. According to Dr. Clarence A. Wood...who describes the object as a primitive torpedo boat, a number of men who left the Southold church on that eventful Sunday morning... took the road that led towards Orient close 'to the Sound shore and finally discovered the strange craft stranded near the old Mulford house. Among these men were Deacon Huntting as well as parson Jonathan Huntting, youthful Alvah Stratton Mulford, Benjamin Reeve Prince and Benjamin Boisseau. Also from Orient, then called Oyster Ponds, came Noah Terry, a man it seems of great courage, for although 67 years of age at the time, he showed the Southold men his utter disdain of British marksmanship by climbing aboard the stranded boat and waving his hat. Eventually, It seems, the British sent a boatload of redcoats ashore to destroy the craft. Meanwhile, Mulford had arrived at his home nearby to find that it had been splintered by one of the missiles fired from the British ships. Fortunately other members of the family, including his grandfather, Deacon Mulford, were at church when the house was struck."[19]

The beached *Turtle*, lying near the old Mulford house

Even Captain Richard Burdett, of the *HMS Maidstone*, reported some details of the incident to the British government, claiming that, on June 25, 1814, he was informed that "the wonderful turtle boat which has been so long constructing at New York by the celebrated Mr. Fulton" had been driven by a gale into the Long Island shore. Burdett further explained the attack by the *HMS Sylph* and his own vessel, and what they found:

> "Upon rounding a point of land, I discovered this newly invented machine lying in a small sandy bay, in a wash of the beach, with a vast concourse of people around it, a considerable part of whom were armed militia, who took their stations behind the banks, to the right and left of the turtle boat, which lay on the beach resembling a great whale..."[20]

Across Noyack Bay, in the coastal village of Sag Harbor, New York, sounds of the intense confrontation reverberated from house to house, and townsfolk became quite convinced that the war had now reached their own backyards:

> "We were returning from Church and thought the first explosion the torpedo brought here last week. The firing is incessant and seems louder and heavier than any we have ever heard before; the tremendous explosions of those deep mouthed thunderers jar the house, windows rattle; how near these messengers of death are we know not–we have yet remained safe from the destroying enemy; the past summer we have been frequently alarmed and once the enemy landed at Sag Harbor, but were soon driven back by the militia stationed there; they soon, as they said, found themselves in a hornet's nest."[21]

A scattering of records down through the years indicate that, following the loss of the *Turtle*, Cornelius Penfold Berrien and his twin brother, Richard, returned to their respective homes in Newtown Village, Long Island; that Joshua Penny retired to Sag Harbor; and that Captain Jeremiah Holmes returned to Mystic, where he and his wife, Ann, raised their nine children. Over time, the two brothers, along with Arthur and George Cullum, continued to manufacture and sell coaches, as well as deal in prime real estate ventures. The Record Office in New York City indicates purchases of large chunks of land by the partners along Reed Street from one Philip Jacob. This property had once been known as the "Old Negro Burying Ground." When Arthur Cullum, his wife, Harriet, and their six children relocated further west to the village of Meadville, Pennsylvania, Cornelius purchased his share of the property. Apparently, the pair had also peddled property in Plattsburgh, New York, a burgeoning vacation area situated along the western shore of Lake Champlain:

> "Will be sold at auction, at the house of Joseph I Green, in Plattsburgh, on the first day of December next, at one o'clock in the afternoon. Lot No. 13, in the second location of Plattsburgh, containing 330 acres of land–Also, Lot No. 86 in the second division, old patent, containing 65 acres of land, lying near Dead Creek–Dated Nov. 25, 1816. Cornelius P. Berrian and Arthur Cullum."[22]

In 1823, brother Richard wrote *The American Telegraph and Signal Book*, printed by published J.W. Bell of New York City, and "intended as a universal register; arranged in the order of classes and grades, for the purpose of communicating any degree of information from one vessel to another, either by day or night, as far as the eye can see, or the ear hear; and to any part of the habitable globe if necessary."

On October 23, 1815, Richard P. Berrien had granted manumission to his only female slave; his brother, Cornelius, had done the same for his only two slaves on August 29, 1823. Four years later, in 1827, at the age of forty-seven, Cornelius took possession of an extremely profitable coach manufacturing firm located at 7 John Street in Manhattan, previously owned and operated by John Bloodgood and Richard P. Lawrence. Just one year later, on April 3, 1828, Cornelius would pass away nearly unnoticed at the relatively young age of forty-nine in Newark, New Jersey, and would be laid to rest in the First Presbyterian Churchyard cemetery in Manhattan. Those who knew him believed that he "had died of a broken heart," having lost both of his youngest sons within the four year period prior to his death. He left behind his wife of twenty-two years, Elizabeth Morris Berrien, who would outlive him by nearly three decades, as well as his youngest daughter, Jane, who would be laid to rest next to her father and brothers at the First Presbyterian Churchyard in December of 1847.

Meanwhile, life continued on for brother Richard, who seldom spoke of his submarine exploits, or about how his brother Cornelius was at the helm of the *Turtle* when the two of them had attempted to sink a British blockader during the War of 1812. In fact, by the time of Cornelius' death, their exploits had largely been forgotten.

By the mid-1840s, the Washington Square section of New York had been transformed from the "potter's field" that the Berrien twins had known so well to an exclusive residential neighborhood. In 1842, the congregation of the Sullivan Street Methodist Episcopal Church congregation, located just to the south, decided to disband and sell its property. Oliver Loveland, a young and prominent member of the Bedford Street Church, admired the structure and convinced other members to join with him in the purchase of the old house of worship. Then, just as the papers were about to be signed, several of the major supporters backed out, fearing the project would fail and they would lose their entire investment.

Loveland was undeterred, however, and "almost alone, assisted only by Dr. S.A. Purdy, he purchased the property for the stipulated price, the two becoming personally responsible for its payment," reported *The New York Times*. It was an extremely risky venture. Neither of the men was financially able to maintain a new church organization, let along the mortgage. "Both of the new owners were at the time of slender means," said *Times*. Financial salvation came from Sylvanus Gedney, a member of the old Sullivan Street church whose "love of the old edifice was too strong to part with it." On December 12, 1842, the three men founded the Sullivan Street Methodist Episcopal Church with just one other member, Richard Penfold Berrien, who would become the First Superintendent of the attached Washington Square School.

Elizabeth Vanderbeek Berrien passed away on June 4, 1862, in Kensico, Westchester County, New York. Twenty-eight months later, Richard P. Berrien died on October 26, 1864, at the age of eighty-five. He was laid to rest alongside his beloved wife in nearby Yonkers. Though he and his brother did not seek notoriety from their submarine adventures during the War of 1812, they certainly left behind a vital link to its development and heritage.

Captain Thomas Johnstone, December 10, 1834

-11-
Thomas Johnstone: *Eagle & Etna*

"Escaped from the Fleet Prison, early this Morning, Thomas Johnson, a Native of Ireland, charged with Debts to a large Amount, and also on a Warrant upon a Charge of a capital Felony committed on the 6th of June last, at Southwold, in the County of Suffolk: He is a Seafaring Man, was the Owner of the Ann Cutter, of Hastings, and has for some Years been a notorious Smuggler; he was some Time ago in the County Gaol of Surrey, charged with a capital Offence, from which he also made his Escape; he is a good-looking well-made, Man, about Thirty-five Years of Age, wears his own Black Hair cropped, is rather pitted with the Small-Pox, and about Five Feet Ten inches high; he has a remarkable small Brown Spot on one of his Eyes, between the Eye-brow and the Eye-lash. Whoever will apprehend him, so that he may be brought back to the Fleet, shall receive a Reward of Two Hundred Pounds from the Warden of, the said Prison. And the Commissioners of His Majesty's Customs do hereby promise a farther Reward of Three Hundred Pounds to any Person or Persons who will apprehend, or Cause to be apprehended, the said Thomas Johnson, to be paid by the Receiver-General of His Majesty's Customs, upon his, the said Johnson's, being taken and recommitted to Prison."[1]

One stormy night in 1802, a broad-shouldered gent, standing just under six feet tall, achieved the believed-to-be impossible by escaping from London's Fleet Prison without the aid of tools or weapons. With Herculean strength he wrenched the bolt on his cell door from its socket with his bare hands. With spider-like agility, he managed to scale a twenty-foot perpendicular brick wall, hanging on to the few projecting ridges with his fingertips and bare toes. Once outside, a carriage whisked him away to nearby Brighton, where he boarded a fast sailing ship bound for the French coast.

Captain Thomas Johnstone, better known in history as "Johnstone the Smuggler" and the "Hampshire Smuggler," was a native of Lymington, Hampshire, England, though in his lifetime he would claim allegiance to England, France, and the United States. Born in 1772, he grew up near the base of an Iron Age hill fort known as Buckland Rings. The town itself began as a Saxon village in the sixth century, when the Jutes arrived in from the Isle of Wight and founded a settlement they called Limentun. The Old English word "tun" meant a "farm or hamlet," while "limen" was derived from the ancient British word "lemanos," meaning "elm-tree."

About 1200, the lord of the manor, William de Redvers, created the borough of New Lymington around the cobblestoned quay and High Street, while Old Lymington comprised the rest of the parish. He gave the town its first charter, which provided the right to hold a market. From the Middle Ages to the time that Johnstone was born, Lymington would be famous for making salt. The saltworks mines, in fact, comprised almost a continuous belt along the coast toward the castle at Hurst Spit. Celia Fiennes, who traveled throughout England on horseback and wrote about her experiences, visited the village in the 1690s. She offered details of how seawater was drawn into clay-lined trenches, where some of the water was allowed to evaporate. The concentrated brine was then pumped by windmills to tanks outside the boiling houses, where it was put into large, copper or iron boiling pans fired by coal brought by barge. As the water was further evaporated, the salt crystals were skimmed off to be dried and stored, before being taken out again by barge to ships for transportation.

Lymington also had a long history of smuggling, beginning with the surreptitious transport of wool to America in the seventeenth century to evade high excise taxes. In 1724, Daniel Defoe wrote of the town: "I do not find they have any foreign commerce, except it be what we call smuggling and roguing; which I may say, is the reigning commerce of all this part of the English coast, from the mouth of the Thames to the Land's End in Cornwall." How the Johnstone family had come to settle here was a part of their distant and colorful past, though they had actually originated 500 miles north in Annandale, County of Dumfries, Scotland:

> "The first trace we find of them is in the reign of Alexander III, when Hugo de Johnstone owned lands in East Lothian, which he bequeathed to his son John de, who gave a portion of them to the Monastery of Sotray, about 1285, 'for the safety of his soul.' His descendants, Thomas, Walter, Gilbert and John, swore fealty to Edward I in 1296–the last mentioned baron being termed, in the deed 'Chevalier of the County of Dumfries.'"[2]

However history hints that the Johnstone family had, for a number of decades, resided in Strathaven, some twenty miles to the east of Annandale. One historian mentioned that the "Parish of Johnstone derived its name from the village and the hamlet from its having become, in Scoto-Saxon times, the 'tun,' or dwelling place, of some person who was distinguished by the name of John. This place afterwards gave the surname to the family of Johnstone, who became a powerful clan in Annandale."[3]

There is little doubt that, however vague the time of their arrival in Dumfries, during the reign of King James VI of Scotland and of England, the Johnstones of Annandale were a very powerful clan. Even during the fourteenth century an immense number of families bearing the name were found in the region, all claiming kinship with the Lord of Lochwood, as the ancestral castle of the Johnstones was called. Furthermore, the expansive clan was "ready at all times to sally forth to war under their chief's banner, either against the King himself, or on predatory incursions on other Border tribes, chief amongst whom were the Maxwells and Gordons." Evidence suggests that, with both of these clans–particularly the Maxwells–the Johnstones waged a hereditary feud, which never rested, and resulted in a great deal of bloodshed across many generations.

One of the strongest traits of the Johnstone clan was that they were united and devoted to their Chieftain, and when a plea came from any part of the family, stalwart fighting men were always forthcoming; they were always true to their family motto, "Nunquam non Paratus," meaning "Never Not Ready." So true this was that in 1585, Lord Maxwell was declared a rebel, and a commission was given to the Laird of Johnstone to pursue and apprehend him. However, two bands of soldiers, which the government had sent to assist him, were utterly destroyed by the Maxwells. During the mission, Lochwood, the chief house of the Johnstones, was overrun and burned by the Maxwells, who blatantly mocked: "Dame Johnstone might have light to put on her hood."

The destruction was a major setback. Lochwood had been erected during a war-torn and turbulent age, standing for decades amid impassable bogs and marshes, making it nearly impregnable. King James VI of Scotland, who is credited with "never saying a foolish thing," said of Lochwood, "that the man who built it, though he might have the appearance of an honest man outwardly, must have been a knave at heart." Indeed, it had been built in the fourteenth century, and the ruins can still to be seen at the north end of the parish of Johnstone.

The leader of the Johnstone clan was so overcome wth disgrace of defeat, being a man of pride and honor, that he died of grief. Still, the feud continued. In 1608 Lord Maxwell invited Sir James Johnstone to a conference, each Chieftain to bring one friend only. When they met at a place called Auchmanhill on August 6, the attending Maxwell fell into a bitter and reproachful argument with Johnstone of Gunmanlie, and Maxwell fired his pistol. As Sir James Johnstone turned round to see what had happened, Lord Maxwell shot him in the back. With the old knight mortally wounded and laying on the ground, Maxwell rode around him on houseback try and kill him, but Johnstone defended himself with his sword until his life and strength failed him.

The feud continued until 1613, when Lord Maxwell was taken prisoner in Caithness, brought to Edinburgh for trial, and by order of the King–who wished to send out a warning to the nobility and disorderly Borderers–publicly beheaded him on May 21, 1613. "Thus," wrote Sir Walter Scott, "was ended by a salutary example of severity, the foul debate betwixt the Maxwells and the Johnstones, in the course of which each family lost two Chieftains, the Maxwells dying, one on the field of battle, and one by the executioner's sword; the Johnstones, one died of a broken heart, and the other by the assassin's bullet."[4]

In about 1616, King James I of England–who had ruled Scotland since July of 1567–offered a free grant of land to any Scottish clansman who would leave Scotland and settle in Ireland, With the "roving spirit of adventure" long associated with the Johnstone clan, Thomas Johnstone, third son of the then Earl of Annandale—our Thomas Johnstone's fifth great-grandfather—stepped forward to volunteer. Thus began the next 150 years of Johnstone family migration.

Thomas Johnstone, transplanted to Scotland, was a Protestant who became Rector of Ballyroney, Drumgooland and Ballynahinch, in the County of Down. He was ordained Deacon by the Bishop of Down and Connor on March 27, 1618; Presbyter by May 4, 1618; appointed Vicar of Drumgooland October 10, 1628; and Curate of Clonduff on May 28, 1634. His eldest son, James, had a son named John, who married a niece of James Mace, Rector of Lisburn.

John Johnstone, smuggler Thomas Johnstone's third great-grandfather, purchased a large farm at Ballinderry, County Antrim, near Portmore, and settled there in about 1670. He had five sons and three daughters. One son, Thomas, a lieutenant in the army and great-great-grandfather to smuggler Thomas, died in America, and a number of his descendants owned large tracts of land in Virginia and Kentucky. One daughter married Laird Catherwood of Ballyvester, near Donaghadee; the second married George Watson of Brookhill, near Lisburn; and the third daughter married John Kelly, of Ballinderry.

At the time that our Thomas Johnstone of submarine fame was born in 1772, his father, Thomas, was a fisherman and a smuggler who had come to ply his trade along the southern coastline of England. The elder Thomas, who often took his son with him to sea, was tragically drowned in 1784. Hence, by the age of twelve, the youngster was helping to support his widowed mother as a "fisherman." In truth, he was already an accomplished mariner, and his familiarity with the English Channel and the coastal waters from Cornwall to Suffolk made him a much sought-after maritime pilot.

In fine family tradition, young Thomas Johnstone began smuggling by the age of fifteen. Soon, he knew every creek and inlet along England's smuggling coastline, and became the best known pilot in the Channel trade. When England went to war with revolutionary France in 1793, the twenty-one-year-old joined the eight-gun privateer, Three Friends, and set out to capture French merchantmen and their heavily supplied vessels in the English Channel. Ultimately, he was captured and thrown into a French dungeon for "safe keeping." While imprisoned, Johnstone spoke so convincingly of his absolute hatred of England that his captors armed him with a lugger and sent him off with dispatches to assist one of their spies in Southampton.

Inevitably, Johnstone betrayed the spy and handed the dispatches over to British officials, who rewarded him by allowing him to keep the French lugger. Seemingly finished with his wartime expeditions, he returned to his home, where he took up the trade of "fishing" once again off the coast of Stonechurch. Every now and again, he accepted a piloting job. In the spring of 1796, while the schooner, *Daisy Miller*, an English navy frigate boarded the vessel and impressed Johnstone and half of his crewmates into naval service.

AMERICAN SUBMARINERS: PRE-CIVIL WAR

Prison cell in New Prison, Clerkenwell

Always the schemer, Johnstone informed the frigate's officers where they might find another "bunch of likely lads" to be "pressed into service," promptly leading them to the New Inn at Warebourne, near London. What he had failed to disclose, however, was that his brother-in-law, Arthur Hudson, was there with his own gang of smugglers, celebrating their most recent profitable venture. The navy impressments squad had been duped into a "hornet's nest," where a fight broke out. Within minutes, the navy men were bruised and battered, reeling back to their frigate and leaving Thomas Johnstone behind. With nowhere else to go, Thomas threw in his lot with his brother-in-law's band of smugglers.

Over the course of the next several months, English excise men made Hampshire so difficult for smugglers that Johnstone made his way first to Sussex, and then to Kent. There, he was recruited by a local squire, Sir Robert Goudhurst, on behalf of Prime Minister, William Pitt the Younger. Pitt had ordered Goudhurst to "find a courageous smuggler" to land General Bertrand Barere, a Frenchman turned British agent. Duty-bound, Johnstone brought Barere discretely across the English Channel hidden in the belly of the three-masted, twenty-five-ton lugger, *Rover*. With Goudhurst's approval, Johnstone brought *Rover* back across the Channel loaded to the gunwales with contraband, thereby diverting local suspicion as to the true purpose of his journey.

In early 1798, Johnstone was imprisoned at the New Prison in Clerkenwell, London, convicted of smuggling, but he escaped soon thereafter. Further periods of imprisonment followed in France, Holland and, eventually, Fleet debtors' prison for owing nearly 11,000 pounds. So notorious were Johnstone's escapades that nearly a quarter-century later, a 1823 publication, *The Historical Gallery of Criminal Portraitures, Foreign and Domestic*, continued to report that "no prison has yet been found strong enough to hold him."[5]

In 1803, Johnstone found himself incarcerated in the jails of Flushing, confined under military guard. Once again, he managed to escape. He made his way to Paris, where he happened to meet an American marine engineer named Robert Fulton, who was in the process of testing his underwater diving apparatus. The timing could not have been better, for Fulton had just received word from the French First Consul that none other than Napoleon was interested in his invention, known in local circuits as the *Nautilus*. Fulton immediately recognized that Johnstone was an experienced mariner, and invited him to become his chief engineer in charge of improvements to the *Nautilus*. Johnstone, it seems, would also participate in a number of test dives in nearby Brest. The smuggler, who had recently escaped debtor's prison and was wanted by taxmen, readily agreed.

With the assistance of Thomas Johnstone, Fulton soon designed a copper sphere that could store two hundred cubic feet of compressed air. Testing the new innovation, the two men went down with one other volunteer in depths of five feet of water, where they remained for six hours without difficulty. The experiment had been a resounding success.

Next on the pair's plan was the development of an explosives delivery system for the *Nautilus*. Their early mine designs were fashioned from various sized copper cylinders, each containing between ten and two hundred pounds of gunpowder. Furthermore, they were each fitted with an innovative gunlock mechanism, which would trigger the detonating charge whenever they came in direct contact with the hard wooden surface of a ship's hull.

Meanwhile, Napoleon was also interested in utilizing Thomas Johnstone's marine expertise. When war with England flared again, he offered the convicted smuggler 2,000 guineas to pilot his invasive fleet of landing barges across the Channel to Britain. Yet, something went terribly awry during the expedition, almost as if they had been informed of the invasion, for the British seemed to be lying in wait for the attack. Somehow, Johnstone managed to evade capture by slipping into Channel waters and swimming to an American schooner. Taking Johnstone as their prisoner, he was then taken to New Orleans, where he was handed over to the British Consul. Some months later, Johnstone was, surprisingly, pardoned by Prime Minister Pitt. It seems that Robert Fulton, who had grown impatient with the French reluctance to purchase his *Nautilus*, had gone to England where he was experimenting with underwater torpedoes. Fulton, in turn, requested Johnstone as his assistant, and Pitt had offered Johnstone the alternative of freedom or trial for treason.

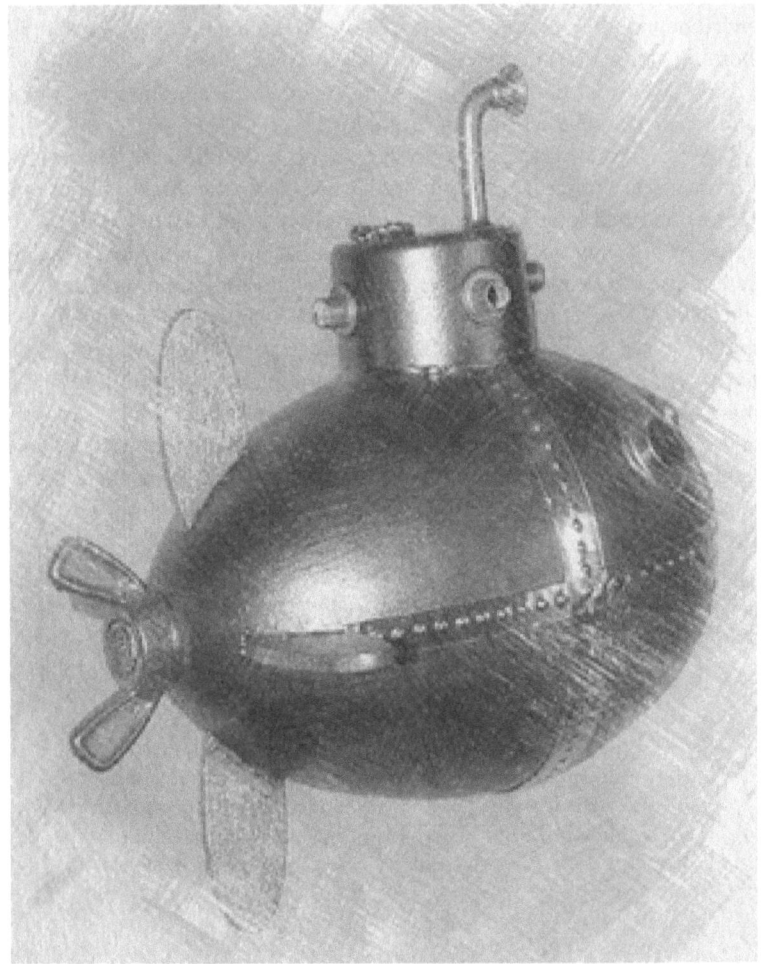

Model of Fulton and Johnstone's copper sphere submarine

So, the man of Scottish heritage, who had been born in England and had, during different times in his life, pledged his allegiance to Britain, France, and America, returned to Dover, England and rejoined Fulton. The pair spent the next few months making and testing innovative underwater explosives–bombs with time fuses, designed to operate like modern day limpet explosives. In use, a swimmer or diver would approach an enemy ship and attach the mine, which was designed with hollow compartments to give it only a slight negative buoyancy, making it easier to handle underwater. In this case, the pair had surmised that such a bomb could be delivered by an unobserved, submerged vessel.

Final experiments were being conducted on the vessel and its explosives when, on October 21, 1805, the Battle of Trafalgar was fought and won by the British Royal Navy against the combined fleets of the French Navy and Spanish Navy. Though Fulton continued to have hopes of selling his inventions, interest in both his submarine and its weaponry began to wane. Still, in all "fairness" to the American inventor, the British government agreed to appoint an arbitration committee to decide the matter once and for all.

When the arbitrators met in August of 1806, those representing the government put miscellaneous sundry questions to the American inventor; questions that had long ago been answered. They inquired, for example, as to whether or not "any one would risk being caught in the submarine vessel and expose himself to being hanged in consequence of using engines not permitted by the laws of war." The men also asked precisely how the submarine might be employed to sweep of the Channel to locate floating bombs. Finally, they asked about the effect of storms on such bombs, and on the chance of a submarine being driven to shore by a storm. These questions were all answered again by Fulton, one-by-one, in a very logical manner, and both questions and answers were recorded in history as "Notes on Observations of the Arbitrators Particularly of Captain Hamilton and Sir Charles Blagden," and attached to Fulton's own copy of his "Descriptions."[6]

These same notes indicate that Robert Fulton made it quite clear that the plans he submitted to the British Government were so far in advance of anything he had proposed to the French that they constituted new plans:

> "But, it may be said that my Experiments have been so Public that no part of my plan is now a Secret, I would ask who has seen the Plans and System which I have exhibited to this Committee where is to be found did any gentleman here know them all or any part of them perfectly before I appeared? It is true there have been Ideas of this subject scattered in the World but the impracticability of any important result has always been attached to them which Idea I perceive has much weight in this Committee."[7]

Furthermore, Fulton urged the Arbitrators that a list of questions, which he would set forth in his notes bearing on the efficacy of his bombs, should be submitted to a second decision-making body of experts, to include Lord George Keith, Commodore E.W.C.R. Owen, Admiral Demet, Captain Seccombe, Captain Salt, Captain King, Lieutenant William Robinson, and none other than Thomas Johnstone himself, then captain of the Nile Cutter. He concluded his appeal to the arbitrators in the following spirited language:

> "Now Gentlemen I beg you to believe that I have not taken these measures nor made use of these Arguments to draw from you either Capital

AMERICAN SUBMARINERS: PRE-CIVIL WAR

or Annuity I am not a Man much governed by a thirst for Money, an honorabel [sic] fame is to me a much more noble feeling, But I like truth candor, and Justice to all Parties concerned with me in this Business, I have therefore used these Arguments for the following reasons. First, That at this meeting it is right for me to Shew [sic] you in the most striking manner in my power what I conceive your danger and should you not see it as I do and future bad consequences should result to this Country the fault will not rest with me but with you and His Majesty's Ministers, and I shall not have to accuse myself of want of Candour [sic]. Second, I have used them to gratify two friends who have been kind to me, and who are more governed by the hope of gain than I am, I have now acquitted myself to this Government and to them, And neither this Government nor they have more to expect of me. Therefore Gentlemen should your award not meet their views of Wealth, I shall feel free to act as I think proper And I will take the fame and Consequences of these Engines on myself Abandoning all calculations of a pecuniary kind, and the whole of the Drawings and Papers here exhibited shall be published within one year with all my Experiments in France and Negotiations with this Government. In fact I will do my utmost to make it a good Philosophic Work and give it to the World. I will then form a Committee of the most respectable Men in America and proceed regularly in Experiments on the large Scale publishing the result from time to time and thus drawing the attention of the ingenious and Enterprising to such Pursuits I shall hope to succeed in my first object that of annihilating all Military Marines and giving liberty to the Seas. Gentlemen a man who has the candour [sic] to give you this in Writing has but little deception or fear in his character and will not abandon so glorious an Enterprise for trifling Rebuffs or mean consideration. At all events whatever may be your Award I never will consent to let these inventions lie dormant Should my Country at any time have need of them, Were you to grant me an Annuity of 20,000 a Year, I would sacrifise [sic] all to the safety & independance [sic] of my Country, But I hope England and America will understand their mutual Interest to well to War with each other. And I have no desire to introduce my Engines into practice for the benefit of any other Nation."[8]

Despite his valiant arguments, Fulton's offer was utterly rejected by the arbitrators. In September of 1806, when the inventor made his way back to America, Captain Thomas Johnstone returned to his mariner way of life. By 1809, then in his late thirties, he joined the British Navy and piloted an invasion fleet of more than 600 vessels, which was the largest expeditionary force that had ever left Britain. Around 40,000 soldiers and 15,000 horses, together with field artillery and two siege trains, crossed the North Sea and landed at Walcheren, Netherlands, and other islands in the estuary of the Scheidt on July 30.

The primary mission was not to reinforce the British army in Portugal, but to provide belated support Austria in its war against the French Empire and to capture or destroy a French fleet being assembled in Antwerp. The British troops were the cream of the British Army, 70% of the units being up to strength

1st Battalions, with a sprinkling of 2nd Battalions. They were faced by a divided French command that consisted mostly of second rate national guard and penal units. Initially, with Napoleon being distracted by the campaign with Austria, the invasion went well. The British were able to capture the islands of Walcheren and South Beveland. But soon the expedition bogged down because of poor planning, divided leadership, and conflicting goals–all exacerbated by little prior intelligence on the climate and topography of the area.

What would later become known as the Walcheren Campaign involved very little fighting, though Johnstone would sustain heavy losses from a disease popularly dubbed "Walcheren Fever," a typho-malarious or paludal-enteric illness. More than 4,000 British troops died in islands–only 106 in combat–and the remainder withdrew on December 9. All in all, the invasion was a failure.

After the war, the British Navy gave Johnstone command of a newly constructed cruiser cutter, *HMS Fox*, and ordered him to clean up the smuggling operation along the British coast. This he did, rather haphazardly, for the next five years. Meanwhile, a scattering of historical documents lend credence to the theory that he also set out to perfect Fulton's submarine concept.

Yet, was he a smuggler, a marine engineer, and a brilliant inventor, or simply a teller of tall tales? Oddly enough, the jigsaw puzzle that would become Captain Johnstone's legacy includes pieces that, when properly assembled, hint at the much more complex portrait. The most important of these snippets remain unpublished, however, and molder in an obscure, dusty corner of Britain's National Archives. When sorted, deciphered, and reassembled, they give credence to an odd statement that first appeared in the *Historical Gallery of Criminal Portraitures*–one that dates back to the construction of Johnstone's submarine not in response to an 1820 urging by wealthy Bonapartists, but to a time three years prior to Napoleon's imprisonment.

It was believed to be sometime in late 1812 or early 1813, after "having exhibited a model of the internal clock-work, or machinery," that the inventive side of Johnstone entered into an agreement with the British Cabinet Ministers to construct a working submarine for the sum of £100,000. The contract specified that his vessel would be "capable of being steered, elevated, and depressed at pleasure, under water, and at the same time affix the torpedo under the bottoms of ships."[9]

What makes this agreement especially interesting is the context of the times and circumstances. In 1812, Great Britain was at war with the United States–and the U.S. had employed Robert Fulton to work on a new generation of wartime weapons. This explains how Johnstone was able to arm himself with a whole series of invitations to various government inside circles, proving that he was formally employed "on His Majesty's Secret Service on submarine, and other useful experiments, by Order." How these trials were actually funded is a different matter. In the confusion of wartime, historical records indicate that Britain's army and navy each assumed that the other would be paying for the submarine's construction. It was a situation ripe for Johnstone's exploitation, something at which the con man was known to excel. To that end, he retained the services of a London engineer who sketched a submarine that was twenty-seven feet long and "in shape much like a porpoise." An inner chamber, six feet square and lined with cork, protected the two-man crew.

A well-versed civil engineer, Thomas Martin, a resident of High Holborn Street in London, was employed to oversee the construction of the actual craft, whose hull would be made of sheet iron. Her general description was "that of a salmon swimming; her length, about twenty feet; and her space in the inner chamber, about six feet square." After several months of work, she was nearly completed:

> "In 1814, this wonderful piece of mechanism was nearly completed at a village on the Thames side, not far from Watlington or Wallingford; and the projector [had] three letters of safeguard, addressed to the magistracy and military commanders of Berkshire and Oxfordshire, signed by the Duke of York, as commander-in-chief, the Earl of Liverpool, and Lord Sidemouth, stating that Captain Johnstone was employed on an experiment that had the sanction of government, and desiring he might not be interrupted."[10]

The vessel's weaponry was quite formidable, and "so intense was the force of the torpedo when discharged, that it acted in all directions with equal force, and that by lodging a single engine against the main pier of each of the bridges over the Thames…and setting the torpedo accordingly, he could toss the whole into the air just as the park and tower guns were being discharged."[11]

In the spring of 1813, Johnstone repeatedly tested his reworked Fulton-designed submarine and torpedo at Woolwich, where it was highly successful. From these experiments, he and those who witnessed them, believed that the vessel would result in "a final termination of naval combats between fleets of men of war and frigates, for no vessel can be secured, by any vigilance, which lies afloat on an open water, against sub-marine assaults."[12]

Yet, since there was no current conflict in progress, Thomas Johnstone's employment of his diving machine in actual combat would have to wait. In the summer of 1813, Lord Thomas Cochrane, a Scottish naval flag officer of the Royal Navy nicknamed the "Sea Wolf," informed Johnstone precisely where "an immense treasure was deposited by the Buccaneers, off the Spanish main, and where there were two or three wrecks, comprising a prodigious mass of bullion and specie."[13] Cochrane further suggested to him that he might be just the person, with his submarine boat and torpedo weaponry, to conduct an unsanctioned salvage operation. It is unknown as to whether or not he pursued riches in the form of sunken treasure.

By 1816, the semi-retired Johnstone was residing in a small cottage that he had purchased along the Vauxhall Bridge Road, in Chelsea, just southwest of

London. Only forty-four years old, he had married a "pretty 18-year-old heiress" and settled down to "quiet wedding bliss," resulting in the birth of a son and a daughter. Meanwhile, he worked in seclusion at his nearby fortress of Battersea, continually improving upon Fulton's submarine concepts, designing a clockwork-powered vessel made of iron and lined with cork and wood. He hoped to proceed with a full-scale prototype, but the tight-fisted Lords of the Admirality absolutely refused to finance the project. To add to his disappointment, Johnstone was arrested in late 1817 on suspicion for working for both the French and the American governments. Again, he was imprisoned, this time in a new jail near London, though he would remain there only a short time:

> "...He watched his opportunity; and at the appointed time, by an extraordinary effort of courage, strength, and activity, he locked up one of the turnkeys, knocked down another, turned the key upon them all, and springing with all the agility of young [Philip] Astley upon a fine fleet horse which stood in waiting near hand, he galloped, ironed as he was, to Battersea; there, in a lonely spot, he was met by a smith who released him of his irons, which were buried in a garden, and he lay concealed at the house of a friend...till the heat of the first pursuit, stimulated by a large reward, was over."[14]

There is absolutely no doubt that each of Thomas Johnstone's submersible designs was primitive–driven by sails at the surface, and relying on oars for motive power when fully submerged. Nor is there anything to suggest that he actually solved the vast number of technical problems that prevented the development of effective submarines during this period. Perhaps the greatest problem he faced was preventing his vessel, once it was submerged in neutral buoyancy, from sinking to the bottom of the sea.

British archives contain correspondence from Johnstone confirming that the boat was fully ready for deployment, and that he was requesting full payment of £100,000 for its completion. They also show, however, that in early 1820, a commission of senior officers led by Sir George Cockburn was dispatched to submit a detailed report on the submarine–not, apparently, to assess its new technology or success, but to estimate how much it actually cost to construct. Cockburn was a serious player in the naval hierarchy of the day, and remains notorious as the man who burned the White House to the ground when Washington fell to British troops in 1814. Though his original report on Johnstone's submarine has vanished, its contents can be assembled from the Royal Navy's decision to shave Johnson's six-figure demand down to a mere £4,735 and a few pennies.

What this indicates without much doubt is that, early in 1820, Johnstone possessed a very real submarine at exactly the same time that, French sources suggest, Bonapartist officers were offering thousands of pounds for just such a innovative vessel. And this belief can be tied, in turn, to two reports. The first, which appeared in the *Naval Chronicle*, describes a trial of Johnstone's vessel on the River Thames:

> "On one occasion, the anchor... got foul of the ship's cable...and, after having fixed the petard [mine], Johnson strove in vain to get clear. He then looked quietly at his watch, and said to the man who accompanied him, 'We have but two minutes and a half to live, unless we can get clear of this cable.' This man, who had been married only a few days, began to lament his fate... 'Cease your lamentations,' said Johnson sternly to him, 'they will avail you nought.' And, seizing a hatchet, he cut the cable, and got clear off; when immediately the petard exploded, and blew up the vessel."[15]

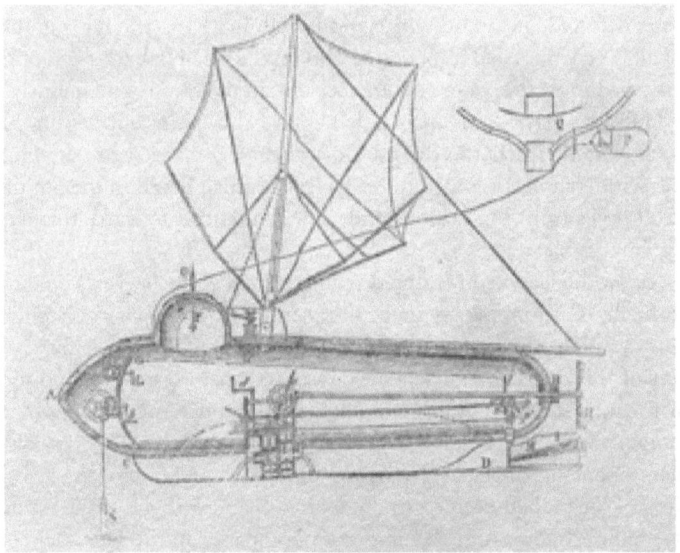

Thomas Johnstone's submarine design

The second account, found in the unpublished memoirs of London artist, Walter Greaves, is a recollection by Greaves' father. The father was a Thames boatman who recalled how "one dark night in November," 1820, the smuggler was intercepted as he attempted to bring his submarine out to sea. Greaves stated that, "she managed to get below London Bridge, the officers boarding her, Capt. Johnson in the meantime threatening to shoot them. But they paid no attention to his threats, seized her, and, taking her to Blackwall, burned her."[16]

In 1820–or so he later "confessed" to authorities–Thomas Johnstone's submarine expertise was resserected when the imprisoned smuggler was offered the sum of £40,000 to rescue the emperor Napoleon from bleak exile on the island of St. Helena. This escapade was to be conducted in an incredible way, carrying Napoleon down a sheer cliff, using a type of bosun's chair, to a pair of submarines waiting off shore. From there, the emperor would be transported to the United States. Johnstone would be expected to design and build the submarines himself.

The sordid tale begins with Emperor Napoleon himself. As the inheritor of the French Revolution–the outstanding event of the age, and the one that, more than any other, caused rich and privileged elites unease–the Corsican had become the terror of half of Europe. As "an unmatched military genius, the invader of Russia, conqueror of Italy, Germany and Spain, and architect of the Continental System," he was–in British eyes at least–the greatest villain of his day. In the English nurseries he was called "Boney," a bogeyman who hunted down naughty children and gobbled them up for dinner; in France, he was referred to as "a beacon of chauvinism." His legend was only diminished after he had been defeated, apparently once and for all, in 1814. Though a grand coalition of all his enemies had imprisoned him on the small Italian island of Elba, he had managed to escape, return to France, and, in the campaign famously known as the Hundred Days, unite his whole nation behind him once again. His final defeat, at Waterloo, left the British Goverment determined to take no further chances with Napoleon. Exiled to St. Helena, a small island in the South Atlantic 1,200 miles from the nearest land, it was intended to make further escape literally impossible.

Yet, while Napoleon endured six increasingly difficult years on St. Helena before finally succumbing to cancer–or, some say, to arsenic poisoning–there were always plots afoot to rescue him. Emilio Ocampo, who offered the best account of this collection of schemes, recorded that "Napoleon's political ambition was not subdued by his captivity…and his determined followers never abandoned hopes of setting him free." Nor did the so-called "Bonapartists" lack adequate financing. In fact, Napoleon's brother, Joseph, who was at one time the King of Spain, had escaped to the United States with a fortune estimated at twenty million francs. And the emperor's popularity in the U.S. was so strong that "the British squadron taking him into exile headed several hundred miles in the wrong direction to evade an American privateer, the *True Blooded Yankee*," which was captained by the notorious American pirate, Joshua Hailey, and sailed under the flag of the revolutionary government of Buenos Aires. Hailey, it was reported, was determined to carry out the daring rescue mission of Napoleon.

The greatest threat of Napoleon's rescue did, indeed, originate in South America. Napoleonic France had been the only power to offer support when the continent sought independence from Spain, and a few patriots were willing to contemplate supporting an escape or, more ambitiously, an invasion of St. Helena. The prospect was attractive to Napoleon as well; if there was no realistic hope of returning to Europe, he could still dream of establishing a new empire in Mexico or Venezuela.

Safely landed on St. Helena in 1815, however, the emperor found himself in what was, in all likelihood, the most secure prison that could have been devised for him. The island was extremely isolated, almost entirely ringed with cliffs and devoid of secure places to drop anchor. It boasted only a limited number of possible landing places, all of which were guarded by a large garrison totaling 2,800 men, armed with 500 cannon. Napoleon, meanwhile, was held at a place called Longwood, a refurbished mansion with extensive grounds in the most remote and dismal portion of the island's interior.

Although the deposed emperor was allowed to retain an entourage, and offered a good deal of freedom within the confines of Longwood's estate, everything else on the island was strictly controlled by St. Helena's stern and officious governor, Sir Hudson Lowe, whose career prospects were intimately tied to the successful security of his famous captive. Longwood was heavily guarded; visitors were interrogated and searched, and the estate was barred to anyone during the hours of darkness. An entire Royal Navy squadron, consisting of eleven ships, patrolled continuously and vigilantly offshore.

So concerned were the British to thwart even the smallest possibility of Napoleon's escape that small garrisons were established on nearby Ascension Island and at Tristan da Cunha, 1,200 miles further out in the Atlantic, designed to forestall the unlikely possibility that these uninhabited volcanic pimples might be used as staging posts for a daring rescue. No single prisoner in history had ever been so closely guarded. "At such a distance and in such a place," the Prime Minister, Lord Liverpool, reported with satisfaction to his cabinet, "all intrigue would be impossible."[17]

And yet—surprisingly, perhaps—the British were correct in their assumption that it was necessary to take extreme precautions. The marines sent to occupy Ascension discovered that a message had already been left on its main beach, which read: "May the Emperor Napoleon live forever!" In fact, when Ocampo summarized his amazingly long list of plots to liberate the emperor, they included efforts to arrange a rescue by fast-moving yacht, a newly designed steamboat, and even a hot air balloon.[18]

Meanwhile, it remained unknown in St. Helena that Thomas Johnstone's diving vessels—named the *Eagle* and the *Etna*—had, indeed, been completed at a secret boatyard on the upper Thames by November of 1820. Where exactly the one-time cohort of Robert Fulton fit into this murky picture of daring plots is difficult to say. Although scarcely adverse to publicity and notoriety, the smuggler of both merchandise and men had always dwelt in the margins between fact and fiction—the latter of which was often of his own invention. Reliable historical accounts of his life are largely absent—even his name is generally misspelled "Johnston" or "Johnson." The one biography of him is a farrago, extracted from the Lee Kong Chian Reference Library of Singapore. Even one of the most prolific literary figures in history, the novelist Sir Walter Scott, was misled about Johnstone's colorful career—writing, incorrectly, that he had piloted Admiral Nelson's flagship at the Battle of Copenhagen. Scott did, however, have a colorful portrait of words to offer in describing Johnstone's exploits:

"Captain Thomas Johnstone, better known as Johnstone the Smuggler, of all the men of the present day, bears, perhaps, in his life and adventures, the closest assimilation with that of Rob Roy. The desperate conflicts, hair-breadth escapes, ready wit, intrepidity, personal prowess, place his endowments nearly on a par with the northern hero. No prison has yet been found strong enough to hold him. His escape from the Fleet prison was scarcely second in perils and difficulties to that of Jack Shepherd from Newgate. And still more arduous was his flight from the cells of a dungeon in Flushing, wherein, on the recurrence of war between England and France, in 1803, he was confined under a military guard. After his escape from the new gaol, in the borough, loaded with heavy irons, a thousand pound reward was offered for his apprehension. The political services he rendered the British government, and particularly the Duke of York, as Commander in Chief, obtained him a general pardon."[18a]

Yet there is, indeed, historical evidence that Johnstone designed and constructed his rescue submarines, and that he spoke openly, after Napoleon's death, about his plan to use them. The most complete version of events, in what is purported to be the smuggler's own words, can be found in an obscure memoir entitled *Scenes and Stories of a Clergyman in Debt*, which was published in 1835, while Johnstone was still alive. The author claimed to have met the smuggler in debtor's prison, where Johnstone agreed to put his tale in his own words. The book contains memoirs of several dramatic episodes that are closely aligned with contemporary accounts–his remarkable escape from Fleet Prison, for example. At the very least, the correspondences lend weight to the belief that the material in *Scenes and Stories* really was written by Johnstone–though of course it does not prove that the plot was anything but a flight of his own personal imagination:

"I constructed two submarine ships, which I intended should be engaged in the meritorious and humane service of rescuing the immortal emperor Napoleon–the greatest man of his age–from the fangs of his jailor, Sir Hudson Lowe. The *Eagle* was of burthen [volume; equivalent to about a third of displacement] of a hundred and fourteen tons, eighty-four feet in length, and eighteen foot beam... The *Etna*–the smaller ship–was forty feet long, and ten feet beam; burthen, twenty-three tons. These two vessels were [manned by] thirty well chosen seamen, with four engineers. They were also to take twenty torpedoes, a number equal to the destruction of twenty ships, ready for action in case of my meeting with any opposition from the ships of war on the station."[19]

Johnstone's narrative passes quietly over the not inconsiderable difficulty of how such small vessels were to make the voyage south to St. Helena, and continues on to their propulsion, with the larger *Eagle* boasting "two engines of twenty-horse power each, the small [*Etna*]...with one engine of ten-horse power." Furthermore, each submersible would possess "high pressure, well arranged, equipped with warlike stores." The expedition would be "ready for action in case of my meeting with any opposition from the ships of war on the station."

AMERICAN SUBMARINERS: PRE-CIVIL WAR

Johnstone did not, however, explain exactly how his submarines would make their way off the coast of the island–the *Etna* so close, in fact, to the shore that it would need to be "well fortified with cork fenders" to prevent being dashed to pieces on the rocks. The plan then called for Johnson to land, carrying "a mechanical chair, capable of containing one person on the seat, and a standing foot-board at the back," and equipped with the enormous quantity of 2,500 feet of "patent whale line." Leaving this equipment on the rocks, the smuggler would scale the cliffs, sink an iron bolt and a block at the summit, and make his way inland to Longwood:

> "I should then obtain my introduction to his Imperial Majesty and explain my plan... I proposed that [a] coachman should go into the house at a certain hour... and that His Majesty should be provided with a similar livery, as well as myself, the one in the character of a coachman and the other as groom.... We should then watch our opportunity to avoid the eye of the [naval patrols on] guard, who seldom looked out in the direction of highest point of the island, and upon our arriving at the spot where our blocks, &c., were deposited, I should make fast one end of my ball of twine to the ring, and heave the ball down to my confidential man...and then haul up the mechanical chair to the top. I should then place His Majesty in the chair, while I took my station at the back, and lowered away with a corresponding weight on the other side."[20]

The rescue of Emperor Napoleon would take place at night, with the emperor boarding the *Etna* and then transferring to the larger *Eagle*. The two submarines would then make sail–they were to be equipped with collapsible masts as well as engines:

> "I calculated that no hostile ship could impede our progress...as in the event of any attack I should haul our sails, and strike yards and masts (which would only occupy about 40 minutes), and then submerge. Under water we should await the approach of an enemy, and then, with the aid of the little Etna, attaching the torpedo to her bottom, effect her destruction in 15 minutes."[21]

Finally, Johnstone explained that the two submerged vessels would eventually resurface and make their way across the Atlantic Ocean. Upon arriving "at a secure and convenient spot on the coast of the United States," he would communicate with "his majesty's government through the medium of my friend and patron, the ever-to-be-lamented Duke of York." Together, they would decide upon "a more suitable and honourable [sic] asylum for his imperial majesty."

Historians might have believed that Thomas Johnstone's story ended there and was, perhaps, filled with only half-truths. However, it does have support from a number of sources. The Marquis de Montholon, a Paris-born general during the Napoleonic Wars, who voluntarily went into exile with Napoleon and published an account of his time on St. Helena years later. Montholon wrote of a group of French officers who planned to rescue Napoleon "with a submarine," and mentions elsewhere that 5,000 or 6,000 Louis d'or were spent on the construction of the vessel.

To further the plausibility of Johnstone's rescue mission, the *Naval Chronicle*, a British periodical published monthly between January of 1799 and December of 1818, mentioned the one-time smuggler in connection with a submarine plot, though this time the sum involved was £40,000, payable "on the day his vessel was ready to proceed to sea." And an even earlier source, the *Historical Gallery of Criminal Portraitures*, published in 1823, added the vital missing link that explained why Johnstone felt competent to construct such a vessel: fifteen years earlier, when the Napoleonic Wars were at their height, it claimed that he had, indeed, worked with the renowned Robert Fulton, who had come to Great Britain to sell his own plans for an underwater boat. Together, these historical records offer creedence to the Johnstone submarine legacy, now largely forgotten by history.

What has been much more difficult to establish in history, however, is whether Fulton and Thomas Johnstone actually met; their association and working relationship is hinted at in several publications, but nothing survives as absolute proof. Johnstone himself was likely the source of a statement that appears in the *Historical Gallery* to the effect that he encountered Fulton in Dover in 1804 and "worked himself so far into [his] secrets, that, when the latter quitted England...Johnstone conceived himself able to take up his projects."[22]

Even more troublesome is the suggestion that the book at the very heart of this historical recollection–*Scenes and Stories of a Clergyman in Debt*–is not precisely what it appears to be. In 1835, a denunciation appeared in the satirical newspaper *Figaro* in London, alleging that its real author was Frederick William Naylor Bayley, now suspected to be a writer of fabrication and fiction, not a churchman, though he certainly spent time in jail for unpaid debts. The same article contained the statement that "the most extraordinary pains have been taken by the publisher to keep...Captain Johnson [sic] from sight of this work." Why make such a claim if, indeed, Thomas Johnstone himself had written the account that appeared under his name?

As time passed, the aging smuggler spent the 1820s bragging about a lengthy succession of projects involving his "amazing" submarine designs. At one point, he was reportedly working for the king of Denmark; at another for the Pasha of Egypt; at yet another to be building a submarine to salvage a ship off the Dutch island of Texel, or to retrieve valuables from wrecks in the Caribbean. Truth from fiction is difficult to sort out. We know that, after emerging from debtors' prison, Johnstone lived for years south of the Thames on a pension of £140 annually. That was scarcely enough to allow his life to be lived to its fullest.

The exiled former French emperor Napoleon Bonaparte died in captivity at St. Helena before Thomas Johnstone could move forward with his daring rescue plan. Likely, this was fortunate because, given the nature of the primitive vessel, he likely would have met a sudden and horrible death at sea. Strangely for a smuggler, he died quietly at home in bed some eighteen years later at the ripe old age of 67. Yet, the Scotsman, who was born in England and pledged allegiance to both France and America, contributed both real and, perhaps, semi-fictional development to submarine evolution.

Lodner Darvontis Phillips

-12-
Lodner Darvontis Phillips: *Marine Cigar*

"(Phillips' submarine), being the most complete invention of its kind with which I am acquainted...it was cigar-shaped, 40 feet long and 4 feet in greatest diameter, and in the course of a few years he so far perfected his arrangements for purifying air, &c., that on one occasion he took his wife and two children with him, and spent a whole day in exploring the bottom of the lake..."[1]

It was a cheerful, sunny Sunday afternoon, July 23, 1916, as a thin mist drifted up from the surface of Lake Michigan. A group of young men made their way slowly past the elaborate exhibit at 208 South State Street, a short distance west of Lake Michigan, talking about life's complications and generally having a good time. All around them, streams of people strolled through the open roadway in a festive mood. Young children were dressed aptly for the occasion, wearing everything from tiny blue-and-white sailor suits to loose-fitting middy blouses and shorts.

It was a festive ocassion for site-seers. The Municipal Pier—now known as Navy Pier—had recently opened to much fanfare and celebration. In fact, the *Chicago Tribune* had boasted on July 5 that "No city in the world has any structure on a water front that compares with the new Municipal pier." In addition to the city view and the cool lake breezes, the pier offered dancing and music, and there was much excitement about the upcoming appearance of famed Chicago conductor, Johnny Hand. And, in future years, it would be an entertainment venue, a university, a naval base, an army base, a convention center, a food storage facility and, in 1921, a race track between airplanes and pigeons (with the pigeons coming out as a concise winner).

People from all over the region were crowding into the city on that particular weekend. They came in streetcars, horse-drawn wagons, broughams, carriages, omnibuses, and motorized public cabs known as "hacks." Along State Street, the newly-designed elevated train crossed the Chicago River into "the loop," so named because of the circular route most trolleys followed as they reached the center of the city. Filling up like packed sardine cans, picnic steamers loaded their anxious passengers just a short walking distance to the northeast.

After having paused momentarily to study the huge display of photographs depicting contemporary tugs, freighters, barges, and tankers, one dashing young man stopped dead in his tracks. Before him lay a weathered, copper-sheathed vessel that was shaped something like a fat cigar. A short ladder led up to an open hatchway, and a sign to the left boasted that, for a mere ten cents, you could "inspect the interior of the *Fool Killer* at your own risk." Nearby, an oversized poster, printed by the Skee-Ball Company of Illinois, boasted:

> "Submarine–'Fool Killer' now on exhibition at 208 State Street. 'The Fool Killer,' resurrected for your inspection is the most intensely interesting exhibit ever shown in Chicago. Every man, woman and child should see it. It is an educational inspiration...After lying for a generation in the mud bottom of the Chicago River, the submarine 'Fool Killer' was discovered by Capt. Deneau–the diver who recovered 250 bodies at the time of the Eastland disaster. This tragic and historic relic is now on exhibition... together with the bones of the man and dog who perished when it sank. Cap. Deneau–Hero of the Eastland–delivers lectures and answers questions through the day and evening...In addition to the talks by Capt. Deneau, Professor Herbert gives an educational discourse every half hour on the history of submarines from the time of Alexander the Great's 'glass barrel' to the present time..."[2]

Hurriedly, the man and his friends dug into their baggy trouser pockets, willing to pay the insignificant price for a chance to share a brief hazard within the stomach of the mysterious whale-like structure.

Indeed, the object of his respect was not a death-trap for a man and his dog at all, but rather a crude diving machine that had recently been discovered lying on the murky bottom of the nearby Chicago River. Accounts claimed divers had found the vessel while attempting to salvage the *Eastland*, a cruise ship that had rolled over at its berth near the Clark Street Bridge. The catastrophe had drowned more than 800 people, all of which were Western Electric employees and their families on their way to a company picnic in Michigan City, Indiana.

But the poster's claim simply wasn't true; the submarine hadn't been discovered until November of 1915, more than four months after the disaster. But at least one of the same rescuers was involved in her discovery–23-year-old professional diver named William "Frenchy" Deneau, who was credited with saving more than 250 drowning victims from the *Eastland*. A local hero, Deneau had made the following claim concerning the rescue:

> "I was standing on the bridge watching passengers board the ship, when suddenly she listed and turned over. I ran to the dock and volunteered to help. We went down as fast as we could get into diving suits..."[3]

According to the *Chicago Tribune*, Deneau had been laying underwater cable a few months later near the Rush Street Bridge on November 23 when a sweep of the dredging shovel uncovered the mysterious vessel beneath three feet of mud. The *Tribune* went on to say:

"The boat is said to have belonged to Peter Nissen, spectacular mariner, who was lost in his revolving vessel while attempting to drift across Lake Michigan...The 'Foolkiller' was so called because it first made its appearance shortly after the Chicago fire, in the days when submarines were unheard of, and drowned its original owner, a New York man, when it made a trial trip."[4]

Sketch of daredevil mariner, Peter Nissen

At first glance, this story seemed plausible. There actually was a "spectacular mariner" named Peter Nissen. A Chicago accountant who dreamed of glory, Nissen had shot the Niagara River rapids on July 9, 1900, and again in 1901 in boats of his own design, respectively called *Foolkiller No. 1* and *Foolkiller No. 2*.

Later he came up with an even more daring notion: he would attempt to roll across Lake Michigan in a hammock suspended inside a giant canvas balloon, which he promotingly dubbed *Foolkiller No. 3*. The craft was little more than a big canvass balloon–the main inner workings were simply a hammock-type seat hung from the axel; Nissen would steer by moving the basket back and forth across the axel. The idea was that the thing would roll over both land and sea.

Peter Nissen's *Foolkiller* entering the Niagara Falls rapids, October 14, 1901

In late November of 1904, hardly the ideal time weather wise for such a risky adventure, he set out across the lake from Chicago–and almost made it. On December 1, the *Foolkiller No. 3* was found collapsed on the beach two-and-a-half west of Stevensville, Michigan. Nissen's body lay a few hundred yards away. He had died of exposure.

But here was one major problem with Frenchy Deneau's tale concerning the submarine on display in Chicago. Unorthodox though Peter Nissen's *Foolkiller* vessels were, none of them even came close to resembling a submarine, and none bore any resemblance to the vessel Deneau had pulled from the Chicago River in 1915. In the voluminous press coverage of Nissen's stunts over the years, there was no mention of his ever having constructed, designed, or owned a submarine. So, where did the odd-looking vessel come from?

Lodner Phillips' first submarine being salvaged near Chicago's Rush Street Bridge

On January 16, 1916, the *Chicago Tribune* ran another story about Deneau's find, this time with the headline "Skulls Found on *Foolkiller*, Old Submarine." Somehow, the story had changed:

> "An unwritten tragedy of the Chicago River was brought to light after twenty-five years yesterday when the bones of a man and the skull of a dog were taken from the mud-coated 'Foolkiller,' the ancient submarine that occupied a berth in the river bed since 1870... The craft was built

in the early '70s by an eastern man and floated. Its first submersion was its last but one. It remained down for twenty years and then was purchased and raised by William Nissen. He made some experiments with it, but one day about twenty-five years ago it disappeared and was not seen again. Deneau, while making some investigations in the muddy bed of the river at Wells Street, came upon the steel vessel deep in the mud...it was finally brought up and towed to the Fullerton Avenue bridge, where Deneau and his helpers set about cleaning it. Yesterday in the mud that crusted the inside of the queer craft were found the skull of a dog and some human bones."[5]

Oddly enough, Peter Nissen, Chicago's forgotten hero, had now become the unknown William Nissen, who was actually alive and living in the city, though the two were not related. The location where the submarine was discovered had also shifted from the Rush Street Bridge to the Wells Street Bridge. The next year, Deneau would be quoted as saying the vessel had been found near the Madison Street Bridge. Finally–and most strangely–some skeletal remains had been found on board; though apparently not until seven weeks after the initial discovery, and three weeks after the sub had been pulled from the water. What was more odd, the bones were not complete, as one would expect if they were the remains of the sub's drowned occupants, but just fragments.

Yet, one part of Deneau's story was true...after lying undisturbed for years, the odd-looking submersible had been brought to the surface, cleaned, and dried out. Although no one had realized it at the time, the unique vessel would later be determined to be the ingenious creation of an unknown inventor, Lodner Darvontis Phillips, a man who had spent a number of years experimenting with underwater crafts. Indeed, to that that time, he was only one of a handful of Americans who would design and construct a workable diving apparatus.

Lodner's family roots can be traced back dozens of generations to the early 1400s and Lord Philip Philipps, who resided at Cilsant in southwest Wales. In 1611, King James I wanted to raise money to meet the rising cost of keeping his army in Ireland, so he hit upon the idea of selling baronetcies (hereditary knighthoods). Sir John Philipps, Thomas', great-great-grandson of Lord Phillips, was one of the privileged buyers. He had married Anne Perrot, granddaughter of King Henry VIII, allowing him to buy a baronetcy to be known as Penbrokeshire at a cost of £1,095. The sum was supposed to cover the cost of keeping thirty soldiers in Ireland for a period of three years.

From that day forward, throughout the seventeenth and eighteenth centuries, the Philips' grew to be the most powerful family in all of Pembrokeshire County, exercising tremendous political, social and economic influence over all aspects of life. They controlled vast estates, and were prominent philanthropists, being particularly supportive of the charity school movement. Patrons of the arts for generations upon generations, they supplied the region with sheriffs, justices of the peace, lord lieutenants, and members of Parliament.

Eventually, William, Lodner's great-great-great-grandfather, was the first Phillips to arrive on American soil, settling in Newport, Newport County, Virginia, in about 1680. Though he had already been married and bore a daughter in Braunton, Devon County, England, the adulterer took a second wife, Susannah Williams, daughter of Roger Williams, nephew of the founder of Rhode Island in 1684. Over the course of the next two decades, they would bring four daughters and three sons into the world. On August 9, 1722, their youngest son, David Phillips, would marry twenty-eight-year-old Mary Bowyer at Christ Church and Saint Peters in Philadelphia, Pennsylvania.

The following year, Lodner's great-grandfather, Benjamin Phillips, was born in Philadelphia, Pennsylvania, and married Elizabeth Oswald in 1745. Much later, at the age of forty-five, Benjamin would become a drum major during the early days of the Revolutionary War, and carried his drum in the Battle of Bunker Hill. After the war, he assisted in surveying and settling the area around Genesee County, New York.

Birth records indicate that David Phillips, Lodner's grandfather, was born in Dunstable, Hillsborough County, New Hampshire, on January 19, 1769. For a number of years prior to 1740, the boundary lines of the province of New Hampshire were in dispute. Massachusetts claimed that the division boundary between Massachusetts and New Hampshire was defined by a line drawn from a point on the Atlantic coast three miles north of the mouth of the Merrimack River, and running on the northerly and easterly side of the river at a distance of three miles from it, to a point three miles beyond the parallel of the junction of the Winnipiseogee and the Pemigewasset rivers. From that point, the boundary cut due west to the Connecticut. This disagreement included all the territory in the present-day limits of Hillsborough (Hillsboro) County, with the exceptions of the town of Pelham and a small portion of the town of Hudson. It also included the whole of Cheshire County, as well as the larger part of present-day Merrimack and Sullivan Counties.

Meanwhile, New Hampshire claimed for her southern boundary a line due west from the same point on the ocean. By this claim, the towns of Pelham, Hudson, Litchfield, Nashua, Merrimack, Hollis, Amherst and all other towns lying within about fourteen miles of latitude were conceded to be within Massachusetts. The ancient town of Dunstable, which contained more than two hundred square miles, and included all of the towns named above and portions of other towns within the claimed limits of New Hampshire, made a part of the county of Middlesex, Massachusets, and had not, before 1740, been regarded by any party as in part the territory of the province of New Hampshire.

On December 28, 1739, the westerly portion of Dunstable was erected into a separate and distinct precinct by the government of Massachusetts, and went by the name of West Dunstable until April 3, 1746, when, in answer to a petition from the inhabitants, about one-half of it was incorporated with full town privileges by the Governor and Council of the province of New Hampshire, and named Holles. In the meantime, the boundary between Massachusetts and New Hampshire had finally been settled in 1741 by the King himself, who ended the controversy in favor of New Hampshire and fixed the present boundary, granting the province a much larger territory than had been claimed previously. In making this decision, communities that had previously held a "corporate existence" in Massachusetts were rechartered by the province of New Hampshire, and new towns were formed from those portions of existing towns cut off from Massachusetts.

By the end of the 1700s, thirty-year-old David Phillips was happily married with five children, all under the age of ten. Census records of 1800 show that Lodner's paternal grandparents were residing in the small town of Plainfield, Cheshire County, New Hampshire, ninety miles northwest of Dunstable. By 1820, documentation indicates that the family had doubled in size to ten children. As a young man, David had chosen to follow in five generations of family footsteps, taking up the profession of leather shoe and boot maker.

During pioneer times in western New York, Lodner's grandfather had come to Genesee County as a land surveyor, making his home about ten miles southeast of Rochester in the tiny hamlet of Perinton Center. The region had rich soil and abundant waterpower, both essential in luring farmers and craftsmen from the rocky hills of New England to the western frontier. It had been William Walker of Canandaigua who had purchased thirty-six square miles of the untamed land, and hired his brother, Caleb, and his cousin, Glover Perrin, to survey the property and divide it into sixty-six equal lots. Each of these 350-acre parcels would be sold to incoming settlers.

Glover Perrin, his family, and his six siblings and their families settled in the area, which became known as Perinton Center when the township was officially incorporated by the New York State Legislature on May 26, 1812. Other settlers soon followed, as word of the region's promise traveled back east. Between 1800 and 1814, all of Walker's lots were sold and the Perinton Center census showed a growth in population from seventy-one to 821 people. A dozen of these newcomers included David Phillips and his wife, along with their six sons and four daughters.

On April 6, 1843, the Free Will Baptist Society was organized in Genesee and Wayne counties, with Samuel Wire, Benjamin Chapman, John D. Robinson, Willard Parker, and David Phillips named as its founders and trustees. The official certificate was recorded on May 6. Soon, the Society would build a meeting-house in the southwesr part of Wayne County, and under the ministry of Reverend Samuel Wire, would hold services regularly for several years. David, Lodner's grandfather, would remain an active member until his death.

Meanwhile, Lodner's maternal grandparents, Eleazer P. and Sarah Putnam Bateman, who had been married on November 8, 1757, had long resided in East Killingsly, Windham County, Connecticut, before relocating to western New York. Prior to the Revolutionary War, Eleazer had served as a magistrate under the English crown, though he remained neutral during the hostilities. Afterward, in 1806, he took his family to Genesee County, New York, where he was active in public life, helped to establish the freemasons in the nearby town of Pittsford, and served as county sheriff and justice of the peace. In fact, maintaining the peace was a fulltime venture throughout the county, particularly with a transient population working on the construction of the Erie Canal:

> "The work was hard, the hours long, living conditions poor, though usually there was food enough. Because of these conditions Egypt was a lively place during the digging of the canal. Eleazer Bateman held court there almost continuously."[6]

Eleazer died at the advanced age of eighty-four years old, after having raised a large family, mostly daughters.

Lodner's father, Cyril Phillips, was a native of Plainfield, Cheshire County, New Hampshire, and had come to the community of Perinton Center, New York, with his parents and siblings in 1814 at the age of fifteen. He would learn the art of leather shoe and boot making from his father, David, a tradition that had been carried on through six generations of the family. There, he met and courted one of the youngest of Eleazer Bateman's daughters, Virena, whose ancestors had come from England and also settled in Genesee County. Described as being somewhat "frail and shy," Virena and many of her siblings were often sick with one ailment or another. Oliver Loud, who would one day become Cyril's brother-in-law by marrying Virena's sister, Charlotte Bateman, had the perfect remedy, and was what locals often referred to as "Perinton Mead," and was advertised to either "kill or cure" the patient:

> "Take the whites of twelve eggs, mix them well in 24 gallons of water, add 40 pounds of honey, boil together one hour. Then put in a little ginger or cinnamon or mace or pimento or a very small quantity of each as may be convenate [sic]. When the mixture is cold add a spoonful of yeast and pour it into a cask which should be full that it may work at the bung…"[7]

Cyril Phillips married Virena at Perinton Center, New York, in 1821 and, on May 18 of the next year, they gave birth to their first son, Addison Joseph. In 1825, Lodner Darvontis was born. Next came brother William Shillingforth, born March 24, 1828. Only sister, Virena, would join them just one year later.

The Phillips children would spend their entire youths in western New York. Their educational opportunities were quite limited, due to the primitive condition of the local schools, and also because their father needed them at home for daily chores. By the 1830s, life in Perinton Center was changing, as the Erie Canal opened up the western portion of the state. The Village of Fairport, an approximately one square mile area within the Town of Perinton Center, was drained of its unhealthy swamps by the new canal, and the north-south route through the village served as a natural highway for farmers to bring produce to the canal. The result was a booming canal town that eventually eclipsed the hamlet of Egypt, as well as the surrounding canal settlements of Knapp's Bridge, Fullam's Basin, and Hartwell's (Bushnell's) Basin. And, with change came money making opportunities for skilled labor and services:

> "There are about seven miles of canal in the town. It cut across the farms and necessitated the building of those low bridges to connect fields and farm buildings. Frequently the state had to build the bridge to secure the right of way. As the route followed went north of the little hamlet of Egypt and the community of Perinton Center, it caused a decided shift in population and enterprise...there were stores, a grist mill and a saw mill, wagon and blacksmith shops, a tannery, a foundry, a nursery, three taverns and a post office."[8]

Growing up near Rochester, situated along the southern edge of Lake Ontario, young Lodner had ample opportunity to study the mechanics of a variety of seagoing vessels, and to dream of unknown creatures lurking below. His father, who had held high hopes that each of his sons would one day grow up to follow in his boot and shoe making footsteps, was disappointed that his middle son would, instead, spend his days tinkering with gadgets and inventions of his own design. Life changed, however, when their mother, Virena Phillips, died in 1834 at the age of thirty-four. Lodner was only eight years old.

Perhaps out of love, perhaps out of loneliness, or perhaps with the need of a mother for his young children, Cyril Phillips would take a second wife, Philena Joy, late in 1835. Attracted by the mystery and promise of the unsettled wilderness, as well as a fresh start, Cyril relocated his second wife and children to LaPorte County, nestled in the northern portion of Indiana, in the spring of 1842. There, he would establish one of the largest boot and shoe factories in the entire Midwest, located in the 200 block of Franklin Street in Michigan City. The community in which the Phillips family had chosen to put down firm roots was, indeed, an excellent export locale for leather footwear:

> "About fifty people lived in Michigan City in 1833. By 1836, the population had swelled to 1,500 and Michigan City had twelve dry goods stores and ten hotels. George and Fisher Ames had a hardware store, and Couden owned a stove, tin, and iron store. Shoes and boots were manufactured in Michigan City, and Addison J. Phillips employed forty cobblers in 1846."[9]

The community would also soon boast a first class train depot, which would help the Phillips Boot and Shoe Company. Constructed on the Lake Shore and Michigan Southern line, which later was the New York Central, the depot's round-headed windows were typical for Italianate buildings, but the drip moldings over them and the vertical board and batten siding were more common on Gothic Revival buildings. The east end of this building was constructed soon after the tracks were first laid through La Porte in 1853.

Furthermore, the community had a lengthy marine history, which included Indian canoes, voyagers, schooners, and sidewheelers. It would be nearby Lake Michigan that would become the underwater proving grounds for young Lodner's submarine expeditions

Described by family members as handsome, not the most lovable, and a "kind of backwards boy," young Lodner shared a mysterious trait with another earlier inventor, Leonardo da Vinci: both had the habit of signing their names completely in reverse. In Phillips' case, he began with the "s" of "Phillips" on the left and ended with the capital "L" of "Lodner" on the right. It would become his trademark.

Incorporating materials found locally, his miniature prototype submersible was made ready for her maiden voyage, which would be conducted in the summer of 1845. Shaped much like "a white fish," she was launched into the cool waters of nearby Trail Creek, which flowed into the calm Lake Michigan harbor, in late July of that year.

Gingerly, young Lodner climbed aboard and closed the hatchway behind him, anxious to explore a world that most had only imagined. Slowly, the crudely constructed craft drifted past the base of Old Lighthouse and out into deeper waters:

> "The hull was covered with sheet copper. It had no apparatus for propelling it except a pole to push it along the bottom of the lake. The pole passed through the hull, the opening being made water-tight with rubber gaskets. A device similar to a crude cylinder was used for submerging and raising the submarine. When the cylinder was filled with water, it served the purpose of making the craft go down. Expelling the water from the cylinder by means of a plunger operated by hand was to give it sufficient buoyancy to rise to the surface. The boat sank in some twelve feet of water about where the harbor now is–pretty near the old lighthouse, but across on the west side of the river. No one was in it at the time. Lodner and his brother, William, afterwards raised it, and taking it up the river, placed it on the bank."[10]

Evidently, Lodner did not believe that his initial design was satisfactory for future deep-water missions, for he simply abandoned the tiny submersible on the very spot where it had been dragged ashore. After weeks of neglect, with its hull weathered and decaying, the tiny vessel mysteriously disappeared.

Lodner would design an evolutionary number of diving crafts during the next several years, with each successive model a bit closer to his liking. One of these was reported to have been found beneath a watery grave in the muddy bottom of the Chicago River, and would later be recovered by a team of salvage divers and put on display in Chicago in 1916. After the public exhibit, this early submersible was sold to Charles W. Parker's Greatest Shows, a well-known traveling carnival. Newspaper accounts followed it westward to Oelwein, Iowa, in May of 1916. The vessel was advertised as "The Submarine or Fool Killer, the first submarine ever built," being exhibited along with "skee ball, a new amusement device." Yet, the intriguing submersible did not receive top billing, and was merely listed among other draws, including "The Electric Girl, The Vegetable King, Snooks, the smallest monkey in the world, the fat girl, and the Homeliest Woman in the World." By the end of June, it was back on display at the Riverview Amusement Park in Chicago, when it disappeared, never to be seen again.

Rendition of Lodner Phillips' first submarine, 1845

Lodner Phillips married Maria Holland in the spring of 1850. Maria appeared in the September 7, 1850 census in the Second Ward of Chicago, Cook County, Illinois, as Mrs. M. Phillips, age twenty-two, having been born and raised in Ireland, and married within the past twelve months. On that same record appears an assumed older sister, as M.J. Holland, age twenty-three, also recorded as being born in Ireland. Both had originated in Dublin, at a time when their father had been in the Irish government service. Little more is known of the Holland family.

By the spring of 1850, Lodner felt that he had developed a near-perfect design for an underwater boat. Yet, he did not have the adequate funds to put it into material form. His father and two brothers, Addison and William, would repeatedly come to his financial rescue, however, agreeing to cosign no less than seven separate loans in order to subsidize the experiments. All moneys borrowed, which totaled $241, were owed to a neighbor, Richard Hewes, with each loan payable within one year's time from the date of issuance. Apparently, however, the notes were not paid in due time, for records indicate that court papers were "served on the written named defendant, Cyril Phillips, by reading..."

As a further embarrassment to the Phillips family, the plaintiff, Richard Hewes, claimed that, since virtually no effort was made to repay the loans, he was entitled to "four hundred and fifty dollars, and the foreclosure of the mortgage and the sale of the Phillips property..."[11] The court agreed, for the elder Phillips was forced to sell a small portion of his holdings to pay off his son's overdue bills.

Lodner's family hoped that the sale of Cyril Phillips' property would turn out to be well worth the hardship that it caused, for a much improved design was completed in the summer of 1851. Under its "Western Correspondence" section, a Batavia, New York, newspaper known as *The Republican Advocate*, reported on the underwater vessel's construction in its July 1, 1851, edition:

> "A citizen is building a diving boat. It is nearly completed. It is of sufficient size to contain all things necessary for life and labor. The officers and crew of the sub-marine exploring boat is to be composed of one man. It is to be sunk and kept at the bottom of the sea by rocks, which can be thrown out when a sail to the surface is desired. Condensed air is to be taken on board for breathing and other purposes. It is to be propelled by machinery, worked by hand. The speed of this singular craft on voyages of discovery or pleasure, is calculated at four miles an hour. Success to the enterprise; and may its bold and enterprising originator never have other than safe and prosperous voyages."[12]

Soon to be known as the *Marine Cigar*, due to its resemblance to a long, pointed stogie, the upgraded model measured forty feet in length and just four feet at its greatest diameter:

"It has two double hatches, one on the top, and one at the bottom, and may have side hatches if required. The upper hatch is sealed down when the vessel is submerged; when the upper hatch is open the bottom one is shut, and vice-versa. It has two sight domes, which are used when the vessel is on the surface and it has four interrupted keels to prevent it turning over when submerged... Should the vessel run into anything, it can be extricated without injury, having on its point or bow a thimble or outer case which is so constructed that by reversing the screw, the boat would be backed, leaving the thimble. Having a glass tube properly marked, the exact depth of water from the surface is always shown. Fresh air is supplied as necessary from tanks containing many atmospheres compressed. The boat is sunk by admitting water into tanks through pipes and is raised by expelling the same. It can be kept stationary or at any required depth of water from 1 inch to 200 feet, and in this lies the secret which makes the boat effective..."[13]

As an added feature, the *Marine Cigar* housed a "secret mode of loading guns" while submerged, which would be ideal for attacking a threatening enemy vessel. Yet, according to its inventor, the craft's true intent was not one of aggressive hostility during war; rather, Lodner hoped that his submarine vessel would be used to examine the submerged portions of damaged ships and wharfs, or to partake in deep-water pearl fishing.

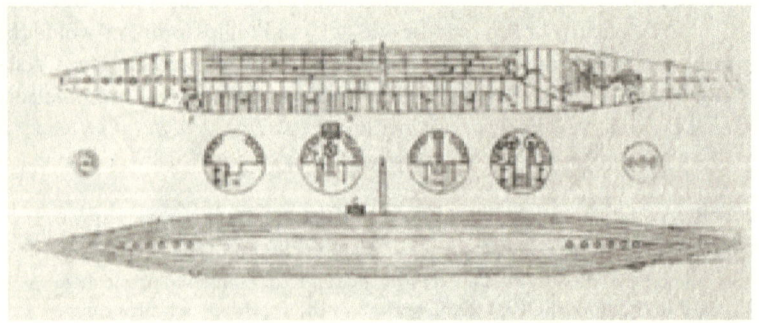

Drawing of Lodner Phillips' *Marine Cigar*, 1851

To propel his unique underwater craft, Phillips had devised two distinct modes of power. The first was described as a simple hand-turned crank; the second was provided "by electromagnetism with a screw," which was "fitted to a shaft on a universal joint by which the rudder is dispensed with."[14]

The lower section of the *Marine Cigar* housed a series of water tanks, and, when all but the middle one was filled, the craft would sit extremely low in the water. An automatic valve allowed the central tank to "fill to the desired amount necessary to attain a determined depth." A lengthy hollowed-out pole, measuring approximately one meter in height, allowed verbal communication with people on the surface at shallow depths. Furthermore, heavy iron weights, attached to a reel and chain system, provided a ready-made anchor. Descriptively, it was reported that:

> "The prow of this submarine offered the particularity of having a sliding spherical joint permitting the introduction and maneuvering of all sorts of instruments: saws, clamps, etc. A series of hub lots allowed the supervision of the operator to these various gadgets. Air pumps forced the air inside the boat to pass through a series of tubes plunged in water tanks and ending in watering can-heads. While going through the water the air cooled off and left its carbonic acid. To maintain the longitudinal balance of the boat, a clock placed in the center of the ship activated the valves and determined the introduction of water either in the forward or rear reservoir. When the ship had regained its horizontal position, the clock was again vertical and the passage of the water from one reservoir to the other stopped."[15]

Lodner Phillips' air-purification system was well ahead of its time, and could maintain purified oxygen for up to ten hours. Lieutenant F.M. Barber, of the United States Navy, later praised him for having "devoted more attention to the subject of purification of the atmosphere in a submarine boat than any of the other inventors."[16]

Phillips claimed that he had conducted a four-hour test dive to the very bottom of Lake Michigan, without the use of an air-hose or outside oxygen supply. His crew had also adequately demonstrated the use of hand-tools underwater, from within the submarine's hull, by managing to saw through a chunk of fourteen-inch square timber. This "introduction and maneuvering of all sorts of instruments" would allow the operator, and crew of "20 to 30 men," to work at salvage operations at any depth, through a ball and socket joint positioned at the far end of the ship's bulkhead. Furthermore, light within the boat's interior would be provided by dead-lights and, when submerged at too great a depth for these to operate efficiently, an illuminating lamp would take their place.

Initially, the *Marine Cigar* could maintain a top speed of 4.5 knots per hour, with two men working the crank of a double-bladed propeller. Later, Phillips hoped to install a coal-burning boiler for generating steam, which, in turn, would run the vessel's unique "electromagnetic" engine. However, the planned apparatus was never put in place and, perhaps, Phillips was fortunate that it wasn't. In practice, the boiler most likely would have raised the interior temperature to an unbearable degree, using up all available oxygen in the process.

On April 7, 1852, Phillips dispatched a letter from his Michigan City home to William H. Graham, a high-ranking official of the U. S. Naval Department, saying:

> "I have made application for a Pattent [sic] for a Submarine boat...and Two Years ago I made application for a Pattent [sic] for the Same through Watson & Renwick as agents to get the Pattent [sic] for me and have not

been able as yet to obtain one. I have made two of these boats Which I have experimented to the Satisfaction of all who have seen me opperate [sic]. I went down in the depth of Water 20 ft. & for which I have travelled [sic] under watter [sic] at the rate of 4 Miles an hour by use of Screw Propeller and now have a machine of the Same Kind which I am confident I can go down with Safety 100 hundred [sic] feet with Safety and Travel 4 or 5 Miles pr. hour. My boat will be completed in about 3 months–then I will be prepared to make experiments for the Navy–or elsewhere. My object in writing to you is this–I understand you are authorized to examine a machine of this Kind and If approved of by You, to purchase for the Navy... I wish you to write me and let me know whether you have one in view–& if So where it was invented & by whom..."[17]

On April 21, 1852, Graham forwarded the following "caustic" reply to Phillips' inquiry:

"Sir. Your letter of the 7th instant in relation to the submarine boat of your invention was referred to the Bureau of Construction &c. the chief of which reports, that 'no authority is known to this Bureau to purchase a submarine boat. The boats used by the Navy go on and not under the water...'"[18]

Employing an uncharacteristic measure of patience and fortitude, Lodner Phillips' patent application was eventually approved on November 9, 1852, for the design and construction of "Steering Submarine Vessels," to be used for the express purpose of "Exploring the Bottoms of Harbors, Rivers, Lakes, and Seas." His detailed drawings included a compressed-air tank for storing oxygen within a limited space, as well as glassed-in portholes. Furthermore, they boasted a hermetically sealed hatchway, positioned on the floor of the submersible, which would allow salvagers the ability to exit and enter at their own discretion whenever a salvage manuever was in order.

After her completion, Phillips' latest model was dispatched almost immediately to the depths of Lake Erie, where she would partake in her first salvage mission–the examination of a sunken steamship known as the *Atlantic*. Devastated in a collision with the *Ogdensburg* on August 20, 1852, the *Atlantic* was thought to be resting approximately one hundred seventy feet down in a location six miles directly south of Long Point, Ontario, Canada.

Soon after she had sunk, divers had been sent down to inspect the wreckage. Indeed, they had managed to pinpoint her approximate location, but had failed in their attempt to salvage some of her most valuable artifacts. Details of Phillips' specific plan to conduct an intricate follow-up salvage operation, using his newest *Marine Cigar*, are sketchy at best. However, the pages of the *Detroit Advertiser* did manage to offer an interested public a few scant details of the planned upcoming mission:

AMERICAN SUBMARINERS: PRE-CIVIL WAR

"A Sub Marine Propeller—We saw yesterday at the Railroad Freight House a curious looking structure of wood and iron, shaped something like a paddle-wheel at one end and an iron flanged steering paddle at the other. On the sides are small Bull's eye windows, filled with very thick glass. The machine, we were informed, is Phillips' Sub Marine Propeller, and came over by the railroad from Michigan City, on its way to pay the *Atlantic* a visit. We know not whether the sub marine was sent to examine her (the Atlantic), hit by the *Ogdensburg* on either the labord or starboard side, which is a point on which there is some question yet."[19]

Drawing of the *Atlantic*, 1852

Lodners' dive to the bottom of Lake Erie resulted in an extremely close call while "attempting to reach the wreck in water one hundred fifty-five feet deep." After submerging about two-thirds of the depth, the inventor found that his vessel was leaking severely, and he was forced to return quickly to the surface. Following repairs, during which the craft was inspected inch-by-inch, he was still not satisfied that she was safe. Hence, he decided to send her down, unmanned, for a brief test run. The *Marine Cigar* was slowly lowered, attached to one end of a hawser, toward the bottom of the lake. Moments later, while attempting to return her to the surface, the hawser-line unexpectedly snapped, and the submarine plummeted quickly to the murky lake floor. Though the location of the *Atlantic* was well documented, the *Marine Cigar* would never be found.

The decision to refrain from taking the boat down himself likely saved the young inventor's life. And, though a number of historians have since claimed that Phillips had gone down with his vessel on that particular occasion, later records prove beyond doubt that such reports were clearly a fallacy.

Following the unfortunate loss of his patented diving vessel, Phillips moved his wife and three children to the city of Chicago. Forced to borrow additional funds to finance a new model, he immediately put his mind toward making a number of improvements. In March of 1854, Lodner took out a loan in the amount of $611.18, using his father, Cyril, and brother, Addison, as co-signers once again. The financing, which was provided by local Michigan City resident, Judson Sawin, a thirty-three-year-old wagon maker who lived with his father, Baptist clergyman, Benjamin Sawin. The entire loan was secured with the full promise that it would be repaid within "eight months...provided we earn it out of the submarine propeller; if not, we promise to pay it one year from the date."[20]

Still unable to make profit from his invention, the note was not paid in time. LaPorte County Court records indicate that, once again, officials attempted to serve papers on Lodner's father and brother on February 8, 1856. Furthermore, it was noted that "Lodner Philips [sic] was not found in his bailiwick."[21] On this occasion, however, the Phillips family was spared from further legal ramifications: seven months later, on September 10, the amount of $676.65 was paid to Sawin, which included the original amount borrowed plus an adequate chunk of interest.

Eventually, on October 14, 1856, Lodner Phillips was granted Patent No. 15,898, for a new invention, which he referred to as his "diving armor." In reality, his newest invention was a completely enclosed reinforced atmospheric diving suit constructed primarily of cast iron, consisting of a barrel-shaped torso with a series of eight ball-and-socket joints. The joints were neatly fashioned at the shoulders, elbows, knees, and hips. Furthermore, the suit boasted a single viewing port, a manhole cover entrance on top, and a lifting eye in the center of the hatch cover for hauling it up and down. Some of the more intriguing features were the waist high hand-cranked screw propeller at the front of the suit, the added manipulators projecting from the waist that extended the operator's reach, and the "buoyancy" balloon attached to the top that surely would have collapsed with increasing depth.

Perhaps most importantly, the apparatus housed a complete built-in air supply, allowing the wearer to descend and remain submerged for lengthy periods of time. Since Phillips' primary purpose for designing his diving armor was for salvage operations, it is not surprising that he had taken the time to install a network of tools attached to the ends of the suit's arms. In his initial patent application, he stated:

> "...the advantages of this machine over all others are first, the operator is freed from all pressure of water at any depth; secondly, he has ample locomotive control over the apparatus; thirdly, he can ascend to the surface on his own account and without the assistance of others. I constructed the bolts of this cap, so that the cap may be loosened and removed by the operator from the inside."[22]

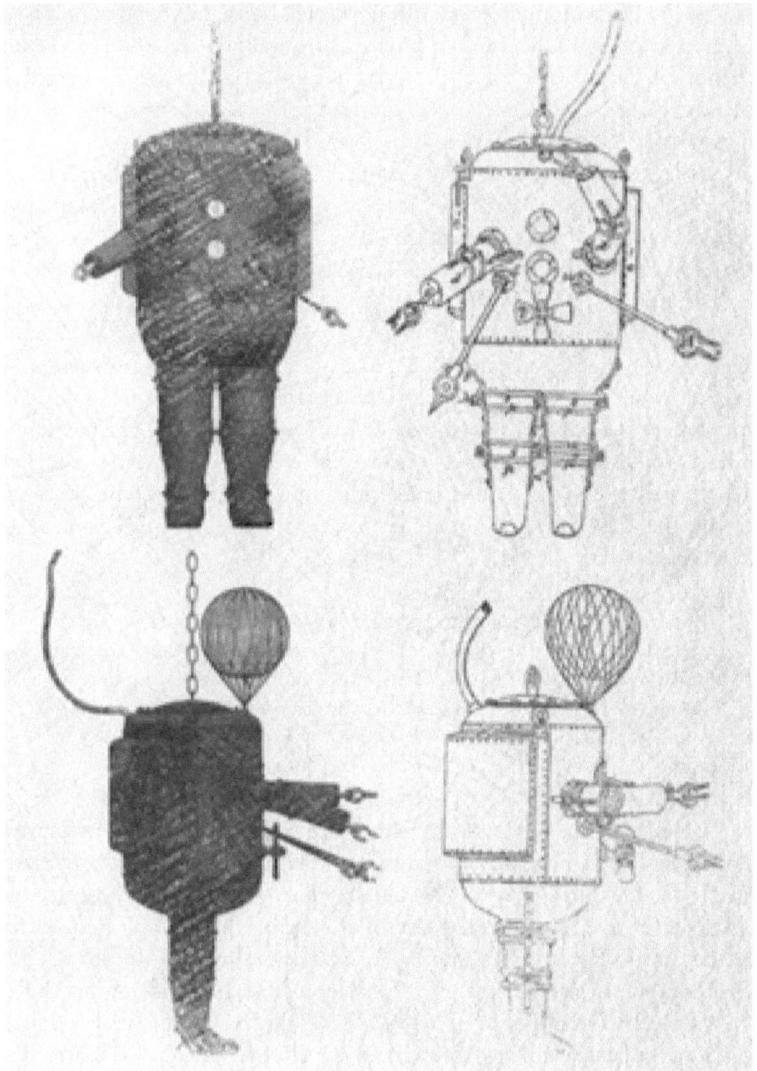

Depiction of patent drawing of the Lodner Phillips' diving armor

Phillips decided to demonstrate his just submarine, in conjunction with the diving armor, before a large audience, which had gathered along the shoreline of the Chicago River. With his poor track record of repaying his debts, the inventor was forced to hand over the cash borrowed for a recently purchased anchor just prior to tossing it overboard from the rear of the diving craft.

After making his submarine stationary in the moving current, Phillips, outfitted in his cumbersome diving suit, jumped from the stern section and descended to the bottom of the muddy river, delighting the crowd of onlookers. Breathing through a tube, he then proceeded to walk the length of the submarine beneath the surface, hooking a series of canvas bags to the submerged anchor. As the bags were pumped full of air from the surface they became buoyant, and the anchor, with Phillips in tow, bobbed to the surface.

With demonstrations such as this, Lodner Phillips slowly began to gain quite a reputation as a "daredevil" in local circles. In fact, his submarine was rudely dubbed the "Fool Killer," due to the prevailing belief that any vessel constructed to dive deep underwater would, eventually, lead to the untimely demise of its operator.

Phillips, who was now more than thirty years of age, continued his efforts to design the perfect diving machine. His plans called for the construction of a vessel that would come fully equipped with an arsenal of weaponry for war. Similar in size and shape to his patented *Marine Cigar*–aside from the fact that its diameter would measure precisely one-eighth its length–his newest model was heavily plated with protective armor on the top. This shield would, in theory, maintain the safety of the submarine's crew from attack by small arms. It also was designed with:

> "...a funnel...for the launching of torpedoes coming in stages through a cylinder with a double closure. An under water cannon, whose opening with automatic closure was attached to the hull by a spherical joint, allowed the shooting of projectiles from bottom to top...a rocket, when launched, dragged along with the help of a cable, (with) a torpedo located ahead and below it."[23]

By early 1862, as Americans found themselves caught up in a Civil War, Phillips approached the Union government, willing to offer them his submarine plans. It was his hope that they would see their way clear to construct such a vessel, which he claimed could destroy ironclad ships carrying supplies into Southern ports. Government officials, however, were initially not interested in his instrument of war, and refused to consider his ideas seriously at that time.

Sometime later, however, between 1862 and 1864, as the war dragged on, Phillips relocated to New York City and presented designs for a submarine squadron to the Secretary of the Navy, Gideon Welles. The first of three models, he explained, would measure approximately forty feet in length. It would possess iron tanks filled with compressed oxygen, which, the inventor estimated, would sustain a small crew of five men for no less than twenty-four hours. The vessel would also be capable of attaching explosives to the underside of enemy ships. And, if this method of attack was not acceptable, a mine which would explode on contact could simply be attached to a length of rope which, in turn, would be dragged from the rear of the submarine.

AMERICAN SUBMARINERS: PRE-CIVIL WAR

Drawing of a Lodner Phillips' early submarine

A second, more elaborate, version of the Phillips submarine was described as being one hundred twenty feet in length, and would be able to transport twenty men for up to five days below the surface. She would be protected by three-inch steel plating, and her steam-propulsion would enable the vessel to travel at a maximum speed of fifteen miles-per-hour on the surface, and eight miles-per-hour while submerged. Designed for harbor and coastal defense, this larger version would come fully equipped with shell rockets that, when fired from the surface, would travel up to three miles. It would also house a newly developed gun that could be fired with accuracy above or below the waterline.

The third and last design was nearly identical to the second, but was two hundred feet in overall length. This added dimension would enable the vessel to carry even heavier armament. Also, it would be able to move further out to sea with no danger to its crew.

To raise the odds that Secretary Welles could not help but be interested, Phillips further claimed that:

> "...all the distinctive features were unequivocally demonstrated by construction of a vessel, forty feet in length, in the year 1850 and by its constant use up to the year 1855...the use of shell rockets upon the water line and the discharging of cannon beneath it...was coincident with the use of the vessel from 1850 to 1855, hulls having been blown to pieces or sunk in more than one instance."[24]

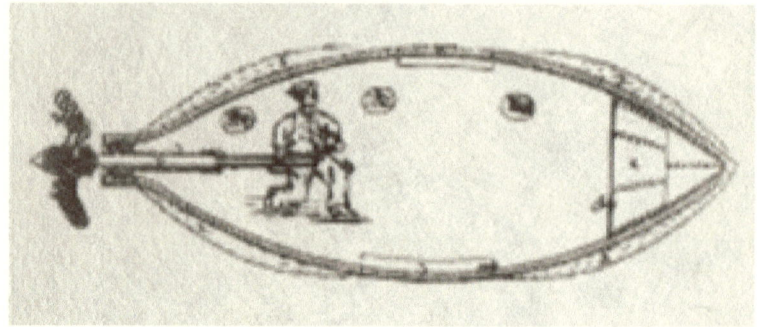

Drawing of a larger Lodner Phillips' submarine

Obviously impressed with the inventor's extensive description, Secretary Welles forwarded the entire outline to the Permanent Commission of the Navy Department, whose job it was to closely study any and all innovative proposals. The Commission was comprised of several prestigious members, including: Alexander Dallas Bache, Superintendent of the U.S. Coastal Survey; Charles H. Dawes, Rear Admiral and Chief of the Bureau of Investigation; Joseph Saxton, Assistant Superintendent of Weights and Measures; and Joseph Henry, Secretary of the Smithsonian Institution.

After carefully examining Phillips' detailed plans, the Commission determined that such an ingenious machine could, indeed, mean devastation to the Southern States' war effort. Speaking on their behalf on June 28, 1864, Admiral Charles H. Davis made a strong recommendation to Secretary Welles that the Navy consider adopting the submarine design submitted by Phillips. Davis described the boat in intricate detail:

> "The first vessel described is of a cigar-shape, forty feet in length, and furnished with tubes filled with compressed air sufficient not only to supplybreathing air for five men for twenty four hours, but also to be used

for the purpose of expelling the water from tanks communicating with the sea, whereby the vessel may be made to rise towards the surface, while it is made to sink by letting the air escape from the tanks into the cabin and readmitting the water, by which the specific gravity of the vessel is increased. By an ingenious contrivance, and the mere loading of a valve to correspond with the required pressure of the water, a given depth below the surface of the sea may be automatically preserved. This vessel, which is to be propelled by means of man-power, is to be rendered serviceable in attaching torpedoes to the side, or exploding them beneath the bottom of vessels, and to be available in sawing, undermining and otherwise removing obstructions through the agency of compressed air as a motive power. The other vessels proposed are of much larger size, to be propelled by steam, and to be armed with shell rockets to be effective at the surface of the water, and with guns worked on or beneath the surface as occasion may require. So many conditions are to be fulfilled in order to make successful application of any plan of submarine warfare, that the problem up to this time, within the knowledge of the Commission, has never been successfully solved, or, if so, has not been practically demonstrated. The Commission, however, would not discourage further attempts, and in consideration of the importance of the invention, and the simplicity and apparent feasibility of the plans proposed by Mr. Phillips... would venture to recommend that an appropriation, sufficient for the construction of one of the smaller vessels, be made for this purpose. In addition to the reasons above mentioned, which have induced us to offer the foregoing suggestion, is the testimony with which we were presented to prove that Mr. Phillips has actually constructed a vessel of this kind, and experimentally tested all parts of the contrivance."[25]

Although few proposals were viewed as being sound by this powerful group during its existence, Phillips had not only managed to gain its attention, but had pushed his inventive foot in through the commission's door. Still, with a tight security on all records of their activities in place, his proposed fleet of submarines never reached the construction phase.

Whether or not the newest version of Phillips submarine design ever made it past the drawing board is a mute historical point, for the Civil War soon ended, and the inventor was forced to resign himself to the fact that his underwater crafts were no longer in high demand. Yet, still hoping to profit from his ventures, he filled his days with the design of other useful devices. They included a machine that could mold plastic fasteners, a plastering device, a steam-powered wagon, a diving bell that could extract treasures from the sea floor, a machine that could card wool, and another that created buttons out of ordinary clamshells.

Lodner Darvontis Phillips devoted his entire life toward the design and construction of the "perfect" submarine. Yet, though "the modest son of a shoemaker was truly a precursor of genius such as...Fulton had been," he never found fame and fortune from his research.[26]

Maria Holland Phillips, the love of Lodner's life, passed away quite unexpectedly in 1862, at the relatively young age of thirty-four, leaving him alone and largely forelorn. Though he tried desperately to continue on without her, he found himself with no one to guide him through emotionally and financially troubled times. He drifted eastward to New York City, working odd jobs and staying in rundown tenement houses. Over time, he lost touch with most of his family and friends.

Lodner Darvontis Phillips died on October 15, 1869, at the age of forty-four. Doctors referred to the cause of death as "phthisis," known in modern times as tuberculosis. At the time of his passing, he was a destitute and lonely man, residing in the seedier portion of lower Manhattan. Laid to rest in an unmarked pauper's grave, located in the Greenwood Cemetery, he was, undoubtedly, the victim of his own futuristic intelligence, creating an amazing diving vessel that was most certainly far in advance of the times. Though it did not bring him fame and fortune, he would go down in history as, perhaps, one of the most important pieces of the American submarine puzzle.

Sketch of Brutus de Villeroi

-13-
Brutus de Villeroi: *Alligator*

"If some one of the large number of experimenters who endeavored to construct submarine boats since that time had contented himself with closely copying the valuable features of Bushnell's vessel, instead of starting out with radically new and untried plans, and without having any experience to guide him, we should have had success to record instead of an almost unbroken list of failures."[1]

As a steady stream of fishermen walked toward their homes during the early evening in the second week of August, 1832, looking forward to relaxation after a long day of harvesting the nets, a slowly-gathering cloud-cover threatened yet another heavy downpour. In the extreme western lowland region of France known as the Loire River Valley, the recent deluge of rains had caused the banks of the country's longest waterway to rise, swell, and, finally, flood out across the landscape. Crops and pastures were inundated with several feet of mucky water. Livestock and farm equipment had been swept away. As had occurred on so many occasions in recent days, businesses and homes had been ruined by Mother Nature's destructive forces. And, once again, the threatening weather had forced an early end to an otherwise good day of fishing.

Though massive field stone walls and thick mud embankments had been constructed and reconstructed here since the Middle Ages, the predictable flooding had repeatedly plagued those living in the valley. Eventually, many of the families, who had resided along this angry waterway for generations, had simply moved away. Those who had opted to remain reinforced their fragile safety by building a series of deep reservoirs in which they hoped the excess water would be forced into and stored. But, despite their massive efforts, life-altering and life-threatening situations had continued to prevail.

As the four-and-one-half-year-old youngster stepped spiritedly along the winding, decades-old dike system walkway, skipping flat stones into the river, large drops of water began to fall. Within minutes, he was listening to the familiar rhythmic pounding sound, as they landed powerfully against the Loire's ever-rising currents.

Even at this early age, the boy was quite certain that the results would be a new series of flood trails carved into the land. Tiring from his muddy-sinking steps, and realizing his chosen path was growing increasingly slippery, he recalled the instructions given to him from father–to pray whenever God's wrath seemed imminent. He paused momentarily to gaze out across the widening river, beginning his silent, innocent plea for reprieve from danger. There, amid the swift, white-foam currents, the silky topside of a strange alligator-like thing captured his attention. He believed that it was a sign from the heavens.

Squinting now, and shielding his eyes from the rain for a better look, he watched in earnest as the unidentified creature moved in his general direction. It was not more than a stone's throw to the east, perhaps as far as one hundred yards from the thriving township limits. Alongside the thing, he saw a man, perhaps thirty-five years of age, standing in a small rowboat, and preparing to climb on the protruding back of the beast. Maybe, thought the boy, he was attempting to kill the monster before it reached the village.

Carefully, the man stepped on top of the thing and made his way toward what appeared to be a gaping wound on its back. Hoping to share his indescribable phantasm with anyone who might be in the vicinity, the youngster scanned his vision up and down the Loire River banks. Seeing no one, he moved his eyes toward the nearby Maritime Canal, a parallel waterway that enabled large, oceangoing vessels to reach the port city of Nantes and the inland city of Tours. To his utter disappointment, he decided that he was the only person in sight, either on land or aboard ship, to see the mysterious creature.

Then, as the bewildered youngster continued to scrutinize the, as yet, unidentified beast from this safe distance, it began to drift away from the river's slippery, muddied bank. He realized that he had a hard-to-swallow tale to share; one that his father and mother would consider a figment of his adventurous imagination. Destined to be the oldest of five children, the seemingly "tall tale" would be shared with younger brother, Paul, and sisters, Anne, Mathilde, and Marie, at a much later time in a drastically different format.

Suddenly, as the youngster looked on in earnest, the curved outer skin of the sea creature disappeared beneath the surface amid a huge swell of bubbles and foam. Hurriedly, the excited and frightened boy rushed toward the security of his family's small cottage, located at No. 2 Quai Jean-Bart, convinced that he had just witnessed the untimely demise of one of his neighbors. But, instead he was fortunate enough to have been privy to submarine history in the making.

Just a few days later, all doubters who had listened to the young boy's "crazy story" would become believers. On August 12, 1832, a public demonstration of the inventor's amazing prototype diving vessel, known then as the *Waterbug*, was conducted at the Nantes docks:

> "There we saw M. de Villeroi enter into a boat made of iron, having the shape and appearance of a fish, ten feet long, three feet wide, which boat was manned by three men, the inventor included. M. de Villeroi, began operations at 3 p.m. After several evolutions on the surface of the water, he began to navigate about one foot beneath the surface of the water, til thirty-five minutes past three; then descended near the bottom of the water, but in a different direction, in order to deceive the boats

which were following him on the surface. At forty-five minutes past three o'clock he returned near the surface of tile water, where, after ten minutes of different evolutions in various directions, he came up on the surface and opened his safety door. At fifty-five minutes past three he made his appearance out of his boat, cheered by all present, having remained with his companions inside of that boat fifty-five minutes without any communication with the exterior atmosphere, and maneuvering his boat with the greatest facility."[2]

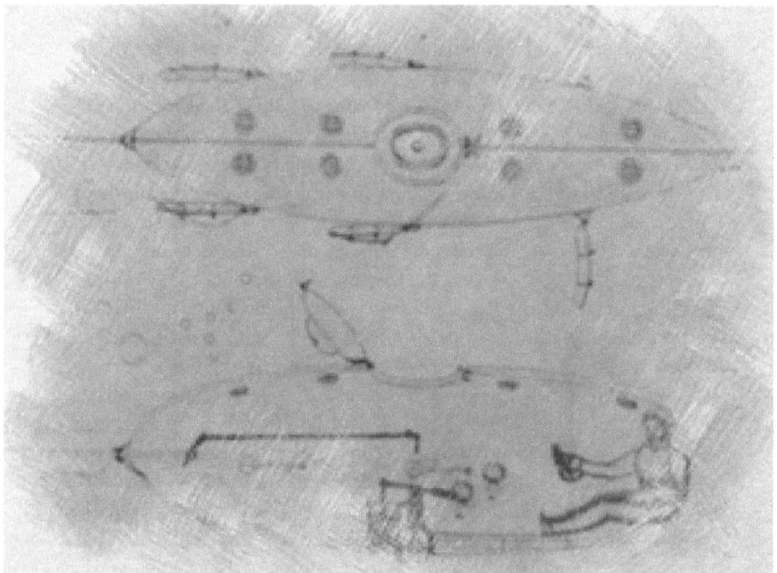

Drawing of Brutus de Villeroi's *Waterbug*, demonstrated in 1833

Years later, the eyewitness, Jules Gabriel Verne, who had been so very young and imaginative at the time, would revisit the day in August of 1832, when he and other Nantes residents witnessed Brutus de Villeroi's amazing underwater invention:

"Mister Robin, our primary schoolteacher, would read pages of our (local) history at the end of the year in the lazy days that separate the Certificate of studies from the summer vacation. As he had a small house in Noirmoutier, he read us the forgotten history of this fabulous man, Brutus Villeroi, the submarine pioneer. This page of our History is also a chapter of the history of the world. On August 10, 1832, on the island of Noirmoutier, in the place called La Claire, occurred a notable event, reported by the academic societies of Vendee and Anjou which overwhelmed their subscribers. Assistant professor Brutus Villeroi was on the island as a substitute [teacher] for the brothers of the Christian school. To attend his experiment he had invited marine engineers, journalists from local and regional newspapers and strong colleagues from his school. Cassocks, military hats, frock coats, the beards of the scholars, and the white skirts of ladies fluttered in a sandy glade at the edge of a forest of mimosas. Brutus Villeroi arrives, transformed into a fisherman, hauling a strange device pushed by two sailors on a handcart. He greets the learned company and declares: 'Ladies, gentlemen, I have the honor to present you my fish-ship which was completely conceived and constructed by me. This boat is unsinkable and has the ability to sail under water.' The gentlemen and ladies look at one-another, stunned. They examined this oblong box which resembled a wooden dolphin, opened by a lid to allow the pilot to enter and which had at both extremities lateral fins comparable to those of a shark. In the front, a thick inner wall of transparent glass was inlaid in the shell to allow the navigator to guide his device under the sea. The speaker continued his explanation: 'I would point out to you that this is in no way comparable to da Vinci's diving bell or to the diving suit drawn by the same inventor. It is not linked up to the earth, and it can sail to a depth of thirty or forty meters under water. I will have the honor to do make this machine move in front of you...' The assistants pushed the cart to the beach, released the hawsers and the ropes that connected it to the hitch, and the fish-ship settled onto the damp sand. The pilot entered carefully, nimbly wedged himself on the seat, waved his arms as a farewell, closed the lid and, vigorously pushed by the two sailors, the fish-ship went under the waves of the Atlantic. The spectators watched, stunned. 'There must be some sorcery,' said a priest. 'Or some deception.' 'Or some unknown propulsion motor in the interior,' said a scholar. 'He will drown himself,' said a lady. And for twenty minutes they watched the sea carefully. The journalist from the *Vendeen Album* who was observing the horizon with a pair of navy binoculars abruptly uttered a triumphant cry: 'I can see him, he has landed on the continent. He is waving at us...' And on the coast of Fromentine, the first conqueror of the crossing of the Gois underwater waved his arms in a sign of victory. A flotilla of fishing boats sailed to escort the fish-ship. A quarter of an hour later he was emerging at the place called La Claire, in front of an enthusiastic and delirious crowd. Brutus Villeroi received the reception that Bleriot had to have known on the Dover cliffs."[3]

Jules Verne would reshape and retell this story in his own literary version years later; of what he had witnessed on that fateful day, publishing a widely-acclaimed fictionalized account. Still, though no one realized it at the time, the greatest portion of that submarine description was based totally on reality.

Meanwhile, hundreds of nautical miles across the Atlantic Ocean, Abraham Lincoln, the Commander-In-Chief of the United States armed forces during the American Civil War, would be faced with the unique opportunity to become involved in the promotion of modern submarine warfare. And, though the man behind the plan to carry out a covert attack against Confederate ships of war was a French-born citizen, the top-secret craft would be both financed with American money and constructed on American soil.

AMERICAN SUBMARINERS: PRE-CIVIL WAR

Jules Gabriel Verne, age 25

By then, the inventive Frenchman, Brutus de Villeroi, who was born Brutus Amedee Villeroi in September of 1797, had designed more than a dozen such experimental vessels. As early as May of 1832, near his hometown of Nantes, France, he had successfully submerged himself in a narrow, ten-foot long prototype for a period of almost two hours. Floating much like an air-filled balloon on the surface, the underwater contraption had rocked gently back-and-forth in the current beneath the rain-flooded waters of the 634-mile long Loire River, which wound its way past his small cottage-style home. Here, in his own ideal proving grounds, de Villeroi had already become convinced that the development and ultimate perfection of his concept would prove invaluable to any nation caught in the clutches of a naval conflict. Only much later, however, would he realize that his unique experiments had captured the imaginative fascination of a spunky neighbor boy named Jules, who would often accompany him during experimental shallow dives.

Though de Villeroi and Verne would never come close to descending to a depth of "twenty thousand leagues under the sea," the pair would become inspirations to many submarine inventors who would follow. Yet, for the French-born designer, the road to success would be filled with numerous pitfalls.

De Villeroi had secured his fascination for adventure and the sea by growing up with men who made their livings on the open waters. At the age of thirteen, he had signed up as a cabin boy, traveling to nearby ports and learning local superstitions from rugged sailors. Finishing school, he had studied law for a time, before following in the footsteps of generations of de Villerois and becoming a fisherman at the age of eighteen. From that day forward, he held his love of the sea very close to his heart.

Yet, to the ridicule of most who knew him, de Villeroi had long described his far-fetched notions of traveling below, not at the surface, of the oceans. Coupling this with the fact that the design and construction of underwater vessels was in its infancy during his early career as an inventor, he was forced to work in total isolation. Thus, confronting the intricate problem of building a solid, watertight, easily submersible and maneuverable craft without access to the accumulated assistance or knowledge of what predecessors in the field had already accomplished, he was, for all intents and purposes, entirely on his own.

Undaunted by the immensity of his experimental undertaking, de Villeroi set out to not only discover for himself the major ingredients required of a sound diving vessel, but to consider any and all likely problems that he might encounter along the way. The task of predicting future catastrophes, by and large, was quite impossible, however, and defects in de Villeroi's forecasts were inevitable. Yet, surprisingly–and perhaps pushing him toward continued experimentation–many other assumptions he made would lead to success. Truly, therefore, he worked long and hard hours within his own, somewhat lonely, personal proving grounds.

Correctly, on the one hand, the future French expatriate turned American hypothesized that any fully-submersible craft must, first and foremost, be totally water tight and, therefore, strong enough to withstand the increasingly immense pressure of depth. This had been emphasized over and over with a number of unmanned tests, conducted with the deployment of ordinary copper boilers. Time and time again, no matter how much reinforced material he employed, the weighted copper confinements had been lowered beneath the currents to greater and greater depths only to be resurfaced with deep indentations and holes inflicted by the immense pressure. Eventually, through further trial-and-error, de Villeroi discovered that reinforced steel beams, placed at strategic points inside, managed to maintain his makeshift unmanned vessels' original shape.

Furthermore, the inventor reasoned, if a submariner was to safely submerge himself inside one of these vehicles, an adequate or replenishable oxygen supply would need to be readily accessible. On numerous occasions during his earliest manned experiments, de Villeroi recorded that he often "grew extremely light-headed and sluggish from a lack of previously breathed air." Though he understood that it was not a perfect solution, he initially opted to install a crude, floating snorkeling device, with one end open to the inside and the opposite end held firmly at the surface by a chunk of cork. Though he was convinced there must be a better way of breathing, it was a concept that would have to be employed until an improved mechanism could be devised.

Experiments with his earliest underwater vessels also proved unmistakably that de Villeroi would be plagued by a number of miscalculations. For example, at first he was of the opinion that his submerged craft could be steered by sight while under the water. However, a few subsequent test runs quickly convinced him that some other means of vision would be necessary to guide the craft's movements. Aside from the fact that refraction of the sun's rays caused him great visual difficulty, he found that the Loire River's fiercely flowing undercurrents were far too turbid and murky. Furthermore, even water that appeared fairly clear at moderate depths on a cloudy day took on the illusion of a dense fog whenever the sun shined, with every tiny suspended particle reflecting the light and, therefore, hindering his legible and accurate sightings. As a further distraction, swells from passing fishing vessels offered his eyes the impression of dozens of moving, twisting prisms flashing rhythmically downward to the mucky river bottom.

Initially, de Villeroi dealt with the visual quandary quite logically, installing a simple compass, which he hoped would pinpoint accurate direction. After taking his craft down at a fifteen-degree angle and then leveling her out at a depth of almost twenty feet, he noted "the compass needle was swinging wildly in an erratic circle." Eventually, after a good deal of arbitrary movement and vibration, the needle came to rest, pointing almost directly north.

De Villeroi incorrectly determined that the oddly-reacting compass must be faulty. After resurfacing, however, the confused experimenter was perplexed to see that that same compass now seemed to be working just splendidly. Several hundred yards off course, and somewhat frustrated, he was stubbornly unwilling to give up. Instead, he decided that the only plausible solution would be to make an accurate sighting before submerging, and then to rely on his keen sense of awareness, direction, and location.

Hard-luck experience also taught de Villeroi that, in his best estimation, a minimum of ten to fifteen percent of the submarine's volume should be out of water while operating at the surface. This was required in order to avoid any risk of floundering in turbulent foam while the hatch was propped open. Eventually, however, after he was safely and securely locked inside, that buoyancy would have to be drastically reduced before the craft was ready to go down. This, he determined, could be accomplished by either admitting water equal in volume to the emerged portion of the craft, or by forcing it under with heavy weights. Since he could figure no credulous technique to let go of these weights, and thus return to the surface, he selected the former idea for use aboard his vessels.

The *Porpoise*, to which de Villeroi's *Waterbug* would be referred by newsmen, was soon equipped with two hand-pumps to force water in and out of her ballast tanks. Furthermore, she was horizontally balanced both above and below the surface by a pair of sturdy wooden rudders, while a small foot-controlled, chain-driven propeller, similar to that of an ordinary bicycle, glided her along the surface and down through the murky depths. On December 16, 1832, an eyewitness report of one of her dives was published in *L'Echo de la Fabrique*:

"In Noirmoutier, we first witnessed the submarine, invented by Mr. Villeroi of Nantes. Mr. Villeroi gave to its machine through shape and propulsion the gift that nature gave to fish. The length is 3.20 meters with its largest diameter being 1.10 meters. Three men can operate it and stay comfortably in it for about an hour. The seas were rough; Mr. Villeroi entered the machine and pushed it to the horizon. The steam submarine first went at along the surface for about half an hour and then dove in 15 to 18 feet of water, where it collected rocks and sea shells from the seafloor. Then during that dive it went in different directions in order to elude some of the crafts that had surrounded it at the beginning of the trial. Mr. Villeroi then resurfaced at some distance and navigated on the surface in different directions, and then after that navigating, which lasted five quarter of an hour, he opened his panel, and showed him self to the public who welcomed him with cheers. From that trial, it seems that he demonstrated that one can, with that machine, wander at will in vast areas either at the bottom or in mid waters with the same speed as would do any regular vessels. One can then go, with a measure of depth, calculated from its density/pressure, in the middle of a harbor or a fleet, unknown of its enemy, burn its ships, by settling under its hulls; exposing them to all kinds of wreckage, by cutting its ties; one can also, with these means, extract salvage objects from the bottom, collect coral, pearl oysters and divers shells. The inventor assures that he can go at will down from 5 to 600 feet of depth; but then, considering the absence of light, one would be reduce to collect the productions of these unknown regions, by randomly manually picking them. While he was in depth of 15 to 20 feet, he clearly distinguished the time on the dial of watch from one end to the other of the craft. Since this machine was made of steel, he could not attempt all the magnetic experiments he wanted, another copper machine would provide him that opportunity. When we were sailing at the surface,' de Villeroi later explained, 'we clearly heard the sound of the waves, and we were illuminated by an oscillating light identical to their undulations; they would even sometimes present us with a surprising effect, similar to a kind of scintillation. When going down to 15 to 20 feet of depth, the visibility gradually went down, and we only had half day light, momentarily interrupted by the probable passage of fish or some marine vegetation."[4]

A few weeks later, after experiencing near disaster beneath the relatively calm waters of the Maritime Canal, de Villeroi came to understand the grave importance of strategically placing the craft's center of gravity. During one particular run, as the *Porpoise* began to become totally submerged and moved steadily on a forward course, she suddenly shifted violently to one side. As he continued to sink more quickly than anticipated, de Villeroi felt an immense amount of pressure on his lungs. Meanwhile, the craft was inclined to a greater angle than he had originally calculated, which he knew might cause her to nose-dive into the muck below. If that should occur, he might, indeed, be stuck, and unable to resurface.

Realizing that such a steep gradient might also cause him to submerge too deeply and lead to an inward collapse of the boat, not unlike the copper boilers that he had experimented with months earlier, de Villeroi frantically began to pump water from her capacity-filled ballast tanks. Slowly, the *Porpoise* began to level off and arch upward, rising to the surface–rear-end-first–once again. Though it had been an extremely close call, the inventor had learned one extremely valuable lesson: that, completely opposite to that of a surface-type vessel, a submarine's center of gravity must be positioned beneath its true center of buoyancy:

> "The surface vessel's centre of gravity is ordinarily above its centre of buoyancy; yet the equilibrium is stable, because, if the vessel is inclined to either side, the centre of buoyancy of the vessel...that is, the geometrical centre of volume of the water which it displaces, and which is the fulcrum around which it revolves, moves toward that side; and owing to the shape of the transverse section above the water's surface, the vessel cannot be so inclined without raising the centre of gravity through a distance corresponding to the inclination. Raising the centre of gravity is equivalent to raising the vessel herself through the same distance. The force tending to raise the centre of gravity is therefore resisted by the weight of the ship, and the distance through which the centre of gravity is raised, at each degree of inclination, multiplied by the weight of the ship, is the measure of her stability. In a submarine vessel the case is quite otherwise..."[5]

Word of the "daring Frenchman" began to spread throughout Europe and across the Atlantic to America. In October of 1835, the *United Service Gazette Army and Navy Chronicle*, detailed dives by de Villeroi that had taken place in Saint Quen, France:

"Experiments are being made at St. Quen with a novel species of submarine vessel, invented by Mr. Villeroi, which is of the shape of a fish, and worked by three men inside, without any communication with the external air. Admiral Sir Sidney Smith, who has now resided so long at Paris as to become, we presume, a naturalized Frenchman, has been appointed by Louis Phillippe one of a committee to examine this curious mechanism. Something similar was proposed some years since to effect the escape of Napoleon from St. Helena."[6]

In 1836, a pair of Dutch naval officers, Anton Lipkens and Olke Uhlenbeckm visited de Villeroi and took a cruise in his latest submarine. The pair documented the experience aboard the "duikboot" (diving boat) in both writings and drawings:

"This three man sub was built by DeVilleroi in France and demonstrated to the Dutch in 1837. Looking for all the world like a species of waterborne insect, it was 10' 6" long by 27" high by 25" wide and displaced about six tons when submerged. It had eight deadlights on top to provide interior light, a top hatch with a retractable conning tower for surface navigation, three sets of duck foot paddles and a large rudder -- all operated from inside the tiny sub. Two hatches allowed a man to put his arms through the side through a leather seal to work outside the sub, although it is not shown how he was able to see what he was doing. There was a small ballast system amidships that appears to use a lever and piston and a 50 lb anchor to allow the sub to hover a fixed distance off the bottom to work."[7]

In 1842, a decade after his amazing demonstration at Noirmoutier, scant historical records find that Brutus de Villeroi had become a professor of drawing and mathematics at the College of Saint-Donatien, where the student Jules Verne had recently registered. The local history saluted this above-the-norm professor as a well-articulated, great innovator. He enjoyed an undisputable reputation among his students.

Although there exists no written testimony or personal manuscript that allows us to shed light on the relationship between the professor and his student, logic tells us that it was likely impossible for the student Jules Verne–whom his friends described as "keeping himself busy by covering his notebooks with plans and models of flying machines," could have ignored his drawing professor. Could this youngster who, according to his fellow students, would sometimes "sketch the outline of a steam elephant bus" on the blackboard, have not shared his visionary dreams with educator Brutus de Villeroi?

Imagine the teacher and the student, within the walls of the old school when they return in October, "under the age-old sycamores as the fall wind strips their crowns of leaves." Further imagine their dialogue in the school yard covered with browning leaves and the first burs of the big chestnuts. With what eagerness did Jules Verne, the child, hear of the unbelievable adventure of the dive under the ocean? Indeed, such conversations would have been pure aberration if thirty years after the school yard and the playground the *Nautilus* did not arise.

After years of further test dives, and several alterations to the *Porpoise*'s original design, de Villeroi was confident that his submarine had been brought to near perfection. With this firmly in mind, he decided that it was time to follow another of his dreams. Traveling by sailing ship, *Panama*, with Master James Hanson as captain, Brutus de Villeroi and his wife, Eulalie de Villeroi, departed from their place of birth in Nantes, traveling first class through Bordeaux across the Atlantic Ocean to America. There, they stepped ashore in the land-of-opportunity's northern metropolis of New York City.

In early 1859, with his concepts of submarine design carefully detailed in writing and sketched on paper, the expatriate Frenchman went about constructing a 35-foot long hull at the "machine works Neall, Matthews, and More," located in the Bush Hill district of Philadelphia. Later, the unfinished vessel was reportedly taken under the wing of one of Philadelphia's most prominent citizens, William Henry Witte.

A noted political figure, who had been a past United States Congressman and a candidate for the Pennsylvania governor's chair, Witte was known as "a man of great natural ability, and what he lacked in classical culture made up by close reading and study and persuasive eloquence." Evidently, he found the project worthwhile enough that he assisted de Villeroi in its completion by inducing "its removal to the Penn Iron Works of Reaney, Neafie, and Company, where it was supplied with a propelling apparatus."

The new *Porpoise* would ostensibly be designed to conduct salvage work, particularly the wreck of the *HMS DeBraak* (Dutch for "The Beagle"), which had sunk off the coast of Delaware in a violent storm in 1798. The *DeBraak*'s origins were somewhat obscure. During the 1780s, she sailed against England under the Dutch flag, operating with a Mediterranean squadron out of Toulon, France. In 1793, she took part in the defense of Willemstad against a French Revolutionary army, and at the end of 1794, *DeBraak* was ordered to escort a convoy of East Indiamen to Batavia. She was rerigged as a brig and re-armed with sixteen 24-pound carronades, beginning her Royal Navy service in under Captain James Drew on June 13, 1797.

The *DeBaark*'s company consisted of eighty-five officers, marines, boys, and sailors. After a period of time on duty in the English Channel, she had been ordered into convoy duty. During the Atlantic crossing, however, she became separated from her convoy off the Azores. At the end of April, she captured a Spanish ship worth £160,000 in prize money and, on May 25, Captain Drew put into Delaware Bay. Shortly after a pilot boarded off Cape Henlopen, she had "a sudden flaw of wind" and capsized. Within minutes, she had sank off the Delaware coast, settling in about eighty feet of water, with the loss of forty-seven of her crew, including Captain Drew, and twelve Spanish prisoners.

Sketch of Stephen Girard, whose estate financed the De Villeroi submarine

The wreck soon became the subject of dozens upon dozens of rumors concerning the amount of treasure the ship purportedly carried when she sank, with estimates of the value eventually reaching $500 million. Financial backing for the construction of de Villeroi's first American salvage submarine was furnished by a relative of the late Stephen Girard, who had reportedly been Philadelphia's wealthiest citizen. Completed in the spring of 1859, the 35-foot submarine saw experimental operations in and around New Castle, Marcus Hook, and Rancocas:

"It has been tried frequently at those points, and marvelous stories are told of the facility with which it can be sunk beneath the waters, again raised to the surface, and propelled and steered ether beneath the surface or upon it...the vessel was intended for all submarine purposes. It had been under water for three hours at a time, and could be moved about at pleasure. The persons in it could leave it while under water, as though it was a diving bell. They manufacture, while under water, they said, the supply of air needed for respiration. Externally it had the appearance of a section of boiler about twenty feet long, with tapered ends, presenting the shape and appearance of an enormous cigar with a boiler iron wrapper, and for all the world like Winan's celebrated steamer in respect to shape. The after end was furnished with a propeller, which had a contrivance for protecting it from damage from coming in contact with external objects. The forward end was sharkish in appearance, and the shark idea was carried out in other respects, as only the ridge of the back was above water, while the tail and snout were submerged. Near the forward end was a hatchway or "man-hole," through which egress and ingress were obtained. This whole was covered with a heavy iron flap, which was made air tight, and which was secured in its place by numerous powerful screws and hooks. Two tiers of glass bull's eyes along each side of the submarine monster, completed its external features, afforded light to the inside, and gave it a particular wide awake appearance. But its Angus eyes did not avail to save it from capture. About twelve o'clock last night the harbor policemen saw a skiff loaded with pig lead move off from South street wharf, in charge of two young men, and they paid a visit to the submarine ship, in which a portion of the same description of lead had already been placed. The submarines with their skiff and lead were seized and brought to the city, and at about two o'clock this morning their iron pet was towed to town and moored at Noble street wharf. The news of the capture soon flew around, and by little after daylight, the rush of people to the spot commenced. All sorts of stories were aloft, and thousands upon thousands gathered at the wharves, scaled the neighboring board piles, and importuned the amphibious policemen, who had the monster in charge, for permission to board her and see how she looked inside. But 'no admission' was the rule, and the interior remained invisible to the millions."[8]

Word of de Vileroi's continued successes soon spread like a prairie fire, westward across the continent. A few months later, a small town newspaper known as the *Hornellsville Tribune*, printed in western New York, ran a remarkable story that had been borrowed from the *Philadelphia Ledger*. It offered a number of details concerning de Villeroi's diving boat, including its design and capabilities:

"Yesterday afternoon, an intelligent experiment took place at New Castle, Del., with a submarine salvage boat, invented by Mr. Villeroi, who descends to the bottom of the river without any arrangement for receiving a supply of fresh air from above, the boat being intended to supply itself with the quantity of air needed while under water, enabling it to remain submerged for any length of time required. As singular as this may seem, the experiment yesterday allowed that it was perfectly practicable, for eight men went down in the boat and remained there an hour and three quarters without any communication from above. The mode of generating air to supply the boat is yet a secret, but it is believed to be by some chemical arrangement. The boat is made of boiler iron, and is perfectly round and shaped somewhat like a fish. It is 35 feet long, 44 inches in diameter, and propelled by a screw 3 feet in diameter. It has two rows of bull's eyes on the top for the purpose of giving light to the interior. On each side, near the bow or head, are placed pieces of iron 18 inches square, which are moved like the fins of a fish, and are intended to direct the boat up or down when under the water. The only place of ingress or egress in this singular boat is through a trap on the top, and when her crew of 13 men enter, it is covered with a heavy iron cap and fastened on the inside, thus shutting out all communication from the outside, and preventing the admission of air. To sink the vessel, after everything has been prepared for a submarine voyage, water is pumped by a machine into large gutta-percha bags, within the boat, until a sufficient quantity has been obtained to sink her, and as soon as this takes place, the screw is set in motion, by means of straps worked by six men, and at the same time the inventor sits near the head, to give it direction by the fins before mentioned. After the boat reaches the spot where it is intended to operate upon the bottom of the river, a trap-door is opened to the bottom of the boat, and the workmen get out, taking with them the means of obtaining a full supply of fresh air from the boat, which is kept stationary by means of a piece of iron in the shape of a cone, which is let down from the bottom. During the experiment yesterday the boat was all submerged with the exception of a few feet at the bow, there not being sufficient weight forward to sink her. All that part in which the persons were entirely submerged, and of course the individuals were cut off from a supply of air from above the water. At this point the experiment was abandoned in consequence of the supplying pump getting out of order. The occupants of the boat after being released from their confinement, looked as cool as those who had been sitting on shore under the shade watching the experiments."[9]

As can be seen repeatedly, Brutus de Villeroi was never shy about "tooting his own horn" when it came to his inventive abilities and his growing celebrity. In fact, when he filled out his 1860 United States Census forms, he likely raised the eyebrows of more than one enumerator when he listed his occupation as "natural genius." Though it was an audacious statement, it most certainly was not idle boasting, for the displaced Frenchman was, without doubt, a visionary engineer with a touch of genius.

On Tuesday, May 14, 1861, de Villeroi's underwater vessel, which had reportedly been docked at various points for the past five months along the Rancocas River–including Marcus Hook, New Castle, and Delanco–was brought southward to the Philadelphia Navy Yard for the purpose of securing a patent. Just two days later, however, on May 16, Philadelphia harbor police stopped and boarded the strange contraption, which they had spotted moving down the river. The thirty-five foot vessel, described as being "sharkish in appearance," had a crew of three, which included its designer, Brutus de Villeroi, Alexander Rhodes, a 30-year-old Frenchman, and Henry Kriner, an American, aged 19. Although the French inventor claimed that he and his crew had been heading to the Navy Yard for underwater tests, officers there disavowed any knowledge of him. Rhodes and Kriner were arrested and escorted to the local precinct, while de Villeroi was held for extensive questioning. Likely, his prototype as described by a local Philadelphia newspaper was so top-secret until that point that not even government officials were prepared to divulge its progress:

> "The Submarine Propeller submitted to our investigation consists of an iron cylinder, cone shaped at the two extremities, about thirty three feet in length, by four feet at its greatest diameter. It is propelled by means of a screw in the stern with two trunions, one on either side resembling some what a whale in the external form and appearance. Light is communicated to the interior by means of glass bulls eyes on the back, thirty six in number. An ellipsoidal section eight inches in height, opening and closing at will, affords entrance and exit to a crew of from six to twelve men, according to the speed required. A corresponding section at the bottom of the boat admits the egress of the divers who breathing by means of tubes attached to the boat are able to perform submarine operations, such as raising sunken cargoes, and attaching torpedoes to the bottoms of hostile vessels. An artificial atmosphere, perfectly respirable by the men is generated by the inventor by a chemical process so that the submerged boat is executes its maneuvers without any connection with the surface. Its entire apparatus is contained in the interior and invisible from the outside."[10]

Though de Villeroi had kept a rather low-profile around the Philadelphia area until now, he would soon be a fairly well-known figure, easily recognizable to a number of city residents. In fact, the French inventor's voyage through local waters may have been nothing more than a publicity stunt to get the Union navy's full attention. If so, his scheme worked out quite well, for a series of published reports began to appear all across the city:

> "Never since the first flush of the news of the bombardment of Fort Sumter, has there been an excitement in the city equal to that which was caused in the upper wards this morning, by the capture of a mysterious vessel which was said to be an infernal machine, which was to be used for all sorts of treasonable purposes, including the trifling pastime of scuttling and blowing up Government men-of-war. For a few days past the police have had their attention directed to the movements, not of a 'long, low, black schooner;' but of an iron submarine boat, to which very extraordinary abilities and infernal propensities were attributed. The

Harbor Police, under the direction of Lieutenant Benjamin Edgar, were directed to be especially spry, and they kept their optics wide open for the mysterious stranger. Yesterday afternoon they stumbled upon a queer contrivance which lay at the lower end of Smith's Island, and proved to be the submarine monster of which they were in search."[11]

Another newspaper, Philadelphia's *Saturday Evening Post*, published the following commentary, along with sketches, in its May 25, 1861, edition:

"We give this week engravings of an aquatic monster which recently caused no small degree of excitement among the very unexcitable citizens of this remarkably sober Quaker City. Our neighbors of the Inquirer well say, that 'never since the Battle of the Kegs has the riverfront of Philadelphia been the scene of such a peculiar excitement. At an early hour in the morning rumors spread like wildfire among the inflammable population crowding our wharves, that a monster, half aquatic, half aerial, and wholly incomprehensible, had been captured by the Harbor Police, and had been safely chained at the foot of Noble street pier. Forthwith the pier became the grand centre of attraction. The crowd increased hourly, the spectators flocking to see the amphibious and ambiguous creature. All sorts of speculations were freely indulged in as to the uses and purposes of the lengthy iron circular continuance, all tending, however, to the belief that it was designed to aid and assist Jeff Davis in the benevolent occupation of transferring Federal vessels of war into flying morsels of wood and iron, i.e., blowing them up, while every one concurred in the opinion that it was 'very like a whale'"[12]

In the days that followed, the inventor gave an astonishing interview to local reporters, claiming his vessel could remain submerged for several hours, utilized an airlock that permitted a diver to exit and enter the boat while submerged, and employed an air purifying device that supplied air to the crew while underwater. After being allowed to see the vessel inside and out, one local Philadelphian described it as follows:

"Externally it had the appearance of a section of boiler about forty feet long, with tapered ends, presenting the shape and appearance of an enormous cigar with a boiler iron wrapper, and for all the world like Winan's celebrated steamer in respect to shape. The after end was furnished with a propeller, which had a contrivance for protecting it from damage from coming in contact with external objects. The forward end was sharkish in appearance, and the shark idea was carried out in other respects, as only the ridge of the back was above water, while the tail and snout were submerged. Near the forward end was a hatchway or 'man-hole,' through which egress and ingress were obtained. This whole was covered with a heavy iron flap, which was made air tight, and which was secured in its place by numerous powerful screws and hooks. Two tiers of glass bull's eyes along each side of the submarine monster, completed its external features, afforded light to the inside, and gave it a particular wide awake appearance. But its Argus eyes did not avail to save it from capture. About twelve o'clock last night the harbor policemen saw a skiff loaded with pig lead move off from South street wharf, in charge of two young men, and they paid a visit to the submarine ship, in which a portion of the same description of lead had already been placed. The submarines with their skiff and lead were seized and brought to the city, and at about two o'clock this morning their iron pet was towed to town and moored at Noble street wharf. The news of the capture soon flew around, and by little after daylight, the rush of people to the spot commenced. All sorts of stories were aloft, and thousands upon thousands gathered at the wharves, scaled the neighboring board piles, and importuned the amphibious policemen, who had the monster in charge, for permission to board her and see how she looked inside. But "no admission" was the rule, and the interior remained invisible to the millions. The harbor men very courteously offered us a peep inside. After dropping from a high wharf into a skiff and then jumping a few feet, we found ourselves upon the back of the iron mystery. After much unscrewing and unhooking, the top of the man-hole was lifted off, and divesting ourselves of coat and hat, we squeezed into the machine, under the gaze of a curious and admiring multitude of about five thousand people. We suddenly found ourselves squatting inside of a cigar-shaped iron vessel, about four feet in diameter. There was a crank for the purpose of operating the propeller already described, apparatus for steering, rods, connecting with fins outside, which could be moved at pleasure, and which had something to do with steadying and sinking the craft. There was a large reel of wire which might be intended for galvanic purposes, pumps, brass faucets, pigs of ballast lead, and numerous other things, which might be intended for either infernal or humane purposes for aught we know. The interior was abundantly lighted by means of the double tier of bull's eyes we have described."[13]

Captain Samuel Du Pont, Commandant of the Philadelphia Navy Yard, ordered a thorough examination of the de Villeroi submarine. Three officers were chosen to board the vessel, interview the inventor and report their finding to Du Pont and the Navy Department. The three were ideally qualified to perform the inspection and review, for they included: senior officer, Commander Henry K. Hoff, an expert in ship design; Commander Charles Steedman, an expert in naval warfare; and Robert Danby, an eminent naval engineer. Together, they scrutinized the submarine and its inventor for the next several days.

The resulting report of July 7, 1861, dispatched from Commander Henry K. Hoff to Captain Du Pont, indicated that "the services of the distinguished French engineer would be very valuable to the government and that the possession of his invention would be of the greatest importance":

"This last idea he has at length carried out, by building his submarine salvage boat according to the following dimensions, viz: 35 feet long, exclusive of the propeller wheel, and 44 inches in diameter, both ends tapering off. It is propelled by a wheel or screw 3 feet in diameter and steered by two paddles. The 36 eyes along the backbone, as it were, are made for the purpose of giving light inside. This boat is capable of diving from 300 to 400 fathoms...and can easily sustain the pressure of water at that depth. It can navigate with eight men underwater during two or three hours, without any communications with the surface of the water, and its crew will breathe as freely as thought in the open air. It can be made to navigate on the water, underwater or a few feet from the surface of the water according to the necessary circumstances. With this salvage boat men can get out at the bottom of the water, work, pick up things and walk about, just as freely as on shore. Having seen the plans and models of the invention, the gentlemen here who have taken the matter in hand felt the utmost confidence in it; but in order to satisfy all, the test was had in the Delaware river, at Marcus Hook on Saturday. Being their invitation, we saw the curious boat which is above described, into which, in our presence, M. Villeroi with five men entered; and it then, with all on board descended into the water remaining beneath the surface one hour and a quarter, during all of which time the boat had no communication with the external atmosphere. Incredible and impracticable as this may seem, it is nevertheless true, as those where on the shore can testify. By what wonderful new invention in science this was achieved we cannot say, and indeed the principle is undoubtedly the most extraordinary discovery of the age. We saw, also, M Villeroi's men (sailors) plunge into the water and disappear, and after entering the boat, reappear on the surface, thus testing the power to enter and quit the boat while she was under water. In fact, from what we saw, we entertain no doubt whatever that M. Villeroi's boat is the grand desideratum for submarine operations."[14]

So convincing was the recommendation, now known as the *Hoff Report*, Du Pont filtered it, along with de Villeroi's plans, up through the appropriate naval bureaucracy. Meanwhile, de Villeroi had taken it upon himself to write to both the Secretary of the Navy, Gideon Welles, and President Abraham Lincoln. The letter to Lincoln was forwarded to the Navy Department. Secretary Welles called upon Commodore Joseph Smith, Chief of the Bureau of Yards and Docks, requesting a report on this submarine. Smith, in turn, claimed that the *Hoff Report* reflected favorably, but that the present submarine was too small to be tested as a weapon. He recommended that a larger version be built on a "no payment for failure" basis. Without much hesitation, de Villeroi agreed, and it was decided that the upscaled version would be constructed with the expert assistance of Martin Thomas, a highly skilled and well-versed shipbuilder from Philadelphia.

Exhibiting his soon-to-be well-known stubborn and independent disposition, however, de Villeroi insisted that he alone be placed in charge of personally overseeing the entire project from start to finish. Though President Lincoln initially objected to the demand, believing that American ingenuity was far superior to that of any Frenchman, the persistent inventor would eventually get his way. A few weeks later, by November of 1861, Martin Thomas (representing de

Villeroi, likely due to citizenship concerns) was ready to agree to the following contract to construct the Union Navy's first submarine vessel:

> "This agreement, made and entered into this first day of November, A.D. one thousand eight hundred and sixty one, between Martin Thomas of one part and the United States by Gideon Welles, Secretary of the Navy on the other part, witnesseth: First: The party of the first part will construct and deliver to the party of the second part within forty (40) days from the date of this agreement, an Iron Submarine Propeller of the plan of M. de Villeroi, at least fifty six inches (56") in width and sixty six (66") inches in height and forty five feet in length, for the sum of fourteen thousand dollars to be paid when completed and delivered, ready for use within ten days after delivery and certificate is in all respects ready for service. Second: The government of the United States will employ M. de Villeroi to superintend the construction of said propeller, as well as in its employment for actual service when required, and agrees to pay him for his full services at the rate of two thousand dollars per annum whilst thus employed, his pay to commence with the date of this agreement: also to pay reasonable wages to the crew of said propeller, and to transport it from Philadelphia to the place or places where the Secretary of the Navy direct it to be used. Third: In case the said de Villeroi shall perform valuable services with said propeller for the United States by the destruction of an enemy's ship or vessel by direction of the Secretary of the Navy and to his satisfaction, then the government of the United States shall pay to the party of the first part a further sum of eighty six thousand dollars ($86,000) subject to and appropriated by Congress. Fourth: The secret of said invention shall be divulged by the inventor, M. de Villeroi, under his solemn oath or affirmation in a written paper subscribed by him to be sealed and deposited with the Chief of Bureau of Yards and Docks, with the certificate thereon of Mr. W. L. Hirst that he has carefully examined the paper and firmly believes it to be of the secret of said invention, not to be opened until after the payment of said eighty six thousand dollars, or the death, disability or dereliction of duty of the inventor shall occur. Fifth: The said invention shall not be used by or the secret divulged to any government, power or individual without the consent in writing of both parties to this agreement."[15]

Delighted, de Villeroi immediately set about the time-consuming task of enlarging his current schematic mechanical drawings to fit Lincoln's request. And, although the Navy had specified that the submarine's construction should take no more than forty days at a cost not to exceed the agreed upon $14,000, the project was destined to suffer from long delays and increasing costs.

The construction phase of the larger diving craft commenced immediately and, within just a few weeks, it had already fallen behind schedule. On December 7, de Villeroi wrote to Commodore Joseph Smith that the vessel was "almost entirely finished," although he also intimated that there may be some problems and the time may need to be extended because of some "delicate pieces of the interior" were not yet finished. He further explained that the ship was entirely different than anything that the Nefie and Levy's shipyard had ever attempted, and that it was scarcely possible for the contractor to appreciate how long it took to build the boat. Furthermore, claimed de Villeroi, the contractor, Martin Thomas, had not scheduled work orders properly.

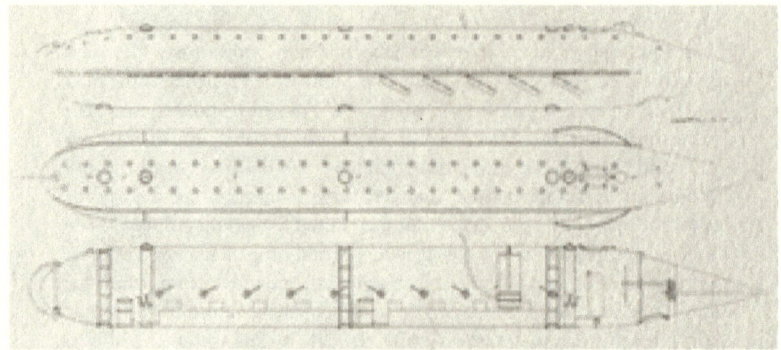

Sketch of the de Villeroi's mechanical drawing

The seeds of disagreement had now been sewn and would disrupt the entire building phase. Enter William L. Hirst, a Philadelphia attorney, who would act as a go between in the growing dispute between de Villeroi and Thomas. Commodore Smith granted a fifteen-day extension on December 10, 1861, the date the boat was originally scheduled to be finished. On the twentieth of the month, Smith received word that the "secrets" were in Hirst's possession and locked in his personal safe.

Commodore Smith took a hard stand on finishing the submarine in a timely fashion, partly because he was working against a deadline of his own. The City of Norfolk had already fallen to the enemy, and word of the conversion of the *USS Merrimac* into the *CSS Virginia* had recently reached Washington. Smith told de Villeroi in no uncertain terms that any contract scheduling difficulties were "no fault of mine." De Villeroi's letter passed on from Hirst to the Navy Bureau asking for an additional fourteen days to finish the work. The inventor claimed that the delays were entirely the fault of the contractor in that money was not forthcoming to allow work at night and on weekends. De Villeroi further stated that more crewmen had to be hired soon so they could be trained in time for full operations. At the end of the letter, de Villeroi informed Commodore Smith that the two of them must correspond directly and not through the contractor to resolve these problems.

Commodore Smith was absolutely furious. He dispatched a scathing letter to de Villeroi on January 3, 1862, spelling out the facts of bureaucratic life. He stated that he would be very happy to correspond directly, but "as for the contract, the Department knows no one but the contractor." He also informed the stubborn inventor that, because of the delays and evident problems, the ship would not be considered received until it had been well and fully tested.

The second extension came and went, and the submarine was still not finished. It appeared now that there were some things the inventor wanted for the boat that Martin Thomas had not provided, and that these parts were needed to produce the "secrets" alluded to in the original contract.

In his own defense, de Villeroi wrote to Smith again on the January 18, 1862, saying rather magnanimously that his payment "is in the glory and successful completion of the work." He went on to say that "after taking on the ballast of lead and some pieces of platina which have not been furnished me" the work would be finished. He felt that, since the completion date and extensions had passed, he and Smith could deal directly with each other, stating "now that you have done away with the contractor, business ought to be between the government and the inventor."

As the coldest part of the winter season set in with all of its fury, Martin Thomas now believed that there was virtually no possibility that the submarine would be completed much before the early spring of 1862. Though greatly disappointed by the delay, President Lincoln thought that there was very little that could be done to speed up the construction process. His assumption was absolutely correct.

Commodore Joseph Smith replied to de Villeroi on January 22, stating that no further money would be forthcoming until the boat was finished and tested. He continued on to state that the government still knew no one but the contractor with respect to competence in constructing the submarine. One week later, he wrote Thomas and laid it on the line with him as well. If the boat was not finished and ready to be shipped aboard the USS Rhode Island in three or four days, the time for using the submarine would have passed. Finally, he stated "the Merrimac is out of dock and ready for trial at Norfolk."

The submarine was reportedly ready for launch on January 29, but according to Martin Thomas, some of the oars that were to be installed for primary propulsion still had to be reworked. A parallel letter from de Villeroi stated the delay was due to ice on the river, something that he had not planned for, nor had control of. In the meantime, the boat would be painted, dark green outside and white inside.

February arrived and the boat had still not been completed. Commodore Smith was getting discouraged with the progress of the project and was becoming more and more concerned with the threat posed by the *CSS Virginia*. A letter to de Villeroi indicated that Smith had little faith in the usefulness of the boat, but did feel it warranted a trial run.

At this point in time, Commodore Smith made a tactical error in judgment. De Villeroi had been asking Thomas for things to finish the boat. He needed the plates of platina (which were silver covered platinum), explosives, and other items. In his letter on the first of February, Smith informed de Villeroi that the contractor, Martin Thomas, was to furnish everything de Villeroi needed to finish the submarine. De Villeroi immediately wrote back that there was a list of things which were required, but had not been supplied and were holding up completion of the boat. These included explosives, two hydraulic jacks, platina, a telescope which could give distances (an invention of de Villeroi's which had not been patented) and a chest of tools. In that correspondence, he complained of an entire litany of things that Thomas had done or not done. These included having what de Villeroi termed "unethical" discussions about his inventions with scientists and not spending enough money to complete the work in a timely manner. The cost of the project, he further said, was very much less than the $14,000 allowed for by the contract. He felt that the boat should be taken by the Navy for completion to keep it safe from harm.

Commodore Smith had had enough, writing to de Villeroi that "the time has elapsed for the completion of the boat and the contract is forfeited. You now decline, as I learn, to give certificate of the completion of the boat because the contractor demurs to furnishing a quantity of costly material, which the chemists say is unnecessary. Therefore work and superintending is stopped and will remain so until you and Mr. Thomas come to terms...If the contractor will deliver the boat in 10 days complete and with your certificate and you and your crew will be there, the government will test the efficiency and if she proves satisfactory, payment will be made. Until there is compliance with these terms, the Department will...consider the bargain as closed."

Meanwhile, as construction continued at a snail's pace, de Villeroi seemingly was able to make splendid use of the lost time. In order to deal with the long-standing, perplexing problem of a vitiated oxygen supply available to a submerged crew, which the inventor had personally encountered during his early experiments, he reasoned logically that there was but three possible solutions to the hazardous dilemma. Eventually, he would become convinced that, perhaps, all three ideas should be incorporated in his vessel.

First and foremost, as a primary source of breathable oxygen, an ordinary, rubber-hosed snorkeling device could be employed to provide fresh air from above. As a second back-up system, he determined that a large quantity of clean inhalation could be carried aboard his submarine, stored safely inside a series of cumbersome, pressurized reservoirs. And, last but not least, a unique filtering system could be devised, which would "purify" spent oxygen.

After much experimentation, the ingenious inventor managed to completely eliminate the first two options in favor of the latter. Before she would even be launched on her maiden voyage, however, he vowed that his Americanized submarine would boast an extremely innovative chemical purification system, which would have the unique ability to actually clean the used inner-air supply of his submarine.

Eventually, Brutus de Villeroi's expertise had resulted in a new "submarine propeller" forty-seven feet long with a crew of twenty-six. One of the many delays in the construction of this boat was his insistence upon the use of certain very expensive chemicals, which he claimed were needed for the air filtration system. The exact means by which de Villeroi "scrubbed" the air of carbon dioxide is unknown, but possibly his system utilized a series of motorized pulleys that drew long sheets of woolen cloth through a bath of lime-impregnated water. This would have served to remove a quantity of CO_2 from the atmosphere of the boat while returning a small amount of oxygen at the same time. The cost of the chemicals was $15,000 (which, in modern dollars, translates to $225,000-$300,000). Little wonder that the Union Navy balked at the expenditure, though de Villeroi intended to install it using private funding.

Unlike other Civil War submarines, the boat designed by de Villeroi was not powered by a central screw propeller; it used a row of nine oars down either side. The paddles of the oars were made in such a fashion as to fold in on the return swing so as to reduce drag. A single crewmen manned each oar, with an officer and a diver completing the compliment of twenty men aboard the ship. As one writer has suggested, the interior of the boat must have resembled that of a "Viking longboat," as the sailors hauled away at the oars.

With his air filtration design now in place, de Villeroi optimistically predicted that the vessel's occupants would be able to remain submerged for up to a maximum of three hours without suffering any difficulty whatsoever. A "doubting" Thomas, the Philadelphia shipbuilder who was supposed to be de Villeroi's partner and co-planner in the construction process, remained skeptical of the claim, vehemently warning that "such a notion is destined to fail not only slightly, but miserably."

Determined to prove that he was right in his seemingly preposterous claim, de Villeroi offered himself as a "guinea pig" for the cause, volunteering to submerge personally for an extended period of time. Thomas weighed the risks of such an unproved adventure. Though he was tempted to take the Frenchman up on his offer, it was ultimately decided that his "expertise" was far too valuable to risk, and the Northern government refused his dangerous proposition.

Still, though he would eventually be forced to admit that a working air-purification system was, indeed, possible, Thomas retained one major concern about de Villeroi's innovative oxygen supply: that it would require careful management and operation by a highly-qualified, expert crew in order to prevent what he referred to as "over-oxygenation." Such an occurrence, he and de Villeroi categorically agreed, would cause those aboard to become mysteriously "over-exhilarated" and at risk of becoming "brain happy." Though such a condition was then believed to cause no permanent ailment, science would eventually define it as "hyperventilation."

Following extensive successful testing of de Villeroi's second American-made and American-financed model by the Union Navy in March of 1862, it was determined that the forty-seven-foot submarine was ready for operations. In the third week of May, however, just a few days before her scheduled completion, de Villeroi's violent and stubborn temper flared out of control once again. This time, he had predictably, perhaps, become embroiled in another heated disagreement with the submarine's hired Philadelphia contractor concerning the intricate specifications of the still unproved breathing apparatus. Ultimately, Martin Thomas threatened to resign from the project.

A frustrated Abraham Lincoln now realized that he would be forced choose between his hand-selected expert builder and the French expatriate who was responsible for the underwater craft's design. Informed by others that the two stubborn men now refused to even speak to one another with a civil tongue, the President was also convinced that he should have followed his initial instincts concerning the Frenchman's insistence to oversee the construction phase of the expensive project. If he had, in fact, refused to agree to the arrangement in the first place, there would be no need to secure de Villeroi's "prior approval" concerning any of the submarine's specifications. Still, on the other hand, he wondered whether or not the craft could be completed without the stubborn inventor heading the project.

Lincoln would never be forced to choose, however, for the decision would soon be made for him. In a further heated disagreement, de Villeroi held steadfastly to his doubtful reservations concerning Thomas' urging to install a mechanical means of submerged propulsion. Though he had earlier agreed to put in place the screw-type propeller extending through a stuffing-box arrangement, the fickled inventor reversed himself. Instead, he now wanted to return to an earlier crude "folding oars" concept. By this point in time, Lincoln's patience had run thin, and de Villeroi was pointedly informed that such a radical change in the design would cost both money and time. In essence, the inventor's stubborn wants and desires were believed to be totally unwarranted and unacceptable.

Disgusted and angry, the hot-tempered Frenchman refused to back down from the dispute. Meanwhile, Lincoln ordered that construction on the vessel continue, uninterrupted or impeded by further squabbling. As final vindication, de Villeroi decided to totally sever his working relationship with the shipbuilder from Philadelphia, the presiding President, and the entire Union government. At the time, however, he made his worst error in judgment to date, believing falsely that he was "indispensable," and that the construction of his craft could not possibly reach conclusion without him. Martin Thomas, however, would determinedly prove worthy of the formidable challenge.

Disillusioned with the entire affair, de Villeroi departed from American soil. While it was initially reported that he had decided to return to his Nantes home in France, a second, more reliable source, later claimed that the inventor had, instead, traveled south to Monterey, Mexico, where he intended to conduct some "undisclosed business." Either way, history records that he stubbornly refused–either in France or somewhere abroad–to become involved in another foreign financed construction project. Still, one small piece of evidence would offer a conflicting testimonial concerning the remainder of the de Villeroi story.

Meanwhile, despite the inventor's estrangement from the Union government, Martin Thomas and his team of experienced shipbuilders continued to work around the clock. Finally, in late May of 1862, the submarine was completed. All that was left to do was to test her under actual battle-worthy conditions.

The *Alligator*, as the new vessel was now known, closely resembled the large, lizard-like American reptile that had given her the name. On the morning of June 19, 1862, she was launched in the Delaware River in front of dozens of Union government personnel. On the same day, an order by the Secretary of the Navy, Gideon Welles, was dispatched to Flag-Officer Louis Malesherbes Goldsborough, U.S. Navy, regarding the submarine propeller:

> "The submarine propeller under contract with Mr. Martin Thomas will leave Philadelphia at 11 o'clock a.m. this day for Hampton Roads, via the [Chesapeake and Delaware] Canal. The boat is under charge of Mr. Samuel Eakins. Mr. Thomas goes to Fortress Monroe with the boat, which is, or should be, manned with twenty men, including the master, who receive $40 per month each, including subsistence. The master receives at the rate of $1,500 per annum whilst employed. If the crew is not full, you can supply deficiencies. She is, or should be, prepared for operation with two torpedoes and all apparatus for submarine work. You will employ her for clearing obstructions in James River, or any other submarine work you may think proper, and supply the powder on Government account. A tug has been hired to tow her to Fortress Monroe, which you can discharge and use one you have already in use, or retain her with the propeller, as you shall judge best. Please report when the propeller arrives, and also when and where she shall operate."[16]

Over the course of the next few days, the *Alligator* was deftly maneuvered around Petty's Island, submerged for brief periods, and resurfaced, proving that all the months of hard work were about to pay off. Then, on June 23, 1862, Flag Officer Goldsborough forwarded the following message to Commander John Rodgers, Commanding Officer aboard the *USS Galena*:

> "I send to you the submarine propeller, in charge of Mr. Samuel Eakins. She will be towed up by tug which brought her from Philadelphia, and which tug you will keep with her until further orders. I also send the U. S. S. Satellite to accompany her, accommodate officers and crew, and render any other service that she can. Let a ration be issued to each one of the crew of the submarine propeller and a strict account kept of the number of rations that may be so issued. The Satellite has 20 barrels of powder on board for the use of the submarine propeller. This contrivance, as I have already intimated to you, should be employed at once up the Appomattox, if it can be of any service whatever there in destroying the railroad bridge at Petersburg , or removing obstructions in our way. It afterwards may be employed to remove the obstructions abreast of Fort Darling (Drewry's Bluff). Make it as useful in every way as you can."[17]

Photo of the Captain Samuel Eakins

Meanwhile, Goldsborough remained unconvinced of the *Alligator*'s true worth, and expressed these sentiments to Gideon Welles in writing:

"A submarine propeller in tow of a tug arrived at Hampton Roads yesterday. She is not prepared for operation with any torpedoes. She required a lot of whisky barrels, twenty barrels of powder, and a steamer to accompany her and the little tug, in order to accommodate powder, men, etc., all of which were promptly furnished. No arrangement had been made to provision her men; I therefore, at the request of the parties, agreed to let each one have a ration per day, the value of which to be deducted from the monthly pay allowed. Today she leaves for James River, accompanied by the tug that brought her from Philadelphia and by the Satellite. Owing to the very light draft of the tug, and for other reasons, it is well to retain her services for the present, and I have given orders accordingly. I have directed Commander Rodgers to use her first in the Appomattox, if she can possibly be applied there to any advantage whatever in the destruction of the bridge at Petersburg , and next in removing the obstructions at Fort Darling. I saw this contrivance yesterday. I hope it may be of service to the Government, but my impression is that it is next to a very useless concern. Thus far no experiments have been made with it of any consequence. Some men went down in it and remained under water three-quarters of an hour, but this they could have easily done in an ordinary diving bell. Beyond this no other experiment has been attempted, as I am informed by Mr. Eakins."[18]

True to the Union philosophy of using the submarine craft to clear obstacles, however, the as yet unchristened submersible headed up the James River in late June of 1862. Unfortunately, since neither the James nor the Appomattox were deep enough to permit the vessel to fully submerge, this first-ever combat sortie of a U. S. Navy submarine had to be called off when the Army retreated from the Peninsula. Returning to Fortress Monroe, Captain Samuel Eakins docked the boat so that she could be redesigned with a central screw propellor and officially christened the *USS Alligator*.

In August of 1862, Lieutenant Thomas O. Selfridge, a veteran of the *USS Cumberland* who had served as skipper of the *Monitor* immediately following its famous battle, accepted command of the submarine only after being promised promotion to captain if he and the *USS Alligator*'s new crew successfully destroyed the newest Confederate ironclad, *Virginia II*. During two weeks of test runs in the Potomac, the *Alligator* proved to be underpowered and unwieldy. In fact, during one particular trial run, the submarine's air quickly grew foul, the crew panicked, and all tried to get out of the same hatch at the same time; prompting Selfridge to call the whole enterprise "a failure." Frustrated and disgusted with submarine warfare, Selfridge was relieved and given command of *USS Cairo*. Apparently, the dream of using this "secret weapon" against the *Virginia II* had been scrapped for an indefinite period of time.

Meanwhile, Assistant Secretary of the United States Navy, Gustavus V. Fox, notified Rear Admiral Samuel F. Du Pont by way of covert message of the intended purpose for the one-of-a-kind underwater craft, explaining:

"We have sent you down the semi-submarine boat 'Alligator' that may be useful in making reconnaissances..."[19]

Driven by Brutus de Villeroi's original screw propeller design, rather than an ordinary set of folding oars as was later proposed, the forty-seven-foot long, four-and-one-half-foot wide *Alligator*, again under Eakins' supervision, spent almost one year's service maneuvering through the murky bottom of the James River, just south of Williamsburg, Virginia. During each of dozens of outings, she transported an ample crew of up to seventeen within her roomy confines. On many occasions, in fact, carefully-calculated plans were formulated to dispatch her on secret missions along the Southern coastline, though her specific destinations were neither divulged nor recorded for posterity's sake. All we do know is that each of her excursions was successful.

In a test run witnessed by President Lincoln on March 18, 1863, the *USS Alligator* made four knots. A letter to Commodore Smith stated the vessel operated admirably. Now, in the spring of the year, there was another task at hand. The commander of the South Atlantic Blockading Squadron was Samuel F. Du Pont, the same officer that had headed the initial investigation of de Villeroi's invention eighteen months before. Now in Port Royal near Charleston, Du Pont had the difficult task of Charleston harbor to crack and, unlike Farrigut, he could not just force passage by running past the forts into the inner harbor. Even there, his ships would have been sitting ducks. In addition, the *CSS Chicora* and *CSS Palmetto State* threatened to lift the blockade by escorting cargo ships past the Union Naval forces off the harbor entrance. In his opinion, the *Alligator* would be ideal for attacking these two ships at their anchorage. Hence, he requested the services of the submarine and was rewarded by orders that the vessel would be towed to Port Royal for his use.

Though the *Alligator*'s covert missions would remain well-guarded from historical record, we do know that either overly-cautious Union officials or the cruel hand of destiny would eventually put an abrupt and untimely end to her top-secret assignments. Acting Master W. F. Winchester had his orders, and his *USS Sumpter* proceeded past Cape Henry in water he later described as "very smooth." By early morning, the *Sumpter*, a wooden screw steamer, was past the Cape Hatteras Lighthouse. The sea water temperature was rising, up to sixty-eight degrees, and the wind picked up until, by 8 a.m., the *Sumpter* was struggling to make headway.

Under the pressure, the ship's engine began to fail. Winchester ordered his crew to set the fore and aft sails, but it didn't seem to help. By noon, when the sailors were finally able to take an accurate reading, the ship was at latitude 34.43, longitude 75.2, and making very little headway:

> "The wind by this time had increased to a very heavy gale from Southward and westward and a very heavy sea."[20]

Soon, the *Sumpter* was plunging under to the foremast, then struggling to get back to the top of the waves. In order to save his vessel from certain disaster, Winchester turned to run with the storm. Yet, the wind blew harder and harder, the waves crested and crashed without easing, and the *Alligator* yanked at the *Sumpter* until one tow line broke entirely. They were quickly reaching a terribly perilous situation:

> "The *Alligator* was steering wildly and threatening to snap the hawser. It being evident we would soon lose her, I called a council of all the Officers."[21]

The question to his council was simple: life or death? The *Alligator*, Winchester feared, would soon pull the *Sumpter* under the waves with her. As the decks rolled under their feet and the timbers moaned, the officers' vote was unanimous: cut her free.

At precisely 6 p.m. on April 2, the *USS Alligator*'s last tow-line was released some fifty miles south of Cape Hatteras. Great gray waves broke over *Sumpter*'s stern and swept the two vessels rapidly apart. Free of the dragging iron weight, the Sumpter drove on, slowly but surely, into the pounding storm. Still, the crew had its hands full with just one ship. An unexpected, though fortunate, break in the weather gave them some valuable time to repair the ailing engine, but within twenty-four hours, the storm had built again. The wind screamed, and "snow fell so thickly that the crew could not see a ship's length distant," Winchester wrote.

The spanker boom, or after sail, of the *USS Sumpter* was completely washed away, the wardroom skylight broke, as two huge waves carried off two of her crewmen. Finally, on the morning of April 6, the wind lessened and the seas dropped. A reading showed that the *Sumpter* now floated at latitude 37.38 and longitude 71.04, well north and east of her last known position. She limped onward toward the New York coastline for repairs, carrying the sub's last commander, Acting Master Samuel Eakins, and crew away from their ship forever. The *Alligator* was never seen again. Apparently, the submarine gauntlet would have to be carried forward by other, future inventors in the field.

More than one hundred years after the American Civil War had reached its climactic conclusion, a letter was discovered buried beneath a mountain of miscellaneous archives. Originally, it had been dispatched via courier to Southern government officials from Monterey, Mexico, a city nestled along the banks of the Santa Catalina River, on April 9, 1863. Ironically, though no one had paid much attention at the time, the letter had accurately predicted the future success of the submarine, describing in general terms a prototype craft designed, constructed, and tested during the previous year:

> "Narciso Monturiol, a scientific Catalonian, has invented a vessel for submarine navigation. She is called "Ictineo" (fish-like vessel). As a man-of-war she can prevent not only the bombardment of the ports, but also the landing of the enemy. If the services Monturiol are secured and the necessary number of vessels built, no Federal squadron would dare to approach our coasts, since an unseen enemy can leave our harbors and destroy their

ships. The "Ictineos" have guns which fire under water and also rams and torpedoes. They can navigate in a depth of about twenty-five fathoms. The want of atmosphere to support animal life in the depth of the seas, which has been the great drawback to submarine navigation, has been obviated. The inventor creates an artificial atmosphere and shutting himself up, like a larva, carries with him the elements of existence. Several of the Spaniards here are...satisfied that he is not an idle talker. He has lately made experiments at Barcelona which prove his success."[22]

Narciso Monturiol

Some historians were inclined to believe that it was highly unlikely that two distinct foreign inventors could devise an innovative air-purification system at about the same time in history, and that "Narciso Monturiol" was a fictitious name. Indeed, they claimed, Monturiol was simply an alias belonging to the transplanted Frenchman, Brutus de Villeroi, who had become so enraged and disenchanted with Union officials that he had later attempted to sell his underwater craft to the Southern forces. Of course, they were wrong.

The first steam-powered submarine in the world, the *Ictineo II*, had indeed been constructed by the Spanish engineer, Narcis Monturiol. Born in Figueres, Catalonia, Spain, on September 28, 1819, this son of a cooper had studied Law and had written manuscripts on the subjects of geography, physics and natural history. Monturiol eschewed law in favor of politics, making a name for himself as a political antagonist and socialist revolutionary. His earliest inventions had included a cigarette rolling machine and a method for mass-producing notebooks. He first conceived of building a submarine to help coral fishermen during the early 1850s and, by June of 1859, the seven-meter-long *Ictíneo* was ready for its maiden voyage. *Ictíneo*'s propeller was hand-driven by a crew of four men.

Monturiol soon began construction of a much larger submarine, known fittingly as the *Ictineo II*, on February 10, 1862. The completed vessel measured seventeen meters long and displaced sixty-five tons. Launched on October 2, 1864, her massive propeller was initially operated by sixteen men. She was outfitted with a single cannon that could be fired while completely submerged, and Monturiol offered the Confederacy his advanced submarine to smash the Federal blockade, but it was not purchased. Owing to its poor performance, Monturiol decided to replace the human power with a 6-horsepower steam engine.

Replica of Narcis Monturiol's *Ictineo*

The *Ictineo II* would be relaunched on October 22, 1867, and while submerged, she was propelled by a one-cylinder machine set in the stern section. The *Ictineo II* completed thirteen submersions to a depth of as much as thirty meters, with the longest one lasting for seven and a half hours beneath the Barcelona harbor. Quite obviously, Monturiol was ahead of his time, and among other things, he invented the double hull as well as the bulb-shaped bow, still used in modern submarine vessels today. In 1868, the *Ictineo II* was seized by its creditors because of financial difficulties, and broken up and sold as scrap metal. Narcis Monturiol died on September 6, 1885.

Meanwhile, we do know that, in the spring of 1863, Brutus de Villeroi wrote the French Government from his home in Philadelphia in the hopes of selling a new design for a 125-foot long, oar-powered submarine. This latest design was far more ambitious than the *USS Alligator*. At the time, de Villeroi had severed his political ties with the United States Navy's contractor, Martin Thomas, feeling totally cheated and insulted. Then, on May 1, 1863, de Villeroi wrote an additional letter to the French Minister of the Navy, attaching copies of the United States Navy's *USS Alligator* blueprints. The purpose of this letter and the blueprints were to show the French Navy his seriousness and credentials as a submarine inventor. This letter also described what de Villeroi deemed to be necessary capabilities for a successful submarine.

On June 7, 1863, the Commission organized by the French government to evaluate de Villeroi's plans deemed the proposal poorly researched, and concluded that the submarine design proposal was not innovative. The Commission further judged the proposal to lack engineering and design explanations. In addition, it noted that while Brutus de Villeroi had referred to additional reports and articles written on his previous submarine designs, those documents were not included for review and evaluation. Finally, the Commission noted that since the French Navy was already waiting for the results from another submarine design, *Le Plongeur*; and, thus, the Commission recommended rejecting Brutus de Villeroi's design.

In summing it all up, the French government added insult to rejection by claiming that de Villeroi's submarine design was "completely unnavigable, the artillery could not work, and the saws would never have any useful purpose." The Commission further decided that no follow-up action should be taken. On June 9, 1863, they informed the inventor of their decision in writing.

Brutus De Villeroi, the self-proclaimed genius of submarine weaponry, died of in relative obscurity of chronic bronchitis in Philadelphia, Pennsylvania, in 1874, eleven years after the *Alligator* had vanished beneath Cape Hatteras, North Carolina, waters. His brief obituary in the Philadelphia Inquirer noted that the inventor's death had been hastened by the "proverbial ingratitude" of the United States government:

"MONS. A. BRUTUS DE VILLEROI—On Monday, June 29th, Mons. A. Brutus de Villeroi died at his residence No. 318 South Fifteenth street, in this city, aged 81 years. He was a native of France, and was educated liberally, and achieved distinction as a civil and naval engineer. At the outbreak of the rebellion, in 1861, M. de Villeroi invented and perfected a novel torpedo boat, a model of which was exhibited on the Rancocas Creek, and for the ingenuity and originality of the invention the Secretary of the Navy, Mr. Gideon J. Welles, rewarded him by appointment in the navy. The perfection of Erikson's monitor rendered the torpedo for the time unavailable, and M. de Villeroi was not handsomely treated by the authorities in Washington. He was discharged and others took the glory and fruits of his labors and studies. He was an accomplished gentleman, and had the courtly manners of one who had mixed in the highest circles. For several years he has been in failing health..."[23]

Though both the vessel and its designer were gone, the historical records concerning the *Alligator* did not vanish entirely. Researchers have turned up tantalizing references to the vessel since at least 1932, when George Eakins, son of *Alligator* commander Samuel Eakins, dispatched a letter to the United States Office of Naval Records and Library, asking for information about his father's unusual ship. On July 13, 1932, a former member of Admiral William F. Sims' wartime staff, Captain Dudley W. Knox, who was then the Officer-in-Charge of the library, responded to Samuel Eakins' request. In a detailed letter, he explained that Navy officials had signed a contract with de Villeroi for $14,000 to build a submarine in 1861. Soon thereafter, Eakins secured a copy of his father's naval orders, which placed him at the helm of the *Alligator*.

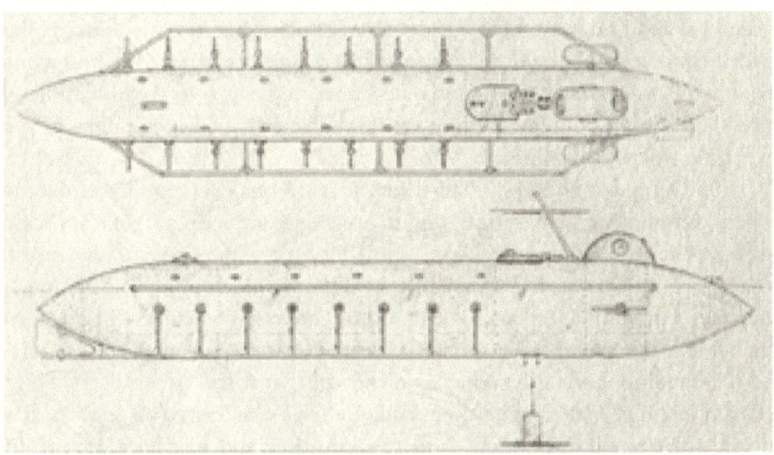

Drawings of de Villeroi's *USS Alligator*

Later, Samuel Eakins' son, George, relocated his family to New London, North Carolina. In 1954 he proudly showed the copy of those same orders to the *Stanly News and Press*, a local newspaper. Less than two decades later, in 1973, the *Daily Press* of Newport News, Virginia, published a story about Katie Eakins,

Samuel Eakins's daughter. The article included a photo of the submariner and a drawing of the *Alligator* from a French history book.

Nearly fifty years later, in June of 2002, information concerning the *USS Alligator* "surfaced" once again when the wife of U. S. Office of Naval Research's Chief of Naval Research, Rear Admiral Jay M. Cohen, discovered an article about the *Alligator* in a Civil War magazine and showed it to him. Cohen proceeded to contact Robert Ballard, the scientist and explorer who had discovered the *RMS Titanic* and the National Oceanic and Atmospheric Administration's National Marine Sanctuary Program Director, Dan Basta, asking for any assistance that they might be able to provide. Basta, in turn, directed marine archaeologist, Bruce Terrell, to conduct research to determine, as near as possible, the most likely area on the sea floor that might contain any extant remains of the sunken submarine. Asked to coordinate with Captain Woody Berzins, who was the ONR's representative on this project, Terrell assessed all available historical sources, and identified as primary resources letters of the acting masters of the *USS Sumpter* and the *USS Alligator* that reported the incident of the loss of the vessel to the Secretary of the Navy.

Eventually, in May of 2004, Catherine G. Marzin, a National Marine Sanctuary researcher, hit an historical "jackpot." While traveling in France to visit family and to investigate French Naval archives in the hope of finding documentation on the submersible, archivists at the Service Historique de la Marine in Vincennes told her they'd found some old naval documents. A few days later in Paris, she found original blueprints for the submarine, left in an aging trunk by Brutus de Villeroi himself, along with several letters of correspondence. "I figured I could find something," Marzin later said of her intensive search, "but I didn't think it would be the blueprints. It was quite exciting." The find would not only help researchers to reconstruct models to scale, but would help determine the *Alligator*'s unique hydrodynamic characteristics, which might help in predicting where she sank.

In December of 2004, a half-dozen adventurous East Carolina University students enrolled in the maritime studies program completed a significant scientific search for the sunken *Alligator*. The main thrust of their search was centered in the "Atlantic Graveyard," a small inlet into the Carolinas off of Cape Hatteras. The area between Cape Hatteras and Cape Lookout was chosen as the focus area because the last recorded spotting of the *Alligator* was along Cape Hatteras, and the conditions when it went down showed that it was "a prospective place to begin looking." Yet, despite their valiant efforts, the lost vessel continued to remain unrecovered. Still, each of these expeditions did manage to prove one thing: if searchers hoped to locate the vessel one day, they must begin by closely examining all the facts surrounding her disappearance.

The *USS Sumpter* was a wooden merchant screw steamer built in 1853 and chartered by the United States Navy during the Civil War. She was considered to be in poor condition by the time she was ordered to tow the *Alligator* to Charleston in April of 1863. The *Sumpter* left Hampton Roads with the submarine in tow on the first day of of the month. The *Alligator* was sealed tightly shut with no crew on board, and she soon encountered rising winds from the southwest that grew to gale intensity by the time she reached Cape Hatteras late in the evening of April 1.

The *USS Sumpter*'s last recorded coordinates with *Alligator* in tow was latitude 34.43, longitude 75.20 at noon on April 2. From there, the *Sumpter* continued to sail into the southwestern winds with fore and aft sails set, and the bow plunging deeply. All the while, she took such a heavy pounding that the engines suffered partial failure and the forward hatches flooded. At approximately six that evening, after breaking one of her two tow hawsers, the *Alligator* was cut free with the intention of returning to its location once the storm had abated.

As fate would have it, by the time the storm had ended at 6:00 p.m. on April 3, the *Sumpter* had been beaten north and was nearly floundering near Cape Henry where she had begun her voyage and was kept from returning to the site of the *Alligator* by a subsequent nor'easter that caused further damage. Two vital points remain significant in any attempt to locate the *Alligator*: she was in a sealed and floating condition when she was lost; and since her intended use as a submarine required her to be leak-free, she may have drifted for some time over some distance before she sank, unless she was severely damaged by the storm. Also, the *Sumpter*'s acting master's report to the Secretary of the Navy suggests that during the storm, the master was concerned that they were in the Gulf Stream and were attempting to sail west to escape its northerly pull.

Before historians can determine precisely where the *Alligator* might be today, they first must understand where the *USS Sumpter* was when she cut the last hawser that sent the submarine adrift. In order to do so, researchers must recreate the *Sumpter*'s voyage through the Captain's letters, and take into account the weather and prevailing currents.

The *Sumpter* was a screw steamer, and on a good day, with no current, she could probably do about 8.5 knots towing the *Alligator*. Furthermore, the two vessels were traveling in the Gulf Stream, while a very strong, southwesterly gale was gusting. The vessels were on a southerly, southwesterly course much of the day. Then, at about 3:40 p.m., the *Sumpter* changed course to the northeast. Her engines were damaged at the time, and her storm canvas was barely keeping her ahead of the seas (after she had come about). And, finally, the heavy wind generated surface current for a Beaufort scale 9 is about 3 to 5 knots.

Using all of this data, a map information plot can be generated to determine the *Sumpter*'s noon location on an NOAA Atlantic Ocean chart. From this fix, a circle with the radius of fifty-one nautical miles can be drawn depicting the area the vessel could have traveled in six hours on a good day doing 8.5 knots. We can use this to assume the maximum area the *Sumpter* could have been when the hawser was cut. Yet, just because we assume the *USS Sumpter* may have set the *Alligator* adrift in this area, it does not necessarily mean she actually sank here. The reason is simple; the *Alligator* was not ready to be scuttled. In fact the crew of the *Sumpter* had every intention of going back to retrieve her. Furthermore, the fact that she was staying afloat the entire time the *Sumpter* was struggling with the heavy seas is a testament to her own seaworthiness.

We do know that after the *Alligator* was set adrift, the wind continued from the southwest, but began to back towards the north. By 6:00 p.m. the following day, a full gale was coming out of the northeast. From wind driven currents, one would assume that the *USS Alligator* may have even made a "comma" shaped track going to the north, then east, then south, and then to the southwest. However, she was also located in the Gulf Stream, which has a prevailing current to the east-northeast off Cape Hatteras. This was probably a much greater factor in her transport than the wind drive currents from the storm. Thus, if the *USS Alligator* did not immediately sink, it is highly unlikely that she is even located within the arbitrary trapezoidal area.

Thus, the mysterious *Alligator* may ever be found. Like a proverbial needle in millions of haystacks, it might depend on mere luck rather than scientific exploration. Still, as information concerning her inventor continues to surface, perhaps the *Alligator* will also be found and brought up from the depths of the sea.

Drawing of James Buchanan Eads

- 14 -
James Buchanan Eads: *Mississippi Diver*

"At the parlement helde at london the 30th yeare of the Reigne of Kinge Henrie the eight, Anno, 1538, it is mentioned in the cronicles that the Lord Cromewell beinge then Lorde Privye Seale & Vicar generall, did chardge all busshopps (through the Realme) that theye whould have the large bible in englische in every parish churche, and withall they should nowe begin to keepe a register booke of all that should be baptised, maried, and buried, in every parishe from thensforth forwarde yearlye."[1]

Around 1900 BC, "Beaker" people arrived on the island from Germany–so called from their distinctive pottery, a sort of Glockenbecher (bell-shaped cup). Initially, they called the Island "Wiht" (weight), meaning "raised" or "what rises over the sea." Eventually, the Romans came in 43 AD and translated Wiht into the name "Vectis," from the Latin "veho," meaning "lifting." The Roman rule started under Vespasian and continued peacefully for over four hundred years. Then came a period of strife starting with the Saxons under Cerdic and Cynric in 530 AD. Many of the natives were slaughtered, and four years after Cerdic's death the government was divided between his two nephews, Stuf and Wihtgar. In 544 Wihtgar died and was buried at Carisbrooke. In 661 AD, Wight changed hands again when it was captured by Wulfhure, King of the Mercians, but it was in 686 AD that the West Saxon King, Caedwalla, conquered it and brought Christianity to the Island.

For nearly two centuries the people of Wight then led a fairly peaceful life until the Danes arrived this far south. In 897 AD their relentless "burning and killing" went on for more than a century, and it was no wonder that the Islanders lived in constant fear. At the time of the Norman Conquest, William the Conqueror granted over lordship of the Isle of Wight to his relative, William Fitz Osbern, who began the construction of a castle at Carisbrooke. The lordship of the Island was passed to the De Redvers family in 1101, with the hereditary rights and privileges that accompanied it, until the Countess Isabella De Fortibus, the last survivor in the family, sold the Island to Edward 1 in 1293 for six thousand marks.

The acquisition of full control of the Island by the crown was important because of the island's vulnerability to invasion. The lordship of the island was now a royal appointment. One of the lords of the island–Henry Beauchamp, Duke of Warwick–was actually given a title of King to the Isle of Wight in 1444 by King Henry VI, who attended the ceremony in person and placed the crown upon his head.

During the Hundred Years' War, the Island, like much of the south coast, became a target for marauding French. The Island's only fortification, the Norman Castle at Carisbrooke, assumed a defensive role for which it was unsuited owing to its central position. Without protection, the French could land on the coast and burn and plunder while ignoring the castle. Towns and villages like Yarmouth, Newtown, and Newport were sometimes attacked and burned to the ground. It is said that in 1377 a party of French fell into an ambush on the outskirts of Newport and were cut to pieces in Dead Man's Lane, now Trafalgar Road. They are supposed to be buried at Noddies Hill, now known as Nodehill or Upper St. James' Street. On the same occasion the French besieged the castle, but, according to legend, retired on the death of their commander, shot from the castle's west wall. Concern about the French attacks could be seen in the frequent modifications made to the castle's defenses throughout the fourteenth century.

James Buchanan Eads has family roots that can be followed back through the shadows of history across ten generations, originating in that isolated and small community of Newport, Isle of Wight, Hampshire, England. It was there, in about 1500, that a man with the surname "Edes"–derived from the Old English word "eade," meaning "abundant wealth"–appeared, married Alice when both were in their mid-twenties, and died on April 12, 1552 in his birth town. Yet, since that time, ancestors have often inquired: what's in a name? Genealogists walking through English historical corridors have claimed that most Parish Clerks employed simple phonetic spellings to surnames. Thus, Edes, Eedes, Eades, and Eads sounded the same, and later became relevant in tracing this particular family's passage through time and place. A change in Parish Clerk or Vicar often resulted in a change in spelling. According to the Hampshire Parish Registers left behind, for example, second generation Lawrence appeared as "Eades" in his marriage record and "Eedes" at birth.

And so it went, with Lawrence Eades marrying Alice James in Newport, and fathering three sons and a daughter–Richard, John, Thomas, and Jane– during the mid-1500s. Each would evolve from Edes to Eades during his or her lifetime. Richard, it seems, was destined to be the most prominent:

> "A product of the Westminster School, Eedes matriculated from Christ Church in 1571. He enjoyed a distinguished academic career, being elected Junior Proctor of the University for 1583, and appointed Canon of the fourth stall of Christ Church in 1586. In the same year he was made Chaplain to Queen Elizabeth, and created Doctor of Divinity in 1589..."[2]

Richard remained Chaplain to Queen Elizabeth's successor, King James I, soon thereafter becoming the Dean of Worcester. He was next selected as a

Bible translator to James, but his personal contribution to the *King James Version* seems to have been precluded by his unexpected death–likely of the plague then ravaging England–in November of 1604.

Richard did manage to offer history a bit of his writing, however, although much of it was more legend than reality:

> "At this time Christ Church contained two playwrights, Richard Eedes, who had produced a tragedy Caesar Interfectus, probably at the same time Gager's Meleager was acted, in 1582, and so in 1583 was every bit as distinguished as Gager (although he would write no more plays)..."[3]

Evidence indicates that Richard's writing seems to have been staged on the same occasion as the first performance of Gager's *Meleager*, in 1582. Only the epilogue of his play survives, however, which is quite regrettable, since such a relatively early example would have been of tremendous interest for the development of the Elizabethan history play. In fact, it has even been suggested to have been a source for Shakespeare's *Julius Caesar*. Other than the Iter Boreale, Eades' only surviving Latin poetry consists of gratulatory verses prefacing various contemporary publications, mainly by other members of his Oxford circle.

Yet, perhaps Richard managed to leave something of even greater value: one surviving sibling, Thomas, who might carry on the family name and heritage. Born on June 4, 1570, the playwright's younger brother had been named after his maternal grandfather, Thomas James. From his marriage to Ann Serle in 1592, came two sons, Henry and Thomas, each of which was born in further northwest, on the English mainland south of London, in the town of West Clandon. After their mother died in the early 1600s, their father remarried, this time to Jone (sic), who gave them a half-brother, William.

After fathering two daughters, Joane and Katherine, Henry I begat Henry II–by then spelled Eads. His only son was born July 10, 1642, in West Clandon. That Henry fathered Henry III, submariner James Buchanan Eades' great-great-grandfather, who was born on March 25, 1668, in nearby Shalford, County Guilford, England. Sadly, at the tender age of fourteen, Henry Eads III's father died and, within two years, the lad had left the rest of his family behind and departed from the port of Deptford bound for the New World. At the time of his departure, on July 14, 1684, he was "bound" over as a servant to Colonel John Lightfoot III for a period of seven years, in order to pay for his eight-week passage to Jamestown, Virginia. By 1691 he had relocated to Maryland, purchasing property on June 10, 1696, and three months later, on September 17, he married Mary Elizabeth Hallett. Together, they would have two sons, Henry IV, born "on the banks of the Shenandoah," and James, who died in infancy.

James Buchanan's grandfather, also named James, was born the third of four sons about 1756 to Henry IV and Mary (Pegely) Eads in Hagerstown, Washington County, Maryland. He married Hannah Clark in 1774, when both were barely eighteen years old. Records indicate that grandfather James was then employed for a short time during the American Revolution as a clerk at the Hughes Iron Works, nestled along a tributary of the Antietam Creek at the base of South Mountain some six miles east of Hagerstown. The operation had been owned and operated by the Hughes family since 1768.

On January 15, 1776, the U.S. Congress created a committee to determine the number of cannon needed by the Continental Army, and a contract for their production was agreed upon with the Hughes Iron Works. Along with a contract with a Mark Bird in Pennsylvania, the Hughes brothers would produce over 1,000 tons of cannon at a price of $10,000. Eventually, James left Hughes when they ceased operation in 1775, working as a farmer in Maryland and raising a family of eleven children, six sons and five daughters. After relocating their entire brood to a small farm near Lexington, Kentucky, for a short time, the Eads family made their way one hundred miles north to an area a few miles beyond the tiny village of Harrison, Ohio, just a few hundred yards west of the Indiana and Ohio border.

Among James and Hannah's passel of children was youngest son, Thomas Clark, born on June 29, 1794. On March 14, 1816, Thomas married Nancy Ann Buchanan, first cousin of James Buchanan, then a young lawyer making his mark in Lancaster, Pennsylvania; and, in the same year that he was first elected to the United States House of Representatives, Nancy and Thomas gave birth to their third child, a son that they would name James Buchanan Eads.

By the time that young James Buchanan was born in Lawrenceburg, Indiana, on May 23, 1820, two sisters—Eliza and Genevieve—had preceded him. The family would move around after that, with one biographer claiming that "James' father never was very prosperous." Attempting to find financial stability, he moved his family first to Cincinnati in 1822 and then back to Louisville in 1829. In 1833, Thomas Eads decided to uproot his family once again, this time believing that St. Louis would be the answer to their economic problems. So, at the age of thirteen, young James boarded the steamboat, *Carolton*, along with his mother and two sisters, while his father remained behind to gather supplies for a general store he planned to open.

Traveling on a steamboat was certainly an imaginative experience for the curious James Buchanan. Fascinated at a very young age by the machinery and mechanics of similar vessels that had run continually along the Ohio River's ninety billion gallons of water that flowed every day past Louisville every day, his father had fed his interest by building James a small workshop. For hours on end, he would tinker away in it, taking apart the family clock, building scale models of steamboats, and even constructing a functional steam engine. As his grandson, Louis How, would later reminisce, a particularly boyish (and ingenious) moment during this childhood occurred when he produced a miniature wagon that mysteriously moved around the room under "its own power." As his mother and sisters gasped, the mischievous youngster soon revealed that the motive power was produced by a single, live rat:

"He had fastened the rat by its tail on a tread-wheel which gave motion to the cart wheels, and a hole had been left open in the narrow cover just out of reach of the rodent, showing a way of escape. The lusty kicking to reach the hole whirled the tread-wheel."[4]

A number of people from all walks of life were aboard the *Carolton*–artists, musicians, writers, entertainers, military men, and political figures–all traveling along with "common" farmers, laborers, businessmen, pioneer families, adventurers, vagabonds, and at least one engineer and future submarine inventor. One writer described the thirteen-year-old as "a thin, wiry boy, with light-brown hair tousled in the wind, gray eyes dancing... His manner was gentle, but his energy was appalling and his pranks legion."[5]

In fact, feeling that he was so "full of the dickens," his father had attempted to corral his antics by actually hiring "a sturdy playmate to take the brunt of his mischief."[6] It didn't work though. Indeed, young James thirst for knowledge seemed unquenchable. He investigated the intricate details of the entire steamboat, from pilothouse to paddle wheel. And now, as they floated past Paducah, Kentucky, his mother looked on with a real sense of pride, seeing her son's immense fascination with the *Carolton*'s mechanics. He intended to design a real working steamboat, he confided in her. Even then, he realized that "it would be much harder to make than the puffing steam engine he had put together three years ago in his workshop... As for the sawmills and fire engines he had (also) made, they were nothing" in comparison to what he would construct one day.[7]

As the *Carolton* continued to make its way along the Ohio River toward Cairo, Illinois–a town named by the Egyptian immigrants who were the first to settled there–young James must have been imagining the journeys of Mark Twain, who claimed:

> "Piloting on the Mississippi River was not work to me; it was play–delightful play, vigorous play, adventurous play–and I loved it."[8]

And then suddenly, as they rounded a sharp bend, he knew that they had reached the mighty river itself. They had left the low flatlands behind, where the "willows bent over the water, dabbling their fingers in it, (where) they moved back from one army of reeds that climbed ashore." Truly, the steamboat had found the Mississippi River:

> "Its waters lashed nearer, rougher, they caught at the boat greedily and fell away from its prow in a boiling double spray. James pressed against the rail, his hands tightening on it... The Mississippi was different than anything people had said about it, more real, more alive. It could be happy, angry, proud or reckless, as though it had thoughts and feelings. It must be the most powerful river in the world–his river."[9]

All too soon the Eads family–minus their father–arrived in the city known as the "Gateway to the West." As the *Carolton* approached the St. Louis riverfront on September 6, 1833, a chimney flue unexpectedly toppled over, and a deadly fire broke out, killing eight people and severely injuring many more. Ann Eads and her three children emerged on a low sandy bank along the riverfront unharmed, but all of their worldly possessions had been lost in the blaze. Save for the clothes on their backs, they suddenly found themselves alone and penniless in a mysterious new place, "and early on a cold morning the family set foot, scarcely clothed, not only in the city of which the young boy was to be one day the leading citizen, but on the very spot, it is said, where he was afterwards to base one pier of his great bridge."[10]

The somewhat destitute family received help and refuge from a few of the old French families among St. Louis' six thousand residents, and Ann Eads met the challenge by renting a house on North Main Street, facing the river along the top of a bluff, and taking in boarders. Meanwhile, young James responded to the adversity with the same hard work and determination exhibited by his mother. Discontinuing his formal education in order to help support his family, he started by selling apples on the street. Soon after, he caught the eye of a boarder in the house his mother had rented, a local business owner named Barrett Williams. After recognizing the outgoing personality of the bright young boy, Williams immediately offered James a job as a clerk at his dry goods mercantile store. The firm, which he co-owned with Andrew Duhring, was situated nearby on Main Street, between Olive and Locust streets. There, young James would deliver packages, carry out the ashes from the fireplace, fetch coal, tidy up a bit, and proudly bring home his pay of three dollars at the end of each week. It was, however, a position that would provide far more than mere income.

Soon thereafter, Barrett Williams discovered his young employee's strong aptitude and overwhelming appreciation for mechanics, and allowed James the privilege to use his own personal upstairs library. Studying a variety of scientific books at night, Eads acquired his first theoretical knowledge of engineering. In this way, without a formal education, he began, during a time when there was no free higher education, to educate himself. From that point forward he was a constant reader not only of scientific works, but all types of books. Hence, during those late-night sessions after the mercantile had closed, he poured through the classics, became a fan of classic poetry, devoured books about geography and history, and most importantly, taught himself engineering and mathematics.

Still, life was not easy for the young boy from Lawrenceburg, Indiana. At the age of sixteen, James suffered a devastating and heartbreaking loss when his eighteen-year-old sister, Genevieve, died on December 13, 1836, from "a consumptive cough." Then, just fifteen months later, his only remaining sister, Eliza Ann, had become deathly ill "from the same dread malady that had carried the younger Genevieve away"; she died at the age of twenty on March 23, 1838. James could often be seen, grieving at their unmarked side-by-side graves near the family home on the bluff. Later, in June of 1853, he would have both of their cremated ashes exhumed and re-interred at the Eads family mausoleum at the Bellefontaine Cemetery in Saint Louis, the same place where his mother had been laid to rest just two months earlier. The tree-lined, quiet resting place was located just a mile or so from his beloved Mississippi River.

At the age of nineteen, reportedly because of both personal health concerns and the dissolving of the mercantile partnership, James reluctantly left Williams and Duhring and accepted a position that would allow him to spend more time in the open air. It was an extremely chilly morning in March of 1839 when he began his next job as a "mud clerk" aboard the steamboat *Knickerbocker*, then laying in wharf at the St. Louis docks, on its way from Cincinnati, Ohio, to "Galena and Dubuque." Finally, he had found his way to the great waterway that would, from that day forward, remain a large part of his existence and identity.

Beneath the large circular cape that he had opted to wear for his first day on the job, James carried with him a miniature steamboat, complete with all of its working parts. It was, in fact, "ready to raise steam on a tin boiler, ingeniously and systematically arranged." Inquiring as to where he might safely store his model boat, he had been led to the vacant locker in mud clerk's room, where he would sleep and dream about the mighty river for the next few months.

In the beginning, his daily routine included wading through the muck of unpaved waterfronts to accept or release freight, clearing away obstacles in the *Knickerbocker*'s way, and securing the boat to shore. As the name implied, a mud clerk would often be given the dirtiest jobs aboard ship. But James' tasks didn't end there, for during the day he would stand watch with the first mate from noon until supper, then turn in while the captain and head clerk took over. At midnight, he would pull himself from his berth to collect freight bills, bargain with the greedy wood yard "pirates" for adequate fuel, all the while maintaining one vigilant eye on the all-night gamblers on board the *Knickerbocker* and the other on the riffraff deck crew always out to break into the vessel's barrels of whiskey. All of this was extremely arduous work, but it offered him the hands-on riverboat experience he craved. Though he received no salary at first, his hard work soon earned him the position of chief clerk–also known as the "purser."

By then, his parents had moved away, this time more than two hundred river miles north to Iowa. Thomas Clark Eads had, in fact, traveled upriver in the spring of 1836, to a place where Eleazer Parkhurst had laid claim to a large tract of land. The elder Eads quickly talked his way into a partnership with Parkhurst, agreeing to help him develop a town site that he had planned. The property, which had been awarded to Parkhurst along with another section of land by virtue of Article VI of the Black Hawk Purchase Treaty of 1832, butted up against the northern edge of Antoine Le Claire's Reserve. The two tiny hamlets, fittingly named Le Claire and Parkhurst, would struggle along economically, side by side, for twenty years before being combined into the single, somewhat sprawling village of Le Claire.

Now living in Iowa, Colonel Thomas Clark and Nancy Ann–known to the rest of the Eads family simply as "Ann"–constructed a dignified home at the end of a winding lane in the northwest corner of Parkhurst. Known as Glen Argyle Cottage–named for the seat of his wife's family clans in Scotland–its long, low, sweeping roofline at the front came down to a full-length porch below. In that roof were a pair of matching dormer windows, the upper portions being semi-circles. In the rear was an L-shaped section, with a matching window and a side entrance, making the entire thirty foot by forty foot structure "one of the wonders of the age." Completed in the winter of 1836-1837, the eager couple moved in the following spring.

Later that same year, the Colonel built a larger two-story frame building near the riverfront, which served as a hotel and meeting place in the village. Historical records state that the Colonel was "a handsome man, always well-dressed, with high hat and cane, and dignified." His wife was described as a "woman of poise and of sweetness of face," with some even saying that "she resembled Queen Mary of Scotland."[11]

Thomas Clark Eads would serve as a postmaster in Parkhurst, a community in search of an identity that was also known for a brief period as Berlin. On June 2, 1842, the Colonel became a candidate for recorder of Scott County. Very politically minded, he was an active Whig party member throughout the 1840s and into the early 1850s, and the *Davenport Gazette* made numerous references to him as a delegate to both county and state conventions.

Drawing of the *Knickerbocker*

Meanwhile, James Eads had opted to remain behind in St. Louis to pursue his Mississippi steamboat career. Whenever the *Knickerbocker* stopped near enough to his parents' Argyle Cottage residence, however, he dropped in for a hasty visit. Yet, the majority of his time was now spent learning the mighty waterway's nooks and crannies. Though he was in awe of the river's elegance and beauty, he remained always cognizant of her destructive power. He had experienced it firsthand aboard the *Carolton* in 1833, and he would see it again when the *Knickerbocker* was ripped to pieces by a snag on December 11, 1839. For the second time in just a half-dozen years, he found himself shivering on shore, watching the boat that had transported him to far places of adventure sink to the muddy bottom of the river. Along with passengers and the rest of the steamboat's crew, he had been picked up "by a passing flotilla of flatboats just as the heavily laden steamer tilted down, the bellow of a few cattle aboard choked in a hungry gurgle of water."[12]

His job aboard the *Knickerbocker* was now over, and James was forced to begin considering alternatives to his present career. He understood–perhaps more than anyone–that the Mississippi River swallowed up steamboats at a rapid pace. In fact, nearly one per week was being sunk or wrecked by her enticing fury; and, along with the vessels' vulnerable hulls, the river took their "valuable engines, boilers, and cargoes." Most recently, "wreckers" were paid quite handsomely by ship owners and insurance companies to salvage these valuable sunken boats and their cargoes. In addition, the law stipulated that anything lying at the bottom of the Mississippi River for five or more years became the property of anyone who could retrieve it. Knowing all of this, James decided to go into the business of salvaging these boats, their machinery, and their freight. Driven less by aesthetics and more by profit, he began to formulate a very concrete plan.

In 1842, after months of design revisions and improvements, twenty-two-year-old, James Buchanan Eads, secured a U.S. patent for a special boat equipped with a diving bell that allowed workers to walk on the dangerous river bottom. In short order, he visited the office of a pair of seasoned boat builders. Calvin Case and William Nelson were somewhat surprised, though intrigued, when the enterprising young man offered to partner with them in his planned salvaging business. In exchange for this "generous offer," all they had to contribute was the construction of his salvage vessel. He had, in fact, brought the detailed sketches for its design with him. The drawings exhibited the details of a diving bell designed to be transported by "a stout twin-hulled boat with a sparse grove of derricks and pumps rising from its deck."[13]

James gave no explanation of his proposed vessel's mode of operation, nor details of exactly how salvaging would be accomplished. Nonetheless, the two men were so enthralled by his concept and assurances that they agreed to provide him with both financial backing and the construction of his vessel. Within weeks, *Sub-Marine Boat No. 1* was being built, and James was looking forward to his first underwater exploration. Yet, as always, his impatience in every new anticipated adventure got the best of him, and he decided that he simply could not wait until she was completed..

So, while James waited for his first diving-bell boat to be completed, he heard of a barge heavily loaded with one hundred tons of pig lead that had sank in the rapids near Keokuk, "where the twinkling of the Star of Empire...(could) be seen by any far-reaching eye, perched upon the farther bluff of the graceful Mississippi." Having contracted with the wreck's owners, James made his way more than 200 miles north of Saint Louis to rescue the freight from fifteen feet of water. At the time, he had no personal experience in the use of diving-armor; but he had hired a skilled diver from the Great Lakes region, who brought his own apparatus to the site of the sunken vessel. Together, the enterprising pair set off on their mission:

> "Obtaining a barge, this was promptly anchored over it and preparations made for the diver to go to work; but the current was found so exceedingly rapid that it was impossible to use the armor with any safety. A belt around the diver's waist was attached by a cord to the bow of the boat to hold him against the current, and a ladder procured on which the diver undertook to descend, but it was impossible for him to control his body in the current."[14]

More determined than ever to rescue the barge's valuable cargo, James traveled by horse and wagon into the town of Keokuk. Boasting a population of barely 150 residents, he hunted for some solution to his problem. Suddenly, while visiting a local drinking establishment, he realized what he needed to do:

> "Determined not to be baffled, Mr. Eads immediately...purchased a forty gallon whisky barrel with which to improvise a diving bell. With several pigs of lead secured around one end of the barrel by a network of ropes, and with that head taken out, a block and tackle attached to the network at the other end and a temporary derrick erected, he was soon prepared to commence the recovery of the cargo. But the diver demurred and would not descend in this dangerous looking apparatus. Mr. Eads then set an example, which he has followed throughout all his varied experience as an engineer, which was never to ask a man in his employ to go where he was unwilling to trust his own life. The bell thus suspended was held against the current by a rope which led up to the bow of the barge, and a strap across the lower end of the barrel was used as the seat for the diver in It. He at once got into the diving bell and ordered his men to lower him down. He .had a trace chain attached to a lead line, the lower end of the trace chain having a ring in it, and with this he was readily enabled to form a loop, which was placed over one of the pigs of lead, and at a given signal it was hoisted up. A small cord sufficed to draw it back to him while he was still in the bell; and in this manner a number of pigs weighing seventy pounds each were recovered before be started to come up... the air-pump all the time supplying him with air. But, in the meantime,

having cleared the space beneath the bell, the guy-line moved it farther and farther up-stream, in compliance with his signals, and instead of the line being slacked out again when his men commenced raising the bell, it was held so far forward that the derrick capsized, having no guy to hold it in the opposite direction. His assistants seized the block and tackle and pulled the whisky-barrel up to the surface of the water by hand. But it was so weighted with the lead around it that they could not raise it higher. Not knowing what was the matter, he waited patiently, the air-pump running with redoubled velocity, supplying him with plenty of air. He soon saw the fingers of a man under the chime of the barrel, and, recognizing this as an invitation, he seized the man's hand and got out from under the barrel, much to the delight of all on board. The derrick was then secured against any possible catastrophe occurring again, and, after a number of successful trips to the bottom, the diver was content to do the remainder of the work..."[15]

Amazingly, the makeshift diving bell had served its purpose well enough, and James was eventually able to recover all of the lost freight. "Fortune," he later said, "favors the brave."

Sketch of *Sub-Marine Boat No. 1*

The business venture proved to be an instant financial success. The small *Sub-Marine Boat No. 1* raced around western rivers, searching for and salvaging lost cargo before his competitors could get to it. Typically, James found the river bottom as intriguing and mysterious as the wrecks themselves, and he likened it to a living being, with "its very wildness, its sudden bars, unexpected canyons and writhing turns, recorded in cryptic code the mild moments of frantic surges of the stream, the joy or anguish, the might and frustration of a giant."[16]

Martha Dillon Eads, Missouri Historical Museum

Meanwhile, James continuously worked to perfect the Eads diving bell, which would come to be known as the *Mississippi Diver*, weighting her with lead, rigging her to air pumps, and equipping her with a small seat. Inside and submerged for lengthy periods of time, his submersible was able to move around the bottom of the river with ease, all the while withstanding fast moving currents. As brazen as he was intelligent, the twenty-three-year-old inventor did much of the diving bell work alone. Already known locally as "Captain" James Buchanan Eads–since he often piloted his own vessels and worked right alongside his crew–James exhibited an honorable commitment to the arduous work of salvaging lost valuables. He was, in all actuality, "practicing what he preached."

As time went by, in fact, he could begin to boast that "there was not a stretch of fifty miles in the twelve hundred between Saint Louis and New Orleans in which he had not stood on the bottom under his diving-bell."[17]

Yet, in spite of his deep appreciation for the river, James held high hopes of love, and all the happiness it brought with it. By then, he had met and become smitten with a young lady named Martha Nash Dillon, "an intelligent, sultry, attractive debutante." With her "brown hair smoothed down at the sides and caught up high on the back of her head in a roll from which curls dangled to her shoulders, her blue eyes discreet," she was the apple of her father's eye, a wealthy businessman from St. Louis named Colonel Patrick Dillon. He was no stranger to the diving bell operator. Martha's mother had died when she was young, and her father had remarried Eliza Eads, James's first cousin. From the very beginning, the Colonel disapproved of his daughter seeing this poor, uneducated country boy, so James and Martha met only as often as they could–in secret:

> "Occasionally James and Martha met at the home of Sue and her husband, Dr. Charles Stevens, a young physician from the East. Now and then, in the summer of 1844, they went so far as to steal a few horseback rides together, and Martha had boldly given James permission to call her 'cousin,' which sent him back to the river warm with hope."[18]

Daringly, James wrote to Martha in September of 1844, eventually broaching the subject of his "high ideals of married happiness." To his surprise and delight, she had the courage to reply, allowing herself to compliment him on his "fine penmanship." James replied again almost immediately, modestly giving the credit for his writing to his pen, which he "enclosed as a gift." It was nothing more than an ordinary brown holder made of wood with a steel point, and it can still be seen within its more than one hundred, sixty-year-old missive that Martha had immediately returned with the following message:

> "How long my father's roof may shelter me, I know not, but while I remain within its precincts my line of conduct is determined upon. Do not use this pen until you have occasion to write to her whom you have selected for your companion as you journey through this vale of life."[19]

Quite obviously, Martha's final comment was provocative to James, who now realized that she must, indeed, love him. He had poured out his affection for "The Sweetest Flower on Rose Hill." After several more weeks of courtship, he finally asked Martha to accept his hand in marriage in June of 1845. She would only agree to do so with her father's approval: "Without his consent I must never be to you more than a friend."[20]

Within a few days time, on another warm June evening, James sat patiently, listening to Colonel Dillon offer his "description of a fire grate on Chouteau Avenue." When the elder man paused momentarily to collect his further thoughts, the nervous but determined suitor asked the all-important question. Martha's father was literally taken my surprise, for he had never suspected that the young diving bell captain, "slender yet muscular, carrying himself with conscious pride, his face ruddy from outdoor work, his eyes deep and unflinching," fancied has lovely daughter.

The elder Dillon decided without hesitation that he would not hear of a union between "his beautiful daughter" and the likes of James Buchanan Eads. In a letter to Martha, James detailed her father's curt response to his request:

> "Well, this is a matter which cannot be decided hastily; though I am afraid Mr. Eads that I can give you no encouragement. I have several objections to make, though not one, personally for I esteem you very much having always found you polite and respectful, and I value your friendship. But in selecting a husband for my daughter I must see that a man knows how to make money, for if he can't make it and save it when he is young, he never will, and I don't know that you can show any evidence of it. It is true you are very young yet, and have plenty time to rise in the world, and I have not doubt there are many families who would be proud to form a connection with you–but I must speak plain to you Mr. Eads, I will acknowledge to you that I am an ambitious man and am anxious to unite my daughter to some one of the families of the highest standing in the country. I am an ambitious man, I wish to marry my daughter to a man that has a name, although you are young and may rise as high as any. Besides I think you are too young for Martha. You have plenty time to think of marrying some years hence, and will no doubt rise… And there is another matter that I want everyone to understand who may wish to marry Martha, and that is, that she will not receive a cent until my death… There is another matter that I am very much opposed to; that is families living together although I must say that I admire your course in taking care of your parents; but Martha is a girl who would put up with a great many things which she would not like, without saying a word…"[21]

James was devastated. The pair, though obviously deeply in love, decided to honor her father's wishes and maintain a respectable distance–at least for the time being. In his melancholy, he decided to go on a "bachelor tour" of the East Coast, visiting the cities of Washington, New York, Philadelphia, Baltimore, and Boston. He describes his tour in great detail to Martha, finding himself completely fascinated by the Patent Office:

> "From this floor you ascend by a spiral flight of white marble steps to the National Gallery, and here is a sight which makes the warm blood of an American bound with pride through his veins, as he surveys the magnificent saloon with its curious and multifarious contents. Earth, Air, and Sea have been ransacked to yield the tribute here. The wonders of the world brought home by the Exploring Expedition are here shown to the curious spectator. You would think there was at least a shipload of them.

The identical press at which Franklin worked in London as a journeyman printer one hundred and twenty years ago, is there. The suit worn by Genl Washington when he resigned his commission at Annapolis 23rd December 1783 to Congress there. The camp chest containing the cooking and eating utensils round which the Hero and his noble companions have sat whilst eating their scanty meal. Imagine, for you can imagine and I cannot describe, the feelings which swell within the breast while viewing this plain little set of furniture...I could spend five days at the Patent Office and find something new and interesting every day."[22]

Still, the young inventor and businessman had already proven time and time again that he was not someone to give up easily on something that he had set his mind to do. So, he persuaded his own mother, Nancy Ann Buchanan Eads, to send a letter to Martha. In August of 1845, she, indeed, dispatched a warm, deliberate, unschooled plea on her son's behalf:

"Dear Martha, you will meet a mother's welcome and shear a mother's love and I do not know anything to mar your happiness; except your father's disaprobation and wear he reasonable in his objections I should advise you and my son to relinquish your clames on each other for the preasent but he is unnreasonable."[23]

Whether it was due to Ann Eads eloquent request or the unrelenting persistence of her son, Martha Dillon would eventually see things his way and marry the man she so desperately loved, against her father's wishes, in October of 1845. Shortly before the wedding, James wrote to Martha:

"I sometimes, when I am in deep reflection, with my head upon my pillow, fear that I may in after years, act like some other men, and treat my wife far less kindly than a heart as confiding and affectionate as yours so richly merits..."[24]

Ironically, perhaps, James realized those early fears of not being up to the task of being an exceptional husband. With the responsibility of supporting not only his wife and their children, and assisting his parents as well, he drove himself quite hard, frequently neglecting his own family. For much of their marriage, in fact, James and Martha would live apart. He had convinced her to live with and look after his parents. While she remained behind in the remote village of Le Claire, Iowa, James quit the salvaging business, left St. Louis, and made his way eastward once again, this time to Pittsburgh, Pennsylvania–a lengthy and arduous journey by steamboat, stagecoach, and train–to learn everything he could about his newest business venture: the production of glass. If he could make it happen in St. Louis, it would be the first of its kind west of the Ohio River, and would make the newlyweds quite wealthy.

James Eads' decision to move away from the salvaging business marked the beginning of a difficult chapter in his life. After leasing a large building in St. Louis, he invested heavily to transform it into a glass factory. But the business struggled from the very start. Within two years, sales remained stagnant and his fellow investors had, one-by-one, pulled out. Suddenly, he found himself with a warehouse full of glass and $25,000 of debt. As he struggled to make financial ends meet, life became one of continual sacrifice for not only him, but Martha. Halfway through her most recent letter, she wrote that she understood that "tho' so deeply immersed in business," he would want news of wife and child. In August of 1846, Martha gave birth to Eliza Ann, the couple's first baby. With a small one to care for, she began to miss James more than ever.

Meanwhile, as he worked around the clock to get his new business venture off the ground, she slowly became overwhelmed by all of the chores and errands associated with managing an extended family on her own: "Today the mere cooking of the meals has occupied no little time. If, when the labor is divided we are so tired, how could poor mother [James' mother Ann] have stood it without any assistance."[25]

The couple continued to write each other tender letters, showing James at twenty-six years of age to be "a keen, experienced, and yet...unsophisticated young man; generous, proud, brave, and courteous; a lover of Nature, of poetry, of people, and of good books; an inveterate early riser; reverend in religion, and yet, while nominally a Catholic, really a free-thinker; sentimental in his feelings almost as if he had lived a century sooner, and at the same time controlling his true and deep emotions, and showing his strong love only to those he loved."[26]

Yet, more and more frequently, Martha begged James to return home to her. Heavily pregnant with their second child, she informed him: "I am not well tonight, but I am much sadder than I am sick, so sad indeed, that laying aside all prudential considerations with regard to your business, I implore...you will come up without delay." The letter today appears water stained–perhaps stained with Martha's tears. In any case, James didn't receive it in time and James Jr. was born in his absence.

In a last ditch effort to become financially solvent, James had no choice but return to salvage work. His creditors must have had confidence in his abilities and integrity, since they advanced him $1,500 to get the diving bell business up and running once again. In 1848, the *Sub-Marine Boat No. 2* was constructed at Cairo, and she would prove eminently successful. Fortunately, Eads decision to return to the business and build a second boat to haul his diving bells was sound, and the financial turnaround began almost immediately. Strong as he was physically, his health was not as good. Yet, even in sickness, James scarcely ceased to toil during the first year or two; and at the end of ten years, not only had all his debts been paid, but his firm would be worth half a million dollars.

Perhaps the hand of fate, though cruel to some, was on the side of James Buchanan Eads. On May 17, 1849, disaster struck St. Louis when the steamer

White Cloud, moored at the foot of Cherry Street, caught fire at the city wharf. Flames soon engulfed the entire downtown area. "There is no telling how many lives are lost," an eyewitness reported, "some burnt, some drowned, and some blown to pieces with powder." Fifteen blocks were utterly destroyed and twenty-nine boats destroyed in a matter of just a few hours.

Drawing of James Buchanan Eads diving bell design

What was a devastating loss for St. Louis proved to be a windfall for James. His *Sub-Marine Boat No. 3* had recently begun building, and he soon found it necessary to hire additional crewmen to help bring up the sunken cargo. Though he worked hard for a living, he still found time to relax. Yet, even in his down time his mind sought something to keep itself occupied: records indicate that he could often be found at night aboard the diving bell playing chess, and in later years he would become unusually adept at that game.

The business of salvaging cargo was full of action. Constantly traveling from here to there and back again; steaming up and down the river, and into its many narrow branches; going wherever a boat was wrecked or burned or run aground, the Diving Bell Submarine hurried off to reach the spot before other wreckers arrived. Under their bell his divers got at the engines, boilers, and freight, while the pumps, worked from above, cleared away the sand; and sometimes by means of great chains and derricks the very hull itself would be lifted and towed ashore. But all along the huge river, which at times would suddenly rise three feet in a single night, and whose strong current played such giant pranks as turning over a wreck in the chains that were raising it, there was need of constant vigilance and watchfulness.

Yet, James felt more on "solid ground" on the Mississippi River than on the shore, and his business increased so much that he was soon running four diving-bell boats at the same time. Winter and summer, the work continued almost nonstop, and the job of cutting out a vessel wrecked in an ice-gorge, or of raising one from beneath the ice, was as trying as walking the river bottom in search of a wreck. James himself, years later, described one of his many experiences:

> "Five miles below Cairo, I searched the river bottom for the wreck of the Neptune, for more than sixty days, and in a distance of three miles. My boat was held by a long anchor line, and was swung from side to side of the channel, over a distance of 500 feet, by side anchor lines, while I walked on the river bottom under the bell across the channel. The boat was then dropped twenty feet farther down stream, and I then walked back again as she was hauled towards the other shore. In this way I walked on the bottom four hours at least, every day (Sundays excepted) during that time."[27]

For a day's work the city of Saint Louis gave him about $80, out of which he paid his own workmen. He was so prosperous that, as he wrote to his wife, there was no need for him to join the rush to California to pan for gold; and his success caused much envy among his rivals. He began to clear the channel of the Mississippi from some of its obstructions, and to even improve the harbor of Saint Louis. To many, he was not only a local celebrity, but a hero.

But the immense amount of salvaging work took him away from Martha and his children for longer and longer periods. And his loving wife was all too aware that it was extremely dangerous and tedious work, and that there was always the very real possibility that James could one day be taken away from her through some terrible accident:

> "Do not dive if you can possibly avoid it. Those horrible boats trouble me. What chance would you have, if an accident should happen while you were below, and you could not succeed in catching to the hook on the [diving] bell."[28]

Yet, Martha did not lose her husband James; she lost her son James. On June 15, 1849, their ten-month-old died. Now, having just given birth to a second daughter, the forlorn mother would only mention her only son's death on a single occasion, obliquely, in a letter two months after she had laid him to rest:

> "Oh James, you surely will not condemn me to a long separation from you this winter. That and my other affliction together are too much for my health and spirits…and I know so well, by my own sad heart, what a mother's feelings are when separated from an only son."[29]

By then, Martha was exhausted with the task of running the household, looking after her ailing mother-in-law, and caring for her own children. From their correspondence it seems that rather than coming home to spend time with his fatigued wife, James sent her to Brattleboro, Vermont, to take a rest at a "water cure," which was then in vogue. On her return trip home, Martha received a letter from her husband. In closing he had written: "I will bid you good night, consigning you with confiding love unto the care of Him who hath sheltered me through many dangers, and blest me with a wife much beyond my deserts. Good bye dearest Mattie."[30]

The letter was his final farewell. Martha died less than two weeks later, on October 12, 1852, of cholera. Whether it was out of grief or guilt over Martha's death, James Buchanan Eads started diving into more dangerous situations than he ever had before; into situations where none of the people who worked for him would agree to go.

On one occasion, James even went down in his diving bell during a time when the mighty river was at flood stage. He later wrote about the experience as if there was very little risk involved:

> "Frequently in the upper part of the river, in low water, the currents cut tortuous channels down many feet lower than the dry surfaces of the sand bars. By the floods these channels are quickly obliterated and filled up when they cross the main current of the full river. During one of these floods I had occasion to descend to the bottom in a current so swift as to require extraordinary means to sink the bell; and although the sand was apparently drifting like a snow storm at the bottom, sixty-five feet below the surface, and was doubtless being swept off of bars that were dry in low water, I feel confident it was really afloat or suspended. This

was near Island No. 10, and in a current much more rapid than any that sweeps by New Orleans. My boat was carried away the next day by the drift-wood; and this constitutes my only experience on the river bottom in flood times..."[31]

And yet, only James truly understood the river's mood and disposition, making him undaunted by the perils below the surface. By the time that *Sub-Marine Boat No. 4* was built in Paducah, Kentucky, in 1851, he had developed his technological array so sufficiently that he could raise entire sunken steamboats. *No. 4* had been outfitted with one of "Grimes' patent pumps," which was one of the most powerful pumps that had ever been invented, and this Eads and Nelson Company had the sole right to use it on all waters of the Mississippi Valley. In fact, over during the next few years, they would manage to raise some fifty steamboats while using the Grimes pump, an accomplishment thought to be impossible in most of those salvage operations. The firm was now earning upwards of $4,000 on individual salvage jobs, and this was during a time when the average annual salary of a skilled tradesman was $500. As his wealth multiplied, Jamrs was slowly discovering that life at the bottom of a river could eventually catch up to a man.

James Eads' Compton Hill mansion

James bought himself a spacious mansion located in the southern part of St. Louis, which he named Compton Hill. Just a year and a half after his first wife Martha died, he decided to remarry, and on May 2, 1854, wed his widowed cousin, Eunice Hagerman Eads, who had three daughters of her own. Although, to some the marriage was one of convenience–after all, Eads did need a wife to help run his household and look after his own two daughters–it seems apparent from their correspondence that Eunice and James were truly an affectionate couple. In one long, loving letter, Eads wrote: "I can not rest day nor night until I shall have the pleasure of seeing you, and enjoying your company. You are all to me, and your happiness is all that I live for."

Eunice Hagerman, James Eads second wife

In 1855, five snag-boats built by the government for removing the Red River raft, costing about $185,000, were bought by Eads and Nelson, and converted into submarine boats to be used for wrecking purposes.

By 1856, *Sub-Marine Boat No. 7* was built at a cost of $80,000, and was undoubtedly the most complete boat of the kind in the world, and was capable of raising the largest vessels. By then, James had come to know the intricate river bottom so well that he went to Washington and proposed to Congress to remove all the snags and wrecks from the Western rivers–the Mississippi, the Missouri, the Arkansas, and the Ohio–and to keep their channels open for years to come. And, he further informed them that he could pinpoint on a map every single wreck then in existence. A bill to clear every waterway he had ever explored passed in the House, but stalled in the Senate, being defeated by Jefferson Davis and others. The next year, because of continued failing health, James finally retired from business, but he carried with him a fortune. He had not succeeded in his purpose at Washington, but his name would long be known there and always remembered.

Drawing of *Sub Marine No. 7*

In 1858, James constructed for himself a rose-arbor at the rear of his Compton Hill estate, designed as a place that he could go to relax and think. Over the course of the next four years he remained as much unoccupied as his busy mind permitted. He was, at any rate, what everyone in St. Louis referred to as "a man of leisure."

As the Civil War approached, the forty-year-old James Eads understood that the western rivers would play an important strategic role in the conflict.

AMERICAN SUBMARINERS: PRE-CIVIL WAR

Uppermost in his mind was the fact that the Mississippi River in particular was a key component in Winfield Scott's "Anaconda Plan," a naval strategy devised to blockade and squeeze the Confederacy "like a coiled snake." Agreeing with Scott, Eads surmised that if the Union could control the Mississippi from New Orleans to St. Louis, it would ultimately control the western theater of war.

President Lincoln realized this as well, referring to the Mississippi River as the "backbone of the rebellion" and the "key to the whole situation." Just three days after the surrender of Fort Sumter, on April 17, 1861, James received an urgent telegram from Washington, D.C. The communiqué had been dispatched by Edward Bates, a former Missouri Congressman and close personal friend of Eads, who had recently been named Attorney General in Lincoln's cabinet:

> "Be not surprised if you are called here suddenly by telegram. If called, come instantly. In a certain contingency it will be necessary to have the aid of the most thorough knowledge of our Western rivers and the use of steam on them, and in that event, I have advised that you should be consulted."[32]

It wasn't very long before Eads found himself standing in front of President Lincoln's cabinet, reviewing river strategy in preparation of war. While there, he enthusiastically backed a proposal to build a fleet of gunboats that could help conquer the lower Mississippi River. Soon, the plan evolved into building an entire flotilla of ironclad gunboats, a type of military vessel never before seen in the western hemisphere.

As bids for the project began to be accepted on August 5, 1861, Eads submitted a bold proposal of his own, easily winning the government contract. Just two days later, he signed an agreement stipulating that he would deliver seven ironclad gunboats at a cost of only $89,600 per vessel. Remarkably, he further promised that they would ready to launch in only sixty-five days. He was so confident in his plan that he even agreed to pay a hefty fine of $250 per boat for each day it was late.

With a due date of October 10, 1861, Eads began work in earnest, quickly contracting with foundries, sawmills, and forges in several states, instantly putting thousands of men to work around the clock. His primary base of operation was the Union Iron Works, a shipyard Eads leased on the southeastern side of St. Louis, in the village of Carondelet. It was here, near the point where the River Des Peres flowed into the Mississippi, that the first ironclad warships ever constructed in the United States came to be a reality.

The ironclad ships were constructed, but not designed by, James Eads. Although he would make a number of significant design improvements to ironclad construction as the war progressed, the initial seven were designed by an engineer named Samuel Pook. Known affectionately as "Pook's Turtles" because of the resemblance they took in the water, these first ironclads were like nothing that had been seen before. At 175 feet long and fifty-one feet wide, the boats squatted low in the water, and each was armed with thirteen cannon poking out of sloped wooden sides covered with 2-1/2 inch iron plate. A crew of 175 would man each gunboat.

Due to financial delays and design issues, James did not manage to meet his self-imposed deadline, though the first–named the *Carondelet*–slid into the Mississippi River just two days later. The *St. Louis* rolled out of the iron works on October 14, 1861, and she would make history, engaging Confederate timber-clad gunboats in the Battle of Lucas Bend in January of 1862. James Eads talked about that event in a letter to Abraham Lincoln:

> "...[the *St. Louis*] was the first armored vessel against which the fire of a hostile battery was directed on this continent and, so far as I can ascertain, she was the first ironclad that ever engaged a naval force in the world."[33]

The Civil War was impacted greatly by the ingenuity of James Buchanan Eads, and a number of historians since have given him much credit for assisting the Union toward victory. From that point forward, he would be invited to consult almost anywhere there were problems with rivers; and, perhaps, his greatest accomplishment was yet to come–the construction of a mighty bridge across America's mightiest river.

Those who knew him did not always understand him; some thought him to be pompous, while others knew him to be an extremely generous man. Yet, above any other human trait, he always exhibited his unbending sense of self-assurance and self-confidence:

> "The love of praise is, I believe, common to all men. And whether it be frailty or a virtue, I plead no exception from its fascination. Yesterday, friends expressed to me their pleasure at the thought that my mind would (be) relieved after testing the bridge. But I felt no relief, because I felt no anxiety on the subject."[34]

Ultimately, following the war, James would live twenty-two years longer, accomplishing more than this author can write in a single chapter. For most of those years he gave speeches, lobbied politicians and entertained investors.

Then, in the spring of 1887, worn out and frail from a lifetime of diligence and hard work, the engineer James Eads propped himself up in his sick bed, revising plans for his latest project. Outside of his window he could hear the sound of the waves crashing onto the sandy beach in Nassau, the Bahamas. His second wife, Eunice, and stepdaughter, Adelaide, fussed over him: in all likelihood, they realized that he didn't have long to live.

Back in the States, a landslide of newsmen wrote about his latest scheme. It was an audacious idea–a multi-track railroad designed to transport entire ocean liners from the Atlantic Ocean across Mexico to the Pacific. The railway would give the United States much easier access to markets in the Far East. In a letter to President Rutherford B. Hayes six years earlier, James had claimed the project would realize certainly "the dream of kings and conquerors during the last 350 years."

For seven long years the inventor had been trying to interest the U.S. Congress in funding the concept instead of two competing ideas for canals—one across Panama, the other across Nicaragua. He had whipped the opposition and the press into a frenzy. The *New Orleans Picayune* referred to his plan as "The Great Ship Railway Raid on the Treasury." The *Chicago Tribune* called him "the most audacious, unprincipled and successful lobbyist the national Capital has ever known."

On March 8, 1887, as his proposed ship railway project was being debated in Congress, James Buchanan Eads collapsed and died. Appropriately, as he took his last breath, his final words were: "I cannot die. I have not finished my work."

LOUIS S. SCHAFER

Portrait of Lambert Alexandre

- 15 -
Lambert Alexandre: *Explorer*

"The Great Fair of the American Institute continues open daily at Castle Garden, from 9 A.M. until 10 P.M. At 12 noon today, Mons. Alexandre makes his demonstration with his sub-marine boat, descending to the bottom of the river with several men–remaining for hours, if required–and ascending on signal, as directed. Bloomfield's celebrated band will enliven the scene at the Garden this evening..."[1]

In the autumn of 1781, a group of Quaker brothers made an offer to purchase a rather small piece of land, once owned by Walloon Jansen de Rapelje, from its current owner, Cornelius Remsen. From the time that the first Europeans had settled here, this property, situated along the riverfront, had been known as "Waal Boght," meaning "Bay of Walloons" or "bend in the river." So impressed with the property were Joshua and Comfort Sands, farmers who had profited from the American Revolution, that they decided to found a community called Olympia on the banks of the East River. The streets were platted and water quality was good. Eight grist mills operated on the East River tides, but the land didn't sell because the Brooklyn Heights palisade prevented expansion.

Later known as Wallabout Bay, John, Samuel, and Treadwell Jackson knew that this was a "sacred" place. They bowed their heads in silent prayer, in fact, each time they remembered that as many as 11,000 American prisoners had died here aboard horrid British prisoner ships, where innocent soldiers, merchants, and traders had been tortured, beaten, and often starved to death during the first five years of the war. Patriots, the Jacksons intended to build Brooklyn's first shipyard on this boggy marshland.

After renaming the property Vinegar Hill, hoping to attract Irish immigrants who remembered the rebellion of 1798, the brothers constructed a series of wooden docks and commenced to build their first merchant ship, the *Canton*, as well as a frigate, the *John Adams*. On February 7, 1801, after nearly twenty years in the shipbuilding business, John Jackson sold the nearly forty-two acres of waterfront property to Frances Child, an agent representing the U.S. government, for an astounding $40,000. Just sixteen days later, the land was resold to the young navy department for five dollars. Then, on May 18 of that same year, the city of Brooklyn transferred all waterfront rights to the site for one dollar.

Once the city had its own navy yard, officials quickly realized they needed a Commandant's House, which was constructed in 1806, designed by the same architect that would construct Washington's Capitol. Conveniently, to satisfy weary sailors, nearby was the Pierrepont gin distillery at the foot of Joralemon Street, situated close to the Livingston brewery. Initially, the navy yard would be utilized to outfit ships for raids against pirates and the British during the War of 1812.

A few years later, on May 20, 1820, the New York Navy Yard–also known unofficially as the Brooklyn Navy Yard–launched the first navy warship, the *Ohio*. Nearly a quarter-century into the 1800s, on July 1, 1824, the government acquired an adjacent thirty-five-acre parcel from Sarah Schenck, the widow, along with other heirs, of Martin Schenck, all members of one of Brooklyn's oldest families. Following the construction of ten more vessels–a pair of frigates, four sloops, two schooners, a brig, and a cutter–the Yard remembered Robert Fulton by launching the first U.S. steam warship assigned to sea duty, the nine-gun, side-wheel steamer dubbed the *Fulton*, which left port on her maiden voyage in the spring of 1837.

Construction of an attached hospital facility began in earnest in 1830; with the main hospital building completed in 1838; and, in 1841, Commodore Matthew Perry was appointed yard commandant. Soon, the first public park–known as City Park–occupied space at Flushing Avenue and Navy Street, just outside the yard's gates. By the late 1840s, the Annex had been developed into a self-contained, walled-in, parcel of land with a gatehouse, a laboratory, and a cemetery whose markers faced Dead Man's Lane.

As the Vinegar Hill district reached the half-century mark of the 1800s, sailors crowded into the commercial and residential areas at a remarkable pace. Carson McCullers, who would write the novel *The Mortgaged Heart* one hundred years later, looked back in time and described the atmosphere of the place in great detail:

> "Here in Brooklyn there is always the feeling of the sea. On the streets near the water-front, the air has a fresh, coarse smell, and there are many seagulls. One of the most gaudy streets I know stretches between Brooklyn Bridge and the Navy Yard. At three o'clock in the morning, when the rest of the city is silent and dark, you can come suddenly on a little area as vivacious as a country fair. It is Sands Street, the place where sailors spend their evenings when they come here to the port. At any hour of the night some excitement is going on in Sands Street. The sunburned sailors swagger up and down the sidewalks with their girls. The bars are crowded, and there are dancing, music, and straight liquor at cheap prices."[2]

Beginning in the late summer of 1850 and continuing throughout the next several months, a number of local newspapers and magazines began to report on an egg-shaped submarine then undergoing testing at the Navy Yard. Construction of the vessel had begun at the nearby "Messrs. Pease & Murphy's engineering works, this city, for the Submarine Exploring Company." The firm was actually founded as James Murphy and Company, and it was owned and operated by three of New York City's finest ship builders: James Murphy, William J. Pease, and William P. Buckmaster. The round-looking craft was the brainchild of Lambert Alexandre, an expatriate recovery and salvage diver from France, whose office was located just a few miles away, across the East River, at 23 Maiden Lane in New York City.

Before coming to America, Alexandre had been a one-time associate of Dr. Antoine Payerne, another submarine experimenter who had constructed a similar vessel in France. Born February 27, 1806, the physician would eventually relocate, first to St. Most Cloisters Grenoble, then to Paris in 1840. His prototype submarine, described as a "bateau-cloche" (diving-boat), would be dubbed the *Belledonne*.

Drawing of the *Belledonne*

Being that the vessels designed by the two colleagues had so much in common, newsmen theorized that, perhaps, Alexandre had "borrowed" the design from Payerne, thus infringing upon his patent. One account by *Scientific America* had gone as far as to note that Alexandre's design had been constructed in France, having been utilized in "the harbor of Cherbourg...[where] one of these machines, forty feet long, is employed daily to remove some submarine rocks which obstruct the entrance to one of the basins."[3]

Payerne and Alexandre had begun their submersible craft experiments four years earlier, in 1842, beginning with a more common diving bell design. Following a number of dives with the bell suspended from the frigate *Success*, the enterprising pair came up with a rather brilliant idea: instead supplying air to the diving bell through an attached India rubber tube, why not place cases containing compressed air inside the belly of the bell and do away with the necessity of an attached tube? During the next few weeks, Payerne and Alexandre descended a number of times in just such an arrangement, once reaching a depth of fourteen fathoms. It was now time to demonstrate the vessel to government officials.

Finding very little interest in France, they traveled to England, and secured the attention of expert military engineer, Sir Charles William Pasley.

It should have been no surprise that the British official, by then a well-respected sixty-one-year-old Major-General with the greatest portion of his career behind him, would be intrigued by the Parisian's invention. Since 1839, Pasley had been in charge of clearing away the wrecks of the *HMS Royal George* from Spithead and the *HMS Edgar* from St. Helens. All of this work could be made much less tedious, Payerne had promised, by using his unique diving bell. The Major-General had, in fact, already witnessed its operation during an exhibition of the vessel at the Polytechnic Institution in London. So, in early August of 1842, Pasley met with the Frenchman to discuss the bell's feasibility. Almost immediately, however, the seasoned British official expressed his doubts about the vessel's value:

> "...as he told the Doctor, though he was satisfied that he could produce good air at any depth, the pressure of from 12 to 15 fathoms of water at the bottom of the anchorage at Spithead would compress the air in a diving-bell so much, that though men might exist in it, they would not be able to work to advantage, being nearly up to their necks in water. Therefore, unless the doctor could get over this difficulty his ingenious and novel invention would not be attended with any practical benefit..."[4]

With a limited amount of diving experience at greater depths, Payerne and Alexandre were initially perplexed by the problem. Yet, after considering the possible solutions, the French doctor surmised that he might utilize an "expedient for removing (water)" from his submerged bell. That "expedient," quite naturally, would be consist "of filling four iron cylinders with condensed air, which was forced into them by a small air-pump, until the gauge proved that the pressure was equal to nine or ten atmospheres." Following a number of experiments, during which the compressed air was pumped into the submerged diving bell, the doctor was ready for a public demonstration. Hence, on Saturday, September 3, 1842, following a brief dive by Dr. Payne and Major-General Pasley, a second team prepared for a more extensive test. Lieutenant George Hutchinson, of the Royal Engineers, joined one of Payerne's assistants, Robert Hardiman, board the vessel. Slowly, they were lowered into the River Thames at Spithead:

> "...air was forced into the forced into the bottom of the diving-bell by one of the small pumps which usually supplies air for a helmet diver. By means of this pump the water was expelled from the lower part of the diving-bell, and replaced by condensed air, which enabled them to descend to the very bottom..."[5]

With the oxygen issue now resolved, it was a very short stretch of imagination that brought both Payerne and Alexandre to the point of designing a self-propelled submarine with the same concept. The Payerne design "was very much the shape of a modern heavy-gun projectile except that it tapered slightly towards the stern, which, instead of being flat like the base of a shell, was slightly convex. It was 35 feet long and about ten feet at its greatest diameter. Inside it wasdivided into two parts by a convex bulkhead, the fore-part constituting the air reservoir and the after portion the room in which the propeller was turned by a hand-crank. The vessel steered by vertical and horizontal rudders, and the divers emerged into the water by means of an air-lock or small chamber in which the air was compressed till its pressure was sufficient to stop the inrush of water when the outer hatch was opened."[6]

Yet, Payerne was still not completely satisfied with his submarine and, with the help of his colleague, Lambert Alexandre, he redesigned the vessel and renamed her the *Pyrhydrostat*:

> "In appearance it was something between a cylinder and an ordinary boat with a convex deck. It was divided by two vertical bulkheads into three compartments. The after one, which occupied half the length of the vessel, contained the engines, driven by steam generated by a sealed-up furnace burning coke, the tanks to be filled for immersion, and a heavy weight which could be lowered to act as an anchor. The centre one, divided horizontally by a deck with a manhole in it, formed the working chamber and the air-lock to give the diver egress, while the foremost one contained merely an extra supply of compressed air..."[7]

In 1854, an English journal would introduce the Payerne submarine to thousands of intrigued readers:

> "The inventor, Dr. Payerne, has not only discovered means to descend to the bottom of the sea and to work there at his ease with a body of operatives, and to remain there as long as he pleases, replacing by chymical proceedings the oxygen absorbed, but he has discovered a method of directing the boat under water by steam, as if it were on the surface. He has engaged to start from any harbour in France and to reach the coast of England, though navigating under water..."[8]

Whether or not Alexandre copied Payerne's sketches, was merely promoting a Payerne-built submarine, or had constructed a vessel of his own design is not known, but his claim that he was the patented owner strongly suggested the latter. In any case, the expatriate Frenchman undoubtedly brought a number of improvements to the table that he had constructed totally on American soil.

Born in early 1805 to Lambert Joseph Alexandre and Marie Elisabeth (Danieux) Alexandre, Lambert Alexandre married Marguerite Van Exter in Liege, Belgium, on June 28, 1843. His mother had not lived to witness the event, for she had died eleven months earlier, in late July of 1842. Tragedy had also struck the Alexandre family a dozen years earlier, not once but twice, when

Lambert had lost his brother Jacques on August 10, 1831, and his sister, Hubertine Josephe, less than a month later, both to small pox.

After burying their two-year-old son, Michel Lambert Alexandre, in late March of 1849, Lambert and Marguerite Alexandre decided to make a fresh start in America, arriving in March of 1850 with their one-year-old daughter, Marie Rosalie, and three-month-old, Henrietta Alexandre. Those who met the submarine designer found him to be a "nervous little man," five-feet-two-inches tall, with a narrow chin, a receding brown hairline, and jet black eyes that seemed to dart around whenever he spoke. Though he never divulged his true family history, anyone who knew him intimately understood that his family roots had traveled through Normandy, France, to Liege, Belgium, during the Middle Ages.

On September 3, 1850, Alexandre submitted a formal application to the United States Patent Office in Washington, D.C., offering "certain new and useful Improvements in Submarine Vessels for the Exploration of the Bottoms of Rivers Lakes and other Bodies of Water." The application not only included specific details of his vessel's proposed design, but offered intricate sketches from a side view, a vertical-longitudinal view, a transverse view, and "a section of fragment upon an enlarged scale of the ribs and panels of the sides of the vessel."

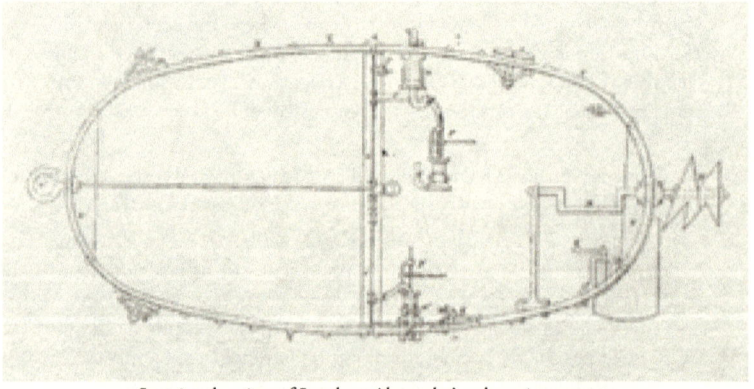

Interior drawing of Lambert Alexandre's submarine patent

The inventor began his patent application by making a comparison between typical diving bell designs and, what he considered, his far superior craft. He then went on to offer further details of his design concept:

> "The invention or discovery of the means by which persons can descend at will and explore the bottoms of rivers lakes and other bodies of deep water and thence at will return again to the surface of the water with facility and safety has long been considered a great desideratum and many devices have at different times and by different persons been contrived for this purpose; some of these have manifested a high degree of ingenuity and skill but none of them have possessed such a degree of adaptation to the general purposes of submarine explorations as to render them prac-

tically useful or capable of superseding the cumbrows and unwieldy but hitherto indispensable diving-bell. The chief reasons of the failure of these attempts have been in my opinion the difficulty of keeping up a proper circulation of air within the vessel and the difficulty of discharging instantaneously the load or ballast by means of which the vessel is forced to sink thus allowing her to rise to the surface with a buoyant force proportioned to the load discharged whenever this operation becomes necessary from some derangement of her machinery. To obviate these defects is the object of my invention which consists first in securing within the working-chamber or cabin of the vessel a pump which is connected by pipes with an airtight compartment from which it can draw air and into which it can compress air at will the connection being such that by moving proper cocks or valves the pump becomes either a suction or a force pump with respect to the airtight compartment or to the cabin."[9]

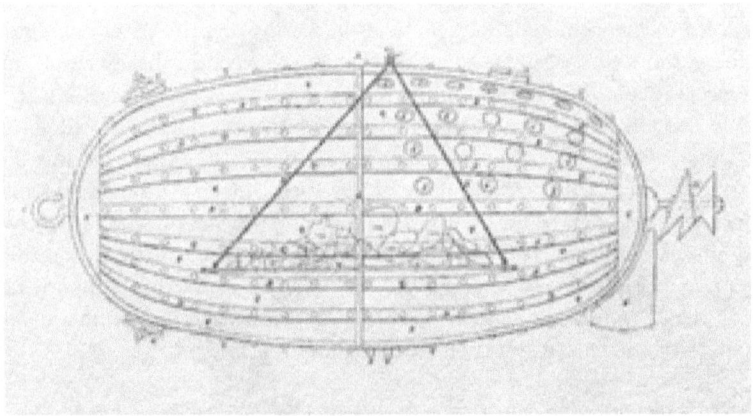

Exterior drawing of Lambert Alexandre's submarine patent

Claiming to displace a minimum of ten tons, Alexandre's submarine measured thirty feet in overall length and eleven feet in diameter at center, and was powered by a single, hand-cranked propeller from within. Of particular distinction was the fact that the oddly shaped vessel could be dismantled in a very brief amount of time for easy portability:

> "My improved submarine vessel has the general form of an egg being an ellipsoid whose long axis is about double the length of its short axis; it is composed of pieces united together in such a manner that they can be separated at will put up in convenient packages for transportation and can with facility be again put together with water and airtight joints to reconstruct the vessel which will then be ready for launching into the water."[10]

The top and sides of the vessel's cabin came equipped with a set of bull's-eyes to admit light. Furthermore, its top and bottom were constructed with one or more man-holes; those on top for the entrance and egress of the crewmen when at the surface of the water, the lower ones for the purpose of gaining access from the interior of the cabin to the earth or other substance at the bottom of the water. In that way, salvagers could "examine, draw in or make fast to any object that may there be met with..."[11]

The interior of Alexandre's vessel was subdivided into several compartments, one of which was a cabin that could "conveniently accommodate several persons." The other compartments were designed for the reception of water to ballast the vessel and to contain a supply of compressed air for the persons in the cabin to respire during the period that the vessel is submerged. The cabin housed force pumps to be utilized by its occupants to keep the air in circulation and, therefore, maintain "a sufficiently pure state for respiration by forcing it through a solution of caustic potash, which absorbs the carbonic acid with which the air has been charged by breathing." The pumps also enabled the crew to keep the water from encroaching upon them by its increasing pressure as they descended to the bottom. These pumps could also be used to eject this ballast-water from the receptacle buoyancy, thus causing it to rise quickly to the surface.

For additional oxygen, the craft would remain connected to the surface by a long air hose, lifted by a hollow copper float. The submarine was built to transport between three and seven able-bodied crewmen, who could remain comfortably submerged for up to seven hours at a time, at pressures up to two-and-one-half atmospheres "without fatigue." In any dire situation, immediate ascent could be provided when hinged, external cast-iron ballast supports held up by chains would be unlatched to drop iron plates stacked upon them. Concerning this emergency arrangement, Alexandre explained:

> "...by this operation the vessel is relieved of so much of her load and as her buoyancy is correspondingly increased she starts instantly toward the surface; as the vessel is thus fully under the control of its inmates they are insured from every danger of detention at the bottom any longer than they choose to remain there. These drop-platforms by which the submarine navigator can at will instantly discharge the ballast and thereby control such effective means for raising the vessel to the surface I deem of the highest importance because it renders submarine explorations for the first time nearly if not quite as safe as sailing on the surface of the water by giving more full and perfect control over the vessel than has heretofore been attained."[12]

Still unsure of whether or not the American government or business investors would take any real interest in his submarine, Lambert Alexandre continued to peddle other ingenious devices. On April 3, 1850, the *New York Herald* hailed a new and extraordinary invention by the enterprising Frenchman. Calling his latest venture "artificial leeches," he had already patented the concept in London, England, in October of 1848. Almost exuberantly, the writer of the article claimed that "they never fail, they give no pain, they cause no trouble, they inoculate with no disease, they do not crawl and scare one, and wriggle and refuse to bite." In fact, proclaimed the article, no longer would American doctors have to import the "horrid reptiles" from Sweden.

Curious buyers wondered what an "artificial" leech might be. Alexandre's creation, also known as "terabdella," resembled the cylinder of a large pin-and-tumbler lock, attached to a glass syringe with a cork plunger, allowing them to be attached to the skin and release blood flow, which could then be pumped into a vile. It was, without question, mechanical "blood letting."

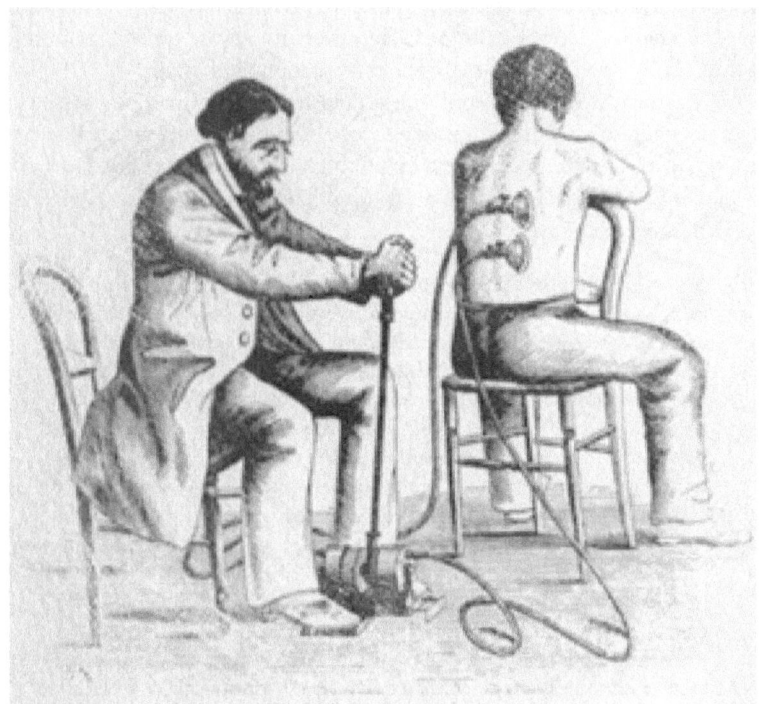

Drawing of Lambert Alexandre's artificial leech process

From his office at 23 Maiden Lane in the heart of New York City, the French inventor peddled a significant number of these patented artificial leech mechanisms. On Tuesday, September 10, 1850, the *New York Daily Tribune* printed an advertisement that claimed his artificial leech machines "possess over the natural leech the advantage of economy, cleanliness and facility of application, and deserve the special attention of country physicians and farmers." Promoting the wiley physician's devices even further, writer Andrew H. Smith flatly stated:

"In the first place the appearance of the animal is repulsive and disgusting, and delicate and sensitive persons find it difficult to overcome their repugnance to contact with the cold and slimy reptile. This is especially the case when it is a question of their application about or within the mouth. Then again, their disposition to crawl into cavities or passages results sometimes in very annoying accidents. Another source of annoyance is that they are often unwilling to bite--the patience of all concerned being exhausted in fruitless efforts to induce them to take hold."[13]

As far away as Boston, Philadelphia, and Washington, D.C., Alexandre's patented artificial leeches were drawing much attention from the medical field. They were described as being "neatly put up in cases, each containing from six to twelve mechanical leeches, triangular lancets...with all the necessary directions for use...easily applied, simple in their construction, and cheap."

Meanwhile, publicity concerning the Alexandre submarine's appeal and hopes in changing the future of warfare spread throughout the city, spilling over the State of New York, and eventually tumbling across the country. On Friday, November 20, 1850, the *New York Herald* published a lengthy account of the vessel's progress and potential uses:

"About five months since, in noticing the progress of arts and manufactures, we mentioned a sub-marine boat, which bid fair to surpass anything that the wildest imaginings would lead us to expect, even from the genius of the present age. This important invention is the result of the application of a law in physics, on a large scale, by Mons. Alexandre, an eminent French civil engineer, which law established the fact that a certain quantity of compressed air, contained within a given space, makes an efficient equilibrium, or in other words, balances the pressure of water so as to prevent it from entering the sub-marine boat... The ingenious and estimable engineer who has contrived this apparatus, by means of it, can descend at will to the bottom of the sea, or examine the bottoms of streams or rivers, in direct contact with their hidden treasures, and with the power of working as well as of moving along at his ease, for hours, and with perfect safety, without inconvenience or suffering, although deprived of all communication, either direct or indirect, with the air... We think that to insurance companies this machine will be invaluable in recovering goods or merchandise from wrecks. It will also be valuable for laying down telegraph wires securely across rivers, etc. For the pearl and coral fisheries, it will undoubtedly, be of immediate and most profitable use, and we may add, that for seeking gold or other valuables lost in wrecks, or for an examination of the hidden dangers at the entrances of harbors... or drafting sub-marine charts, it will be found most important...it is our firm conviction that the sub-marine boat of Mons. Alexandre will rank with the application of steam to boats by Fulton, and be an honor to America, while it should immortalize the inventor."[14]

Writing in 1851, one reporter from *Scientific America* described the innovative craft as a "very excellent and ingenious invention," further warning that "with such a vessel as this, no enemy's fleet could be safe on our coast." Meanwhile, Alexandre's submarine, now known as the *Explorer*, was believed to have a number of latent, unintended value to the medical world:

> "...it is stated that lime water is employed to purify the atmosphere in the *Explorer* when it becomes impure by the carbonic acid gas expelled from the lungs of the operators. It has been found by experiment that when the apparatus is working in a current, there is not the least occasion for the lime water...The carbonic acid is heavier than the common atmosphere, and also combines more readily with water, therefore it drops down into the current, in which the men work, at the bottom of the machine, and is carried off; this is an important scientific fact well worth treasuring...as it proves to us that a vessel of water placed upon a stove answers more than one beneficial purpose, viz., to send moisture through the atmosphere; it also absorbs impurities which may be in it. Running streams in cities and villages, upon the same principle, tend to promote health by absorbing impurities from the atmosphere, as well as carrying them off by mechanical contact."[15]

Tragedy during the winter of 1850, though indirect, placed Alexandre's ongoing submarine experiments on hiatus for a time, forcing him to rethink which machine shop might be engaged to put the finishing touches on his underwater craft:

> "On Monday, Feb. 4, 1850, a two-hundred horse power boiler, situated in the basement of A.B. Taylor & Co's printing press and machine works in Hague Street exploded, burying in the debris of the large building 120 persons, who had just commenced work for the week, and of this number 64 of the employees lost their lives, including the person in charge of the engine and boiler. The explosion was a most terrific one, and was heard distinctly as far up town as Fiftieth Street, three miles from the scene of death and disaster."[16]

During the ensuing investigation into the accident, experts offered evidence before the coroner's jury that "Messrs. Pease & Murphy (the manufacturers of the boiler) were deeply responsible in selling the boiler, knowing its imperfections, and after it had been in the open air for more than one year."[17] The inquest also placed blame on A.B. Taylor and Company, "for using more steam than they were informed the boiler would bear," as well as the Milligan and Walker Company, for allowing the boiler "to go out of thejr shops or hands, knowing it to be in an imperfect condition."

Though the matter would, apparently, end with no further legal actions, Alexandre decided to move his *Explorer* project to another New York iron works firm, identified in local newspapers as "Messrs. Secor and Underhill." Uninterrupted by the tragic accident, the *New York Sun* reported on October 22, 1851, that the submarine would be ready for its final testing phase in just a few days. With a public exhibition scheduled in the East River, the paper further claimed that "the most perfect confidence is entertained as to the success of this means of the submarine exploration, and its success is a guarantee of a rich reward."[18]

In actuality, "Secor & Underhill" were two distinct firms working collaboratively to complete distinct parts of the submarine project. Jeronimus S. Underhill, owner of the Dry Dock Iron Works in Greenpoint, Brooklyn, had facilities to build boilers, but was forced to subcontract all machine work, castings, and forgings. Described as a "sharp, shrewd businessman," Underhill desired to work with only the best in the business. William Perine, his longtime friend and partner, was the first to come to mind when he was asked to take over the Alexandre submarine project. Perine, who had recently been a partner in name only at "Perine, Secor & Company," recommended the Secor family.

Together, Alexandre and Underhill agreed, though they must have realized they would be working with a firm that had very little experience in construction iron vessels of any kind. Aside from their father, Francis, who was the primary owner of the current "Secor and Company," the firm employed sons Charles A., James F., Thorne, Henry R., and Zeno Secor. Credentials and experience could only be found with the elder Francis, who had once been employed as a foreman by Henry Eckford's shipyard when that firm had constructed a number of ships during and after the War of 1812:

> "It was Eckford's extraordinary ability to design, lay down, and build ships, ranging in size from a very small schooner to the largest frigates, working in a wilderness and in severe winter weather with sick or dissatisfied labor, and to do all this in extremely short periods of time, that maintained American superiority on Lake Ontario. From a naval shipbuilding point of view, the outstanding men of the War of 1812 were Eckford and the Browns, Adam and Noah. Through the efforts of these three, the Navy held control of the lakes and prevented the British from invading the North and Northwest... No officer or constructor of the Navy accomplished more. There were no competitors to the Browns and Eckford among the navy yards, or in the contract shipyards along the coasts, [even though] on the lakes... building was made infinitely more difficult than on the coast because of climate and geographical conditions, to say nothing of scarcities of labor and some materials."[19]

Raised by a father who put in long hours in managing shipbuilding projects, the Secor brothers had "operated as shipwrights specializing in the making of spars, as ship chandlers, and as builders of sectional dry docks." Despite brother James Secor's assertion that they had all had shipbuilding experience, and that they had "made large profits and succeeded in accumulating fortunes," their credit was somewhat dubious and their credibility somewhat questionable. In fact, when Alexandre first met the family, several members were residing together in a cramped boarding house that was in desperate disrepair.

AMERICAN SUBMARINERS: PRE-CIVIL WAR

As 1851 came to a close, weather in New York City turned bitterly cold, delaying work on the submarine for a period of time. Then, during the first few days of January, heavy snow was followed by freezing rain and high winds, making a wintry mess across the city. Finally, on January 3 of the new year, snow fell throughout the entire day, to a depth in excess of eight inches. Nearly everything in the City came to a complete standstill.

Meanwhile, Lambert Alexandre began to think that, perhaps, he and his family might remain in the United States, at least for the foreseeable future. Business was improving, and he was beginning to realize more and more interest in his submarine *Explorer*, perhaps as an ideal vessel that could be employed to recover lost merchandise from sunken cargo ships or explore unknown regions below the surface. Other interested parties now believed that she might even be utilized for clearing obstructions in shallow water harbors.

With all of this weighing heavily on his mind, and little time to spare, the forty-six-year-old inventor decided to get out of the patented artificial leech business and concentrate his efforts at marketing his submarine. To that end, he placed the following advertisement in local newspapers:

> "Agent Wanted–for a profitable business, with no risk whatsoever. Mr. Lambert Alexandre, having his time fully taken by his submarine costs operation, will put his stock of patent artificial leeches into the hands of a responsible and industrious person. Goods to be accounted for only when sold. Apply personally, between 3 and 5 o'clock p.m., to Lambert Alexandre, 23 Maiden Lane, third story."[20]

Within just a few days, he had handed the business over to someone he felt was competent to make a profit for them both. Now, Alexandre could concentrate on refining what most interested him.

A public demonstration of the submarine *Explorer* took place on Friday, March 5, 1852, at the New York Navy Yard. As the large crowd gathered, including the general public, naval personnel, select dignitaries, and newsmen, the craft could be seen moored a slight distance from the docks where the water was about thirty-five to fifty feet deep. Almost immediately, Alexandre, slight in stature though wiry in his seemingly constant movements, stepped nimbly from a rowboat out onto the top of the vessel, followed by three anxious assistants. One by one, they climbed inside, and the top manhole was secured with heavy bolts. On shore, Commodore William D. Salter gave the signal by way of an electric telegraph connected to the craft, and within ten minutes the submarine floated some distance from the docks and began its descent, quickly disappearing below the surface of the calm waters.

A general hush fell over the onlookers, with the vessel remaining totally submerged for what seemed like hours. As moments passed, more and more in the crowd grew increasingly anxious, now convinced that something had gone terribly wrong. After eleven or twelve agonizing minutes, Commodore Salter once again gave the signal, and within a few moments the *Explorer* broke the surface like a humpback whale about twenty feet west of where she had disappeared. The experiment, which had lasted less than thirty minutes total, was reported to be "perfectly satisfactory by the officers of the Navy Yard who were present." In fact, the only person who seemed disappointed was Alexandre himself, who later commented that he "had not been allowed to remain under water for a sufficient length of time to thoroughly test the capacity of his boat."[21]

Still, everyone present had been genuinely impressed by the demonstration, as details of the event were shared with the public at large through the media all across the city:

> "This apparatus is made of boiler iron, and in shape resembles an egg. The whole length is 30 feet, with a diameter in the centre of about 11 feet, tapering from this to each end, to the diameter of 7 feet. Attached to the outer sides, near the bottom of this machine, are heavy weights, so that, with the addition of 150 gallons of water which can be pumped into the tank located inside, at the pleasure of the operator, the machine can be lowered at once, without much trouble. On one end there is a screw propeller, by which a man on the inside can move the machine along when under water, and a rudder to guide it to any point required. At the top there are two places of ingress, so arranged as to exclude air when closed, and at the bottom there are several plates that can be removed at pleasure, through which the work is done. The inside is divided into two apartments—the one at the stem being 10 feet in length, in which is arranged the means of raising or lowering the machine; and here are four force-pumps, which are so arranged as to be used for either water or air; there is also in this room a battery, by which communication can be had with those above the surface, by the same process as the magnetic telegraph; or, in case of accident, there are small buoys, about 10 inches in diameter, which can be sent to the surface by being passed through the trap at the bottom of the machine, and to these a rope can be attached, to draw up anything that may be required. In this room they have also the means of purifying the air, so that, with the air in the air chamber, which can be introduced at any moment, and the purifying means, a person can remain under water all day, if necessary, and without suffering as divers do in any other way before known, from the great pressure of air which is forced to them through pipes leading from the surface. In the front room is the air-chamber and the principal water tank, and also arrangements for operating, as in the other. The weight on the sides is so arranged that the occupant can let it go in case of necessity, and then the machine will rise to the top of the water at a speed of ten feet per second. The machine is the invention of M. Alexandre, a Frenchman, and the most perfect submarine boat we have ever seen."[22]

If Lambert Alexandre hoped to sell the entire concept of underwater exploration to the public, the time now seemed ripe, for they were increasingly clamoring for more detailed information and, perhaps, even a first-hand view of his amazing machine. Still, it would never be possible to offer inexperienced divers the opportunity to climb aboard and submerge. Yet, in true circus-like style, an article appeared in the pages of the *New York Herald*, describing the experience to such a great degree that ordinary citizens might at least feel like they were taking part in an actual dive:

> "The submarine boat is…wholly constructed of sheet iron, connected by rivets; and weighs about 24,000 pounds without ballast, and 78,000 pounds with ballast; on its sides, there are numerous orifices, filled with bull's eyes for the admission of light; at the stern it id provided with a propeller and a rudder, by which the men in the interior can propel and guide it without difficulty. The interior is divided into two separate compartments–one occupying two-fifths of the vessel (which is called the cabin)–the other three-fifths being occupied by two large reservoirs, to which are attached two pairs of pumps, either for air or for water uses. The whole operation of the submarine boat depends upon the displacement of a certain quantity of condensed air, and in taking in or throwing off a greater or less body of water by means of the pumps. In descending, the water pumps are first called into play to force into the water chamber and sufficient quantity of water, so as to overcome the equilibrium, which keeps the boat floating, and to sink it. After arriving at the bottom, so much of the condensed air in the reservoir is admitted into the cabin as to establish a balance between the pressure of the water and that of the atmosphere, thereby preventing the water of the river from entering into the cabin when the two hatchways at the bottom of the vessel are opened. The equilibrium being established, the hatchways are then opened, and the submarine soil is exposed to the workmen within, who then can operate either by mining rocks or fishing for pearls…"[23]

In an effort to drum up business and income, advertisements began to appear all over the area, with Lambert Alexandre offering his submarine diving services for a fee to anyone so inclined. Suggestions offered by the inventor included "pearl fisheries, gold searches, or all other purposes to which the boat can be applied." Any interested parties could visit him any morning between the hours of ten and twelve, at his office located at 131 Fulton Street, even if they were simply wanting to purchase a "leisurely outing."

Meanwhile, persistently attempting to peddle his underwater invention, Alexandre found exhibit and demonstration space at the upcoming 25th Annual Fair of the American Institute of the City of New York, which would be open to the public at Castle Garden, a sandstone structure completed one year before the War of 1812. The Alexandre exhibit would run from Tuesday, October 5, through Friday, October 29, 1852. Spread across twenty-five acres, the waterfront property was nestled against the southern tip of Manhattan Island, and had served as a promenade, exhibition hall, opera house, and outdoor theatre since

July 3, 1824. Most recently, the Garden had been the site of a pair of extraordinarily successful concerts given for charity by the Swedish soprano, Jenny Lind, to initiate her American tour managed by Phineas Taylor Barnum, as well as a performance by European dancing star Lola Montez, who had performed her notorious "tarantula dance" for a tantalized crowd–mostly men.

For the Annual Fair, embossed invitations were printed and mailed to guests weeks before the festivities opened. Signed by John A. Bunting, Chairman, as well as the Secretary of the Board of Managers, John W. Chambers, and Corresponding Secretary, Adoniram Chandler, the personalized invites would become somewhat of a collector's item almost overnight.

The annual event was an enormous undertaking, with the total number of exhibitors–excluding the cattle show–reaching nearly 2,300. The increased number of applicants requesting space to exhibit their inventions in working motion forced the organizers to enlarge the machine room by sixty feet in length at a cost of $400. Aside from the additional space, moving exhibits were furnished with an ample 25-horsepower steam boiler, able to manipulate one-hundred-and-eighty feet of shafting line through a series of pulleys. Even though they believed this would be enough, it proved both inadequate and unacceptable to the high demand. Yet, instead of competing with other exhibitors inside, Alexandre decided to take his audience to the banks of the nearby river:

> "Yesterday a great crowd assembled outside of the west end of the building, in order to witness the promised descent of M. Alexandre and friends, in the newly invented submarine boat. They were naturally anxious to see a machine of which so much has been said, and this anxiety was likewise manifested by men belonging to vessels lying in the river, for they came off to the scene in boats. The machine lay about ten yards from the Garden, and in appearance was…like a large tank, of an elongated ellipse shape, and dotted with bull's eyes, for giving light to the person's inside. In length it was about thirty feet, and ten feet in diameter at its greatest transverse section… As the appointed hour drew nigh, the gentlemen selected to descend in the vessel got down the hatchway. The party included Mr. [Lambert] Alexandre (the inventor), Mr. [August] Mauritz (manufacturer, Centre street), Captain Politier and Mr. Jose (operating gentlemen), Mr. Abram Baseford (manufacturer, Centre street), and Mr. Ullman (storekeeper, Bowery). Everything was made water tight, the boats cleared off, and all anxiety was exhibited by the spectators to see the machine descend. Time wore away, however, and still the curious looking tank lay on the water. The audience began to manifest impatience, and very many uttered uncomplimentary sarcasms. At length the machine disappeared under the water, and after the lapse of five minutes, reappeared. Again it descended and remained submerged thirty minutes. When it came up, there was a general rejoicing, for a great many persons had hinted their suspicions that it had sunk to the mud. A cheer saluted the adventurous party… In answer to the questions which were addressed to him, he said the machine had descended forty-five feet, and

then sloped down an embankment forty-two feet more. After the people had satisfied their curiosity in that respect, they spread themselves over the building to observe articles of another description..."[24]

Attendance at the 1852 Fair was unexpectedly large, with total net receipts at Castle Garden indicating 100,000 paid admissions. Taking into consideration the number of members who were furnished with free family tickets, the number of delegates from various kindred associations coming from all across the U.S., the "extreme liberality of the managers in granting free admissions to distinguished individuals from abroad," and free access granted to exhibitors, final estimation of the number of attendees was more than 500,000 during the entire twenty-five-day extravaganza.

Depiction of Alexandre's submarine Explorer at of Castle Garden

Lambert Alexandre could not have been more pleased, for not only had literally thousands of potential customers witnessed the operation of his invention, but he had been awared one of only ninety gold medal handed out in honor of exceptional achievement. However, his excitement and pride soon turned to outrage and disappointment when he read a critical critique by one of the local New York reporters:

"...when the enthusiasm had a little abated, opinions were given forth that the experiments would have been more satisfactory if Mr. Alexandre had given a practical illustration of the benefits which his machine is said to render in the way of finding sunken articles, for as it was there had only been a demonstration of the possibility of remaining under the water for thirty minutes. We hope Mr. Alexandre will take this hint in his next experiment..."[25]

It may have been the beginning of the end for Lambert Alexandre's submarine experiments. In spite of its technological advances, the French expatriate's vessel seems to have received very little future interest, evidenced by a 1854 newspaper correspondent who wrote that the submarine "is now lying at the foot of Tenth Street and East River, where it has been abandoned for over a year." Ultimately, no one really knows what became of the valuable submarine.

On June 2, 1855, Lambert Alexandre stood before a New York Superior Court judge, requesting to become a naturalized citizen of the United States. Standing in as his required witness was twenty-four-year-old, Albert Crouze, who listed his address as 117 Sullivan Street in New York City. The request was granted, and the one-time Frenchman proudly became an American.

Still tinkering with ideas and inventions for both above and underwater vessels, Alexandre applied for and was granted another patent on January 28, 1856. While still residing in New York City, he managed to devise an entirely innovative method of moving vessels through the water. His innovation was published in a detailed patent application for "improvements in propelling vessels." In it, the inventor explained that:

"The nature of my said invention consists in the construction of certain parts, which regulate the motion of buckets which perform the duty of propelling or carrying a vessel forward in the direction of its length without introducing the deficiencies and imperfections hitherto experienced by the use of paddle wheels, screws, or other known devices for that purpose...viz. the great amount of friction, resistance, and loss of power caused by the paddles...when emerging from the water. To accomplish the object to the greatest possible extent, and to remove the impediments above mentioned, my improvement proposes the employment of a system of submerged buckets placed within and under the vessel, and made to slide lengthwise between suitable frames and slides; an alternative reciprocating motion being imparted to said buckets by a direct acting or other suitable engine. Each bucket is moreover of such a construction and so connected to the rod or rods by which it is moved that it can revolve one-quarter of a circle upon trunnions [sic] set in the before mentioned slides, for the purpose of allowing said bucket to move through the water edgewise and horizontally presenting very little surface to the water..."[26]

Alexandre's most recent patent application was witnessed by two of New York City's finest and reputable men. They were Lemuel W. Serrell and Thomas

G. Harold, who held their own patents on a variety of machines, including one for a carding, one for making kettles, a dredging machine, one for sawing logs, and an improved photographic plate vice. Later, Serrell would become a well-respected patent attorney, representing a number of clients, including the well-respected, Thomas Edison.

On February 15, 1856, Alexandre applied for a U.S. passport, which would allow him to travel freely to England and France, and back again. It would provide him the rare opportunity to present his inventions at a variety of venues throughout the world. Yet, in reality, Alexandre had absolutely no intention of maintaining his permanent home in the United States, and when he traveled to Europe later that summer, he never returned.

On the evening of May 26, 1857, the Society of Telegraph Engineers and Electricians brought their meeting to a close with the President's Annual Conversazione. The meeting rooms were "decorated with many choice works of art, and there was also exhibited a large and interesting collection of mechanical models." Aside from Moritz Pillischer's achromatic microscopes and improved stereoscopes, Henry Clifford's "new and superior method of lowering boats" into the water, and specimens of various new modes of laying and connecting train rails, the engineers received a brief glimpse of Lambert Alexandre's newest creation, the "sillographe":

> "Among those (inventions) especially attractive were M. Lambert Alexandre's self-acting log, for indicating and registering the speed of ships. This invention, in its simplest state, is called the sillometer, and visibly indicates, with mathematical accuracy, the speed of a ship in its smallest variations, a hand on the dial following all the variations of the ship's course. When the instrument both indicates and records or registers the speed, it is named sillographe, and writes down by itself all the variations of speed, which the sillometer only marks."[27]

On February 25, 1858, Alexandre surfaced briefly once again, when he applied for a patent on an apparatus that provided "signals for preventing accidents on railways." Little is known of what became of the inventor's work during the next several years, although his whereabouts can be traced to a modest home in Paris, where he lived quietly with his family for the next fifteen years.

On April 20, 1872, the final words were heard from the aging inventor, as he dispatched a letter from his home to Adolphe Ernest Ragon, of Upper Westbourne Terrace, in the County of Middlesex, Paddington, England. In it, he commented on Ragon's "new or improved case for railway and other tickets, fitted with a memorandum paper or advertisement sheet." Though Alexandre then seems to simply vanish from history, the Frenchman who had brought his innovations to America left us with a number of applications used aboard diving vessels for several decades to come.

Portrait of Jonathan Avery Richards

Portrait of John Wesley Wolcott

- 16 -
J. Avery Richards & John W. Wolcott: *Deep-Sea Diving Bell*

"They make quite a favorable report of their doings 'down below.' The air was perfectly pure and easily breathed–they were as comfortable as they would have been in a small, close room. They could see objects, by calculation, from 15 to 20 feet, in all directions. The arms worked perfectly easy. The light was sufficient for them to read a newspaper, and see the small figures on an ivory thermometer..."[1]

Experimentation in salvage diving in America reached a "fever pitch" during the mid- to late-1830s. New York's monthly magazine, *The Knickerbocker*, reported in its "Gossip with Readers and Correspondents" section that its editors had grown quite enthusiastic with the subject of submarine exploration. In one particular issues, published in September of 1838, a reporter recounted the intriguing "performance of 'A Man in Sub-marine Armor' off the Battery," during which a diver described as an "uncouth agglomeration of four limbs" appeared to be "very much like a robustious beer-barrel on skids."

To the majority of eyewitnesses present on that eventful September day in 1838, the strange looking diver was remembered quite readily. He wore:

"...an inverted head-piece, or hat, like a topsy-turvy iron pail, with a small glass-door with hinges in front. This was attached to an India-rubber jacket, terminating near the middle of the body in a strong copper hoop, which was screwed to another and corresponding hoop, fastened to the caoutchouc 'trowserloons,' which terminated in bronze or brass 'leggin,' and impervious boots. He had a long cord in his 'mailed right hand,' and there was a small engine hose coiled up on the deck, which he alluded to as 'that air-pipe.' This was wormed into the top of his hat; and over the rail he went, after a bow to the crowd on the Battery, and a wave of his hand, neither of which could have ever been learned from a French dancing-master..."[2]

Jonathan Avery Richards III, who would always be referred to by family, friends, and business associates as "J. Avery," was a notable American submariner who came from a long line of powerful and wealthy men. His sixth great-grandfather was Sir Edward Richards I, who had been born to one Richard Richards of Yaverland, Isle of Wight, England, in 1568. In 1605, Sir Edward became High Sheriff of County Hampshire, a region that was pressed snugly up against the southern coastline of England. Soon after marrying Bridget Mitchell, daughter and co-heir of John Mitchell of Stamerham, County Sussex, in 1606, the couple moved to Southampton. There, Edward I and Bridgett would give to birth four sons, including John, Germain, Edward II, and Richard. Following Bridget's death, Edward I married a second time, to Jane Martin, who was J. Avery's sixth great-grandmother. Jane bore Edward I two children: son Edward II and daughter Cecily.

On May 20, 1628, at the grand age of sixty, Edward I was knighted by King Charles I at the Palace of Whitehall in London. A few months later, he was stricken by a mysterious illness, which was described in the following passage:

> "Old Mr. Edward Richards of Yaverland, having been long sick, fell into a trance, in which he continued 2 days and nights without speaking or taking any sustenance. They all expected every hour when he would depart out of this world. Doctor Lewkenor, his physician, left him as a dead man, came to me and told me he was past hope of recovering. Three of his children with divers others to the number of 10 persons, continued in his chamber, expecting when it would please God to call him, and they put all things in order for his burial, for he had been long sick before he fell into the trance. But, at the end of the 2 nights and days, he awaked and roused himself up in his bed. They demanded of him how he did. He replied, 'Reasonably well,' and told them that he had either seen a vision or one had told him, being in the trace, of divers things: amongst other things that he should recover out of this, his long sickness, and should live (he being then aged three score years) and see all those in the room buried before him, which fell out accordingly. His 2 sons, John and German, were the last: German died at Portsmouth suddenly, being well, and dead in 2 days. Sir John died some 3 months after, and the old man some 6 months after. Although I give small credit to dreams, yet thus it fell out unhappily."[3]

Edward II, son of Sir Edward I, was born about 1585 in Southampton, County Hampshire, England, near the confluence of the River Test and the River Itchen. The area, having been inhabited since the Stone Age, then held a monopoly on the export of wool to the Mediterranean and on the import of sweet wine. During son Edward's childhood, the port went into decline, soon becoming a more convenient stop for buccaneers that plundered Spanish ships in the English Channel and out in the deeper waters of the Atlantic Ocean.

Little is known of J. Avery Richards' fifth great-grandfather, Edward II, except that he was educated at the Free Grammar School of the Mayor, Bailiffs and Burgesses of the Towne and County of Southampton. The school had been established by a wealthy gent named William Capon, who's last will and testament provided £100 toward the "erection, maynetenance and fynding of a gramer scole" in the town. At the age of twenty-four, son Edward II married Barbara Warden, and they were known to have had two sons; Nathaniel was born in 1607, while Edward—named after his father and grandfather—was born in 1609.

Free Grammar School of the Mayor, on New Street

Although his name does not appear on the ship's passenger list, it is believed that Edward Richards III came to America with brother Nathaniel aboard the *Lyon*. With William Pierce, Master, at the helm, the ship departed from London on June 22, 1632, and arrived in Boston on Sunday, September 16 "after a voyage of eight weeks from Land's End, although the passengers had been aboard for twelve weeks. They had five days of east wind and fog, but no disaster. There were one hundred and twenty-three passengers of which fifty were children, all in good health."

Edward III resided with his elder brother in Cambridge, Massachusetts, until 1636, when Nathaniel opted to relocate to the nearby planting area of Hartford. Meanwhile, Elder John Hunting of Watertown had decided on moving to an area known as Dedham, and Edward III had become betrothed to Susanna Hunting, whom he married September 10, 1638. She was Elder Hunting's sister, and chose to live near her brother in Dedham, rather than living with strangers in Hartford. Edward III dutifully agreed with her wishes, for he apparently much "preferred her pleasure to the society of his brother."

The "closed corporate community" of Dedham was just three years old when Edward III and Susanna arrived in 1639. When incorporated, residents hoped to name the town "Contentment," but the Massachusetts General Court overruled them and the community was named after a hamlet in County Essex, England. Like so many other settlements in the Massachusetts Bay Colony, Dedham was inhabited by men who were both proprietors and settlers, for they owned specific home lots in the town, worked certain fields and pastures in common, and held the remaining vast acreage of the land grant in trust to be granted to future community members. Richards had to obtain approval from these "town fathers" in order to own land in Dedham. He also had to accept civic responsibilities, such as road building, militia duty, and "fence viewing."

Once approved, Edward Richards III, described in the town record as a "shoemaker," purchased a twelve-acre lot in the town center in 1639, the year after he married Susanna. By making that transaction, he officially became a "proprietor," committing himself to much more than building a house, raising a family, and making a living. He was, in essence, an investor buying "twelve shares of the town," much like a stockholder buys shares in a company. The township proprietors set a self-imposed limit to their numbers, the economic benefit of which was a secure knowledge that, in future years, they and their descendents would control enough acreage for each to live well and to see future generations prosper. In essence, they were attempting to ensure wealth and prestige.

On January 1, 1643, Edward joined other Dedham proprietors in a unanimous vote to authorize the first taxpayer-funded public school as "the seed of American education." They hired the Reverend Ralph Wheelock as its first teacher, agreeing to pay him twenty pounds annually to instruct the youth of the community. Not only would both of Edward's sons be taught here, but generations of Richards would learn alongside students whose descendents were destined to become presidents of Datmouth College, Yale University, and Harvard University. Among them would be an enterprising lad who would contribute immensely to the evolution of American submarine development.

As already stated, Edward Richards III's twelve acres were his proof of part ownership in the company town, and for the remainder of his life he collected "dividends" on them. He received grants of meadow and marshland, upland and pasture. His beginnings were those of a small stockholder, and the returns on his investment over time were also relatively small: five acres of woodland here, two acres of swamp there. These small lots accumulated, however, so that by 1653, fourteen years after Edward III's arrival in Dedham, his holdings totaled more than fifty-five acres. His relative economic standing in the town had also risen, from twentieth to twelfth highest among the seventy-eight property holders. As his financial status improved, so did the prestige of the civic positions he held, beginning as the mundane though necessary fence-viewer and moving up to influential roles as selectman and constable.

Sometime between 1653 and 1657, Edward III made the one major land purchase of his lifetime: a 150-acre tract situated south of the Charles River, known as "Mr. Cook's Farme." By this one act he guaranteed his family's economic security for several generations, as well as establishing himself as one of Dedham's three most powerful citizens. Though history did not record how much he paid for this property–since the deed of sale has been lost–an earlier deed for the same land records a cost of sixty-seven pounds, fourteen shillings for the "farm, part meadow, part upland…next Charles River as it lyeth…bounded betwixt a little brooke and certain Rocks."

By the time that Edward III died on August 25, 1684, he and Susanna had given birth to three daughters and two sons in alternating fashion: Mary, John, Dorcas, Nathaniel, and Sary. The eldest, John, lived in a nearby house that he had built for his family, while Nathaniel shared the homestead with his father. Edward III's holdings were quite impressive, including: a half-cellared house and its furnishings plus other buildings on the home lots; the "remainder of Mr. Cook's Farme"; and acreage in seven other locations throughout the Dedham region. Edward's will listed sizeable cash and "country pay" bequests, and instructed John and Nathaniel to divide the real estate, valued at £161, at the time of their mother's death. Finally, "in case my son Nathaniel do bring up one of his Sons to learning I give to that Grandchilde Sixty pound toward it."

Born on November 25, 1648, son Nathaniel Richards was J. Avery's third great-grandfather. By the time he had reached very young adulthood, he had earned a reputation as a skilled hunter by killing wolves for the bounty, as well as for the dastardly deed of "sitting out of order" at the meetinghouse. Just prior to marrying Mary Aldis on December 12, 1678, at the age of thirty, he was granted township lumber to build an addition on his father's house.

Soon, family patterns began to repeat for Nathaniel. His eight children were born at a rate of one every one or two years, until he had added five sons and three daughters to the Richards clan; initially, he became a fence viewer in outlying areas, hoping to eventually work his way up the social ladder; and he began to pay taxes on the homestead edition that he had built with his own two hands, which was, in fact, his family's new home.

Despite some of this "sameness" of his life, by the middle of the 1680s, Dedham had changed drastically. No longer was it a "fragile outpost of the colony's frontier," nor was it a "closed corporation." No longer was there proprietary power reserved to the elite, enabling them to reject newcomers considered "indigents" from settling there. As a result, the community had tripled in population in less than three decades. Families bought and sold land freely, and the era of property dividends was all but over. Nathaniel, and his brother John, in fact, received their final allotment of thirty-five acres each in 1687.

As time passed, and Nathaniel's sons reached adulthood, he set them up on their own eighty-acre plots across the Charles River. Third son, James, born on February 24, 1683, married Hannah Metcalf, daughter of Deacon Jonathan and Hannah (Kendrie) Metcalf, in 1706. The two would raise a large family of eleven children. Among them was Ebenezer, J. Avery's great-grandfather, who was born on January 12, 1719. He was just eight years old when his grandfather, Nathaniel, "died very suddenly while sitting in his chair…in his seventy-ninth year." During his lifetime, the elder Richards had added wealth to the family fortune, had been an "upstanding member of the community," and had died very well respected.

Ebenezer, who married Thankful Stratton, had eight children, and their last son, Jonathan I, was born on August 17, 1760. At the age of sixteen, he enlisted in the Massachusetts Militia under Captain Ebenezer Battles, taking part in a number of confrontations against the British during the Revolutionary War. On March 4, 1776, he participated in the Battle of Dorchester Heights, less than a dozen miles from his Dedham home. With other brave locals, the volunteers were able to liberate the town of Boston and its surrounding lands from British occupation without a single shot being fired. In 1777, he joined Colonel Aaron Smith and marched to Stillwater, New York, to oppose the forces of General Johnny Burgoyne in battle. During the next several months, Jonathan Richards would also proudly serve "as a substitute" for Andrew Cunningham in Colonel William McIntosh's regiment and Captain Thomas Mayo's company.

After the war, Jonathan I married Hepzibah Colburn on May 5, 1785. While giving birth to her second child, she died unexpectedly from complications. Though heartbroken, the thirty-tear-old veteran would marry once again, this time to Sarah Avery on January 4, 1791. Sarah had recently "taught the Middle School of the First Parish," while Jonathan I, now a Deacon, "was master in the First Parish, West School" for the next few years. Oddly, they would name their firstborn Hepzibah, after Jonathan I's first wife. After giving birth to a second daughter, Sally, their only son, Jonathan Avery II was born on April 6, 1797.

Jonathan Avery Richards II, J. Avery's father, was baptized in the First Church in Roxbury on April 16, 1797. He was destined to grow up in the wealthy family tradition, remaining in the Roxbury (Rocksbury) and Boston area all of his life. By the age of twenty-one, he had become a well-respected bookkeeper at a local bank in Boston. On November 23, 1820, he married twenty-three-year-old, Nancy Davis Gore of Roxbury, daughter of Paul and Mary (Kenney) Gore. Together, they would produce two children: Mary Adelaide was born one day after Christmas in 1821, and Jonathan Avery III in the Spring of 1823, on April 19.

While their mother managed the home front, father Jonathan remained heavily involved in both community and civic affairs. He served for a number of years in the Massachusetts State militia, eventually rising to the rank of Lieutenant-Colonel. Later, he would represent the community of Roxbury in the State Legislature. Finally, he was ordained as a Deacon of the First Church of Roxbury on June 3, 1838, a position that he would serve faithfully for three years. Sadly, he died on his only son's twenty-second birthday, April 19, 1845, at the relatively young age of forty-eight.

Meanwhile, J. Avery and Mary Adelaide attended classes at the Roxbury Townhouse School, which was founded on August 30, 1830. A few years later, J. Avery went to work as an apprentice for Joseph Milner Wightman in nearby Boston. Wightman, the son of James Pountney Wightman, a poor immigrant tailor, was a self-made businessman. His father had died when he was only ten years old, leaving Joseph's mother, Martha, to raise him, an older sister, and three younger brothers. Four years later, in 1826, the fourteen-year-old youngster became a machinist's apprentice with a firm owned by John Codman and Timothy Claxton, a pair of mathematical and philosophical instrument makers.

Codman and Claxton's partnership lasted for only three years, after which Claxton became the sole proprietor until 1835. In the summer of that year, near tragedy struck when the thriving business was completely destroyed by a mysterious fire. Since he was fully insured, however, he was able to rebuild. Understanding that it would be difficult to keep up with the increasing workload, Claxton decided to go into partnership with his one-time apprentice, Joseph Milner Wightman, who Claxton later described as his "right hand man."

In 1837, the two enterprising individuals would present a number of unique machine improvements at the prestigious Exhibition and Fair of the Massachusetts Charitable Mechanic Association. Examining their sectional model of a steam engine, a pneumatic apparatus for schools, a table air-pump, a larger air-pump, and "orreries," Claxton's and Wightman's work was judged to be quite remarkable, earning them a silver medal and the following review:

> "The sectional model illustrates the mechanism of the high and low pressure engines. The pneumatic apparatus, for schools, furnishes the means of performing, in a satisfactory manner, all the common experiments in this branch of natural philosophy, at a small expense. The table air-pump is simple in construction…it has a single barrel, which is worked upon its piston in a vertical direction, by means of a lever. This arrangement is thought to give the instrument several advantages over that of the common construction. This pump is also easily kept in repair, and, for general use, is considered superior to any that has fallen under the notice of the Committee. The large air pump is similar in construction to the table pump, and designed for experiments on a larger scale. The orreries are well made, and sold at a moderate price. Claxton & Wightman deserve great credit for the improvements they have introduced in the manufacture of Philosophical Apparatus. Many of their articles have been either invented, or greatly improved by them."[4]

In the autumn of 1837, Claxton returned to his native England, and the firm of Claxton and Wightman became the firm of Joseph Milner Wightman. The sole proprietor, who now began to supply educational institutions with a large amount of scientific instruments, now needed to hire an apprentice of his own. To fill the void, he decided to employ fifteen-year-old J. Avery Richards in the spring of 1838.

Without hesitation, J. Avery paid the annual $1 dues and joined the Mechanic Apprentices' Library Association, "a club of young apprentices to mechanics and manufacturers…whose object is moral, social, and literary improvement." Some historians would later describe it as "the first of the kind known to have been established in any country." During his association with the group, they "[met] quarterly; …[had] nearly 200 members, and a library of about 2000 volumes; connected with which [was] a reading room, gratuitously supplied with the best newspapers and magazines of the city, and a cabinet of natural history. In addition to these advantages, the association [had] lectures and debates in the winter, and a social class for the study of elocution in the summer."[5]

Portrait of Joseph Milner Wightman

Over the course of the next four years, J. Avery would spend every free hour studying mechanical drawings and other published library materials that might lead him to not only make improvements of Wightman's scientific instruments, but create inventions of his very own. In its annual report to Congress, the Smithsonian Institution's Board of Regents expressed what J. Avery would learn as a paid member of the Mechanic Apprentices' Library Association:

> "The association consists entirely of apprentices to mechanics and manufacturers–of course embracing only minors... The affairs of the institution have been very ably and successfully conducted by its youthful

members. The association occupies two rooms in Phillips Place, opposite the head of School Street; the one for reading and lecture-room (say 30 feet by 40) the other (say 30 by 15) for library and conversation room. The library is well selected to promote the intellectual culture of the class for whom it was intended. The reading department contains the principal newspapers and periodicals of the city, and many from different parts of the country, and is in a most flourishing condition. A cabinet of minerals and curiosities has been commenced; an annual course of free lectures is supported by the institution; an elocution class has been formed, the exercises of which consist in the reading of original compositions, declamation, and debate... The library is open three hours every Tuesday and Saturday evening. About 10,000 volumes are lent out annually."[6]

Between his work experience with one of the most brilliant mechanical innovators of the times, and his long hours spent at the mechanics library, J. Avery was able to gain valuable insight into the design of scientific instrumentation of all types. In fact, he earned his own personal recognition at the Third Exhibition and Fair of the Massachusetts Charitable Mechanic Association, held in September of 1841:

"J. Avery Richards, in Boston, an Apprentice to Mr. Wightman. A Stomach-pump, which the Committee have marked No. 1. It is a very good piece of mechanism, even supposing it to have been from the hands of an experienced workman; but more remarkably so, as it was made by a lad of eighteen years old, in his third year of apprenticeship."[7]

In 1845, J. Avery joined forces with a number of Boston citizens that worked diligently to improve the water delivery system into the City. The result would be the development of the Cochituate Water Works, a system created by the construction of Lake Cochituate Dam to provide a reservoir for water supply to Boston via the fourteen-mile Cochituate Aqueduct. Lake Cochituate was the first major water supply system built for the city, and replaced the previous inadequate usage of Jamaica Pond. In January of 1850, J. Avery would be selected as the first Water Registrar, a prestigious position on the Cochituate Water Board committee that he would hold for the next seven years.

It would seem that J. Avery followed in his father's footsteps when it came to patriotic sentiments and civic duty. During his early twenties, he was connected to the military service, holding the commission of lieutenant of the New England Guards. The position was not simply a volunteer situation, for each member was mandated by the group's constitution, revised in January of 1839, to be in good standing among the membership of the Guards:

"Any citizen of the age of 18 years and upwards, who may wish to become a member of the Company, shall be admitted if recommended by the Investigating Committee at any meeting of the corps, five-sixths of the members present voting in his favor, and no member shall be discharged from the Company by his own request, unless his request be in writing addressed to the Commanding Officer, nor unless five-sixths of the members present vote in favor of his discharge."[8]

Quite regularly, J. Avery and his fellow Guards could be seen marching throughout the city on parade days, with a band playing music from *Bunker Hill Quick Step*, a lively tune composed by Boston organist, pianist, compiler, and teacher, Charles Zeuner, specifically for their use and enjoyment. A few years later, J. Avery would join the Massachusetts Independent Corp of Cadets. Though the name implied some sort of military organization, it would be remembered more for its many "social functions and sumptuous balls."

Throughout this period of his life, J. Avery had begun to incorporate his intricate scientific knowledge to the design of the diving bell, imagining that such improvements were now available that would make it possible to dive deeper than any man had previously gone. Working with a local machine shop, he designed his bell from two large hemispherical pieces of cast iron bolted together by sixteen flanges. Situated at the upper extreme of the ball was a collar boasting a removable hatchway, large enough to serve as a door for up to three crewmen. At the entrance's outside center was welded a single eyehook, through which a strong chain could be strung, thus allowing the hatch to be raised and removed. A similar sized rounded hole, minus the hatch, was designed at floor level, which would allow crew members to exit the vessel during a shallow-water dive.

About midway down the sides of the sphere were a series of four rounded, thick glass portholes, one every ninety degrees, so that the crew could see outside the bell. Each window had a matching shutter on the outside, which could be opened and closed laterally from within by a handle extending through a stuffing box arrangement. Just below one of these portholes was a ball and socket "working rod," by which external objects could be manipulated, moved, or even picked up. At its extended end a number of tools, including "a hook, pike, scoop, forceps or other shape" could be utilized, depending upon what might be needed for a particular salvage maneuver. The entire contraption could be worked from the inside.

On the opposing side of the bell was a "flexible arm," which could be used in conjunction with—or instead of—the ball and socket arrangement. Constructed of "caoutchouc," or India rubber, it was in the form of a conical tube, fortified on its inside by a coil of wire rings "of sufficient strength to resist compression." In theory, a crewman from within the bell could readily slip his arm through the tube and manipulate it manually.

From his work with Joseph Wightman, Richards had surmised that, by attaching a lengthy air-tight flexible leather "suction hose" to a pump at the surface of the water, fresh air could be forced downward to any depth, while a second pump could be used to extract stale oxygen. In his design, these hoses were attached at the upper ends of the diving bell. In an emergency, if the pumps failed, air could also be forced to circulate by way of a "bellows, fan-blower, or other similar means." Cocks were installed upon the air pipes in case of any hose failure that would otherwise allow water inside.

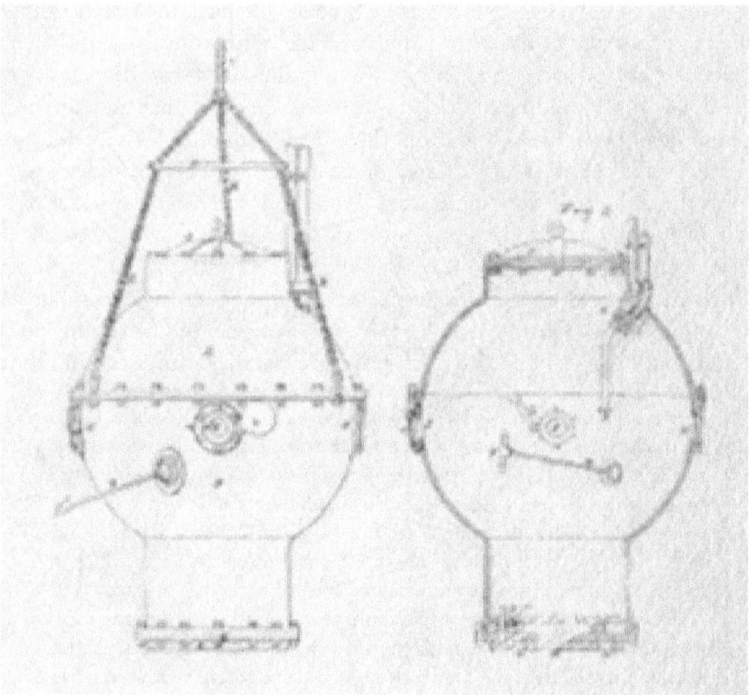

Patent drawing of J. Avery Richards' *Deep-Sea Diving Bell*

By late summer, 1848, the prototype model had been completed, submerged without a crew, and was ready for a manned test. Local newspapers publicized the upcoming event:

> "The *Boston Transcript* gives an interesting description of a new diving bell, the invention of Mr. J. Avery Richards, of that city. It is a closed instrument of cast iron, and weighs 6000 pounds, with space enough in the well-room for a thousand pounds of lead ballast, if required. Its form is an elongated globe, 7 feet in height by 5 in diameter, with glass windows on four sides, and two arms of a peculiar construction passing through its sides, at the control of the operator. With these arms articles can be hooked up or grappled, and a chain cable attached to a sunken wreck. There are tubes for the admission of fresh and to cary [sic] off the foul air, and for conversation. The interior is spacious enough to contain three persons, and two can work in it conveniently, remaining in it any necessary length of time, with perfect ease and safety."[9]

On Tuesday, August 1, 1848, all was ready for an initial test dive demonstration. Outfitted with the Richards *Deep-Sea Diving Bell*, as well as the necessary pumps and air hoses, the light sloop *Noddle* made her way carefully out into Boston Harbor near Minots Ledge Lighthouse, creeping along the lee shoreline of Cohasset. Long known to locals as Lighthouse Channel, the treacherous waterway ran between the Brewster Islands and the northern reaches of the community of Hull, was sometimes narrow, winding, and not always deep. It was out past Long Island Head Lighthouse, in much deeper waters, that Captain Joseph Cumminsky set the *Noddle*'s anchor. Three men, including J. Avery Richards, Samuel Remsell, and Edward A. Child, walked out onto a platform that extended over the edge of the low-slung scow. There, with the hatchway collar of the diving bell sitting snugly like a peg in a block from below, they climbed aboard, the hatch was closed, and the three men waited patiently for the ten iron bolts to be fastened tightly from the outside. Sealed within, she was rigged and hoisted downward below the sloop's deck, her ballast allowing her to sink steadily downward and out of sight. Local newsmen reported what they witnessed from above:

> "Yesterday, the Bell was taken on board the Lighter sloop Noddle. Capt. Cumminsky, who, with the inventor and his assistants, proceeded down to Light House Channel, where the instrument was rigged and hoisted overboard, and sank to the depth of one hundred and twenty-six feet, where it remained one hour. When hoisted up and opened it was found to be perfectly tight, notwithstanding the immense pressure to which it had been exposed at that great depth. Everything being satisfactory to Mr. Richards and his party, Mr. Samuel Rumrell, who has had some experience with sub-marine apparatus, in company with Mr. E.A. Child, entered the Bell, and the head was screwed on, and let down ninety-five feet. A free conversation was kept up with them through a tube 133 feet in length. They were very anxious to be let down to the bottom, 126 feet, but it was thought prudent not to let them lower, the rigging not being suitable in case of any accident, and not working quick enough from so great a depth..."[10]

Once the Richard's diving bell was brought to the surface, those inside were extracted and, within moments, began to offer details of their adventure. Richards explained that their air supply "was perfectly pure and easily breathed," and that "they were as comfortable as they would have been in a small classroom." Through the vessel's view ports, they could readily see objects estimated to be fifteen to twenty feet away. The arms, which would be employed for salvage purposes during any typical dive, seemed to operate without issue.

Inside, the light was sufficient to "read a newspaper, and see the small figures on an ivory thermometer." On deck of the *Noddle*, the temperature had been eighty-six degrees; at a depth of ninety-five feet, the thermometer had read a comfortable sixty-eight. When the trio was at their deepest point, a bell was struck with a hammer, and "the blows were distinctly heard by those in the sloop, but the sound seemed to come from a very great distance." When they had reached seventy feet, they "passed into a stratum of deep green water which slightly dimmed the light in the bell." Richards compared it to "the effect of a cloud passing over the sun." Finally, when asked if they had encountered any difficulties, Remsell said that the "only annoyance...was from a large sculpin, who was detected several times rather saucily looking in at one of the windows."

Patent drawing of J. Avery Richards' *Deep-Sea Diving Bell* aboard the *Noddle*

Overall, Richards was convinced that his deep diving design could "bear a pressure of 200 pounds to the square inch," thus enabling his crew to safely "attain a depth of 200 feet with perfect safety." Until that particular day in August of 1848, in fact, the deepest recorded dive in history aboard any bell had been about seventy feet. Hence, the advantages of his vessel over all others was marketed as its unique "capability of being worked in deep sea, its simplicity (of design), the ease with which it can be operated, the view it affords of objects, the comfort and perfect safety it secures to the operator, and the indefinite time she can remain under water."[11]

In need of a steady stream of financing to support the construction of additional diving bells, as well as pay for upcoming improvements and expeditions, Richards turned to long time friend and business associate, John Wesley Wolcott. A Boston-based financier, and co-partner in the Gardner, Wolcott, and Company Bank, Wolcott had come from a long line of English and American clothiers and investors. His eighth great-grandfather, Thomas Wolcott, had listed his occupation as a "tucker" and "fuller," which essentially meant that he handled newly woven wool cloth and prepared it for sale by soaking and beating it by means of a water driven mill. His name appeared on a number of tax rolls during the 1520s and 1530s, as well as several wills. Having been born around 1487 in the village of Tolland, County Somerset, England, he married Margaret Welling, and together they gave birth to four sons. His eldest, Thomas "the younger," followed in his father's footsteps, carrying on the career as a well-respected tucker.

Three generations later, John Wolcott I, John Wesley's fifth great-grandfather, brought the woolen-draper trade to America in the 1630s after his first wife, Mary Wrentmore, had died unexpectedly. Arriving aboard the *Recovery*, which had sailed from Weymouth, Dorsetshire on March 31, 1633, John was admitted as a freeman at Waterford, Massachusetts. Almost immediately, he began the lengthy process of accumulating wealth. Within that first year, he owned property in the neighboring township of Cambridge, and had purchased and resold the Higginson-Roger Williams house in Salem. Shortly after his arrival in America, he married Winnifred Crawford, a widow, by whom he had a daughter, Sarah, and a son, John II, in 1636.

Two generations later, John Wesley's great-great-grandfather was born in Brookfield, Massachusetts, in 1694, though a fateful chain of events threatened to cause a break in the Wolcott family links:

> "Early on the morning of October 13, 1708, John Wolcott, a lad of about 12 or 14 years old, was riding in search of the cows, when the Indians fired at him, killed his horse under him and took him prisoner.... John Wolcott, the lad above mentioned, was carried to Canada, where he remained for six or seven years, during which time, by conversing wholly with the Indians, he not only entirely lost his native language, but became so naturalized to the savages, as to be unwilling for a while to return to his native country. Some years afterwards, viz. in March 1728, in a time of peace, he and another man having been hunting, and coming down the Connecticut River with a freight of skins and fur, they were hailed by some Indians; but not being willing to go to them, they steered for another shore. The Indians landed at a little distance from them, several shots were exchanged, at length Wolcott was killed."[12]

When great-great-grandfather, John, miraculously returned from Canada still alive in 1718, he was given a hero's welcome and forty acres of land. The following year he was granted another one hundred acre plot, a year later another seventy, and the year after this another seventy acres. In 1724 his father gave or sold him forty-one additional acres at Brookfield, in which he is referred to as a "husbandman," or farmer. Three years later, on October 12, 1727, he married Dinah Walker, the sister of his younger brother's wife. With more than 320 acres of property, some considered him "well-off."

The cruel hand of fate or destiny seemed to have it in for John and Dinah's happiness, however, for it was only a few months later that he walked up the Connecticut River on a hunting expedition from which he never returned. On June 14, 1728, his grieving wife–believed to be a widow–delivered a healthy baby boy, whom she named John after his missing father. A few years later, in 1730, the "widow" married Peter Rice, also of Brookfield. It is this writer's opinion, based on historical and DNA evidence, that John IV probably did not die along the Connecticut River in 1728, as had been reported in history, but instead returned to the Indians with whom he had lived for so many years. The subsequent tale of his death in a fight with the natives was probably a fabrication to explain his deliberate disappearance.

The upper Connecticut River, where John Wolcott IV of Brookfield went on his final hunting expedition in 1728, led right up to New Hampshire. An account of settlers at Charlestown, New Hampshire, being captured by Indians in 1754, explained that they had been taken up the Connecticut River to Canada. On the first day of their abduction, they were moved ten miles up the river "to the upper end of Wilcott's Island," where they crossed the river on rafts. It seems a likely spot to have harbored John Wolcott IV, a native Indian wife, and their children. John is said to have been fluent in the Algonquin language, which was spoken by the native people of this area. If all DNA indications are accurate, John apparently spent the latter part of his life as a hunter and trapper on the upper Connecticut River, avoiding contact with his Brookfield wife and son, and instead residing happily ever after with another wife.

So, the fifth John in a long line of Wolcotts grew up without his biological father in the town of Brookfield, Massachusetts, though he did not stray from the "righteous path." When he was but fifteen years old, Peter Rice married his mother and gave him legal guardianship. Raised with humility and patriotic sentiments, John would one day marry Experience Walker, the daughter of his uncle Jonathan Wolcott, in 1748. They would have eight children and, though one of his sons would become the sixth generation John, the grandfather of John Wesley Wolcott of diving bell fame was a brother named Solomon.

In 1756, when his youngest was less than a year old, patriotic fervor overcame great-grandfather John. So, at the age of twenty-six, he left his wife and four young children behind to serve in Captain John Burke's company during the French and Indian War. One year later, he marched in relief of the captured Fort William Henry in Captain Ezekial Upham's company. After the war, he returned home, became an avid farmer, had four more children, and raised the entire brood on the Wolcott family homestead in Brookfield.

Over the course of twenty-one years, John and Experience Walker had three daughters and five sons. Solomon, their third child, was born on September 10, 1753. On May 3, 1775, he and his brother, Timothy, enlisted for eight months as corporals in Captain John Granger's company, Colonel Ebenezer Learned's Regiment. The two marched from Brookfield to the Lexington Alarm in early June. Afterward, the Regiment was adopted into the Continental Army. On the 17th of the month, Solomon and Timothy Wolcott fought alongside one another and other brave men in their unit at a battle that took place near Bunker Hill and Breed's Hill in Boston.

At the age of twenty-four, when the war had ended, Solomon married Lydia Bodwell of Methuen, Massachusetts, who was already heavy with child. Like each of the three generations of Wolcotts that came before him, they would have exactly eight children. Their eldest was Timothy, born just seven months after they had shared their vows.

Little is known about John Wesley's father, Timothy, who was born two days before Christmas in 1778, in Brookfield, Worcester County, Massachusetts. At the age of twenty, he married sixteen-year-old Jane Wellcome. He would preach the gospel for forty-five years as a devout reverend at the local Unitarian Church and, in 1817 he would publish a hymn book entitled "A Sellection [sic] of Hymns & Spiritual Songs for Those who Wish to Praise God." Over the course of twenty-four years, Timothy and Jane would have five sons and four daughters. Their youngest son, John Wesley, was born on the last day of July, 1819, in Portland, Cumberland County, Maine.

Timothy, it seems, was a wanderer of sorts, relocating his entire family from Portland, Maine, more than fifty miles southwest to Somersworth, New Hampshire, during the 1820s. From there they would move northward to Bridgton, Maine, and eventually south to Kennebunkport. John Wesley married Lucy Edgecomb on April 11, 1843, in Poland, Androscoggin County, Maine. Though he was heartbroken when she died within twelve months, he would marry a second time to Henrietta Louise Eustis on June 11, 1845. His second marriage would produce five children, all of which were born in Boston.

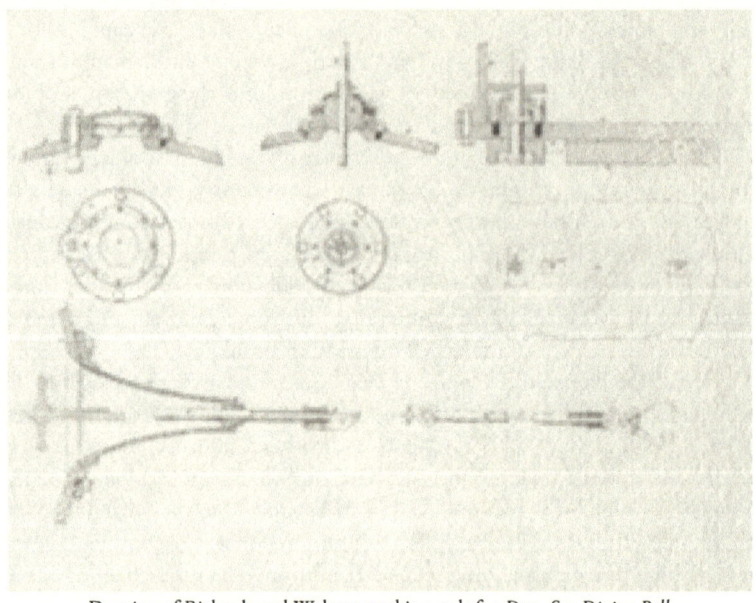

Drawing of Richards and Wolcott working rods for *Deep-Sea Diving Bell*

On April 3, 1849, J. Avery Richards and John Wesley Wolcott were granted Patent Number 6,250, for their *Deep-Sea-Diving Bell*. The enterprising pair did not attempt to say that they had invented the bell, but instead "claim[ed] as our invention, is the combination of working rods with the diving bell, by means of ball and socket, or their equivalents..."

AMERICAN SUBMARINERS: PRE-CIVIL WAR

Inexplicably, however, though historical record does document a number of further events in each of their lives, little more is offered about their promising diving contraption during the next several seasons. J. Avery retained his steady job working as an assistant to treasurer John H. Rend of the Bay-State Iron Company. Situated at 95 Water Street in South Boston, the firm boasted that they were "manufacturers of plate iron, ship plates, armor plates, and rail road iron." Described by those who knew him as "a great favorite, being genial, unaffected, and well-informed," he would later be promoted to clerk and treasurer of the growing company, two very demanding and time-consuming positions he would still hold in February of 1883 when the company financially failed, "partly due to the general dullness in the iron trade and the agitation of the question of changes in the tariff, (though) its immediate cause is understood to be the refusal of banks in this city to make further loans of money."[13]

Drawing of Bay-State Iron Company

Richards also had a number of other responsibilities and interests in his life, perhaps keeping him far to busy to pursue the risky venture of underwater exploration. He continued as Boston's Water Registrar, a position he had held on the Cochituate Water Board committee since 1850. Amid this very "workaholic" lifestyle, he fell in love with and married sixteen-year-old, Minnie Marie Bancroft, daughter of Thomas and Mary Davis Bancroft, on October 29, 1853. Their first daughter, Minnie, was born on June 9, 1855. Census records from 1860 indicate that the three of them resided in the 12th Ward of Boston, with a sixty-five-year-old, Mary Davis Bancroft, and a servant, Ellen Wench, who acted as a housekeeper and caregiver for their five-year-old daughter and Minnie's widowed mother. A second daughter, Mary Anne, came along the following year.

Despite the fact that he already seemed to have enough to keep him busier than the average head of household, J. Avery joined a small group of other prominent Boston investors to found a company called the Suffolk Iron Works on March 17, 1854. This was done to further his diving bell pursuits:

> "Be it enacted by the Senate and House of Representatives, in General Court assembled, and by the authority of the same, as follows: Sect. 1. John D. Richardson, Josiah Dunham, Jr., J. Avery Richards, their associates and successors, are hereby made a corporation, by the name of the Suffolk Iron Works, for the purpose of manufacturing castings and machinery, in the city of Boston; and for these purposes, shall have all the powers and privileges, and be subject to all the duties, restrictions and liabilities, set forth in the thirty-eighth and forty-fourth chapters of Revised Statutes. Sect. 2. Said corporation may hold real and personal estate, necessary and convenient for the purposes aforesaid, not exceeding in amount two hundred and twenty thousand dollars. Sect. 3. No shares in the capital stock of said corporation shall be issued for a less sum or amount, to be actually paid in on each, than the par value of the shares which shall be first issued. Sect. 4. This act shall take effect from and after its passage."[14]

Meanwhile, John Wesley Wolcott's life took a much different pathway during the mid- to late-1850s. Partnering with Henry Joseph Gardner in the "note brokerage business" to form "Gardner, Wolcott, and Company," the two pooled their assets and connections, turning them into a series of lucrative investment schemes.

Wolcott could not have chosen a more colorful and well-known partner. Born on June 14, 1818, in Boston, Massachusetts, son of Henry, a physician, and Clarissa (Holbrook) Gardner, Henry Joseph Gardner had obtained his early education in private schools, including Phillips Academy in Exeter, New Hampshire. After graduation from Bowdoin College in 1838, he entered the mercantile business as partner in a dry goods firm in Boston. Eventually he acquired sole proprietorship of the business, the name of which became Henry J. Gardner and Company. He married Helen Elizabeth Cobb of Portland, Maine, on November 21, 1843. Within a decade, he had fathered four sons and three daughters.

In 1850, Gardner entered local politics in Boston, serving as a member of the Boston Common Council in 1850, 1853, and 1854, and as president in 1852 and 1853. He served in the Massachusetts House of Representatives from 1851 to 1852, and as a delegate to the Massachusetts Constitutional Convention in 1853. In the general election of November 13, 1854, Gardner, with 81,503 votes, was elected Governor of Massachusetts as the American or "Know-Nothing" Party candidate. Although semi-secretive, this party attracted large numbers of supporters who feared foreign influence in the United States and Roman Catholic domination. When the votes had been counted, a celebration among party members had ensued, and their boastful attitude was published in the pages of the *Daily Evening Journal*:

"The people of the Old Bay State have spoken, and from Berkshire to Cape Cod, are heard the voices of her native born children, declaring for the perpetuity American institutions, and American liberties. The descendants of the heroes of Bunker Hill, Lexington, and Concord, have spoken in a voice of thunder, in favor of Americans ruling America. Gardner is, no doubt, elected by the people, and they have driven his base slanderers and perjured maligners, to their hiding places, and from which they will never emerge. The legislature is safe, thus giving us an American senator. Surely, this is glory enough for one day. The heart of the Old Commonwealth is still true to the principles of its old revolutionary fathers, and it has administered a rebuke to one bitter foe of Americanism [Isaac Davis, Democratic candidate for Congress], that will show him in what estimation his assertions are held by the citizens of his own home. Everywhere the Americans have stood shoulder to shoulder, and cheered each other on to a victory that is unprecedented in the annals of political warfare. We have swept the State, without the aid of the Press, without public discussion, and in spite of ermined libellers, and the opposition of three mighty, powerful political organization [Democrats, Whigs, Free Soilers]. We selected our candidate for Governor, without bringing his name before the public, and without having the opportunity of even discussing his claims and his position. But we remembered at the polls our obligations, we fought for principles, not men, and the ruins and wreck of three political parties lay scatttered at our feet. The Bible is now secure in the spot where our fathers placed it, new safeguards are now sure of being reared around our American Institutions, and the warm pulsation of the people's heart beats only for freedom, temperance and Protestantism. Civil and religious liberty has accomplished a triumph, which sinks into insignificance, any political victory ever achieved by any party within this commonwealth. Let every American rejoice, not for the triumph of men, but for the glorious victory of principles. But while they rejoice, let them be generous to their defeated opponents, so that the honor of the victory be not tarnished by an unmanly abuse of a defeated foe. While we, as Americans, are exultant, let us not be overbearing, for it is the victory not of a party, but of the people, whose only aim and desire is to ensure the perpetuity of those institutions, for which our father's [sic] fought, and which we have to-day shown ourselves worthy to inherit, and able to perpetuate."[15]

It was almost immediately after leaving office on January 6, 1858, that Gardner returned to his dry goods business and rejoined financial forces with John Wesley Wolcott, with whom he had been in business throughout his three terms in office. Their bank was located at 46 State Street in central Boston. But it wasn't long before Wolcott found himself in hot water and, as is typically the case with "guilt by association," so did Gardner.

Wolcott's problems began during a financial panic in the autumn of 1857. It was at that time that Middlesex Mills, a large manufacturing corporation headquartered in Boston, failed. In looking over the account books, a committee of creditors discovered an expenditure of $87,000 for the ostensible purpose of affecting the passage by the U.S. Congress of the Tariff Act of 1857, by which the duty on wool was reduced, thus lowering the cost of manufacturing woolens. An investigation by Congress ensued when it was found that the sum of $74,000 of this expenditure remained in the hands of Wolcott, of which he gave no account.

Criminal investigation of the matter began on January 15, 1858, when the U.S. House of Representatives agreed to the following resolution:

> "Resolved, That a committee of five Members be appointed to investigate the charges preferred against the Members and officers of the last Congress growing out of the disbursements of any sum of money by Lawrence, Stone & Co., of Boston, or other persons, and report the facts and evidence to the House, with such recommendations as they may deem proper, with authority to send for persons and papers."[16]

The five-member committee was, on January 18, constituted as follows: Benjamin Stanton, of Ohio; Sydenham Moore, of Alabama; John C. Kunkel, of Pennsylvania; Augustus R. Wright, of Georgia; and William F. Russell, of New York. It was their job to review the testimony of a number of witnesses, including Wolcott, and consider their individual levels of involvement. On February 12, 1858, with the recommendation of the committee, the U.S. House of Representatives dispatched the Sergeant-at-Arms to arrest Wolcott for contempt in refusing to answer a question that he contended was "inquisitorial."

Yet, suspicions were even more serious than contempt of Congress. The committee in the report to the House went on to say that, as they have evidence that the firm of Lawrence, Stone & Co. paid to Wolcott, early in March of 1857, the sum of $58,000 in two payments, one of $33,000 and the other of $25,000, which constituted a part of a charge of $87,000, which appeared on the books of the Gardner, Wolcott, and Company firm to have been expended in procuring the passage of the tariff of 1857. The members of the House believed it to be very material and important to the elucidation of the matter referred to them to know from Wolcott whether he admits the receipt of any such sum; and if so, how it was expended. In other words, they suspected Wolcott of illegal doings in using the money to make illegal payoffs to members of Congress in an attempt to sway the vote. Wolcott denied all allegations.

Though the House voted on March 22 to release him from custody, a number of regional newspapers had already passed judgment about the case. In one such report, the insinuations were quite direct, claiming that "Wolcott was, until recently, a clerk and salesman for the large commission dry goods house of Francis Skinner & Co., on a moderate salary of $300 or $400 per annum; all at once he loomed up into large proportions as a 'capitalist.'"[17]

Finally, one reporter summed the entire matter up nicely when he wrote: "Money wipes out many stains, but it won't, in such a community as this, restore the confidence to the 'banking-house' of Gardner, Wolcott, & Company..."[18]

But it wasn't total financial ruin for John Wesley Wolcott. He continued to reside at his primary family estate in a suburb known as Dedham-Readville, located just south of Boston, though he also invested some of his wealth in a prime piece of real estate eight miles further south. He named the property the "Blue Hill Farm," since it was located among the Blue Hills, so named by early European explorers who noticed the bluish hue on the slopes when viewed from a distance as they sailed along lengthy Charles River. In actuality, the bluish tint came from the presence of sodium-rich riebeckite in the stone. More than 10,000 years before the Europeans arrived, Native Americans had made their home in the hills. The natives referred to themselves as Massachusetts, or "people of the great hills." There, at Blue Hill, Wolcott began to raise an expensive breed of cattle, imported from County Ayr, in Scotland. Soon, his cows, with their distinctive orange to dark brown markings, were being bred for farmers all over the region.

John Wesley Wolcott's Brunswick Hotel, built by Peabody and Sterns

John Wesley Wolcott hired one of the most prominent architectural firms—Peabody and Stearns—to design "the finest hotel in the world." The team of Robert Swain Peabody and John Goddard Stearns Jr. had a prolific architectural reputation throughout the northeast, having secured more than one thousand commissions and building a vast and vibrant repertoire, from warehouses to retail stores, banks, schools, railroad stations, libraries, playhouses, and country houses. One million dollars was poured into the Brunswick Hotel's construction, with red brick and sandstone being mortared together on the corner of Boylston and Clarendon Streets. Completed in 1874, it was enlarged in 1876, and was one of the first hostelries in the U.S. designed to be fireproof. This probably was due to the lesson taught by the great Boston fire of 1872. It also boasted the "finest passenger elevator in hotel service," and there was to be found a "private bath with every suites, a convenience unheard of until that time. In other words, it was an architectural masterpiece.

If Wolcott had soiled his reputation with the banking scandal, he had, by now, regained favor. One of the first historic events connected with the Brunswick was the *Atlantic Monthly* dinner, held there on December 17, 1877, in celebration of John Greenleaf Whittier's seventieth birthday, at which there were present the most eminent American authors of the time:

> "The Brunswick was the scene last night of such a gathering of "literary fellers" as is seldom if ever seen in this country. Among the guests who assembled to do honor to the Quaker poet were such men as Henry W. Longfellow, Ralph Waldo Emerson, Oliver W. Holmes, Charles Dudley Warner, Thomas W. Higginson, R.H. Stoddard, Benjamin H. Ticknor, John Weiss, E.P. Whipple, Francis H. Underwood, George E. Waring, J.T. Trowbridge, Edward Abbott, James R. Osgood, Horace E. Scudder, G.P. Lathrop, S.J. Barrows, J. Boyle O'Reilly, Samuel L. Clemens, H.S. Noyes, Luigi Monti, Charles Elliot Norton, W.H. McElroy, Edward H. Knight, A.G. Houghton, William A. Hovey, J.B. Greenough, G.C. Hill, William F. Apthorp, W.H. Bishop, W.H. Babcock, William M. Baker, Sylvester Baxter, C.C. Buel, Mr. Bugbee, Hezekiah Butterworth, T.G. Cary, C.P. Cranch, Arthur Dexter, Charles Wyllys Elliott, Charles Fairchild, Arthur Gilman, D.A. Goddard, Professor Greene, T.S. Perry, T.C. Rich, Arthur Searle, John Trowbridge, J. Hammond Trumbull, Joseph Wharton, Edward Wheelwright and others. And last, but not least, to the great surprise and delight of all, Mr. Whittier himself was there. The beautiful dining hall in the new wing of the hotel was the scene of the festivities, the tables being laid with over sixty covers. On the walls were a portrait of Whittier, wreathed in English ivy, and an oil painting of his Amesbury home. The tables were beautifully decorated with flowers."[19]

The same year President Hayes and his family occupied a suite at the Brunswick while the President attended the Commencement exercises at Harvard. On his return from his trip around the world, in 1879, General Grant attended a complimentary dinner given for him at this hotel. Two Massachusetts Governors, Rice and Talbot, made the hotel their home after their terms of office; President Arthur also was a guest at the hotel, as were the Dukes of Argyll and Sutherland.

Wolcott continued to rebuild his empire and reputation throughout the remainder of his life. As major financial investment were concerned, the Hotel Vendome came next, standing proudly in the Back Bay district at the corner of Commonwealth Avenue and Dartmouth Street in Boston. Completed in 1881, it was, perhaps, the most opulent of all hotels of the times. Designed by Charles Whitney, when completed the eight-story structure boasted a total cost of one million dollars from start to finish:

"Its fronts are of white Tuckahoe and Italian marble, with elaborately carved windows and doors. The roof and towers are of wrought iron, covered with slate. The floors are laid upon iron beams and brick arches, and all the interior partitions are of incombustible material... with its basement story and mansard roof, [it] is eight stories in height. On the first floor is the rotunda and the various public rooms. The rotunda is paved with English encaustic tiles, in colors and patterns harmonizing with the furnishings; and it is finished in hard woods, cathedral glass, and frescowork. There are five great dining rooms, an elegant banquet-hall...and several grand parlors..."[20]

Meanwhile, just a few blocks away, the true inventor of the *Deep-Sea Diving Bell* remained involved in a number of business ventures of his own. Continuing to assist in the construction Boston's infrastructure, J. Avery Richards joined forces with John H. Reed and Thornton K. Lothrop to form the South Boston Freight Railway Company in May of 1868. The firm was granted the right to "construct, maintain and use a street railway, with suitable turnouts, and with such tracks and brauch tracks as the board of aldermen may, from time to time, permit; the rails of said tracks to be of such pattern as the board of aldermen may prescribe, and to be also suitable for railway freight cars in common use; commencing on the easterly end of First street in South Boston, thence through First street to I street; thence through I street to Second street; thence through Second street to Dorchester street; thence across Dorchester street to First street; thence through First street to Federal street; thence across Federal street, Foundery street and the square between said street and avenue to land of the Old Colony and Newport Railroad Company, there to connect...with the tracks of the Boston, Hartford and Erie Railroad Company...also commencing at the junction of First and Granite streets, thence through Granite street to Mount Washington avenue; thence through Mount Washington avenue to Federal street, and thence on Federal street to East street, there to connect with the tracks of the Marginal Freight Railroad Company..."[21]

The passenger ship, *SS Atlantic*, which could use sails as well as coal-fired steam for power, was forced to reduce speed due to strong headwinds. She had been making her way from the River Mersey in Liverpool and Queenstown to New York, her nineteenth voyage, but opted to alter course to replenish bunkers and provisions in Halifax, Nova Scotia. Reportedly making a speed of about twelve knots,, she steered a wrong course, and was not sounding for depths or making correct allowances for the strong coastal currents.

At 2:40 a.m. in the pitch black night of April 1, 1873, the steamer crashed into the rocks of Mars Head, off Peggy's Point Lighthouse. Officers and crewmen immediately rushed on deck, and tried to lower the ten lifeboats by chopping the ropes with axes, but the lifeboats were washed quickly away, as the ship was sinking and the seas washed over the deck. Twenty people were killed on the deck when the bow on the foremast came loose and turned. Many more drowned on the half-deck when the entrance was blocked by panicking passengers trying to get up. With few exceptions, married men refused to leave their wives and children behind, preferring to die with them, even though they could have been rescued by climbing up the rig. Rocket distress signals were fired every minute or so, but without any results. The top of a rock, which was sticking up over the surface, was about forty yards away from the ship.

Depiction of the SS *Atlantic* disater, by Currier and Ives

The horror of the event unfolded below deck as hundreds of mostly women and children desperately struggled to reach safety. By then, the SS *Atlantic* had rolled over on her port side toward the sea. Desperate to save lives, Quartermaster John Speakman succeeded in taking the signal halyards to the rock off shore. Third Officer, Cornelius Brady, followed, and together they hauled a heavier 200-foot rope from the sinking ship to the rock. About 250 men were able to use this tenuous link, plus three other ropes, to make the forty-yard journey from the vessel to the rock. Of the 957 passengers and crew on board, 283 people drowned almost immediately, and another 262 succumbed to the bitter cold, some dropping from the decks, rigging and spars into the icy waters below.

Within one day, the *Deep-Sea Diving Bell* was called into action. With J. Avery Richards overseeing the entire operation, she was removed from storage, loaded aboard a schooner, rigged, and floated to the rocky cove southwest of Halifax. One of the men, who would take the bell down for its initial dive to explore the wreck, exited the submerged vessel in a rubberized suit to search for bodies. After making his first inspection, he offered the following account:

"The air from above, which is furnished through the rubber tube, comes with a hissing sound, producing a strange feeling. I shudder at the thought of being immersed so deeply, and how slight an accident would insure instant destruction. All around the objects looked weird-like, the glasses in the casque magnifying the already bloated forms into twice their size. The waters are very cold, and a chilly feeling creeps over me at first, but as I proceed it wears away, and I enter upon the task I have undertaken with more nerve than I fancied I possessed. The immense hull lies well down on the port side, which is broken in several places from contact with the reef. Fish were swimming around, eagerly devouring the particles of food which are to be picked up. Picking my way toward the hull, I catch hold of a rope and scramble up the deck. The place where I have descended is where the ship parted, and a sectional view of the hull and cargo is obtained. The forward hatch is open, and I peer down the hold. Oh, what a spectacle is presented? The cargo has broken bulk and lies heaped up in a confused mass; bodies of men and women, bruised and torn, are jammed among the cases and crates. It is a horrible sight to look upon, and the magnifying power of the orbs through which I gaze upon it renders it all the more horrible. Fishes swim in and out among the corpses and boxes, feasting on the dead. Limbs are strewn around, having been broken off from the bodies by the continual action of the waters, which, when agitated, drive against the ugly pieces of the broken hull that stick up here and render my movements very hazardous. Having seen enough of this part of the sunken horror, I proceed toward one of the steerage cabins, in which all the women and children were drowned as they lay in their bin… Having seen enough of the horrors beneath the water on that fatal reef–horrors of the deep, which will never be erased from my vision–I decided to ascend, and motioned accordingly to the men who were above in the boat, and pumping down to me the necessary supply of air to sustain life; in a few minutes I was once more at the surface, gazing upon the light of heaven and experiencing a sensation of relief at having left the chambers of death in the cabins of the ill-fated *Atlantic*."[22]

By midday of April 4, 167 bodies had been recovered from the frigid waters and, after five more days of searching for remains, J. Avery Richards announced that there were no more. Next, a thorough inventory was conducted, with a number of victims being positively identified. The remains of the more affluent were dutifully claimed by sorrowing friends and relatives, who brought them home for burial.

On a spot overlooking Sandy Cove near the village of Terence Bay, the Reverend William Johnson Ancient stood solemnly over a mass grave. Two hundred, seventy-seven, mostly women and children, would be laid to rest in simple coffins provided by the Canadian Government and the White Star Line. Behind him stood local fishermen and their families, newsmen, government officials, relatives, friends, and strangers, all praying for the souls of the victims. Among them was J. Avery Richards. Less than a mile away, Father James Quish, the priest from Prospect, performed a similar service for the Catholic victims.

Reverend William Johnson Ancient overseeing the mass funeral

A dispatch from Philadelphia on April 3rd stated that 336 survivors had been brought to Halifax, and another seventy-seven had been "taken up by the *SS Lady Head*." Fearful that they would further strain the limited resources of the tiny village of Terence Bay, a small band of these survivors made the difficult nineteen-mile journey to Halifax on foot. From there, the survivers gathered together and were transported to Portland, Maine, aboard the steamer *Falmouth*, and then by rail to Boston.

Little else is known of the *Deep-Sea Diving Bell*. Ironically, though J. Avery Richards and John Wesley Wolcott had long since abandoned their partnership and close relationship, they died within six weeks of one another: J. Avery of acute nephritis just one day before his sixty-second birthday on April 22, 1885, and sixty-four-year-old John Wesley of pneumonia on June 4, 1885. Just beyond the vine-covered twin spires that mark the somber entrance to Boston's Forest Hill Cemetery, one could walk among the more than 3,650 graves. There, within a short distance of one another, you can find each of their tombstones. Ironically, each had left the exploratory nature of deep diving behind them as they matured, only to explore more pressing aspects of their lives.

Portrait of Edgar William Foreman

Sketch of Henry Beaufort Sears

- 17 -
Edgar William Foreman & Henry Beaufort Sears: *Nautilus*

"It consisted of an arched corridor of apparently interminable length, gloomily lighted with jets of gas at regular intervals... There are people who spend their lives there, seldom or never, I presume, seeing any daylight, except perhaps a little in the morning. All along the extent of this corridor, in little alcoves, there are stalls of shops, kept principally by women, who, as you approach, are seen through the dusk offering for sale...multifarious trumpery... So far as any present use is concerned, the tunnel is an entire failure."[1]

In the mid-1820s, when Edgar William Foreman was born, Sir Marc Isambard Brunel, engineer and inventor, was at the forefront of civil engineering. His most remarkable undertaking was the construction of the Thames Tunnel from Rotherhithe to Wapping. Work had begun in 1825 when Edgar was not yet old enough to even remember but, due to repeated flooding and cave-ins, the tunnel would not be completed until he was eighteen years old. With no answers to these construction problems, the project had been abandoned for several years.

In December of 1834, Brunel succeeded in raising enough money–including a loan of £247,000 from the Treasury–to continue construction. By August of 1836 an improved and heavier bore shield had been assembled, allowing digging to safely resume. Young Edgar, then twelve years old, was made aware of the project's progress by way of conversations he overheard between his father and grandfather, William, who lived in nearby Shadwell Parish of East London. On a few occasions, Edgar had been taken to visit the dig site. There, he chanced to witness an amazing machine that could actually transport workmen below the surface of the River Thames for hours at a time. His father had called it a "diving bell."

The use of diving bells in marine civil engineering had taken a major step forward when Edgar's father was a young boy. It was in 1807 that John Rennie had taken over the improvements to Ramsgate harbor. He made further improvements to the use of the diving bell in actual construction activities including an overhead gantry bell handling system and the ability to hoist large building blocks under the bell and then into position underwater. His cast iron bell design weighed a cumbersome five tons (5,091 kg), however, making work slow and deliberate. Rennie had installed solid glass, cast bull's eyes on the top to admit light, and the feature would later be utilized in harbor construction works all over the world. His son, Sir John Rennie the Elder, who later took over the business along with his brother George, hoping to become the principal manufacturer of diving bells in Great Britain.

Sir John Rennie's diving bell, used to build the Thames Tunnel

By the early 1840s, cast iron Rennie diving bells—just like the one that Edgar saw—had already been supplied to the majority of the Royal Navy's dockyards and primary harbors. In 1838, Colonel Charles Pasley of the Royal Engineers decided to adapt a Rennie bell, borrowed from the local dockyard, in a valiant attempt to clear the wreck of the brig *William*, which was obstructing navigation of the Thames at Gravesend. In short order, the project became not only a construction site, but a salvage operation. It was unsuccessful, however, because the current played havoc with the bell-handling requirements, and the job had to be finished by a group of "helmet divers."

The following year Pasley began work on clearing the wreck of the *Royal George* at Spithead, Portsmouth. This time he decided to modify the Rennie bell to overcome the problem of tides causing the submersible to be "thrown violently about." His idea was to give the submersible a hydrodynamic profile by the addition of "boat-ends." However, his prototype was built at great expense and the resulting bell was so large and unwieldy that it took over forty men to operate. Following an abortive trial on May 14, 1839, from *HMS Anson* in the Medway, just off the Thames, Pasley was forced to revert to helmet divers. When Edgar Foreman had learned of these repeated failures, his imaginative mind began to formulate a plan to create a more workable diving bell design.

More than 50,000 people—including the eighteen-year-old and his family—walked through the River Thames tunnel from Wapping to Rotherhithe on the day that it opened, March 25, 1843. By then, he had come to realize that his own diving bell design would require a good deal of money. Though his parents, Jonathan and Mary Ann, lived quite comfortably among the wealthy and poor alike, they had not come from upper class forebears.

Depiction of the Thames Tunnel

From its earliest beginnings, the Foreman name was well documented across Scotland and England. The first recorded spelling was that of Robert Foreman, which was dated in 1301 in the Yorkshire Pipe Rolls, during the reign of King Edward I. Other early examples included Alan Forman and Robert Fourman in the 1327 Subsidy Rolls of Yorkshire, while Sir William Foreman (also written as Forman) was Lord Mayor of London in 1538. Edgar William Foreman's direct lineage can be traced back generations to Jeremiah and Mary Foreman, his great-great-grandparents, who brought four children into the world–Jeremiah, Jr., Elizabeth, Mary, and John–in the Parish of Saint John, situated in what was then known as the Wapping district of East London. The family would remain in this marshy region, hemmed in by the River Thames to the south and a major route known as High Street to the north, for several decades to come.

Wapping's proximity to the river had offered generations of Foremans a strong maritime influence. All around them were sailors, mast-makers, boat-builders, block-makers, instrument-makers, victuallers, and representatives of all the other trades that supported the seafaring way of life. The riverfront was also the site of 'Execution Dock', where pirates and other water-borne criminals faced death by hanging from a gibbet constructed close to the low water mark. As an example to the young, their bodies would be left dangling until they had been submerged three times by the tide.

After Queen Anne came to the throne in the early 1700s, under the terms of the Acts of Settlement designed to ensure the Protestant succession, the "New Churches in London and Westminster Act" of 1711 was passed, establishing a Commission to build fifty new houses of worship in populous districts. The royal agenda was as much political as pious, to control the working classes with imposing edifices towering over their homes and reminding them of the national religion. This was particularly needed, it was believed, in the "East End," where immigration was taking hold and there were many dissenting conventicles. Each of these grand structures would be funded from a tax on coal. In theory, this would provide an unending budget to work with, but only twelve—including "Saint George-in-the-East"—would ever be completed. All ran tremendously over budget, and the royal scheme came to an end.

When the Saint George-in-the-East church opened in 1729, parts of Wapping were still semi-rural, with open fields and an unsanitary sewage system, but the area was beginning to develop. Like his father and grandfather before him, Jeremiah Foreman, Jr. worked as a well-trained and licensed "lighterman," so-called because it was his job to transfer goods between ships and quays in the River Thames aboard flat-bottomed barges known as "lighters."

Merchants who were building houses near the docks, or who came from further away, attended Sunday mass in their carriages. By the first day of January in 1738, when Edgar William's great-grandfather, John Foreman, was born, only seven of the 2,484 inhabitants of London that "kept coaches" lived in the Saint John parish, and access to the church remained socially segregated. By 1800, an average of 500 to 600 baptisms were conducted each year—rising to over 1,000 by the time of Edgar William's birth, before "daughter churches" were built. With 400 to 600 burials each year, death kept an even pace.

Edgar's grandfather, William Foreman, was born on January 24, 1768, and was baptized fourteen days later. By then, his parents, John and Ann Foreman, had managed to move north of the "continual street, or a filthy strait passage, with alleys of small tenements or cottages, built, inhabited by sailors' victuallers," into the Shadwell district of London. Here, in a neighborhood known as "Sun Tavern Fields," young William lived just a stone's throw away from Shadwell Spa, whose warm sulphuric waters were used to treat the sick, as well as for its salts used by calico-printers to fix their dyes. Within this maritime hamlet, William grew up amid small shops filled with tanneries, breweries, wharves, smiths, and dozens of taverns. In fact, his own father was a rope maker, who hoped that his son would one day carry on the family tradition. It was not to be, however, for the youngster developed much different plans for his life as he grew toward adulthood.

Jonathan Foreman, Edgar's father, was born to William and Mary Foreman in the last decade of the eighteenth century, and christened on December 9, 1796. Raised in a small, overcrowded cottage with his two sisters and one brother, the youngster had exhibited a particular interest in the field of physiology early on, sometimes wandering the River Thames waterfront, discovering shells of sea urchins, fish bones, and worn out remains of dead animals. As he grew older, he avoided the pressure put upon him by his peers to join them as a "resurrection-boy," willing to disinter the recently deceased in exchange for the going rate. Children's bodies, which were sold by the inch, were worth "six shillings for the first foot, and nine [pence] per inch for all it measures more in length." During shortage of supply, adults brought between ten and twenty guineas apiece.

By the time that Jonathan Foreman had met and married his bride, Mary Ann, the twenty-four-year-old had become an up-and-coming surgeon, and the newlyweds had relocated to a well-to-do area of south London known as Pimlico. As a result of an increase in demand for property in the previously unfashionable West End following the Great Plague and the Great Fire, Pimlico had become quite ripe for new homes and young careers. In 1825, Thomas Cubitt was contracted by Lord Grosvenor to further develop the region, which, up to this time had remained a marshland. Ingeniously, he had devised a method of draining the muck by using soil excavated during the construction of Saint Katherine's Dock.

Soon, new homes began to dot the landscape. The largest and most opulent houses were raised along Saint George's Drive and Belgrave Road, the two principal streets, as well as near Eccleston, Warwick and Saint George's Squares. Lupus Street contained similarly grand houses, as well as shops and a hospital for women and children. Smaller-scale properties, typically of three stories, lined the side passages, including Ranelagh Street, where the Foreman family had come to live. A newspaper article described the best parts of the district as "genteel, sacred to professional men... not rich enough to luxuriate in Belgravia proper, but rich enough to live in private houses." Its inhabitants were "more lively than in Kensington...and yet a cut above Chelsea, which is only commercial."[2]

Jonathan Foreman and his wife, Mary Ann, seemed to fit right in with these "genteel" residents of Pimlico. The couple gave birth to their first child, a son named Frederick, in 1822. Younger brother, Edgar William, was born in the autumn of 1824, and was soon followed by Charles in 1829 and only sister, Sarah Anne, in September of 1831. Christening records indicate that each of the Foreman children were baptized in the Roman Catholic Parish of Saint George, located in Hanover Square, London, England, within a month of their births.

As young Edgar matured, he and his elder brother, Frederick, began their formal education at the local Pimlico Grammar School. Opened in 1830, it was a "handsome structure, in front of which is a well-executed portico of two Doric columns between pilasters, supporting a pediment decorated with triglyphs and dentals." Though Edgar was but six years of age, he was more than ready to attend the ominous-looking structure, located at 22 Ebury Street, just a few minutes walking distance southwest from their home. Designed for boys only, it would provide him with what was then known as a "classical education," comprised of a three-part process of training the mind. The early years of school would be spent in absorbing facts, systematically laying the foundation for advanced study. In the middle grades, Frederick and Edgar would be trained to think carefully and meticulously through arguments. And, during their high school years, they would learn to express themselves more pointedly, applying all that they had learned in their earlier years of formal education. This classical pattern was known then as the "trivium."

As time went by, Edgar's parents became increasingly concerned about the dangerous deterioration of the entire community developing around the their children:

> "There had arisen in the lower portion of the district assigned to S. Paul's, amid the marshes of Pimlico, near the Hospital and to the east of Ebury Street, a series of deplorable slums, which extended down to the river...those gardens, which in still earlier times had belonged to the Earl of Ranelagh, attracted to their nightly shows, amid fashionable sin and frivolity, the princes and nobles of the land. But in that neighbourhood most unfashionable sin and brutal degradation reigned... There the streets were rugged and but half made, undrained, unpaved. The houses were not old but already ruinous. The foul sewer, which drained half of Western London, and had been originally 'The Serpentine River,' ran, open and uncovered, full of filth of every sort down to the Thames, between starved, half-decayed trees whose branches produced leaves that could be numbered. The appropriately named 'Nell Gwynn's Court' looked down, in defiance of cholera, upon this flowing tide of abomination, and delighted in filth and foulness both of body and soul, which neither the Sanitary nor the Ecclesiastical Commissioners had been cruel enough to put to flight. The inhabitants matched, naturally enough, their surroundings. Men, women and children were half clad, without shoes, dirty, ragged, reckless. Their lot seemed so low and miserable that they were careless with despair and without power to desire to be otherwise than they were. The low lodging-houses were dens for profligates and thieves. The small beer-shops were receptacles for the veriest dregs of society. Street rows were incessant. Drink and gambling flourished. Dirty, disorderly, ill-conditioned children filled the streets. Blasphemy met the ear at every turn."[3]

In the early spring of 1838, Jonathan, Mary Anne, and their four children set sail on an twenty-three-day journey to America. Edgar's parents had had enough of the encroaching "dregs of society" and "dirty, disorderly, ill-conditioned children." They had, albeit somewhat unsuccessfully, tried vigilantly to raise them in a manner as close to upper class as they possibly could.

When they arrived in early autumn, New York City's 300,000 people resided in twenty-two distinct wards, each uniquely comprised of various cultural groups. Initially, the family moved into a home in the 17th Ward, just west of what was known as the Bowery, by far the most crowded and largest with ten percent of the city's population. Initially, it seemed, despite their hopes, the Foreman parents had not brought their children safely into the "American dream":

> "Increasingly refined sections of the city emerged in proximity to neighborhoods defined by deepening poverty. Many New Yorkers who stayed in Manhattan's lower wards as settlement spread north lived in crowded, dark apartments in buildings that were often converted churches, breweries, or single-family homes. Called rookeries, such units were precursors of the tenements that dominated working-class housing in New York later in the century. Many uptown neighborhoods developed specific residential identities, while poorer areas continued to mix commerce and residences. The result was overcrowding–and not just of humans. Horses and scavenging pigs contributed to the "messiness" of the poorer wards, and the refuse left by such animals mixed with the noxious byproducts of local tanneries, slaughterhouses, and distilleries to dirty the streets and foul the air. Human waste was collected in privies. Usually located behind or in the gaps between buildings, privies typically were shared by more than a dozen families, and almost always were overflowing. Municipal sanitation services were extremely limited, and African-American workers held the exclusive privilege of emptying privies for low wages. In summer months, the stench was overwhelming, and disease commonplace."[4]

During the late 1830s and early 1840s, Jonathan Foreman continued to practice medicine at New York City Hospital, the entrance of which was situated opposite of the termination of Pearl Street, while his wife was in charge of raising the children and making certain that they were educated properly. The elder Foreman also became active in the "Know Nothing" movement, an anti-immigrant sentiment driven by fears that the country was being overrun by Germans and Irish, who did not uphold Anglo-Saxon values. Meanwhile, Edgar William, Charles, and their younger sister, Sarah Anne, had exhibited a deep interest in art, which would develop into careers in architectural drawing. All three would attend classes and lectures at the National Academy of Design in New York City.

The decade of the 1840s brought a number of changes to the city of New York and the Foreman family. To Edgar, the town of the mid-nineteenth century must have seemed somewhat provincial–a sprawling city with few public parks, whose monotonous grid-plan and architecture were in no way comparable to London or any of the other great European capitals. True, it was growing rapidly: the great exodus from Northern Europe had begun, following the potato famine of 1845 in Ireland and the revolutions of 1848. Incredible as it seemed to old-timers, the little town of 60,000 souls of 1800 was, less than a half-century later, a sprawling metropolis of over a half-million inhabitants.

The July 30, 1850, U.S. census, as reported by Assistant Marshall, Isaac H. Brown, of the 7th Ward of New York City, New York, indicated that twenty-eight-year-old, Frederick, twenty-one-year-old, Charles, and nineteen-year-old, Sarah Anne, all lived together with their parents, along with their twelve-year-old brother, Henry, who had been born in New York just months after the Foremans had arrived. A few months earlier, Jonathan had invested a great deal of wealth in the purchase of the old Atlantic Hotel, with the idea of making his fortune in real estate. Located at 5 Broadway in lower Manhattan, the grand old mansion had once been the home of Robert Livingston, member of the Continental Congress and chancellor of New York State. Decades later, on Saturday, April 24, 1830, the *New York Evening Post* announced the mansion's transition into a place of respite for both permanent residents and travelers alike:

> "M'Neil Seymour, late of the Franklin House, New York, and formerly of the Marlborough Hotel, Boston, begs leave to inform his old friends and the public generally, that he will open a house of entertainment, on the 1st of May ensuing, at No. 5 Broadway, in the city of New York, to be called the Atlantic Hotel. The situation, being near the Battery and opposite the Bowling Green, is one of the most pleasant and eligible in the city. The house is spacious and commodious, and will be...in a style of convenience and elegance rivaling any similar establishment in New York. There will be ample accommodation for families; and every pains will be taken to render the establishment in all respects worthy the support of genteel company from every part of the Union and from abroad. From his long experience in the business, and his extensive acquaintance, the advertiser flatters himself that he shall be favored with a liberal share of public favor."[5]

When business dropped off in the early 1840s, Seymour was forced to auction all of the hotel's contents, including handmade "carpets, oil cloths, mahogany sofas, chairs...center and card tables, piano fortes, hall lanterns, astral and mantel lamps, large gaming tables," his entire assortment of bedroom furnishings, and even "a large quantity of German silver spoons and forks...kitchen furniture, including a first rate mangle."[6]

The building was sold for delinquent taxes in a chancery sale for $10,400, virtually empty, to William C. Anderson in September of 1844, only to be resold to Jonathan Foreman in the summer of 1850. Yet, ownership and operation of the grand old building proved no small task for the Foreman family, who were forced to refurnish and refurbish the ailing mansion. Possessing ninety-five feet of street frontage and measuring 180 feet deep, the brick structure was four stories high and contained no less than eighty-five rooms to outfit. The entire project took well over a year-and-a-half and, when completed, Jonathan had invested $65,000 in purchasing the structure, $25,000 for adequate furnishings, and a good deal more to renovate its interior. Still, as advertised, soon enough he was ready for business:

> "Atlantic Hotel, No. 5 Broadway, opposite the fountain–This old and favorite hotel, having been entirely refurbished in every department, is now ready to receive families and gentlemen for the winter…J. Foreman"[7]

To Edgar, the Atlantic Hotel and all of Broadway represented the living symbol of America, the "open road" later described by Walt Whitman, along which streamed the vast procession of humanity. Once known as "Great George Street," which it was called until long after the War for Freedom, the thoroughfare was already over two miles long, extending from Bowling Green to Union Square. When Grace Church was begun in 1843, it would stand at the "head" of the street, for it was then assumed that Broadway would not extend much above Tenth Street. Gradually, however, it would look down upon a city rushing far beyond it, reaching out into places where "a few years since cattle grazed, and orchards dropped their ripened fruits."[8]

Even before his father opened the hotel for business, however, twenty-six-year-old, Edgar had struck out on his own, renting a room at a boarding house in Brooklyn, New York, owned by sisters, Jane and Anna Long. Unlike the posh residential district that he was accustomed to down in lower Manhattan, this was a working-class area nestled against the opposite side of the East River waterfront. Some of the worst slums in New York City stood here, within a stone's throw of City Hall and the offices of the major metropolitan newspapers. As in other parts of the city, people like Edgar, who filled the tenements and boarding houses, struggled with a host of problems brought on by rapid urban growth and industrialization. Some managed to cope, while others did not.

Edgar found work as a freelance architect and artist, earning additional income peddling his own drawings, as well as the work of others, at the firm of Jones and Newman. At this point in his seemingly undetermined career, he was competing with a growing number of young men producing numerous drawings and lithographs, greatly demanded by a growing publications industry attempting to satisfy the interests of a public eager for more visual illustrations of the world. In early 1847, he completed a tinted lithograph, signed in the lower left corner, depicting the Rainbow Coffee House at 27 Beekman Street, between Nassau and William streets. It proudly advertised for the proprietor, William Foreman, a full menu of lunches and dinners. Furthermore, it stated:

> "The Subscriber, having become Proprietor of the above well known House, takes this opportunity of ensuring the Patrons of the establishment and the public in general that every effort will be made to render the Rainbow one of the most popular places of resort in the City. The House is filled up with all the modern improvements–Hot, Cold, and Shower Baths. Rtc. The Lodging Rooms are all a good size, and neatly furnished,

and will be let to respectable Gentlemen at such prices as cannot fail to give satisfaction. Robinson's Celebrated Ale, brewed expressly for the Rainbow, will still maintain its preeminence, and the Eating department will be of the best kind. The principal journals of the Old Country, together with the City papers, will be found on the tables..."[9]

Lithograph, *Rainbow Coffee House*, by Edgar William Foreman

As early as 1848, for twenty-five cents per copy, Jones and Newman offered a small number of Foreman originals, promoted as a "Pictorial Directory of New York, exhibiting a...series of colored elevations, of all the dwellings, stores, and public buildings fronting on the principal streets, beginning with Broadway, the chief of all."[10]

On May 31, 1848, an advertising seeking canvassing appeared in the *New York Daily Tribune*:

"A Rare Chance–several enterprising, active young men, of genteel address, are wanted, as canvassing agents, for an important interesting work of art, just published. Enquire of E.W. Foreman, at the lithographic establishment of Jones & Newman, 128 Fulton Street, upstairs."[11]

Later that summer, Edgar William joined forces with fellow artist, Eliphalet M. Brown, Jr., to produce a piece of work known as *New York and Environs, from Williamsburg*. It was a chromolithograph exhibiting Brown's figure drawing talent and Foreman's coloration skills. At the time, Brown was working with his brother, James, in a small, but successful, studio on Broadway. Together, the men were on friendly terms with the likes of Samuel Morse and Napoleon III, apparently traveling in influential circles. Still, they continued to work locally with Jones and Newman, as well as Currier and Ives and Matthew Brady, producing demographic portraits and marine lithographs.

New York and Environs from Williamsburg, by Foreman & Brown

From Edgar's and Eliphalet's depicted vantage point of "New York and Environs," one was able to see sections of both the East and Hudson Rivers, the famed United States Navy Yard (housed at the old Wallabout), every settled Manhattan neighborhood covering the areas of lower Manhattan to Murray Hill, and even traces of the New Jersey shoreline. What is more significant in the drawing's detail was that the artists managed to capture nearly every kind of ship in operation during the 1840s, including steamboats, three-masted war vessels, and recreational sail boats. Perhaps most notable is the work's inclusion of both brick and brownstone buildings, particularly since 1848 marked a year when the latter type of structure was becoming increasingly popular among extremely wealthy property owners.

For Edgar, artwork barely paid the bills. Always thinking of inventive ways to find wealth, he had developed an updated design of his submersible craft, which he often bragged "might be used to salvage sunken vessels and harvest pearls." Yet, though the concept seemed sound, he still had not secured the means to build such an innovative craft. It was at this point in his life, however, that good luck shined down upon him, for in the spring of 1851, Henry Beaufort Sears came to the Foreman hotel, hoping to rent a room. Aware of his son's aspirations, Jonathan introduced the two young men, and they became instant friends and eventual business partners.

Henry Beaufort Sears, then an enterprising merchant, came from a long line of European Sears surnames, most likely from Holland, though definitive lineage cannot be established. Still, his great-great-great-great-great-grandfather, Richard Sears, who was born in about 1590 in Amsterdam, Netherlands, first appeared in New England colonial history with the mention of his name in the records of the Plymouth colony tax list of 1633, when he was one of forty-four persons there assessed nine shillings in corn at six shillings per bushel. From Plymouth, he seems to have crossed over to Marblehead, Massachusetts, and was taxed there, as shown by the Salem list, in 1637 and 1638. He also had a grant of four acres of land "where he had formerly planted," from which it appears that he may have been in that plantation at some previous time.

In 1639, Richard Sears joined the colonists under Anthony Thacher and traveled to Cape Cod, where the group founded the town of Yarmouth. His first home was built on Quivet Neck, and afterwards he built a second house a short distance to the northwest. In 1643, the name of Richard Sears appears once again in the list of inhabitants of Yarmouth "liable to bear arms." Records further indicate that he was made freeman in 1652, grand juror in 1652, took the oath of allegiance and fidelity in 1653, was constable in 1660, and representative to the court in Plymouth in 1662. Along the way, Richard had married Dorothy Jones, sister of Anthony Thacher's second wife, Elizabeth, and had given birth to three sons–Knyvet, Paul, and Sylas–and one daughter, Deborah (Paddock).

Still, it is not certain that Dorothy Sears was his only wife, or the mother of all–or even any–of his children. Indeed, there is some discrepancy indicating that he was previously married, and that all of his children may have been born of a former wife. Eventually, in 1664, seventy-five-year-old Richard purchased, for twenty pounds from "Allis, widow of Governor William Bradford," a tract of land at Sesuit. It was here that he lived out the remainder of his life with his aging wife, until his death in August of 1676.

The Sears family lineage can be followed through Captain Paul Sears, son of the aforementioned Richard, to Samuel, then Judah, and on to Henry Beaufort's great-grandfather, David. After marching with Captain Seth Brigg's company at Lexington, David settled down with his second wife, Susannah (Handy), in Rochester, Massachusetts, where they would raise their children, Prince, Susannah, Alice, Acsah, and David Jr.

Prince Sears, Henry's grandfather, moved twenty miles northwest of Rochester to Taunton, Bristol County, Massachusetts, in 1793, where he married Sally Tucker on April 20 of that year. Jonathan Prince Sears, Henry' father, was born there on April 23, 1797. Within just six months, Jonathan's father, died, leaving his mother all alone to raise the newborn baby, along with his older sister, Sally. The day before his twenty-fifth birthday, on April 22, 1822, he was married to Nancy H. Francis by Reverend Bartlett Pease at Dighton,

Bristol County, Massachusetts. During the next half-dozen years, they would give birth to a son, Henry Beaufort, and two daughters, Francis Everett and Elvira FitzAlan.

Henry Beaufort was born on May 24, 1825, and grew to maturity amid a colonial industry that had developed along the Three Mile River, in a house constructed in the Westville section. During the Federal Period, from 1775 to the time of his birth in 1825, Taunton had been characterized by the dominance of iron manufacturing, exploiting the natural resource found in the nearby bogs. This industrial growth brought skilled ironworkers from England and Scotland who helped to introduce the use of bituminous coal to the iron manufacturing process. In 1800, local manufacturers were shipping more than eight hundred tons of ironware and seven hundred tons of rails to various larger ports along the eastern seaboard annually. The introduction of large stone cotton mills ushered in a new era for Taunton along the Three Mile in the early 1800's.

Jonathan and Nancy Sears raised there three children with strong religious morals, attending the nearby Westville Congregational Church, which had been constructed the year prior to Henry's birth. The elder Sears was "a successful merchant, and his children were given an appropriate education at a schoolhouse, which was within walking distance on Worcester Street.

Less than two months after his eighteenth birthday, on July 1, 1842, Henry began his training at the West Point Military Academy as a cadet. Among his illustrious classmates were George B. McClellan, Thomas J. "Stonewall" Jackson, Nelson Davis, and George Pickett. When all fifty-eight graduated four years later, most were promoted to the army just in time to take part in the war with Mexico. Prior to serving his country, however, Henry married fifteen-year-old, Harriet Louiza Clitz, on October 6, 1846, in New York City.

Reaching the rank of Second Lieutenant, Sears took part in a twenty-day battle at the primary Mexican beachhead seaport of Vera Cruz in March of 1847. Unquestionably the strongest fortress in the entire Western hemisphere at the time, boasting a Mexican garrison of 4,390 men defending forts Santiago, Concepción, and San Juan de Ulúa, the entire battalion was under the command of Brigadier General Juan Esteban Morales. Following heavy bombardment from U.S. forces, all Mexican troops surrendered. The U.S. had suffered minimal casualties, with only thirteen deaths.

Following the Defense of Convoy at Paso de Ovejas on August 10, 1847, the National Bridge on August 12, and Cerro Gordo on August 15, Sears was promoted to the rank of Brevet First Lieutenant for "gallant and meritorious conduct in several affairs with guerrilleros." After seeing action at Las Animas, serving as Division Quartermaster at Huamantla, and fighting at Atlixco, the war came to an abrupt and unexpected end. Afterward, Sears served as the Division Acting Assistant Adjutant-General in Washington, D.C., and at Fort Macon, North Carolina, from December 8, 1848, before turning in his resignation from active duty on June 30, 1849. For the remainder of his life he would be known as "Major" Sears, though his highest military rank was Second Lieutenant. This was, in all likelihood, more of a self-promotion than an actual title.

The July 15, 1850, U.S. census, as reported by Assistant Marshall, Stephen Angar, indicates that twenty-six-year-old Henry resided with his eighteen-year-old wife, Harriet, and their one-year-old daughter, Ella, in the West Ward of Newark, New Jersey. Living with them was his fifty-seven-year-old mother, Nancy, and twenty-eight-year-old youngest sister, Elvira. Later that year, Henry Sears moved his entire extended family to the Atlantic Hotel, owned by Jonathan Foreman, who continued working on its renovation and was not yet ready for its grand opening. However, he respected and liked Henry and his family so much that he agreed to allow them the priviledge of moving in ahead of schedule.

Often, throughout 1852, as Edgar William Foreman and Henry Beaufort Sears relaxed in each others company during the evening hours, their conversation would turn to Edgar's idea for the construction of a submersible bell that could be utilized to salvage lost cargo from sunken vessels. Intrigued, and knowing that the only thing that the young inventor lacked was adequate funding, Henry suggested that he could provide the financial backing. Agreeing to the arrangement, the partners set about finding and hiring the ideal iron works to put the concept into concrete form.

Edgar Foreman and Henry Sears began the construction phase of the submersible in February of 1852, building what the latter would refer to as a "model successfully constructed to exemplify the principle" of the Foreman diving bell. As earlier agreed, Henry provided the capital and early marketing scheme, while Edgar provided the brains. Interestingly, their version of a submersible would be one of the first to incorporate compressed air and water ballast chambers, as well as the ability to move itself below the surface.

Yet, tragedy struck on Thursday, July 8, 1852, seemingly putting an abrupt end to Edgar and Henry's diving experiments:

> "Edgar W. Foreman was drowned while bathing in Long Island Sound, near New-Rochelle, on Thursday, the 8th last, in the 27th year of his age. Mr, Foreman was a young gentleman of rare genius, fine attainments, prepossessing manners and amiable disposition, and the announcement of his departure to the land of spirits will shock a large circle of attached friends in this City. Mr. F. was bathing with a party, and venturing out farther from the shore than any of the others, with his bathing-dress on, dove into deep water, soon after which he rose to the surface and made a feeble effort to swim, but almost immediately sunk from the sight of his bewildered and agonized friends. His lifeless body was recovered after an hour's search. Mr. Foreman was a good swimmer, and his singular death can only be accounted for on the supposition that he was suddenly taken with cramp in his limbs or with a fit. Previous to his death, Mr. F. was engaged in carrying forward some interesting experiments with the diving bell, and in addition to bringing sorrow to the hearts of his many devoted friends, his death may prove a serious loss to science."[12]

Among the onlookers who stood helpless on shore was his friend and business partner, Henry B. Sears, who had "loved the deceased as an own brother."

Edgar was buried in the Trinity Church Yard on Boston Post Road, known locally as the "Huguenot Burying Ground." He was laid to rest not only among the community's most prominent French Calvinistic founders, but common "merchants, seamen, editors, social activists and members of the clergy." On his granite tombstone was inscribed this simple message:

"Edgar William Foreman, d. 8 July 1852, in his 27th yr. Son of Jonathan Foreman and Mary Anne"[13]

Henry B. Sears knew that work on the diving machine should go on, if not only for the sake of science, but in honor of his deceased partner. Meanwhile, he also attempted to follow his attorney's advice in arranging a legal agreement addressing ownership of the craft's design, though Foreman family members seemed not to offer their full trust and confidence in him.

Improvement of the submersible continued without Foreman's expertise, and it wasn't long before Sears became involved in a major salvage operation. On August 12, 1852, just over one month after his partner had been buried, a group of passengers had boarded the steamer *Atlantic*. Mastered by Captain Pettey, the ship departed from Buffalo, New York, bound for Detroit later that evening. The total number of passengers was 576, comprising 132 Norwegian immigrants, a number of Germans, and the rest Americans. About two o'clock in the morning of August 20, while the majority of passengers slept, the *Atlantic* collided with the *Ogdensburg*. One survivor offered the following chilling details:

"I left Valders, Norway, April 5th, 1852, with my wife and two children— Ole a son by my first wife and Gunil, a daughter by my living wife. It was fortunate for us that we had no knowledge of the danger and adversity that were to meet us on our way, otherwise we should hardly have started on the trip. Already on the second day we were met by an omen of ill-indication for a safe journey; namely, the ship that was to carry us had already gone. Before another ship came, nine weeks had passed… A large number of people and goods of every description were now crowded together onto a large boat called the *Atlantic* and at eleven o'clock it moved off on Lake Erie. There were many people and all wanted to find a place to sleep. As many as found room went down into the cabins, but many had to prepare their beds upon the deck. I, and my family, were among the latter. The deck was crowded with every conceivable thing: baggage, new wagons, and much other stuff. So we lay down to rest but sleep was not of long duration. When it was near midnight we were awakened by a loud crash and saw a large beam fall down upon a Norwegian woman of our company. It crushed several bones and completely tore the head off a little baby that lay at her side. Another ship had collided with ours and knocked a large hole in the side of the *Atlantic* so that a flood of water rushed into the cabins and people came up as thick and fast as they could crowd themselves. It seemed as if even the wrath of the Almighty had a hand in the destruction. The sailors became absolutely raving and tried to get as many killed as possible. When they saw that people crowded up they struck them on the heads and shoulders to drive them down again. When this did not help, they took and raised the stairway up on end so the people fell down backwards again. Then they jerked the ladder up on the deck. All hopes were gone for those that were underneath... People rushed frantically from one end of the boat to the other. The trap doors were torn open and goods and people were swept into the water... My wife and children and I were miraculously saved; although swept into the water as the ship sank, with much swimming around with my wife and children on my back, we were picked up by the other ship. When I discovered that all of my family were alive, I was full of joy, as if I had become the richest man in the world, despite the fact that we had lost all of our goods."[14]

Local papers wrote first-hand accounts of the disaster, which were republished as far away as Philadelphia, Boston, Chicago, Detroit, and New York. Estimates put the dead at more than 500, many of whom remained trapped aboard the sunken vessel. Within days, Henry B. Sears learned that her sinking was no mere accident:

"The *Atlantic* sailed out from Buffalo in the evening at eleven o'clock and to sight the Propeller *Ogdensburg* that belonged to a competitive company. Between these there was a bitter enmity and the captain of the *Atlantic* became desirous of running over the *Ogdensburg* and sinking it. All the lights were turned out so that the act of running down the rival company's boat would be unnoticed. At the last moment the *Ogdensburg* had time to turn hastily aside to escape the *Atlantic* and advanced a short distance, but in anger at this attack, the *Ogdensburg* turned and with a mighty spring, pushed a big hole in the *Atlantic*'s side so that the water soon caused the boat to sink. The loss of life is estimated at about 300, of whom 60 were Norwegians. A trial of the officers of each ship was held with the result that the *Atlantic* was blamed for the misfortune. Mr. Pettey, the captain of the *Atlantic*, was arrested and taken to Milwaukee..."[15]

Almost immediately, Sears forwarded a written proposal to the owner of the sunken vessel, Eber Brock Ward, the "steamship king of the Great Lakes" and Detroit, Michigan's, first millionaire. Sears offered to use his diving vessel to salvage both bodies and valuables of the sunken ship. His was not the only such salvage offer. Details appears in a number of publications, including the *Syracuse New York Daily Journal*:

"Mr. Sears, of New York, one of the gentlemen who forwarded to Mr. Ward, the owner of the *Atlantic*, a proposition to raise the wreck of that boat, is the inventor and patentee of a new and apparently a very scientific machine adapted to such labor. The machine, by which he proposes to raise the wreck, is an improved Diving Bell, by which he is enabled to descend in any depth of water and to work in from twenty-five to thirty fathoms. It is so arranged internally that by the mere turning of a valve it commences and continues its descent to the bottom. It there affords free communication with any object there situated. While submerged it can be freely moved in any direction either in still water or in the strongest currents, so by its use the entire bed of a river may be explored from its source to its mouth. When desired, by turning a valve, it commences its ascent. There is no suspension from above, but the machine is perfectly independent in its action. It is the joint invention of Mr. H.B. Sears and E.W. Foreman, late of New York..."[16]

Portrait of Eber Brock Ward, owner of the sunken *Atlantic*

Henry Sears threw himself into his work on completing his diving bell, attempting to be the first to reach the ill-fated *Atlantic*. The concept of clearing obstacles for the building of bridges or running salvaging operations of sunken vessels was not new, but in the era of sails, unless the ship foundered on shore or in very shallow water, there was little chance of retrieving anything from the wreck. Inland rivers and lakes had far less depth, but if a boat were lost in deep water—as was the *Atlantic*—it was believed that the hulk and its contents would typically lay there for eternity. For want of wealth—and not humanistic concerns—Henry Beaufort Sears was determined not to allow that to happen in this particular case.

By 1850, sunken vessel were nearly in every North American waterway, up and down the inland rivers and tributaries, either obstructing passage or hiding treasure. Without the ability to disinter them—like the grave robbers of London and New York—from their watery graves, the old boats remained as a constant reminder of the typical fate of seafaring men. They also harbored ghosts, if Mark Twain is to be believed:

> "More than one grave watchman has sworn to me that on drizzly, dismal nights, he has glanced fearfully down that forgotten river as he passed the head of the island, and seen the faint glow of the spectre steamer's lights drifting through the distant gloom, and heard the muffled cough of her 'scape-pipes and the plaintive cry of her leadsmen."[17]

The diving bell had been utilized for salvage operations in America as early as 1838 by William Thomas of St. Louis, but its improvement was attributed to James Buchanan Eads. Going from clerk to inventor, he had adapted the submersible, and went into business for himself in 1842. Constructing what he called "bell boats," bearing the name *Sub-marine*, he was extremely successful at retrieving sunken hulks.

Insurance companies immediately realized the value of Eads' work, and put large amounts of coverage on all covered boats. Like treasure hunters, salvage companies received a portion of what they recovered, ranging from twenty to seventy-five percent. Sadly, this was not the case for the *Atlantic*, which was totally uninsured. Still, there were a number of interested parties willing to pay a great deal of money to the man that could successfully recovered valuable machinery, as well as treasure, from the sunken vessel. Without question, this would nor be an easy task:

> "The wreck lies four miles above Long Point, and three miles from lake shore. She is in twenty-seven and a half fathoms of water; her upper deck being twenty-one and a half fathoms below the surface. A small schooner is moored over her, with signal lights at her masthead..."[18]

After thoroughly demonstrating his diving bell concept, however, the owner of the sunken *Atlantic* opted to hire another team of divers to salvage his vessel. All efforts would fail for the time being, and it would be more than twenty years before she was raised.

Just weeks after returning from Lake Erie, a detailed application for the *Nautilus* Diving Bell, as the Foreman and Sears invention was called, was submitted to the U.S. Patent Office. As agreed to by his dead partner's parents, it named Edgar as the inventor, his father, Jonathan, as the administrator of his deceased son's invention, and Henry B. Sears as the legal "assignor." In general terms, the description provided presented an overview of the vessel's primary construction and mode of operation:

> "This invention is intended for effecting exploration and other operations below the surface of water, and is in that respect analogons to other machines devised for the same purpose. The nature of this invention consists in so combining with a reservoir of condensed or compressed air at the surface, and in connection with the diving chamber, an arrangement of sliding blocks or movable pulleys attached to an anchor and the diving chamber that motion and direction may be given to the diving chamber..."[19]

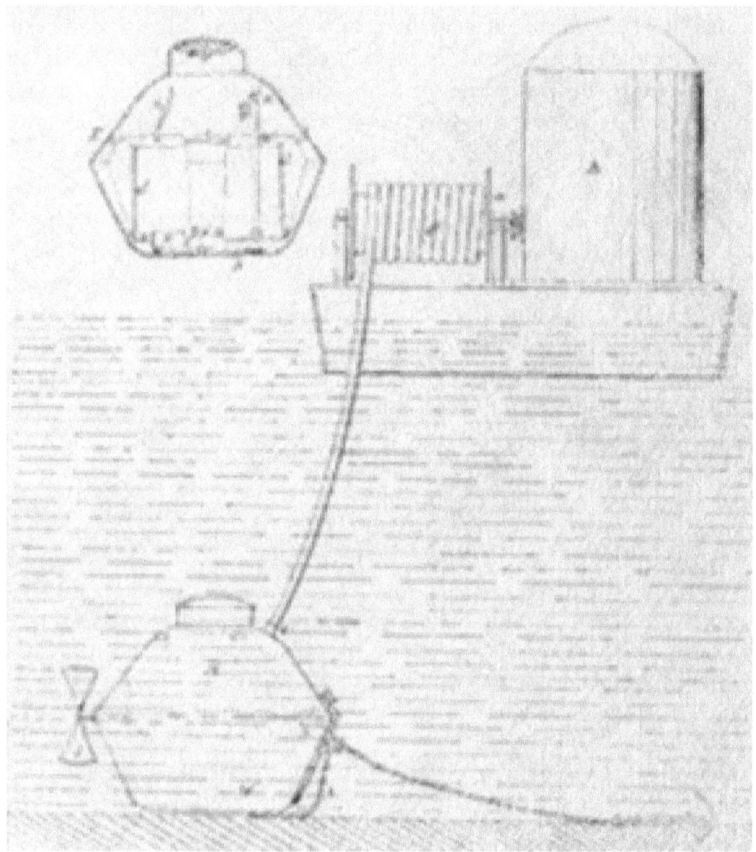

Patent drawing of the Foreman and Sears diving bell, *Nautilus*

The outer shell of chamber of the vessel itself was in the shape of to bowls, or cones, one flipped upside-down on top of the other and joined at the rims. At the upper-most portion of the vessel was a manhole opening, where workmen could enter prior to submersion and seal the opening with bolts from inside. At their feet was a similar manhole encircled by a rim, or lip, which could also be sealed and unsealed by bolts from within. The use of the rim was "to retain within the vessel any object the explorers may take in through the bottom," as well as "to keep in place the ballast which, for convenience, is arranged here forming a seat for the divers."[20]

Around the lower sides of the chamber were a series of both air and water reservoirs for "regulating the gravity" of the *Nautilus*. Each tank was connected to the next by two sets of pipes—one for supplying air and the other for pumping water in and out. The air supply came via a flexible India rubber tube connected to a large tank at the surface of the water, either by "shore or supported by means of a boat or float," which regulated the buoyancy of the vessel. A second flexible air tube extending to the outside of the craft could be attached to "one or more divers operating with armor exterior to the diving chamber," with these workmen "regulating their own supply of air and obviating the necessity of a pump at (the) surface." Finally, both the inside tanks and exterior armor could expel or discharge used oxygen when needed.

Outside the *Nautilus* was "an arrangement for anchoring it to the bottom of the river for holding it in place or to afford the means of shifting its position." The chain leading to the anchor could be reeled in or out, depending on what might be needed, thus allowing the vessel to be held firmly to the bottom or to float upward a few feet. On the opposite side of the *Nautilus* was what was described as a "propeller rudder" fashioned from a "common screw, fixed upon a shaft passing through (the hull)...having a crank to revolve it." This would allow operators from within to propel the craft in "a certain arc in various directions, (with) the anchor forming the center point."[21]

After describing quite specifically how the *Nautilus* was constructed, the patent application then detailed its general operations while in use:

> "The diving chamber floating upon the surface of the water is anchored so as to stand over the bed of the wreck or other object to be explored, as nearly as may be. The reservoir is then charged by means of an air pump with as much air as may be necessary according to the depth to be attained. The flexible tube is attached (and) the workmen enter with such tools as they require and the top is shut down and fastened. The tanks at first contain only air at the pressure of one atmosphere, the cock is...opened (allowing) water to flow into the tanks and force the air out, which decreases the buoyancy of (Nautilus) so much that it sinks. As the chamber descends, the (second) cock is opened, so far as to allow a sufficient amount of air to be sent in from the reservoir to supply the inhalation, and also to counterbalance the pressure of the water outside for the ascertaining of which proper gages [sic] may be employed. The

specific gravity of the vessel may be regulated for any depth of water it is to go to, by properly proportioning the water and air in the tanks so that it may be held in suspension at any depth the operators may please; the up and down motions are thus effected. The traversing motion along the bottom is by means of the anchor and rudder... As soon as the chamber is over the proper spot, the cover to the (bottom) hole is taken off, the water being kept back by the pressure of air from within. The workmen can then operate."[22]

While the craft was submerged, light could be admitted to the inside by way of heavy plate glass panels, or "bull's-eyes," inserted into the top and sides of the hull. When the salvage work had been completed, the bottom manhole would be resealed from within, and the vessel would be forced to rise to the surface once again by simply "emptying the tanks of water and filling them with air." The patent was officially approved as number 9,965 on August 23, 1853.

In September of 1853, the *New York Tribune* provided a great deal of detail about the submersible already being tested at the Brooklyn Navy Yard:

"The machinery of the 'Nautilus Submarine Company,' experimented with on Wednesday at the Navy Yard, was invented nearly two years since by Mr. E. W. Foreman and Mr. H. B. Sears. In its earliest developments, Mr. Foreman, a gentleman of great promise, died, and the machine was perfected, and introduced by Mr. Sears, the Superintendent of the Company. The machine is of peculiar contraction, being in fact a mechanical nautilus, having the power of ascent and descent at will, entirely independent of suspension. In connection with the machine at the surface, is a reservoir of condensed air, which, according to depth of water, may contain from 20 to 120 pounds pressure of air to the square inch. This compression is produced by a powerful pump capable of throwing 4,000 cubic feet air per hour. By an interior arrangement of tanks, etc., a variable buoyancy may be given to the machine; capable of lifting weights of ten or more tons; it can be held in suspension at any point of ascent or descent, thus allowing stones to be raised clear from the bottom, then transported and deposited in any precise spot; movement being effected in any direction whatever by a series of three cables and anchors worked from the inside, ascent and descent are effected in a most rapid manner. This facility of descent, change of buoyancy and power of movement under water, render this machine of great value for all sub-marine purposes. The whole bed of a river may be explored from bank to bank–treasure, pearl shells, corals, sponges, and all products under water may be easily gathered and sent to the surface without requiring the machine to rise to the surface. Foundations of piers may be prepared and then built upon, obviating all crane work for raising and lowering stone, as all work of lifting, transporting, and depositing is done by the machine itself..."[23]

The news article went on to explain that the *Naulitus* could also be instrumental in salvage work of sunken vessels by actually attaching lengthy straps to their wooden hulls and "raising them by applying points of support directly to the timbers of the ship."

Meanwhile, trying to get over the tragedy of Edgar's death and attempting to commemorate his life, his sister, Sarah Ann, carried on his earlier interest in architectural art and linear drawing. She enrolled in coursework at the National Academy, becoming quite talented both artistically and architecturally in her own right. During the time spent at the Academy, in late 1853 and the early months of 1854, Sarah befriended Jacob D. Blondel, who maintained a small studio of his work near the Foreman home. Through him she also became acquainted with James Henry Cafferty, founder of the New York Sketch Club and occasional book illustrator, who supplemented his meager income by peddling artists' supplies to classmates at the Academy. Yet, Sarah's closest friendship was with portraitist Theresa Heller, who lived quietly with fellow artist, Joseph Vollmering. Though the two would later claim to be legally married, they seldom associated with others outside their close circle of friends at the Academy.

In the early summer of 1854, in response to a newspaper advertisement seeking classroom instructors, Sarah traveled from her parents' home in New York City to the growing midwestern community of Sandusky, Ohio. The ad had been placed in a number of publications by architect Sheldon Smith, principal of Smith's Commercial College and Academy of Design. Walking confidently up the three flights of stairs to his office in the Romanesque Revival limestone and sandstone building, which stood on the corner of Columbus Avenue and Water Street, Sarah interviewed for the position as a teacher of painting and linear drawing. Smith, who had brought his family to the northern Ohio community in 1853, must have liked what he saw in the young, vivacious lady, for he hired her almost immediately.

Although Sheldon Smith was the primary designer and architect, he would often collaborate with a number of his teachers–including Sarah–on building design projects. In the summer of 1854, for example, he designed and constructed a Gothic Revival style, mastic covered home att 334 East Washington Street in Sandusky for the proprietors of the Exchange Hotel. Other projects credited to Smith and his proteges included entire commercial blocks built for Hector Kilbourne, a Freemason and surveyor who had laid out the original plat map for the city of Sandusky.

During her first year as a classroom instructor, Sarah Foreman happened to meet German-born Philip Willner, a handsome, blue-eyed, black-haired, twenty-six-year-old professor of both music and Romantic languages. The couple was immediately enamored with one another, and they were married in the summer of 1855. The newlyweds decided to take an extended European vacation and honeymoon abroad. Philip, however, had difficulty securing a proper passport, and wrote a follow-up letter to his original application, addressing it directly to William L. Marcy, Secretary of State, in Washington, D.C.:

"Hon. Sir...About two months ago I sent to the Department of State (under your address) my naturalization documents with a full description of my person for the purpose of having a passport for Europe issued me, but to this time my humble request has not been complied with. As I am soon to take my departure you would greatly oblige me by having the passport submitted to me at the earliest convenience. I omitted to state in my first letter that a lady will accompany me, which I assume ought to be mentioned in the passport. Your obediently, Sandusky, Ohio, June 15, 1855, Philip Willner."[24]

Heavy with unborn child, Sarah and Philip set sail from London, England via first-class steerage for the three- to four-week return journey to New York City and the home of her parents, hoping to arrive before the baby's expected birth:

"The steerage occupied the whole of the 'tween decks. Single and double and upper and lower berths were arranged all around the sides of the ship. As far as possible, families were placed together and the women passengers given all the privacy possible in the limited space available. The steerage was reached by ladders at the fore and main hatches, which were always open except in bad weather, and ventilators through the deck and a wind sail or two furnished the fresh air to the steerage. Should weather become stormy and the sea heavy the hatches were closed and the poor emigrants had to make the best of their surroundings until the weather moderated."[25]

Tragically, Sarah would not live long enough to raise a family. On May 2, 1856, during their journey home from British-controlled Madras, Chennai, India, aboard the packet ship *Devonshire*, she died of small pox. Local New York newspapers reported the sad and unexpected circumstances surrounding the twenty-four-year-old's death:

"At sea, on board the ship *Devonshire*, on the passage home, on Friday, May 2, Sara Foreman Willner, the beloved wife of Phillip Willner, and only daughter of Jonathan and Mary Anne Foreman, of this city. Her remains were solemnly committed to the deep."[26]

Devastated by the loss of one of his fondest teachers—and frustrated by the slow, ongoing construction of one of his most cherished projects—Sheldon Smith left Sandusky and moved his family northward, to Detroit, Michigan. Meanwhile, widower Phillip Willner was forced to pick up the pieces of his shattered life. Within a year-and-a-half, he had been remarried, relocated to Newton, Massachusetts, and been hired as a professor of German at the Pemberton Square English and French School for Young Ladies in nearby Boston. Until his death at the age of eighty-seven on the day after Christmas in 1915, he would stay in close contact with the Foreman family, always remembering the unexpected passing of his beloved first wife and their unborn child, which was to be named "Edgar" in honor of Sarah's deceased brother.

Sketch of Captain Henry Lewis Tibbals, who tested the *Nautilus* for safety

Throughout much of 1855, Henry B. Sears had been employed as a consulting engineer for the Philadelphia, Wilmington and Baltimore Railroad, during the planning stages of constructing a bridge across the Susquehanna River. Since April of 1836, the railroad company had used a train ferry operation to transport railroad cars over the Susquehanna from one side to the other. It was hoped that the project would one day span the 3,270 feet across the waterway, connecting Havre de Grace, Maryland, on the west bank with Perryville,

Maryland, on the east. It was Sears' belief that his *Nautilus* could accomplish a good deal of the rock moving work necessary to complete the expansive bridge. He chose a well-respected seaman, Captain Henry Lewis Tibbals, to test his newest iron diving bell, *Nautilus*, for the Havre de Grace bridge project across the Susquehanna River.

The stories about Captain Tibbals' diving bell adventures are impossible to corroborate, though historical evidence indicates that he had personal intimate knowledge of such dives. We also know that he was born in Middleton, Connecticut, on December 18, 1829, spending most of his boyhood at sea. At ten he was a cabin boy on a brig, a job that paid him seven dollars a month. By the age of twenty he had become a master sailor of another brig on a voyage to the West Indies. Writer James McCurdy states:

> "His later voyages involved carrying a cargo of railway iron for the pre-canal railroad crossing of the isthmus of Panama and testing the first diving bell in the United States, which led him to Mexico, where he was granted the salvage rights to the Spanish ship *San Pedro* by Governor General Santa Anna. The frigate had blown up in Mexican waters in 1814 with a cargo containing three million dollars in silver. Using the diving bell, Tibbals dove in one hundred feet of water and retrieved sixty-eight thousand dollars before a change in the Mexican government halted the operation. He then traveled to Panama and Acapulco, where he dove for pearls."[27]

After thoroughly inspecting the *Nautilus*, Tibbals gave it a resounding stamp of approval, and the bell was used in successfully building the bridge abutments.

In December of 1855, Henry B. Sears was a keynote speaker at a meeting held before the New York Geographical Society on the subject of "sub-marine exploration." He offered his attentive audience a general overview of diving bell history, discussing the improvements of the *Nautilus* design. By then, he had not just one *Nautilus*, but a fleet, which he claimed were valuable to both "the naturalist and the commercial world." He further explained his submersibles' primary advantage over all others being "that in using it, reservoirs of condensed air are employed...(that) remain on the surface of the water, where they are anchored..." Over time, Sears continued to garner widespread publicity, although he had yet to land that large salvaging contract that he had so stubbornly pursued for so long.

As time passed the *Nautilus* was receiving more and more attention from the media. Promoted as both a type of salvaging vessel and a pearl-harvesting craft, those interested in commercial development also saw the *Nautilus* as an inexpensive way to deepen the shallow portions of the obstructed Atlantic Dock. Situated in South Brooklyn, near the South Ferry, facing what was called Butter Milk Channel, the landing area offered Brooklyn a clear advantage over Manhattan commercial shipping. When completed, in fact, the Docks–inspired by the great London and Liverpool Docks in England–were magnificent, with over forty acres of basin protected on all sides against winds, huge grain elevators, and hundreds of warehouses with safe on and off loading at water's edge. As a promotional piece pointed out, "insurance can be effected at lower rates here, than on the New York side," and access to Manhattan was relatively easy: "The direct communications to, and from these Warehouses, is by the New Ferry from the foot of Hamilton Avenue...and requires but twelve to fifteen minutes to go from the Atlantic Docks to the Custom House, the Banks, and Exchange on Wall Street."[28]

Yet, everyone knew that the Butter Milk Channel had earned its name from a group of dairy farmers who, in years past, would cross the treacherous narrows by boat to sell their milk to Manhattan markets. Tidal currents in the channel were notoriously strong–strong enough, some said, "to churn the milk into butter." After the opening of the Erie Canal, cargo ships literally jammed all New York ports, and developers had recently determined that further dredging of the Butter Milk Channel was necessary, reasoning that deeper equaled less churning. It was with this in mind, in the middle of this "mile-long tidal strait between Brooklyn and Governors Island," that Henry Sears conducted public demonstrations of the *Nautilus*:

> "Yesterday at the Atlantic Dock, Brooklyn, on board the bark *Emily Banning*, some interesting experiments were made with one of the *Nautilus* Machines recently invented by Major Henry B. Sears, formerly of the U.S. Army. A large number of distinguished ship-builders, engineers, and several scientific public men were present. The machine with which the experiments were to be made, was in readiness at the hour appointed. It was lying in the water, a short distance from the *Emily Banning*. Its copper-covered summit appeared above the surface. By means of a rope attached, the machine was soon brought close beside the bark, and the top or 'man hole' being opened, preparations were made for a descent. Four gentlemen present joined the inventor in the first descent. Other descents were subsequently made, in which nearly all the party participated. The machine used would accommodate twelve. After witnessing the safe return of several parties, our reporter felt no hesitancy in adding himself to the number of daring voyagers. Descending through the 'man hole,' he found himself within an enclosure some twelve feet by ten in dimensions, elliptical in shape, completely air-tight, with a few circular windows at top, the whole neatly painted, and an abundance of bars and bolts, evidently endeavoring to give the utmost evidence possible of security. Thermometers, gauges, screw levers and other implements for use presented themselves in abundance. Communicating with the outside was an air tube and a speaking trumpet. A body of air was first let in, the density being increased or diminished at will, according to necessity, from the use of reservoirs of condensed air. A sensation of pressure is first felt on the drum of the ear by the ingress of air, but is only temporary. The descent was begun by touching a valve. The rapidity, or slowness, or depth of descent was shown as being entirely under the control of those having

charge of the machine. The direction of the machine in any given course was also shown as being subject to the will of the manager. Our reporter was submerged about ten minutes, and at the bottom, a distance of thirty feet under the surface, found he could…read and write with perfect ease. The ascent was, likewise, made by touching a valve. The place of experiment did not admit of course of that extended trial of the capacity of the machine, which is claimed for it by the inventor. At an informal meeting held subsequently, Major Sears stated at length the different uses to which the machine could be applied and its perfect security. After which, a resolution was unanimously passed, expressing satisfaction at the exhibition and entire belief in its adaptability to every variety of submarine operations. The *Emily Banning*, from which the experiments were made, sets sail this week with four of the *Nautilus* machines for the Pacific to engage in the Pearl fisheries."[29]

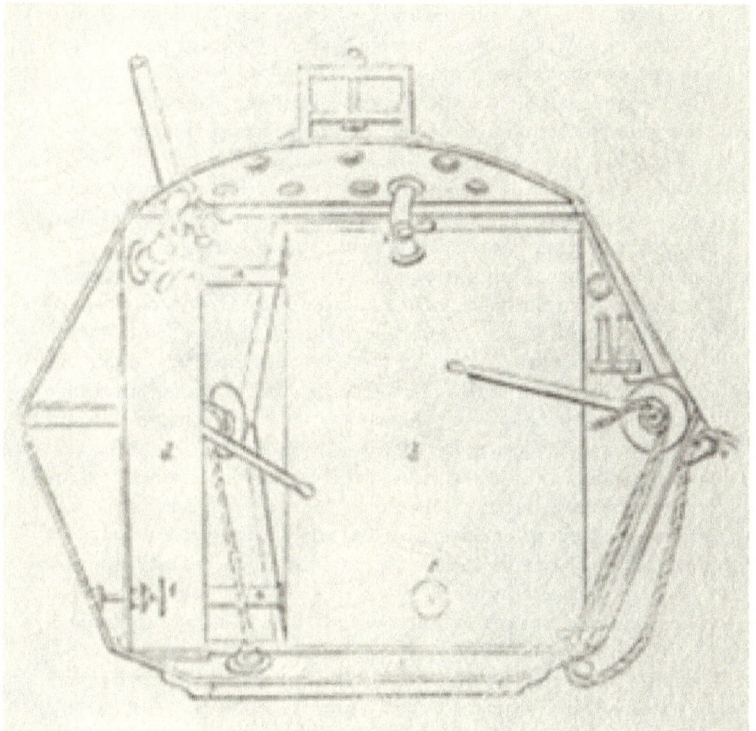

Sketch of *Nautilus*, in the Artizan, 1855

Though the reporter was, undoubtedly, impressed with the invention, there was absolutely no mention in the article of Edgar William Foreman. In fact, the writer referred only to Sears as the inventor, which deeply offended the Foreman family. Two days later, an article appeared in the *New York Times*, rebuking both the article's author and Henry Sears for not giving credit where credit was due. Sears quickly determined that the criticism, signed "Justico," had been written by one of the Foreman brothers. Specifically, it stated that "repeated reference is made to Major Henry B. Sears as the 'inventor' of the Diving-bell used on that occasion...whatever credit belongs to the inventor, per se, is due, I believe, to the inventor, Edgar W. Foreman, deceased–Mr. Sears being, as always understood, simply the assignee of the patents issued for the invention."[30]

Sears was extremely unhappy at the accusation, and decided to forward a carefully worded response to the editors, which was printed the next day:

> "I must trespass on your columns for a few words in reply. In April, 1852, feeling the great want of new machinery for sub-marine purposes, while boarding in the family of Mr. Foreman, I made an arrangement with the late Edgar W. Foreman to unite with me in securing , if possible, the desired end. I was to pay all expenses of experimenting, etc., and if we were successful in our research, the results were to be equal between us as co-inventors. We had just reached the crude principle, having one model successfully constructed...when on 9th [sic] July, same year, Mr. Foreman was drowned at New-Rochelle. We were joint inventors–as survivor, I was entitled and advised by my counsel to take the matter in my own hands as such survivor. I visited the father of deceased; said that I desired no change to take place in consequence of the mournful accident; that the only way in which his son's name could be connected with the machine, was by waiving my claim as co-inventor, and allowing the patent to be taken in his name. This proposition, with an expression of great feeling, was accepted by the father. I had all the proofs of co-inventorship, but I loved the deceased as an own brother, and was desirous that he should have more reputation if the thing was successful than if he had lived. The model, as developed at the time of Mr. F's decease, was not susceptible of practical application. For two years and a half I have improved, added new features, conquered obstacles which seemed insurmountable, and have produced a finished whole. I have received able assistance from my Engineers. They have all received their due meed of credit. The model, with principle as first developed, is now at my office, where all can judge whether I may be considered as the inventor of the finished machine. I have never failed to mention, with deep feeling, the assistance rendered me in the first instance by the deceased Mr. F., or to admit that his mind, practically trained, was perhaps superior to my own. That the article signed 'Justice' should, under the circumstances, have emanated from a member of Mr. F.'s family I regret. I know the feeling entertained by the father of the deceased gentleman to be at variance with this view..."[31]

Whether or not Edgar Foreman's own father disagreed with accusations made by another of his sons is debatable. However, this exchange was the beginning of the end of the earlier close relationship shared by Sears and the Foreman family.

Apparently, Sears' plan to set sail for Baja California's pearl fishery, where black pearls had long been harvested by Native American free divers, was delayed for several months. In February of 1856, the *New York Daily Tribune* reported "the bark *Emily Banning* arrived at Acapulco on the 24th December for supplies. She is engaged in pearl fishing and wrecking, and has been successful, as she had on board $20,000 worth of old silver and pearls. Until Dec. 12, she was engaged in surveying the pearl grounds from Panama to Acapulco... having arrived at the Bay of Panama in the latter part of October. The machinery used on board the *Emily Banning* is the *Nautilus* machine, owned by the Nautilus Submarine Company..."[32]

In actuality, it was the Nautilus Pearl Fishing Company, which had been incorporated by the State Legislature in Wilmington, Delaware, on January 30, 1855. Though little else is known regarding the cultivation of Baja pearls, Sears remained quite active in his adventures. In early March of 1855, the schooner *Searsville*, measuring 108 feet in length and twenty-seven feet in breadth, was completed in Dennis, Massachusetts. With her home port designated as St. George, Maine, she had been constructed for the express purpose of transporting all *Nautilus* submersibles to various destinations.

In April of 1855, the *New York Times* reported that the *Searsville*, under the command of "Captain Sears," had recently returned from Trinidad "loaded principally with old iron guns and an anchor, from the remains of Spanish men-of-war that were burnt in the Gulf of Paria, near the Port of Spain, in 1797." Diving in about thirty-six feet of water, the *Nautilus* had managed to recover ninety iron cannon and a pair of bronze six-pounder guns, all of which were shipped back to New York for scrapping at the city's iron foundries. Across town, at the failing Atlantic Hotel on lower Broadway, Jonathan Foreman conducted an auction on Saturday, April 28, 1855, selling what was left of his furniture and fixtures. He read local newspapers with bitterness and, perhaps, ironic displeasure that Henry Sears, the man he had trusted with his son's genius, had completely forgotten who had actually invented the *Nautilus*.

Meanwhile, Henry Sears seemed to be making his fortune, for on May 15, 1855, it was reported that the Nautilus Submarine Company was exploring the wreck of the frigate *San Pedro*, which had been blown up near the island of Margarito, Venezuela, in 1815. Understanding that between $2,000,000 and $3,000,000 of treasure had been lost, Sears immediately went to work:

> "Some three hundred thousand dollars have been taken up; the men now engaged in the attempt have described the affair as literally shoveling up dollars. Two months, it is said, will be sufficient to take up every vestige of the *San Pedro*, and the captain reports he has another vessel near him in the same depth of water, 56 feet, with fifty thousand dollars on board in specie, and another with fifteen thousand dollars, both of which he will take up before proceeding on his voyage."[33]

Always the promoter of his diving vessel, Henry Sears put on a large-scale demonstration at Glen Cove, New York, situated along the north shore of Long Island, on Thursday, November 13, 1856. Literally dozens of people not only witnessed, but participated in, a series of short dives to the bottom of Long Island Sound. The first dive "was made by Major Sears, the inventor, Hon. Erastos Brooks and Samuel Hallett, Esq. of Hornellsville, President of the American-Nautilus Company." They went down to a depth of twenty-two feet, and remained below the surface for seven or eight minutes.

Hallett, it seemed, had "earned" his way into the office of President of the American-Nautilus Company. Earlier in 1856, his aspirations led him to run for Congress and, though he lost this race, soon opened a bank in New York City. "Samuel Hallett and Company" had their offices at 53 Beaver Street where, along with his wife's brothers, Frank M. and George W. McDowell, and his wife's sister's husband, Nirom M. Crane, invested in a few choice projects. Two had been the Atlantic and Great Western Railroad, and the other, the *Nautilus*.

Samuel Hallett, President of the American-Nautilus Company

Also present for the mid-November demonstration at Glen Cove were a number of well-respected men in their respective fields, including: John Parker Hale, Senator from New Hampshire; George Washington Patterson, Lieutenant Governor of New York and Harbor Commissioner; Hon. Seth C. Hawley, Commissioner of Code on New York; Daniel C. McCallum, Superintendent of the Erie Railroad; Simeon S. Post, Chief Engineer of the Ohio and Mississippi Railroad; Allan Campbell, Chief Engineer of the New York and Harlem Railroad; James Gay, Chief Engineer of the U.S. Navy; John McLeod Murphy, Chief Engineer of the Brooklyn Navy Yard; Benjamin Franklin Delano, Naval Constructor; Joseph Jesse Comstock, Captain of the mail steamer *Baltic*; Christopher Heiser, Manager of Castle Garden; Thomas Colden Ruggles, Civil Engineer; and Julius H. Kroehl, submarine inventor:

> "The company formed to work this invention had chartered the steamship *Champion*, and invited the press and many of the leading celebrities of our State to a grand excursion... Starting from Peck ship ferry at 10:00 a.m., Glen Cove was reached, after a beautiful sail, about noon. In mid stream we found a large schooner lying at anchor, with steam engine on deck, and on mooring near her we learnt this apparatus was used for forcing compressed air into the receiver which supplies the *Nautilus*. At a few yards from the schooner we observed floating, like a huge porpoise in the water, the *Nautilus*... in external form (she) is almost round, or as Senator Hale aptly termed it, 'a water balloon.' It is about ten feet in diameter, by seven feet deep, and weighs ten tons... In order to test the 'feeling' in the *Nautilus*, 100 persons went down...of whom forty were ladies. We ourselves entered the trap set for us with feelings of misgiving... The iron door was screwed down, and immediately on descending a noise like the near letting off of steam dinned our ears; but this very unpleasant sensation was relieved by going through the operation of swallowing. We got down before we knew it, and the engineer lifted the door of the bottom and disclosed to us about six inches of muddy water. When we had gratified our curiosity...and obtained a number of shells as relics, the door was replaced and we shot up to the surface... Everybody was more than satisfied, though few understood the rationale of the invention or the peculiarities of its construction as compared with the diving bell..."[34]

Undoubtedly, a vast number of improvements had been made to the *Nautilus* design in the four years since Edgar William Foreman had drowned. In fact, it was no longer a mere diving bell controlled entirely from a mother ship above. Instead, it was operated completely from within, quite independent of the outside world. Henry Sears explained some of these improvements to the crowd at Glen Cove, New York, on that warm November day:

> "The *Nautilus* is not made or got up for a stock company to speculate on, but for practical purposes. It is made to travel on the bottom of the waters, to gather pearls, to collect gold from the beds of rivers, to gather the untold wealth of old ocean... (We), the inventors, had expended much time and large sums of money in bringing this machine to its present perfection. Immense and unknown difficulties were met with at every step. The first apparatus that we constructed could move up and down in the

water, but that was all; we could not get it to lift weights; for as soon as we got any heavy body to the surface, down it went from us. These difficulties were also attended with danger, the Nautilus having been shut up out of the water, at the outset, four feet from the surface, and all thought that those inside the machine were done for except the inventor, who knew they were safe, if they only had the proper amount of compressed air with them. The properties of air and water were not in the slightest degree understood when we set out; we had, therefore, everything to learn–to construct a science, in fact. We had to rid ourselves of the various difficulties incidental to the condensation of air, and more important than this, the latent heat of the air. Our pumps could not stand the pressure we put upon them, for iron melted and leather burnt up. We went to Europe to obtain pumps, which would compress air to the extent of 44 lbs. to the square inch, but the philosophical men of that continent sent us for answer that our request was an impossibility. But we have a pump now–you saw it working today–which, instead of 44 lbs., compresses air 200 lbs. to the square inch, and that pump is also our invention... A great feature in the machine is that it is independent of all outside influence or assistance, for it is managed from the inside alone..."[35]

Newspapers all across America were now giving Henry Sears the highest of accolades, believing that his *Nautilus* would alter the very course of the nation's history. One reporter summed it up with an extremely supportive explanation:

"We feel a national pride in the success of this great work. Heretofore the palm of superiority in mere mechanical invention has been universally conceded to our countrymen by other nations, but we have been denied a claim to discovery in works demanding a knowledge of the hidden and mysterious laws of nature's arcane. We challenge the world to produce more astounding results than those embodied in the electric telegraph, and this new invention of the *Nautilus*. It is not merely the machine itself, but the acquired knowledge in relation to the before unknown properties and laws of air and water, now for the first time developed, and which hereafter will be the basis for still further discovery; but in a commercial point of view alone the invention is one of the most important of the century, and the name of Major Sears will reflect glory on his country and be classed with those of Franklin, Morse, and others, as a benefactor of his race."[36]

Meanwhile, the team of board members of the American-Nautilus Company prepared for an extensive trip to England, where they planned to both demonstrate and promote the *Nautilus* in front of a number of prominent officials. Slowly but surely, the "doubting Thomases," who had initially believed that Samuel Hallett and other investors had risked far too much money in the project, were changing their opinion one-by-one:

"We, with many others, for a time, thought that Mr. Hallett had made a mistake in investing money in the perfection of the *Nautilus*; that his enthusiasm had for once obscured his judgment, and we looked, not for an explosion, certainly–but that the *Nautilus* scheme would at last burst like the thousand bubbles that float to the surface. We have come to regard the *Nautilus* as one of the fixed facts of the times, which, instead of impairing is to add largely to the fortunes of those who have aided by their means in perfecting it…"[37]

Henry B. Sears, now falsely given credit as "sole inventor" of the *Nautilus*, traveled with his primary investor, Samuel Hallett, and his pump-designer, John Williamson, to London in 1857, where he shared his expertise with the Society of Arts and conducted lengthy demonstrations at Victoria Dock. Ironically–and, perhaps, unknowingly–the trio was exhibiting the creation of a man, Edgar William Foreman, who had been born just a few miles west of these same docks thirty-two years earlier.

In its June 14, 1857, publication, the well-respected English civil engineer, Robert Stephenson, shared the following with a *London Era* reporter:

"The *Nautilus* Machine–and I am speaking from personal and careful examination–appears to possess so many qualifications as a diving-bell (a machine which has hitherto been confined to very limited practical operations), that I may truly say it may be called a universal diving-bell. I assure you that I could not help feeling very much interested in what had been told me of its usefulness. They are distinct classes of mechanical genius; one distinguished for extreme ingenuity in minute details, applicable to many processes of the highest value in civilized society; but I think the highest class of mechanical talent and genius is brought to bear in completing those mechanical contrivances that may be called rough and ready machines. Every mechanic in this room will fully appreciate what I mean. I consider this one of such rough-and-ready machines, and I must say the *Nautilus* Diving-bell appears to me to combine the highest class of mechanical skill with that high class of ingenuity in detail to which I have referred… The Nautilus was applied to…work, and I have no doubt the meeting will be surprised to learn the fact that an amount of work which had previously occupied a period of three weeks and four days, was performed by the *Nautilus* in two days and two hours with the same number of men employed daily…"[38]

The *Nautilus*, after "doing duty" to complete success and acceptance in the River Thames, now traveled to Paris, where it was engaged "by the Government to perform important subterranean services on the marine fortifications of the French seaboard." Local news reported its public demonstrations:

"An immense crowd lined the western parapet of the Pont Royal this afternoon, to witness the performances of the '*Nautilus*' diving-bell, which has lately been brought here from London. Mr. Hallett, the President of the Nautilus Submarine Company, had issued cards of invitation to several French, English, and American gentlemen connected with science or literature, to 'assist' at the experiment."[39]

Meanwhile, just as quickly as the fervor had begun and expanded all across America and Europe over the *Nautilus*, widespread interest began to unexpectedly subside. With the rumblings of unrest driving the North and South toward civil war in America, the public turned its attention away from the promising peacetime submersible. On September 17, 1858, the following personal advertisement appeared in the pages of the *New York Herald*:

"If Mary Anne Foreman, formally of Pimlico, London, or either of her sons, Frederick or Edgar, who left there about 1838, for New York, should see this, they will meet old friends on board the ship *Salsette*, at De Berg's wharf, Williamsburg; or any person knowing their whereabouts, and who would communicate the same, will confer an obligation."[40]

It is unknown whether or not any of the remaining Foreman family members responded to the search, however, for life had changed drastically for all of them since leaving Pimlico twenty years earlier.

As war approached, the Foremans could not hide their strong opposition to the Union, believing that owning slaves was a God-given right. By January of 1861, Jonathan and Mary Anne were living at the six-story New York Hotel, located at 88 Broadway between Washington and Waverly Place. For months, the establishment had been favored by successionist visitors from slave states, and had refused to exhibit patriotism by flying the American flag. The elder Foreman had counted himself among this group. Believed to be a hotbed of Confederate spies during the upcoming war, it had been the first to introduce room service and the ala carte menu for the very wealthy in 1853. Decades later, on January 19, 1891, its grand dining room would be the site of the Confederate Veteran Camp of New York First Annual Dinner, with Varina Howell Davis, First Lady of the Confederacy.

Jonathan Foreman continued to follow the news about the *Nautilus*, along with the political unrest of the times. He often expressed his bitterness about how Henry Sears "had stolen his beloved son's life work" to anyone that would listen. On February 19, 1861, the *New York Herald* published a piece on President-elect Abraham Lincoln's upcoming visit to New York City. The English immigrant, now sixty-three years old, agreed with what the article editorialized to him and other Southern sympathizers:

"What will Mr. Lincoln do when he arrives? What will he say to the citizens of this great metropolis? Will he kiss our girls, and give a twirl to the whiskers which he has begun to cultivate? Will he tell our merchants, groaning under the pressure of the greatest political convulsion ever experienced in America that 'nobody is hurt' or that 'marching troops into South Carolina' and bombarding its fortresses is 'no invasion'?"[41]

On the day that he arrived, "almost everywhere flags were flying. All the principal hotels, except the New-York Hotel displayed the national banner, and from many private houses it was flung to the breeze." Looking down from his window, Jonathan Foreman thought he'd never see the day when an entire city would honor such a despised man. Edgar's father died on Saturday morning, June 15, 1861, on the uppermost level of the six-story New York Hotel. Though he had anticipated it, his son's submersible *Nautilus,* designed more than a decade earlier, had not brought him any sort of fame or fortune.

By the time of his passing, the North and South were two months into civil war, and Henry Beaufort Sears opted to remain in Liverpool with his family. He did not attend Jonathan's funeral. Over the course of the next two decades, he would invest his time and money in a number of other inventive schemes, applying for several unique patents along the way. Undoubtedly, it was more fortune than fame that motivated him and, if nothing else, no one could deny that his intelligence and drive had brought him this far in life.

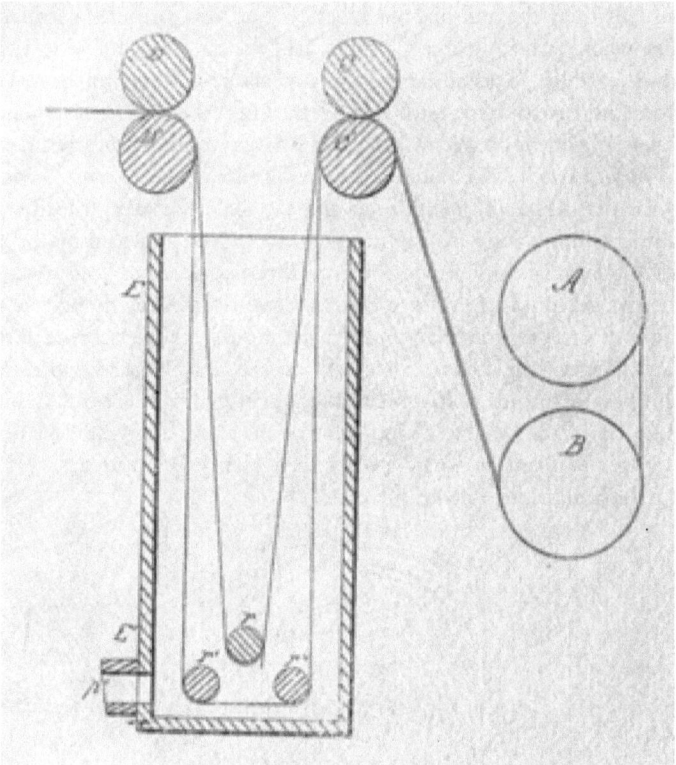

John Scoffern's sheathing and coating machine

In August of 1860, feeling swindled by business partner Wilson Ager, Sears had filed a lawsuit with the New York Supreme Court in an attempt to recoup more than $1,600 owed him for his investment in the development of a rice cleaning apparatus. While the case was still pending, the Sears family decided to avoid the Civil War by leaving the divided United States. On August 25, 1861, the *New York Times* announced his departure, along with his wife, Harriet Louiza, and children Ella, and Harriet, all of whom left New York City on the *SS Edinburgh* enroute to Liverpool. He understood full well at the time that they would never return.

One-and-a-half years later, in December of 1863, Henry applied for and was granted a patent in Liverpool for a similar, though somewhat improved, machine capable of "cleansing or dusting rice and other grain." Apparently, by this point in time, he had changed directions entirely, feeling there was much money to be made in the area of agriculture and other "above-water" ventures.

In 1867, Sears joined in partnership with John Henry Johnson in the creation of a unique machine for grinding wheat and other grain into flour. Just a few months later, in January of 1869, history records that John Scoffern had assigned a patent to Sears for a machine used for "sheathing and coating ships' bottoms." By then, the transplanted American had also partnered with Drysdale Carstairs–whose father, George Carstairs, had been a successful wine merchant in Leith–in forming "Carstairs and Company," a rice-milling firm located a half-mile from the River Mersey at 12 to 22 Burlington Street in Liverpool. This financial arrangement between Carstairs and Sears would last nearly a decade.

On January 5, 1877, a notice was published in the *London Gazette*, dissolving the partnership of Henry Sears and Drysdale Carstairs. It further stated that "all debts due to and by the firm will be received and paid by the undersigned, Drysdale Carstairs." Apparently, the fifty-two-year-old Sears was wealthy enough that he could see his way clear to semi-retirement, though he would never be very far away from planning his next money-making scheme. Just three years later, however, he died unexpectedly, on February 12, 1880, in Liverpool, leaving his entire fortune to his children. Though the initial concept to build an improved, self-maneuverable diving bell had been the brain-child of his close friend, Edgar William Foreman, it had been Henry Beaufort Sears who had turned the concept into a major success.

Johnny B. Green, portrait

- 18 -
Johnny B. Green: *Lake Erie Diver*

"The propeller had stopped to make repairs after the accident, and now when her crew were apprised of the dreadful condition of those who had been in the *Atlantic*, by the cries, shrieks and lamentations of the drowning people, the *Ogdensburg* promptly steered for the spot, and was the means, under divine Providence, of saving about two hundred and fifty of the unfortunate who still survived. Hundreds were battling with the waters, and while the sympathizing crew of the propeller were [sic] dragging some aboard of that vessel with all possible dispatch, many others sunk into the abyss of waters, and were seen no more. From the most authentic statements it appears that more than three hundred lives were lost."[1]

Bruce H. Weaver was a typical, upper-middle-class resident of Greensboro, North Carolina, whose great-grandparents had set sail from Norway in the mid-1800s and had made their way across the Atlantic Ocean to America. From their landing site near Quebec City, they had traveled on to Buffalo, New York, across the Great Lakes, eventually settling in the unincorporated town of Koshkonong Prairie, Wisconsin. By the time that more than a century had passed, Weaver had heard all of the often-repeated Norwegian family stories about some sort of shipwreck that had occurred during their journey, though he did know how much credence could be put to such a tale. After all, he could find no information in history books about such a catastrophe. Yet, though he could not decipher much of it, he continued to treasure a yellowing diary that his maternal great-grandmother, Marit, had written in her native tongue about their migration. "Atlantic" appeared throughout the fading document, though Weaver had assumed that it was a reference to that treacherous ocean.

More than a century and a half later, on a fateful Sunday morning in 2008, a visiting summer minister took the pulpit at Weaver's Lutheran Church in Greensboro, North Carolina. A friendly transplant from Norway, who spoke both English and Norwegian, the young preacher spoke at length to the parishioners about the homeland and their cultural heritage. Something in the conversation made Weaver remember his great-grandmother's diary, and he asked the traveling minister if he might assist him with a more accurate and detailed translation of the mysterious document. Intrigued, the man of the cloth readily agreed to meet with him at his home, where he might examine the journal firsthand. Little did the two men realize at the time that both family history and immigrant heritage was about to be untangled like a fine-toothed comb pushed through soft hair.

As the two men devoured the written words, they were absolutely mesmerized. Oldemor (meaning great-grandma), Marit Haave–which some family members pronounced as "Hove"–had been born in 1813 in Vestre Slidre, nestled between the high mountains along the Oppland fylke of southern Norway. In 1845, at the age of thirty-two, she had married Ole Alfson Rodvang, had given birth to two children, and had struggled to put enough food on the table on their small farm. Soon after the great potato famine arrived from Ireland, Ole decided that America might be a more prosperous place to raise their children. Marit's husband and his three brothers–Finkel, Barbo, and Knud–pooled their savings and paid a large sum of money to local resident, Steven Olsen, a provider of immigration services. Olsen promised to bring them across the Atlantic Ocean to New York City, where they would then travel on to Koshkonong Prairie, Wisconsin. The group grew over the next few months, reaching nearly one hundred travelers. They were all instructed to limit their luggage to one steamer per family, filled with nothing but clothing, food for the trip, and any other treasures that they could not bring themselves to leave behind. One item that Marit decided to make room for was her personal diary.

An extremely bitter winter presented the Rodvang's with their first obstacle, as snow and mud impeded their progress by wagon to the coastal city of Drammen. Ongoing weather delays caused them to miss their scheduled ship boarding by a single day. They waited there for further instructions, with almost nine weeks passing before a second vessel–a sloop-rigged lumber hooker named the *Argo*–was secured for their passage to America. Yet, there was another problem–she was docked in Christiana (today Oslo), which was a two-week journey by land from Drammen. Yet, Marit and Ole understood that they had no other alternative, so they climbed aboard a flatbed wagon once again, and made the overland journey.

Once safely aboard the *Argo*, the Norwegian travelers quickly learned how inadequate the vessel was for a trans-Atlantic voyage. The five-year-old ship's heavy, metal-wrapped hull caused it to move painfully slow through the choppy waters of the North Atlantic. To make matters worse, her waterline length of only 58.9 feet and relatively narrow beam of 14.4 feet caused the vessel to wallow through the massive waves, rocking like a porch swing to-and-fro in a heavy wind. Overcrowded, overheated, and continuously uncomfortable, the eight-week journey proved to be nothing but misery, particularly for the Rodvang children and others their age, who suffered terrible bouts of seasickness, vomiting, and diarrhea. Yet, the Norwegian migrants proved themselves up to the task, with all arriving alive and in relatively good spirits in the port of Quebec. Though it wasn't New York City, as had been promised, the tired and hungry passengers recited Lutheran prayers, thankful that they were exiting the stench-filled belly of the *Argo*.

AMERICAN SUBMARINERS: PRE-CIVIL WAR

Suddenly, an accident occurred as they disembarked from the compact vessel. A friend and neighbor from Valdres, Thorsten Nilsen Majestad, fell overboard as he was bringing his baggage down the gangplank. It was "right pitiful for the others to see how he struggled," for they had no means whatsoever with which to save him. Arrangements were finally made for dragging the port bottom. Eventually, he was found, but by then it was too late. The incident was all the more tragic, since he had a wife and three children, who mourned their lost husband and father.

Captain Olsen on the *Argo* contracted with a local firm to transport the remaining emigrants and their baggage on to Milwaukee at a cost of seven dollars each. It took two weeks of steamboat, train, and wagon rides to move the hoard on to Buffalo, New York, where the next phase of their trip would be aboard a much roomier, cleaner ship known as the *Atlantic*. Scheduled to depart during the second week of August on its way to Detroit, Michigan, the steam-powered vessel had been constructed in Newport (presently Marine City), Michigan, in 1848, and had been enrolled under the laws of the United States of America at the port of Detroit on May 29, 1849. The *Atlantic*, mastered by Captain Joseph Byron Pettey, primarily served the passenger trade, carrying U.S. citizens between her ports of call, and immigrants to points further west. The original owners of the vessel were Samuel Ward and his nephew, Eber Brock Ward, who jointly owned and operated a firm known as the E.B. and S. Ward Steamship Line.

Drawing of the *Atlantic* Steamer

Along with 426 other deck passengers and 146 cabin passengers, the Rodvang family climbed aboard the *Atlantic* on August 20, 1852. They were pleased to see how "beautiful and ornate" she was compared to the *Argo*, boasting eighty-five clean and fresh staterooms. As they descended down into the large steerage section, they could hear happy sounds of upper-deck wealthier passengers enjoying the summer evening, with smells of fine cooking permeating the late afternoon and evening air. Soon, darkness enveloped them.

Within a few minutes, the ship's steam engines came to life. Nothing about the voyage seemed ominous to the array of first- and second-class passengers, as they enjoyed the vessel's comforts. There was a slight "surface haze, the moon and stars shown brightly through a dark sky," and first-class travelers enjoyed a luxury meal, fine wines in the upper saloon, and dancing to music being played by the live orchestra. As the hour approached midnight, the *Atlantic*'s paddle wheels provided rhythmic rumbling for easy sleep. Marit and Ole had settled in comfortably near an interior bulkhead below deck, with their six-year-old daughter, Ambjorg, and two-year-old son, Ole, sleeping between them.

Without watning, as the *Atlantic* was making her way through the rather calm Canadian waters of Lake Erie, she collided with the eastbound flag-vessel propeller, *Ogdensburg*. As a result, though Captain Pettey had assumed there was but minimal damage, the grand steamship began to take on an immense amount of water. Her position was approximately three miles southwest of the tip of Long Point, Ontario, and between six and seven miles from the boundary between the U.S. and Canada. Though Pettey attempted a desperate run toward shore, it soon became clear that the ship would not make it. Below them was to nearly one hundred, sixty feet of water:

> "The propeller struck the *Atlantic* forward of the wheel, on the larboard side; the shock was so little felt on board the steamer, that she continued her course without any apprehension of danger; and, as the propeller had reversed her engine before the collision took place, the crew of it did not suppose that any serious mischief had been done to the other. However, before the Atlantic had proceeded two miles, it was discovered that she was sinking rapidly. The passengers were all in bed at the time, and when they were aroused from their slumbers to be informed of their perilous condition, the scene of confusion and dismay, which followed is beyond all the powers of language to describe... As soon as the startling intelligence was communicated to the passengers, all were assembled on deck, to meet or avoid the fate which threatened them. The poor Norwegians, who were generally ignorant of the English language, could scarcely be made to comprehend the cause of the alarm, but observing the consternation, which prevailed among the other passengers, they became wildly excited, and threw themselves into the water in spite of every effort to restrain them. The other passengers listened to the exhortations of the captain, and became perfectly calm, assisting to throw overboard settees, chairs, mattresses, and other buoyant articles, which might be the means

of supporting them in the water when the boat went down... The dense obscurity of the night, the damp and chilling atmosphere, the terrific hissing of the water as it rushed through the gaping leak upon the furnaces, in which every spark of fire was soon extinguished, the shrieks and cries of the affrighted women and children who remained on board, and the still more distressing exclamations of those who were struggling in the water, all these circumstances combined to make a scene of horror which appalled even those who could have met their own fate with fortitude and intrepidity."[2]

The sudden jolt had startled the Rodvang family awake. Making their way quickly above deck, they pushed toward the stern of the sinking ship, in an opposite direction from which the rest of the steerage class passengers were moving. Suddenly, Ole turned to his wife and whispered: "We need to get into the water and away from the boat." Then, without speaking another word, he grabbed Ambjorg tightly to his chest and slipped over the side rail with a wooden stool grasped in his left hand. Realizing that she was unable to swim, Marit looked on fearfully as her husband and daughter slowly drifted away into the darkness. Frantic and alone, she found her way through the screaming throng to the hogging-arches that guarded the *Atlantic*'s paddle wheels. There, gripping fast to her two-year-old tearful son, she floated upward as the ship sank beneath them, eventually latching on to a piece of steel bracing attached to the smokestack. It was there that she dangled, holding on to Ole with the ferocity of a mother whose only mission was to save the life of her son.

After two desperate hours of clinging to the side of the sinking *Atlantic*, the *Ogdensburg* suddenly appeared alongside and began to take on upper-class passengers and crew from the stern section. In the commotion of pleading for help, a strong arm unexpectedly circled Marit's waist and lifted both her and little Ole to safety. Her savior was the *Atlantic*'s bursar, Julius Morvine, the last person to leave the sinking vessel before she disappeared into the black abyss. Once she had reached safety aboard the *Ogdensburg*, Marit was overjoyed to be reunited with her husband and daughter, who had safely made it aboard the rescue ship as well. The accident and its aftermath would later be described by a number of the survivors:

> "Like two dogs that have tangled viciously but briefly and then backed of to survey the damage wrought, the ships drifted apart after the collision, neither, apparently, seriously holed. But minutes later a begrimed and frightened fireman sought out the Captain to report that the *Atlantic* was looding below with water spurting up through the engine-room gratings. Captain Pettey gave the 'abandon ship' order and the crew began their orderly routine of lowering boats and assigning seats. But the terrified Norwegians, who understood no English, panicked at the shouted orders and began to jump overboard. By now the water had reached the fires and huge clouds of steam began spurting up from the skylights and

companionways. In this eerie scene of disaster the *Atlantic* made her final plunge, leaving the surface of the lake cluttered with wreckage, trunks and drowning passengers...almost 300 people, many of them hapless immigrants, either went down with the ship or drowned while waiting rescue. The *Atlantic* went to the bottom some four miles off Long Point in 155 feet of water."[3]

Sadly, of Steven Olsen's Norwegian group of immigrants, only about one-half survived; sixty-eight had perished, including two of Ole's brothers, Finkel and Barbo, along with their wives and four small children. On September 26, ten months after leaving Norway, Ole and Marit Rodvang would finally arrive in Koshkonong Prairie, Wisconsin. A few years later, they would push even further west into Iowa, where they would purchase an eighty-acre farm for $120. Over time, it would expand to 246 acres of prime real estate. The elder Ole died in March of 1884, and was laid to rest in the Washington Prairie Lutheran Cemetery, a few miles southeast of the town of Decorah, Iowa, in Winneshiek County. Ambjorg, who had been miraculously snatched from the Lake Erie waters with her father, married Torger Landsrud and gave birth to ten children before being trampled to death by a bull in a freak farm accident in August of 1900. When Marit died at the age of eighty-nine on January 4, 1902, her handwritten diary was passed on to her only surviving child, Ole, who could speak and read only English. From him it found its way into the possession of Ambjorg's eldest daughter, Olena, and eventually to Ambjorg's grandson, Bruce Weaver. It would be more than 100 years before her poignant words would be interpreted and her life's journey clearly remembered.

Henry Wells & William G. Fargo

Though the sinking of the *Atlantic* was believed by most to be one of the greatest tragedies in American history, a few viewed the event simply as a "business setback." Since there existed no rail lines running along the south shore of Lake Erie, the American Express Company had suggested the use the *Atlantic* to transport its gold, cash, and other valuables to the Northwest Territory. Two of its most vocal representatives, in fact–Henry Wells and William Fargo–had been successful of convincing their board of directors of the scheme. And to them, though the large loss of lives was tragic, it was not nearly as "tragic" as losing the wealth of their investment company.

So, as the Rodvangs and dozens of other families dealt with their immense grief and recovery, Wells and Fargo decided to secure an experienced salvage diver to recover their lost safe. Their first choice was a man from Silver Creek, New York, named Johnny B. Green, born to Peter and Mary Eliza Green in 1826 on a small farm near the township of Lachine, Canada. Nestled a few miles southwest of Montreal, the community got its name from the French "La Chine," meaning "China." Early European explorers had hoped to uncover a route from New France to the Western Sea and, from there, on to China–hence, its auspicious name.

Johnny's family had relocated to the U.S. side of the Saint Lawrence River when he was just eight years old. The Greens–which now included younger siblings, Andrew and Lucy–settled more than 100 miles upriver near Ogdensburg, New York. The elder Green, who had migrated to Canada with own his parents from France, worked from sun up until sun down, trying to make a living as a produce farmer, growing potatoes, corn, and beets. And it was here that young Johnny first became acquainted with, and comfortable in, swimming in the deep waters of the nearby river:

> "Our new farm was situated near the river St. Lawrence, and it was in the waters of this noble river that I first learned to swim. I mastered the art with more than ordinary ease; and I once practiced it to perfection..."[4]

By the mid-1830s, Ogdensburg had already become a strategic location for shipping. Nestled at the confluence of the Oswegatchie and St. Lawrence Rivers, earliest settlers had found a natural, deep harbor wide enough for larger vessels and possessing sufficient flow along the Oswegatchie to power mills of all types. After construction of a mission, the community's founder, Abbe Francois Picquet, had designed and built a dam across that waterway in order to power the first sawmills. As young Johnny reached his teenage years, he was amazed to witness the launching of the community's first steam ferry in 1839, which made daily round trips between Ogdensburg and Prescott, Ontario.

While Johnny was still a young schoolboy, the Green family moved once again, this time southwesterly to Oswego, New York. In Colonial days, much of the pine around that region had been cut and shipped to England, where it had been utilized in the manufacture of masts and spars. Lumber continued to be a thriving local business when Johnny arrived in the early 1840s, but the chief lumber trade was through importation. Posts, staves and squared timbers were the major items received, and nearly all the lumber brought into Oswego was being cut and shipped from the vast forests along the northern shores of Lake Ontario. Vessels were typically brought to anchor offshore, where the timber and staves had been collected for shipment. The timbers were then floated out to the vessels and the staves brought out in scows. Upon arriving in Oswego, each vessel was then unloaded directly into canal boats for further shipment, or deposited at the local lumber mills for further processing.

Occasionally, there were accidents and acts of vandalism out in the harbor, with ships being grazed by other vessels or goods being taken illegally. It should come as no surprise then that it was here that Johnny would make his first successful dive for money, recovering "a box of soap and a clock–two articles that had been stolen and thrown into the water." Later, he wrote about this early commercial underwater experience:

> "As the weather was fine and diving a sport in which I greatly delighted, I at once decided to try my art in the search. I divested myself of my garments, and dove for the bottom of the river. I sank about fifteen feet– half way–when I began to feel a little timid, and I instantly rose to the surface...I plunged down again, and swam to the bottom...and with me as I returned to the surface, I brought a bar of soap... Encouraged by this prize...I continued diving with renewed vigor, and was soon rewarded by finding and recovering the clock; and, in doing so, my last submersion lasted one minute and a-half, a longer time than I had ever remained under water before."[5]

As a teenager, Johnny began to gradually earn enough money to make a living by salvaging freight from the harbors and river inlets. Back in Ogdensburg, he recovered sixteen tons of Spanish pig lead that had been lost aboard a sunken schooner in 1837. And, in the early part of September of 1841, at the age of fifteen, the youngster was asked to search for the remains of his first drowning victim at Oswego:

> "...it was at this date that I was first called upon to search for a more precious freight than I had ever before, in the hasty conception and adoption of my profession, conceived of undertaking...it was the body of a fellow being. A boy of about sixteen years had fallen from a canal boat the previous day, and his body could not be found... After diving several times, but without success, I at last found the body. The hands were gripping a stick of protruding timber at the bottom of the river–it was with much effort that I released their hold..."[6]

In the early summer of 1845, Johnny traveled by wagon from Oswego back to Ogdensburg, where he dove for the wreck of a British gunship lost during the War of 1812. It turned out to be a lucrative venture, with the youngster recovering "cannon, swords, balls, muskets, and various other implements of war." By his early twenties, he had gained a reputation as a diver who "never dove with an air link to the surface" in shallow waters; instead, he simply held his breath. In deeper, colder waters, he was known to wear a primitive wetsuit made up of three old sweaters layered on top of one another. All in all, the arrangement helped to protect him from colder waters at greater depths.

In the autumn of 1847, after having salvaged "everything in the harbor of Oswego worth the arduous labor of raising," Green traveled to New York City for the first time before returning to the area of his birth near Quebec, Canada. By then, he was deeply smitten with a young girl from Chelsea, Massachusetts, the fourteen-year-old daughter of wealthy shipwright, Philip Jennings. Yet, Grace Ann Jennings was far too innocent to cavort with the likes of Johnny Green, so he was forced to worship her from afar–at least for the time being.

Unknown to the Jennings family, Johnny decided to wed another, more out of necessity than love. Records indicate that he married eighteen-year-old "spinster," Ann Brady, the daughter of James and Catherine (Keegan) Brady, on October 22, 1849. By the time that the marriage became official at Saint Paul's Chapel for Mariners, located at Rue Champlain in the Loretteville district of Quebec, Ann had already given birth to a daughter, a fact that she kept secret from the strict Anglican Church officials. In any case, it is unknown as to whether or not the child, Adelia, was actually Johnny's daughter, though he cared for her–at least financially–as if she were his own.

Apparently, accepting the responsibilities of marriage and fatherhood, Johnny took fewer and fewer chances in his diving career, often going long stretches without taking on a single risky salvaging job. Yet, something kept drawing him back to the deep waters of the Great Lakes. Leaving Ann and baby Adelia behind in Quebec with her family in 1849, he again decided to travel to New York City to seek his "fame and fortune." During the journey southward along the Hudson River, near a small town by the same name, a sloop ran into a canal boat and "instantly sank in thirty-four feet of water," taking "the captain, his wife, and one hand…to the bottom with it."[7] The twenty-four-year-old diver, well known throughout New York by then, managed to dive down, remove the top of the cabin, and bring each victim back to the surface one-by-one. Again, local papers referred to Johnny Green as a "hero."

Remaining in New York City for a time, Johnny could find very little work as a professional diver and salvage man. Instead, he used his skills as a machinist, which he had learned at D. Talbott and Company in Oswego, as well as a ship repairman, a skill in which he "often went beneath the surface of the water, and corked vessels, when they leaked at the bottom but not sufficiently to warrant taking them into dry dock."[8]

Census records indicate that, by the end of July, 1850, Johnny Green found himself living without his wife and daughter at to home of his aging parents on West Bridge Street in the 3rd Ward of Oswego, New York, along with his younger brother, Andrew, and two younger sisters, Lucy and Mary. By then, his sixty-year-old father, Peter, had retired from the produce growing business, and his two sons were responsible for providing the family with an adequate income in order to make ends meet. Both, in fact, listed their professions as "sailor," with each hiring themselves out as first mates aboard various Great Lakes paddle wheelers traveling between Oswego and Cleveland, Toledo, and Detroit.

Meanwhile, hoping to make a better future for Ann and Adelia, Johnny had continued to painstakingly save much of his earnings, and began turning whatever he owned into ready cash:

> "I found, after eleven years of toil and exposure, not only on the seas but beneath the seas, I had laid by the sum of seven thousand dollars. With this little amount, I had decided to procure...a home in 'The West,' on which I hoped to spend the remainder of my life. And I saw nothing foreshadowed in the future, which would debar that realization–my golden wish."[9]

Yet, his "golden wish" would never come true. On Monday, July 12, 1852–the same summer that the *Atlantic* sank–Johnny Green was aboard the recently constructed paddle wheeler, *City of Oswego*, along with his wife, daughter, brother, his sister-in-law, and her parents. Built in Buffalo by George Stephen Weeks, who had moved his family and shipbuilding business from Clayton, New York, the wooden screw-driven propeller, boasting two decks and ornate trimmings, had been launched just one month earlier on June 15. She was 138 feet long, 24.8 feet at her widest beam, and weighed in at a hefty 357 tons. With ten in his party, Johnny and his entourage was traveling westward to Detroit, where they hoped to begin a new life. Without much warning, something went terribly awry:

> "At about midnight I was aroused by a heavy shock and a sudden crash. The thought of a collision flashed across my mind... We were run into by the Steamer *America*, bound for Buffalo; and our boat was filling with water..."[10]

The *City of Oswego* had been struck severely on her starboard side. It took only a few precious minutes for her to sink to the bottom of the lake in about forty feet of water, with her position just above Willoughby, Ohio, a community situated about twenty miles east of Cleveland. The man, who had made quite a name for himself by executing literally dozens of dives to recover both drowning victims and merchandise, was horrified by what he witnessed and heard:

> "All now was confusion, and fright; women shrieking for help, children calling on their parents to save them, while others were imploring God to have mercy on them. Many of the passengers were now first steping [sic] from their state-room, and, as they did so, and beheld the sullen waters enveloping the vessel's edge, such shrieks of horror rung upon my ears as I never, never wish to heat again."[11]

Though Johnny managed to swim to safety, his twenty-two-year-old wife, Ann, and his three-year-old daughter, Adelia, were among the helpless victims, along with his sister-in-law's parents and about a dozen other passengers. Though he made three valiant attempts to locate them, remaining "under water for such a length of time that...blood gushed from...(his) eyes, ears, lips and under... (his) nails," he was unable to bring any of them safely to the surface. Tirelessly and relentlessly, beginning at dawn on the following morning, he would spend countless days living and sleeping along the beach near the sunken wreck, diving repeatedly to locate their lifeless remains:

> "In the morning, myself, brother and friends, returned to the place of the collision, and I again dove to the wreck...for fourteen days I watched the shore of Lake Erie, dayly [sic] traveling for miles that extent bordering the vicinity of the wreck, waiting for the bodies of those near and dear ones, that were lost on that woeful night..."[12]

Throughout the remainder of his life—and beyond in historical records—there would remain some confusion as to whether or not Ann was, in fact, Johnny's wife. Indeed, a few records have indicated that she was the spouse of Johnny's brother, Andrew. However, Canadian marriage records, Johnny's second marriage cerificate, and a book written by Green himself, have since confirmed the "mistake." It is clear from each of these reports that it was Johnny himself who purposefully clouded the issue—in effect, it is now believed he did so in order to guard a well-kept secret from the woman who had always been his true love.

Commercial divers working on the nearby shipwreck of the steamer *Griffith*, which had burned and sank in about fifteen feet of water a few miles off shore during the summer of 1850, chanced to meet the distraught Johnny Green during one of his desperate dives to recover remains of the victims. They looked on in amazement as he went down time and time again, refusing to give up on his quest. A few were moved by his personal anguish, and invited him to use their "submarine armor" to conduct his relentless search. The apparatus was "constructed of copper and India rubber...that part constructed of copper was to protect the head," which the party of divers referred to as the "helmet." Johnny later detailed the unique costume:

> "It (the helmet) was of oval form, quite large in comparison with the head, and had a window in front, and one on each side, for the diver to see through. The rubber covered all the remainder of the body, except the hands, and its dimensions were sufficient to admit an ordinary sized man, with three suits of woolen clothes, which amount was necessary to keep the body warm while under water. At the top of the helmet was attached the pipe, through which air from the surface, by means of an air-pump, was forced into the armor, keeping it constantly inflated. At the waist of the helmet in front was the escape pipe, for letting off the impure air into the water... There was also in the helmet a valve, which, in case of leakage

of the supply pipe, would instantly close and prevent the air from passing out; and another on the end of the escape pipe, which the water would instantly close on rushing into the pipe,"[13]

Submarine Armor described by Johnny Green

Aside from this unusual protective suit, the salvagers were also employing a diving bell composed primarily of brass, which was also linked to the surface with a rubber hose. Johnny later described the bell in some detail:

"The diving-bell commonly in use resembles nearly a large box deprived of its bottom. Its ordinary length is about six feet, its breadth five and a half, and its height four feet and a half. To avoid the necessity of fastening weights to make it descend, it is formed of cast-iron; and being made in one piece, and very thick, there is no danger of Sea water forcing itself through the sides or top. It is also airtight. The thickness of the sides of the bell prevents also its being fractured, should it by any accident receive a heavy blow. In the top of the diving-bell is a round aperture, communicating by a number of small circular holes with the interior, where the holes are all covered and closed by a piece of thick leather, which acts as a valve, and admits air. A strong leather hose is screwed on to the external aperture, and from two holes near its sides rise two strong chains, uniting in a ring, by which the whole machine is to be suspended. In the top also are cemented twelve very thick lenses, for the purpose of admitting light. At the ends of the bell are two seats, placed at such a height, that the top of the head is but a few inches below the upper part of the bell; and in the middle, about six inches above the lower edge, is placed a narrow board, on which the feet of the divers rest. On one side, nearly on a level with the shoulders, in a small shelf, with a ledge, to contain a few tools, chalk for writing messages, and a ring, to which a small rope is tied. A board is connected with this rope; and after writing any orders on the board with a piece of chalk, on giving it a pull, the superintendent above, round whose arm the other end is fastened, will draw it up to the surface, and, if necessary, return an answer by the same conveyance. 'Our compliments to our friends above water;' was the little, memorandum written by the author of this brief notice, when he formed one of a happy party at the bottom of the sea. 'Health and prosperity to the ladies and gentlemen inhabiting the region of fishes,' was the answer which was received to it in less than three minutes..."[14]

Johnny Green also noted that, on the inside top of the diving bell was a contrivance by which stone was suspended for added buoyancy. The weight of the entire suit was approximately four tons, though air trapped inside made it seem much lighter when submerged. A leather hose was connected with a double condensing pump, worked by four men on an anchored flatbed at the surface. In order to allow the bell to be repositioned, it was suspended by a "windlass purchase-tackle," which was fixed on a moveable four-wheel iron box. These wheels moved along a stationary iron railway, which was fixed upon another platform, allowing it to move back and forth in any direction. Thus, by way of two iron railways–"established on beams and supported by piles, the lower being fixed in the direction of the length of the wall, and the upper being on the lower moveable plane"–it was possible to move the diving bell to any position that might be required.

On only his second dive with this arrangement, the diving bell and its unique air pump allowed Johnny to remain submerged for nearly six hours, a length of time "unprecedented in the annals of diving." Eventually, by using this apparatus, he recovered the remains of his wife, his daughter, his other family members, and the other drowned passengers:

"...I was rewarded by finding all the bodies of those for whom I searched, and sent them to their relatives, or had them decently interred...Having performed these last rites to the dead, I at once looked around me for an opportunity to earn a subsistence, for my trunk had been found in the mean time, rifled of my little fortune in gold, and even my clothes. I stood in the world empty handed... But I had willing hands, a bold heart, and knew there was something for them to do...with me there was no such thing as fail."¹⁵

Johnny, in fact, put to good use what he had learned from "the old divers" salvaging the *Griffith*, for he would incorporate both protective submarine armor and the diving bell in the majority of future deep diving adventures.

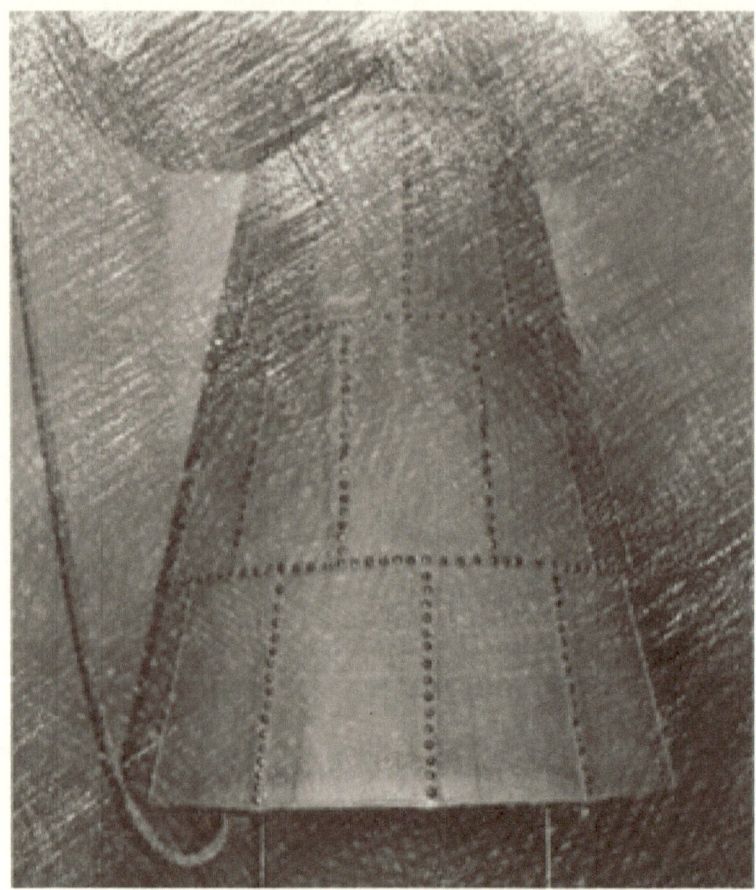

Diving Bell described by Johnny Green

Soon enough, the New York diver, and those that had introduced him to the armor and bell, had formed "a mutual company, with the understanding that the spoils should be divided pro-rata." Since he did most of the deep dives personally, Johnny was virtually the only man among them who knew exactly how much wealth was below the surface. Understanding full well the importance of setting aside money for the future, he actually stashed some of his findings below the surface in a series of hidden "submarine vault(s)...in Lake Erie," which he planned to retrieve secretly at some future date. In essence, he was 'robbing" his own business partners of their fair share of the booty.

Meanwhile, just after midnight on Friday, August 20, 1852, the ill-fated westbound passenger steamer, *Atlantic*, was on its deadly collision course with the eastbound propeller-driven package steamer, *Ogdensburg*, just off Long Point, a lengthy peninsula that jutted out into the middle of Lake Erie from Port Rowan, Ontario. Under informal rules of the road, by which the majority of shipmasters operated at the time, the *Ogdensburg* was the "vessel of burden," and she was expected to give right of way to the *Atlantic*. A commonly recited ditty helped sailors recall this vital navigational rule: "If to starboard red appear, 'tis your duty to keep clear."[16]

Hence, it was believed that the sailors aboard the *Ogdensburg* should have been able to see the *Atlantic*'s "red," or portside, running lights off their starboard bow. And it was their responsibility to steer clear of the approaching passenger steamer. Degress McNell, first mate aboard the *Ogdensburg*, failed to do so, however, falsely believing that the *Atlantic* was still an hour away, and so he kept his vessel steaming on course, full speed ahead.

Suddenly spotting the *Atlantic* directly in his path, coming out of the foggy mist like an apparition, McNell thought that she seemed to change "course, turning to the north as if trying to pass in front of, rather than behind, the *Ogdensburg*." The first mate immediately signaled the engine room to reverse engines full, simultaneously shouting for his wheelsman to turn hard to port. The stern of the *Ogdensburg* began to "squat" as the engine suddenly changed from "full ahead" to "full astern." The *Ogdensburg*'s whistle happened to be inoperable at the time, and McNell rushed out onto the hurricane deck shouting as loudly as humanly possible, pleading with the other vessel to turn hard to starboard. But it was far too late to avert the inevitable, and he looked on in horror as the bow of the *Ogdensburg* rammed the *Atlantic* hard in her defenseless port side, between the steamer's bow section and her paddle box, directly amidships. The *Atlantic*, valued at around $75,000, went down quickly with her cargo and baggage, worth an additional $75,000, taking between 150 and 300 passengers with her to their watery graves.

In less than a week, salvage divers from around the eastern United States began to arrive like "buzzards to a carcass." It was reported by local news media that "a number of piratical cruisers...are prowling in the vicinity...watching for opportunities to plunder the dead as they rise to the surface." A handful of experienced divers were also on hand, hoping to salvage the sunken American Express Company safe that had been on board the fallen vessel. Rumors claimed that it contained "a vast fortune" in cash and gold. Among these specialists were submariner Lodner Darvontis Phillips and diving bell expert Henry Sears.

Atlantic and *Ogdensburg* collision

Within ten days, Johnny Green and Professor Benjamin Maillefert had also arrived at the Lake Erie site, along with the rest of their crew aboard the steamer, *Fox*. On Monday, September 13, Johnny made his initial dive. Though he felt quite comfortable at a depth of 105 feet, the pressure on his breathing hose malfunctioned and he was forced to return to the surface. A week later, he made a second series of attempts to reach the lost safe:

> "Notwithstanding the somewhat unfavorable condition of the weather and the roughness of the water, it was determined to make an attempt to reach the wreck on Saturday morning, in order to test the capacity of the new hose. Mr. Green therefore arrayed himself in the marine armor and started on his second trip to the bottom of Lake Erie. He descended without any difficulty and landed directly in the interior of the steamer's smoke-pipe, the top and sides of which he felt with his feet and hands. He was then elevated again some little distance, and alighted the second time on the braces, following down until he got onto the cross-braces. He did not however succeed in making a firm footing on the deck, owing to the unsteadiness of the small steamer used upon the occasion, which communicated too much motion to the hose and ropes. There was much risk of the intrepid diver getting entangled in the ropes and wood-work so as to be unable to extricate himself or to tear the dress, and being again elevated, he descended a third time along side and clear of the wreck. He now went down fourteen feet below the upper deck and even with the guards. His head being one hundred and thirty-nine feet below the surface of Lake Erie. This is the deepest dive ever made, one hundred and twenty-six feet being the greatest depth ever before reached. The new hose was found to be perfectly successful; the diver felt quite at ease and went down and up without the slightest injury to dress, pipes or man. The marine armor consists of a perfectly air-tight India rubber dress, topped by a copper helmet with a clear, thick plate of glass in front. The pipes, which supply and exhaust the air, lead from the top of this helmet. The pumping

requires much labor; four, and sometimes six men being employed upon it at the same time, and compeller to work hard at that. A great pressure of air is experienced by the diver upon his lungs, equal to 75 lbs. to the inch, and very few individuals could bear it for any length of time. When first going into the dress the sensation of oppression is very overcoming, but passes away in a great measure after entering the water. When a depth of ten feet in reached in the descent, the dress becoming entirely emptied of air and collapsed to the body, causing a pressure all over the diver equal to the heft of a ten pound weight, excepting as to the head, which is protected by the copper helmet. The difficulty in breathing now becomes great, and a painful sensation is experienced by the diver, the jaws becoming distended, and the head seemingly splitting. This continues until after descending another ten or twelve feet, when the pain is relieved, the diver feels comfortable, and experiences no further inconvenience. When about sixty feet below the surface, hundreds of legitimate inhabitants of the water surround the diver, nibbling at their strange visitor as though he were 'food for the fishes.' After reaching seventy-five feet, all is perfectly dark–a black, impenetrable darkness -- and an electric flame plays around the inside of the helmet, caused by the friction of the pump. At about one hundred and sixty feet the water is very cold being in the present season within four or five degrees of freezing."[17]

Ultimately, Green and Maillefert would fail in their quest to recover the American Express Company safe. On Green's first dive, as stated, his air pump apparatus had malfunctioned, and he was immediately brought back to the surface. The pump was repaired and Johnny made a second attempt, but found himself inside the *Atlantic*'s upright smokestack. Again, his surface crew hauled him back to the *Fox*. And then, on the third dive, he managed to reach the sunken vessel's deck, where he spotted the fallen vessel's bell and other debri, only to have his air hose actually break as he felt his way toward the cabin where the safe was believed to be. Once again, he was fished out, and Maillefert decided that enough was enough, and the entire crew–including Johnny Green–steamed back to Buffalo, New York.

During the winter of 1852-53, Johnny salvaged the 497-ton steamboat, *Erie*, caught fire, burned and sank on the night of August 9, 1841, off Silver Creek, New York. Captained by Thomas Jefferson Titus, she was on her way from Buffalo to Chicago when an explosion was heard and "almost immediately the whole vessel was enveloped in flames." She had taken 242 passengers–mostly German immigrants trapped near her steerage section–down with her. It was later suspected that several cans of turpentine, used just a few days earlier when she had received a fresh coat of paint, had accidentally ignited. It was later reported:

"The lake was a bit rough and the boat was over a mile from shore. The captain and crew stuck to their posts in the fire and heat. Hundreds maddened by fear leaped into the lake to swim to the distant shore. The flames spread with rapidity, the dry timbers of the vessel burning like matchwood. Down in the boiler-room nameless heroes stuck to their work and the captain and the wheelsman at the helm headed the fated steamer to the shore. Soon all that remained of the gallant pleasure vessel was a blackened hull. The screams ceased, the flames died out and the thousands of watchers on the bluffs ashore knew all was over. One of the gallant men aboard was a wheelsman, George Fuller. He stuck to the helm after all others had succumbed and in the blazing pilot-house held the boat straight for shore, thus enabling many to save their lives. He lost his own life in the flames..."[18]

The following morning the shore was lined with dead bodies as far as the eye could see, some drowning and others burned beyond recognition. There were a number of extremely wealthy German immigrants aboard and it is supposed that over $300,000 in money was lost in the disaster. Volunteers from all of the lakeshore towns joined forces in gathering up the remains from the strand, giving them each a proper burial. Even today in various cemeteries, particularly Silver Creek and Sheridan, there are scores of graves marked simply: "A life lost on August 9, 1841, on the steamship *Erie* near Silver Creek."

Until Johnny Green arrived in the region, a number of divers had failed in their quest to locate and salvage the sunken wreck. On Wednesday, September 14, 1853, the *Buffalo Daily Republic* reported the following:

> "The steamer *Southerer*, Capt. Hayes, returned this morning from the wreck of the steamer *Erie*, off Silver Creek. The celebrated diver, John Green, and his partner Mr. Quigley, came down on the *Southerner*. From the former we learn that they anchored over and commenced operations on the wreck of the *Erie* on Monday. Mr. Green decended in his diving apparatus and remained under water four hours. He succeeded in placing a chain around the bow of the vessel and making it fast to a buoy. He also fastened a chain aroun the cylinder, and his partner placed a third chain around the stern of the vessel. She lays on a hard bottom, and no doubts are entertained but that she will be raised. Mr. Green brought up with him several lumps of silver that had been melted, which he found near the engine. As soon as weather permits, Mr. Bishop's derrick will be brought from Grand River, and an attempt made to raise her."[19]

During his numerous dives to locate the sunken riches of the *Erie*, Johnny Green only managed to secure about "seven hundred dollars, mostly in five franc pieces–a better percentage than we often get from many a bank on terra firma." Eventually he gave up the quest and, from there, traveled on to the West India Islands in the hopes of finding and salvaging gold from a British man-of-war, the *Sovereign*, which was lost along the Silver Banks in 1773. Though Johnny could find but a single milled silver dollar, it was estimated that she had gone down with "eighteen tons of Spanish milled dollars."

Meanwhile, Johnny still could not quite bring himself to admit that he had been "defeated" by the *Atlantic* wreck, writing later:

"It is said that there is nothing on earth to which man will so eagerly cling, as to gold. That it occupies his thoughts by day–his dreams by night; and, true to this passion, that wealthy safe at the bottom of Lake Erie had been rife in my mind, during all my adventures on the Silver Banks…"[20]

Eventually, in the summer of 1855, Johnny returned to Boston, where he secured an aging schooner, the *Yorktown*, and a crew of eighteen able-bodied men. Together, in mid-August, they returned to the area where the *Atlantic* had gone down, quite determined to salvage the safe that would make them all rich. After several days of taking bearings and soundings, they believed that they had located the precise spot where the wreck lay–some five miles south of the extreme end of the Long Point peninsula. They lowered iron grappling hooks, snagging onto the sunken vessel and securing buoys up above. Finally, Johnny was ready to dive. On his first attempt, he used a small diving bell to reach the deck of the vessel, which he found covered in about eight to ten inches of muck. Five days later he made a dive without use of the bell–a decision that he would come to regret for the rest of his life:

"…Green descended by means of a line, which having a grapple on the end, became attached to something below. He was dressed with three pair of flannel drawers, three shirts, also flannel, three pair of woolen pants, three coats, and three pair of woolen stockings, surmounted by his submarine armor; on his feet he had a pair of stodgy shoes, with a lead sole 1/2 or 5/8 of an inch thick, and a belt of 80 lbs of shot around his body, to sink him, and the breast piece cannot weigh less than fifty pounds. Taking hold of the line he descended, finding it perfectly so that he could see all around him to the depth of sixty feet, when it grew dark, and for the balance of his fearful journey amid the caverns of the deep, he was guided solely by the line, until at a depth of 140 feet, when he struck bottom, or something which he soon made out to be the wheel house, of the ill-fated boat; grouping-along, he slid on the hurricane deck, from thence to the guards of the boat; by poking around he discovered the precise position of the boat and found himself not far from the sought for office, and made fast the end of the line which he carried down with him, to a stanchion near the gang way, and giving the signal he ascended, carrying with him a piece of the wheel-house which he had secured, (a piece of which, about 8 inches long, 4 inches wide, and 1-1/4 inch thick, was sawed off and presented to me by the captain of the Yorktown.) He had gone down, in all, 152 feet, and remained just 40 minutes…he soon stood on the deck, feeling his way along, he reached the third window, which being unbroken he shattered it, and reaching in his hand at last laid it upon the much coveted safe, just in the position it had been described to him. Not being able to reach far enough to make his line fast, he again ascended for a hook to hook through the handles; reaching the deck he made known his success and requirement, and as no hook was ready, sat down until one could be secured to a line. As they were about ready he rolled over, saying he was sick…"[21]

A horrible pain tore through Green's upper body, and he soon lost all feeling in his lower extremities. Realizing that he was in dire straights, having been overcome by this unidentifiable illness, they quickly removed his diving clothes, buoyed the line leading to the safe, and took the Yorktown as fast as the aging schooner could be coaxed to move back to Port Dover, Ontario. Determining that "he could not live," there was nothing that a pair of local hospital physicians could do to diagnose him or treat him. Yet, resting comfortably throughout the night, the diver seemed to improve somewhat by morning. Slowly, over the course of several days, Johnny's condition steadily improved. When he was strong enough to travel, they sent him on to a specialized clinic in Boston for treatment of his paralysis. Though it wasn't known at the time, Green had suffered an extremely violent episode of what would come to be known in diving circles as decompression syndrome, or the "bends." The condition occurs when dissolved gases, primarily nitrogen, come out as bubbles with changes in pressure. Though not understood at the time, Johnny's affliction affected every part of his body, including joints, lungs, heart, skin, and his brain. He would, in essence, never be the same.

After five months of persistent physical therapy, Johnny was actually able to move around with crutches. By the following summer, he was able to walk, though he was still in a great deal of pain. Yet, even "in this crippled state, (he) was loth [sic] to give up the trial," and he returned to Buffalo, New York, in June of 1856 and, by July, was prepared to make another attempt at salvaging the *Atlantic*'s metalic safe. Oddly, however, when he and his crew arrived, they discovered that the grappling line and buoy that Johnny had attached leading to the vessel's cabin was missing. Though he believed it to be somewhat preposterous, it appeared that some "form of thievery or piracy" had taken place, perhaps within the past few days:

> "On diving to the wreck on the fourth of July, I reached the spot where I left the safe the previous year, and imagine my disappointment, when I found that the prize for which I had almost lost my life once, and risked it again, was gone. Crippled as I was, I worked myself along to the next door–a stateroom–in which there was a trunk containing seven hundred dollars in gold. The trunk was also gone. I felt for the safe again. It was gone...all my efforts for nothing...never did I rise to the surface with such a heavy heart. On emerging, I was again paralyzed, prostrating me equally to my former shock. I was immediately brought to Buffalo, and by treatment which I was then familiar with...I was restored to my present disabled state..."[22]

Soon enough, Green learned precisely who had discovered his marker, followed his grappling line down to the murky depths, and had retrieved the booty before him; it was a man named Elliot Perry Harrington, someone that Green was well aware of. In fact, he further came to realize that Harrington had "succeeded in raising the safe on the twenty-seventh of June," the very same day that Johnny and his crew had set sail for the wreck.

Johnny B. Green, the one-time tugboat captain and now famous salvage diver who was truly "a day late and several thousand dollars short," would always regret that he had reached the *Atlantic* just a few days after the safe had been recovered. Though he did actually marry the true love of his life, Grace Ann Jennings, in Boston, Massachusetts, on August 24, 1854, their wedded bliss was extremely short-lived. Within a year of tying the knot, he had suffered his terrible bout with the bends, and she had been forced to face the fact that he would never be physically able to dive again, let alone give her the children she had dreamed of for so long. Suffering from constant pain, debilitating unhappiness and discontentment pervaded his entire existence. Unable to live with his anguish, Grace would eventually leave him in 1861, sadly having their marriage legally annulled. Eventually, in December of 1865, she would marry Andrew J. Pierce in Chelsea, Massachusetts, with whom she would live out the remainder of her years.

After finally losing the love of his life, Johnny would slowly tumble in and out of deep depression for years thereafter. He drank whiskey heavily on most days, and eventually lost his final battle with hopelessness and despair. On the evening of October 16, 1868, alone at his home in Buffalo, New York, he committed suicide by swallowing cyanide. He was only forty-two years of age at the time. In the pages of its November 28 publication, the *Buffalo Express* summed up his tumultuous life in the following manner:

> "John G. [sic] Green, the diver, whose unhappy death by his own hand… was in his time the principal actor in a little drama, the story of which is an illustration of the fact that as we unconsciously tread every day on the graves of past generations, so we daily meet in every walk of life those whose hearts are the living tombs of buried hopes. Early in life he became deeply attached to a young lady in Chelsea, Massachusetts, the beautiful and accomplished daughter of a wealthy citizen. The attachment was reciprocated, and although while the father of the lady looked with no favorable eye upon what he considered an unequal engagement, he wisely forbore from active opposition. In return, Green pledged himself never to claim the hand of his affianced until he had accumulated sufficient to enable him to retire from a vocation so full of peril in its nature and uncertain in its results. Lighted on by the star of hope he became the most daring and enterprising submarine operator of his time, now plunging down among the weird yet strangely beautiful caves of the tropical seas, which held the wrecked galleons of Spain, and then exploring the bottom of Lake Erie for the sunken treasures of our inland commerce. Such enterprise brought its reward, and he was able to look upon the consummation of his hopes as very near at hand. When he undertook to rescue the treasure from the sunken steamer *Atlantic* he meant that it should be his last job of diving, and he communicated this fact with radiant face to the few friends who shared the cherished secret of his life. He entered

enthusiastically upon the task, and this very impatience proved his ruin. Daring the progress of his work he impudently insisted on descending while warm, against the remonstrance of his comrades. The result is well known. He was seized with paralysis and was dragged to the surface more dead than alive. From that attack he never recovered. He dragged out the miserable remnant of his life a melancholy wreck in health and hopes. Moody and disconsolate, he sought in the intoxicating glass temporary relief from the sorrow, which oppressed him. At length he rashly ended his misery and life altogether, and found in the suicide's grave the peace he vainly sought elsewhere."[23]

Benjamin Sylvester Maillefert

- 19 -
Benjamin Sylvester Maillefert: *Aerostatic Tubular Diving Bell*

"This termagant humor is said to prevail only at half tides. At low water it is as pacific as any other stream. As the tide rises, it begins to fret; at half tide it rages and roars as if bellowing for more water; but when the tide is full it relapses again into quiet, and for a time seems almost to sleep as soundly as an alderman after dinner. It may be compared to an inveterate hard drinker, who is a peaceable fellow enough when he has no liquor at all, or when he has a skin full, but when half seas over plays the very devil. This mighty, blustering, bullying little strait was a place of great Difficulty and danger to the Dutch navigators of ancient days; hectoring their tub-built barks in a most unruly style; whirling them about, in a manner to make any but a Dutchman giddy, and not unfrequently [sic] stranding them upon rocks and reefs. Whereupon out of sheer spleen they denominated it Hellegat (literally Hell Gut) and solemnly gave it over to the devil. This appellation has since been aptly rendered into English by the name of Hell Gate; and into nonsense by the name of Hurl Gate, according to certain foreign intruders who neither understood Dutch nor English…"[1]

For almost 200 years, incoming and outgoing ships had made their way past into the treacherous waters of the East River, maneuvering around outcrops, shoals, and rocky masses through the narrow straits connecting New York City's waterfront to the Long Island Sound. One of the worst areas of all known as Hell Gate, where the Harlem River waters crashed briskly together with those of the East River, and where the latter waterway connected to Long Island Sound. Undoubtedly, its name grew out of its reputation of dangerous currents and "tidal rips that ebbed and flowed through the rocks." One historian would describe the treacherous waterway in the following fashion:

> "When the tide rises on the eastern seaboard it sets into New York Harbor and, farther to the north-east, into Long Island Sound. At New York Bay it splits at the tip of Manhattan, one current pushing up the Hudson and through the Harlem River, the other entering the East River. Here, with the horizontal movement impeded by the opposite flow of the Harlem River and the narrowness of the channel up to the Sound, the huge basin of Hell Gate begins to fill. The waters, like wild beasts, circle their confines, impatient for the chance to escape. The downcoming flow of the Harlem River is then stopped by the strength of the escaping currents

and sent back up through Little Hell Gate and the Bronx Kills, and the channels to the west, like a sluiceway, is filled with swift seething water racing up to the Bronx shore. This flow continues for hours, building up to a high tide along the East River shore. Then at a time when other waters would settle into slack, the downcoming tide, which has been delayed four hours by the distance and the drag of the Long Island Basin, begins its relentless drive—and the struggle for mastery is on. Four hours after entering the sound this tide has changed the flow of the river which is now down the narrow 'sluiceway' from the Bronx and down Little Hell Gate Channel into Hell Gate Basin, counterclockwise around Millrock and as far down the river as the upcoming tide will allow. To this confusion of ebbs and flows, currents and eddies, add the rocks, reefs, and the freakish whims of the winds. At ebb tide the process was reversed, but no less confusing."[2]

Early European explorers, beginning with Dutchman Adriaen Block–whose only memory can be found in the naming of Block Island–made their way through the menacing rip tides and jagged rock underbelly, using only sails, their wits, and prayer. They would keep a constant eye on the water's movement, with their "ship's lifeboats, anchors, and grappling hooks always at the ready." Over time, sailors who threaded their way through the intricate maze gave colorful names to the underwater obstacles: "Pot Rock, Greater and Little Mill Rocks, Hen and Chickens, Frying Pan, Negro Head, Bald Headed Billy, Bread and Cheese, the Hog's Back, Flood Rock Island, and others."[3]

Truths and fables began to swirl around the Hell Gate history, much like the waters themselves. Writer Washington Irving would later contribute to the growing folklore:

> "In the midst of this perilous strait, and hard by a group of rocks called 'the Hen and Chickens,' there lay in my boyish days the wreck of a vessel which had been entangled in the whirlpools and stranded during a storm. There was some wild story about this being the wreck of a pirate, and of some bloody murder, connected with it, which I cannot now recollect. Indeed, the desolate look of this forlorn hulk, and the fearful place where it lay rotting, were sufficient to awaken strange notions concerning it. A row of timber heads, blackened by time, peered above the surface at high water; but at low tide a considerable part of the hull was bare, and its great ribs or timbers, partly stripped of their planks, looked like the skeleton of some sea monster. There was also the stump of a mast, with a few ropes and blocks swinging about and whistling in the wind, while the sea gull wheeled and screamed around this melancholy carcass. The stories connected with this wreck made it an object of great awe to my boyish fancy; but in truth the whole neighborhood was full of fable and romance for me, abounding with traditions about pirates, hobgoblins, and buried money..."[4]

AMERICAN SUBMARINERS: PRE-CIVIL WAR

During the 1840s and early 1850s, one out of fifty vessels that attempted to negotiate the gauntlet was either damaged or sunk. Annually, 1,000 ships ran aground, costing merchants hundreds of thousands of dollars. Finally, the New York Harbor Commission requested Federal assistance in opening up the Hell Gate. The report requesting aid for removing obstructions to navigation blatantly stated: "For several years there has been a gradual but constant increase in the tonnage of vessels engaged in foreign commerce...and their draft is still increasing. It is imprudent to send a ship of the largest class to sea."[5]

One demolitions expert in particular, Professor Benjamin Sylvester Hogarth Maillefert, was identified as someone who might alter the course of the brisk and dangerous one-mile stretch of waterway. Maillefert had, indeed, already gained diving and explosives notoriety in his own right. Born to a French father and Spanish mother in Barcelona, Spain, on November 11, 1813, his family had migrated to southern England in about 1820. At the age of thirty, he married Elizabeth Schmidt, and by 1846 they had found their way to Nassau, on the Island of New Providence in the Bahamas, with their newborn daughter, Josephine Antoinette, in tow. Described by local islanders as outgoing and daring, Maillefert was "of an active turn...(and) had previously passed a life of considerable adventure, a decided spice of romance being mixed up in his career."[6]

The following year, in early 1847, the cargo ship *Sybella*, sailing out of Boston to the Bahamas loaded with cotton and iron, ran aground in the shallows and sank near the Berry Islands. Maillefert, a self-proclaimed expert with underwater explosives, persuaded local officials to hire him to "blow up the wreck," in order to allow salvage divers a means to get at her lost cargo. Initially, explosive charges were placed by Maillefert's crew beneath the ship's belly, between her planks and the underlying rock, and detonated galvanically from above. Eighty such "torpedoes" were fired during a three-week period, though the attempts seemed to inflict little damage to the sunken *Sybella*'s hulk.

Still, the professor did discover something very intriguing in the course of the operation: though the wrecked vessel remained quite intact, the rocks that were below her hull had been obliterated by the explosions. This, in fact, suggested an entirely novel theory to blowing up structures and rocks below the surface of water–instead of placing the charges beneath the intended target, Maillefert now believed that he should position them above his target. And his hypothesis proved correct, for with just a single depth charge, the *Sybella* "was completely shivered into fragments," thus allowing easy access to her hull. Later, one of his divers would describe the explosives used by Professor Maillefert:

> "A canister is prepared, containing powder in proportion to the size of the rock to be blasted. If the rock is a very large one, three hundred pounds is often used. In the side of the canister are inserted two wires, enclosed in gutta-percha. The ends of the wires enter the can, and are united with a small platina wire, and the finest powder is used about this wire as priming... The other ends of the wire are attached to a boat lying at

a safe distance from the spot where the explosion is to take place. By working a battery, the powder is ignited, and instantly is seen, over the rock, or place of the powder, a semi-globular volume of fire,, some twenty feet in diameter, and ten feet high. This consequently forms a vacuum of about the same dimensions; and it is the common belief, that, as the water presses from all sides on its centre, to fill the vacuum, it breaks the rock into pieces. Some, however, are inclined to think it is the shock of powder acting on the rock at the same time it acts on the water. There 'is an immense body of water moved, why not allow the powder to remove a little rock as well as so much water? The effect is so tremendous on the water, that it often throws it into the air two or three hundred feet, and kills fish five hundred feet from the place of blasting..."[7]

Sketch of Maillefert's blasting technique

During the next four months, Maillefert used his newly discovered technique to blast away more than 900 tons of coral off Rockfish Shoal at the entrance to Nassau Harbor. Having complete success there, he was "determined to repair to the United States...with the idea of making his second great effort at the famous Hell Gate," which had long presented hazards to incoming vessels looking to unload at New York docks. In October of 1849, he relocated his wife and daughter to the City of New York, determined to "sell" his blasting techniques to city officials. For nearly two years his attempts to convince the city's decision makers that his unique methods were not "absurd" fell on deaf ears. However, slowly but surely he persuaded a small contingency of backers to endorse his methods. Led by merchant and philanthropist, Moses Henry Grinnell, along with "public-spirited citizen" and newspaper editor, Ebenezer Meriam, the Professor was introduced to U.S. Navy Lieutenant, Maxwell Woodhull, Assistant to the Coast Survey, and Washington A. Bartlett. Slowly, Maillefert was working his way up the political ladder, which, indeed, took time to climb. Becoming convinced of his plan, Woodhull helped him up to the next rung by dispatching a letter to his superior, Alexander Dallas Bache, Second Superintendent of the U.S. Coast Survey. As the "most dominant figure in American science prior and during the Civil War, Bache was definitely the final decision maker:

"Permit me to introduce to you Mr. B. Maillefert, a gentleman of experience in matters of removing rocks and obstructions from harbors and rivers; he is possessed of sufficient means to perform what he engages in."[8]

The committee was prepared to offer Maillefert a contract: no more than $16,000 to $20,000 for the removal of four major rock obstructions, including Pot Rock and Way's Reef at Hell's Gate, as well as Diamond and Prince's Reef out in New York Harbor. In addition, the professor stated the he was "willing to break or scatter, and remove if necessary, the whole of the…shoals in the depth of 30 feet at low tide." Thus, in early August of 1851, Maillefert began the underwater mining process by attacking "the principle obstruction" in the East River, Pot Rock. The first blast shattered four feet from the top and, within a four-month period, he had managed to detonate 301 charges "being a total of 27,981 pounds of powder, at an expense of about $6,000 to blast 19 feet of rock off the top of the 235 by 75 foot boulder."[9]

Sketch of obstruction known as Pot Rock

As the operation continued throughout February and into early March of 1852, Maillefert's activities began to attract a good deal of attention from the general public. Though it all started out with more skepticism than credibility, his gradual success eventually began to change the minds of doubters. In fact, working from dawn until dusk on most days, in the middle of the busy river at the very heart of the city, crowds of onlookers began to get a sense that the submarine blasters might, in fact, be making some real progress. And, it didn't hurt Maillefert's growing reputation that the local news media kept close track of the entire operation, reporting on the step-by-step process that the professor's team employed:

"A large float is anchored in the channel about eight feet from the rock. Precisely at high water, there being but three or four minutes' cessation of the current, the large tin canister is carried from the float and sunk upon the top of the rock. The boat returns to the float, bringing up the end of the wire attached to the canister, Mons. Maillefert attaches the wire to his battery and completes the circuit. Instantly a report is heard, and the mass of waters over the rock rise into the air. There seems to be a solid body of water, perhaps twenty feet in diameter, rising to a height of fifteen or twenty feet, and then towering up in broken fragments and jets twenty or thirty feet higher..."[10]

On Friday, March 26, 1852, Maillefert's team experienced what he already understood all too well–that a single mistake while working with dangerous explosives could be utterly disastrous. At about two o'clock in the afternoon, after having detonated one charge on a protrusion known as the "Frying Pan," the explosives crew prepared to detonate a second charge. They operated from two vessels, with Maillefert and his brother-in-law, William Smith, in a Francis Metallic Lifeboat containing a galvanic battery on a seat in the stern section. In the other vessel, an ordinary wooden lifeboat, were Captain Theodore Southard, two laborers, Joseph Martin and John Whalen, and four 125-pound explosive charges. When all was ready, one of the charges was lowered onto the top of Frying Pan rock, and Captain Southard handed Maillefert the wire, which he believed was attached to the sunken explosive. Yet, instead, it was attached to a second cylinder lying in the belly of the wooden lifeboat:

> "Not suspecting the unfortunate blunder of young Southard's, Mr. Maillefert and his brother-in-law rowed off some forty yards from the other boat, and fired the charge. The effect of the explosion of 125 lbs of gunpowder closely packed in an iron cylinder, were of course, terrific. The boat containing Southard and his companions was blown to atoms, and its occupants sent flying high through the air. Of one man, no trace has been discovered. Of another, a headless, armless, legless trunk was picked up by a rowboat and taken to Steven's Point, where it now is. Southard himself was very seriously injured, both externally and internally. He was blown to a considerable distance, and picked up by the crew of a sloop, which was passing, who conveyed him to Astoria, where he and his two unfortunate companions resided. His physician, Dr. A.H. Stevens, speaks favorably of his condition, but it is to be feared that his wounds are fatal...."[11]

Indeed, within a few days, Captain Southard died of his injuries. The massive explosion had also blasted Benjamin Maillefert and his brother-in-law, William Smith, nearly one hundred and fifty feet into the air, with the former suffering massive bruises and burns, loss of his sight, and a badly broken shoulder. Williams, meanwhile, who was more shielded by the metallic lifeboat, suffered only minor abrasions.

In late March of 1852, a formal inquest into what the media now termed the "Hurl Gate Catastrophe" was conducted, in an effort to determine whether or not Maillefert should be held accountable in the deaths of his three crew members, one of which was never found. Those on the investigating panel listened to testimony from brother-in-law, William Smith and Maillefert's wife, Elizabeth, who had been on shore at the time of the accident. As further testimony, they took a deposition from an eyewitness named James Low, who had refused to pick up the bodies when asked to do so, claiming "they should have been blown to hell long ago."

Sketch of the Hell Gate accident

Finally, the inquisition jury heard from Professor Maillefert himself, who was forced to testify from his bed. After a few short minutes of considering all evidence and testimony given, the jurors offered the following verdict:

> "That the said Theodore Southard and Joseph Martin were killed by the accidental explosion of a canister of powder suspended by the side of a boat. They attach not the slightest blame to Mr. Maillefert, or his assistants..."[12]

Benjamin Maillefert's recovery took several months, with his lost eyesight eventually returning. In mid-June of 1852, he returned to work. Fourteen months later, in August of 1853, he would complete his blasting work in Hell Gate, having pulverized much of Pot Rock, Diamond Reef, and a massive obstruction near the entrance to the harbor at New Haven, Connecticut. Indeed, his efforts had almost completely dismantled the whirlpool that had grounded so many ships. By then he had even patented his method of "improvement in blasting rocks under water." In essence, he had made quite a name for himself throughout the eastern half of the country.

Meanwhile, just after midnight on Friday, August 20, 1852, the ill-fated westbound passenger steamer, *Atlantic*, was on its deadly collision course with the eastbound propeller-driven package steamer, *Ogdensburg*, just off Long Point, a lengthy peninsula that jutted out into the middle of Lake Erie from Port Rowan, Ontario. Under informal rules of the road, by which the majority of shipmasters operated at the time, the *Ogdensburg* was the "vessel of burden," and she was expected to give right of way to the *Atlantic*'s right-of-way. A commonly recited ditty helped sailors recall this vital navigational rule: "If to starboard red appear, 'tis your duty to keep clear."[13]

Hence, it was believed that the sailors aboard the *Ogdensburg* should have been able to see the *Atlantic*'s "red," or portside, running lights off their starboard bow. And it was their responsibility to steer clear of the approaching passenger steamer. Degress McNell, first mate aboard the *Ogdensburg*, failed to do so, however, falsely believing that the Atlantic was still an hour away, and so he kept his vessel steaming on course, full speed ahead.

Suddenly spotting the *Atlantic* directly in his path, coming out of the mist like an apparition, McNell thought that she seemed to change "course, turning to the north as if trying to pass in front of, rather than behind, the *Ogdensburg*." The first mate quickly signaled the engine room to reverse engines, shouting for his wheelsman to turn hard to port. The stern of his ship began to "squat" as the engine changed from "full ahead" to "full astern." The *Ogdensburg*'s whistle was inoperable at the time, and McNell rushed out onto the hurricane deck shouting as loudly as humanly possible, pleading with the other vessel to turn hard to starboard. But it was too late, and he looked on in horror as the bow of the *Ogdensburg* rammed the *Atlantic* hard on her port side, between the steamer's bow section and her paddle box, directly amidships. The *Atlantic*, valued at $75,000, went down with her cargo and baggage, worth an additional $75,000, taking between 150 and 300 passengers with her to their watery grave.

In less than a week, salvage divers from around the eastern United States began to arrive like "buzzards to a carcass." It was reported by local news media that "a number of piratical cruisers...are prowling in the vicinity...watching for opportunities to plunder the dead as they rise to the surface." A handful of experienced divers were also on hand, hoping to salvage the sunken American Express Company safe that had been on board the fallen vessel. Rumors claimed that it contained "a vast fortune" in cash and gold. Among these diving specialists were submariner Lodner D. Phillips and diving bell expert Henry Sears. On Monday, August 30, 1852, the *Buffalo Daily Republic* printed the following report:

> "Mr. Maillefert, of Hell-gate-rock-destroying notoriety, has visited the wreck, or the point where it lies, and believes it praticable [sic] to raise her. He has returned east for his sub-marine apparatus, to raise the safe of the American Express Company."[14]

AMERICAN SUBMARINERS: PRE-CIVIL WAR

Within ten days, Maillefert had returned to the Lake Erie site, along with Johnny Green and the rest of his crew aboard his personal steamer, *Fox*. On Monday, September 13, Johnny made his initial dive. Though he felt quite comfortable at a depth of 105 feet, the pressure on his breathing hose malfunctioned and he was forced to return to the surface. A week later, he made a second series of attempts to reach the lost safe:

> "Notwithstanding the somewhat unfavorable condition of the weather and the roughness of the water, it was determined to make an attempt to reach the wreck on Saturday morning, in order to test the capacity of the new hose. Mr. Green therefore arrayed himself in the marine armor and started on his second trip to the bottom of Lake Erie. He descended without any difficulty and landed directly in the interior of the steamer's smoke-pipe, the top and sides of which he felt with his feet and hands. He was then elevated again some little distance, and alighted the second time on the braces, following down until he got onto the cross-braces. He did not however succeed in making a firm footing on the deck, owing to the unsteadiness of the small steamer used upon the occasion, which communicated too much motion to the hose and ropes. There was much risk of the intrepid diver getting entangled in the ropes and wood-work so as to be unable to extricate himself or to tear the dress, and being again elevated, he descended a third time along side and clear of the wreck. He now went down fourteen feet below the upper deck and even with the guards. His head being one hundred and thirty-nine feet below the surface of Lake Erie. This is the deepest dive ever made, one hundred and twenty-six feet being the greatest depth ever before reached. The new hose was found to be perfectly successful; the diver felt quite at ease and went down and up without the slightest injury to dress, pipes or man. The marine armor consists of a perfectly air-tight India rubber dress, topped by a copper helmet with a clear, thick plate of glass in front. The pipes, which supply and exhaust the air, lead from the top of this helmet. The pumping requires much labor; four, and sometimes six men being employed upon it at the same time, and compeller to work hard at that. A great pressure of air is experienced by the diver upon his lungs, equal to 75 lbs. to the inch, and very few individuals could bear it for any length of time. When first going into the dress the sensation of oppression is very overcoming, but passes away in a great measure after entering the water. When a depth of ten feet in reached in the descent, the dress becoming entirely emptied of air and collapsed to the body, causing a pressure all over the diver equal to the heft of a ten pound weight, excepting as to the head, which is protected by the copper helmet. The difficulty in breathing now becomes great, and a painful sensation is experienced by the diver, the jaws becoming distended, and the head seemingly splitting. This continues until after descending another ten or twelve feet, when the pain is relieved, the diver feels comfortable, and experiences no further inconvenience. When about sixty feet below the surface, hundreds of legitimate inhabitants of the water surround the diver, nibbling at their strange visitor as though he

were 'food for the fishes.' After reaching seventy-five feet, all is perfectly dark–a black, impenetrable darkness -- and an electric flame plays around the inside of the helmet, caused by the friction of the pump. At about one hundred and sixty feet the water is very cold being in the present season within four or five degrees of freezing."[15]

Though a number of so-called "expert divers" claimed that Johnny had not, in fact, managed to reach the sunken vessel, believing her to be at too great a depth for any man to survive such a dive. On one such attempt, however, he proved that he had made it to the lake bottom by bringing up an artifact; the ball that had been attached to the top of the *Atlantic*'s flag staff.

That remnant was then handed over to Henry Wells, co-founder of Wells Fargo and the American Express Company. Wells, in turn, commemorated the sunken ship quite fittingly by placing it on public display at the top of a flag pole standing in front of his Aurora, New York, mansion. Known as Glen Park, he had moved his family from New York City to the small village on the eastern shore of Cayuga Lake, one of New York State's Finger Lakes.

The structure was described as being "of Tuscan villa architecture...the outer walls are of blue limestone, the inner of brick with a chamber between, rendering them impervious to dampness and making the rooms cool in summer and warm in winter. The partitions of the main building are of brick from the foundations upward. The halls and rooms are spacious and sunny, commanding charming views from each window." The home would later be donated to Wells Seminary–renamed Wells College–and used as a residence hall for women.

Ultimately, Benjamin Maillefert, Johnny Green, and the rest of the crew would fail in their quest to recover the American Express Company safe. On Green's first dive, as stated, his air pump had malfunctioned, and he was immediately brought back to the surface. The pump was repaired and Johnny made a second attempt, but found himself trapped inside the *Atlantic*'s upright smokestack. Again, his surface crew hauled him back up to the *Fox*. And then, on the third dive, he managed to reach the sunken vessel's deck, only to have his air hose break as he felt his way toward the cabin where the safe was believed to be. Once again, he was fished out, and Maillefert decided that enough was enough, and his entire crew–including Johnny Green–steamed back to Buffalo.

Benjamin Maillefert returned to primary business of blasting submerged rocks, working his trade during the next several months at Louisiana's Red River to clear the rapids leading upriver to Natchitoches. Johnny Green, meanwhile, joined the Boston Wrecking Company and traveled to the West Indies to search for the fallen British man-of-war, *Sovereign*, which had sunk near the Silver Banks, about seventy-five east of Turk's Island in 1773. The two men would not work as partners ever again.

Over the next several years, Benjamin Maillefert did not remain in close contact with Johnny Green, his one-time close friend and primary diver. Perhaps it was because he had little time, since he was both raising five children

AMERICAN SUBMARINERS: PRE-CIVIL WAR

and designing improvements to his diving apparatus. Arthur, Lizzie, Adam, and Charley were born like clockwork, two to three years apart, beginning in 1854 and leading up to the start of the Civil War. Meanwhile, on March 30, 1858, Maillefert, then living with his growing family in Astoria, New York, submitted a patent application for "Improvements to Diving Bells":

> "The object of the invention is to establish a communication between the interior of a diving bell and the surface of the water, so that the divers may be permitted to come out of the bell and above the surface of the water without raising. This invention consists in the combination with the bell of an air reservoir...for the purpose of facilitating the moving of the machine."[16]

Indeed, Maillefert had long envisioned a number of unique uses for his diving bell, and hoped to capitalize financially. On December 8, 1859, the *Sacramento Daily Union* published a story titled "A Submarine Oyster Saloon":

> "Monsier Maillefert, who removed the rocks at Hellgate, East River, New York, proposes to build a mammoth diving-bell, with which to work the mammoth oyster beds discovered in Long Island Sound. Parties may then enjoy the pleasure of taking the oysters from their beds and devouring them at a depth of six fathoms (80 feet) below the surface of the Sound."[17]

By then, Maillefert had become friends with a man named Levi Hayden, whose background, in many ways, was as diverse and colorful as his own. Born in 1813 in Springfield, Otsego County, New York, he was left an orphan when he was only nine years old. He was then apprenticed at the age of sixteen to a house and ship joiner, Elijah F. Reed, of Hartford. After reaching the age of majority in 1833, he spent the next two years "in the embryo city of Chicago," building houses and sleeping in the only apothecary shop in the fledgling city.

Starting in the summer of 1835–and lasting for more than a decade–Hayden sailed throughout the world, hired on as a ship's carpenter and mail agent. Beginning aboard the new steamer, Bangor, which plied its trade between Boston and Bangor, Maine, he moved on to the whaling vessel, *Cyrus*, the following year, fitted out in Nantucket and bound for the Pacific Ocean. Over the course of the next four seasons, he traveled to Callao, the Marquesas Islands, Tahiti, and eventually Pitcairn Island, the home of the descendants of the mutineers of the English ship, *Bounty*:

> "The only survivor of the original party found there by Mr. Hayden was the Tahitian wife of Fletcher Christian, the chief of the mutineers. The colony comprised about 100 persons. He became much interested in them, and has since made mention of them in some published notes. He was presented with two old Bibles of the Bounty, which were well worn in the instruction of the children..."[18]

Over the course of the next two decades, Hayden engaged in shipbuilding and repair in New York City, where he eventually met and went into business with Professor Maillefert. Incorporating with capital of $50,000, they "commenced the reduction of Coenties Reef and other rocky obstructions," as well as sunken wrecks that interfered with navigation.

Maillefert's *Aerostatic Tubular Diving Bell*

In pursuit of sunken treasures and cargo, the enterprising pair incorporated an innovative diving bell design that had been the brainchild of Professor Maillefert. Known as the *Aerostatic Tubular Diving Bell*, it was a rather large cast-iron, boat-shaped vessel that could be lowered from the surface, positioned precisely, and actually float just a few inches above the bottom or directly above a sunken wreck. Pressurized from a pump, the two men could then be lowered down into the floating arrangement's long, narrow reinforced tube that extended all the way to the surface. The tube, also serving as an airlock, was described in detail by the *Monthly Nautical Magazine and Quarterly Review*:

"The new *Aerostatic Tubular Diving Bell*, invented by B. Maillefert, the well known submarine engineer, is considered the most advantageous submarine apparatus of the present age. By this valuable invention, a secure, permanent, and instantaneous communication with the bottom of rivers and harbors is obtained, thus rendering submarine operations comparatively easy. By it, foundations for piers, light-houses, etc., can be laid at much less expense and less labor heretofore, and the divers can devote their entire attention to the work they have to perform, and need not be under a constant apprehension of accidents, as is the case when working in diving-bells of any other description. Mr. M. has succeeded in accomplishing the great desideratum which has ever been looked for in the art of diving, namely–that of enabling the diver to be perfectly independent of outside attendance, inasmuch as he can at any time go in or out of his bell without disturbing either the men above or the bell below from the position in which it is fixed, and in this respect it is unlike any other apparatus used, where, in all cases, the courageous diver is more or less at the mercy of those above, who oftentimes cannot assist him, through some disarrangement in the machinery, gears, etc., and the poor fellow is left to perish."[19]

Aside from its easy entrance and exit through the tube, with divers getting in or "out in less than two minutes," Maillefert's invention allowed "uniform light" to be admitted at any depth below the surface through that very same tube. Furthermore, with no less than four air-cocks, the funnel acted as a buoy, and it was physically incapable of capsizing–at least in calmer waters. Finally, with one end open at the surface, those assisting from above could readily communicate with those working below the surface. Hence, as the *Monthly Nautical Magazine* wrote, a diver is able to "ask for anything he wants, without any extra exertion on his part to talk louder than usual."

Hence, Maillefert's unusual diving bell design boasted working space inside that was conical in shape and provided space enough for two men. Meanwhile, the outer shell was circular with its chimney-like stack at the center. Ultimately, in 1859, the professor began the New York Submarine Engineering Company, situated at 68 Cedar Street in lower Manhattan, with business partner, Levi Hayden. Soon, the pair offered their diving bell design for sale in four distinct sizes. In an 1860 prospectus, the firm peddled a 1,000-cubic-foot diving bell for a mere $3,200, as well as one half that size for $2,600. The venture, however, would never be financially lucrative.

In order to make financial ends meet, the enterprising pair became involved in clearing underwater river obstructions throughout the eastern United States. Though the work was tedious, it sometimes provided unexpected scientific rewards. In the autumn of 1860, for example, while they and their crew were busy deepening the channel of the Red River Falls near Alexandria, Louisiana, they discovered the remains of a mastodon in the rocks below. The beast's teeth measured four-and-one-half inches in length, and its tusks were six inches in diameter. Understanding the value of the discovery, the professor and Hayden carefully preserved their find and delivered it to a local paleontologist.

LOUIS S. SCHAFER

Depicting of New York Submarine Engineering Company blasting a vessel at Core Sound

In the early months of the Civil War, Maillefert and Hayden remained quite active, being utilized by a number of Union commanders in the field for their keen knowledge of explosives. When General Ambrose Burnside learned that the Confederates were building ironclad ships at Norfolk, Virginia, he planned an expedition to destroy the Dismal Swamp Canal locks to prevent transfer of the ships to Albemarle Sound. Maillefert and Hayden were given three wagons of powder in order to get the job done, though the mission ended as an utter failure when a concentration of fire by Confederate muskets and artillery stopped the advance of 8,000 Union soldiers under the command of General Jesse Lee Reno.

The patriotic pair was then dispatched to "clear out all obstructions from the canals and other channels in the direction of Norfolk, for the passage of the fleet." This was quickly accomplished by the employment of submerged charges. So pleased was General Burnside that he wrote the following recommendation:

"I most cheerfully certify and acknowledge the good and valuable services rendered my department by Prof. B. Maillefert and Capt. L. Hayden, engineers of the New York Submarine Engineering Company, by their very efficient plan of submarine can blasts. The great dispatch with which they removed all manner of sunken obstructions from the channels of the Neuse and Pamilco [sic] Rivers: Core, Croatan, and Currituck Sounds; the Albemarle and Chesapeake Canal, etc., etc., making ample and speedy channels for the passage of our gunboats and transports, elicited my warmest commendation, and greatly facilitated my operations in the department. I therefore warmly recommend them for their skill and practical application of knowledge to other departments or individuals requiring similar services..."[20]

In mid-December of 1863, Maillefert and Hayden submitted an application to the United States Patent Office, which was approved on January 5 of next year. In it, they described their design for a unique "diving room," which could be attached the end of a vessel:

"This invention consists in providing, in the interior of a vessel propelled by steam, sails, or other means, a fixed working chamber with an open bottom, and into which air is compressed, as in a diving-bell, to permit persons to operate within it below the surface of the water, so as to be protected (by the water) from an enemys [sic] projectiles. It also consists in the combination, with such chamber, of an airlock so arranged below the surface of the water as to permit persons to pass through it on their way to and from the working-chamber. To enable others skilled in the art to construct and use our invention, we will proceed to describe it.... We propose generally to apply our invention on board a vessel of the monitor class or an armor-plated vessel of light draft. The working-chamber should, for greater convenience of operation, be arranged immediately at the end of a vessel, and is made airtight at its top and sides, but open at the bottom to the water, said bottom being on a level with or at a convenient distance above the level of the bottom of the vessel. In the example represented the bottom of the chamber is sufficiently above the bottom of the vessel to allow the passage under it of a boom...which works through a horizontal passage formed in the bottom of the vessel, the said boom being intended to carry out to a suitable distance beyond the end of the vessel canisters of gunpowder for blowing up pilings or other solid obstructions, or to be furnished with hooks or other grappling apparatus for tearing away torpedoes, chains, or other obstructions, which can be torn away by the propulsion of the vessel in a proper direction, the said boom to be worked by men within the chamber. This chamber may be also used for making examinations of the channel or for placing charges of gunpowder or for applying other means of removing obstructions than those above mentioned. To permit men to operate within the said chamber below the water-line, the chamber is supplied with compressed air by air-pumps or other means, by which the level of the water within it is depressed below the natural level outside of the vessel. To provide for the entrance and exit of men to and from the said working-chamber without coming on deck, we arrange the air-lock behind or on one side of the chamber, with an air-tight door or man-hole between it and the chamber, and a similar door or manhole between it and the interior of the vessel. When the working-chamber is not being used, the door or man-hole is closed. When persons desire to enter the working-chamber, they enter the air-lock by the door or man-hole and then close it, and afterward open the door or manhole to enter the working chamber. On leaving this working-chamber and passing into the air-lock, they close the door or man-hole before opening. This air-lock is like that used in many diving-bells, except that it is arranged on a level with, instead of below the bell or working-chamber..."[21]

Just a few weeks earlier, Maillefert had also proposed the use of explosive charges to clear the obstructions in the channel between Fort Sumter and Charleston. Each of these "torpedoes," he explained, "will be provided with a clockwork arrangement, which shall determine the exact time of firing; they are to contain 110 to 125 pounds of gunpowder each."[22]

Having witnessed a demonstration of the "depth" charges, a number of Union officials expressed positive opinions of the design. In fact, on February 16, 1864, Rear Admiral John A. Dahlgren, dispatched the following message to Maillefert from his Flagship Steamer, *Philadelphia*, then anchored in Port Royal Harbor, South Carolina:

> "Sir: Having witnessed the action of your time torpedoes, I think they may be serviceable in operating against the rebels at Charleston and elsewhere. If, therefore, you will make without delay 100 of the same kind and deliver them at the New York navy yard I will cause you to be paid at the same rate as charged for those tried...$350 for each..."[23]

The very next day, however, on February 17, the Confederate submarine, *H.L. Hunley*, utilized a spar torpedo to sink steam sloop of war, *Housatonic*. The *Hunley* went down to the murky bottom with the *Housatonic*, not to be seen again for nearly 150 years. As a result of the attack, Dahlgren's wooden vessels kept up their steam and moved further out to sea out of reach each evening. And, even though he had ordered Maillefert's explosive charges, Dahlgren would never utilize them to penetrate the obstructions.

After the War, Benjamin Maillefert was hired at the Torpedo Station along the James River, where he assisted other naval officers in removing Confederate percussion torpedoes. He also agreed, through various written contracts, to assist in the removal of torpedoes and sunken vessels, which continued to hamper peacetime commerce. Under a contract signed on April 15, 1873, the professor agreed to pay the sum of $50 to purchase, salvage, and remove the wreck of the experimental monitor, *USS Keokuk*, which had gone down near Morris Island during the First Battle of Charleston Harbor. Initially named the *Moodna* (often misspelled as the *Woodna*), she had been launched in December of 1862 as one of the first warships to be entirely of iron construction, with wood used only in her decking and as filler in her iron cladding. Yet, after being struck more than ninety times–the majority of which struck her at or below the waterline–her thin composite armor proved to be no match for enemy projectiles.

AMERICAN SUBMARINERS: PRE-CIVIL WAR

Maillefert working with other personnel at the James River Torpedo Station

Within weeks, Maillefert won a bid to clear the wrecks of the *Weehawken*, the *Housatonic*, and the ill-fated *Hunley* submarine, all of which had become dangerous to vessels navigating the channel. Employing helmeted diving gear, he and his crew were able to successfully plant charges above the two larger vessels. Still, after nearly a decade of being submerged, they had both been half-buried in sand and "frozen in place by coral-like growth." As a further hindrance to the entire demolition, the waters in the harbor were so murky that divers were unable to see their own hands in front of their faces. Lacking artificial underwater lighting–which would not be invented for decades–they found it literally impossible to locate the fallen submarine, and the U.S. Navy reported that "the torpedo boat...could not be found."

Later, in September of that same year, Maillefert agreed to remove a number of other wrecks blocking the harbor, along with a portion of Bowman's Jetty. One was the wooden screw steamer, *USS Isaac Smith*, renamed the *CSS Stono*, after her capture on January 30, 1863. Later, when the Confederates abandoned the city on June 5 of that same year, she had burned and scuttled near Fort Moultrie. A second vessel was the *Prince of Wales*, a British schooner that had been captured on December 24, 1861, and was later set afire by Union sailors when Confederate riflemen forced them to abandon ship. Finally, Maillefert agreed to remove the *Juno*, a Confederate steamer that "had broken apart during a storm," sinking so quickly that "most of the surprised crew had drowned."

Though he was now approaching the age of sixty, Maillefert continued his precarious underwater work as an engineer throughout the early 1870s. Still, diving was not the only source of personal danger and public notoriety. While engaged in a project to remove obstructions from the James River in mid-February of 1871, he had an unexpected close call while staying at the Spotswood House Hotel on Main Street in Richmond, Virginia:

> "Being one of the first to wake up at the alarm of fire I lost no time in partly dressing and...I turned my attention to others in need of help, and on my fourth trip up to the second floor was fortunate (or unfortunate) enough to find in bursting a room door open two gentlemen side by side, enjoying the effects of Christmas spirituality. After trying, but in vain, to wake them up to the reality of their awful position I turned one out of bed, and he, being awakened so suddenly and seeing the flames in all their ghastliness through the influence of malt extract, took me, no doubt, for some intruder, and not being prepared or willing to submit to intrusion, straightaway, with energy worthy of a better cause, threatened to mash me, and with sundry adjectives went to bed again. Finding no time was to be lost I used force, and for a time a fierce struggle was carried on in this room of death. I was now under, not on top. Finally, after being scratched and kicked unmercifully, I got the best of this life-wrestling, and dragging the poor fellow through the hall, flung him headlong down the narrow stairs into the arms of some men who happened to be there. Returning to his companion I found him beyond help–the flames had caught their unconscious prey."[24]

Steregraphic image of Maillefert's Sub-Marine Exhibition on Lake Otsego

Later that same year, Maillefert traveled throughout the country demonstrating his unique methods of underwater blasting. In August of 1871, he found his way to Cooperstown, New York, along the southern banks of Otsego Lake. There, his "Sub-Marine Exhibition" was "witnessed by a large number of highly interested spectators" who had gathered to see the blast. In order to ensure that those who had failed to see the event first-hand, a local photographer, Washington G. Smith, managed to capture an image for posterity's sake.

By 1874, the sixty-one-year-old professor was keeping himself extremely busy in Charleston Harbor, salvaging the many Civil War wrecks that remained there. His work was slow and tedious, involving blasting the wrecks and then lifting up the pieces without the use of diving bells. Major James W. Cuyler, U.S. Army Corps of Engineers, reported on his progress in cleaning up the harbor:

> "Mr. Griffin raises his stone by a pair of grappling-irons, worked by a whip by manpower, on a small flat, and can raise stone from 1½ to 2¼ cubic yards in size. Mr. Maillefert works on a larger scale, using a large scow, on which is a heavy 'tongs' or set of claws, run by steam-power, and can take up stone from 3 to 4 cubic yards in size. The locality is most unfavorable for the work. Owing to exposure to heavy seas and a contracted channel-way, giving strong currents, varying with the winds and the different stages of the tide, it was found impossible to do any work but for about an hour on either side of the slack-water time, so that the work has progressed but slowly; scarcely as rapidly as the importance of it called for…"[25]

As the months passed, it became increasingly obvious that Maillefert's progress was unacceptable. One observation was made about five hundred yards east of Bowman's Jetty, extending from "Sullivan's Island across the channel to Drunken Dick Shoal, a length of about 370 yards." The greatest low-tide depth in that region was measured to be about fifteen feet, making the area impassable by a number of heavier vessels. In fact, it was further reported that "there was no perceptible improvement…notwithstanding Mr. Maillefert's dredge-steamer had then been at work nearly a year."[26]

As a result, it was determined that "no further appropriation is now recommended for containing this work." Unfortunately, by 1876, Maillefert was completely bankrupt, desperate for money, and his health had taken a turn for the worst. He was forced to retire to his home in Astoria from the business of underwater salvage and obstruction clearing.

Yet, age could not quiet the professor's inventive mind. In March of 1880, he joined forces with Henry Ehlers of New York City to apply for a patent on "a process and apparatus for refrigerating and making ice," in which compressed air from a pump passed through a cooling mechanism supplied with a constant stream of cold water. From there, the air passed on to a chamber, expanding with the presence of steam supplied in a jet stream, bringing the air and steam particles of "moisture into intimate contact" and making ice. The entire process was considered ingenious for the times. The patent was granted in late August of that same year.

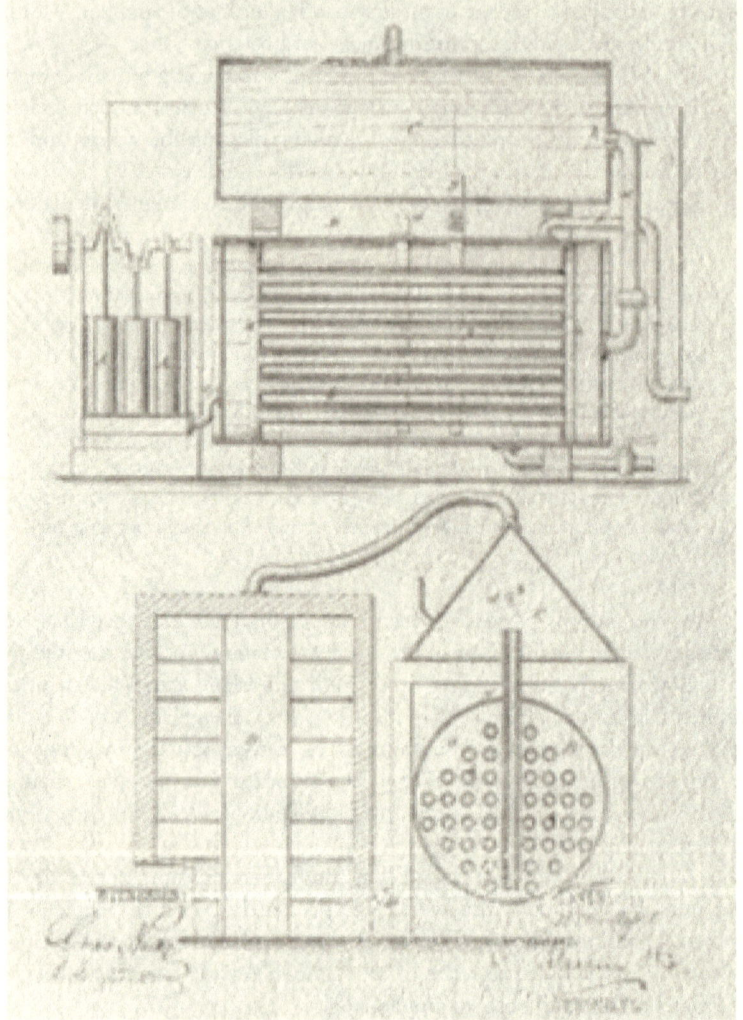

Patent drawing of Maillefert's ice making machine

Benjamin Maillefert health continued to deteriorate over the next several months. Though he had cancer, records would indicate that he died on August 8, 1884, of typhoid fever, and was laid to rest in Thomasville, Davidson County, North Carolina. Two years later, however, his remains would be exhumed and reburied in the family plot at the Saint Michaels Cemetery, situated in the East Elmhurst section of Queens, New York. His only commemoration–more a historical comment than an obituary–was printed in the *New York Times* a few days after his death:

AMERICAN SUBMARINERS: PRE-CIVIL WAR

"Prof. Benjamin S. H. Maillefert was a member of the firm of B. Maillefert & Co., who obtained a reputation in their experiments with surface blasting, which was applied by them to the Hell Gate work. He was engaged in this work as far back as 1855. Their implements for surface blasting consisted simply of a boat and iron rod, to feel the bottom with and to let down charges with an electric battery. The firm obtained a contract to clear away Pot Rock and Sheldrake Reef, the contract ending on January 1, 1870. The result of their labor was not entirely satisfactory, as during the summer the rock was blown away only so as to give a depth from 12 to 20 feet, while the contract called for 25 feet. The Government then took charge of the work under Gen. Newton. Prof. Maillefert since then led a quiet life, not engaging in any business."[27]

Even though the *New York Times* failed to make mention of a number of other vital contributions to American diving, historical records certainly indicate precisely how important those contributions were in the evolution of submarines.

Portrait of Elliot Perry Harrington

- 20 -
Elliot Perry Harrington: *Lake Erie Sub*

"When the diver alighted upon the deck, he was saluted by a beautiful lady, whose clothing was well arranged, and her hair elegantly dressed. As he approached her, the motion of the water caused an oscillation of the head, as if gracefully bowing to him. She was standing erect, with one hand grasping the rigging. Around lay the bodies of several others as if sleeping. Children holding their friends by their hands, and mothers with their babies in their arms were there."[1]

Such sensationalized reports began to appear and reappear in a number of 1856 publications across the country, including the *National Magazine*, the *Detroit Advertiser*, the *Frank Leslie's Illustrated Newspaper*, and *Scientific America*. Though highly intriguing and truly amazing to anyone who envisioned the deep seas as a world of wonder, they had all been completely and utterly fabricated. For a brief while, the identity of the "diver" who had "alighted upon the deck" would remain a total mystery. Yet, soon enough, the name of Elliot P. Harrington would begin to become quite well-respected.

Indeed, until then, Harrington had been somewhat of an unknown to the realm of deep salvage work. Though he appeared to be nothing more than a common farmer, he had come from a long line of renowned ancestors, beginning some three centuries earlier in Stepney, Middlesex County, along the eastern section of London with his seventh paternal great-grandfather, Sir John Harrington. Known in historical records as "the Poet," John Harrington had been born about 1525 and was married to Etheldreda (Malte) Dyngley, the natural–though publicly unacknowledged–daughter of King Henry VIII. At the time of her birth, the King had bribed John Matle, the royal tailor, to claim Etheldreda as his own illegitimate daughter, though Matle never actually married Etheldreda's mother, Joan, the royal laundress. John had, however, made a very profitable marriage, securing from the union not only the Manor of Kelston, but four other manors in Somerset. These wealthy properties had been taken from Bath Priory and given to Etheldreda by the King. Either way, though she died without carrying on the royal bloodline, John was not forgotten, and was eventually attached to the services of Princess Elizabeth.

Soon, John the Poet was remarried to Isabella Markham, daughter of Sir John Markham, Knight of Cobhane and one of the princess' ladies. In 1554, with Mary's accession, John and his wife were imprisoned in the tower, along with Princess Elizabeth. Later, with Elizabeth on the throne and John's position secure, he began the building of one of the great manor houses of that day at Kelston. The fact that John the Poet was the son of John Harrington and Elizabeth Mutton is proved by the statement in *National Biography*, in which several pages are devoted to the life and accomplishments of John the Poet. It is stated that John, who died at Worms in 1613 (son of James, first Lord of Harrington) was a cousin of John Harrington 'the Writer' (son of John the Poet). This gives them a common grandfather in the John who married Elizabeth Mutton and shows their youngest son to have been John the Poet.

John Harrington the Poet's son, known in historical records as John the Writer, was born in Kelston, Somerset County, in August of 1561 and educated in law at Eaton and King's College in Cambridge. He grew up to become a courier, a master of art, and "a prolific muse writer." He became a prominent member in the court of Queen Elizabeth I, and was affectionately known as her "saucy Godson." After marrying Mary Rogers, daughter of George Rogers of Cannington, in 1583, he fell out of favor with the often opinionated queen and was banished from her court for what were termed "racy" interpretations of both French and Italian works. In fact, he was told not to return until he had fully translated a particular lengthy poem by Ludovico Ariost, entitled *Orlando Furioso*. After literally years of work on the immense project, he managed to complete the task in 1591.

At about the same time, John Harrington III also devised Britain's first flush toilet. Called the Ajax—a "jakes" being an old slang word for toilet—it was initially installed at his manor in Kelston, and later used at the castle to Elizabeth I's "great satisfaction." In 1596, under the pseudonym of Misacmos, John the Writer published a book about his invention, called *A New Discourse upon a Stale Subject: The Metamorphosis of Ajax*. The book, which made political allusions to the Earl of Leicester, greatly angered the Queen, who believed it to be a coded attack on the "stercus," or "excrement," that was poisoning society with torture and state-sponsored "libels" against his relatives, Thomas Markham and Ralph Sheldon. After the publication of this work John was again banished from the court, though the Queen's mixed feelings for him may have been the only thing that saved the Writer from being tried at Star Chamber. The work itself enjoyed considerable popularity throughout England and beyond.

It was the next Harrington generation, John the Writer's son, John IV, who brought his wife, Ann (Clinton) Harrington, to America. Landing in Boston aboard the *Elizabeth* in about 1630 with their two sons, Robert and Benjamin, records indicate that the elder Harrington died in an accidental drowning in Boston Harbor within a few months of the family's arrival. Hence, Benjamin, submariner Elliot Harrington's fourth great grandfather, came of age with his three siblings without their father as a role model. Unable to raise the three boys in a proper manner, the widow Ann sent them to live with their uncle in Rhode Island. Records indicate that Benjamin acquired a twenty-five-acre parcel of land in Providence on January 19, 1654, along with his close friend and distant relative, John Clawson.

During the next six years, the two friends had a falling out. On the night of January 4, 1661, Clawson was attacked from behind a thicket of barberry bushes, near the north burial ground by an Native American named Waumanio, whom Clawson "supposed to be instigated there" by Benjamin Harrington. Clawson's chin was split open by a blow with the broad axe, and from the gaping wound he soon died, but not before he had pronounced a strange curse upon his suspected murderer. As legend records, generations of Harrington's believe that the dying man's words were strangely fulfilled, "that he (Harrington) and his prosterity might be marked with split chins and be haunted with barberry bushes" from that day forward. By these words it was believed that the descendants of the murderer were marked by the "excavated or furrowed chin which caused the curse of Clawson to be kept in remembrance," and a number of arguments were caused by "huskings and frolics" whenever mention of the words "Barberry bushes" were spoken around any member of the Harrington clan.

Meanwhile Waumanio confessed to the horrific attack on Clawson and was sentenced to be executed by hanging, while Benjamin Harrington, who had been initially charged as an accessory, was cleared by the jury and the court. A century and four generations later, Job Harrington, the eldest of twelve children, was born to Stephen and Patience (Eldred) Harrington in the town of Pownal, tucked into the southwest corner of Vermont in Bennington County. In 1804, he was commissioned from Lieutenant to Captain and, eventually, came to reside in the town of Climax, Kalamazoo County, Michigan.

Chautauqua Creek near Harrington Road

One of Captain Job Harrington's fourteen children, Larkin–submariner Elliot's father–was born on January 22, 1800, in Otsego County, New York. After marrying Abigail Houghton, son Elliot Perry was also born there on April 19, 1824, the second of eight children–four sons and four daughters. The family would relocate to a farm near the tiny crossroads town of Volusia, situated just a few miles south of Westfield, New York, in 1825. The journey was typical of the times, with the Harrington family packing everything of value in an old, wooden wagon, with "a good ox team the reliable propelling force."

There, Elliot grew up on a large wooded chunk of property, helping his father cut and trim old-growth trees at the family owned saw mill, nestled along what was known as Harrington Road. The old dirt two-track pathway branched eastward where Lyon Road made an abrupt turn southward near the Porter family farm and graveyard, coming to an abrupt end along the west side of the ever winding Chautauqua Creek. In 1846 and 1847, Elliot attended the Chautauqua County Teachers' Institute, with aspirations to become an educator in western New York. Yet, that all seemed to change on February 8, 1849, when, at the age of twenty-five, Elliot married his already pregnant eighteen-year-old cousin, Emmeline Leticia Maxion. Emmeline, who had been born in Ypsilanti, Washtenaw County, Michigan, on March 8, 1830, would give him two sons sandwiched in between two daughters; Ada Francis, William Murray, Forest Deville, and Alice Mabel–the latter of whom everyone affectionately referred to as "Allie."

Porter graveyard, where Ada Francis is buried

Elliot and Emmeline struggled mightily after their first child was born in September of 1849, trying desperately to keep food on the table. Yet, in spite of their hopes and aspirations, young Ada Francis came down with a severe case of cholera during the early weeks of 1852. She died on March 22, and was laid to rest in the Porter graveyard, next to her first cousin and namesake, Frances Harrington, who had died when just a baby fifteen years earlier.

Elliot–who would identify himself at different times as a "wheelwright," a "millwright," a "farmer," and a "submariner operator"–initiated his diving career at the age of twenty-eight. Beginning in childhood, he had exhibited a remarkable gift for mechanical work, constantly tinkering with simple machines, improving them or making something entirely new from parts, and he "seemed to understand mechanical bearings at sight." His friends would claim that he seemed "destined to take up submarine work," since he was "as much at home in the water as on land." So, when the 355-ton screw sloop, *Oneida*, capsized while under sail amid a horrific gale and went down with nineteen hands just a few miles east of Barcelona, New York, on November 10, 1852, it was natural for him to traverse the seven miles northward from the family farm to the site of the sunken ship and attempt to secure the valuable cargo that had gone down. Elliot was completely successful in this, his initial diving venture, bringing up the *Oneida*'s entire shipment of flour, along with a number of other valuables.

The same storm that had swept across the Great Lakes during that two-day period resulted in the complete or partial loss of fifty-four other vessels, creating a literal windfall for salvage divers throughout the Midwest. Hence, during the next several months, Harrington plied his diving skills in the harbors, rivers, and inland lakes of New York, Ohio, and Michigan, with a number of successful attempts to salvage both cargo and human remains. An adequate income from his expertise was slowly developing into a steady career.

In 1853, a propeller-driven vessel named the *Princeton*, mastered by Captain Charles D. Ludlow, sank just west of Van Buren Point, New York. Heavily loaded with a cargo of dry goods, stoves, hardware, and an assortment of agricultural implements, she had been dispatched from the Erie railroad unloading dock at nearby Dunkirk, some eight miles to the northeast. Resting at the sandy bottom at a depth of about eighty-five feet, the local press reported on salvage efforts conducted by a local diver:

> "With consummate skill the *Princeton* was unloaded and the young Chautauquan (Harrington) gave back to the Erie railroad a large portion of the cargo which had been delivered to the ill-fated steamer..."[2]

In the spring of 1855, Elliot had taken his twenty-three-year-old wife and two young children from Volusia, New York, to Washtenaw County, Michigan, so that they might visit her parents in Ypsilanti while he took a vacation from his hectic diving schedule. Yet, catastrophe and the need for his diving skills seemed to follow him no matter where he went. On June 2 of that year, a sheep farmer named William Briggs, from Scio Township, just west of Ann Arbor in Washtenaw County, Michigan, drowned while washing his sheep in a small lake near the Briggs family farm. Reportedly, he had "swam across it some forty rods, and upon returning was... seized with cramps and sank near the middle." The *Ypsilanti Sentinel* offered the following press on the accident and subsequent efforts to recover his body:

> "All efforts to recover the body being fruitless. Messrs. (Elliot) Harrington and (Lodner) Philips were sent for to search with their submarine armor... Accordingly, on Thursday last, they made numerous descents, at various depths, discovering most singular irregularities of bottom, and curious formations. In some places the plummet will strike bottom in a short distance. A few feet off, down it goes to an almost unfathomable depth. Sometimes upon arriving at what seemed to be the bottom, the diver's feet rest upon nothing, and down he goes into impenetrable darkness and a soft mass of mingled water and sediment, until prudence warns him against further progress. Down sixty-five feet from the surface went Mr. Harrington, in the vain search for solid bottom, and still his lead sank through 'deep obscure." At one time the plummet will show a current which carries the line rapidly away from the perpendicular, again it swings around, indicating a whirling eddy..."[3]

Harrington and Philips made a number of daring efforts to recover the remains, but it was all to no avail, for the body was never found. Still, a headstone was erected in Ann Arbor's Forest Hill Cemetery to commemorate the life of William David Briggs, placed there by his grieving wife, Harriet.

In the winter of 1855-56, Harrington brought together a team of sailors and mechanics to assist him with maintaining his surface search vessel, air pump apparatus, and diving bell. They included: Martin Quigley, a forty-five-year-old "carpenter" and "architect" from Portland, Chautauqua County, New York; Charles O. Gardner, a twenty-eight-year-old machinist, also from Portland; and William M. Newton, a twenty-seven-year-old mechanic, who had recently relocated from Poland, Chautauqua County, New York, to Detroit, Michigan. Working aboard an aging schooner that Harrington had recently purchased, the four friends set off to make an attempt to recover the *Atlantic*'s sunken riches:

> "It is the afternoon of June 18th, 1856, and the schooner *Fletcher* has just dropped anchor off the western tip of Long Point. She has sailed from either Dunkirk or Barcelona, with evidence supporting the latter port and...the names of at least four of those aboard have come down to us. Perhaps there were others, but it is established that Elliott [sic] P. Harrington of Volusia, Charles Gardner and Martin Quigley of Chautauqua, and William Newton of Detroit, Michigan, were aboard, and these four men, treasure-bent probably, took no 'outsiders' along. In the past weeks they had dragged for and located the sunken Atlantic, which, for almost four years had been resting upon the bottom of Lake Erie and, although at least four previous efforts by others to raise the safe from the wreck had failed, these four men, with abounding faith in themselves, believed the

seemingly impossible could be done. They knew the ship rested in 170 feet of water, a discouraging depth to even the most bold-hearted of divers and yet they were ready to sacrifice time, money and even life to bring the treasure to the surface. They were not to be deterred by the awful pressure of water at the depth of 175 feet, nor of the darkness and cold certain to envelope them. They knew the strong box reposed just where the purser of the sunken ship told them it did–in his stateroom or cabin, just abaft the pilot house on the port bow. No door led to it from the deck and the only way access to the room could be gained was through a window. Danger was written in every move, yet that afternoon they calmly went about their work of preparation. In one respect they were favored. Lake Erie was enjoying a period of calmness. The surface was as calm as a millpond; ideal weather for diving. On the morrow, Elliott [sic] Harrington was to make his first descent into the unknown... And now with a riding light in the deck of the *Fletcher* and with one of the quartette to stand watch, the others sought sleep for the night, hoping Lake Erie would continue her spirit of calmness and that the 19th of June, 1856, would be favorable for their first efforts to be made in tearing from the grasp of Davy Jones, the $35,000 he had now held for 4 years..."[4]

Indeed, the following morning, Thursday, June 19, dawned bright and calm across Lake Erie, ideal for a safe dive. After all mechanics of the pump were checked and rechecked, the foursome prepared to go down. Finally, Harrington donned his somewhat cumbersome diving suit. Known as "submarine armor," it had been designed by Thomas Foster Wells and John Emery Gowen, Boston business partners. To Harrington's team, the suit appeared to be coal black, indicative of the fact that "the usual outer layer of canvas" had been discarded by the diver, leaving the rubberized "Macintosh cloth" exposed beneath. When he was certain that all was in place, Harrington gave the customary hand signal, indicating that he was ready to begin his slow descent:

> "...encased in Wells & Gowen's submarine armor, (Harrington) made his first descent. This armor is made of two layers of canvas and one of India rubber, the rubber occupying the middle. It is loose and flexible, and of course resists no pressure. From in front of the mouth proceeds a tube composed of nine alternate layers of canvas and rubber, with a copper wire coiled inside to prevent collapse. This is flexible too, and being as long as the depth to which the diver goes, and the upper end being in the open air, secures proper respiration. The aperture is three eights of an inch in diameter..."[5]

Though they could not hear him through his diving helmet, Quigley, Gardner, and Newton fully understood the signal. With leaden shoes strapped securely to his feet, and additional weights tied around his torso, Harrington gave one final tug on the rope. Aside from the "check," or signal line in his hand, the rope and India rubber breathing tube would be his only lifelines to the surface.

Drawing of Wells & Gowen submarine armor, circa 1855

Over the side went Harrington, immediately disappearing beneath the murky water's surface:

> "...he was governed by the wreck-line, and struck the promenade deck about forty feet aft the state-room where the Express Company's safe was, which was in the third state-room aft the wheelhouse on the larboard side. He remained on deck but one minute. After descending from 50 to 70 feet, depending upon the clearness of the air above, all is dark to the

diver, and he is governed entirely by feeling... The greatest caution as to entangling lines must be used, and Mr. Harrington went each time outside the stanchions, moving, as he advanced, his wreck line, so that with each dive he advanced nearer the stateroom. The second dive he was three minutes upon deck; the third four; the fourth seven..."[6]

Yet, despite his repeated efforts, Harrington did not strike pay dirt, for the safe remained just out of his reach. As the afternoon waned, the foursome decided to call it a day. On June 20, Harrington made four more dives:

"Sunrise on the morning of June 20th, 1858, revealed another "flat" spell on the surface of Lake Erie. The day came on both hot and clear and Elliott [sic] Harrington early began his activities of the second day's diving into the paralyzing cold and stygian darkness of 170 feet of water off Long Point. On the day before he had actually reached the deck of the sunken *Atlantic* and had fought his, way through cold, blackness and slime in his brief descents in trying to locate the purser's stateroom, the third room abaft the wheel-house on the port side of the sunken ship. The day had closed and the treasure still remained hidden below. With this his descent of the second day came a prowl of four minutes on the promenade deck. Harrington could stay no longer and he was hauled to the surface, rested, and made ready for the second. Now he was down seven minutes, edging his way forward on the object of his search, smashing at either wood or glass as he trudged along. Always as the steel bar crashed through an object, he knew he was at a stateroom window, if nothing gave way, he realized he was hitting wood. To the surface again, there to rest and dive once more. Down now for the third dip. It was afternoon and he withstood the pressure and cold on that descent of three minutes, edging forward still breaking windows, still crashing the steel bar into wood. Hauled to the surface, rested again and down now for the fourth and last time that day. This would make eight dives in two days and we wonder at the stamina of the man making those descents into the depth of water. Below this fourth time for six minutes a total of twenty minutes that day and fifteen the day before. Thirty minutes of actually walking upon the deck of the *Atlantic*, how Harrington must have smiled to himself as he completed his work of that fourth dive on the second day for it was on this descent that he locate beyond any contradiction, the window of the purser's room. Half the battle had now been won, but serious and painstaking work remained; no door led in the room and no other way of entering it existed save through the small window. A blow from the steel bar removed the glass and thus he now stood almost squarely before the prize. The *Atlantic*'s purser had told him where it would be found, adding that a chain was affixed to its top and if contact were made and the box dragged to the window, it might small enough to be pulled through the opening and onto the deck. Thus closed the labors of the second day. They had been fruitful, the exact spot where the money rested was known and so it was that on the night of June 20th, 1856, the four young men aboard the salvage ship *Fletcher* discussed their plan of attack for the morrow. Weather indications were favorable and it appeared Lake Erie was in the embrace of one of those 'flat' periods, when for days the surface is like a millpond. Ideal days for diving and though Davy Jones still held the treasure, his hold upon it was now fast becoming insecure and if the present weather held, the seemingly impossible might be accomplished."[7]

Like Johnny Green before him, Elliot Harrington intended to use a "boom derrick" to lift the hefty safe to the deck of the *Fletcher*. Having heard of Green's miraculous recovery and intentions to dive for the *Atlantic* once again, the wily Harrington had picked up the pace of his own dives. On his very next attempt, he had followed the grappling line once again down to the fallen vessel and had found the opposite end attached to the ship exactly where Johnny Green had left it. Unable to see, he felt his way along the deck where he finally put his hands on the safe. Quickly, he attached cables to it that were pulled by the steam-powered hoist aboard his salvage boat. Yet, when the steam engine had given the safe a powerful tug, the steel strongbox had moved so suddenly that Harrington was unable to get completely out of its way. Fortunately, it was only a slight glancing blow to his temple, for if it had been "head on," it likely would have killed him.

On June 22, 1856, the "perilous work was done," and the four men stood aboard the schooner *Fletcher* in celebration as they pried open the twenty-eight-inch by eighteen-inch by sixteen-inch iron chest. Inside they found an estimated $5,000 worth of gold, $31,000 worth of bills, and six watches, two of which were solid gold. Yet, reportedly, the iron chest had not been waterproof:

> "Water had entered the box in those forty-six months of submersion in Lake Erie and the paper money was not in good condition. Nevertheless, it was capable of being counted and the men found themselves in possession of thirty-one thousand dollars in paper money. This, with the gold coins, totaled thirty six thousand dollars, which verified the rumor, which spread at the time the *Atlantic* went down of her taking with her to the bottom, thirty-five thousand dollars in money. Nothing now remained but to divide the treasure and as to the actual money, it was divided into four equal parts, or about nine thousand dollars to each of the four men engaged, it was a liberal reward for that brief half week of labor, dangerous as it had been and the success of the exploit soon reached the public; newspapers acclaimed it as well they should and the four men seemed set for life. Nine thousand dollars was quite a sum of money in those days... and one in possession of a nest egg of that size could well consider himself free from want..."[8]

The four jubilant salvagers were not able to celebrate for very long. In actuality, whether they realized it or not, they had failed to follow the precise letter of the law after salvaging the sunken safe. Legally they were mandated to go before a United States court, relate what they had done to rescue the valuables, and take an order as to the disposition of the gold and money inside. Capitalizing on their legal error, the American Express Company would opt to take the matter to a Buffalo, New York, court, where they had "obtained an injunction against the spending and keeping of this money by the men who had recovered it." Ultimately, the Company demanding the return of what they believed was rightfully theirs.

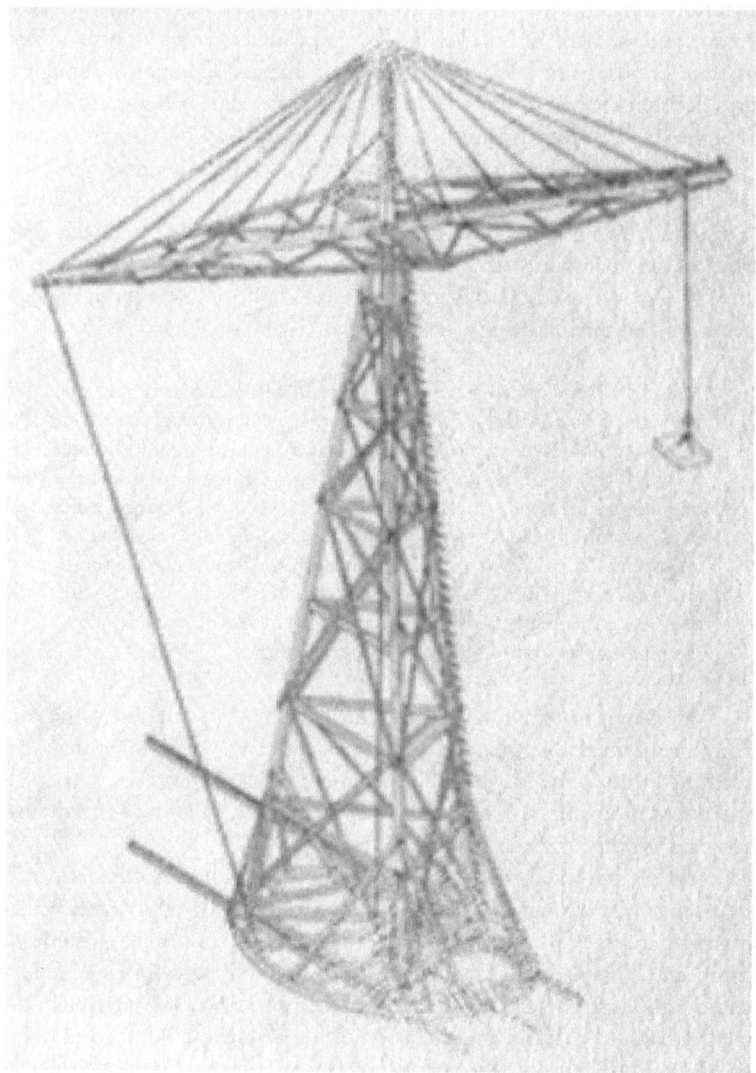

Drawing of a boom derrick used by Harrington aboard the *Fletcher*

When their day in court finally arrived, Harrington embarrassingly admitted that about $2,800 had been destroyed when he had "tried to dry it in his mother's kitchen stove." A compromise for the remainder of the recovered money was reached, with the salvage crew keeping just the $5,000 in gold, $2,000 in notes from the Bank of Erie, and the two gold watches–which were now "mysteriously missing." The rest of the recovered gold script, including a share drawn from the Government Stock Bank of Ann Arbor, the Burlington Bank of Vermont, and the Bank of America in Chicago, as well as $4,600 worth of Michigan State Bonds, went back to the American Express Company. Though the court's decision seemed to put an end–at least for the time being–to the lengthy saga of the *Atlantic*'s lost treasure box, it wasn't the finality of Harrington's career.

In late September of 1856, Harrington received an unexpected letter from a treasure hunter living in New Jersey, asking the experienced diver to join him on a diving expedition. Indeed, Harrington was intrigued, and shared the text of the invitation with John W. Barnes, editor of the *Grand River Times*, printed in Grand Haven, Michigan. A few weeks later, on October 8, the newspaper published the following article, entitled "Kydd, the Pirate":

> "A man in New Jersey has written a letter to Mr. E,P. Harrington, the celebrated diver, that he has an instrument that will unvaryingly point out metal, even if it is 300 feet under water. He says he has found, through the use of this machine, the safe of the steamer Lexington, and also the long sought for 'Kydd vessel.' Of the last, he says, she is about 30 miles from New York... He has been over the spot, and has bored through her deck several times. He writes quite confidently, and wants Harrington to go down and join him in an expedition to recover the lost treasure. The vessel lays under ten feet of mud, and about twelve feet of water over that. The mud can be scraped off with a dredge, he thinks...."[9]

Yet, even if Harrington had been intrigued by the possibilities, the editor of the *Times* seemed to scoff at the notion that such vast wealth might have been rediscovered with some 'hair-brained" metal-detecting contraption, stating: "Let those in search of a pirate invest their money." Besides, Elliot had already made other plans for the immediate future.

Still disappointed by the court's decision in favor of the American Express Company, Harrington packed up his wife and two young sons, William and Forest, and moved them nearly 600 miles west to the fledgling, somewhat insignificant, crossroads village of Charles City, Iowa. Situated in Floyd County, straddling the eastern bank of the Cedar River, the town had originally been named "Charlestown" after the eldest son of Joseph Kelly, a hunter and trapper from Monroe, Wisconsin, who was the area's first known white settler in 1850. The name changed, first to "St. Charles" and eventually to "Charles City," in order to avoid duplication of other Iowa community names. Charles City had recently become the seat of Floyd County, when it was established in 1851 and officially organized in 1854. Floyd County, meanwhile, had been named for Sergeant Charles Floyd, a member of the Lewis and Clark Expedition.

The Harrington family settled into a modest home on the west side of St. Charles Township, where Elliot took up the trade of carriage maker. Always interested in local causes and, perhaps being proactive about any future family deaths, he had helped to establish the Charles City Cemetery Association on December 29, 1857, for "the purpose of purchasing and platting a piece of ground for the internment of the dead, and to superintend the sale of the lots." Harrington was called upon to be one of its first trustees, and had a hand in purchasing the Association's first eighty acres for $340–later to become the western most portion of the Riverside Cemetery as it expanded eastward. The plan was to recoup the initial investment by the selling of burial plots, though it is believed that a number of local citizens were interred before the Association broke even.

As time passed, the Harringtons gradually became a larger part of the Charles City everyday fabric. During the local July 4, 1858, St. Charles City celebration, he became a local celebrity when he entertained a large group of locals with his diving prowess. The *St. Charles City Republican Intelligencer*, owned and published by Azro Benjamin Franklin Hildreth, reported on the events:

> "E.P. Harrington made an exhibition, in the Cedar River, of the celebrated 'Diver,' a sort of armor to be used in diving into water."[10]

From there his popularity grew rapidly. Just a few days later, on July 7, Deacon Nicholas Fleenor of nearby Rock Grove City resigned as the Floyd County Coroner, and Harrington was selected as his successor. In August, he was popularly elected on the Republican ticket as one of St. Charles City's constables, a peace officer given full authority to uphold law and order throughout the growing community. Then, on October 1, 1858, he became one of the founders of the St. Charles "Blue Lodge of Masons," No. 141, soon becoming a Master Mason and being appointed to the position of the group's first treasurer. And, though he was now far removed from his career as a salvage diver, the Iowa press did not let its citizens forget Harrington's amazing accomplishments. On February 10, 1859, the *Dubuque Weekly Times* printed the following:

> "Mr. E.P. Harrington...is the gentleman who dived one hundred and seventy feet to the wreck of the *Atlantic* in Lake Erie, in June, 1856, and rescued the safe of the American Express Co., which contained $46,000! He made eighteen descents to the wreck, and was on the boat in all, one hour and thirty-nine minutes. The longest he was down at any one time, was eleven minutes. He could see nothing, it being tenfold darker than midnight, a hundred feet from the surface..."[11]

As civil unrest fast approached, the Masons of Floyd County, Iowa–including Elliot Harrington–gathered together to discuss possible military action by its local citizens. They agreed that "defense and action are sometimes necessary to patriotism," as was represented by their own words:

> "While the older States of this Union have been concerned in the French and Indian war, King Philip's war, the Revolutionary war, the war of 1812, the Black Hawk war, the Mexican war, the Mormon skirmish and the war of the great Rebellion, the young State of Iowa has been concerned almost exclusively in the latter, and Floyd County only in the great Rebellion, with the collateral frights from the Indians. Following the chronological order, however, compels us first to notice the Military Company of 1859..."[12]

Aligned with that printed notice, a number of able-bodied men of St. Charles gathered together at a meeting conducted in the Cheney and Brackett Hall on July 18, 1859, for the expressed purpose of "organizing a military company." Gustavus B. Eastman called the meeting to order and, within a few moments, the group had selected newspaper owner, Azro B.F. Hildreth, as its Chairman, and attorney, William B. Fairfield, as its Secretary. Familiar with the writing process, Hildreth had soon drafted articles of agreement for the sole purpose enrolling new members:

> "We, the undersigned, hereby form ourselves into a military company, for the purpose of exercising in the manual drill, as prescribed by the United States regular service, and for such other purposes and acts as may be proper to a military organization, under such style and name as shall hereafter be determined."[13]

Indeed, one of those who initially signed the agreement, along with dozens of others, was Elliot P. Harrington. The group immediately approved the company name as the "City Light Guards," elected Eastman as their Captain, and organized a smaller sub-committee to draft and report a constitution. During the very next meeting, held amid a display of fine martial music, Harrington was selected as the group's Second Sergeant.

The 1860 census records, taken on July 26, indicate that Elliot–still a "carriage maker"–continued to reside in St. Charles City, Floyd County, Iowa, with his wife Emmeline, seven-year-old Murray (apparently the first name of "William" was not reported correctly), four-year-old Forest, and a six-month-old daughter named Allie. Not only had he become a successful businessman and active political figure, but his involvement in the upcoming war effort had grown to active duty proportions. And, when conflict finally broke out in April of 1861, he would be one of the first to offer his services and diving expertise to the Union's war efforts. By the time that he would be "officially" drafted by the United States on July 1, 1863, the thirty-nine-year-old had already provided more than two years of vital expertise to the service of his country.

It was during those first two years of the conflict that Elliot would become attached to the steamer *Dirigo*, captained by Leonard Barnes Pratt, making a name for himself as an extremely competent and inventive diver. In early 1862, the *Dirigo* was called to Norfolk to assist in raising the celebrated Confederate battleship *Merrimack*, but "the current was found so strong that nothing of this kind could be accomplished." By the end of the summer, the Confederates had managed to put in place obstructions in the Neuse River in North Carolina by sinking a number of vessels. There were nine wrecked vessels in all–six of them "lightships"–making it literally impossible for Union vessels to pass safely up and down the waterway, and Harrington was asked to remove them in any way that he saw fit. He agreed, enlisting his brother, Charles Murray, to assist him.

Meanwhile, Elliot fully understood the value of the sunken lightships. More than forty years earlier, the U.S. Government had begun funding construction and conversion of vessels to be utilized as floating beacons marking dangerous shoals, reefs, and shifting channels along inland and open shipping lanes. In essence, lightships served where lighthouse construction was unfeasible. During the beginning of the Civil War, however, they were also used as prizes of war, quarantine vessels, store ships, troop transports, rescue vessels, and–as in the case of Confederate defense measures–river obstructions.

In considering the options of salvage, Harrington had soon convinced Captain Pratt to attempt a rather unorthodox plan; instead of blowing them out of the water with depth charges, as was typical, he stated that he could make "his way into the holds of the sunken craft," where he would carefully locate "the holes that had been bored to let the water in to sink them," plug them up with wood and tar, close any gaping seams, make tight the hatchways, and "set pumps in motion, and so in a comparative short time…(get) them afloat, good crafts for the use of the United States Government."[14]

Soon, Captain Pratt had also convinced the commanding officer of the *USS Hetzel*, Henry K. Davenport, of the seemingly outrageous scheme, who, in turn, dispatched a letter to Acting Rear-Admiral, Samuel Phillips Lee, Commander of the North Atlantic Blockading Squadron in Norfolk, Virginia:

> "There are a number of vessels sunk in the Neuse River (they were put there by the enemy to prevent our approach to the city), which might be worth something to the Government. Captain L.B. Pratt, of the wrecking steamer *Dirigo*, proposes to raise them without cost to the Government on condition that he receives half their value. I recommend that he be permitted to go to work upon them."[15]

Believing in the possibilities, permission was granted by the Acting Rear-Admiral at the end of July. To begin the operation, Harrington was asked to tackle the raising of a lightship named the *Royal Shoal*. Apparently, the mission turned out to be a success, as indicated from a communiqué sent from Commander Davenport to Acting Rear-Admiral Lee:

> "In accordance with the suggestions contained in your letter of July 24, 1862, I contracted with Captain Pratt, of the wrecking steamer *Dirigo*, for raising one of the light vessels sunk in the Neuse River. I went down to see the vessel, accompanied by two gentlemen conversant with such matters, and they gave me their opinion that she was worth raiding at the price named. She has been raised and is now anchored off the wharf. She has a quantity of mud and filth in her and will require considerable repairs. I have suspended operations on the others until this one (*Royal Shoal*, light-boat) is sufficiently overhauled to admit of my judging whether it would be prudent to contract for raising the other two..."[16]

Next on the list was an unnamed brig, measuring an estimated 100 feet in length, and scuttled approximately three miles below New Bern as part of the Fort Point blockade. Another brig, which was situated about three miles above New Bern, obstructed the shipping lane at about a twelve-foot-depth. She had been scuttled next to an unidentified schooner. Within a few days, both were re-floated. In September of 1862, Commander Davenport sent the following report to Acting Rear Admiral Lee:

> "I have the pleasure to inform you that I have succeeded with the force at my command, assisted generously by the army, in raising the steamer (*Isaac N.*) *Seymour*, which was sunk up the Neuse River. The *Seymour* is now upon the ways, and I hope in the course of a few days to have her ready for service... I had a proposition made to me by the Submarine Company to raise her for $10,000, which was declined, and I am happy to believe that the expense to the Government will be trifling compared with this sum."[17]

By the end of 1862, all obstructions in the Neuse River had been successfully removed, and Harrington turned his attention to other vital matters plaguing the progress of the Union's war efforts. Reviving a pedal-powered submarine concept that had been shared with him by his one-time colleague, Lodner D. Phillips, he dispatched a detailed letter to Rear-Admiral Samuel Francis Du Pont, United States Navy, dated May 11, 1863, offering his services for operations behind enemy lines in Charleston Harbor:

> "I am aware that many plans have been suggested for overcoming the obstructions in Charleston Harbor, and that probably you may lack confidence in any new one. Still, I am anxious to present to you one of my own, which I have entire confidence in, which I trust you would consider entitled to careful consideration, if I should succeed in conveying my ideas plainly. I have had twelve years of experience as a diver; have had enough to do in that line to render me familiar with all underwater operations. I raised the American Express safe from the wreck of the steamer *Atlantic*, in Lake Erie, at a depth of 170 feet of water, and have succeeded in several other undertakings of the kind, which had been abandoned

and declared impracticable by others. Among my experiences was one with a submerged small propeller, driven by hand power, capable of being supplied with air by means independent of all outside help. With it I can make 1½-miles per hour at a depth of 80 feet or less, and could conduct operations outside of it at any given depth with success. From my former experience with the craft, and my acquaintance with the whole subject, I am satisfied that I can construct a small propeller with which, aided by from four to five men, I can, without help from others and without being observed by the enemy, follow the channel at Charleston, cut the wires of torpedoes, cut any cables, or network, or chains, saw off any piling, or overcome any other impediments likely to be met with. While doing so, a telegraphic operation may be kept up with any monitor that may be detailed for that purpose and lying at a distance, so that my own movements can be regulated or made known at any time. I am aware that it looks like a hazardous and doubtful undertaking, yet, after much experience, I have such faith in it that I should be very glad to lay the details before you and leave it for your consideration; some difficulties that would be at first strike an outsider as insuperable, I am confident can be overcome. Having so much faith in it, I would respectfully ask of you the favor to grant me a personal interview and allow me to detail my plans..."[18]

According to reliable sources throughout the Northern States, Elliot P. Harrington would earn a hefty "price on his head" for carrying out this dangerous mission successfully. Reports indicated, however, that there was a bounty soon thereafter in an amount between $5,000 and $8,000, to be paid in gold to anyone who could bring him to Confederate headquarters—either "dead or alive." Yet, Harrington was not captured, for he survived the War in one piece and no one ever collected the Confederate reward. In June of 1865, the forty-one-year-old returned to his home in Charles City, Iowa, where he set about establishing a peacetime diving enterprise.

During the early 1860s, Kansas City had acquired the dubious nickname of "Gullytown" because of its deep trenches that had been cut into the limestone bluffs to make way for streets and buildings. Still, the small, muddy town had a good deal of potential since it was strategically located on the confluence of the Missouri and Kansas Rivers. Nonetheless, its growth had long been severely hampered without the most important form of transportation across the Missouri River—a railroad.

The idea of constructing a bridge over the Missouri River, however, would require an act of the United States Congress. That law came in the form of an "omnibus railroad bridge act," passed in the early summer of 1866. Kansas City had been chosen as the site of the bridge—rather than one of its upstream rivals—due to the intense and prolonged lobbying on the part of a group of its civic leaders. Much was at stake, they reasoned, for their assumption was that the town that first bridged the Missouri would become the commercial hub in the southern Midwest.

Octave Chanute, a young, self-trained civil engineer employed by the Chicago and Alton Railroad, was hired to oversee the supervision of the Kansas City Bridge. A native of Paris, France, Chanute had migrated to the United States with his family at the age six. Prior to his arrival in Kansas City, he had overseen construction of a drawbridge over the Illinois River, at the time the longest railroad drawbridge in the world. Later, he had designed the original stockyards in Kansas City and Chicago, platted the town of Lenexa, Kansas, helped design the elevated train system in New York City, and was even a pioneer in aviation. He had also mapped rail lines in southeastern Kansas for two different railroad companies. When four contiguous towns along the route merged, the new town was given the name of Chanute, in honor of the engineer's important work in that part of the state.

At the start of his newest project in February of 1867, Chanute faced an extremely formidable task. The Missouri River had long been considered "unbridgeable," due to its unusually swift currents, shifting channel, propensity to flood, and its "scour"–the churning turbulence at its sandy bottom. Also weighing heavily on Chanute's mind were the conflicting demands of safety and innovation. He was undoubtedly aware that, in the period between 1850 and 1865, no less than twenty-five bridge failures had occurred across the United States annually. Further compounding the challenge, the town of just a few thousand residents was on the edge of the frontier, largely isolated from the industrial and transportation support available to large-scale engineering projects in bigger cities in the east. Indeed, special tools needed for the job had to be fabricated at a machine shop near the site.

Early on, to combat the underwater challenges, Chanute was forced to consider exactly how to construct the bridge's support system. He knew right from the start that the superstructure would rest on seven piers built of locally quarried limestone. Three of the piers would stand on bedrock, though designing and building the foundations for the additional four "channel piers" presented a critical challenge. Chanute considered a number of different techniques for underwater construction and, in 1868, published a series of reports on seventeen European bridges whose foundations had been built with the use of pneumatic tubes, or "caissons." He particularly admired the Kehl Bridge in Germany, erected across the Rhine in 1858 between Alsace and Baden. Despite his fascination with its pneumatic caissons, however, he ultimately chose open caissons for the construction of the underwater foundations of the Kansas City Bridge.

Chanute turned to diver, Elliot P. Harrington, for assistance with this part of the project, and Harrington quickly agreed. Soon, the experienced diver had gathered together some of the best in the business throughout the Midwest. Aside from Elliot himself, they included: Peter Scully, a thirty-five-year-old Irish immigrant from Saint Louis, Missouri; George A. Bailey from Boston, Massachusetts; Captain Joseph Battles, former master of the light boat *Brandywine,* from Cohasset, Massachusetts; James H. Phillips, from Ypsilanti, Michigan, who had gained attention by repairing damaged locks along the Saint Mary's Canal in 1866; William C. Perry, an engineer and machinist from Detroit, Michigan; James W. Van Norman, a former sailor from Detroit, Michigan; James H. Cowing, from Rives Junction, Michigan; Moses Torrance, of Kansas City, Missouri; and, perhaps the most experienced of all, John S. Quinn, an Irish immigrant and expert diver throughout the Great Lakes region, then living in Detroit.

On May 8, 1869, *Harper's Weekly* published an article, entitled "Submarine Divers," which detailed the group's work on the Kansas City Bridge:

> "Our illustration represents eight submarine divers recently employed under E. P. Harrington, Submarine Engineer (from whom we receive the photographic representation from which our engraving is made), engaged in laying the foundation of the Kansas City Bridge over the Missouri River. A strong wooden caisson, 70 feet long by 22½ feet wide, was constructed, and in this a masonry pier was built. The sand beneath the caisson was removed by dredges, and the courses of masonry were laid as the caisson sank. This process was carried on successfully until the caisson was lowered to within four feet of the bedrock, when a close layer of boulders was encountered. The services of the submarine divers were required to remove these one by one, they working for a whole month, night and day, at a depth of about fifty feet below the surface of the water with 3000 tons of masonry above them."[19]

Drawing of Harrington's divers depicted in *Harper's Weekly*

By the end of the 1860s, Elliot had returned to the Ypsilanti area of Michigan with his wife and three surviving children. There, the family moved into an upscale home along Prospect Road near Prospect Cemetery, which was soon to be transformed into Prospect Park. The now famous diver, desperate to make a respectable living in order to support his family, would become involved in a number of far-fetched schemes, including deep-sea fishing, manufacturing and selling shoes, and even competing in an International Collar and Elbow wrestling championship against renowned fighter, James Hiram McLaughlin. The two men were wrestling for a belt "four feet long, white on the outside with blue edge; also, with a silver plate in front." Harrington was soundly defeated.

Within a few years, the entire Harrington family had moved once again, this time thirty miles eastward to Springwells Township, just outside of the city of Detroit. Six miles northwest, within walking distance of the Detroit River at 628 Sixth Street, he maintained a business front for his diving ventures. Elliot's father, Larkin, died on August 16, 1872, followed by his mother, Abigail, on July 12, 1878. Meanwhile, Elliot continued to be heavily involved with the business of salvaging, as well as with his interest in improving the workability of machines. During the early 1870s, he invented and patented a three-valve pump to provide a more reliable supply of air to underwater workers. Then, on December 21, 1875, he was granted a patent for an automatic railway car coupler:

> "This invention has relation to improvements in automatic car-couplers, wherein an arrow headed coupler, adapted to be received into, an open draw-bar, is held by corresponding vibrating spring-actuated barbed arms against being withdrawn out of the said draw-bar; and it consists in means, substantially as hereinafter-described, whereby the said barbed arms are simultaneously separated to allow of the withdrawal of the arrow-headed coupler, thereby permitting the latter to be drawn out of the draw-bar, and the previously-coupled cars to be separated..."[20]

In June of 1879, Elliot gave a diving exhibition in Bay City, Michigan, attended by more than one hundred onlookers. Afterward, as he relaxed on a wharf near the Saginaw River bridge, a young boy rattled past on a velocipede. Suddenly, Harrington had a thought: perhaps he could design just such a machine that could move across the surface of the water. The following day, he returned to his workshop in Detroit and busied himself with just such a project. By the middle of August, his "aquatic velocipede" was finished. On August 18, he conducted a trial run across a large pond in Richard H. Hall's Brickyard, at 406 Jefferson Avenue. A few days later, a *Detroit Free Press* reporter became the first to witness the amazing invention, and he wrote the following news article:

> "The machine is in the form of a bicycle and is propelled by either the feet or hands or both. The wheel is of galvanized iron, hollow and airtight, and of great buoyancy. The 'tire' consists of two flanges, six or seven inches apart; inside are the buckets or paddles, which propel the wheel. These buckets contain both air and water chambers. The wheel is four feet in diameter and has pedals for the feet and cranks for the hands. In the relative position of the small wheel of the bicycle are two wooden 'fishes,'

to which is attached a lever. They act as a rudder and also help to support the weight of the rider. The machine is steered precisely as a velocipede is. It weighs about seventy-five pounds and Mr. Harrington asserts that it has a buoyancy of five hundred pounds..."[21]

During the interview, Harrington boasted that he was "going to Cleveland on it some day," and invited the reporter to join him for the trip. The reporter declined, claiming a "predilection to sea-sickness."[22]

Elliot P. Harrington would never attempt the journey, however, for he died just two months later, on Friday, October 31, 1879, at the age of fifty-five. He was laid to rest near the graves of his parents in the small Volusia, New York, cemetery, just a stone's throw away from the place where he had grown up. His life's story, compacted into a single paragraph, appeared in the pages of the *Westfield Republic* a few days later:

> "Elliot P. Harrington was the eldest son of the late Larkin and Abigail Harrington... His parents moved to this town when he was one year old. At an early age he developed a remarkable degree of mechanical skill; and among his many effects of his genius he made an excellent bass violin, upon which he played in the church choir many years. At an early age he showed a great fondness for the water, which resulted in the crowning effort of his life–submarine diving. He was one of the first to enter into the diving and wrecking business, going into the deepest water of any man living... I need not undertake to name the wrecks he visited, or the hundreds of thousands of treasure brought to light, or the vessels raised by him. He has been brought to the surface nearly suffocated many times, and once when the air hose burst he was brought up almost lifeless, his eyes pressed from their sockets. His was the venturesome wrecker's life, and no wonder he broke down; he had nerves or steel or he could not have survived the half he did. He has saved many lives from drowning. He invented many useful things connected with his calling... He received many tokens of appreciation for his bravery and worth. Socially he was always cheerful and happy, taking a lively interest in athletic sports, in which he excelled. He was upright and honest in deal, and generous to a fault. In his last sickness he expressed a desire to come near his childhood's home and be buried there, and in accordance with this wish his brother, C.M. Harrington, came with him from his home in Detroit, Mich., to Volusia, N.Y. He was accompanied by his wife and one son..."[23]

Following his burial, Emmeline returned to Michigan, where she would live as a widow until the age of eighty-five. She died on February 5, 1915, and was laid to rest in the Woodmere Cemetery in Detroit.

On Saturday, June 21, 1884, a reporter from the *Jamestown Evening Journal* spoke intimately with Lewis Todd Harrington, the fifty-three-year-old younger brother of the then deceased, Elliot P. Harrington. It was during that interview that Lewis, then a resident of the town of Mayville, New York, and the ex-sheriff of Chautauqua County, proudly showed the reporter a gold watch that he had acquired when his older brother had passed away. Engraved on one side of the case that it was kept in was a simple inscription:

> "Presented to E.P. Harrington by the American Express Company, as a reward for his heroic effort in recovering their safe from the wreck of the steamer *Atlantic* on the 19th of August, 1852. The *Atlantic* was wrecked and sunk in Lake Erie, and on the 22d day of June, 1856, Mr. Harrington performed the miraculous feat of diving to the wreck and fastening a cable to the safe, at a depth of one hundred and seventy feet from the lake's surface."[24]

With a bit of sadness in his eyes, Lewis explained that the case was "made from gold coin that was in the safe at the time of the wreck." As he turned it over to its opposite side, the reporter could see a second engraving—that of a diver in a sweeping downward plunge. It would always remain a fitting memorial to a brother that had already been largely forgotten for his brave and somewhat amazing underwater exploits.

Portrait of George Henry Felt

AMERICAN SUBMARINERS: PRE-CIVIL WAR

- 21 -
George Henry Felt: *Felt Submarine*

"When I was young I longed to write a great novel that should win me fame. Now that I am getting old my first book is written to amuse children. For, aside from my evident inability to do anything 'great,' I have learned to regard fame as a will-o-the-wisp which, when caught, is not worth the possession...but to please a child is a sweet and lovely thing that warms one's heart..."[1]

At the beginning of the 1900s, a disillusioned man who had failed at nearly everything he had ever attempted. wrote that letter to his sister. His best-known book had begun to take shape when a group of young children, led by his own four sons, waylaid him one evening in their modest flat. Working as a beat reporter for twenty dollars a week, his family had been forced to move into a wretched house in the rundown Humboldt Park section of Chicago with no bathroom or running water. His devoted wife, Maud, offered sporadic embroidery lessons to area housewives for ten cents an hour. About the only recreation their four sons had was listening to their father's fanciful fairy tales.

On this particular occasion, the man sat down with the children encircling him and began to talk with his usual animation. He gave little thought as to what he was describing, making it all up as he went along. His story detailed the childhood of a little Kansas girl named Dorothy who was carried away by a violent cyclone to a strange land, where she met a live scarecrow, a man made of tin, and a cowardly lion. One of the children asked, "What was the name of this strange land?" Stumped, the storyteller looked around for some inspiration. In the next room were his personal filing cabinets, and one bore the letters O to Z. "The Land of Oz," he exclaimed, unaware that he had just added a new word to the English language.

In their journey along the Yellow Brick Road across the Land of Oz to the Emerald City, Dorothy and her companions came to a field of poppies, whose stupefying fragrance put the flesh-and-blood travelers into a deep trance, thus preventing their further progress. It was only the intelligence of the Scarecrow and the devotion of the Tin Woodman that found a way to invoke higher powers to get them out of the field and back on the path to the center of Oz.

Indeed, L. Frank Baum, the Theosophist author of *The Wonderful Wizard of Oz*, was quite familiar with such mystical occurrences. In fact, he had read and reread Madame Helena Blavatsky's spiritual guidebook, *The Voice of the Silence*, which had been purchased a decade earlier. Like *The Wonderful Wizard of Oz*, *The Voice of the Silence* described a quest-journey, one during which a pilgrim must pass through three Halls–Ignorance, Learning, and Wisdom. In the second of those Halls, the pilgrim's soul finds "the blossoms of life, but under every flower a serpent coiled." In a note on that passage, the author identified the second Hall as "the astral region, the psychic world of super-sensuous perceptions and of deceptive sights… No blossom plucked in those regions has ever yet been brought down on earth without its serpent coiled around the stem. It is the world of the Great Illusion."[2]

Portrait of L. Frank Baum

Portrait of Madame Helena Petrovna Blavatsky, 1877

Like Baum's book, Blavatsky's *The Voice of the Silence* was written "for those ignorant of the dangers of the lower iddhi," or psychic powers. In writing, those powers were symbolized by the blossom with a serpent coiled around its stem or by a field of poppies, whose fragrance overpowers human minds and submerges people into narcotic sleep. The danger of the lower iddhi, however, is that their attractiveness can entice people away from their purpose in life and preoccupy them with spiritually irrelevant phenomena and with ego-gratifying distractions. All of this was described by Baum in his tale about Oz, in a way that the young children might understand the spiritual message.

The investigation of unexplained natural laws and latent human powers was a major intent—though not the primary one—of a largely unknown group calling itself the Theosophical Society from its earliest conception. Committed to the serious study of the world's religious traditions, their work would touch the lives of countless people throughout history. Besides L. Frank Baum, they would include Irish writer, James Joyce, as well as a number of leading political figures that later joined Mahatma Gandhi in the India-independent movement half a world away:

> "Today everybody knows the word karma. Now, everybody talks about mind-body-spirit connections in their lives. People everywhere talk about the unity of life around the world—and how we should do away with notions of class and race and religious bias. We can trace the popularity of a lot of those ideas back to this little group of people listening to lectures in their rooms in New York in 1875 and saying: 'This stuff is going to be important. We should study this stuff. We should tell other people about it'."[3]

The impetus to establish such a far-reaching society came from a lecture given at one of Madame Blavatsky's soirées by a little-known engineer-architect and mathematician, George Henry Felt, who spoke on the subject of "The Lost Canon of Proportion of the Egyptians." Though only seventeen or eighteen people were in attendance on that fateful September 7, 1875, evening, his lecture would be long remembered for explaining the mysteries of the geometrical symbolism on the wall of an Egyptian temple. Felt also claimed to have discovered how Egyptian priests invoked and commanded spirits of the elements of earth, water, fire, and air. That claim, as well as Felt's promise to demonstrate it, elicited much interest in others at the meeting and led to a proposal to establish a group to pursue such deep mystical matters, as well as more generally the investigation of how science and religion are connected. The group would come to be called the Theosophist Society, and would impact thinking far and wide.

Throughout much of his life, George Henry had experimented with a host of inventive ideas, among them the concept of underwater exploration. Born in Boston, Massachusetts, on September 21, 1831, to Willard and Elizabeth Leuman (Glover) Felt, he had come from a long line of creative and enterprising men and women. In fact, his lineage can be traced back across seven generations to his fifth great-grandparents, William and Mary (Smith) Felt, who raised three sons and two daughters on William's modest income from plying his dual trades as a farmer and basket maker. The couple's eldest child, George, was born first, on February 28, 1601, and grew up on the family's farm nestled between the villages of Heath and Reach and Leighton Buzzard, in Bedfordshire, England. Aside from tending crops and delivering baskets, he was in charge of watching over his younger siblings. Little did he realize at the time, but he was destined to be the first Felt to carry the family name to America.

The tiny dual towns of Heath and Reach were originally two small hamlets in the Royal Manor of Leighton, and records have been found for Heath in 1220 and Reach in 1216. Meanwhile, nearby Leighton Buzzard was a mere speck of a place situated two miles north along the Chiltern Hills, between Luton and Milton Keynes. There are a number of theories concerning the derivation of its name, but the most likely is that "Leighton" came from the Old English Lĕah-tūn, meaning 'farm in a clearing in the woods.' The "Buzzard" portion was later added by the Dean of Lincoln, in whose diocese the town lay in the 12th Century. Having two communities referred to as "Leighton" and seeking some means of distinguishing them, the Dean added the name of his local Prebendary, Theobald de Busar, to the end of the town name. With the passage of time, "Busar" became "Buzzard," and the town became known as Leighton Buzzard.

George, who was submariner George Henry's fourth great-grandfather, grew to manhood and married Elizabeth Wilkinson, daughter of widow Prudence Wilkinson, whose home in Charlestown was on the south side of Mill Hill, nearly adjoining that of her son-in-law. Whether they married in Charlestown, or were already married when they arrived in America, is cause for debate, but it is most probable that they had already tied the knot and brought children with them to the New World. Though history remains uncertain, tradition holds that the two arrived with John Endicott, reaching Salem, Massachusetts, in September of 1628. What is known is that they were not among the earliest settlers in Charlestown, arriving sometime after the first one hundred people or so, who had relocated with Thomas Graves from Salem and laid the town's foundation.

The original community of Charlestown, incorporated on June 24, 1629, was laid out in two-acre divisions, and each male settler was granted one of these parcels on which to build a homestead and plant a few crops. We have the testimony of immigrant George Felt himself that, in the year of his advent, the town had already been named, for in 1681 he described himself as about eighty years of age, and further testified "that the town of Charlestown gave him an house plott of two acres of land lying in the common on the left hand as you go to Cambridge betwixt the ground that was Rice Morrisses and Goble's, which is now in the hands of Thomas Welch Senr, which plott was given him about forty-eight years since."[4]

On February 10, 1634, a town order creating a board of select men was written and officially adopted by the majority of Charlestown male residents:

> "In consideration of the great trouble and chearg [sic] of the Inhabitants of Charlestowne by reason of the Frequent meeting of the townsmen in generall [sic], and yt [sic] by reason of many men meeting things were not so easily brought unto a joynt [sic] Issue: It is therefore agreed by the sayde townesmen joytly [sic] that these eleven men whose names are written on the other side [sic], with the advise of Pastor and teacher desired in any case of conscience, shall entreat of all such busines [sic] as shall concerne [sic] the townsmen, The choise [sic] of officers excepted, and what they or the greater part of them shall conclude of, the rest of the towne [sic] willingly to submit Unto as their pper [sic] act, and these 13 to contineu [sic] in imployment [sic] for one yeare [sic] next ensuing the date hereof, being dated this: 10th of February 1634."[5]

There were thirty-three signers of this order, among them immigrant George Felt. It should be noted that his signature, which can still be found upon a number of the historical records of Charlestown, was written "Felch. This, or "Feltch," is thought to have been the original spelling of the family surname, which was easily and naturally contracted into "Felt" over time. All the descendants of George, as the first to arrive in America, would use the shortened version.

Between 1630 and 1645, George and Elizabeth gave birth to three daughters and four sons. Moses, born on October 20, 1641, was their fifth child, and he was extremely close to his brother, George Jr., who was but one year older. Records hold that George Jr., and Moses, together with their younger brothers, Aaron and Peter, acquired large tracts of land in the extreme northeast of New England, much if which included several islands in the Casco Bay, just east of Falmouth, Maine. Records indicate that, in 1673, the town "granted to George Felt Junr [sic] the lower Clapboard Island," lying in the bay about a mile off his house, "with the priviledges [sic] thereunto belonging excepting liberty for any inhabitants of the Towne to fetch stones from thence or for 'fowling'..."[6]

Casco Bay was the westernmost of the great bays of Maine, eighteen miles from headland to headland. The product of glaciers, it was speared by a series of points extending in a generally southerly direction. Beyond the points were the islands, many laying on the same axis after being chopped off the peninsulas by the dull but indefatigable knife of the sea. Maine had thousands of islands—a survey found 2,000 of uncertain ownership alone—and if its coastline were stretched taut it would reach southward to the Panama Canal. But nowhere was it more jagged and idiosyncratic, nor its waters more jammed with the potsherds of glaciation, than in Casco Bay. In fact, the *Maine Times* claimed that there were 768 islands and ledges visible above the nine- to ten-foot high tides. This count goes back at least to 1700, when an English document reported:

> "Sd bay is covered from storms that come from the sea by a multitude of islands, great and small, there being (if report be true) as many islands as there are Days in a Yr..."[7]

In 1682, Joshua Felt, great-great-grandfather of George Henry Felt, was born in the same Casco Bay area of Maine, to Moses and Hannah (Maine) Felt. Two years later, his aging grandfather, George Sr., conveyed all that was left of his acreage at Casco Bay to his son and grandsons. On June 22, 1688, the eighty-seven-year-old pleaded for financial assistance from the town, claiming:

> "...that it is my grief that I am compelled to trouble yo [sic] Excellency at this time—But having about eighteen years since purchased of one Jn' Phillips of Boston, Gent., late Deceased, a farme [sic] or Plaintaintion [sic] at a Place called the Great Cove (in Casco Bay) containing about two thousand acres of upland and marsh as by a firm Deed under s' Phillips hand and seale [sic], for which I then paid him sixty pounds money,

and improved s' Farme [sic] or plaintation [sic] severall [sic] years before I bought it so that the whole time of my occupying it was about one and twenty years, But some time after the late Indian Warr [sic] it was withheld from me by some of the inhabitants of s' Town of Caskoe [sic] Bay and being by s' warr [sic] much impoverished I could not recover it out of their hands. I also am now forced to suffer for want of convenient care taken of me in my present distresse [sic] being about Eighty seaven [sic] years old and very crasy [sic] and weak..."[8]

Joshua Felt married Anne Wolcott on January 15, 1712, in a quiet ceremony at her parents' home in Lynn, Massachusetts. During the next dozen years they would give birth to three sons and one daughter. Eventually, on April 17, 1729, long after Joshua's parents had relocated to Rumney Marsh in the Township of Boston, his father, Moses, conveyed to Joshua for a mere £150 "all my lands lying & being in Boston afores...with the dwelling house." This was, undoubtedly, his entire estate, and was handed over for such a reasonable price with an understanding "that he was to be cared for by Joshua for the remainder of his life."[9]

For all of his life, Joshua would remain a cooper by trade, acquiring a considerable amount of land in and around Lynn. Soon after his first wife, Anne, died in 1736, he married again, on this occasion to Dorcas (Gould) Buxton, widow of Anthony Buxton of Salem. She bore him no additional children.

Joshua and Anne's youngest son, Jonathan, had been born on June 3, 1719, in Lynn, Massachusetts, and had later relocated to Attleboro, Bristol County, snuggled up against the western border of the State. There, on February 5, 1747, Jonathan married Lovewell Wells, and they soon moved to the Dedham area, situated just southwest of Boston. Prior to Lovewell's death on August 8, 1764, she gave birth to ten children. In less than a year's time, Jonathan would marry his second wife, Mary Withington, who would raise his earlier children and give him four more.

Among this army of Felt children, Benjamin, who was George Henry's grandfather, was born on October 12, 1752, in Dedham, Norfolk County, Massachusetts. He later settled in Milton, Norfolk County, Massachusetts, and married Waitstill Capen, daughter of Robert and Mary Jane (Lyon) Capen of Canton, Massachusetts. As so many Felt wives before her, Waitstill would die long before her husband, on April 30, 1804. And, like so many Felt men before him, Benjamin would marry again, the second occasion being on June 3, 1805, to Jerusha Hunt, daughter of Brinsmead and Abigail (Matthews) Hunt of Milton. We know that Benjamin had bravely served six days at the time of the Lexington alarm, beginning on April 19, 1775, in the South Dedham Company commanded by Captain William Bollard.

On May 7, 1796, Willard Felt, the youngest of six sons, had been born to Benjamin and Waitstill Felt in Milton, Massachusetts. He married Elizabeth Leuman Glover, daughter of Oliver and Lydia Barrett (Lewis) Glover, on December 18, 1824, in Milton, Norfolk County, Massachusetts. There, they would live long and prosperous lives, carrying on the family tradition by raising four boys: Willard Leuman, David Wells, Edwin Mead, and George Henry.

George Henry Felt was born in Boston on September 21, 1831. Third youngest of the four boys, George's extended family lineage had, by then, become well-known and prosperous printers and stationers. Under the business name Willard Felt and Company, they settled into building known as Stationers' Hall, located at 82 State Street in midtown Boston. There, the elder Felt joined forces with Charles Ellms, publishing a number of successful titles, including a series known as *The American Comic Almanac, with Whims, Scraps, and Oddities*, *The Yankee: the Farmer's Almanack for the Year of Our Lord and Saviour 1834*, and *The People's Almanac*.

In late 1833, Willard Felt sold the Boston-based business to his clerk, Thomas Groom, and took his wife and three sons, George, Willard, Jr., and David, to live in New York City. There, Felt opened another publishing house by the same name. The New York location, situated at 191 Pearl Street in southeast Manhattan just a few blocks from the East River, was purchased from Nathaniel and Harvey Weed, brothers who had owned and operated N&H Weed Dry Goods. Incorporated in early 1835, with the addition of sons Willard Jr., and David, Willard Felt and Company would remain in business at this location until 1887.

Aside from this, Willard purchased a piece of property at Number 14 Maiden Lane, near Broadway, in the heart of the City. There, he opened his paper warehouse, advertising stocking "constantly on hand, a complete assortment of…Premium Account Books, which for a series of years have taken the highest premium at the Fairs of the American Institute." Furthermore, the firm claimed to have "a large assortment of English and French Stationary, of superior quality, comprising every variety of articles in their line, (with) particular attention to lithographing notes, drafts, bills of exchange, bonds, certificates of stock, and drawing and engineering materials in great variety."[10]

During the 1840s, David and Willard Jr., parted ways, becoming rivals in the stationary business, with David founding David Felt and Company and brother Willard establishing Willard Felt and Company. The 1850 census, recorded on August 17, indicated that the elder Felt continued to reside in the 18th Ward of New York City in the County of York. By then, Willard was fifty-two years old and his wife, Elizabeth, was forty-eight. All four of their sons, each listed with the same occupation of "stationer" like their father, were still officially living at home, ranging in age from fourteen to twenty-three. Willard Jr., the eldest, had studied law at the University of New York, graduating six years earlier and had been admitted to the bar in 1849. David Wells Felt, next in line, had graduated from the same university in 1845, and had married Mary C. Farrar of New York in 1849. Tragically, his wife would later die in Melbourne, Australia, in 1853, while giving birth to their second child. Fourteen-year-old brother, Edwin, was also destined to attend the University of New York law school, would graduate from that institution in 1856, and would be admitted to the bar just two years later. Meanwhile, eighteen-year-old, George Henry, who is said to have attended "select schools of New York City," did not likely attend the same university as his brothers, since "a letter from the Archives Assistant of New York University indicates that he was not a registered student there." Instead, he was already dabbling in his childhood interest area of engineering and machine design, exploring his own inventive nature and tinkering with the improvement of a number of agricultural implements.

Two days after his twenty-third birthday, on September 23, 1854, George Henry married Mary Anne Frain, daughter of John and Elizabeth (Nesbit) Frain. They moved into a two-story flat located at 244 West 135th Street, situated in the Harlem district of New York City. Over the course of the next two decades, they would give birth to four daughters and four sons. As the Civil War approached, however, the elder Felt's career as a mechanical engineer brought him toward the concept of building a workable submarine as an offensive explosives delivery system. And, he reasoned, if his own government was not interested in the idea, then perhaps another country would be. Soon enough, his experiments and concept drawings would take him across the Atlantic Ocean to Europe.

George Henry would walk the quarter mile or so, west from the family home, to a small, out-of-the-way shed situated along the wharves of the nearby Hudson River. There, he would labor amid a great deal of shrouded secrecy, solemnly and privately perfecting his compact diving machine. Modeled after the concepts German inventor, Wilhelm Bauer, Felt's prototype vessel would be constructed of riveted sheet iron, approximating the size and shape of a small sperm whale. Inside, Felt's sketches indicated that propulsion would be executed through the design of a two-man-power treadmill driving an exterior propeller. As in a few other submarine designs up to that time, the diving boat's buoyancy would be controlled by a pair of small ballast tanks.

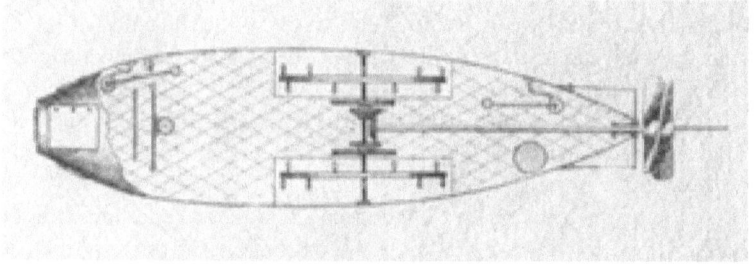

Drawing of the Felt submarine design

George Henry Felt believed that his underwater vessel, once fully submerged, would be able to reach a maximum speed of four knots at a maximum depth of one hundred feet. It would be designed to transport an armament of eight heavy guns, each of which could be fired repeatedly at the surface of the water. While beneath the surface, delivery of a contact explosive device would be achieved by way of a lengthy spar hoisting a bomb, constructed from a wooden cask, hoisted out in front of the vessel. This would allow the ship the ability to "ram" its prey without being seen by the enemy. Yet, prior to the actual building of his war ship, Felt would need to secure the interest of a nation wishing to foot the immense bill. Since the U.S. government seemed to be only slightly "half-heartedly interested," he hoped to gain the attention of either France or England. In early 1856, he presented the idea formally to the French government. He received no immediate response.

Time passed slowly, and the Felt family understood that war was coming soon. Even though George Henry attempted to perfect and peddle his submarine concept, he also began working on a host of other schemes, some related to warfare and others not. Unable to support his expanding family with his inventive ideas, he also spent much of his time improving the art of breeding and showing prized horses. By 1857, records indicate that he and his wife, Mary Anne, were living with their youngest child next door to his brother David, just outside of the family town of Feltville, described as a "quasi-Utopian mill town."

In 1844, David, George Henry's uncle who ran a portion of the family stationery businesses with his father and brothers in both Manhattan and New Orleans, had begun to purchase large tracts up property in the Watchung Reservation area of New Jersey, primarily from the descendants of Peter Willcocks, an Englishman who was the first settler in the area. Moving there from Long Island around 1736, Willcocks had constructed a dam along the Blue Brook in order to power his rudimentary sawmill operation. The four brothers, who had long been members of the Unitarian Church, began snatching up chunks of property from Willcocks' descendants–which would eventually total more than 760 acres–along with the water rights to the Blue Brook. From the outset, their plan was to establish a thriving stationery factory there.

Between 1845 and 1847, David Felt had retrofitted the property along the Blue Brook, which would become the base of operations for his soon-to-be-established company community. With this in mind, he enlarged the mill, rebuilt the dam, and installed new machinery for the manufacture of paper, the printing and binding of books, and the production of stationery. One of the most innovative improvements was the installation of a dye-house and equipment for making marbleized paper, a technique in which the brothers had recently developed a special interest.

Due to the area's remote location and poor road conditions, the Felts needed to import and house workers to live on site. On the property, they built a large mansion for the Felt family, twenty-four houses for workmen and their families, a boardinghouse for unmarried women, a schoolhouse, church, company store, a large storehouse, a blacksmith shop, and a barn. The homes were built in the Greek Revival-style, particularly evident in features such as the symmetry of each design, the use of small rectangular windows to light the top floor of most of the homes, the presence of simple wooden window and doorway moldings, and plain fireplace mantels. These simple, but functional, dwellings were divided at the center, creating two-family, side-by-side accommodations. Each side had its own fireplace and staircase, and was functionally independent.

Drawings of the housing units in Feltville, still standing

The Felt dry goods store was a focal point of the community. It carried general merchandise for the residents and was patronized by the farmers living outside of town. The second floor was used for holding religious services. The Felts believed that worship was an important aspect of village life, and they provided ministers, priests, and rabbis to conduct religious services at minimum of once per week. Austin Craig, a non-denominational minister, was hired to remain in full-time residence within Feltville. The family's incorporation of a school and religious services in the village demonstrated that they were concerned with developing a well-rounded community serving a variety of families.

At the brook's edge, a three-bay garage-like structure stood adjacent to the mill, housing a team of ox-drawn wagons that transported the Felt family's stationary paper products thirty-five miles to their Manhattan base of sales. By 1850, more than 175 people called Feltville their home, and they all worked within the single business of "felting," or making paper.

Within a few years, David and the other Felt brothers had nearly perfected the entire process of felting in the manufacturing of thin wooden fiberboards. Sheets of slurry–best described as thin, sloppy mud-like substances made of wood fibers, water, and a bit of rags–were rolled out and deposited onto a moving drip-screen, allowing the excess water to drain away. This semi-drying process left behind a wet mat known as a felt, which was then fed into a hot air drying compartment. The screen moved ever-so-slowly through a 300-400 foot-long drying house, exiting the opposite end as hardened paper. These sheets then came off the screen onto rollers and moved along toward hand-powered cutters, where it was trimmed into uniform, usable pieces.

According to a transcript printed later during the Civil War, George himself was "engaged in the manufacture of paper." If so, he had a hand in the entire Felt family paper operation, which was soon producing the following products in mass quantities: blank-books, stationery, writing paper, general book-printing and book-binding, marbleized paper for books, and the publication of advertising materials and posters. All publications bore the imprint "Stationers Hall Press, Feltville, N. J., David Felt and Co., Stationers and Printers."

Feltville survived for only fifteen years. In 1860, uncle David, its primary founder and promoter, turned sixty-seven years old. He convinced the rest of the Felt family that they should sell the entire property to Amasa Foster and return the business to New York City. Why David wanted to sell the family business and leave New Jersey was not entirely clear to historians, but there are a number of theories. His advancing age and lack of direct heirs willing to reside in Feltville may have been a major consideration. His brother, Willard, who managed the New York City operations, was extremely ill at this time, and David may have been compelled to keep his retail operations running rather than the maintaining the increasingly expensive Feltville factory site. Aside from all that, the operational setup was becoming outdated, as new factories were beginning to be run by steam-power rather than water. Also, these new factories were much closer to cities and transportation routes, making it much easier to get goods to market. Finally, the impending Civil War must have put a tremendous strain on the entire business, as well as trade with the southern states, although this theory may be more coincidence than fact. Indeed, Willard Felt, George Henry's father, passed away in 1862 at the age of sixty-six, something no one in his immediate family seemed quite prepared to deal with.

The Felt family all reached the same conclusion, knowing it was time to abandon the Feltville project. Amasa Foster would retain title to the dying community until 1864, when he sold the land and its buildings to Samuel P. Townsend. There, Townsend attempted to manufacture sarsaparilla, grow commercial fruit crops, produce silk, and cultivate tobacco for cigars, each venture failing in succession. Over the course of almost twenty years, ownership of the town would change hands no less than six times. For a short period, Feltville was completely abandoned and, it was during this time that George Henry and family began referring to it as the "Deserted Village."

Meanwhile, civil conflict seemed imminent. As early as 1858, the ongoing argument between the North and South over the issue of slavery had led southern leadership to discuss a unified separation from the United States. By 1860, the majority of the slave states were publicly threatening secession if the Republicans, the anti-slavery party, won the presidency. Following Republican Abraham Lincoln's victory over the divided Democratic Party in November of 1860, South Carolina immediately initiated secession proceedings. On December 20, the State's legislature passed the Ordinance of Secession, which declared "the Union now subsisting between South Carolina and other states, under the name of the United States of America, is hereby dissolved." After the declaration, South Carolina set about seizing forts, arsenals, and other strategic locations within their own borders. Over the course of the next six weeks, five more Southern states–Mississippi, Florida, Alabama, Georgia, and Louisiana–had each followed South Carolina's lead.

On April 12, 1861, the bloodiest four years in American history was put into motion when Confederate shore batteries under General Pierre Gustave Toutant-Beauregard opened fire on Union-held Fort Sumter in South Carolina's Charleston Bay. During the next thirty-four hours, fifty Confederate guns and mortars launched more than 4,000 rounds at the poorly supplied fort. On April 13, U.S. Major Robert Anderson surrendered the fort. Two days later, President Lincoln issued a proclamation calling for 75,000 volunteer soldiers to quell the growing Southern "insurrection."

Feeling it his duty, George Henry registered for military duty at Staten Island, New York, on July 31, 1861. On August 28 of that same year, as war raged between the North and South, he was mustered into the service of the Union army, quickly moving up the ranks to become a First Lieutenant in the Fifty-fifth Regiment Infantry, Company I, of the New York State Volunteers. Known as the "Guard de La Fayette," it was primarily made up of French residents from New York City. At the beginning of the war, when the Massachusetts Sixth Regiment passed through the City on its way to Baltimore and Washington, its members were "guests" of the Fifty-fifth. Patriotism overcame the New Yorkers and, as early as April 17, 1861, a unanimous vote had been given to offer support to save the Union. George Henry was among the voting ranks.

The Regiment impatiently waited for several weeks before receiving equipment and marching orders. Each of these came in early autumn, and the men set out to join other forces already in the seat of war. In October, while they awaited instructions, orders to join the army in the field of battle finally arrived. For some time thereafter they were stationed at Fort Gaines in Maryland, attached to General Don Carlos Buell's division. By November of that same year, George Henry Felt had joined the Signal Corp, and had been assigned the precarious duty of retrieving any and all Northern deserters that he could find.

On January 1, 1862, George Henry was transferred to Company K. One week later, he attended a flag ceremony with his regiment at Tennallytown, near Washington. Among the distinguished individuals present were President Abraham Lincoln, Mary Todd Lincoln, General James Shields, General Erasmus D. Keyes, General John J. Peck, and editor Nathanial Parker Willis. Colonel Fred A. Conkling offered the presentation address on behalf of the friends of Lieutenant William A. Wood, donors of an embroidered, tri-color flag:

"From the earliest period of recorded history a sentiment of attachment and veneration for their national ensigns has inspired the hearts of every people. The Romans threw themselves on their knees before their standards, swore by them, adorned them with garlands perfumed with incense, and believed them to be the veritable gods of their legions. In time of peace they deposited them in their temples of worship. To lose them in battle was accounted the deepest infamy, while to capture those of the enemy was regarded as the highest glory of the soldier. Sometimes at the moment in an engagement when a column wavered, the commander would order the ensigns to be thrown among the enemy, and the soldiers, roused to almost superhuman exertions to recover them, turned the tide of battle, victory once more perching upon the Roman eagles… But the occasion, like the flag, is thick with the clustering memories of the past. Reminiscences of glory and achievement belong to this day as indisputably as to any day in our military calendar. The 8th of January is signalized as one of America's epochs. It was on the eighth of January 1815, that an American soldier, grim and earnest in his purpose, but plain and simple in his methods, closed in triumph a brief and brilliant war with the first military and naval power in the world. It was on the same 8th of January that an example was given to our country of the doing of great deeds, the fulfillment of great destinies, the attainment of great results, with means apparently the most inadequate, with preparation the most scanty and imperfect, in spite of poverty and straitened resources on every side. It has been on the 8th of January in every year, from then till now, that the sons and daughters of every State in the Union have commemorated the valiant policies and measures of the President as well as the conquering deeds of the soldier, whose name is forever associated with this day. In this year, for the first time, the anniversary is half lost sight of, amid strange sounds and great realities and still greater presentiments. We have not the accustomed jubilee and festive dalliance, nor have we a completed contest. 'We stand waiting for an advance, halting in impatient expectation of the onset, pausing in an interval which divides from results which, in their importance to mankind, have no paragons in history. We have need to recur to the 8th of January to start into life the sleeping energies of the nation, to quicken the laggard movements and harden the determinations of those whom peace has almost unfitted for the stern exigencies of war. The ceremony for which we have assembled falls well on this marked and memorable day. There is scarce a prouder day to American arms; and its anniversary is honored by this array of brave men, who have left their homes to defend, on distant battle-fields, the life and honor of their country…"[11]

A tumultuous applause echoed across the crowd as Conkling finished his memorable speech. President Lincoln, upon departing from the grounds, found his carriage surrounded by the Fifty-fifth Regiment, George Henry Felt among them. They continued to cheer enthusiastically, prompting Lincoln to comment that "if the Garde Lafayette intended to fight as well as they had entertained and pleased him," he knew they would do exceptionally well, and "had no fears at all on this point."

George Henry spent the remainder of 1862 in Tennallytown, breaking camp when the army of the Potomac moved forward in an effort to conquer the Confederate capital of Richmond, Virginia. By then, the Fifty-fifth had joined the forces of General Darius Nash Couch. Records indicate that George Henry and his comrades in arms took part in the siege of Yorktown, beginning on April 5, 1862. Following the forced evacuation of that post, they moved on toward the Rebel capital, taking part in the Battle of Williamsburg, where seventeen of George Henry's comrades were killed or wounded. Next, they marched on to fight at the Battle of Fair Oaks, led by Brigadier-General, John J. Peck:

> "At half-past one o'clock, June 30th, the Fifty-fifth was called out under arms, formed in line of battle and posted, by your order, in advance of our camp. Some minutes after, General Keyes, passing in front of the regiment, said that he designed it to go and save a battery placed in the first line, and which the regiment ahead were no longer able to support... General Keyes...spoke a few words, saying that he counted on the 'red caps' when the Fifty-fifth, led by General Naglee, charged bayonets upon the enemy at 'double quick,' in magnificent style and, after having taken the position assigned to it, maintained it alone and without any support, under so murderous a fire that in a few moments we had about fifty men hors du combat, among whom were five officers. Two horses were wounded, and mine fell under me, pierced by three balls..."[12]

The American Civil War, being the first in a number of military innovations, was also first in the extensive use of the electric telegraph for all possible wartime purposes, although there was no military telegraph organization in the nation at the outbreak of the conflict. Its army did have one signal officer, Albert James Myer, who had introduced his visual system of communication into service months earlier. From this extent, the United States Army was ahead of its time from all other countries.

At Fort Duncan, Texas, where Myer had served as an assistant surgeon, he inquired in 1856 as to whether or not the government might be interested in his signaling system, which, he explained, grew out of an interest in military communications that went back to 1851. No action was taken until 1859, when a board headed by none other than U.S. Lieutenant Colonel Robert E. Lee gave the qualified endorsement to Myer's scheme. From this followed a great deal of field-testing of the aerial signaling method, conducted by Myer and Second Lieutenant, Edward Porter Alexander.

The equipment commonly used in Myer's visual system consisted of flags for daytime and torches burning turpentine at night. There was a red, a white, and a black flag, with a white center in both the red and black flags and a red center in the white flag. With green, dark, or any earth-colored backgrounds, the white flag was to be used; with a sky exposure, the black flag was to be used; and with broken, or mixed backgrounds, the red flag was be used.

The red flag, or signal, was intended by Myer to be primarily incorporated at sea, on vessels in motion. In that way, the flag's red color would be exposed against the woodwork, rigging, or sails, of the vessel, and at other times against the sky or water. The red flag was also recommended for use when snow formed part of the background. On the other hand, the white flag or signal was believed to "be best, and was used in nine instances out of ten." The staffs, to which all flags were attached, were constructed of hickory, with four tapering joints fitted together by brass ferrules. The joint having a six-inch brass guard at its upper end was installed to protect it from the flames of the flying torch, which was attached to this joint for night signaling. A foot torch served at night as a point of reference. These messages were read from great distances by the use of a field glass, or telescope.

Though somewhat complex to understand, positive results of these tests led to an act of Congress on June 21, 1860, which authorized the appointment of one signal officer with the rank of major, over the objections of then Senator Jefferson Davis, and authorized $2,000 for signaling equipment expenditures. Myer's assignment to the post quickly followed, and he made his way to New Mexico to put his system in place. There he earned the respect and friendship of Major Edward Richard Sprigg Canby who, though he approved of Myer's overall scheme, questioned his plan of having all army officers instructed in the complex system of signaling. Instead, Canby suggested that signal operations in large commands "should be confided to officers and men especially selected" for this type of duty. Soon, Myer would reluctantly adopt this same opinion.

A total of 146 officers would be "commissioned in the Corps" during the war. Twenty "declined the appointments offered them, and some ten or twelve resigned from the army soon after the reorganization was effected." In addition, approximately 297 acting signal officers served in the wartime Corps, but some of them for only very brief periods. The total number of enlisted men who served at one time or another was about 2,500. In mid-1863, 198 officers, besides Myer, and 814 enlisted men graced the rolls of the Signal Corps.

Acting as an oversight to the Signal Corp, examining bodies were set up to evaluate and manage, the primary one being known as the "Principal Board." Myer received the principal board's unanimous recommendation for appointment as the Colonel and Chief Signal Officer, and the lieutenant-colonel position went to William J.L. Nicodemus. Much dissatisfaction resulted from the actions of the examining boards, however, as hopes for advancement were repeatedly frustrated, with some officers even finding themselves reduced in rank. Among the disgruntled was George Henry Felt.

An outgrowth of the Principal Board's examining procedures in 1863, was an intriguing court of inquiry, and it deserves some attention as part of historical record of George Henry Felt. Myer's objected vehemently to a Signal

Corps commission recommendation for Felt, who was a first lieutenant and acting signal officer, questioning his "character as a gentleman...efficiency as an officer, and (overall) moral character." In reality, Myer was worried that Felt might receive credit and recognition for inventing a simpler, improved signaling system; one that would likely make Myer's system obsolete. The court of inquiry held hearings over several days on the matter of and cleared Felt of the charges raised. It was a remarkable situation, that during the hearings, two signal officers sought to throw doubt on Myer's veracity. Two other signal officers claimed that a code issued by Myer had actually been stolen, since it was nearly identical to a rocket code devised by Lieutenant Felt. In fact, Felt had already filed a patent request for just such an arrangement on August 15, 1863:

> "Be it known that I, George H. Felt, of the city, county, and State of New York, have invented a certain new and useful improvements in Rockets; and I do hereby declare that the following is a full, clear, and exact description of the same... This invention is more especially designed for signal rockets for military and other operations. It consists first, in the application to or within a rocket of a Roman candle for the purpose of discharging stars of the same or different colors one after the other, and thereby enabling a greater variety of and more distinct signals to be produced. It consists secondly, in making the stars of the Roman candle with cavities in their upper ends containing charges of gunpowder or other suitable explosive substance for the purpose of driving out the balls from the case and igniting them at the same time. It consists thirdly, in so combining a balloon with a rocket as to make it keep suspended for a time or retard the descent of a Roman candle or other fire-work discharged from the rocket for the purpose of making a signal, whereby such fire-work is rendered visible for a longer period and the signal enabled to be better understood than if it descended quickly. It consists fourthly, in the novel construction and arrangement of a series of divergent spiral passages in the bottom of the rocket, for the purpose of obtaining its rotary motion by the escape of the gases eliminated in the combustion of the charge, and thereby dispensing with the stick heretofore commonly used to guide and steady the flight of the rocket..."[13]

Three months later, Lieutenant Felt alleged he had been denied fair examination by the Principal Board, and carried formal charges forward against Myer to the Adjutant General of the Army, Seth Williams, the burden of which was that Myer had made false statements. Felt also filed charges against Lieutenant Colonel William J.L. Nicodemus, at the same time, claiming that the War Department refused to act on all these charges. Complaining to the Adjutant General on September 21 of the inactions taken, Felt also commented extensively on the weaknesses of Myer's visual signal system. In addition to this, he stated that he had notified Myer as early as July of 1862, that Myer's signal code was "unsafe," and that he had offered a code of his own invention as an alternative.

Although Myer denied Felt's claims, it was true that after Chancellorsville an officer had complained that "the corps is distrusted, and considered unsafe as a means of transmitting important messages. It is well known that the enemy can read our signals when regular code is used, and it is equally evident...that our cipher is unsafe and cannot be trusted..." By then, however, Myer had a cipher disk under development. Although he claimed its use was "habitual" by late August of 1863, chief signal officers in the field were not informed until September 10 that disks would be distributed for general use. From that point forward, important messages would be in cipher, said the directive, since "there is evidence, at this office, that the enemy can read our messages sent in the usual way."[14]

During the court of inquiry hearings, a number of witnesses stepped forward to testify on George Henry's behalf. Sworn statements of support were offered by Colonel Charles S. Merchant, First Lieutenant Charles R. Deming, and Lieutenant Peter H. Niles:

> "In pursuance of instructions received from Lieut. Geo. H. Felt, I fired seven (7) rockets at this camp on the night of March 20, 1863... Notwithstanding the very unfavorable night, the weather being very thick, and, as we supposed, impossible to distinguish any lights at that distance–eighteen (18) miles–even with the aid of a glass, the rockets were very distinctly visible with the naked eye, and messages sent by them could have been seen at a much greater distance. It would have been impossible to have seen a torch that night at a distance of four (4) miles, with our most powerful glasses. I consider these rockets a very valuable acquisition to our present means of signaling, as it becomes available when every other means of communication fails."[15]

As the telegraph began to become more and more prominent during the second half of the Civil War, George Henry Felt realized that his own signaling system would soon become obsolete. Shelving that, as well as his submarine concept for the time being, he continued to work on a number of other unique inventions. On July 24, 1863, Special Order 329 was issued by the War Department, giving George Henry permission to be "mustered out of service to date August 15th 1863 to which time he has leave of absence to close his accounts. No payment will be made him till he has satisfied the Pay Department that he is not indebted to the Government."[16]

Thus, George Henry Felt's brief military career came to an abrupt end. Likely, some type of injury was the primary cause, judging from the inclusion in his records of an Office Casualty Sheet, dated July 2, 1863. No details of the injury were given, however.

On September 25, 1864, George Henry filed another formal application with the U.S. Patent Office. He was granted the patent on October 11 for automated "improvements in reefing and furling sails" to be used aboard ocean-going vessels, "by means of ropes arranged in the form and manner of lacings...the said lacings remaining stationary and the sail being reefed by the yard being lowered all arranged and combined as specified."[17]

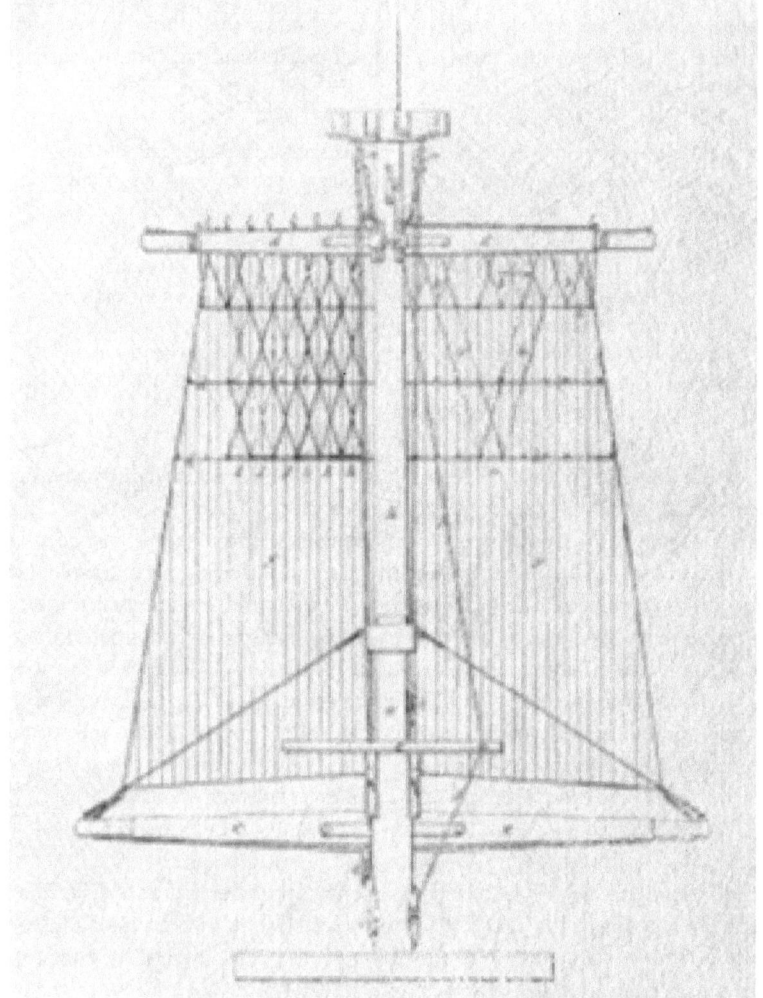

Drawing of George Henry Felt's patented reefing anf furling sails

After the Civil War had ended, George Henry Felt returned to the West Farms, Bronx, New York homestead. In late February of 1866, he patented an "Improved Plug for Blasting," which promised to make the job of detonating rock much more efficient. Meanwhile, he published *The Therapeutic and Chemical Properties or the Active Medicinal Principles of Cod Liver, Determined and Separated* in 1868. In September of 1870, the family purchased property at 130th and 6th avenues in New York City for $25,000, and that year's census recorded that he was a chemist, living with wife, Mary Anne, his sons, Willard, Henry, and George Jr., and his daughters, Elizabeth, Anna, and Maria.

At the same time, George Henry continued his work on the design of a submersible attack vessel, spending several months perfecting its weaponry. On June 26, 1874, he submitted a patent application for an "Improvement in Breech-Loading Ordinance":

> "My invention consists in the novel construction and application of an elastic breech-plug, composed of vulcanized rubber or other suit able similar elastic material, combined with wrought-iron or steel, or other suitable metal appliances, for the purpose of securely closing the breech of a cannon in the bore thereof, when the same is run entirely through the cannon; said plug being so constructed, proportioned, and applied in the bore of the cannon as to have sufficient frictional surface against the metal surface of the bore of the breech as to prevent the plug, when properly screwed up, from being blown out of or moved longitudinally bodily in the breech when the charge of powder is exploded therein."[18]

By this time in his life, George Henry had become heavily involved in an occult group known as the Hermetic Brotherhood of Luxor, said to be a distant forebear of modern-day spiritualism. In actuality, its foundation had been laid by the mediumistic manifestations of Maggie and Kate Fox in Hydesville, New York, in 1848. Within a few years, the reputation and teachings of these two "spirit rappers"–widely known as the Fox sisters–had spread throughout much of the Western world. In fact, in the words of Alfred Russel Wallace, "other mediums were discovered in different parts of the country, as if a special development of this abnormal power were then occurring." Such "mystics," who purportedly could speak directly to the spirits, traveled throughout America, demonstrating their wonders by conducting spiritual encounters through séances.

Psychics and so-called "sensitives" were soon found among all classes of people, and the forthcoming revelations and physical manifestations shook the very foundations of the established religious authorities. By 1850, spiritualist "revealers" bloomed like the Hebrew prophets of old, and occasionally some figure of eminence made public admission of his or her interest in, and strong adherence to, Spiritualism. Horace Greeley, editor of the *New York Tribune*, was one of the most outspoken, testifying to the genuineness of the "rappings" produced by the Fox sisters, and editorially exonerating them from charges of fraud.

John Worth Edmonds, a Justice of the New York Supreme Court known for his profound integrity, defended other mediums in the press. Nathan Pitcher Tallmadge, a former Governor of Wisconsin, publicly supported the claims of such mediums. Other believers in the spiritualist concept included William Cullen Bryant, George Bancroft, James Fenimore Cooper, Nathaniel Parker Willis, Sojourner Truth, and William Lloyd Garrison. During the next several years, hundreds of people came forward, claiming the ability to communicate with the spirit world. In fact, sufficient interest in spiritualism developed to support the establishment of dozens of journals entirely devoted to its phenomena and its interpretation.

The "not-so-secret" secret Hermetic Brotherhood of Luxor is believed to have begun its most serious work in early 1870, with George Henry and Mary Anne Felt two of its most outspoken advocates. According to its teachings, human sexuality was closely aligned with spirituality and vice versa, from the celibacy of Catholic priests and the strict rules of evangelical Christian marriages to transgressive tantric practices that deliberately broke taboos. From its beginnings, the "H.B. of L."–as it was then known–struggled to find a dependable universal formula for balancing physical pleasure and religion. Both its male and female members believed they had found that universal formula, but there was much more to their belief system than instructions in lovemaking. Through the Hermetic Brotherhood of Luxor, history glimpses how secret societies were initiated, both assisting and undermining each other, sometimes simultaneously. We also learn how the roots of American metaphysical religion directly impacted the overall culture of post Civil War America.

A practical occult order that taught the correct use of the "magic mirror for scrying," the Hermetic Brotherhood of Luxor promised initiates that they would learn how to communicate with secret and even discarnate masters by means of astral projection. Theirs was not a mere correspondence course by U.S. mail; students would, instead, receive step-by-step astral instruction as well. Why not promote contact through disembodied masters, when mediums were wowing the nation with channeled spirits speaking from beyond the grave?

On the evening of September 7, 1875, a group of ladies and gentlemen assembled in the home of Madame Helena Petrovna Blavatsky, one of the most well-known and controversial spiritual leaders of the times. Blavatsky had been born as Helena von Hahn on July 31, 1831, in Yekaterinoslav (renamed Dnepropetrovsk in 1926), Russia, the daughter of Colonel Peter von Hahn and Helena de Fadeyev, a renowned novelist. On her mother's side, she was the granddaughter of the gifted Princess Helena Dolgorukov, a noted botanist and writer. After the death of her mother in 1842, eleven-year-old Helena moved to her maternal grandparents' house at Saratov, where her grandfather held the respected position of Civil Governor.

History has recorded that Helena was an exceptional child, and at an early age was aware of being different from those around her. She loved to surround herself with mystery and assured her playmates that in the subterranean corridors of their old house at Saratow, where she used to wander about, she was never alone, claiming she had companions and playmates that she referred to as her "hunchbacks." She was often discovered in a dark tower underneath the roof where she put pigeons into mesmeric sleep by stroking them.

Helena's possession of certain psychic powers puzzled her family and friends. At once impatient of all authority, yet deeply sensitive, she was gifted in many ways. Remembered as a "clever linguist, a talented pianist and a fine artist," she was yet a fearless rider of half-broken horses. Once, while out riding, she fell from the saddle and her foot became entangled in the stirrup. She claimed that she ought to have been killed outright before the horse was stopped, "but for the strange sustaining power she distinctly felt around her, which seemed to hold her up in defiance of gravitation." According to the diary of her sister, she showed frequent evidence of somnambulism as a child, speaking aloud while she walked in her sleep. When awake, she often claimed to see eyes glaring at her from inanimate objects or from phantasmal forms.

At a very early age, Helena sensed that she was in some way dedicated to a life of service, and was aware of a special guidance and protection. Nadezhda Fadeyeva, Helena's aunt, later wrote of her niece's early years:

> "In childhood, all [of Helena's] likings and interests were concentrated on the people from lower estates. She preferred to play with the children of domestics but not with equals... She always needs attention to prevent her escape from home and meetings with street ragamuffins. And at a mature age she irrepressibly reached out to those whose status was lower than her own, and displayed a marked indifference to the 'nobles,' to which she belongs by birth."[19]

As an adult, Helena claimed visions of a phantom protector whose imposing appearance had dominated her imagination. Her powers of make-believe were so remarkable that she could actually cause hallucinations in playmates by her vivid storytelling. She was also known for her violent temper and her ability to swear in several languages. This behavior was, no doubt, intensified as a result of her drug addiction to hashish. She traveled all over the world lecturing and practicing the occult, but her greatest impact would be through her writings.

Arriving in New York City on July 7, 1873, Helena quickly gained local notoriety. Over the course of the next several months, she continually consorted with a number of prominent politicians and upstanding citizens, which culminated in the historical meeting of a small group of dignitaries in early September of 1875. They had come together to listen to a lecture by George Henry Felt, whose recent discovery of the geometrical figures of the Egyptian Kabbalah (Cabbala) was "regarded as among the most surprising feats of the human intellect." Among the interested parties was Colonel Henry Steel Olcott, a man of sterling worth who had acquired considerable renown during the Civil War, had served the U.S. Government with distinction, and was at the time practicing law in New York. Also present was William Quan Judge, a young Irish attorney, who was destined to play a unique role in the future Theosophical work.

Several other learned individuals, as well as wide range of public figures, were on hand to hear Felt's speech. They included: Charles Sotheran, bibliographer, antiquarian, and reporter for the *New York World*; Dr. David E. De Lara, a "learned old gentleman of Portuguese-Hebrew extraction," a venerable Jewish scholar and traveler of repute; newspaper reporter, Herbert D. Monachesi, and author of an article entitled *Proselyters from India*, a lucid piece detailing the formation of the Society; William Livingston Alden, an editorial writer and humorist with *The New York Times*; Henry J. Newton, inventor of the dry-plate method in photography and president of the New York Society of Spiritualists; Charles Carleton Massey, an English barrister-at-law; Dr. William Britten and his wife, Emma Hardinge Britten, who later authored a well known book entitled *Nineteenth Century Miracles*; well respected New York physician, Dr. Charles E. Simmons; a Philadelphia physician, professor at a medical college, and student of alchemy named Seth Pancoast; an English barrister and Doctor of Laws, John Storer Cobb, who was educated–according to unverified sources–at "Oxford, Heidelberg and Paris"; James H. Hyslop, a college student who would later rise to prominence as the leader of official Psychical Research in America; and, finally, Henry M. Stevens, editor of the *New York Observer*, who had come to appreciate George Henry Felt's research into Egyptian mythology and his "discoveries" in relation to the Kabbalah. This led Stevens to introduce Felt to Madame Blavatsky, who was extremely interested in similar subjects.

During his presentation, George Henry disclosed a solution to the Egyptian and Greek "Canon of Proportion," a law to which artists were mandated to regularize dimensions and scale. According to that law, the human body (as depicted in their art) must not exceed eighteen units length to the hairlines, and just under nineteen units to the top of the head. The bellybutton was to be drawn at eleven units length. This was, in fact, beginning the measurement from the soles of the feet. Felt further explained that he considered the Kaballah of the Egyptians to be "a geometrically and mystically arranged figure, intimately connected with all the works of nature, both animate and inanimate." Though somewhat baffled by Felt's discussion, Henry J. Newton would recall:

> "I was among the guests at the lecture, and there met a large company of persons who were interested in the study of the occult. I was full of the keenest interest, and was expecting a treat, which I did not realize. The lecture was very disappointing as it was not at all what was expected, but was a dry dissertation on geometry and ancient mathematics generally, without reference to cabala. The whole thing was flat and would have fallen and remained so if it had not been for one statement made near the close of the lecture. The lecturer referred to the methods used in Egypt and India in connection with their mysteries and said: 'They produce the phenomena of so-called materialization by a combustion of aromatic gum and herbs, instead of a seance of persons to draw the necessary power from. I have produced these phenomena in that way, and can do it again.'"[20]

The positive key to George Henry's presentation, however, was that he spoke not only about the symbolism of the geometric figures of the ancients, but also claimed to have discovered how the Egyptian priests by evocation could make contact with the elemental beings, or "creatures evolved in the four kingdoms of earth, air, fire, and water, and called by the kabbalists gnomes sylphs, salamanders, and undines." He further claimed that these "elements are peopled with beings invisible to the eye," and that he would make them appear for all the world to witness via his own invention. Newspapers throughout the region soon offered boasting details of George Henry's amazing claim, describing how the Theological Society's members refused to align themselves with "mere mundane" spiritualists of the times:

> "Without claiming to be a theurgist, a mesmerist, or a Spiritualist, our Vice-President (Mr. George Henry Felt) promises, by simple chemical appliances, to exhibit to us, as he has to others before, the races of beings, which, invisible to our eyes, people the elements. Think for a moment of this astounding claim! Fancy the consequences of the practical demonstration of its truth, for which Mr. Felt is now preparing the requisite apparatus! What will the Church say of a whole world of beings within her territory but without her jurisdiction? What will the academy say of this crushing proof of an unseen universe given by the most unimaginative of its sciences? What will the l'ositivists say, who have bean prating of the impossibility of there being any entity which cannot be weighed in scales, filtered through funnels, tested with litmus, or carved with a scalpel? What will the Spiritualists say when through the column of saturated vapor flit the dreadful shapes of beings whom, in their blindness, they have in a thousand cases revered and babbled to as the returning shades of their relatives and friends! Alas, poor Spiritualists–editors and correspondents–who have made themselves jocund over my impudence and apostasy. Alas, sleek scientists, over-swollen with the wind of popular applause! The day of reekoning [sic] is close at band, and the name of the Theosophical Society will, if Mr. Felt's experiments result favorably, hold its place in history as that of the body which first exhibited the 'Elementary Spirits' in this nineteenth century of conceit and infidelity, even if it be never mentioned for any other reason."[21]

At the time George Henry offered his research to those who would soon join the newly found Theosophical Society, he had already been openly promoting his "Canon of Proportion" for more than three years. In fact, he had even reached a publishing agreement with one major firm–James R. Osgood and Company, of Boston. Indeed, it was not the first time that he had lectured about it, for he had presented his findings and thesis to a number of audiences, large and small. The *Liberal Christian* had covered one of those sessions, offering a description of the geometric figure that was apparently at the heart of George Henry's theory:

> "First, he [Felt] explained the diagram which unlocks the Cabala. It consists of a circle with a square within and without, containing a common triangle, two Egyptian triangles, and a pentagon, forming the Star of Per-

fection. This diagram he applies to the Pictures, Statues, Doors, Hieroglyphics, Pyramids, Plains, Tombs, and Buildings of ancient Egypt, and shows that they agree so perfectly with its proportions that they must have been made by its rule."[22]

Drawing of Felt's Canon of Proportion geometric figure

The ensuing discussion was, not accidentally, the exact subject of the occult forces of the early historical magician. Felt went so far as to claim that he had tested these magical powers personally and could thus—with gnomes, sylphs, Undine, elves, and the like—connect to this other world. As proof, he promised to publicly demonstrate this at an undisclosed later date. These conversations inspired the imagination of the audience at Madame Blavatsky's flat, and brought Henry Steel Olcott to the idea of organizing a group to study such things. Thus, Felt's lecture was the impetus for the founding of the Theosophical Society.

The following day, September 8, George Henry became a signatory to the Memorandum for the Society and, at a meeting on October 30, he was elected vice president of the group. However, due to his unwillingness or inability to demonstrate his purported power to "consort with the spirits," criticism soon prevailed in the press, putting pressure on the Theosophical Society in general—

and Colonel Henry Steel Olcott in particular—to repair the group's increasingly damaged reputation:

> "The bare announcement of such an association 'sounded in the ears of some of the leaders of the contending forces of theology and science like the blast of a distant trumpet to the struggling armies in a battle'—consequently, unless the Colonel [Olcott] deceives himself in regard to the feelings of scientific leaders (say Mr. Darwin) and men prominent in theology (such as the Pope, for instance), we have a right to believe that the society will be able to furnish the world with some very astonishing facts before long."[23]

Although there were rumblings of doubt beneath the surface, members of the young Society continued to defend George Henry to the press:

> "This is certainly a good prospect as well as a good prospectus for the Theosophical Society, and when Mr. Felt shall have produced his elementary spirits the scientific world, whose eyes are now blinking with the approach of dawn, will open them wide and accept the truth. All jarring and war shall cease between science and religion, and the High Priest of the Theosophical Society, if such being there be, shall be seated on a tripod and crowned with…leaves of the ribes grossularia."[24]

Photograph of Helena Petrovna Blavatsky and Henry Steel Olcott

Despite repeated urgings by Colonel Olcott and other Society members requesting that George Henry fulfill his promise of a public demonstration of magical powers, the one-time submarine inventor failed to comply. Eventually, the he became more and more reclusive, no longer taking part in the Theosophical Society meetings, and attending his final gathering sometime in late 1876. By then, it had become painfully obvious that he was not in a position to provide the required evidence that he had promised for so long. This was, for many members, a tremendous blow and a sound reason to leave the group. Later, George Henry was officially voted out of his position as vice president in disgrace, though it is historically unclear whether or not this resulted in his expulsion as a member.

In the June 19, 1878, letter sent to of *The Spiritualist*, published in London, George Henry offered his side of the story. Remarking how he came to his discovery of spirits while working on drawings of Egyptian Zodiacs, he wrote:

> "I satisfied myself that the Egyptians had used these appearances in their initiations… My original idea was to introduce into the Masonic fraternity a form of initiations such as prevailed among the ancient Egyptians, and tried to do so, but finding that only men pure in mind and body could control these appearances, I decided that I would have to find others than my whisky-soaked and tobacco-sodden countrymen, living in an atmosphere of fraud and trickery, to act in that direction."[25]

George Henry's "elemental spirit research" was slated for publication, as was *The Egyptian Kaballah*, but was never actually printed and distributed. It has since become, perhaps, the single most famous lost document of the Victorian occult revival. The only known copy of his manuscript for *The Egyptian Kaballah* was kept by James R. Osgood, who would later be credited with founding Houghton, Mifflin, and Company, as well as representing the writings of Walt Whitman and Mark Twain. Sadly, however, Felt's precious work was stored in Osgood's warehouse in Boston, and it burned along with that warehouse in the Boston Fire of November 9, 1872. Having collected a significant number of pre-paid subscriptions for the work, and having no means to repay those subscribers, George Henry suppressed this fact for many months. Although he eventually found a new publisher for the material, J.W. Bouton, it would appear that he never completed the replacement manuscript.

Meanwhile, George Henry continued work on his submarine concept, as well as a number of other inventive projects. In August of 1874, his work was deemed to be so impacting and vital that he was elected into the membership of the prestigious American Association for the Advancement of Science. By June of the following year, he had taken his concepts to England, pursuing–and eventually being awarded–a number of patents for his non-military inventions. Still, he was unable to find interest for his submarine designs, which had long since been improved with the installation of both a compressed air supply and armaments. In February of 1880, the near-fifty-year-old was awarded a U.S. patent for liquid gas pump improvements:

"Now, my invention may be stated to consist in an improved arrangement of return tubes or ducts extending from the reservoir to the cylinder and opening into the sides of the cylinder at points behind the piston when near the end of its stroke, through which a quantity of the water is returned under pressure to the cylinder, thus avoiding all air-clearance, and at the same time rendering the back-pressure from the reservoir effective on the back or retreating side of the piston as an auxiliary to the steam-pressure inV compressing or forcing out the charge in front of the piston, whereby air or gas may be compressed to a greater density or water pumped to a greater height than would be otherwise possible."[26]

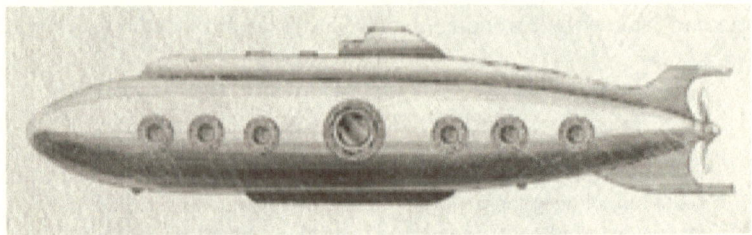

Drawing of the all-improved Felt Submarine

Almost simultaneously, George Henry's spiritualist working material that had been destroyed in Osgood's Boston-based warehouse, had been reconstituted. The materials, including drawings, printers' proofs and plates for illustration, were among his personal effects that were sold on September 11, 1883, to cover back rent that he owed to the Eagle Storage facility on West 33rd Avenue in New York. Those personal effects were purchased by an agent of a well-respected American bookstore known as Brentano's.

Throughout the later 1880s, George Henry concentrated his submarine development efforts on altering its primary mode of propulsion. Instead of human pedal-power, he hoped to install a series of rechargeable galvanic batteries. By November of 1889, he had managed to earn no less than four patents in this area of development, with particular attention to the electrode construct.

George Henry Felt died on Tuesday, December 4, 1906, without ever having realized overall success in his submarine designs:

"George Henry Felt died on Tuesday at his home, 448 St. Nicholas Avenue. He was 75 years old, and is survived by a widow and eight children. His is the first death in the family. Mr. Felt celebrated his golden wedding two years ago. He was an Inventor, and before the civil war Invented a breech loading cannon. During the war, when attached to the Signal Corps, he invented the Felt rocket, which was used in that arm of the service. Mr. Felt enlisted at the beginning of the war with the Fifty-fifth New York Zouaves, and served to the end (error). He was a thirty-second degree Mason."[27]

Unknown by most of history, Brentano's bookstore had held onto the Felt manuscript and materials for more than a quarter-century, well beyond George Henry's death. The Felt diagrams derived the golden section and other root rectangles from the circle. It was in 1914, in fact, that they were sold to a New York doctor named Clarence W. Lieb. At that time, Lieb received some accounting from Brentano's of the provenance of the materials.

Lieb stored Felt's materials, and left them untouched until 1932, when Viola de Gruchy–a young female student of Dynamic Symmetry, a canon of proportion–became one of his patients. On learning of her work, Lieb loaned de Gruchy the Felt materials with the mutual understanding that de Gruchy could one day publish them. De Gruchy worked on these materials until the late 1930s, when she solicited assistance from her teachers, who put her in touch with Claude Chandler Bragdon, a Rochester designer, architect and occultist. Recognizing the value of the materials, Bragdon attempted to collaborate with de Gruchy–unsuccessfully–in arranging and extending the Felt materials for publication. At the time of Bragdon's death on September 17, 1946, it is believed that de Gruchy was in possession of the manuscript and its supporting materials. Again, the materials had, by then, formally changed hands and were 'owned' by a "Miss Felt," who had sought their return either directly or through agents, executors, or heirs. Sadly, nothing more can be found concerning their current whereabouts.

Yet, in spite of history losing track of George Henry Felt's lecture materials, perhaps everything was not lost. In fact, an earlier reference to his occult work has recently been uncovered within the pages of a May 26, 1872, issue of the *New York Dispatch*:

> "In the last issue of the *Dispatch* we briefly noticed this most interesting subject as presented by Brother George Henry Felt. Since then we have been present at several conversations of distinguished brethren and scientists with Bro. Felt, and we can only repeat our original opinion that it is the most wonderful and startling discovery of the age. Bro. F. has been advised to give the result of his discoveries to the public in a permanent form, and we avail ourselves of the agreeable privilege of assisting this laudable endeavor so far as our province as journalists may permit. From his prospectus issued in this connection we make the following extract: 'Kaballah,' according to the Hebraic style, had a very distinct signification from that in which we understand it, the word being an abstract, and meaning reception, a doctrine received by oral transmission. It existed in the earliest traditional ages and in it the secrets of nature and the mysteries of religion, and the meaning of the divine revelations were expressed by occult figures, signs or words, or by common words, signs or figures having a mystical or hidden meaning. According to tradition, this Kaballah of the Egyptians was a geometrically and mystically arranged figure, intimately connected with all the works of nature, both animate and inanimate, which had been revealed to man in the very earliest ages; but

what the Kaballah originally consisted of, or was composed, or anything relating to it, seemed to have been lost. All traditions agreed, however, in this, that the Kaballah would not only be a perfect system of proportion and a complete key to all the works not only of art in the early ages, but of nature itself; that it would also elucidate the origin of language, not only printed or written, and hieroglyphical or figurative, but even spoken language, thus showing the hidden and true meaning of the Old Testament, and also the true meaning of the New Testament. Being a complete key to works of Nature, it explains the origins of species and their different relations, in giving a system of proportion that exists in all her works and operations, and their different ramifications or parts. The Grecian Canon was a system of proportion brought from Egypt by Grecian sculptors and architects about B.C. 360, and in which they fashioned their statues of the human figure and their architectural works. The proof of its correctness is shown through all Nature and Art, and it is Positive; the work is written without using technical terms and plainly, so that any child of twelve years can understand it; the geometrical problems are reduced to the simplest elements, so that all can understand them without a previous knowledge of that science, as being a work of vital interest to every person; the writer thought it should be adapted to the comprehension of all. The Kaballah being a geometrical figure, the actual measurements of which are even established through all Nature and Art, the proof be positive, and cannot be for a moment gainsaid."[28]

The *New York Dispatch* article exhibits, perhaps for the first time, an extended and clear explanation of the lecture he offered on September 7, 1875, to a handful of people. According to historical records, however, George Henry's book would have been far more detailed, containing more than 1,000 illustrations and issued in ten parts covering sixty-four pages. Sadly, the submarine inventor and Theosophist took a number of secrets with him to the grave.

AMERICAN SUBMARINERS: PRE-CIVIL WAR

Chapter Bibliographies

Prologue

1. McCurdy, Edward, *Leonardo da Vinci's Note-Books: Arranged and Rendered into English with Introductions*, Empire State Book Company, 1923, p. 76.
2. *Eclectic Magazine of Foreign Literature, Science, and Art*, "Glaucus; or The Wonders of the Shore", W.H. Bidwell, New York, New York, 1855, p. 220.
3. Aristotle, *Problemata*, 360 B.C.
4. Ibid.
5. Translated by George Rawlinson, *Herodotus, The Persian Wars, Book 8 – Urania*, Random House, New York, New York, 1942.
6. Mangus, Olaus, *Historia Om de Nordiska Folken, Seelig*, Stockholm, Sweden, 1976.
7. *The Penny Magazine of the Society for the Diffusion of Useful Knowledge*, "Trajan's Palace in the Lake of Nemi," Charles Knight and Company, London, England, January 19, 1839, p. 23.
8. Taisnier, John, *Opusculum de Motu Celerrimo*, taken from the *Technica Curiosa, sive Mirabilia Artis* by P. Gaspar Schott, Nurnberg, Germany, 1664, p. 393.
9. Bourne, William, *Inventions or Devices–Very Necessary for All Generalles and Captaines, or Leaders of Men as wel by Sea as by Land*, London, England, 1578, p. 78.
10. Bacon, Francis, *Novum Organum Scientiarum*, volume II, Sherwood, Neely, and Jones, London, England, 1818, p. 167.
11. Napier, John, *Document written by John Napier*, Lambeth Palace Library, c 1594.
12. Pegelius, Magnus, *Thesaurus Rerum Selectarum Magnarum, Dignarum, Utilium, Marinus, per Genere Humane*, 1604.
13. Van Drebbel, Cornelius, *Personal Diary*, National Archives, Washington, D.C., 1620.
14. Bishop, Farnham, *Story of the Submarine*, The Century Company, New York, New York, February, 1916, p. 6.
15. Mersenne, Marin, *Correspandance du P. Marin Mersenne religieax minime*, dated December, 1640, edited by P. Tannery and C. de Ward, Paris, France, 1932-1988, pp. 435-436.
16. Ibid.
17. An engraving with explanatory text in Dutch and French, Municipal Archives, Amsterdam, the Netherlands, 1653.
18. Hautefeuille, Abbe Jean de, *The Art of Breathing Underwater*, 1681.
19. Ibid.
20. Sinclair, George, *The Principles of Astronomy and Navigation*, Heir to Andrew Anderson, Printed to His most Sacred Majesty, Edinburgh, Scotland, 1688.
21. Halley, Sir Edmund, *The Art of Living Under Water; Or, A Discourse Concerning the Means of Furnishing Air at the Bottom of the Sea, in Many Ordinary Depths*, 1716, pp. 492-499.
22. Falck, Nikolai D., *A Philosophical Dissertation on the Diving Vessel Projected by Mr. Day, and Sunk in Plymouth Sound*, London, England, 1775, p. 2.
23. Ibid., p. 6.
24. *The Annual Register, or a View of the History, Politics, and Literature for the Year 1774*, J. Dodsley, London, England, 1782, p. 247.
25. Ibid.

26. Abbot, Willis J., *Aircraft and Submarines: The Story of the Invention, Development, and Present-Day Uses of War's Newest Weapons*, G.P. Putnam's Sons, New York, New York, 1918, p. 245.
27. Falck, Nikolai Detlef, *A Philosophical Dissertation on the Diving Vessel Projected by Mr. Day, and Sunk in Plymouth Sound*, London, England, 1775, p. 9.
28. Ibid., p. 22.
29. Ibid., p. 23.

Chapter 1

1. Norwood, Richard, *The Journal of Richard Norwood, 1639-1640, Surveyor of Bermuda*, introduction: Wesley Frank Craven and Walter B. Hayward, Scholars Facsimiles and Reprints, New York, New York, 1945, pp. 3-4.
2. Glover, Lorri & Daniel Blake Smith, *The Shipwreck That Saved Jamestown: The Sea Venture Castaways and the Fate of America*, Henry Holt and Company, New York, New York, 1866, p. 3.
3. Law, Florence F., *The Parish Church of St. Andrew's, Shalford: Its Association with Families Whose Coat of Arms are on the Font, and Shields in the East Window*, Princeton University, 1898, p. 46.
4. Zacharie, Larrie Benton, *Roger Northwode, Lord Warden of the Cinque Ports*, Betascript Publishing, London, England, 2012, p. 6.
5. Ibid., p. 8.
6. Law, Florence F., *The Parish Church of St. Andrew's, Shalford: Its Association with Families Whose Coat of Arms are on the Font, and Shields in the East Window*, Princeton University, 1898, p. 46.
7. Norwood, Richard, *The Journal of Richard Norwood, 1639-1640, Surveyor of Bermuda*, introduction: Wesley Frank Craven and Walter B. Hayward, Scholars Facsimiles and Reprints, New York, New York, 1945, p. 4.
8. Games, Allison, *Migration and the Origins of the English Atlantic World*, President and Fellows of Harvard College, Cambridge, Massachusetts, 1963, p. 17.
9. Norwood, Richard, *The Journal of Richard Norwood, 1639-1640, Surveyor of Bermuda*, introduction: Wesley Frank Craven and Walter B. Hayward, Scholars Facsimiles and Reprints, New York, New York, 1945, p. 42.
10. Bunyan, John, *Grace Abounding: With Other Spiritual Autobiographies*, Oxford University Press, New York, New York, 1998, p. 129.
11. Norwood, Richard, *The Journal of Richard Norwood, 1639-1640, Surveyor of Bermuda*, introduction: Wesley Frank Craven and Walter B. Hayward, Scholars Facsimiles and Reprints, New York, New York, 1945, pp. 51-52.
12. Ibid., p. 42
13. Callam, G. Marion Norwood, *The Norwoods III: A Chronological History*, Gadds Printers, Worthing, England, 1997, pp. 131-132.
14. Games, Allison, *Migration and the Origins of the English Atlantic World*, President and Fellows of Harvard College, Cambridge, Massachusetts, 1963, p. 85.
15. Wilkins, John, *The Mathematical and Philosophical Works of the Right Rev. John Wilkins*, Press of John Wilson and Son, Boston, Massachusetts, 1869-70, p. 173.
16. Jarvis, Michael J., *In the Eye of All Trade: Bermuda, Bermudians, and the Maritime Atlantic World, 1680-1783*, University of North Carolina Press, Chapel Hill, North Carolina, 2010, pp. 22-23.
17. Ibid., p. 24.

18. Callam, G. Marion Norwood, *The Norwoods III: A Chronological History*, Gadds Printers, Worthing, England, 1997, p. 132.
19. Sanderson, Roberto, Foedera, *Conventiones, Literae et Cujuscunque Generis Acta Publica inter Reges Angliae*, London, England, April 2, 1632, pp. 365-366.
20. Games, Allison, *Migration and the Origins of the English Atlantic World*, President and Fellows of Harvard College, Cambridge, Massachusetts, 1963, p. 137.
21. Jarvis, Michael J., *In the Eye of All Trade: Bermuda, Bermudians, and the Maritime Atlantic World, 1680-1783*, University of North Carolina Press, Chapel Hill, North Carolina, 2010, p. 501.
22. Lefroy, Sir John Henry, *Memorials of the Discovery and Early Settlement of the Bermudas or Somers Islands, 1511-1687*, vol. II, Longmans, Green, and Company, London, England, 1879, p. 59.
23. Mercer, Julia E., *Bermuda Settlers of the 17th Century: Genealogical Notes from Bermuda*, Genealogical Publishing, Baltimore, Maryland, 2008, pp. 139-140.
24. Jarvis, Michael J., *In the Eye of All Trade: Bermuda, Bermudians, and the Maritime Atlantic World, 1680-1783*, University of North Carolina Press, Chapel Hill, North Carolina, 2010, p. 209.

Chapter 2

1. Winthrop, John, *The History of New England from 1630 to 1649*, Thomas B. Wait and Son, Boston, Massachusetts, 1826, p. 73.
2. Randall, John, *Broseley and Its Surrounding. Being a Complete History of Broseley, Willey, Barrow, Benthall, and Linley; with notices of Remarkable Events, Facts, Phenomena, and Manufacturers*, The Salopian and West-Midland Journal Office, Madeley, Salop, England, 1879, p. 18.
3. Ibid., pp. 18-19.
4. Mead, Edwin D., "Pilgrims Ports in Old England," *New England Magazine, An Illustrated Monthly*, New Series, Vol. 25, America Company, Boston, Massachusetts, December, 1901, p. 396.
5. Hart, Edward Bushnell & Edward Channing, "Extracts from John Winthrop's History of New England," *American History Leaflets, Colonial and Constitutional*, No. 31, A. Lovell & Company, excerpt from April 5, 1630, p. 3.
6. Hosmer, James Kendall, *Winthrop's Journal: History of New England, 1630 to 1649*, vol. 7, Issue 1, Charles Scribner's Sons, New York, New York, 1908, p. 31.
7. Ibid., p. 33.
8. Ibid., p. 49.
9. Hale, Edward E., "Edward Bendall and the Mary Rose," *New England Magazine, An Illustrated Monthly*, vol. 1, Boston, Massachusetts, September, 1889 to February, 1890, p. 520.
10. Ibid.
11. Oath of Freeman, Massachusetts Bay Colony, ca. 1634.
12. White, Albert Beebe, *Source Problems in English History*, Harper & Brothers Publishers, New York, New York, October 16, 1637, p. 269.
13. *Note-Book Kept by Thomas Lechford, Esq., Lawyer In Boston, from June 27, 1638, to July 29, 1641*, John Wilson and Son, Massachusetts Bay, Cambridge, Massachusetts, 1885, p. 73.
14. Hosmer, James Kendall, *Winthrop's Journal: History of New England, 1630 to 1649*, vol. 2, Issue 1, Charles Scribner's Sons, New York, New York, 1908, pp. 9-10.

15. Hale, Edward E., "Edward Bendall and the Mary Rose," *New England Magazine, An Illustrated Monthly*, vol. 1, Boston, Massachusetts, September, 1889 to February, 1890, p. 521.
16. Ibid, pp. 521-522.
17. Ibid., p. 522.
18. Ibid., p. 523.
19. Ibid.
20. Winthrop, John, *The History of New England from 1630 to 1649*, Thomas B. Wait and Son, Boston, Massachusetts, 1826, p. 74.
21. *Suffolk Deeds*, Rockwell and Churchill, City Printers, Boston, Massachusetts, 1880.
22. Hale, Edward E., "Edward Bendall and the Mary Rose," *New England Magazine, An Illustrated Monthly*, vol. 1, Boston, Massachusetts, September, 1889 to February, 1890, p. 524.

Chapter 3
1. Sherbrook, Michael, *Account of the Spoilation of Roche*, 1590.
2. Lewis, Roy Hartley, *Antiquarian books: an insider's account*, Arco Publishing, Inc., 1978, pp.138-139.
3. Ibid.
4. Wilde, Mrs. E.E., and Christy, Mrs. Archibold, *Ingatestone and the Essex Great Road with Fryerning*, Oxford University Press, London, England, 1913, p. 171.
5. Bremer, Francis J. *John Winthrop: America's Forgotten Founding Father*, Oxford University Press, New York, New York, 2003, p. 193.
6. Tinniswood, Adrian, *The Rainborowes: One Family's Quest to Build A New England*, Basic Books, the Perseus Group, New York, New York, Part 3, Chapter 17, 2013.
7. Trask, William Blake, *Suffolk Deeds, Liber II, 12 libb*, Rockwell and Churchill City Printers, Boston, Massachusetts, 1883, p. 46.
8. Hagerman, James J., *The Hagerman Collection: State Papers, Domestic Series, 1655*, vol. 104-136, Major Nehemiah Bourne, in a letter to William Molins and Abel Richardson dated February 9, 1655, p. 426.
9. Page, William, *The Victoria History of the County of Essex*, vol. II, Archibold Constable and Company Limited, London, England, 1907, p. 286.
10. Hagerman, James J., *The Hagerman Collection: State Papers, Domestic Series, 1655*, vol. 104-136, Major Nehemiah Bourne, in a letter to William Molins and Abel Richardson dated February 9, 1655, p. 451.
11. Ibid,, p. 460.
12. Ibid., p. 442.
13. Ibid., p. 546.
14. Letter sent from Joseph Falkener, Ordinance Officer, to Robert Blackborne, *The Hagerman Collection: State Papers*, dated September 10, 1655.
15. Smith, Denis, *Civil Engineering Heritage: London and the Thames Valley*, London, England, 2001, p. 109; from the diary of John Evelyn, recorded July 19, 1661
16. Hagerman, James J., *The Hagerman Collection: State Papers, Domestic Series, Charles II, 1663-1664*, in a letter dated August 1, 1663, p. 225.
17. Ibid., in a letter dated August 6, 1663, p. 232.
18. Birch, Thomas, T*he History of the Royal Society of London*, vol. II, 1761, p. 55.

19. Watkins, Walter Kendall, *Colonial Wars: A Quarterly Magazine*, vol. 1, Issues 1-4, "Robert Willis, Gun-Diver and His Introduction of the Diving Bell into Old England from New England," Society of Colonial Wars, Boston, Massachusetts, December, 1913, pp. 126-127.

Chapter 4

1. Bray, William, *Memoirs Illustrative of the Life and Writings of John Evelyn*, G.P. Putnam & Sons, New York, New York, 1870; Luttrell, Narcissus, *A Brief Historical Relation of State Affairs from September 1678 to April 1714*, vol. II, University Press, Oxford, England, 1857.
2. Tordesillas, Antonio de Herrera, *Historia general de los hechos de los Castellanos en las islas y tierra firme del Mar Oceano (General History of the Deeds of the Castilians on the Islands and Mainland of the Ocean Sea)*, Madrid, Spain, 1601-1615.
3. Percy, George, Observations *Gathered out of a Discourse of the Plantation of the Southern Colony in Virginia by the English, 1606*, published in 1608.
4. Bradford, William, *History of Plymouth Plantation*, written between 1630 and 1647.
5. Ingram, Reverend James, *The Anglo-Saxen Chronicle* (translation), London, England, 1823.
6. The family connection between William and Robert Phips was established by a letter written in 1693 by Sir Henry Ashurst. Ashurst was well acquainted with both Sir William Phips and Constantine Phips. Constantine, Ashurst mentioned, was Sir William's "Coszen." The relationship is further reinforced by the use of the same coat of arms by the two branches of the family. A family pedigree was compiled by Elias Ashmole in 1664 for Constantine's oldest brother, Francis Phips Jr., who was then a student at Cambridge. It included the family coat of arms granted to Robert Phips, and this same coat of arms later appears on the marble monument to Sir William Phips in the London church where he was buried, on the family tomb in Charlestown, and on the wax seal attached to his will.
7. Thorpe, Benjamin, *The Anglo-Saxon Chronicle*, Rolls Series, Longman Publishing, London, England, 1861
8. Baker, Emerson W. and John G. Reid, *The New England Knight: Sir William Phips, 1651-1695*, University of Toronto Press, Toronto, Ontario, Canada, 1998, p 171.
9. Ibid.
10. Toppan, Robert Noxon, *Edward Randolph; including his Letters and Official Papers from the New England, Middle, and Southern Colonies in America, 1676-1703*, vol. III, Published by the Prince Society, Boston, Massachusetts, 1899, p. 262.
11. Roberts. Oliver Ayer, *History of the Military Company of the Massachusetts, 1637-1738*, vol. I, Alfred Mudge & Son, Printers, Boston, Massachusetts, 1895, p. 224.
12. Clifford, Barry, and Paul Perry, *Expedition Whydah*, Harper Collins Publishers, New York, New York, 1999, p. 28.
13. Letter written by William Phips to the Earl of Nottingham at Whitehall, London, England, dated October 12, 1692.
14. Drake, Samuel Gardner, *The History of Boston*, Oliver L. Perkins Publishing, London, England, 1852.

Chapter 5

1. Griswold, Charles, "Submarine Navigation," *The American Journal of Science*, Series 1, Volume 2, Lyme, Connecticut, 1820.
2. Felt, Joseph B., *The Ecclesiastical History of New England; comprising not only Religious, but also Moral, and other Relations*, Congregational Library Association, Boston, Massachusetts, 1855, p. 407.
3. Howe, Henry, *Memoirs of the Most Eminent American Mechanics*, Derby Publishing, New York, New York, 1847, p. 136.
4. Bushnell, David, in a letter addressed to Thomas Jefferson, dated October 13, 1787, the New Haven Colony Historical Society, New Haven, Connecticut.
5. Dr. Benjamin Gale, a letter Silas Deane, November 9, 1775..
6. Holland, John P., "Submarine Navigation," *Cassier's Magazine*, vol. XII, London, England, May-October, 1897, p. 547.
7. Ibid., p. 549.
8. Letter mailed to John Adams, dated April, 1776.
9. Cross, Wilbur, *Challengers of the Deep*, William Sloan Associates, New York, New York, 1959, p. 22.
10. Holbrook, S. H., *Lost Men of American History*, MacMillan Publishing, New York, New York, 1948, pp. 62-70.
11. Ibid., pp. 67-68.
12. Washington, George, in a letter to Thomas Jefferson, September 26, 1785, *Papers of Thomas Jefferson*, vol. 13, Library of Congress, Washington, D.C. Printed in Thomas Jefferson, *The Papers of Thomas Jefferson*, ed. by Julian Boyd, et al., 34 vols. to date, Princeton: Princeton University Press, 1950-, 8: pp. 555-57.
13. Delpeuch, Maurice, *La Navigation Sous-Marine: A Travers Les Siecles*, Paris, France, 1907.
14. Hargraves, George, letter to Thomas Jefferson, dated August 4, 1814, *The Papers of Thomas Jefferson, Retirement Series*, November 1813 to September 1814, Princeton University Press, 2010, p. 512.

Chapter 6

1. Clark, William Bell, *Naval Documents of the American Revolution*, vol. 2, part 1 of 9, United States Government Printing Office, Washington, DC, 1966, p. 15.
2. Stark, Charles Rathbone, *Groton, Conn. 1705-1905*, Palmer Press, Stonington, Connecticut, 1922, p. 196.
3. Letter written by Mrs. Elisha Miner, *Brown Alumni Journal*, Brown University, Brown Alumni Magazine Company, Providence, Rhode Island, March, 1911.
4. Stockwell, Thomas B., *A History of Public Education in Rhode Island: From 1636 to 1876*, "Brown University," Providence Press Company, Providence, Rhode Island, 1876, p. 217.
5. Meredith, Austin, *Kouroo Contexture*, "The Reverend James Manning," 2008, p. 7.
6. Bronson, Walter Cochrane, *The History of Brown University, 1764-1914*, Brown University Publishing, Providence, Rhode Island, 1914, p. 40.
7. Rhode Island Historical Society, *Collections of the Rhode Island Historical Society*, vol. VII, Kellogg Printing Company, Providence, Rhode Island, 1885, p. 282.
8. Bronson, Walter Cochrane, *The History of Brown University, 1764-1914*, Brown University Publishing, Providence, Rhode Island, 1914, p. 43.

9. Crafts, William Francis, *The Crafts Family: A Genealogical and Biographical History of the Descendents of Griffin and Alice Craft, of Roxbury, Mass. 1630-1890*, Gazette Printing Company, Northampton, Massachusetts, 1893, p. 114.
10. *Brown Alumni Monthly*, vol. XI, Brown University, Brown Alumni Magazine Company, Providence, Rhode Island, March, 1911.
11. Clark, William Bell, *Naval Documents of the American Revolution*, vol. 2, part 1 of 9, United States Government Printing Office, Washington, DC, 1966, pp. 13-14.
12. Ibid., pp. 13-15.
13. Ibid., p. 14.
14. Ibid.
15. Ibid.
16. Ibid., pp. 14-15.
17. Ibid. p. 15.
18. Ibid, p. 79.
19. Ibid. pp. 79-80.
20. National Archives, Washington, DC, *Franklin Papers*, Letter written from Benjamin Franklin to George Washington, dated July 22, 1776.
21. National Archives, Washington, DC, *Franklin Papers*, Letter written from George Washington to Benjamin Franklin, dated July 30, 1776.
22. Peterson, Harold Leslie, *Arms and Armor in Colonial America, 1526-1783*, Stackpole Company, Harrisburg, Pennsylvania, 1956, pp. 217-218.
23. United States Continental Congress, *Journals of the American Congress from 1774-1788*, vol. II, Way and Gideon, Washington, DC, 1823, p. 114.
24. National Archives, Washington, DC, Letter written from Joseph Belton to the Continental Congress, dated May 7, 1777.
25. Ibid.
26. National Archives, Washington, DC, Letter written from Joseph Belton to the John Hancock, dated May 8, 1777.
27. National Archives, Washington, DC, Letter written from Joseph Belton to the Continental Congress, dated June 14, 1777.
28. National Archives, Washington, DC, Letter written from Joseph Belton to the Continental Congress, dated July 10, 1777.
29. National Archives, Washington, DC, Endorsement to the Continental Congress, dated July 10, 1777.
30. Massachusetts Historical Society, Boston, Massachusetts, *Papers of John Adams*, vol. 6, Letter from Joseph Belton to the First Joint Commission at Paris, dated April 17, 1778.
31. Library of Congress, Washington, DC, Letter from Benjamin Franklin to Hamelin, dated February 28, 1779.
32. American Philosophical Society, Philadelphia, Pennsylvania, Receipt written to Joseph Belton, dated February 13, 1779.
33. Massachusetts Historical Society, Boston, Massachusetts, *Papers of John Adams*, vol. 6, Letter from John Adams to Jonas Belton, September 10, 1779.

Chapter 7
1. Fulton, Robert, *A Treatise on the Improvement of Canal Navigation*, London, England, 1796, preface, p. x.

2. *New York Post*, February 26, 1815; *The Monthly Magazine or British Register*, vol. 41, Phillips, Sir Richard, Princeton University, London, England, February 1, 1816, p. 95.
3. Engle, William Henry, *Notes and Queries: Historical, Biographical, and Genealogical*, Fourth Series, Volume II, Harrisburg, Pennsylvania, 1895, p. 158.
4. Philip, Cynthia Owen, *Robert Fulton, A Biography*, Franklin Watts, London, England, 1985, p. 4
5. Ibid., p. 6.
6. Dickenson, H.A., *Robert Fulton*, New York, New York, 1913, p. 23.
7. Sutcliffe, Alice Crary, *Robert Fulton: True Stories of Great Americans*, The MacMillan Company of Canada, Toronto, Ontario, 1915, pp. 134-135.
8. Fulton, Robert, *A Treatise on the Improvement of Canal Navigation*, London, England, 1796, p. 86.
9. Ibid., p.89.
10. Letter addressed to the Executive Directory of Paris, dated December 31, 1797.
11. Dickinson, Henry Winram, *Robert Fulton, Engineer and Artist: His Life and Works*, Ballantyne, Hanson & Company, Edinburgh, Scottland, 1914, pp. 76-77.
12. Sutcliffe, Alice Crary, "Robert Fulton in France," *The Century Illustrated Monthly Magazine*, vol. 76, Century Company, New York, New York, May to October, 1908, p. 935.
13. Parsons, William Barclay, *Robert Fulton and the Submarine*, Columbia University, New York, New York, 1922, p. 28.
14. Holland, John P., "Submarine Navigation," *Cassier's Magazine*, vol. XII, New York, New York, May-October, 1897, p. 551.
15. Letter addressed to Citizens Monge and Laplace, members of the National Institute, dated November, 1800.
16. Letter addressed to the French Minister of Marine, dated December 3, 1800.
17. Thurston, Robert H., *Robert Fulton: His Life and Its Results*, Dodd, Mead, and Company, New York, New York, 1891, p. 76.
18. Holland, John P., "Submarine Navigation," *Cassier's Magazine*, vol. XII, New York, New York, May-October, 1897, p. 551.
19. Sutcliffe, Alice Crary, *The Clermont*, New York, New York, undated, p. 86.
20. Thurston, Robert H., *Robert Fulton: His Life and Its Results*, Dodd, Mead, and Company, New York, New York, 1891, p. 79.
21. Parsons, William Barclay, *Robert Fulton and the Submarine*, Columbia University, New York, New York, 1922, p. 46.

Chapter 8
1. Hurd, Duane Hamilton, *History of New London County, Connecticut: with biographical sketches of many of its Pioneers and Prominent Men*, J.W. Lewis and Company, Philadelphia, Pennsylvania, 1882, p. 42.
2. *Annals of Congress, House of Representatives, 12th Congress, 2nd Session*, March 3, 1813, p. 1346.
3. Roland, Alex, *Underwater Warfare in the Age of Sail*, Indiana University Press, Bloomington, Indiana, 1979; Jenkins, Mark Collins & Taylor, David A., *The War of 1812 and the Rise of the U.S. Navy*, National Geographic, Washington, DC, 2012, p. 222, 224.

4. Hurd, Duane Hamilton, *History of New London County, Connecticut: with biographical sketches of many of its Pioneers and Prominent Men*, J.W. Lewis and Company, Philadelphia, Pennsylvania, 1882, p. 41.
5. Hoyt, Albert H., *The New England Historical and Genealogical Register*, vol. 28, New England Historic, Genealogical Society, Boston, Massachusetts, 1874, p. 288
6. Caulkins, Frances Manwaring, *History of New London, Connecticut*, Case, Tiffany and Company, Hartford, Connecticut, 1852, p. 576.
7. *Annual Report of the American Historical Association for the Year 1898*, Government Printing Office, 1899, Washington, DC, p. 145.
8. Stark, Bruce P., *New London County, County Court Files, Inventory of Records*, Connecticut State Library, 2008.
9. Tombstone of Phebe A. Halsey Goddard. Preston City Cemetery, Preston, Connecticut.
10. Labensky, Alfred, "Samuel Holden Parsons Lee and Yellow Fever in New London," *Records and Papers of the New London County Historical Society*, Bingham Paper Box Company, New London, Connecticut, 1906, p. 115.
11. Statutes at Large, volume 2, statute 2, Chapter 47, p. 816.
12. "The Torpedo: to the editor of The War," *Kentucky Gazette*, John Scudder, Jr., August 10, 1813.
13. Ibid.
14. Dudley, William S., *The Naval War of 1812: A Documentary History, Volume II, 1813*, Naval Historical Center, Department of the Navy, Washington, DC; letter sent from Sir Thomas Hardy to Admiral Sir John B. Warren, dated June 26, 1813, p. 162.
15. *Niles' Register*, volume IV, p. 337; Barnes, Lieutenant-Commander J.S., Submarine Warfare, Offensive and Defensive, D. Van Nostrand, Publisher, New York, New York, 1869, p. 47.
16. Allison, Robert J., *Stephen Decatur: American Navel Hero, 1779-1820*, University of Massachusetts Press, Amherst, Massachusetts, 2007, p. 134.
17. "Increase Wilson Had First Plant in New London for Iron Products," *The Day*, New London, Connecticut, February 13, 1904, p. 7
18. Dudley, William, *The Naval War of 1812: A Documentary History, Volume II, 1813*, Letter from Robert Fulton to Commodore Stephen Decatur, dated August 5th 1813, Naval History Center, Washington, DC, 1902, p. 211.
19. Ibid., Letter from Commodore Stephen Decatur to Robert Fulton, dated August 9th, 1813, p. 212.
20. Allison, Robert J., *Stephen Decatur, American Naval Hero, 1779-1820*, University of Massachusetts Press, Amherst, Massachusetts, 2005, p. 144.
21. Tucker, Spencer, Stephen Decatur: *A Life Most Bold And Daring*, Naval Institute Press, Annapolis, Maryland, 2005 pp. 131-132; letter from Stephen Decatur to Secretary William Jones, dated July 2, 1813.
22. Green, Samuel H., *Connecticut Gazette*, July 21, 1813.
23. Penny, Joshua, *The Life and Adventures of Joshua Penny, A Native of Southold, Long Island, Suffolk County, New York*, published by the author, New York, New York, 1815, [pages not numbered].
24. Ibid.
25. Ibid.

26. *Gentleman's Magazine and Historical Chronicle*, from July to December, 1813, vol. 114, part the second, Nichols, Son, and Bentley, London, England, 1813, p. 285; Sueter, Murray Fraser, *The Evolution of the Submarine Boat, Mine and Torpedo*, Gieve, Matthews and Seagrove, Limited, London, England, 1907, p. 25.
27. Adams, James Truslow, *History of the Town of Southampton (east of Canoe Place)*, Hampton Press, Bridgehampton, Long Island, 1918, p. 195.

Chapter 9

1. Thurston, Robert H., *Robert Fulton*, Dodd, Mead & Company,
2. Gilder, Richard Watson, *The Century Illustrated Monthly Magazine*, vol. LXXVII, The Century Company, New York, New York, p. 764.
3. Letter from Robert Fulton to the French Legislature, dated 1803.
4. Parsons, William Barclay, *Robert Fulton and the Submarine*, Columbia University, New York, New York, 1922, p. 56.
5. Ibid.
6. Thurston, Robert H., *Robert Fulton: His Life and Its Results*, chap. V, Dodd, Mead, and Company, New York, New York, 1891, (pages not numbered).
7. Ibid., (pages not numbered).
8. Ibid., (pages not numbered).
9. Ibid., (pages not numbered).
10. "Editor's Table," *The New England Magazine*, vol. 23, Warren F. Kellogg, Publisher, Boston, Massachusetts, 1901, p. 126.
11. McCabe, James Dabney, *Great Fortunes and How They were Made; or the Struggles and Triumphs of Our Self-Made Men*, George Maclean Publishing, New York, New York, 1871, pp. 267-268.
12. *New York Evening Post*, January 8, 1808
13. Letter written by Robert Fulton to Joel Barlow, Clermont State Historic Site, Germantown, New York, 1808.
14. Fulton, Robert, "Torpedo War and Submarine Explosions," *The Magazine of History*, William Abbatt, New York, New York, 1914, p. 183.
15. Ibid., p. 185.
16. Thurston, Robert H., *Robert Fulton: His Life and Its Results*, chap. IV, Dodd, Mead, and Company, New York, New York, 1891, (pages not numbered).
17. Philip, Cynthia Owen, *Robert Fulton: A Biography*, Franklin Watts Publishing, London, England, 1985, p. 204.
18. Report from the Committee of the Institute, dated April 11, 1810.
19. Holland, John P., "Submarine Navigation," *Cassier's Magazine*, vol. XII, New York, New York, May-October, 1897, p. 551.
20. Philip, Cynthia Owen, *Robert Fulton: A Biography*, Franklin Watts Publishing, London, England, 1985, p. 253.
21. Letter written by Harriet Livingston Fulton to her second cousin, Robert the Chancellor, Clermont State Historic Site, Germantown, New York, 1812.
22. Barnes, John Sanford, *Submarine Warfare, Offensive and Defensive: Including A Discussion of the Offensive Torpedo System*, D. Van Nostrand, Publisher, New York, New York, 1869, p. 42.
23. Ibid., pp. 229-230.

24. Autographs, Manuscripts and Broadsides from the Stock of the late George D. Smith, Anderson Gallaries, New York, New York, "Memorandum of an Agreement Entered into this Twenty-second Day of July, 1813," signed by Robert Fulton and Samuel Swartwout.
25. Letter written by Robert Fulton to Secretary of the Navy, William Jones, dated May 8, 1812 [actually 1813].
26. Letter written by John Poo Beresford to Colonel Samuel Boyer Davis, dated March 16, 1813.
27. Contract written by Robert Fulton and signed by P. Dubayle, Robert Fulton, and James Welden, dated July 28, 1813.
28. Thurston, Robert H., *Robert Fulton: His Life and Its Results*, Dodd, Mead, and Company, New York, New York, Chapter 5, 1891, pp. 98-100; Colden, Cadwallader David, *The Life of Robert Fulton*, Kirk & Mercein, New York, New York, 1817, p. 233-235.
29. Chapelle, Howard I., *Fulton's "Steam Battery": Blockship and Catamaran*, Smithsonian Institute, Washington, DC, 1966, pp. 141-142.
30. "Sticking to Their Native Soil in Connecticut," *New York Times*, July 27, 1913.
31. Ibid.
32. Piper, Nancy, *Republican Compiler*, Gettysburg, Pennsylvania, June 23, 1829.
33. Colden, Cadwallader David, *The Life of Robert Fulton*, Kirk & Mercein, New York, New York, 1817, p. 257-258.

Chapter 10

1. Towner, Ausburn, *A Brief History of Chemung County, New York*, A.S. Barnes and Company, New York, New York, 1907, p. i.
2. *Niles Weekly Register*, volume 4, Saturday, July 3, 1813, p. 288.
3. Lee, Francis Bazley, *Genealogical and Personal Memorial of Mercer County, New Jersey*, volume 2, Lewis Publishing Company, New York, New York, 1907, p. 796
4. Ibid., p. 798.
5. Ibid.
6. Armbruster, Eugene L., *The Ferry Road on Long Island*, New York, New York, 1919, p. 9.
7. Stratton, Ezra M., *The World on Wheels; or Carriages with their Historical Associations from the Earliest to the Present Time*, Benjamin Blom, Inc., New York, New York, 1972, p. 415.
8. Ibid., p. 418.
9. Ibid., p. 419.
10. Howells, William Dean, *Impressions and Experiences*, "An East Side Ramble," Harpers & Brothers, New York, New York, 1896, p. 131.
11. *The Daily Advertiser*, vol. XVI, issue 4689, dated February 21, 1800. p. 4.
12. Minutes of the Common Council of the City of New York, 1784-1831, volume VII, New York, New York, 1917, p. 396.
13. Guernsey, Rocellus Sheridan, *New York City and Vicinity during the War of 1812-15*, vol. 1, Charles L. Woodward, New York, New York, p. 139.
14. Guernsey, Rocellus Sheridan, *New York City and Vicinity during the War of 1812-15*, vol. 1, Charles L. Woodward, New York, New York, pp. 283-87; Jenkins and Taylor, *The War of 1812*, pp. 90-91; *Connecticut Gazette*, September 15, 1813.
15. *New York Evening Post*, July 26, 1814.

16. Letter written from Doctor Ebenezer Sage to Dr .William Crawford, Gettysburg, Adams County, Pennsylvania, dated July 24, 1814; Mulford, Anna, *A Sketch of Dr. John Smith Sage*, J.H. Hunt, Printer, Sag Harbor, New York, 1897, pp. 69-70.
17. Mulford, Anna, *A Sketch of Dr. John Smith Sage*, J.H. Hunt, Printer, Sag Harbor, New York, 1897, pp. 68-69.
18. *Niles Weekly Register*, vol. 6, Saturday, July 9, 1814, p. 318.
19. Suffolk County News, Sayville, New York, April 28, 1950, p. 12.
20. Flexnor, James Thomas, *Steamboats Come True: American Inventors in Action*, Fordham University Press, Bronx, New York, 1992, p. 356
21. Mulford, Ann, "Sketch of Dr. John Smith Sage" (a pamphlet); Adams, James Truslow, *Memorials of Old Bridgehampton*, privately printed, Bridgehampton, Long Island, 1916, pp. 146-147
22. *Plattsburgh Republican*, October-December, 1816.

Chapter 11

1. "Five Hundred Pounds Reward," *London Gazette*, London, England, November 29, 1802.
2. McDowell, William, *History of the Burgh of Dumfries*, Robert Anderson, Printer, Glasgow, Scotland, 1824, p. 43.
3. Chalmers, George, *Caledonia; or A Historical and Topographical Account of North Britain from the Most Ancient to the Present Times*, vol. iii, Paisley: Alexander Gardner, London, England, 1888, p. 179.
4. Scott, Sir Walter, *Border Minstrelsy*, "Lord Maxwell's Good Night"; Rease, Howard, *The Lord Wardens of the Marches of England and Scotland*, Constable and Company, Ltd., London, England, 1913, p. 57.
5. Brown, John, *The Historical Gallery of Criminal Portraitures, Foreign and Domestic*, Printed by I. Gleave, Manchester, England, vol. II, 1823, p. 494.
6. Parsons, William Barclay, *Robert Fulton and the Submarine*, Columbia University Press, New York, New York, 1922, p. 124.
7. Ibid., p. 125.
8. Ibid., p. 125-126.
9. Brown, John, *The Historical Gallery of Criminal Portraitures, Foreign and Domestic*, Printed by I. Gleave, Manchester, England, vol. II, 1823, p. 495.
10. Ibid.
11. Ibid., p. 496.
12. Ibid.
13. Ibid., p. 497.
14. Ibid., p. 504.
15. *The Nautical Magazine: A Journal of Papers on Subjects Connected with Maritime Affairs*, vol. II, "Voyages and Maritime Papers," Simpkin, Marshall and Company, London, England, 1833p. 189.
16. Pocock, Tom, *The Terror Before Trafalgar: Nelson, Napoleon, and the Secret War*, Naval Institute Press, Annapolis, Maryland, 2002, p. 227.
17. Catlereaugh, Robert Stewart, *Memoirs and Correspondence of Viscount Castlereagh, Second Marquess of Londonerry*, John Murray, London, England, 1853, p. 434.
18. Ocampo, Emilio, *The Emporer's Last Campaign: A Napoleonic Empire in America*, University of Alabama Press, Tuscaloosa, Alabama, 2009.

19. Percy, Reuben, *The Mirror of Literature, Amusement, and Instruction*, vol. xxv, J. Limbird, London, England, 1835, p. 271.
20. Ibid.
21. Ibid., p. 272.
22. Brown, John, *The Historical Gallery of Criminal Portraitures, Foreign and Domestic*, Printed by I. Gleave, Manchester, England, vol. II, 1823, p. 494.

Chapter 12

1. Barber, F.M., "Lecture on Submarine Boats and their Application To Torpedo Operations," *U. S. Naval Torpedo Station*, Newport, Rhode Island, 1875, pp. 21-22.
2. Poster advertising the 'Fool Killer" in Chicago, 1915; Old Lighthouse Museum, Michigan City, Indiana.
3. *Chicago Daily Tribune*, July 25, 1958.
4. *Chicago Tribune*, November 24, 1915.
5. *Chicago Tribune*, "Skulls Found on Foolkiller, Old Submarine," January 16, 1916.
6. *The Herald Mail*, "A Look Back At the Erie Canal," Fairport, New York, April 25, 1957, column 2, p. 9.
7. Loud, Oliver, *The Western Almanack*, "Perinton Mead," Egypt, New York, 1820.
8. *The Herald Mail*, "A Look Back At the Erie Canal," Fairport, New York, April 25, 1957, column 2, p. 9.
9. Mueller, Rose Anna, *Michigan City*, Arcadia Publishing, Chicago, IL, 2005, p. 55.
10. Harris, Patricia A. G., "The Great Lakes First Submarine, L. D. Phillips' Fool Killer," Inland Lakes, Chicago, Illinois, 1986, p. 164.
11. LaPorte Court of Common Pleas, Michigan City, Indiana, February 10, 1859.
12. *The Republican Advocate*, Batavia, New York, July 1, 1851.
13. Harris, Patricia A. G., "The Great Lakes First Submarine, L. D. Phillips' Fool Killer," Inland Lakes, Chicago, Illinois, 1986, p. 36.
14. Ibid., p. 36.
15. Ibid., p. 14.
16. Barber, F. M., "Lecture on Submarine Boats and their Application To Torpedo Operations," *U. S. Naval Torpedo Station*, Newport, Rhode Island, 1875.
17. Phillips, Lodner D., in a letter written to William H. Graham, dated April 7, 1852; Michigan City Historical Society, Michigan, City, Indiana.
18. Graham, William H., in a letter written to Lodner D. Phillips, dated April 21, 1852; Michigan City Historical Society, Michigan City, Indiana.
19. *Detroit Advertiser*, Detroit, Michigan, September, 1853.
20. LaPorte County Court of Common Pleas, Michigan City, Indiana, record dated March, 1854.
21. Ibid., record dated February 8, 1856.
22. Patent 15,898, application dated October 14, 1856, U.S. Patent Office, Washington, DC.
23. Pesce, L., *La Navigation Sous-Marine*, Vuibert & Noney, Paris, France, 1906.
24. Harris, Patricia A. G., "Great Lakes First Submarine, L. D. Phillips' Fool Killer," Inland Lakes, Chicago, Illinois, 1982, p. 30.
25. Admiral Davis Report, June 28, 1864, in Letter book of the Permanent Commission, Record Group 45, Entry 366, National Archives.
26. Pesce, L., *La Navigation Sous-Marine*, Vuibert & Noney, Paris, France, 1906.

Chapter 13

1. Holland, John P., "Submarine Navigation," *Cassier's Magazine, Engineering Illustrated*, vol. VII, May-October, Louis Cassier and Company, London, England, 1897, p. 552.
2. Undated news clipping, "Miscellaneous Letters Received by the Secretary of the Navy," September 1861, Record Group 45, National Archives, Washington, DC.
3. Birard, Guy, "Jules Verne in Nantes," 1842 (French version).
4. *L'Echo de la Fabrique: Naissance De La Presse Ouvriere Lyon*, December 16, 1832.
5. Holland, John P., "Submarine Navigation," *Cassier's Magazine, Engineering Illustrated*, vol. VII, May-October, Louis Cassier and Company, London, England, 1897, p. 543.
6. Homans, Benjamin, *United Service Gazette Army and Navy Chronicle (1835-1842)*, volume 1, Washington, DC, October 15, 1835, p. 336.
7. Lipkens, Anton and Olke Uhlenbeck, "The Duikboot," documents found at the Dutch National Library, The Haag, Netherlands.
8. *Philadelphia Evening Bulletin*, May 17, 1861.
9. *Hornellsville Tribune*, "Submarine Experiment," Hornellsville, New York, September 29, 1859, p. 1.
10. Hoff, Commander Henry K., United States Navy, July 7, 1861, Bureau of Yards and Docks, National Archives and Records Service, Washington DC, RG71, Miscellaneous Letters Sent and Received, 1861-1863, Report on de Villerio Sub, July 7, 1861.
11. *Philadelphia Evening Bulletin*, Philadelphia, Pennsylvania, May 17, 1861.
12. *Philadelphia Saturday Evening Post*, Philadelphia, Pennsylvania, May 25, 1861.
13. *Philadelphia Evening Bulletin*, Philadelphia, Pennsylvania, May 17, 1861.
14. Report from Commander Henry K. Hoff, USN, to Captain S. F. Dupont, Commanding Officer of Naval Station Philadelphia, July 7, 1861.
15. Contract between Martin Thomas and Gideon Welles, Secretary of the U.S. Navy, Bureau of Yards and Docks, National Archives and Records Service, Washington, DC, Item 42, Record Group 71, dated November 1, 1862.
16. Welles, Gideon, Secretary of the Navy, letter dispatched to Flag-Officer Louis Malesherbes Goldsborough, June 19, 1862, National Archives and Records Service, Washington, DC.
17. Goldsborough, Flag-Officer Louis Malesherbes, letter dispatched to John Rodgers, June 23, 1862, National Archives and Records Service, Washington, DC.
18. Goldsborough, Flag-Officer Louis Malesherbes, letter dispatched to Gideon Welles, June 24, 1862, National Archives and Records Service, Washington, DC.
19. List of Papers, National Archives, Washington, DC, dated March, 1863, p. 32.
20. Winchester, Acting Master W. F., in a letter written to Secretary of the Navy Gideon Welles, April 9, 1863, National Archives and Records Service, Washington, D.C.
21. Ibid.
22. List of Papers, National Archives, Washington, DC, dated April, 1863, p. 735.
23. *Philadelphia Enquirer*, Philadelphia, Pennsylvania July 3, 1874.

Chapter 14

1. Brayley, Edward Wedlake, *A Topographical History of Surrey, Ville de Lyon*, London, England, vol. V, 1850, p. 149.

2. Woods, Anthony, *A Briefe View of the State of the Church of England as it Stood in Q. Elizabeths and King James his Reigne, to the Yeere 1608*, edited by John Harington under the title Nugae Antiquae (London, 1779, reproduced by Hildesheim, 1968), Wood's notes, pp. 749-750.
3. Eads, Donald LeRoy, *Genealogy of Edes; Eedes; Eades; Eads Family, 1500-2008*, Fawnskin, California, 2012, p. 9.
4. Dorsey, Florence L., *Road to the Sea: The Story of James B. Eads and the Mississippi River*, Pelican Publishing Company, Gretna, Louisiana, 1947, p. 8.
5. Ibid., p. 2
6. Ibid.
7. Ibid., p. 3.
8. Meltzer, Milton, *Mark Twain Himself: A Pictorial Biography*, University of Missouri Press, Columbia, Missouri, 1960, p. 149.
9. Dorsey, Florence L., *Road to the Sea: The Story of James B. Eads and the Mississippi River*, Pelican Publishing Company, Gretna, Louisiana, 1947, p. 3.
10. How, Louis, *James B. Eads*, Houghton, Mifflin and Company, New York, New York, 1900, p. 3.
11. Snyder, Charles E., "The Eads of Argyle," *Iowa Journal of History and Politics*, vol. 42, State Historical Society of Iowa, Iowa City, Iowa, 1944, p. 78.
12. Dorsey, Florence L., *Road to the Sea: The Story of James B. Eads and the Mississippi River*, Pelican Publishing Company, Gretna, Louisiana, 1947, p. 15.
13. Ibid.
14. Youmans, Edward L., "Sketch of James B. Eads," *Popular Science Monthly*, D. Appleton and Company, New York, New York, 1886, p. 546.
15. Ibid.
16. Dorsey, Florence L., *Road to the Sea: The Story of James B. Eads and the Mississippi River*, Pelican Publishing Company, Gretna, Louisiana, 1947, p. 19.
17. How, Louis, *James B. Eads*, Houghton, Mifflin and Company, New York, New York, 1900, p. 12.
18. Dorsey, Florence L., *Road to the Sea: The Story of James B. Eads and the Mississippi River*, Pelican Publishing Company, Gretna, Louisiana, 1947, p. 20.
19. Ibid.
20. James Buchanan Eads Collection, Letter from Martha Dillon to James B. Eads, dated July 5, 1845, National Churchill Museum, Westminster College, Fulton, Missouri.
21. James Buchanan Eads Collection, Letter from James B. Eads to Martha Dillon, dated June 24, 1845, National Churchill Museum, Westminster College, Fulton, Missouri.
22. James Buchanan Eads Collection, Letter from James B. Eads to Martha Dillon, dated August 12, 1845, National Churchill Museum, Westminster College, Fulton, Missouri.
23. James Buchanan Eads Collection, Letter from Ann Buchanan Eads to Martha Dillon, dated August 20, 1845, National Churchill Museum, Westminster College, Fulton, Missouri.
24. James Buchanan Eads Collection, Letter from James B. Eads to Martha Dillon, dated August 22, 1845, National Churchill Museum, Westminster College, Fulton, Missouri.

25. James Buchanan Eads Collection, Letter from Martha Dillon to James B. Eads, dated April 5, 1847, National Churchill Museum, Westminster College, Fulton, Missouri.
26. How, Louis, *James B. Eads*, Houghton, Mifflin and Company, New York, New York, 1900, p. 13.
27. Eads, James Buchanan, *Mouth of the Mississippi: Jetty System Explained*, Times Print, St. Louis, Missouri, 1874, p. 22.
28. James Buchanan Eads Collection, Letter from Martha Dillon to James B. Eads, dated September 13, 1848, National Churchill Museum, Westminster College, Fulton, Missouri.
29. Ibid.
30. James Buchanan Eads Collection, Letter from James B. Eads to Martha Dillon, dated September 27, 1852, National Churchill Museum, Westminster College, Fulton, Missouri.
31. Eads, James Buchanan, *Mouth of the Mississippi: Jetty System Explained*, Times Print, St. Louis, Missouri, 1874, p. 21.
32. Boynton, Charles Brandon, *The History of the Navy During the Rebellion*, vol. 2, Letter sent from Attorney General Edward Bates to James Buchanan Eads, dated April 17, 1861, Applewood Books, Bedford, Massachusetts, 1868, p. 498.
33. Dorsey, Florence L., *Road to the Sea: The Story of James B. Eads and the Mississippi River*, Pelican Publishing Company, Gretna, Louisiana, 1947, p. 61.
34. *St. Louis Republican*, St. Louis, Missouri, speech given by James B. Eads, July 4, 1874.

Chapter 15

1. *New York Times*, New York, New York, October 14, 1852.
2. McCullers, Carson. "The Mortgaged Heart," Snyder-Grenier, (1955) *Ellen M. Brooklyn!: an Illustrated History*, Temple University Press, Philadelphia, Pennsylvania, 1996, p. 159.
3. *Scientific America*, "The Submarine Explorer," Number 12, Volume VIII, New York, New York, December 4, 1852, p. 89.
4. Percy, Sholto, *Iron: An Illustrated Weekly Journal for Iron and Steel, The Mechanics' Magazine*, vol. XXXVII, J.C. Robertson Publishers, London, England, 1842, p. 260.
5. Ibid., p. 261.
6. Field, Colonel Cyril, *The Story of the Submarine: From the Earliest Ages to the Present Day*, J.B. Lippincott Company, Philadelphia, Pennsylvania, 1908, p. 224.
7. Ibid., p. 225.
8. Field, Colonel Cyril, *The Story of the Submarine: From the Earliest Ages to the Present Day*, J.B. Lippincott Company, Philadelphia, Pennsylvania, 1908, p. 80.
9. Patent application, submitted by Lambert Alexandre, United States Patent Office, Washington, DC, September 3, 1850.
10. Ibid.
11. Ibid.
12. Ibid.
13. Smith, Andrew H., *Medical Record*, "An Artificial Leech," volume 4, November 1, 1869, p. 406.
14. *New York Herald*, "Sub-Marine Boat," New York, New York, November 20, 1850.

15. *Scientific America*, "The Submarine Explorer," Number 12, volume VIII, New York, New York, December 4, 1852, p. 89.
16. *New York Times*, "Fixing the Responsibility," November 4, 1900.
17. Ibid.
18. *New York Sun*, "The Sub-marine Propeller," October 22, 1851.
19. Chapelle, Howard I, *The History of the American Sailing Navy: The Ships and Their Development*, W.W. Norton & Company, Inc., New York, New York, 1949, pp. 307-308.
20. *New York Herald*, New York, New York, January 3, 1852
21. *New York Times*, New York, New York, March 8, 1852
22. Ibid.
23. Bennett, James Gordon, *New York Daily Herald*, vol. XVII, no. 66, New York, New York, March 7, 1852.
24. *New York Herald*, "The Fair at the American Institute," New York, New York, October 14, 1852.
25. Ibid.
26. Patent submitted by Lambert Alexandre, United States Patent Office, witnessed by Lemuel W. Serrell and Thomas G. Harold, Washington, DC, January 28, 1856.
27. *The Civil Engineer and Architect's Journal*, volume XX, R. Groombridge and Sons, London, England, 1857, p. 197.

Chapter 16

1. Sherman, Richard U., Editor, "New Diving Bell," *Oneida Morning Herald*, August 2, 1848.
2. Agnew, John Holmes, "Gossip with Readers and Correspondents," *The Knickerbocker*, vol. 49, February 1837, p. 209.
3. Hannah, Mary, *A Royalist's Notebook: The Commonplace Book of Sir John Oglander, Kt of Nunwell 1622 - 1652*, transcribed and edited by Francis Bamford, Constable and Company, London, England, 1936, pp. 77-78.
4. *First Exhibition and Fair of the Massachusetts Charitable Mechanic Association*, Button and Wentworth, Boston, Massachusetts, September 18, 1837, pp. 27-28.
5. Alcott, William Andrus, *The Moral Reformer and Teacher on the Human Constitution*, vol. 1, Light & Horton, Boston, Massachusetts, Sept., 1835, p. 291.
6. *Fourth Annual Report of the Board of Regents of the Smithsonian Institution*, Printers to the Senate, July 30, 1850, p. 120.
7. *Third Exhibition and Fair of the Massachusetts Charitable Mechanic Association*, Isaac R. Butts, Boston, Massachusetts, September 20, 1841, p. 47.
8. Green, Samuel Abbott, *Constitution of the New England Guards*, Fifth Edition, printed by the Daily Times Office, Boston, Massachusetts, January, 1839, p. 3.
9. Sherman, Richard U., Editor, *Oneida Morning Herald*, August 2, 1848.
10. Ibid.
11. Ibid.
12. Wolcott, John B., *The Wolcott Family Society*, "Chapter II: The Descendents of John Wolcott of Watertown, Massachsetts, 1599-1638" updated August of 2012.
13. *New York Times*, "Failure in the Iron Trade," February 13, 1883.
14. An Act to incorporate the Suffolk Iron Works, Massachusetts Senate and House of Representatives, Chapter 0098, State Library of Massachusetts, March 17, 1854.

15. *Daily Evening Journal*, "Massachusetts Revolutionized: H.J. Gardner Elected Governor by the People," published by David Higgins, G.M. Nichols & George S. Plaisted, Worcester, Massachusetts, November 14, 1854.
16. Smith, Henry H., *Digest of Decisions and Precedents of the Senate and House of Representatives of the United States*, Government Printing Office, Washington, D.C., 1894, p. 264.
17. *Daily Alta California*, San Francisco, California, July 1, 1858, p. 1.
18. Ibid.
19. *Boston Daily Globe*, Boston, Massachusetts, December 18, 1877.
20. Bacon, Edwin M., *King's Dictionary of Boston*, Moses King Publisher, Cambridge, Massachusetts, 1883, p. 237.
21. An Act to incorporate the Boston Freight Railway Company, Massachusetts Senate and House of Representatives, Chapter 0175, State Library of Massachusetts, May 1, 1868.
22. *Madison County Times*, Chittenango, New York, April 10, 1873.

Chapter 17
1. Hawthorne, Nathaniel, "Up the Thames," *The Complete Works of Nathaniel Hawthorne*, vol. 7, Houghton Mifflin Company, Boston, Massachusetts, 1863, pp. 291-296.
2. *The Pimlico Design Guide: A Guide to Alteration of Buildings in the Pimlico Conservation Area*, 2004.
3. Bennett, F., *The Story of W.J.E. Bennett*, chapter IV, Longmans, London, England, 1909.
4. *Cholera in Nineteenth Century New York*, "New York in 1832," online source, found at: http://www.virtualny.cuny.edu/cholera/1832/cholera_1832_set.html.
5. *New York Evening Post*, New York, New York, April 24, 1830.
6. *New York Morning Courier*, New York, New York, April 13, 1842.
7. *New York Daily Tribune*, New York, New York, January 19, 1854.
8. Lamb, Martha J., *The Magazine of American History, with Notes and Queries*, vol. XXIII, Historical Publications Company, New York, New York, 1890, p. 208.
9. Foreman, Edgar W., "Rainbow Coffee House 27 Beekman St. between Nassau and William Street, William, Proprietor," New York, New York, c. 1846.
10. Edgar W. Foreman, *The Illuminated Pictorial Directory of New York*, Jones & Newman, Lithographers, New York, New York, 1848.
11. *New York Daily Tribune*, New York, New York, May 31, 1848.
12. *New York Daily Tribune*, "Drowned," New York, New York, July 10, 1852.
13. Tombstone of Edgar W. Foreman, Trinity Church Yard, New Rochelle, New York.
14. Eldsmoe, Amund O., *Hjalmar Rued Holand*, "The Norwegian Settler's Story," Moscow, Wisconsin, July, 1901.
15. Ibid.
16. *Syracuse New York Daily Journal*, "The Wreck of the Atlantic, Syracuse, New York, September 3, 1852.
17. Twain, Mark, *Life on the Mississippi*, Chatto & Windus, Piccadilly, London, England, 1883, p. 179.
18. *Buffalo Daily Republic*, "The Wreck of the Altantic," Buffalo, New York, August 30, 1852.

AMERICAN SUBMARINERS: PRE-CIVIL WAR

19. Foreman, E.W., Diving Bell, Patent No. 9,965, United States Patent Office, Washington, D.C., August 23, 1853.
20. Ibid.
21. Ibid.
22. Ibid.
23. *New York Daily Tribune*, New York, New York, September 13, 1853.
24. Letter sent from Phillip Willner to William L. Marcy, Secretary of State, dated June 15, 1855, National Archives and Records Administration, Washington, D.C., Collection Number 566612.
25. *New York Times*, "Days of the Old Packet Line," New York, New York, December 13, 1891.
26. *New York Daily Tribune*, New York, New York, May 10, 1856.
27. McCurdy, James, *By Juan de Fuca's Strait: Pioneering Along The Northwestern Edge Of The Continent*, Binford & Mort, Portland, Oregon, 1937.
28. Snyder-Grenier, Ellen M., *Brooklyn!: An Illustrated History*, Temple University Press, Philadelphia, Pennsylvania, 1996, p. 144.
29. *New York Times*, New York, New York, December 27, 1854.
30. *New York Times*, New York, New York, December 30, 1854.
31. Ibid.
32. *New York Daily Tribune*, New York, New York, February 6, 1856.
33. *The Artizan: A Monthly Journal of the Operative Arts*, vol. XIII, London, England, 1855, p. 129.
34. *New York Herald*, New York, New York, November 15, 1856.
35. Ibid.
36. Ibid.
37. *New York Evening Express*, New York, New York, January 22, 1857.
38. *New York Daily Tribune*, New York, New York, June 26, 1857.
39. *London Daily News*, London, England, September 17, 1857.
40. *New York Herald*, New York, New York, September 17, 1858, p. 8.
41. *New York Herald*, New York, New York, February 19, 1861.

Chapter 18

1. Lloyd, James T., *Lloyd's Steamboat Directory, and Disasters on the Western Waters*, James T. Lloyd & Company, Cincinnati, Ohio, 1856, p. 149.
2. Ibid., p. 148.
3. Boyer, Dwight, *Great Stories of the Great Lakes*, Dodd, Mead and Company, New York, New York, 1966, p. 44.
4. Green, John B., *Diving With or Without Armor: Containing the Submarine Exploits of J.B. Green*, Faxon's Steam Power Press, Buffalo, New York, 1859, p. 10.
5. Ibid.
6. Ibid., pp. 11-12.
7. Ibid., p. 16.
8. Ibid.
9. Ibid., p. 17.
10. Ibid., p. 18.
11. Ibid.
12. Ibid.
13. Ibid., pp. 20-21.

14. Ibid., p. 55.
15. Ibid., p. 19.
16. *Punch or the London Charivari*, vol. 53–56, "Fancies for the Fleet," London, England, November, 1867, p. 216.
17. *The New York Times*, New York, New York, September 23, 1852, p. 3.
18. *Buffalo Morning Express*, "Wreck of the Steamer Erie," Buffalo, New York, May 21, 1903, p. 10.
19. *Buffalo Daily Republic*, "Wreck of the Steamer Erie," Buffalo, New York, September 14, 1853.
20. Green, John B., *Diving With or Without Armor: Containing the Submarine Exploits of J.B. Green*, Faxon's Steam Power Press, Buffalo, New York, 1859, p. 40.
21. Ibid., pp. 42–43.
22. Ibid., p. 44.
23. *Daily Milwaukee News*, Milwaukee, Wisconsin, November 6, 1868, p. 4.

Chapter 19

1. Irving, Washington, "The Money Diggers: Hell Gate," *The Works of Washington Irving*, vol. 2, Peter Fenelon Collier, 1897, p. 410.
2. Rust, Claude, "Hellgate's Infamous Past," *Military Engineer*, November-December, 1971, pp. 410-411.
3. Irving, Washington, "The Money Diggers: Hell Gate," *The Works of Washington Irving*, vol. 2, Peter Fenelon Collier, 1897, p. 410.
4. *Documents of the Senate of the State of New York*, vol. 1, C. Van Benthuysen, Albany, New York, 1857, p. 150.
5. Hunt, Freeman, "Submarine Blasting," *Merchants' Magazine and Commercial Review*, vol. 30, New York, New York, 1854, p. 191.
6. Green, John B., *Diving With and Without Armor: Containing the Submarine Exploits of J.B. Green, the Celebrated Submarine Diver*, Faxon's Steam Power Press, Buffalo, New York, 1859, pp. 57-58.
7. Meriam, E., *New York Municipal Gazette*, vol. 1, Anti-Assessment Committee of New York, New York, New York, 1848, p. 1108.
8. Delgado, James P., *Misadventures of a Civil War Submarine: Iron, Guns, and Pearls*, Texas A&M University Press, College Station, Texas, 2012, p. 32.
9. Ibid., p. 33.
10. *Albany Argus*, "Deadly Accident," Albany, New York, March 29, 1852.
11. *The New York Times*, "The Hurlgate Catastrophe: The Inquest and the Verdict," March 31, 1852.
12. Ibid.
13. *Executive Documents Printed By Order of the Senate of the United States*, Second Session, Thirty-Fifth Congress, William A. Harris, Printer, Washington, DC, 1859, p. 57.
14. *New Orleans Daily Crescent*, October 19, 1859, p. 5.
15. Hayden, Jabez Haskell, *Records of the Connecticut Line of the Hayden Family*, Case, Lockwood, & Brainard Company, Windsor Locks, Connecticut, 1888, p. 214.
16. *U.S. Nautical Magazine and Naval Journal*, Oliver W. Griffiths, New York, New York, 1857, p. 47.
17. Ibid.
18. Ibid., p. 48.

AMERICAN SUBMARINERS: PRE-CIVIL WAR

19. *Hayden, Jabez Haskell, Records of the Connecticut Line of the Hayden Family*, Case, Lockwood, & Brainard Company, Windsor Locks, Connecticut, 1888, p. 216.
20. *Improved Diving-Room Fixed at the End of a Vessel*, Patent No. 41,078, Benjamin Maillefert and Levi Hayden, January 5, 1864.
21. *Official Records of the Union and Confederate Navies in the War of the Rebellion*, United States Navy Department, Washington, DC, 1902, p. 139; Letter sent from Benjamin Maillefert to Rear-Admiral John A. Dahlgren, Commander of the South Atlantic Squadron, dated November 27, 1863.
22. *Official Records of the Union and Confederate Navies in the War of the Rebellion*, United States Navy Department, Washington, DC, 1902, p. 326; Letter sent from Rear-Admiral John A. Dahlgren, Commander of the South Atlantic Squadron, to Benjamin Maillefert, dated February 16, 1864.
23. *Hoosier State Chronicles*, vol. 15, February 16, 1871.
24. *Annual Report of the Chief of Engineers to the Secretary of War*, vol. 2, Government Printing Office, Washington, DC, 1874, p. 4.
25. *Report of the Secretary of War*, vol. 2, Government Printing Office, Washington, DC, 1876, p. 431.
26. *New York Times*, August 12, 1884.

Chapter 20

1. *New York Times*, New York, New York, July 23, 1856.
2. *Westfield Republic*, Westfield, New York; Hall, F.A., "Elliot P. Harrington: A Sketch of One of Westfield's Pioneers," read at the Chautauqua Society of History and Natural Science annual meeting, Fredonia, New York, September 15, 1915, p. 7.
3. Littell, E., *The Living Age*, vol. 43, Littell, Son and Company, Boston, Massachusetts, 1855, p. 280.
4. *Dunkirk Evening Observer*, Dunkirk, New York, February 12, 1944, p. 4.
5. *Friends' Intelligencer*, vol. 13, William W. Moore, Philadelphia, PA, 1857, p. 350.
6. Ibid.
7. *Dunkirk Evening Observer*, Dunkirk, New York, February 12, 1944, p. 7.
8. Ibid., p. 5.
9. *The Grand River Times*, Grand Haven, Michigan, October 8, 1856, p. 1.
10. Gaylord, W.P., *History of Floyd County, Iowa*, Inter-State Publishing Company, Chicago, Illinois, 1882, p. 650.
11. *Dubuque Weekly Times*, Dubuque, Iowa, February 10, 1859.
12. Gaylord, W.P., *History of Floyd County, Iowa*, Inter-State Publishing Company, Chicago, Illinois, 1882, p. 418.
13. Ibid.
14. *Westfield Republic*, Hall, F.A., "Elliot P. Harrington: A Sketch of One of Westfield's Pioneers," read at the Chautauqua Society of History and Natural Science annual meeting, Fredonia, New York, September 15, 1915, p. 7.
15. *Official Records of the Union and Confederate Navies in the War of the Rebellion*, United States Navy Department, Washington, DC, 1902, p. 83; letter sent from Henry K. Davenport to Acting Rear-Admiral Samuel Phillips Lee, dated September 22, 1862.

16. *Official Records of the Union and Confederate Navies in the War of the Rebellion*, United States Navy Department, Washington, DC, 1902, p. 117; letter sent from Henry K. Davenport to Rear-Admiral William Branford Shubrick, dated October 4, 1862.
17. *Official Records of the Union and Confederate Navies in the War of the Rebellion*, United States Navy Department, Washington, DC, 1902, pp. 82-83; letter sent from Henry K. Davenport to Acting Rear-Admiral Samuel Phillips Lee, dated September 22, 1862.
18. *Official Records of the Union and Confederate Navies in the War of the Rebellion*, United States Navy Department, Washington, DC, 1902, p. 187; letter sent from Elliot P. Harrington to Acting Rear-Admiral Samuel Francis DuPont, dated May 11, 1863.
19. *Harpers Weekly: A Journal of Civilization*, New York, New York, vol. 13, May 8, 1869, p. 295.
20. Harrington, Elliot P., patent application 144,537, United States Patent Office, Washington, DC, submitted on November 11, 1873.
21. *Detroit Free Press*, "A Detroit Diver's Invention," August 21, 1879.
22. Ibid.
23. *Westfield Republic*, Westfield, New York, November 12, 1879.
24. *Jamestown Evening Journal*, Jamestown, New York, June 21, 1884, p. 1.

Chapter 21

1. Baum, Lyman Frank, *The Annotated Wizard of Oz*, W.W. Norton and Company, New York, New York, 1973, pp. xxvii.
2. Blavatsky, Helena Petrovna, *The Voice of the Silence*, William Quan Judge, New York, New York, 1889.
3. *Read the Spirit*, "Intereview on Madame Blavatsky, Interfaith Pioneer & Theosophy Founder," July 30, 2009.
4. Morris, John E., *The Felt Genealogy: A Record of the Descendents of George Felt of Casco Bay*, Case, Lockwood & Brainard Company, Hartford, Connecticut, 1893, p. 9.
5. Hurd, Duane Hamilton, *History of Middlesex County, Massachusetts: with Biographical Sketches of many of its Pioneers and Prominent Men*, vol. III, J.W. Lewis and Company, Philadelphia, Pennsylvania, 1890. P. 205.
6. Morris, John E., *The Felt Genealogy: A Record of the Descendents of George Felt of Casco Bay*, Case, Lockwood & Brainard Company, Hartford, Connecticut, 1893, p. 27.
7. Haynes, William, *Casco Bay Yarns*, D.O. Haynes & Company, New York, New York, 1916, p. 166.
8. Morris, John E., *The Felt Genealogy: A Record of the Descendents of George Felt of Casco Bay*, Case, Lockwood & Brainard Company, Hartford, Connecticut, 1893, p. 18.
9. Ibid., p. 34.
10. Colton, G.W., *David Rumsey Historical Map Collection*, New York, New York, 1857.
11. *Documents of the Assembly of the State of New York*, Ninety-First Session, vol. xi, no. 148, C. Van Benthuysen & Sons, Albany, New York, 1868, pp. 54-56.
12. Ibid., p. 57.

13. Felt, George H., "Improvements in Signal-Rockets," patent US39636A, U.S. Patent Office, Washington, D.C., August 25, 1863.
14. Felt, George H., letter written to Brigadier General L. Thomas, August 14, 1863 (two letters encluding charges), 28, September 21, 1863, LR, 152-F (1863), RG 94, Washington, D.C.
15. Niles, Peter H., letter written to Captain W.J.L. Nocodemus, Georgetown, Washington, D.C., March 23, 1863; Proceedings of a Court of Inquiry, convened by Special Order No. 65, Willard Felt and Company, New York, New York, 1863.
16. George Henry Felt's military records, National Archives, Washington, D.C.
17. Felt, George H., "Reefing and Furling Sails," patent 44620, Annual Report of the Commissioner of Patents, U.S. Patent Office, Washington, D.C., October 11, 1864.
18. Felt, George H., "Improvements in Breech-Loading Ordinance," patent 159170A, U.S. Patent Office, Washington, D.C., January 26, 1875.
19. Sinnett, Alfred Percy, *Incidents in the Life of Madame Blavatsky*, George Redway, London, England, 1886, p. 28.
20. Newton, Henry J., comments written following George Henry Felt's lecture, New York, New York, September 7, 1875,
21. *The Daily Graphic*, "The Theosophists Speak Out: What They Will Do, and How They Will Do It," New York, New York, December 27, 1875, p. 443.
22. Wiggin, James Henry, *The Liberal Christian: an Independent Journal of Religion, Literature, Science and Art*, "The Cabala," September 25, 1875, p. 1.
23. *The Daily Graphic*, "The Theosophists Speak Out: What They Will Do, and How They Will Do It," New York, New York, December 27, 1875, p. 443.
24. Ibid.
25. Felt, George Henry, letter dated June 19, 1878, addressed to the Spiritualist; appeared in Henry Steel Olcott's *The Old Diary Leaves, 1878-83*, Kessinger Publishing, Whitefish, Montana, 2003.
26. Felt, George H., "Felt Pump," patent US224668A, U.S. Patent Office, Washington, D.C., February 12, 1880.
27. Obituary, George Henry Felt, *New York Times*, New York, New York, December 6, 1906, p. 9.
28. *New York Dispatch*, New York, New York, May 26, 1872.

Index

-A-

Abbott, Edward 420
Abenaki Indians 100
Abercromby, James 139
Abigail 39
Adams, Alexander 79
Adams, John 125, 143-4, 158, 379, 570-1
Adams, Samuel 142, 144
Admiral Decrea 175, 181
Aerostatic Tubular Diving Bell 489, 500
Africk, George 209
Ager, Wilson 462
Albany Gazette 229
Alcester, John 73, 74
Alden, William Livingston 557
Aldis, Mary 403
Aldworth, Robert 96
Alexander, Edward Porter 549
Alexander III 270
Alexander the Great 5, 290
Alexandre, Henrietta 384
Alexandre, Hubertine Josephe 384
Alexandre, Jacques 384
Alexandre, Lambert 378, 379, 381-97, 580-1
Alexandre, Lambert Joseph 383
Alexandre, Marguerite 383-4
Alexandre, Marie Elisabeth 383
Alexandre, Marie Rosalie 384
Alexandria 5, 501
Allen, John 82
Alligator 209, 315, 339-43, 346-50
Allyn, Joseph 143
Allyn, Mary 143
Ambrose 56-8, 75, 502
America 474
American Civil War 308, 311, 318, 337, 343, 348, 374, 376, 462, 492, 499, 502, 507, 524-5, 543, 546-7, 549, 552-3, 555-6, 584
American Comic Almanac, with Whims, Scraps, and Oddities, The 542
American Express Company 471, 479, 481, 496, 498, 521-3, 526, 532
American Revolution 120, 128, 188, 203-6, 249, 356, 379, 524, 570-1
American Telegraph and Signal Book, The 265
American Turtle 113, 121-8, 130-32, 188, 203-4
Ames, Fisher 298
Ames, George 298
Anaconda Plan 375
Ancient, William Johnson 423, 424
Anderson, Robert 547
Anderson, William C. 434

Andros, Edmund 106
A New Discourse upon a Stale Subject: The Metamorphosis of Ajax 512
Angar, Stephen 440
Anna, Santa 451
Annual Register 24, 565
Antinomian Controversy 62
A Prospect of and the Most Famous Parts of the World 40
Apthorp, William F. 420
aquatic velocipede 530
Arbella 56-60
Argo 466-7
Ariel 242
Ariost, Ludovico 512
Aristotle 4, 5, 565
Arnold, Benedict 70, 136, 156, 205
Arnold, William 75-6
Artemisium 4
Arthur, Chester A. 94, 255, 265, 273, 420, 499
artificial leeches 386-8, 391
Astor, John Jacob 241
Atlantic 441-4, 465, 467-71, 474, 479-85, 496, 498, 516, 519, 522-3, 526, 532
Atlantic Monthly 420
A Treatise on the Improvement of Canal Navigation 172, 571, 572
Avery, James 137
Avery, John 142, 143
Avery, Margaret 138
Avery, Sarah 142, 404

- B -

Babcock, William Henry 420
Bache, Alexander Dallas 310, 492
Bacon, Francis 11-12, 565, 582
Badlesmere, Joan de 32
Bailey, George A. 528
Baker, William M. 420
Baldwin, Abraham 129-30
Balloon 192
Baltic 457
Bancroft, George 554
Bancroft, Mary Davis 415
Bancroft, Minnie Marie 415
Bancroft, Thomas 415
Barber, F.M. 303, 577
Barber, Joseph 197
Barere, Bertrand 273
Barlow, Joel 179, 215, 228, 230, 246, 574
Barlow, Ruth 236, 246
Barnes, John W. 522
Barnum, Phineas Taylor 394

Index

barometer 120, 183
Barrett, Richard 190
Barrows, Samuel June 420
Bartlett, Washington A. 492
Bass, Henry 142-3
Basta, Dan 348
Bateman, Charlotte 297
Bateman, Edward 96, 100
Bateman, Eleazer 296-7, 359
Bateman, Sarah Putnam 296
Bateman, Virena 297-8
Bates, Edward 375, 580
Battle of Bunker Hill 203, 295
Battle of Copenhagen 283
Battle of Dorchester Heights 403
Battle of Hastings 93
Battle of Lake Erie 242
Battle of Portland 86
Battle of the Kegs 188-9, 330
Battle of Trafalgar 276
Battles, Ebenezer 403
Battles, Joseph 528
Bauer, Wilhelm 543
Baum, L. Frank 535-8, 586
Baum, Maud 535
Baxter, Sylvester 420
Beauchamp, Henry 353
Beekman, Margaret 227
Belledonne 381
Belton, Ebenezer 139, 142
Belton, Hannah 139, 142
Belton, Israel 159
Belton, John 159
Belton, Jonas 138-40, 150, 158, 571
Belton, Joseph 134-7, 139-47, 149-50, 152-7, 159, 571
Belton, Mary 139, 142
Belton, Mary Morgan 139
Belton, Sarah 137, 139-40, 142
Belton Submarine 135, 145
Belton Tavern 140
Bendall, Anne 56, 59, 62
Bendall, Ephraim 71
Bendall, Freegrace 62-3, 70-1
Bendall, Grace 56
Bendall, Hopefor 70-1
Bendall I, Edward 54
Bendall II, Edward 55
Bendall III, Edward 50-2, 54-7, 60-1, 63, 65, 67-71, 80-1, 85, 567-8
Bendall, Jane 71
Bendall, Mary 64, 70
Bendall, More Mercy 70
Bendall, Reforme 70

Bendall, Restore 71
Bendall, Sarah 55
Bendall's Dock 63, 81
Bendall, William 56
bends 484-5
Benethall, Edmund 54
Benethall, Hugh 53
Benethall, Robert 53, 54
Benjamin, Asher 193
Benthall, Lawrence 54
Benthall Manor 54
Benthall, William 54
Beresford, John Poo 238-9, 575
Bermuda Company 43-4, 46, 48
Bermuda Triangle 103
Bermuda Tub 29, 41, 44, 45, 47
Bermúdez, Juan 29
Bernard, Bona Fitz 32
Berrien, Agnes 251
Berrien, Amy Scudder 251
Berrien, Catherine 251
Berrien, Cornelius II 252, 253
Berrien, Cornelius III 233, 248-62, 265-6
Berrien, Cornelius Jansen 250, 251
Berrien, Elizabeth Morris 266
Berrien, Elizabeth Vanderbeek 266
Berrien, Jane 266
Berrien, John 251, 253
Berrien, Nicholas 251
Berrien, Peter 253
Berrien, Pieter 251
Berrien, Richard 233, 248-9, 253-7, 260-1, 265-6
Berzins, Woody 348
Bickham, James 164
Biddle, James 199, 241
Bird, Mark 356
Bish, Henry 104
Bishop, William Henry 420
Blackborne, Robert 82, 86, 568
Black Hawk Purchase Treaty 359
Black Hawk War 524
Blackstone, William 59
Blake, Christopher 22, 24
Blake, Robert 85
Blathwayt, William 109
Blavatsky, Helena Petrovna 535, 537-8, 555-7, 559-60, 586-7
blockader 259, 266
Block, Adriaen 116, 490
Blondel, Jacob D. 448
Bloodgood, John 265
Bodwell, Lydia 413
Boisseau, Benjamin 264

Index

Bollard, William 541
Bolles, John 205
Bonaparte, Joseph 282
Bonaparte, Napoleon 179, 181-2, 184, 187, 218, 234, 274, 278, 281-6
Bonaventura, Edward 29
Borelli, Giovanni Alfonso 18
Boston Harbor 51, 59, 102-3, 124-5, 410, 512
Boston Tea Party 143, 144
Boston Transcript 409
Boughton, Francis 39
Boughton, Rachel 39
Bounty 499
Bourne, Nehemiah 79, 81-2, 568
Bourne, Robert 79
Bourne, William 10-11
Bowen, Ann 48
Bowen, Richard 45
Bowsprit 147
Bowyer, Mary 295
Bradford, Allis 438
Bradford, William 92, 438
Bradley, Stephen Rowe 237
Bradstreet, Simon 57, 102
Brady, Ann 473
Brady, Catherine Keegan 473
Brady, Cornelius 422
Brady, James 473
Brady, Matthew 437
Bragdon, Claude Chandler 563
Brandywine 528
Breed's Hill 413
Brents, William Jr. 236
Bridgewater 104
Brigg, Seth 438
Briggs, Harriet 516
Briggs, William David 515, 516
Brinckerhoff, Abraham 251
Bringhurst, Joseph 170
British Museum 2
Britten, Emma Hardinge 557
Britten, William 557
Bronson, Isaac 241
Brook, Baron 116
Brooks, Erastos 456
Brounley, Isabel 94
Brown, Adam 242, 245, 258
Brown, Charles 226
Browne, Anne 56
Browne, John 82
Brown, Eliphalet M. Jr. 437
Brown, Isaac H. 434
Brown, John 95-6, 100
Brown, Margaret Haywood 95

Brown, Nicholas 141
Brown, Nicholas Jr. 141
Brown, Noah 241-2, 245, 258
Brown, William 203
Bruen, Sarah 256
Brunel, Marc Isambard 427
Bryant, William Cullen 554
Buchanan, James 356
Buchanan, Nancy Ann 356, 367
Buckmaster, William P. 381
Budd 209
Buel, Clarence Clough 420
Buell, Don Carlos 547
Buffalo Daily Republic 482, 496
Buffalo Express 485
Bunker Hill 413
Bunker Hill Quick Step 408
Bunting, John A. 394
Burden, George 52, 81
Burdett, Richard 264
Burgoyne, Johnny 404
Burke, John 413
Burnside, Ambrose 502
Burr, Aaron 237
Burr, Jonathan 47
Bury St. Edmunds Grammar School 54
Bush, David 130
Bushnell, Alice 114
Bushnell, David 112-3, 116-20, 122-5, 128-31, 150, 177, 188, 203
Bushnell, Edmond 115
Bushnell, Elizabeth 114, 116
Bushnell, Ezra 117, 120, 124-5, 128
Bushnell, Francis 114-5
Bushnell, Francis III 115-6
Bushnell, Joan 114
Bushnell, John 114-5
Bushnell, Martha 116
Bushnell, Nehemiah 116
Bushnell, Nicholas 114
Bushnell, Pharis 114
Bushnell, Rebecca 114
Bushnell, Richard 114, 116
Bushnell, Roger 114
Bushnell, Sarah 114, 116
Bushnell, Thomas 114-5
Bushnell, William 116
Bushnell, William III 116-7
Bushnell, William Jr. 116
Busshenell, Alice 113
Busshenell, Joan 113
Busshenell, John 113
Busshenell, William 113
Butterworth, Hezekiah 420

Button, John 61
Buxton, Anthony 541
Buxton, Dorcas Gould 541

- C -

Cafferty, James Henry 448
Caldicott, Charles 39
Calvert, Cæcilius 151
Calvert, Charles 151-2
Cambridge Agreement 56
Cameley 93-4
Campbell, Allan 457
Campos, Juan 98
Canby, Edward Richard Sprigg 550
Canton 379
Capen, Mary Jane Lyon 541
Capen, Robert 541
Capen, Waitstill 541
Capon, William 400
Car of Neptune 230, 243
Caroline 196-7
Carolton 356-8, 361
Carondelet 375-6
Carstairs, Drysdale 462
Carstairs, George 462
Cary, Thomas Greaves 420
Cassey, Agnes 54
Cassey, Thomas 54
Catherwood, Laird 272
Cavendish, Elizabeth 104
Cavendish, William 44
Cerdic 353
Chambers, John W. 394
Champion 457
Chandler, Adoniram 394
Chanibre, George 75
Chanibre, Hester 75
Chanute, Octave 528
Chapman, Benjamin 296
Chapman, Rebecca 116
Charles 57, 82, 87-8
Charles River 60, 63, 67, 77, 402, 403
Charlestown 59-60, 63-4, 77, 80, 413, 522, 539-40, 569
Charybdis 125
Chase, Thomas 142, 143
Chaumont, Jacques-Donatien Le Ray 157
Chauncey, Isaac 236, 242
Chealsea Meadows Submarine 269
Chicago Tribune 289-90, 293, 377, 577
Child, Edward A. 410
Child, Frances 379
China 242

Christian, Fletcher 499
Church, Benjamin 108
City of Oswego 474
Clapham, J.H. 91
Clarke and Lake Shipyard 97
Clarke, Anne 75
Clarke, John 75
Clark, Hannah 355
Clark, William 523
Clawson, John 513
Claxton, Timothy 404-5
Clemens, Samuel L. 420
Clermont 227, 572, 574
Cleverly, Stephen 142-3
Clifford, Henry 397
Clinton, Ann 512
Clitz, Harriet Louiza 439
Clymer, George 145
Coast Defense Society 241
coasters 259
Cobb, Helen Elizabeth 416
Cobb, John Storer 557
Cochrane, Thomas 279
Cockburn, George 198, 280
Coddington, William 57
Codman, John 404
Cohen, Jay M. 348
Coit, Benjamin 197
Coit, Erastus 197
Coit, Farewell 197
Colburn, Hepzibah 404
Colden, Cadwallader B. 247
Coles, Agnes 75
Coles, William 75
Colt, Samuel 212-3
Columbus, Christopher 91, 448
Commerce 196
Company of Mine Adventurers 71
Comstock, Joseph Jesse 457
Coney, Richard 104
Conkling, Fred A. 547-8
Connecticut Gazette 208, 212, 573, 575
Connecticut River Museum 131
Constantinople 16
Continental Army 118, 145, 192, 203, 206, 356, 413
Conway, Fulke 162
Cooke, Peyton 172
Cooper, James Fenimore 554
Corneliszoon, Cornelis 119
Cotton, John 62
Couch, Darius Nash 549
Cowing, James H. 529
Coytmore, Thomas 80

Index

Crafts, Thomas 142-3
Craig, Austin 545
Cranch, Christopher Pearse 420
Crane, Nirom M. 456
Crawford, Peter 130
Crawford, Winnifred 412
Crispin, William 86
Cromwell, Oliver 21, 353
Crouze, Albert 396
CSS Palmetto State 342
CSS Stono 505
CSS Virginia 334-5
Cubitt, Thomas 431
Cullum, Arthur 255, 265
Cullum, George 255, 265
Cullum, Harriet 265
Cumminsky, Joseph 410
Cunningham, Andrew 404
Curtenius, Peter T. 255
Cuyler, James W. 507
Cyrus 499

- D -

Dahlgren, John A. 504, 585
Daily Evening Journal 416
Daily Press 347
Daisy Miller 272
Dale, Charles 247
Danby, Robert 331
Danett, Thomas 67
Danieux, Marie Elisabeth 383
Dauphin 197
Davenport Gazette 360
Davenport, Henry K. 525, 526
Davenport, John 52
da Vinci, Leonardo 1, 6-7, 299, 318, 565
Davis, Charles H. 310
Davis, Jefferson 550
Davis, John 65, 67
Davis, Nelson 439
Davis, Samuel 137
Davis, Samuel Boyer 239, 575
Dawes, Charles H. 310
Dawes, William 144
Day, James 22-26, 63, 66, 141, 167-8, 565-6, 573, 580
Dearborn, Henry 241
Decatur, Stephen 199, 205-6, 212, 241, 258, 573
Declaration of Independence 141
Dee, John 10, 36
Deep-Sea Diving Bell 399, 409-11, 414, 421-2, 424

Defoe, Daniel 104, 270
Delano, Benjamin Franklin 457
De Lara, David E. 556
Deliverance 31
de Lorena, Guglielmo 8
de Marisco family 93
Deming, Charles R. 552
Demologos 243-5
Deneau, William 290, 292-4
de Redvers, William 270
De Re Militari 6
de Son, Monsieur 16, 17
Detroit Advertiser 304, 511, 577
Detroit Free Press 530
Devonshire 449
Devotion, John 117
Dexter, Arthur 420
Dillon, Martha Nash 364-5, 367
Dillon, Patrick 365
Dirigo 525-6
diving armor 2, 306-7
diving bell 2, 5, 9, 12-13, 19-20, 31, 36, 42, 46-7, 69, 81, 92, 311, 318, 327, 341, 361-6, 368-71, 381-2, 384, 408, 410, 413-4, 416, 427-9, 440, 443-5, 451, 457, 462, 476-9, 483, 496, 499,-501, 516
Diving Bell Submarine 370
diving suit 8, 13, 20, 306, 307, 318, 517
Diving Tub 51, 68-70, 91, 103, 105
Dixon, Jeremiah 151
Dobbins, Daniel 242
Dodson, Francis 99
doglock gun 95
Dolgorukov, Helena 555
Domesday Book 47-8, 54, 75, 94, 138
Doolittle, Isaac 120
Dorothea 224, 231
Douglas, Alexander 197
Drebbel, Cornelius Jacobszoon 11, 14, 18, 36, 119
Dubuque Weekly Times 523
Dudley, Joseph 109-10
Dudley, Thomas 57
Duhring, Andrew 358-9
Duke of Albemarle 104, 106-7
Duke of Argyll 420
Duke of Sutherland 420
Duke of York 151, 279, 284-5
Duke William of Normandy 93, 135
Dunham, Josiah Jr. 416
Du Pont, Samuel Francis 331-2, 341-2, 526
Dyngley, Etheldreda Malte 511
Dyngley, Joan 511

Index

- E -

Eads, Eliza Ann 356, 358, 368
Eads, Eunice Hagerman 372
Eads, Genevieve 356, 358
Eads, Hannah Clark 355
Eads, Henry 355
Eads, Henry I 355
Eads, Henry II 355
Eads, Henry III 355
Eads, Henry IV 355
Eads, James Buchanan 352-9, 361-77, 444, 579-80
Eads, James Jr. 368, 371
Eads, Jane 354
Eads, John 354
Eads, Jone 355
Eads, Lawrence 242, 354
Eads, Martha Dillon 364, 366-8
Eads, Mary Pegely 100, 355
Eads, Nancy Ann 358, 360, 367
Eads, Richard 354-5
Eads, Thomas 354-6
Eads, Thomas Clark 356, 359-60
Eads, Thomas James 355
Eads, William 355
Eagle 57, 125-6, 128, 199, 200-6, 257, 283-5, 562
Eakins, George 347
Eakins, Katie 347
Eakins, Samuel 339-41, 343, 347-8
Earl of Leicester 512
Earl of Stanhope 172, 216
Earl of Warwick 116
Eastland 290
Eastman, Gustavus B. 524
Eaton, Joseph 141
Eckford, Henry 390
Edes, Alice 354
Edes, Benjamin 143
Edgar, Benjamin 330
Edgecomb, Lucy 414
Edison, Thomas 397
Edmonds, Alfred Russel 554
Edsall, Elizabeth 251
Edsall, Samuel 251
Edwards, Morgan 141
Egyptian Kaballah, The 561
Ehlers, Henry 507
Elbridge, Gyles 96
Elbridge, Thomas 96
Eldred, Patience 513
Eliza 196
Elizabeth 512

Ellery, William Jr. 140
Elliott, Charles Wyllys 420
Ellisonn, John 81-2
Ellms, Charles 542
Elmes, William 201-2
Emerson, Ralph Waldo 420
Emily Banning 452-3, 455
Emperor Caligula 9
Emperor Charles V 10
Endicott, John 59, 66, 77, 539
Enforcement Act 198
Englefield, Francis 114
English Gentleman's Magazine 119
Erie 481-2
Etna 283-5
Euboea 4
Eustis, Henrietta Louise 414
Evans, Samuel 241, 245
Evelyn, John 87, 91, 568-9
Evolution of the Submarine, Mine & Torpedo, 213
Explorer 379, 389, 391-2, 395, 580-1
Eyton, Petronilla 53
Eyton, Roger 53, 54

- F -

Fadeyeva, Nadezhda 556
Fadeyev, Helena de 555
Fairchild, Charles 420
Fairfield, William B. 524
Falck, Nikolai Detlef 22, 25
Falkener, Joseph 86
Falmouth 424
Fame 197
Faneuil Hall 51, 61, 81
Fargo, William G. 470, 471, 498
Farrar, Mary C. 542
Felt, Aaron 540
Felt, Anna 554
Felt, Anne Wolcott 541
Felt, Benjamin 541
Felt, David 544, 546
Felt, David Wells 542, 544-5
Felt, Dorcas Gould Buxton 541
Felt, Edwin Mead 542-3
Felt, Elizabeth 554
Felt, Elizabeth Leuman Glover 538, 541
Felt, Elizabeth Wilkinson 539-40, 542
Felt, George Henry 534-5, 538-48, 550-3, 555-63, 570, 586-7
Felt, George Jr. 540, 554
Felt, George Sr. 538-40
Felt, Hannah Maine 540
Felt, Henry 554

Index

Felt, Jerusha Hunt 541
Felt, Jonathan 541
Felt, Joshua 540, 541
Felt, Lovewell Wells 541
Felt, Maria 554
Felt, Mary Anne Frain 543-4, 554-5
Felt, Mary C. Farrar 542
Felt, Mary Smith 538
Felt, Mary Withington 541
Felt, Moses 540-1
Felt, Peter 540
Felt Submarine 535, 562
Felt, Waitstill Capen 541
Felt, Willard 554
Felt, Willard Leuman Jr. 542
Felt, Willard Sr. 538, 541-2, 546
Felt, William 538
Field, Joseph 143
Figaro 286
Fish, Nicholas 257
Fitch, John 173
Fleenor, Nicholas 523
Fletcher 516-7, 519-21
Flower, Samuel 170
Floyd, Charles 523
Fool Killer 290-300, 308, 577
Foolkiller No. 1 291
Foolkiller No. 2 291
Foolkiller No. 3 292
Foreman, Alan 429
Foreman, Ann 430
Foreman, Charles 433-4
Foreman, Edgar William 426-37, 440-1, 443-5, 447-50, 453-5, 457, 459-62, 582-3
Foreman, Elizabeth 429
Foreman, Frederick 431-2, 434, 460
Foreman, Henry 434
Foreman, Jeremiah 429
Foreman, Jeremiah Jr. 429-30
Foreman, John 429, 430
Foreman, Jonathan 431-5, 438, 440-1, 445, 449, 455, 460-1
Foreman, Mary 429, 431
Foreman, Mary Ann 431
Foreman, Mary Anne 432, 441, 449, 460
Foreman, Robert 429
Foreman, Sarah Ann 448
Foreman, Sarah Anne 431, 433, 434
Foreman, William 429-31, 435
Fortescue, John William 109
Fortibus, Isabella de 353
Fortification or Architecture Military: Unfolding the Principall Mysteries Thereof, in the Resolution of Sundry Questions and Problemes 43

Foster, Amasa 546
Fourman, Robert 429
Fournier, Georges 15
Fowler, John 211
Fox 480, 497-8
Foxcroft, Alice Hodson 52
Foxcroft, George 52
Foxcroft, Richard 52
Fox, Kate 554
Fox, Maggie 554
Frain, Elizabeth Nesbit 543
Frain, John 543
Frain, Mary Anne 543
Francis, Nancy H. 438
Frank Leslie's Illustrated Newspaper 511
Franklin 196
Franklin, Benjamin 121, 144-5, 150, 157-8, 169, 367, 457, 523, 571
Franklin, William Temple 157
free diving 2, 15
Freeman's Oath 61
French and Indian War 252, 413
Frese, Fred 131
Frink, Andrew 206
Frink, Nathan 206
From Sea to Sea: 350 Years of East Hampton History 212
Fuller, George 482
Fulton 380
Fulton, Abraham 166, 172
Fulton, Alexander 163
Fulton, David 163
Fulton, Doctor Robert 162
Fulton, Elizabeth 162, 166, 172
Fulton, Harriet 234-5, 246
Fulton, Hugh 163
Fulton, Isabella 166, 172
Fulton, James 162-3
Fulton, John 162-3
Fulton, John III 162-3
Fulton, John Jr. 162
Fulton, Julia 234-5
Fulton, Margaret 162, 172
Fulton, Mary 163, 165-6, 172
Fulton, Richard 162
Fulton, Robert 129, 160-73, 175-6, 178-9, 181, 183-5, 189, 205-6, 214-5, 217-34, 236-47, 258, 264, 274-8, 280, 283, 286, 311, 380, 572-6
Fulton, Robert Barlow 230, 247
Fulton, Robert Sr. 164, 166
Fulton the First 246
Fulton, Thomas 162-3
Fulton, William 162-3

Index

- G -

Gage, Thomas 144
Gale, Benjamin 150, 570
Galileo 18
Gallatin, Albert 198
Gandhi, Mahatma 538
Gann, John 212
Gardiner, John 208
Gardner, Charles O. 516-7
Gardner, Clarissa Holbrook 416
Gardner, Helen Elizabeth Cobb 416
Gardner, Henry 416
Gardner, Henry Joseph 416-7
Garrison, William Lloyd 554
Gates, Horatio 156
Gates, Thomas 31
Gay, James 457
Geddes, John 201
Gedney, Sylvanus 266
General Armstrong 242
Geus, Averill Dayton 212
Gibbons, William 77
Gillan, Benjamin 80
Gillespie, James 163-4
Gilman, Arthur 420
Girard, Stephen 326
Glasgow 18-9, 100, 576
Glaucus 2, 3, 565
Glover, Elizabeth Leuman 538, 541
Glover, Lydia Barrett Lewis 541
Glover, Oliver 541
Goddard, Calvin 193
Goddard, David A. 420
Goddard, George 194
Goddard, Hezekiah 193-4, 197, 205
Goddard, Hezekiah Willard 195
Goddard, Jeremiah Henry 194
Goddard, Sally 196
Goldsborough, Louis Malesherbes 339-40, 578
Goltzius, Hendrick 119
Good Intent 103
Goodwin, John 36
Gore, Mary Kenney 404
Gore, Nancy Davis 404
Gore, Paul 404
Goudhurst, Robert 273, 274
Goulding, Percival Jr. 47
Gowen, John Emery 517
Gower, Jane 71
Gower, John 71
Graham, William H. 303-4, 577
Grand River Times 522
Granger, John 413

Grant, Joane 75
Grant of Norbrooke 75
Grant, Ulysses S. 420
Grassingham, Robert 82-4
Grasso, Ella 131
Graves, Thomas 539
Great Awakening 139
Great Fortunes 228, 574
Greaves, Walter 281
Greeley, Horace 554
Green, Adelia 473-5
Green, Andrew 471, 473
Green, Ann 474-5
Green, Ann Brady 473
Green, Grace Ann Jennings 485
Green, John 159, 482
Green, Johnny B. 464-5, 471-8, 480-5, 497-8, 520
Green, Joseph I. 265
Green, Lucy 471, 473
Green, Mary 473
Greenough, James B. 420
Green, Samuel 208
Griffith 475, 478
Grinnell, Moses Henry 492
Groom, Thomas 542
Grosse, Isaac 52
Grosvenor, Gerald 431
Gruchy, Viola de 563
Guilford Covenant 115
Guinevere 94
Gunmaker's Company Proof House 159

- H -

Haave, Marit 465-6, 468-70
Hadleigh Heath 54-6
Hagerman, Adelaide 376
Hagerman, Eunice 373
Hailey, Joshua 282
Hale, John Parker 456
Hallett, Mary Elizabeth 355
Hallett, Samuel 456, 458-9
Halley, Edmond 1, 19-20, 92, 105
Hallick, Catherine 159
Hall, Richard H. 530
Halsey, Abigail 191
Halsey, Daniel 190
Halsey, Deborah 191
Halsey, Elijah 191
Halsey, Elizabeth Wheeler 190
Halsey, Esther 189, 191, 194
Halsey, Experience 191
Halsey, Ezekiel 191

Index

Halsey, George Washington 191, 196
Halsey, Harriet 191
Halsey, Isaac 190
Halsey, Jeremiah 187, 189, 191-4, 206
Halsey, Jeremiah Shipley 187
Halsey, Jerusha 191
Halsey, John Jay 191, 196
Halsey, Joseph 190
Halsey, Mary 191
Halsey, Nathan 191
Halsey, Phoebe 191, 194
Halsey, Polly 191
Halsey, Recompense 191
Halsey, Sally Ayer 191, 196
Halsey, Samuel 190
Halsey, Sarah 191
Halsey, Silas Plowden 186-7, 189, 191, 195-7, 199, 202-3, 205-8, 210, 212-3, 258
Halsey Submarine 187, 204-5, 213
Halsey, Thomas 190-1
Halsey, William 190-1
Halsey, William Pitt 191, 196-7
Hamelin, Mathieu 158
Hamilton, Alexander 249
Hamilton, Paul 189
Hammond, Elizabeth 99
Hancock, John 144, 154, 571
Hand, Johnny 289
Handy, Susannah 438
Hanson, James 325
Hardiman, Robert 382
Hardy, Thomas Masterman 199, 200, 202, 207-8, 210-1, 213, 250, 259, 573
Hargraves, George 130
Harold, Thomas G. 397
Harper's Weekly 529
Harrington, Abigail Houghton 514, 530-1
Harrington, Ada Francis 514-5
Harrington, Alice "Allie" Mabel 514, 524
Harrington, Ann 512
Harrington, Ann Clinton 512
Harrington, Benjamin 512-3
Harrington, Charles Murray 525, 531
Harrington, Elizabeth Mutton 512
Harrington, Elliot Perry 484, 510-32, 585, 586
Harrington, Emmeline Leticia Maxion 514, 524, 531
Harrington, Forest Deville 514, 522, 524
Harrington, Frances 515
Harrington, Isabella Markham 511
Harrington, Job 513-4
Harrington, John I 512
Harrington, John III (Writer) 512
Harrington, John II (Poet) 511, 512

Harrington, John IV 512
Harrington, Larkin 514, 530-1
Harrington, Lewis Todd 531-2
Harrington, Patience Eldred 513
Harrington, Robert 512
Harrington, Stephen 513
Harrington, William Murray 514, 522, 524
Haslett, Joseph 238
Hautefeuille, Jean 17-8
Hawkins, Thomas 79-80
Hawley, Seth C. 456
Hayden, Levi 499-503, 584-5
Hayes, Rutherford B. 377, 420
Haynes, John 62, 100
Haynes, William 100
Hedger, Thomas 64
Hedges, Reuben 212
Heiser, Christopher 457
Helios 3
Heller, Theresa 448
Hell Gate 125, 489-92, 495, 509, 584
Henry, Joseph 310
Herbert, Thomas 176
Hermetic Brotherhood of Luxor 554-5
Hero 259
Hewes, Richard 301
Higginson, Thomas W. 420
Hildreth, Azro Benjamin Franklin 523-4
Hill, G.C. 420
Hill, Margery 138
Hinnman, Benjamin 192
Hirst, William L. 333-4
Hispaniola 91, 98, 101, 104, 110
Historical Gallery of Criminal Portraitures, Foreign and Domestic, The 274, 278, 286
History of New London County, Connecticut 213
H.L. Hunley 504-5
HMS Anson 428
HMS Bulwark 262
HMS DeBraak 325
HMS Edgar 382
HMS Endymion 260
HMS Fox 278
HMS La Hogue 260
HMS Maidstone 261-2, 264
HMS Nimrod 262
HMS Poictiers 238-9
HMS Ramillies 200, 202, 204-5, 207-8, 210-211, 213, 259
HMS Royal George 382
HMS Saturn 259
HMS Sylph 261-2, 264
HMS Trident 259
Hoff, Henry K. 331, 578

Index

Hoff Report 332
Holland, Maria 301, 312
Holland, M.J. 301
Holmes, Ann 265
Holmes, Jeremiah 212, 259-60, 265
Holmes, Oliver Wendell 420
Hood, Robin 96
Hooke, Robert 87
Hooker, Thomas 62
Hopewell 57
Hopkins, Stephen 141
Hornellsville Tribune 327
Hornet 199, 211
Hotchkin, Beriah 169
Houghton, Abigail 514
Houghton, A.G. 420
Housatonic 504-5
Hovey, William A. 420
Howell, Edward 190
Howe, Richard 150
Howett, Samuel 86
Howe, William 125
Hudson, Arthur 273
Hudson, Ralph 61
Hull, John 98
Hull, Mary Spencer 98
Hulls, Jonathan 173
Hundred Years' War 354
Hunt, Abigail Matthews 541
Hunt, Brinsmead 541
Hunting, John 401
Hunting, Susanna 401-2
Huntington, Samuel 193
Hunt, Jerusha 541
Huntting, Jonathan 263-4
Hurd, D. Hamilton 213
Hurlock, G. 43
Hutchinson, Anne 62-3
Hutchinson, George 382
Hutchinson, William 62
Hydna 4-5
Hyslop, James H. 557

- I -

Ictineo 343-6
Ictineo II 345-6
Ingram, Sarah 116
Irish, Thomas 135
Irving, Washington 490, 584
Isaac Newton 526
Isabella 91-2, 166, 172, 353, 511

-J-

Jackson, John 379
Jackson, Samuel 379
Jackson, Thomas J. "Stonewall" 439
Jackson, Treadwell 379
Jacob, Philip 265
James, Alice 354
James & Mary 104
James River Torpedo Station 505
Jamestown 29-31, 38, 91-2, 355, 531, 566, 586
Jamestown Evening Journal 531
Jeames, John 74
Jeames, Jona 74
Jefferson, Thomas 130, 198, 225, 481, 570
Jenner, Thomas 102
Jennings, Grace Ann 473, 485
Jennings, Philip 473
Jewell 56
John Adams 379
Johnes, Ann 190
Johnes, Edward 190
Johnson, Arbella 57
Johnson, Isaac 57, 59
Johnson, John Henry 462
Johnstone, Gilbert 270
Johnstone, Hugo de 270
Johnstone, James 271-2
Johnstone, John 272
Johnstone, John de 270
Johnstone the Smuggler 269, 284
Johnstone, Thomas 268-86
Johnstone, Walter 270
Joles, Thomas 99
Jones, Dorothy 438
Jones, Jacob 199, 241
Jones, Thomas 65, 67
Jones, William 206, 212, 238, 241, 573, 575
Journal, The 36, 566
Jover and Son 159
Jover, William 159
Joyce, James 538
Joy, Philena 298
Judge, William Quan 556
Julius Caesar 355
Juno 505

- K -

Kabbalah 556, 557, 564
Kantreyn, John 53-4
Keeble, Robert 87
Keith, George 276

Index

Kelly, John 272
Kelly, Joseph 522
Kendrie, Hannah 403
Kersey 54, 56
Kessler, Franz 13
Keyes, Erasmus D. 547, 549
Keynes, Maynard 91
Kilbourne, Hector 448
King Arthur 94
King Charles I 40, 45, 82, 400
King Charles II 87, 101, 103-4
King Edward I 429
King Edward II 74
King George's War 139
King Guthrum 55
King Hakon 8
King Henry II 53
King Henry III 55
King Henry VI 354
King Henry VIII 73, 114, 294, 353, 511
King James I 14, 29, 36, 38, 162, 271, 294, 354
King James II 104, 106, 163
King James VI 270-1
King Louis XI 6
King Philip IV 97
King Philip's War 136, 524
King William I 94
King William III 110, 163
Kinward, Joan 114
Knepp, John 101, 102, 103
Knickerbocker 359-61, 399, 581
Knight, Edward H. 420
Knight, Francis 96
Knights Templar 93
Knox, Dudley W. 347
Kriner, Henry 329
Kroehl, Julius H. 457
Kunkel, John C. 418

- L -

La Blanchiseuse 171
Lady Strange 192
Lake Erie Diver 465
Lake Erie Sub 511
Lake Nemi 9
Lamb, John 137
La Navigation Sous-Marine: A Travers Les Siecles 129, 570
Landgrave, Charles 119
Landsrud, Ambjorg 470
Landsrud, Olena 470
Landsrud, Torger 470

Laplace, Pierre Simon 179-85, 572
Lathrop, George Parsons 420
Latrobe, Benjamin H. 216
Laud, William 62
Laurel 82, 86
Lawrence, Richard P. 265
Lay, William 204
Leacraft, Thomas 46
Learned, Ebenezer 413
Leary, Joseph 131
Lechford, Thomas 66, 567
L'Echo de la Fabrique 322, 578
Lee, Abner 203-4
Lee, Deborah 204
Lee, Elizabeth Sullivan 203-4
Lee, Ezra 126-7, 188, 203-4
Lee, Henry Sullivan 204
Lee, Jane 203
Leek, Ben 212
Lee, Phoebe 203
Lee, Polly 204
Lee, Robert E. 549
Lee, Samuel 195
Lee, Samuel Holden Parsons 194-9, 203-5, 573
Lee, Samuel Phillips 525-6
Lee, Thomas 203
Leland, John 94
Leonidas 197
Le Plongeur 346
Lethbridge, John 22
letter-of-marque 188
Leverett, John 88
Lewis, Jacob 199, 241
Lewis, Lydia Barrett 541
Lewis, Meriwether 523
Lewis, Morgan 241
Lewkenor, George 400
Liberal Christian 558
Liberty 53, 82-7, 126, 141-3, 253-4
Lieb, Clarence W. 563
lighters 25, 80, 430
Lightfoot, John III 355
Lincoln, Abraham 318, 332, 333, 335, 338, 342, 375-6, 460, 539, 547-8
Lincoln, Mary Todd 547
Lipkens, Anton 324
Livingston, Harriet 227-30, 574
Livingston, John 247
Livingston, Margaret Maria 230
Livingston, Robert 227, 230, 434
Livingston, Robert R. 227
Livingston, Robert R. Jr. 227
Livingston, Walter 227, 230
London Era 459

599

Index

London Gazette 462
Long, Anna 435
Longfellow, Henry W. 420
Long, Jane 435
Lord Argyle 19
Lord Maxwell 271, 576
Lord of Lochwood 270
Lord of Toppesfield 55
Lord Sandwich 24-5
Lord Stanhope 218
Lothrop, Thornton K. 421
Loud, Oliver 297
Loveland, Oliver 266
Lowe, Hudson 283-4
Low, James 495
Loyall Nine 142-3
Ludlow, Charles D. 515
Luttrell, Narcissus 91
Lydia 197
Lyell, Mary 71
Lynde, Stephen 71
Lyon, Mary Jane 541

- M -

Macedonian 5, 199, 211
Macon's Bill Number 2 198
Madison, James 187, 198, 207, 225
Magnus, Olaus 8
Maillefert, Adam 499
Maillefert, Arthur 499
Maillefert, Benjamin Sylvester 480-1, 488-9, 491-509, 585
Maillefert, Charley 499
Maillefert, Elizabeth Schmidt 491, 495
Maillefert, Josephine Antoinette 491
Maillefert, Lizzie 499
Maine, Hannah 540
Maine Times 540
Majestad, Thorsten Nilsen 467
Malatesta, Sigismondo Pandolfo 6
Manning, James 140-1, 570
Manning, Margaret 140
Manowormet 96
Marcy, William L. 448
Margaret and John 39
Maria 22-6, 230, 301, 312, 554
Marine Cigar 289, 301-5, 308
Marine Torpedo 121
Marine Turtle 121
Markham, Isabella 511
Markham, John 511
Markham, Thomas 512
Martha 371

Martin, Jane 400
Martin, Joseph 494, 495
Martin, Thomas 279
Mary Rose 64-7, 69-70, 81, 567-8
Marzin, Catherine G. 348
Mason, Charles 151
Mason-Dixon line 152
Massey, Charles Carleton 557
Mather, Cotton 97, 107
Mather, Deborah 203
Matle, John 511
Matthews, Abigail 541
Maule of Melgum 19
Maxion, Emmeline Leticia 514, 524, 531
Mayflower 57, 92
May, Henry 29
Mayo, Thomas 404
McCallum, Daniel C. 457
McClellan, George B. 439
McCullers, Carson 380
McCurdy, James 451
McDowell, Frank M. 456
McDowell, George W. 456
McElroy, William Henry 420
McIntosh, William 404
McIntyre, William 200-1
McLaughlin, James Hiram 530
McNell, Degress 479, 496
Mechanic Apprentices' Library Association 405
Medici, Lorenzo de 6
Meleager 355
Merchant, Charles S. 552
Meriam, Ebenezer 492
Mersenne, Marin 15, 21, 565
Merton College 32
Metcalf, Hannah 403
Metcalf, Jonathan 403
Mexican War 524
Miller, Ben 212
Miner, Elisha M. 140
Miner, Mercy W. 140
Minister of Marine 174-5, 179, 181-2, 572
Minister to the Directory 175
Mississippi Diver 353, 364
Mitchell, Bridget 399
Mitchell, John 400
Mitchill, Samuel L. 241
Mohegan Sachem Uncas 115
Monachesi, Herbert D. 557
Monck, Christopher 107
Monge, Gaspard 179, 181-5, 572
Monoxe, Elizabeth 32
Monoxe, Richard 32
Montez, Lola 394

Monthly Nautical Magazine and Quarterly Review 500-501
Montholon, Marquis de 285-6
Monti, Luigi 420
Monturiol, Narciso 343-6
Moodna 504
Moore, Sydenham 418
Morales, Juan Esteban 439
Morgan, James 137-9, 237
Morgan, John 137-8
Morgan, Joshua 137
Morgan, J.P. 138
Morgan, Margaret Avery 138
Morgan, Mary 138
Morgan, Miles 138
Morgan, William 137, 138
Morris, David 172
Morris, Elizabeth Bruen 256
Morris, John 256
Morris, Sarah Bruen 256
Morris, Thomas 241
Morse, Samuel 437
Mortgaged Heart, The 380
Morvine, Julius 469
Mother Shipton 113
Mott, John 259
Muddy River 64, 115
Mulford, Alvah Stratton 263-4, 576
Murphy, James 381
Murphy, John McLeod 457
Mute 215, 240-2, 244-5, 258
Mutton, Elizabeth 512
Myer, James 549-52

- N -

Naglee, Henry Morris 549
Napier, John 12, 565
Napoleon III 437
Napton 74, 75
Narborough, John 101, 104, 106-7
Narragansett Bay 136
Nash, George 156
Nash, Robert 52
National Biography 512
National Magazine 511
Nautile 234
Nautilus 161, 174-184, 240, 246, 274-5, 325, 427, 444-7, 450-3, 455-61
Nautilus Submarine Company 447, 455, 460
Naval Chronicle 281, 286
Nehântick 137
Nelson, Horatio 225, 283
Nequasset 96

New London Bilious Pills 195
New London Gazette 212
New Orleans Picayune 377
Newport Mercury 141
New Providence 100, 491
Newton, Henry J. 557
Newton, Isaac 42
Newton, William M. 516-7
New Washington Association 237
New York and Environs, from Williamsburg 437
New York Daily Tribune 387, 436, 455
New York Dispatch 563-4
New York Evening Post 260, 434
New York Herald 386, 388, 393, 460
New York Observer 557
New York Post 161, 572
New York Sun 389
New York Times 266, 453, 455, 462, 508-9, 557
New York Tribune 447, 554
New York World 556
Niagara 242
Nicodemus, William J.L. 550-1
Niles, Peter H. 552
Nineteenth Century Miracles 557
Nissen, Peter 291-2, 294
Nock, Henry 159
Noddle 410
Noddle's Island 63
Non-Importation Act 198
Non-Intercourse Act 198
North Atlantic Blockading Squadron 525
North River Steamboat 227-9, 230, 233, 245
Northwode, John de 32
Northwode, Roger de 32, 566
Northwode, Stephen de 31
Norton, Charles Elliot 420
Norwood, Andrew 40, 45, 47
Norwood, Anne 40, 45, 48
Norwood, Edward 33
Norwood, Elizabeth 40, 45, 48
Norwood II, John 32
Norwood, Matthew 40, 48
Norwood, Rachel 40
Norwood, Richard 28-9, 31, 33, 36, 40-1, 44, 46-48, 566
Norwood, Roger 32
Norwood's System of Navigation 48
Nowell, Increase 57
Noyes, Henry S. 420
Nuestra Señora de la Concepción 98, 101
Nuestra Señora de la Limpia y Pura Concepción 104

Index

- O -

Ocampo, Emilio 282
Oceanus 3
Ogdensburg 304, 441-2, 465, 469, 471-2, 479-80, 496
Ohio 380
Okehocking Indians 169
Olcott, Henry Steel 556, 559-60, 587
Oliver, John 67
Olsen, Steven 466-7, 470
Oneida 515
Operation Phips 106
O'Reilly, John Boyle 420
Orion 197
Orlando Furioso 512
Orpheus 210
Osbern, William Fitz 353
Osborn, Lewis 212
Osgood, James R. 420, 558
Oswald, Elizabeth 295
Our Lady of the Immaculate Conception 98
Owen, E.W.C.R. 276

- P -

Paddock, Deborah 438
Paine, Thomas 145
Panama 325
Pancoast, Seth 557
Papin, Denis 20-1
Parker, Charles 300
Parker, Richard 64
Parker, Willard 296
Park, Esther 189
Parkhurst, Eleazer 359
Parkman, Elias 79
Park, Paul 194
Parsons, Samuel 126
Parsons, William Barclay 215
Pashebeshauke 116
Pasley, Charles 382, 428
Patience 31
Patterson, George Washington 456
Paul Jones 242
Payerne, Antoine 381, 382-3
Peabody, Robert Swain 419
Pease, Bartlett 438
Pease, William J. 381
Peck, John J. 547, 549
Pegelius, Magnus 12
Pegely, Mary 355
Pendragon, Uther 94
Penfold, Elizabeth 252
Penfold, John 253
Penn, William 86, 151
Penny, Joshua 208-11, 261, 265, 573
People's Almanac 542
Pepys, Samuel 88
Pequot Indians 137
Percy, George 92
Perine, William 390
Perrin, Glover 296
Perrot, Anne 294
Perry, Matthew 380
Perry, Oliver Hazard 241-2
Perry, Thomas S. 420
Perry, William C. 529
Pettey, Joseph Byron 441-2, 467-9
Philadelphia 504
Philadelphia Ledger 327
Philipps, John 294
Philipps, Philip 294
Phillips, Addison Joseph 297-8, 301, 306
Phillips, Benjamin 295
Phillips, B.J. 262
Phillips, Cyril 297-8, 301, 306, 580
Phillips, David 295-7
Phillips, George 57
Phillips, James H. 528
Phillips, Lodner Darvontis 288-9, 293-312, 479, 496, 516, 526, 577
Phillips, Maria 312
Phillips, Virena 297-8
Phillips, William 295, 301
Phillips, William Shillingforth 297
Phipps, Constantine Henry 97
Phipps, Johannes 93
Phipps, Richard 93
Phips, Anne 94
Phips Diving Tub 91, 103, 105
Phips, James 94-7
Phips, Margaret 94
Phips, Mary 110
Phips Point 96, 99-100
Phips, Richard 94
Phips, Robert 94, 569
Phips, Thomas 94
Phips, William v, 90-95, 98, 100, 102-106, 109-10, 569
Pickett, George 439
Picquet, Abbe Francois 471
Picton Castle 93
Pierce, Andrew J. 485
Pierce, Grace Ann Jennings 485
Pierce, William 401
Pilgrims 14, 92, 567
Pillischer, Moritz 397

Index

Pinke, Joan 113
Pitt, William 191, 196-7, 220-1, 273-4
Planter 115
Plunging Boat 222
Pocahontas 31
Pook, Samuel 375
Pook's Turtles 375
Pope Nicholas III 114
Porcupine 242
Porpoise 210, 322-3, 325
Porter, David 245
Poseidon 125
Post, Simeon S. 457
Poverty Island 120, 124
Pratt, Leonard Barnes 525-6
Pratt, Phineas 117, 119-20
Prince, Benjamin Reeve 264
Prince of Neifchatel 242
Prince of Wales 505
Princess Elizabeth 511-2
Princeton 515
Principia Mathematica 42
privateers 242, 252, 259, 272, 282
Problematum 4-5
Proctor, Thomas F. 156
Proselyters from India 557
Purchas, Samuel 39
Purdy, S.A. 266
Putnam, Israel 124-5
Putnam, Sarah 296
Pykenham, Archdeacon 55
Pynchon, William 60
Pyremon 241
Pyrhydrostat 383

- Q -

Quasi War 198
Queen Anne 430
Queen Elizabeth I 10, 29, 354, 512
Queen Mary of Scotland 110, 360
Quenell, Ferris 114
Quigley, Martin 482, 516-7
Quincy, Edmund 62
Quinn, John S. 529
Quish, James 423

- R -

Ragon, Adolphe Ernest 397
Rainbow Coffee House 436
Ramillies 187, 200, 202, 204-5, 207, 208, 210-1, 213, 259
Randolph, Edward 100, 101, 569

Rapelje, Walloon Jansen de 379
Raritan 230
Reed, Elijah F. 499
Reed, John H. 421
Remsell, Samuel 410
Remsen, Cornelius 379
Rend, John H. 415
Rennie, George 428
Rennie, John 427-8
Rennie, John the Elder 427
Reno, Jesse Lee 502
Republican Advocate 301
Resolution 43, 100, 150
revenue cutters 198, 249
Revere, Paul 144
Rhodes, Alexander 329
Rice, Alexander Hamilton 420
Rice, Dinah Walker Wolcott 412
Rice, Peter 412
Richards, Bridgett 400
Richards, Cecily 400
Richards, Dorcas 402
Richards, Ebenezer 403
Richards, Edward I 399-400
Richards, Edward II 400
Richards, Edward III 400-03
Richards, Germain 400
Richards, Hannah 403
Richards, Hepzibah 404
Richards, James 403
Richards, Jane 400
Richards, John 400, 402-3
Richards, Jonathan Avery III 398-405, 407-11, 414-6, 421-4
Richards, Jonathan I 403-4
Richards, Jonathan II 404
Richards, Mary 402, 403
Richards, Mary Adelaide 404
Richards, Mary Anne 415
Richards, Minnie 415
Richards, Minnie Marie Bancroft 415
Richards, Nathanial 206-7
Richards, Nathaniel 400-03
Richardson, John D. 416
Richardson, Thomas 253
Richards, Richard 399-400
Richards, Sally 404
Richards, Sarah 404
Richards, Sary 402
Richards, Susanna 401-2
Rich, Thomas C. 420
Riker, John Lawrence 199-200, 205-6, 257, 259
Rimini 6

603

Index

Rittenhouse, David 156
River Thames 12, 114, 138, 281, 382, 427-31, 459
RMS Titanic 348
Robinson, John D. 296
Robinson, William 276
Rodgers, John 236, 339, 578
Rodvang, Ambjorg 468-70
Rodvang, Barbo 466, 470
Rodvang, Finkel 466, 470
Rodvang, Knud 466
Rodvang, Marit Haave 465-70
Rodvang, Ole Alfson 466, 468-70
Rodvang, Ole Jr. 468-70
Rogers, George 512
Rogers, Mary 512
Rogers, William 141-2
Rolfe, John 31
Rose of Algiers 101-3
Ross, George 164, 171
Rotterdam Boat 16-7
Rover 274
Royal Africa Company 71
Royal George 428
Royal Ship of Khufu 78
Royal Shoal 525-6
Royal Society 1, 87-8, 568
Roy, Rob 284
Ruggles, Thomas Colden 457
Rumsey, James 173
Rush, Benjamin 145
Russell, William F. 418
Rutgers, Henry 241

- S -

Sacramento Daily Union 499
Sage, Ebenezer 211, 576
Sallie 201
Salmon, Charles 101, 103
Salsette 460
Salter, William D. 391
Saltonstall, Richard 57
Sands, Comfort 379
Sands, Joshua 379
Sanford, Nathan 241
San Pedro 451, 455
Santo Domingo 91, 98
Sargent, Luther 212
Saturday Evening Post 330, 578
Sawin, Benjamin 306
Sawin, Judson 306
Sawyer, John 212
Saxton, Joseph 310

Saye, Viscount 116
Scarlett, Jane 60
Scarlett, Samuel 71
Scenes and Stories of a Clergyman in Debt 284, 286
Schmidt, Elizabeth 491
Schonborn, Johann Philip von 15
Schott, P. Gaspar 10, 565
Scientific America 381, 388, 511, 580-1
Scoffern, John 462
Scorpion 242
Scott, Robert 172
Scott, Walter 271, 283
Scudder, Amy 251
Scudder, Horace E. 420
Scudder, John 199, 205-6, 573
Scully, Peter 528
Scyllias 4
Seabury, Samuel 137
Seafort 80
Seale, Charles William 156
Seaman's Companion 48
Seaman's Practice 40, 43-4
Searle, Arthur 420
Sears, Acsah 438
Sears, Alice 438
Sears, David 438
Sears, David Jr. 438
Sears, Deborah 438
Sears, Dorothy Jones 438
Sears, Ella 440, 462
Sears, Elvira FitzAlan 439-40
Sears, Francis Everett 439
Sears, Harriet 462
Sears, Harriet Louiza 439-40, 462
Sears, Henry Beaufort 426-7, 437-45, 447, 450-62, 479, 496
Sears, Jonathan Prince 438-9
Sears, Judah 438
Sears, Knyvet 438
Sears, Nancy H. 438-40
Sears, Paul 438
Sears, Richard 438
Sears, Sally 438
Sears, Sally Tucker 438
Sears, Samuel 438
Sears, Susannah 438
Sears, Susannah Handy 438
Sears, Sylas 438
Searsville 455
Sea Venture 30-1, 566
Second Continental Congress 152, 155
Secor, Charles A. 390
Secor, Francis 389-90

Index

Secor, Henry R. 390
Secor, James F. 390
Secor, Thorne 390
Secor, Zeno 390
Selfridge, Thomas O. 341
Serle, Ann 355
Serrell, Lemuel W. 396-7, 581
Seymour 526
Seymour, M'Neil 434
Seymour, William 162
Sforza, Francesco 6
Shawmut 63
Sheepscot River 96, 99
Sheldon, Ralph 512
Shepherd, Jack 284
Sherbrook, Michael 73
Shields, James 547
Shippen, Peggy 70
sillographe 397
Simmons, Charles E. 557
Sims, William F. 347
Sinclair, George 18-9, 100, 565
Sizer, Jonathan 205
Skinner, Francis 418
Skipwith, Fulner 216
Smith, Aaron 404
Smith, Andrew H. 387
Smith, Elizabeth 139
Smith, George 169
Smith, John 78, 92, 143, 163, 218-9, 576
Smith, Joseph 164, 332-6
Smith, Mary 163-5
Smith, Sheldon 448-9
Smith, Sidney 324
Smith, Susanna 163
Smith, Washington G. 507
Smith, William 494
Somers, George 30, 40
Somers Island Company 38
Sons of Liberty 142-3, 253
Sotheran, Charles 556
Soulby, Anne 52
Southard, Theodore 494-5
Southeil, Ursula 113
Southerer 482
Southwell, Robert 101
Sovereign 482, 498
Speakman, John 422
Speed, John 40
Spencer, Daniel 98
Spiritualist, The 561
SS *Atlantic* 421, 422-3
SS *Edinburgh* 462
SS *Lady Head* 424

Stamp Act 142, 252
Stanborough, Ruth 191
Stanly News and Press 347
Stanton, Benjamin 418
Stanton, Sarah 191
Stark, Aaron 136
Stark, Jonas 136
Stark, Mehitable Shaw 136
Stark, Sarah 136
Stately 209
St. Charles City Republican Intelligencer 523
Stearns, John Goddard Jr. 419
Steedman, Charles 331
Stephenson, Robert 459
Stevens, Charles 365
Stevens, Henry M. 557
Stevens, Sue 365
Stiles, Ezra 140
Stites, Richard 141
St. John 114
St. Louis 376
Stoddard, Ralph 137
Stoddard, Richard Henry 420
Stokes, John 86
Stoudinger, Charles 245
Stoughton, William 108, 110
Strachey, William 31
Stratton, Rebecca 116
Stratton, Thankful 403
Strickland, J.W. 156
Strong, John 212
Stuart, Arabella 162
Sub-marine 444
submarine armor 475, 478, 483, 516-8
Sub-Marine Boat No. 1 361, 363
Sub-Marine Boat No. 2 368
Sub-Marine Boat No. 3 370
Sub-Marine Boat No. 4 372
Sub-Marine Boat No. 7 374
Submarine Exploring Company 380
Success 57, 381
Sueter, Murray Fraser 213
Sullivan, Elizabeth 204
Susannah and Thomas 102
Sussex 82
Sutcliff, Alice Crary 227
Swarthwout, Samuel 206
Swartwout, John 237
Swartwout, Robert 237
Swartwout, Samuel 237, 238, 239
Sybella 491
Symonds, Henry 81
Syracuse New York Daily Journal 442, 582

Index

- T -

Taisnier, John 10
Talbot 56-7
Talbot, Thomas 420
Tallmadge, Nathan Pitcher 554
Tartar 252
Taylor, Alan 91
Tegg, Thomas 202
terabdella 387
Terhune, Geesje 256
Terrell, Bruce 348
Terry, Noah 264
Tethys 3
Thacher, Anthony 438
Thacher, Elizabeth 438
Theosophical Society 537, 558-61
Therapeutic and Chemical Properties or the Active Medicinal Principles of Cod Liver, Determined and Separated, The 553
The Washerwoman 171
The Yankee Torpedo 201
Thomas, Martin 332-6, 338-9, 346, 578
Thomas, William 444
Thompson, Charles 141
Tibbals, Henry Lewis 451
Ticknor, Benjamin H. 420
Tigress 242
Tilehurst 113-4
Time of Dissolution 73
Titus, Thomas Jefferson 481
torpedo 122, 132, 176, 180, 187-9, 202, 205,-7, 211-3, 223-4, 226, 232-4, 236-8, 245-6, 258-61, 263-5, 278-9, 285, 308, 347, 504-5
Torpedo Act 188-9, 199
torpedo boat 234, 236, 245, 258-9, 263, 264, 347, 505
Torpedo War 226, 574
Torrance, Moses 529
Townsend, Samuel P. 546
Treaties and Conventions, Letters, and the Journal of Public of any kind by the King of England 41
Trial 57, 79
Trigonometrie or the Doctrine of Triangles 40
Trott, George 143
Trowbridge, John 420
Trowbridge, John Townsend 420
True Blooded Yankee 259, 282
Trumbull, J. Hammond 420
Truth, Sojourner 554
Tucker, Daniel 38
Tucker, Sally 438
Tucker, William 39
Tully, Elias 117
Turell, Daniel Jr. 99
Turner, Robert 60
Turtle 258-63, 265-6
Twain, Mark 357, 444, 561, 579

- U -

Uhlenbeckm, Olke 324
Underhill, Jeronimus S. 389, 390
underwater explosives 117, 118, 183, 188, 222, 226, 230, 234, 275, 491
Underwood, Francis H. 420
United Service Gazette Army and Navy Chronicle 323
United States 199, 211
University of Oxford 32
University of St Andrews 18
Upchurch, Mary Jane 97
Upham, Ezekial 413
USS Cairo 341
USS Cumberland 341
USS Galena 339
USS Hetzel 525
USS Isaac Smith 505
USS Keokuk 504
USS Merrimac 334-5, 525
USS Sumpter 342-3

- V -

vacuum pump 15
Valturio, Roberto 6
Vanderbeek, Elizabeth 256, 266
Vanderbeek, Geesje Terhune 256
Vanderbeek, Solomon 256
Van Der Heyden, Jan 17
Vander Wonde, Cornelius 15
Vane, Henry 79
Van Exter, Marguerite 383
van Mander, Karel 119
Van Norman, James W. 529
Varnum, James Mitchell 141-2
Vendeen Album 318
Verne, Anne 316
Verne, Jules Gabriel 317-20, 324, 325, 578
Verne, Marie 316
Verne, Mathilde 316
Verne, Paul 316
Verrazzano, Giovanni 136
Villeroi, Brutus Amedee de 314-5, 317-9, 324-5, 328-9, 336, 341, 345-6, 348
Villeroi, Eulalie de 325

Index

Virginia Company 29, 31, 36-7, 39-40
Virginia II 341
Visitation of Warwick 74
Voice of the Silence, The 535-7, 586
Vollmering, Joseph 448
Volney, Constantin François de Chasseboeuf, comte de 182, 184
von Guericke, Otto 15
von Hahn, Helena 555
von Hahn, Peter 555

- W -

Wadham, Dorothy 75-6
Wadham, Nicholas 75
Walker, Caleb 296
Walker, Dinah 412
Walker, Experience 413
Walker, William 296
Wallace, Alfred Russel 554
Walley, John 99
Ward, Andrew 193
Ward, Eber Brock 442-3, 467
Warden, Barbara 400
Ward, Samuel 141, 144, 149, 467
Waring, George E. 420
Warner, Charles Dudley 420
War of 1812 187, 205, 237, 242, 250, 258, 266, 380, 390, 393, 472, 524, 572-3, 575
Warren, John Borlase 198, 200, 202, 573
Warren, William 103
Warrington, Samuel 241
Warwick Patent 116
Washington, George 128, 150, 191, 196, 203, 367, 456, 571
Waterbug 316-7, 322
Watson, George 272
Waumanio 513
Weaver, Bruce H. 465, 470
Weber, Burt 106
Webster, John Clarence 109
Weed, Harvey 542
Weed, Nathaniel 542
Weehawken 505
Weeks, George Stephen 474
Weiss, John 420
Welcome 80
Welden, James 206, 237, 239-40, 258, 261, 575
Wellcome, Jane 414
Welles, Gideon 308, 310, 332-3, 339-40, 578
Welling, Margaret 411
Welling, Thomas 210-1
Wells, Henry 143, 470-1, 498

Wells, Lovewell 541
Wells, Thomas Foster 517
Wench, Ellen 415
West, Benjamin 169, 171-2
Westfield Republic 531
West, John 169, 171
Whale 57
Whalen, John 494
Wharton, Joseph 420
Wheeler, Anna 191
Wheeler, Elizabeth 190
Wheelock, Ralph 402
Wheelright, John 63
Wheelwright, Edward 420
Whipple, Edwin P. 420
White Cloud 369
White, John 96-7, 100
White, Joseph 207
White, Mary Phips 100
White, Nathaniel 43-4
Whitfield, Henry 114
Whitman, Walt 435, 561
Whitney, Charles 420
Whittier, John Greenleaf 420
Widow's Row 205
Wightman, James Pountney 404
Wightman, Joseph Milner 404-6, 408
Wightman, Martha 404
Wilkins, John 21, 566
Wilkinson, Elizabeth 539
Wilkinson, Prudence 539
Wilkinson, William 46
Willcocks, Peter 544
Willes, Jona 75
Willes, Richard 74-5
Willes, Thomas 75
Willes, William 75
William 428
William and Francis 57
Williams, Barrett 358-9
Williams, Jonathan 236
Williams, Laban 197
Williamson, John 459
Williams, Richard S. 259
Williams, Roger 295, 412
Williams, Seth 551
Williams, Susannah 295
Williams, William 141
William the Conqueror 94, 162, 353
Willis Diving Bowl 73, 85, 87
Willis, John 75-7
Willis, John Jr. 76
Willis, Mary 75, 81, 88
Willis, Nathanial Parker 547

Willis, Nathaniel Parker 554
Willis, Robert 72-88, 569
Willis, Samuel 81
Willis, Sarah 77, 79, 88
Willner, Philip 448-9
Willner, Sarah Foreman 448-50
Wilson, Increase 205, 573
Wilson, John 60, 62, 566-7
Windham Bilious Pills 195
Windsor Castle 225
Wingfield, Edward 92
Winthrop, Adam 56
Winthrop, John 52, 56-7, 59-60, 65-6, 77-8, 567-8
Wire, Samuel 296
witchcraft 46, 108
Withington, Mary 541
Witter, Elizabeth 47
Witter, James 48
Witter, John 45
Witte, William Henry 325
Wolcott, Anne 541
Wolcott, Dinah Walker 412
Wolcott, Experience Walker 413
Wolcott, Henrietta Louise Eustis 414
Wolcott, Jane Wellcome 414
Wolcott, John I 412
Wolcott, John II 412
Wolcott, John IV 412-3
Wolcott, John V 412
Wolcott, John VI 413
Wolcott, John Wesley 398-9, 411-4, 416-20, 424, 541, 581
Wolcott, Jonathan 413
Wolcott, Lucy Edgecomb 414
Wolcott, Lydia Bodwell 413
Wolcott, Margaret Welling 411
Wolcott, Mary Wrentmore 412
Wolcott, Oliver 241
Wolcott, Sarah 412
Wolcott, Solomon 413
Wolcott, Thomas I 411
Wolcott, Thomas II 411
Wolcott, Timothy 413
Wolcott, Winnifred Crawford 412
Wonderful Wizard of Oz The 535-6
Wood, Clarence A. 264
Woodhull, Maxwell 492
Woodna 504
Woodruff, John 190
Wood, Timothy 251
Wood, William A. 547
Wooley, Robert 190
Wooster, Abraham 139

Wrentmore, Mary 412
Wright, Augustus R. 418
Wulfhure 353
Wyllis, George 77
Wyllys, Ambrosius 75
Wyllys, Richard 75
Wyllys, Robert 73, 74, 75

- Y -

Yale, David 70
Yale, Elihu 70
Yankee: the Farmer's Almanack for the Year of Our Lord and Saviour, The 183-4 542
Yorktown 242, 483
Young Hornet 259
Young Teazer 201
Ypsilanti Sentinel 516

- Z -

Zeuner, Charles 408
Zeus 125